Handbook of
Enterprise
Integration

BOOKS ON SOFTWARE AND SYSTEMS DEVELOPMENT AND ENGINEERING FROM AUERBACH PUBLICATIONS AND CRC PRESS

CAD and GIS Integration
Hassan A. Karimi and Burcu Akinci
ISBN: 978-1-4200-6805-4

Applied Software Product-Line Engineering
Kyo C. Kang, Vijayan Sugumaran, and Sooyong Park, eds.
ISBN: 978-1-4200-6841-2

Enterprise-Scale Agile Software Development
James Schiel
ISBN: 978-1-4398-0321-9

Handbook of Enterprise Integration
Mostafa Hashem Sherif, ed.
ISBN: 978-1-4200-7821-3

Architecture and Principles of Systems Engineering
Charles Dickerson, Dimitri N. Mavris, Paul R. Garvey, and Brian E. White
ISBN: 978-1-4200-7253-2

Theory of Science and Technology Transfer and Applications
Sifeng Liu, Zhigeng Fang, Hongxing Shi, and Benhai Guo
ISBN: 978-1-4200-8741-3

The SIM Guide to Enterprise Architecture
Leon Kappelman, ed.
ISBN: 978-1-4398-1113-9

Getting Design Right: A Systems Approach
Peter L. Jackson
ISBN: 978-1-4398-1115-3

Software Testing as a Service
Ashfaque Ahmed
ISBN: 978-1-4200-9956-0

Grey Game Theory and Its Applications in Economic Decision-Making
Zhigeng Fang, Sifeng Liu, Hongxing Shi, and Yi LinYi Lin
ISBN: 978-1-4200-8739-0

Quality Assurance of Agent-Based and Self-Managed Systems
Reiner Dumke, Steffen Mencke, and Cornelius Wille
ISBN: 978-1-4398-1266-2

Modeling Software Behavior: A Craftsman's Approach
Paul C. Jorgensen
ISBN: 978-1-4200-8075-9

Design and Implementation of Data Mining Tools
Bhavani Thuraisingham, Latifur Khan, Mamoun Awad, and Lei Wang
ISBN: 978-1-4200-4590-1

Model-Oriented Systems Engineering Science: A Unifying Framework for Traditional and Complex Systems
Duane W. Hybertson
ISBN: 978-1-4200-7251-8

Requirements Engineering for Software and Systems
Phillip A. Laplante
ISBN: 978-1-4200-6467-4

Software Testing and Continuous Quality Improvement, Third Edition
William E. Lewis
ISBN: 978-1-4200-8073-5

Systemic Yoyos: Some Impacts of the Second Dimension
Yi Lin
ISBN: 978-1-4200-8820-5

Architecting Secure Software Systems
Asoke K. Talukder and Manish Chaitanya
ISBN: 978-1-4200-8784-0

Delivering Successful Projects with TSPSM and Six Sigma: A Practical Guide to Implementing Team Software Process^SM
Mukesh Jain
ISBN: 978-1-4200-6143-7

Handbook of
Enterprise
Integration

Edited by
Mostafa Hashem Sherif

CRC Press
Taylor & Francis Group
Boca Raton London New York

CRC Press is an imprint of the
Taylor & Francis Group, an **informa** business

AN AUERBACH BOOK

Auerbach Publications
Taylor & Francis Group
6000 Broken Sound Parkway NW, Suite 300
Boca Raton, FL 33487-2742

© 2010 by Taylor and Francis Group, LLC
Auerbach Publications is an imprint of Taylor & Francis Group, an Informa business

No claim to original U.S. Government works

Printed in the United States of America on acid-free paper
10 9 8 7 6 5 4 3 2 1

International Standard Book Number: 978-1-4200-7821-3 (Hardback)

Library of Congress Cataloging-in-Publication Data

Handbook of enterprise integration / edited by Mostafa Hashem Sherif.
　　p. cm.
　　Includes bibliographical references and index.
　　ISBN 978-1-4200-7821-3
　　1. Management information systems. 2. Information technology--Management.
3. Enterprise application integration (Computer systems) 4. Business
enterprises--Computer networks. I. Sherif, Mostafa Hashem.

T58.6.H34134 2010
658.4'038011--dc22
2009024351

Visit the Taylor & Francis Web site at
http://www.taylorandfrancis.com

and the Auerbach Web site at
http://www.auerbach-publications.com

Contents

SECTION I: Introductory Chapters

SECTION II: Technologies for Networking, Network Management, and Quality Assurance

SECTION III: Software and Service Architectures

SECTION IV: Enterprise Applications

SECTION V: Standards

SECTION VI: Management of Integration

SECTION VII: Conclusions

Figures

Tables

Listings

Introduction

It is now well accepted that companies accrue a significant competitive advantage when their systems, even those that are independently designed and built, can work together harmoniously without requiring extensive retrofits. Although business and/or political drivers are often the impetus for technology planning in enterprises, changes in business plans or in legislation may have significant repercussions on production and support systems. Furthermore, in a networked configuration, with advanced automation and computerization of processes and procedures, the task of maintaining compatibility over all affected interfaces when changes are continuous is very costly, if not overwhelming.

Accordingly, the designers of integrated systems face the following three simultaneous tasks:

- To bring existing systems together by masking their heterogeneity so that they can contribute successfully to business processes
- To design and implement new systems that can be assembled or reconfigured quickly in response to business and operational needs
- To establish procedures for managing smooth migrations from the legacy systems, that is, with minimum perturbations to existing operations

The chapters of this current volume are reflections on the precedent themes from different perspectives, based on direct knowledge of, and experience with, the design, implementation, and operation of enterprise systems. The authors come from various professional backgrounds, both industrial and academic, with valuable hands-on experience. They represent disciplines ranging from information and communication technologies, manufacturing and process engineering, through to project management and marketing. Their contributions highlight the significant ways by which cross-enterprise and intra-enterprise collaborations have changed in the last decade. The target audience, however, remains the same: practicing professionals as well as graduate students of software engineering, information management, system modeling, and business administration. Similarly, the goal is to provide a comprehensive picture of the technological, business, and project management aspects of enterprise integration in today's environment.

The handbook is divided into seven sections that can be read more or less independently. The introductory section consists of two chapters. The first chapter is a general guide to the subject of enterprise integration with a map to the various contributions of the volume and how they tie together and to business strategy, infrastructure development, and software architectures. The second chapter challenges the reader to use the analogy with biological systems to understand how system integration fits in the whole industrial ecology through symbiosis and competition in a Darwinian sense so that strategies, whether related to business or technology, could be congruent with the niche in which the organization resides.

The chapters of the next section relate to the technological foundations of system integration. They deal with the technologies for networking, network management, and quality assurance. One chapter is devoted to the effects of next generation networks and the next generation operation support systems on the evolution of enterprise applications and their management architectures. The challenges of integrating mobility, including service discovery and the security aspects, are addressed using context management through the appropriate middleware. Quality management is discussed at two levels: before deployment from the point of view of risk management and following deployment by observing the actual performance through network monitoring. A chapter presents the various Java-based platforms for enterprise servers and enterprise applications.

The five chapters of Section III present the various architectures of software service that are now considered to manage the bewildering complexity of enterprise systems. The centralized architecture of the mainframes was followed by several generations of distributed architectures, each taking advantage of the exponential increase in density-integrated circuits as well as their processing speed and memory storage. There are currently more than a dozen software architectural styles that need to be handled and integrated. The architectures need to consider cross-enterprise integration as well, to take into account Business-to-Business (B2B) integration scenarios that are more and more common because of the Internet. The various approaches to achieve this integration—Enterprise Resource Planning (ERP), enterprise application integration, software-oriented architecture, and Web services— are considered. Model-driven engineering is a relatively new concept of system design based on modeling and analysis of enterprises to link the vision and decisions at the strategic level to the design and implementation of the final service delivery systems. The starting point could be the modeling for the business processes or even at a higher level of abstraction by considering the exchange of economic values among the business partners to take into account their goals from the collaboration. The reader may notice some slight variations in the points of views and definitions across the various chapters of this section. This is to be expected in an interdisciplinary activity in full effervescence; it is hoped that in the next few years, these disagreements will be settled and common points of views will emerge. However, all approaches have adopted the UN/CEFACT Modeling Methodology to define the exchanges and the processes that are mobilized during business collaboration.

Section VI deals with practical matters concerning the migration from legacy systems to the Web, the various architectures for computer telephony integration, customer relationship management, as well as the integration of Radio Frequency Identification (RFID) in enterprise information systems and global electronic commerce.

Clearly, it would be beneficial to envision interoperability beforehand, as each system is being conceived. This depends also on interface standards at various levels, whether for the communication networks or the applications that intercept, analyze, and interpret the exchanges before using them as inputs to the processes for the execution, and control and planning of business and industrial processes. The final level concerns the internal executive decision support systems that extract the essence of all these actions to prepare for the short- and long-term. Section V deals with several standards for production management, in particular the ISO 15531 MANDATE standard; the standards for international trade and enterprise interoperability and B2B electronic commerce, particularly X12 and EDIFACT; the UNIFI (Universal Financial Industry Financial) messages; ISO 20022; UBL (Universal Business Language); Electronic Business (using) Extensible Markup Language (ebXML); Web Services; and the various financial dialects of XML.

Good management is essential for the success of complex undertakings. The focus of Section VI is on the management of system integration projects, whether related to known applications such as ERP systems or to emerging technologies such as RFID. Because many new forms of collaboration are built around the notion of virtual teams, the lessons learned from the numerous studies on the subject are condensed in a few key points to assist team leaders in carrying out their responsibilities. Finally, possible ways to salvage integration projects when they begin to falter are presented in a chapter reproduced from the second edition of *Enterprise Systems Integration* (2002).

The final section summarizes the main points of the book and discusses some recent trends related to system of systems engineering and integrated delivery networks in healthcare systems.

Composing this handbook took almost 20 months. I would like to acknowledge the patience and enthusiasm of all contributors who graciously agreed to modify their contributions over and over. Finally, I would like to end by recognizing the vision of John Wyzalek who guided the project from its inception.

Mostafa Hashem Sherif
Tinton Falls, New Jersey

Editor

Mostafa Hashem Sherif has been with AT&T in various capacities since 1983. He has a PhD from the University of California, Los Angeles; an MS in the management of technology from the Stevens Institute of Technology, New Jersey; and is a certified project manager for the Project Management Institute (PMI).

Among the books Dr. Sherif authored are *Protocols for Secure Electronic Commerce*, CRC Press, second edition (2003); *Paiements électroniques sécurisés*, Presses polytechniques et universitaires romandes (2006); and *Managing Projects in Telecommunication Services*, John Wiley and Sons (2006). He is a co-editor of two books on the management of technology published by Elsevier Science and World Scientific Publications in 2006 and 2008, respectively. He is also a standards editor for the *IEEE Communications Magazine*, an associate editor of the *International Journal of IT Standards & Standardization Research*, and a member of the editorial board of the *International Journal of Marketing*.

Contributors

Ehab Al-Shaer
School of Computer Science,
  Telecommunications and
  Information Systems
DePaul University
Chicago, Illinois

Koichi Asatani
Department of Computer Science and
  Communications Engineering
Kogakuin University
Shinjuku, Tokyo, Japan

Jean-Luc Barraud
Schneider Electric, Automation—
  OEM Sensors and Safety
L'Isle d'Espagnac, France

Bernhard Bauer
Department of Computer Science
University of Augsburg
Augsburg, Germany

Paolo Bellavista
Department of Computer Engineering
University of Bologna
Bologna, Italy

Ygal Bendavid
Department of Mathematics
  and Industrial Engineering
Montreal, Quebec, Canada

David Bennett
Department of Technology
  Management
Aston Business School
Aston University
Birmingham, United Kingdom

Michel Bigand
Department of Computer Science
  and Project Management
Central School of Lille
Villeneuve d'Ascq, France

Dario Bottazzi
Department of Electronics,
  Information and Systems
University of Bologna
Bologna, Italy

Mario Bourgault
Department of Mathematics and
  Industrial Engineering
Polytechnic School of Montréal
Montréal, Québec, Canada

Raouf Boutaba
David R. Cheriton School of
  Computer Science
University of Waterloo
Waterloo, Ontario, Canada

Dario Bruneo
Department of Computer Engineering
University of Messina
Messina, Italy

Maria-Victoria Bueno-Delgado
Department of Information
  Technologies and Communications
Polytechnic University of Cartagena
Cartagena, Murcia, Spain

Zehra Cataltepe
Department of Computer Engineering
Istanbul Technical University
Istanbul, Turkey

Ben Clegg
Aston Business School
Aston University
Birmingham, United Kingdom

Antonio Corradi
Department of Computer Engineering
University of Bologna
Bologna, Italy

Sergio Costas-Rodríguez
Information Technologies Group
University of Vigo
Vigo, Pontevedra, Spain

Anne-Françoise Cutting-Decelle
Department of Computer Sciences
    and Modelling Methodologies
Central School of Lille
Villeneuve d'Ascq, France

Prasanta Kumar Dey
Aston Business School
Aston University
Birmingham, United Kingdom

Yurdaer Doganata
IBM T. J. Watson Research Center
Hawthorne, New York

Nathalie Drouin
Department of Management
    and Technology
University of Quebec at Montreal
Quebec, Montreal, Canada

Esteban Egea-López
Department of Information
    Technologies and Communications
Polytechnic University of Cartagena
Cartagena, Murcia, Spain

Bettina Fricke
Convios Consulting
Augsburg, Germany

Joan García-Haro
Polytechnic University
    of Cartagena
Cartagena, Murcia, Spain

Caroline Gervais
Department of Management
    and Technology
University of Quebec at Montreal
Quebec, Montreal, Canada

Felipe Gil-Castiñeira
Department of Telematics
    Engineering
University of Vigo
Vigo, Pontevedra, Spain

Francisco Javier González-Castaño
Information Technologies Group
University of Vigo
Vigo, Pontevedra, Spain

Birgit Hofreiter
Institute of Information Systems
University of Liechtenstein
Vaduz, Liechtenstein

Christian Huemer
Institute of Software Technology
    and Interactive Systems
Vienna University of Technology
Vienna, Austria

Mirko Jahn
InterComponentWare AG
Walldorf, Germany

Lev Kozakov
IBM T. J. Watson Research
    Center
Hawthorne, New York

Binnur Kurt
Omega Training and Consultancy
Istanbul, Turkey

Philipp Liegl
Institute of Software Technology
and Interactive Systems
Vienna University of Technology
Vienna, Austria

Chang-Yang Lin
Department of Computer Information
Systems
College of Business and Technology
Eastern Kentucky University
Richmond, Kentucky

Lin Lin
Nortel
Belleville, Ontario, Canada

Ping Lin
Nortel
Belleville, Ontario, Canada

Jean-Jacques Michel
IDPICONSEIL
Maisons-Alfort, France

Rebecca Montanari
Department of Electronics,
Information and Systems
University of Bologna
Bologna, Italy

Jörg P. Müller
Department of Informatics
Clausthal University of Technology
Clausthal-Zellerfeld, Germany

John P. Murray
Retired
Femrite Drive
Monona, Wisconsin

Kathleen Naasz
Centenary College
Hackettstown, New Jersey

P. G. L. Potgieser
ABN AMRO
Amsterdam, the Netherlands

Antonio Puliafito
Department of Computer
Engineering
University of Messina
Messina, Italy

Daniel A. Rodríguez-Silva
Department of Telematics
Engineering
University of Vigo
Vigo, Pontevedra, Spain

Stephan Roser
Department of Computer Science
University of Augsburg
Augsburg, Germany

Roberto Saracco
Telecom Italia Labs
Torino, Italy

Marco Scarpa
Department of Computer
Engineering
University of Messina
Messina, Italy

Rainer Schuster
Institute of Software Technology
and Interactive Systems
Vienna University of Technology
Vienna, Austria

Mostafa Hashem Sherif
AT&T
Middletown, New Jersey

Alessandra Toninelli
University of Bologna
Bologna, Italy

Klaus Turowski
Department of Business Informatics
and Systems Engineering
University of Augsburg
Augsburg, Germany

Mehmet Ulema
Department of Computer
Information Systems
Manhattan College
Riverdale, New York

Javier Vales-Alonso
Department of Information
Technologies and Communications
Polytechnic University of Cartagena
Cartagena, Murcia, Spain

Jin Xiao
David R. Cheriton School of
Computer Science
University of Waterloo
Waterloo, Ontario, Canada

Bob Young
Department of Mechanical
and Manufacturing
Engineering
Loughborough University
Loughborough, United Kingdom

Angelo Zaia
Inquadro Srl
University of Messina
Messina, Italy

Marco Zapletal
Electronic Commerce Group
Institute of Software Technology
and Interactive Systems
Vienna University of
Technology
Vienna, Austria

Xuemei Zhang
Alcatel–Lucent
Murray Hill, New Jersey

Acronyms

3GPP	Third Generation Partnership Project
ACK	Acknowledgment
ACL	Access Control List
ADL	Architecture Design Language
ADSL	Asymmetrical Digital Subscriber Line
AIAG	Automotive Industry Action Group
AIDC	Automatic Identification and Data Capture
AIM	AOL Instant Messaging
AJAX	Asynchronous JavaScript and XML
ALE	Application-Level Events
AM	Amplitude Modulation
ANSI	American National Standards Institute
ANX®	Automotive Network eXchange
API	Application Programming Interface
ARIS	ARchitecture for integrated Information Systems
ARP	Address Resolution Protocol
ARQ	Automatic Repeat Request
ASN.1	Abstract Syntax Notation Number One
ASP	Application Service Provider
ASR	Automatic Speech Recognition
ATM	Asynchronous Data Transfer
B2B	Business-to-Business
B2BUA	Back-to-Back User Agent
B2C	Business-to-Consumer
BAM	Business Activity Monitoring
BGP	Border Gateway Protocol
BI	Business Intelligence
BIS	Bank of International Settlements
BPA	Business Process Analysis
BPEL	Business Process Execution Language
BPEL4WS	Business Process Execution Language for Web Services
BPM	Business Process Management
BPR	Business Process Reengineering
BPSS	Business Process Specification Schema
BRI	Basic Rate Interface
BSI	Business Service Interfaces
BSS	Business Support System
BTO	Built to Order

BTS	Built to Stock
CA	Collision Avoidance
CAD	Computer-Aided Design
CAM	Computer-Aided Manufacturing
CBPC	Common Business Process Catalogue
CCITT	Comité Consultatif International Téléphonique et Télégraphique
CCS	Common Channel Signaling
CCXML	Call Control Extensible Markup Language
CD	Collision Detection
CD	Committee Draft
CDMA	Code Division Multiple Access
CEFIC	Conseil Européen des Fédérations de l'Industrie Chimique
CEPT	European Conference of Postal and Telecommunications
CGI	Common Gateway Interface
CHAP	Challenge-Handshake Authentication Protocol
CHIN	Community Health Information Network
CIM	Common Information Model
CIM	Computation-Independent Model
CIM	Computer-Integrated Manufacturing
CIM	Computer-Independent Model
CIMOM	Common Information Model Object Manager
CIMOSA	Computer-Integrated Manufacturing Open Systems Architecture
CLR	Common Language Runtime
CLS	Continuous Linked Settlement
CMMI	Capability Maturity Model® Integration
CMOS	Complementary metal oxide semiconductor
CMTS	Cable Modem Termination System
CNGI	China's Next Generation Internet
COPS	Common Open Policy Standard
CORBA	Common Object Request Broker Architecture
CoS	Class of Service
CPA	Collaboration Protocol Agreement
CPN	Colored Petri–Net
CPP	Collaborative Protocol Profile
CPPA	Collaboration Protocol Profile and Agreement
CRC	Cyclic Redundancy Check
CRM	Customer Relationship Management
CRT	Cathode Ray Tube
CSCF	Call Session Control Function
CSMA/CD	Carrier Sense Multiple Access with Collision Detection
CSS	Cascading Style Sheet
CSU	Channel Service Unit
CTC	Concurrent Technologies Corporation
CTI	Computer Telephony Integration
CUG	Closed User Group
DARPA	Department of Advanced Research Project Agency

DBMS	Database Management System
DCE	Distributed Computing Environment
DCF	Distributed Coordination Function
DCOM	Distributed Component Object Model
DEC	Digital Equipment Corporation
DEDICA	Directory-Based EDI Certificate Access and Management
DHCP	Dynamic Host Configuration Protocol
DHCP-PD	DHCP Prefix Delegation
DIS	Draft International Standard
DMTF	Desktop Management Task Force/ Distributed Management Task Force
DNS	Domain Name System
DOCSIS	Data Over Cable Service Interface Specifications
DOD	Department of Defense (US)
DODS	Data Object Design Studio
DOM	Document Object Model
DOS	Disk Operating System
DSL	Digital Subscriber Line
DSS	Decision Support Systems
DSSS	Direct Sequence Spread Spectrum
DSU	Data Service Unit
DTD	Document Type Definition
DTMF	Distributed Management Task Force
DTT	Digital Terrestrial Television
DVB-H	Digital Video Broadcasting-Handheld
DWDM	Dense Wavelength Division Multiplexing
EAI	Enterprise Application Integration
EAN	European Article Number
EAP	Extensible Authentication Protocol
EAS	Electronic Article Surveillance
ebXML	Electronic Business (using) Extensible Markup Language
ECM	Enterprise Content Management
EDI	Electronic Data Interchange
EDIFACT	Electronic Data Interchange For Administration, Commerce, and Transport
EIS	Enterprise Information System
EIS	Executive Information System
EJB	Enterprise JavaBeans
EMF	Element Management Function
EPC	Electronic Product Code
EPC	Event-driven Process Chain
EPCIS	EPC Information Services
EpMF	Enterprise Management Function
EPR	Endpoint Reference
ERP	Enterprise Resource Planning
ESB	Enterprise Service Bus

ETL	Extract, Transform and Load
eTOM	Enhanced Telecom Operations Map
ETSI	European Telecommunications Standards Institute
FCC	Federal Communications Commission
FDIS	Final Draft International Standard
FDMA	Frequency Division Multiple Access
FEC	Forward Error Correction
FFA	Function Failure Analysis
FHSS	Frequency Hopping Spread Spectrum
FinXML	Fixed Income Markup Language
FIXML	Financial Information Exchange Markup Language
FM	Frequency Modulation
FMC	Fixed-Mobile Convergence
FMEA	Failure Mode and Effects Analysis
FOREX	Foreign Exchange
FP	Function Points
FpML	Financial Products Markup Language
FSA	Frame-Slotted-ALOHA
FSK	Frequency Shift Keying
FTP	File Transfer Protocol
FTTH	Fiber to the Home
FXML	Financial Exchange Markup Language
GERAM	Generalized Enterprise Reference Architecture and Methodology
GPRS	General Packet Radio Service
GPS	Global Positioning System
GRAI	Graphs with Results and Actions Inter-Related
GSM	Global System for Mobile Communications, Originally Groupe Spécial Mobile
GTAG	Global Tag
GTIN	Global Trade Item Number
GUI	Graphical User Interface
HD	High Definition
HDLC	High Level Data Link Control
HDTV	High Definition Television
HF	High Frequency
HGWC-FE	Home GateWay Configuration Functional Entity
HL 7	Health Level 7
HMMP	HyperMedia Management Protocol
HPMM	Hierarchical Passive Multicast Monitor
HR	Human Resource
HrFs	Heuristic Risk Factors
HRM	Human Resource Management
HSDPA	High Speed Data Packet Access
HSUPA	High Speed Uplink Packet Access
HTML	HyperText Markup Language
HTTP	HyperText Transfer Protocol

IAB	Internet Architecture Board
IATA	International Air Transport Association
ICANN	Internet Corporation for Assigned Names and Numbers
ICCI	Innovation Co-Ordination, Transfer and Deployment Through Networked Co-Operation in the Construction Industry
ICMP	Internet Control Message Protocol
I-CSCF	Interrogating Call Session Control Function
I-CSC-FE	Interrogating Call Session Control Functional Entity
ICT	Information and Communications Technology
IDE	Integrated Development Environment
IDN	Integrated Delivery Network
IEC	International Electrotechnical Commission
IEEE	Institute of Electrical and Electronic Engineers
IESG	Internet Engineering Steering Group
IETF	Internet Engineering Task Force
IFTM	International Forwarding and Transport Message
IFX	Interactive Financial Exchange
IGMP	Internet Group Management Protocol
IHE	Integrating the Health Care Enterprise Initiative
IIOP	Internet Inter-Object Request Broker Protocol
IJSSE	International Journal of System of Systems Engineering
IL	Intermediate language
IMAP	Internet Message Access Protocol
IMS	IP Multimedia Subsystem
IN	Intelligent Network
INS	Intentional Naming System
IOS	Inter-Organizational Information Systems
IP	Internet Protocol
IPCP	Internet Protocol Control Protocol
IRML	Investment Research Markup Language
IRTF	Internet Research Task Force
IS	International Standard
ISDN	Integrated Services Digital Network
ISO	International Organization for Standardization
ISOC	Internet Society
ISP	Internet Service Provider
ISTH	International Standards Team Harmonization
ITIL	Information Technology Information Library
ITIL	Information Technology Infrastructure Library
ITU-R	International Telecommunication Union–Radiocommunication Sector
ITU-T	International Telecommunication Union–Telecommunication Standardisation Sector
IUID	Item Unique Identifier
IVR	Interactive Voice Response
J2EE	Java 2 Platform, Enterprise Edition

J2ME	Java 2 Micro Edition
JAAS	Java Authentication and Authorization Service
JAF	JavaBeans Activation Framework
Java EE	Java Platform, Enterprise Edtion
Java ME	Java Platform, Mobile Edition
Java SE	Java Platform, Standard Edition
JAXP	Java API for XML Processing
JAXR	Java API for XML Registries
JAX-WS	Java API for XML Web Services
JCA	Java EE Connector Architecture
JCP	Java Community Process
JDBC	Java Database Connectivity
JEE	Java 2 Platform, Enterprise Edition
JIT	Just-in-Time
JMS	Java Message Service
JMX	Java Management Extensions
JNDI	Java Naming and Directory Interface
JSP	Java Server Page
JSR	Java Specification Request
JTA	Java Transaction API
JTS	Java Transaction Service
JVM	Java Virtual Machine
KPIs	Key Performance Indicators
LACES	London Airport Cargo EDP Scheme
LAN	Local Area Network
LCD	Liquid Crystal Display
LCP	Link Control Protocol
LDAP	Lightweight Directory Access Protocol
LES	Logistic Execution Systems
LF	Low Frequency
LMS	Library Management Systems
LOC	Lines of Code
LPDP	Local Policy Decision Point
LSN	Large Scale Networking
LTE	Long Term Evolution
MAC	Media Access Control
MAN	Metropolitan Area Network
MANDATE	MANufacturing DATa Exchange
MANET	Mobile *Ad-hoc* NETwork
MDA	Model Driven Architecture®
MDDL	Market Data Definition Language
MES	Manufacturing Execution System
MIB	Management Information Base
MIDAS	Middleware of Intelligent Discovery of Context-Aware Services
MIME	Multipurpose Internet Mail Extensions
MIMO	Multiple Input Multiple Output

MIT	Massachusetts Institute of Technology
ML	Maximum Likelihood
MLD	Multicast Listener Discovery
MOF	Managed Object Format
MOM	Message-Oriented Middleware
MOWS	Management of Web Services
MPCMF	Market, Product & Customer Management Function
MRM	Multicast Reachability Monitor
MRPII	Manufacturing Resource Planning
MSP	Media Service Provider
MUWS	Management Using Web Services
NACF	Network Attachment Control Function
NAK	Negative Acknowledgment
NAT	Network Address Translation
NCLOC	Non-Comment Lines of Code
NDP	Neighbor Discovery Protocol
NED	Nano Emissive Display
NewsML	Electronic News Markup Language
NGN	Next Generation Network
NGNM	Network Generation Network Management
NGOSS	Next Generation Operation Support Systems
NHPP	Non-Homogenous Poisson Process
NIC	Network Interface Card
NIS+	Network Information Service Plus
NIST	National Institute of Standards and Technology
NMF	Network Management Function
NMS	Network Management System
NNI	Network-to-Network Interface
NOC	Network Operations Center
NOS	Network Operating System
NPD	New Product Development
NSD	New Service Development
NTM	Network Trade Modell
NTP	Network Time Protocol
NTT	Nippon Telegraph and Telephone Corporation
NWDA	National Wholesale Druggists Association
OAGi	Open Application Group
OASIS	Organization for the Advancement of Structured Information Standards
ODBC	Open Database Connectivity
ODC	Orthogonal Defect Classification
ODETTE	Organization for Data Exchange and Tele-Transmission in Europe
ODU	Optical Data Unit
OFDM	Orthogonal Frequency Division Multiplexing
OFX	Open Financial Exchange

OGC	Office of Government Commerce (UK)
OLED	Organic Liquid Emission Display
OLEDB	Object Linking and Embedding Data Base
OMA	Open Mobile Alliance
OMG	Object Management Group
ONS	Object Name Service
OOS	Out-of-Stock Reduction
OSF	Operation System Function
OSGi	Open Service Gateway Initiative
OSI	Open Systems Interconnection Model
OSPF	Open Shortest Path First
OSS	Operations Support Systems
OSS/J	OSS through Java
OTC	Open the Counter
OTU	Optical Transport Unit
OWL	Web Ontology Language
P2P	Peer-to-Peer
PABX	Private Automatic Branch
PADI	PPPoE Active Discovery Initiation
PADO	PPPoE Active Discovery Offer
PADR	PPPoE Active Discovery Request
PADS	PPPoE Active Discovery Session-Confirmation
PADT	PPoE Active Discovery Terminate
PAM	Pulse Amplitude Modulation
PAN	Personal Area Networking
PAP	Password Authentication Protocol
PBX	Private Branch Exchange
PCF	Point Coordination Function
PCIM	Policy Core Information Model
P-CSCF	Proxy-Call Session Control Function
P-CSC-FE	Proxy Call Session Control Functional Entity
PDA	Personal Digital Assistant
PDP	Policy Decision Point
PEP	Policy Enforcement Point
PERA	Purdue Enterprise Reference Architecture
PGP	Pretty Good Privacy
PHP	Hypertext Preprocessor
PIB	Policy Information Base
PIM	Protocol Independent Multicast
PIM	Platform-Independent Model
PIP	Partner Interface Process
PLC	Power Line Communication
PM	Phase Modulation
PMBOK	Project Management Book of Knowledge
PMI	Project Management Institute
PON	Passive Optical Networking

POP	Point of Presence
POP	Post Office Protocol
POTS	Plain Old Telephone Service
PPP	Point-to-Point Protocol
PPPOE	Point-to-Point Protocol over Ethernet
PRI	Primary Rate Interface
PS	Production System
PSK	Phase Shift Keying
PSM	Platform-Specific Model
PSTN	Public Switched Telephone Network
QAM	Quadrature Amplitude Modulation
QoS	Quality of Service
QPIM	QoS Policy Information Model
RACF	Resource and Admission Control Function
RADIUS	Remote Authentication Dial in User Service
RBAC	Role-Based Access Control
RDBMS	Relational Database Management System
REST	Representational State Transfer
RFC	Request for Comments
RFID	Radio Frequency Identification
RIA	Rich Internet Application
RIM	Registry Information Model
RIP	Routing Information Protocol
RIXML	Research Information Exchange Markup Language
RMI	Remote Method Invocation
ROI	Return on Investment
RPC	Remote Procedure Call
RS	Registry Services
RSA	Rivest, Shamir, and Adleman's Public-Key Encryption Algorithm
RSVP	Resource Reservation Protocol
RTCP	RTP Control Protocol
RTLS	Real-Time Locating Systems
RTP	Real-Time Transport Protocol
RTSP	Real-Time Streaming Protocol
RTT	Round Trip Time
S/MIME	Secure Multipurpose Internet Mail Extensions
SAAJ	SOAP with Attachments API for Java™
SaaS	Software as a Service
SAML	Security Assertion Markup Language
SAR	SIP Archive
SASL	Simple Authentication and Security Layer
SCE	Service Creation Environment
SCM	Supply Chain Management
SCOR	Supply Chain Operation Reference
SCP	Service Control Point
S-CSCF	Serving-Call Session Control Function

S-CSC-FE	Serving Call Session Control Functional Entity
SDH	Synchronous Digital Hierarchy
SDK	Service Development Kit
SDMA	Space Division Multiple Access
SDP	Service Data Point
SDP	Service Discovery Protocol
SDR	Session Directory
SED	Surface-Conduction Electron-Emitter Display
SEF	Service Element Function
SEI	Software Engineering Institute
SFA	Sales Force Automation
SGML	Standard Generalized Markup Language
S-HTTP	Secure HyperText Transfer Protocol
SID	Shared Information and Data Model
SIP	Session Initiation Protocol
SITA	Société Internationale de Télécommunications Aéronautiques
SITPRO	Simplification of International Trade Procedures
SLA	Service Level Agreement
SLP	Service Location Protocol
SLSes	Service Level Specifications
SME	Small and Medium Enterprise
SMF	Service Management Function
S–MIDAS	Secure–Middleware for Intelligent Discovery of Context–Aware Services
SMS	Short Message Service
SMTP	Simple Mail Transfer Protocol
SNA	Systems Network Architecture
SNMF	Service Network Management Function
SNMP	Simple Network Management Protocol
SOA	Service Oriented Architecture
SOAP	Simple Object Access Protocol
SODA	Service Oriented Device Architecture
SONET	Synchronous Optical Network
SoS	System of Systems
SoSECE	System of Systems Engineering Center of Excellence
SOX	Sarbanes-Oxley Act
SPRMF	Supplier/Partner Relationship Management Function
SQL	Structured Query Language
SRD	Short Range Devices
SRM	Supplier Relationship Management
SRMF	Service Resource Management Function
SSO	Single Sign-On
SSP	Service Switching Point
STEP	Standard for the Exchange of Product Model Data
STPML	Straight through Processing Extensible Markup Language
SwA	SOAP with Attachment

SWIFT	Society for Worldwide Interbank Financial Telecommunication
TAPI	Telephony API
TCP	Transmission Control Protocol
TCP/IP	Transmission Control Protocol/Internet Protocol
TDCC	United States Transportation Data Coordinating Committee
TDI	Trade Data Interchange
TDMA	Time Division Multiple Access
TEDIS	Trade Electronic Data Interchange System
TEF	Transport Element Function
TIA	Telecommunications Industry Association
TINA	Telecommunication Information Networking Architecture
TINA-C	Telecommunication Information Networking Architecture Consortium
TLOC	Total Lines of Code
TLS	Transport Layer Security
TMF	Telecommunication Management Forum
TMForum	TeleManagement Forum
TMN	Telecommunication Management Network
TNA	Technology Neutral Architecture
TNMF	Transport Network Management Function
ToS	Type of Service
TQM	Total Quality Management
TRMF	Transport Resource Management Function
TSO	Transport Segmentation Offload
TSP	Telephony Service Provider
TTL	Time-to-Live
TTS	Text-to-Speech
TWIST	Transaction Workflow Innovation Standards Team
UA	User Agent
UAC	User Agent Client
UAS	User Agent Server
UBL	Universal Business Language
UBSPSC	United Nations Standard Products and Services Code
UCC	Uniform Code Council
UCM	Use Case Map
UCS	Uniform Communication Standards
UDDI	Universal Description, Discovery and Integration
UDP	User Datagram Protocol
UHF	Ultra High Frequency
UM	Unified Messaging
UML	Unified Modeling Language
UMM	UN/CEFACT Modeling Methodology
UMTS	Universal Mobile Telecommunications System
UN/CEFACT	United Nations Centre for Trade Facilitation and Electronic Business
UN/ECE	United Nations Economic Commission for Europe

UNI	User-to-Network Interfaces
UNIFI	Universal Financial Industry Message Scheme
UN-JEDI	United Nations Joint Electronic Data Interchange
UN-TDI	United Nations Trade Data Interchange
UPCC	UML Profile for Core Components
UPnP	Universal Plug and Play
URI	Uniform Resource Identifier
URL	Uniform Resource Locator
VAN	Value Added Network
VDSL	Very High Speed Digital Subscriber Line
VID	Virtual LAN Identifier
VoiceXML	Voice Extensible Markup Language
VoIP	Voice over IP
VPN	Virtual Private Network
W3C	Word Wide Web Consortium
WAN	Wide Area Network
WAR	Web Archive
WBEM	Web-Based Enterprise Management
WCAG	Web Content Accessability Guidelines
W-CDMA	Wideband Code Division Multiple Access
WD	Working Draft
WEP	Wired Equivalent Privacy
WfMC	Workflow Management Coalition
WiMAX	Worldwide Interoperability for Microwave Access
WINS	Warehouse Information Network Standard
WMS	Warehouse Management Systems
WS-BPEL	Web Services Business Process Execution Language
WS-CDL	Web Services Choreography Description Language
WSCI	Web Service Choreography Interface
WSDL	Web Service Definition Language
WSDL	Web Services Description Language
WSDM	Web Services Distributed Management
WSI	Web Services Interface
WSMO	Web Service Modeling Ontology
WSN	Wireless Sensor Network
WSRP	Web Services for Remote Portlets
WSTF	Web Services Transaction Framework
WWW	World Wide Web
XACML	Extensible Access Control Markup Language
xBRL	Extensible Business Reporting Language
xCBL	XML Common Business Library
XFRML	Extensible Financial Reporting Markup Language
XHTML	Extensible Hypertext Markup Language
X-KISS	XML Key Information Service Specification
XKMS	XML Key Management Specification
X-KRSS	XML Key Registration Service Specification

XML	Extensible Markup Language
XMPP	Extensible Messaging and Presence Protocol
XPDL	XML Process Description Language
XSD	XML Schema Definition
XSL	Extensible Stylesheet Language
XSLT	Extensible Stylesheet Language Transformation

Section I

Introductory Chapters

1 Defining Systems Integration

Mostafa Hashem Sherif

CONTENTS

The scope of systems integration in enterprises has expanded from a focus on the flow of materials in shop floors to the infrastructure for manufacturing, distribution, and communication as well as business applications and administrative processes. It encompasses exchanges among business partners involved in paperless transactions. It may also cover structural realignments in organizational design and technology. Today almost every major organization spends significant efforts in integrating and streamlining systems of various types after mergers, acquisitions, or splits. Some of the motivations clearly revolve around technological issues, while many originate from initiatives to enhance quality, to reduce costs, and to improve the efficiency of operations and decision support in response to competitive pressures and/or legislative mandates for providing timely and accurate information [1].

WHAT IS SYSTEMS INTEGRATION?

Computer intelligence was added into organizations in bits and pieces, as hardware and software building blocks became available, to automate specific administrative and business processes but without an overriding master plan. Each department added its own custom-built applications, built specifically for its own use, without coordination with other functions or departments. With the passage of time, organizations accumulated isolated computer silos, each with their specific hardware, software, access procedures, data formats, and processing tools. Navigating through enterprise information systems to complete transactions or to assist in strategic planning became a time-consuming and an error-prone endeavor, with significant effects on the customer-facing functions as well as the internal processes. Customer care typically touches on many departments responsible for order tracking, credit approval, service provisioning, account maintenance, billing and collections, and returns or repairs. Enterprise information systems typically collate data from multiple sources—within and outside the enterprise—to present a coherent picture of the business dynamics in terms of the enterprise's customers, suppliers, competitors, and its own strengths and weaknesses.

To bring some order into a chaotic situation, enterprise systems integration started as a vehicle and a methodology to bring disparate systems together through a common front-end and mask the underlying computer and communication infrastructure. It has evolved into a systematic redesign of the information architecture, within enterprises and across enterprises, to ensure the flexibility and extensibility of the applications by design, in addition to their interoperability. Both aspects coexist in initiatives for systems integration, even when they are not explicitly stated.

System integration is closely related to enterprise integration, which "is concerned with facilitating information, control, and material flows across organizational boundaries by connecting all the necessary functions and heterogeneous functional entities (information systems, devices applications, and people) in order to improve communication, cooperation and coordination within this enterprise so that the enterprise behaves as an integrated whole, therefore enhancing its overall productivity, flexibility, and capacity for management of change (or reactivity)" [2]. One important distinction is that the scope of system integration may extend outside the boundary of the enterprise to cover suppliers, customers, banks, and other parties involved in electronic commerce.

DRIVERS FOR SYSTEMS INTEGRATION

A combination of several factors have stimulated and facilitated systems integration projects. These are: advances in computer networks and information processing, globalization, the need for organizational agility to cope with competition and rapid development, market positioning through the customization of products and services, and regulatory compliance. It should be emphasized that the various integration drivers interact with each other and their effects are usually combined. For example, both technological advances and deregulations have resulted in a worldwide competitive environment with new patterns of collaboration and partnerships that enterprise information systems have to contend with.

PROGRESS IN COMPUTER NETWORKING AND INFORMATION PROCESSING

Computers were first introduced as stand-alone systems to improve data processing functions in selected applications, such as process control, financial transactions processing, and business and administrative automation. At first, computerization accelerated work procedures without modifying the established ways of operation. With experience, it became apparent that individual computer systems could be tied together to avoid the cost and delays due to rekeying the same data repeatedly and incurring unnecessary transcription errors. The availability of large transmission capacities in a secure and reliable telecommunication infrastructure, the description of which is the focus of Chapters 3 through 10, was a strong incentive to connect remote computers together, while advances in microprocessor technology and software engineering transformed computers into productivity tools for workers and individuals. Computers became integrated into production systems to optimize the scheduling of materials by coordinating planning, scheduling, and execution. Toyota, for example, introduced just-in-time (JIT) techniques to connect shop floors with the back office and to provide its suppliers and partners with advanced visibility into parts designs, engineering measures, and inventory levels. Similarly, with the use of bar codes—and much later radio frequency identification (RFID) tags, the retail environment became another source of feedback to the supply chain, thereby improving the inventory management and production scheduling. In fact, as discussed in Chapters 19 and 20 of this Handbook, radio tagging, that is, the automatic reading of the identification information, is making asset verification much easier. With Electronic Data Interchange (EDI) standards, systems could be designed to improve the efficiency of communication among the different departments within the same enterprise as well as with its commercial partners. Finally, efficient disaster recovery plans are built on the capability for quick reorganization and coordination of activities in response to emergencies.

Enterprise Application Integration (EAI) was one of the first architectural concepts to bring together the various heterogeneous applications and information systems of an enterprise. The goal was to integrate the various platforms, tools, and applications spread across various departments and areas separated by organizational boundaries, so that they could access the same data and communicate using a common protocol. As a term coined by industry consultants, the definition of EAI remains fuzzy. For some, it is a way to achieve *ex post* interoperability of proprietary applications developed at different terms and with a variety of technologies. For others, the term covers an integration *ex ante* by defining common standards for the design of flexible distributed applications.

Service-Oriented Architecture (SOA) is a new blue print for system integration for the start of the design by moving away from monolithic applications, with their own embedded data tied to specific processes and their business rules. SOA is based on the experience gained from distributed computing and object- and component-based designs. Its basic premise is to group business functionalities in well-defined and self-contained functions or "services." Here, a service is defined as a logical representation of a repeatable business activity that has a specified outcome and does not depend on other services, unless it reuses them or it is composed of other services [3]. To maintain this independence, each service is responsible for updating the data it uses. Furthermore, the services are not necessarily under the control of a single administrative entity and they communicate using an Enterprise Service Bus (ESB), rather than through function calls from the body of the programs. By design, the applications are made to be modular and independent of the input data; the data they need are verified and authenticated separately and are accessed through standardized interfaces. Similarly, the business rules are defined and processed outside the applications. With dynamic service composition, services and workflows do not have to be defined at design time, but can be adapted later to fit the context of the service consumer. As a result, the binding of an application with the data it processes and the business rules it applies is made at run time under the control of an external entity supervising the workflow. Finally, legacy software programs, computing devices, and networking resources that were not designed as loosely coupled components are encapsulated via standardized common interfaces.

SOA encourages the reuse of existing software components, whose providers list their locations on a network and the description of their services in a directory (also called registry or service broker) so that potential consumers could discover them and query them with standardized exchanges [4–6]. A precise contract defines the access conditions to a service, the rules to launch it, and the end-conditions that must be validated for the result to conform to the service user's expectations. The contract and its functional clauses are described in standardized languages. To increase flexibility, rule definition is separated from service definition to allow the reuse of the same set of services under changing rules. The sequencing of the workflow (choreography) and coordination of message exchanges between the services (orchestration) are under the control of an external entity, the orchestration engine, which executes the rules describing the business logic and/or composes them on the fly using exchanges with a rule engine. SOA enhances organizational agility, because the workflow can adapt quickly to the needs by changing the service composition of existing services in response to the environmental changes. Learning can be absorbed through modified business rules to reflect gained competency without changing the core services.

As a way to provide networked services, SOA is related to Web services, in the sense that both use XML-based protocols but opinions differ on the exact nature of their relationship. Some authors consider that SOA has to rely on Web services while others tend do decouple XML specifications from SOA pointing to the extreme verbosity of XML-based documents, which could be a drawback when efficiency is needed.

It may be useful to consider SOA as the transposition of concept of intelligent networks (INs) for telecommunications to computer engineering. In fact, an IN is also an architecture to establish and manage a distributed environment that supports real-time network services and end-user applications, such as roaming and location-dependent services in mobile networks. To do so, IN uses a layered architecture to shield the network services and the end-user applications from the network infrastructure. Various network services are formed by different combinations of common building blocks. Also, the cooperating networking platforms would communicate among themselves and with outside applications using standard interfaces and protocols [7]. It should be noted, however, that IN uses the common sense meaning of a "service," while SOA has its own peculiar definition.

GLOBALIZATION

Exchanges among partner enterprises have long relied on proprietary electronic networks for business-to-business transactions. Initially, each industrial sector devised its own rules for automated and structured exchange independently. The explanation is quite simple: in networked services, rivalry does not prevent the parties from cooperating on reasonable terms and conditions to take advantage of the network externalities (i.e., the value of the service offered increases with the number of participants to that network). For example, the Automotive Industry Action Group defined the rules for the North American car industry in 1982, while the European manufacturers formed ODETTE (Organization for Data Exchange and Teletransmission in Europe) in 1984. SITA (Société Internationale de Télécommunications Aéronautiques— International Society for Aeronautical Telecommunications) was established among airline companies to exchange data-concerning airline reservations and schedules, tariffs, and so on. SABRE or Amadeus was established to link travel agents, airline companies, hotel chains, and car rental companies. The SWIFT (Society for Worldwide Interbank Financial Telecommunication) network was established in 1977 to exchange standardized messages that control the international transfer of funds among banks. Various national and regional bank settlement systems were established to transport interbank instructions and financial flows. Many of these systems were later updated to conform with EDI specifications.

New communication and information technologies have allowed companies to split up tasks and to disperse the locations of their execution. More recently, enterprises in advanced countries have concentrated on benefiting from wage differentials to move some of their production facilities and to use service desks in various places around the world to offer continuous 24-h customer care. Outsourcing has been used to off-load supplementary activities to specialized providers, to reduce labor costs, and as an antiunion strategy. Each phase of the outsourcing movement depended on the availability of integrated enterprise systems worldwide. First, manufacturers delocalized their factories or sourced their components from a variety of global producers. Next, the supply chains were restructured as enterprises focused on their core competencies and outsourced nonessential activities and even some internal operations, such as payroll and pension plan administration, human resources administration, and information technology (IT) support. Nowadays, service industries are splitting functions, such as accounting or customer interface, and distributing them to providers on a worldwide basis. This distribution ensures round-the-clock operation and increases the performance by seeking expertise wherever it may be. In fact, it is estimated that today around 75% of large companies throughout North America and

Europe have outsourced the management of human resources. The downside, however, is the increased vulnerability of their supply chains and communication networks to risks outside their control.

Globalization has a direct effect on the management of project teams due to the distributed and long-distance nature of the collaboration. Chapter 26 discusses recent findings on how to improve team performance in a virtual environment.

One effect of outsourcing is that it increases the need for interoperable and flexible IT systems. Integration of proprietary, project-specific solutions is costly and adds delays and risks of lock-in to a given manufacturer or technology. This has stimulated the search for new ways to put together enterprise systems that are more flexible and more responsive to changes in the business needs.

NEED FOR ORGANIZATIONAL AGILITY

The combined effects of deregulation, globalization, and new technologies have changed the landscape in many industries and highlighted the need for organizational agility. The need to shorten product development times has stimulated concurrent engineering as a method to facilitate the rapid development of integrated solutions without excessive costs or delays by engaging the various functional disciplines in tandem rather than in sequence. In the service industries, particularly in networked services such as telecommunications, airlines, or banking, new services from large companies depend on hundreds of computer support systems, many of which with different architectures and operating under different models, to handle aspects of order entry, provisioning, installation, quality management, and so on.

The first important consequence is that constant communications must be maintained among the various functional departments, irrespective of the information architecture within each. With mobility, the strict boundaries among three service spheres of information processing: the home, the enterprise, and on the road, are becoming more and more blurred. The second is that this communication and information-processing architecture, including its operations support systems, needs to be quickly reconfigurable to adapt to changes in the environment or whenever a new service is introduced. This would reduce the time and effort needed to consolidate the distinct systems into a flexible and an "evolvable" structure.

In knowledge-intensive industries, collaboration among parties arises from the distributed nature of knowledge among many highly specialized firms. Consequently, we have witnessed a growing trend in the use of noninternal resources through hybrid governance structures such as partnerships, strategic alliances, and joint ventures. Open innovation, a term coined by Henry Chesbrough in his 2003 book [8], underlines the fact that enterprises can pick and choose the most suitable technology, irrespective of whether it came from within their boundaries. Other terms describing this phenomenon are: the "virtual company environment" with its formal and informal networks or "community of practice." For emerging technologies or applications, in particular, various parties to a project are bound temporarily to share skills, cost, and partial access to each other's information systems. Thus, although the competitive advantage of knowledge-intensive firms stems largely from their own resources and capabilities, their ability to collaborate with other companies in R&D

and complementary functional areas is increasing in importance. The management of such an organization demands a disciplined process for coordination and sharing the data as needed without excessive rules or laxity. Collaboration among suppliers, vendors, and customers adds new risks that proprietary information and trade secrets will be divulged. It should be evident that this type of arrangement is substantially different from the typical supply management, the purpose of which is to reduce inventory or enhance response to market conditions.

PERSONALIZATION OF PRODUCTS AND SERVICES

One way in which firms have been competing is by devoting more resources to offer a personalized attention to their customers by exploiting what IT can offer. This driver for system integration concerns the capability of tailoring a specific product or a service offer to an individual's profile. For example, in call centers, Computer Telephony Integration benefited from advances in the telephone signaling where the calling phone numbers could be transmitted with the call setup information, as well as from the development of Interactive Voice Response systems that would understand what callers punch on their keypads or their voice instructions. In this way, an incoming call could be routed to the most suitable operator equipment with synchronized information extracted from the various enterprise databases, to identify the callers profiles, their account status, the reason for the call, and so on. Selling functions could be added as well to suggest new products or services that would suit the customer's profile. Chapter 17 gives an overview of the various phases in the evolution of the integration of telecommunications and IT applications in enterprise networks. The focus of Chapter 18 is on applications from a sales, marketing, and call center perspective.

Traditionally, marketing was used to identify the characteristics and the needs of a certain segment of potential users to tailor the product or service to them. This new personalization focuses on individuals' expectations, and needs and wants based on their locations or their environment. Many organizations today allocate their resources in relation to their customers' lifetime "value" and loyalty. As a strategy, they track the choices their customers make and use them to refocus their offer mix. Data warehouses store the integrated information culled from any number and variety of data sources to assist in defining these profiles. Management of the data warehouses requires software and intelligent infrastructure to extract the necessary knowledge. Yet, these databases may be distributed among several entities and have different formats so that a service provider would have to negotiate access with each entity separately and then convert the data to a common format. The promise of SOA and Web Services is that most—if not all—of these negotiations would be automatic and on-line and that very little data conversion would be needed by using a common format.

LEGAL ENVIRONMENT AND REGULATORY COMPLIANCE

Governments and regulations have played a significant role in encouraging systems integration. The European Commission spurred European organizations and businesses to use electronic exchanges in the course of their commercial activities and various European customs authorities have harmonized and automated their procedures. Similarly, in the United States, the Federal Acquisition Streamlining Act in October 1994 required the use of EDI in all federal acquisitions. The Expedited Funds Availability Act in 1990 obliged U.S. banks to make the funds of deposited checks available within a certain interval and, indirectly, forced banks to establish the necessary mechanisms to exchange information and reduce the chances of fraud.

Deregulation is another way governments have indirectly encouraged enterprise integration. For example, the deregulation of telecommunication services in most countries has broken vertically integrated service providers by mandating open interfaces and more transparent cost-based pricing. These open interfaces need to be standardized to facilitate systems integration. Chapters 21 through 23 illustrate the applications of current standards in manufacturing, international trade, and business-to-business electronic commerce.

OVERVIEW OF ENTERPRISE SYSTEMS

System integration in enterprises deals with the following three main aspects: planning and scheduling, execution control, and finally financial analysis [9]. Although the exact details of planning and scheduling depend on the nature the service or the product offered, the general requirements concern interoperability, distributed organization, ability to handle heterogeneity, dynamic structure, scalability and fault tolerance. The purpose of these requirements is to assist in the transition from monolithic solutions to a loose federation of interoperable systems, without negative effects on the performance in terms of reliability, availability, and security.

Enterprise Resource Planning (ERP) systems are company-wide information systems that integrate the back office functions used for the exchange of business information (financial, human resources, payroll and other applications, manufacturing, distribution and supply chain management, etc.) to increase the productivity and remove inefficiencies. The goal is to integrate applications and databases and offer a unified user interface across the enterprise. In manufacturing, ERP evolved from Manufacturing Resource Planning (MRPII) systems, which were used to plan and schedule the raw materials. Today's ERP packages, such as SAP R/3, Baan, Oracle, PeopleSoft, and so on, are very general and need to be configured for each enterprise. Although their architecture and exact content may differ from one vendor to another, they all include several modules. Customer Relationship Management (CRM) defines a methodology and a set of tools to support automated processes over the various channels reaching customers, including call centers. The functions covered typically include order taking, order processing, pricing with any discounts and capturing, storing, and analyzing and interpreting customer-related data. The scope of Supplier Relationship Management (SRM) systems is an enterprise's interactions with the organizations that supply the goods and services, such as requisitioning, purchasing, and receiving of supplies. One major component of SRM is the Logistics Execution System that connects processes involved in procurement, order processing, production, storage, inventory management, shipping, and sales. Manufacturing Execution Systems support the production processes in what is sometimes called intelligent manufacturing. The key part is Warehouse Management Systems that handle the movement and storage of materials in a warehouse environment, including tracking, shipping, receiving, and storing.

The above description gives an idea of the effort required to customize ERP packages to the needs of a given firm or administration. The extent of customization determines the magnitude of that effort in terms of time, resources, costs, and so on.

The purview of internally facing systems is the technical and business aspects of operations. Business Support Systems take from where CRM have stopped to deal with customer-related processes such as receiving orders, processing bills, invoicing, collecting payments, and so on. In the case of telecommunication operators, Operations Support Systems typically handle the technical aspects of the day-to-day operations. For example, they handle the network-facing aspects such as the provisioning of equipment and circuits, the management of faults whether reported by the end-users or signaled by the network elements, the verification that performance conforms with the service levels agreed, the recording of usage for accounting purposes and the securing of the physical aspects, and the network records and database. The business aspects cover order fulfillment—possibly across multiple geographic regions or countries, legal entities, currencies, suppliers, and customers—invoices and business flows, and remote order entry. Part of these activities involves the capability to reconcile invoices, billings, payments, and account statements from the enterprise's banks. Planning may rely on historical records, when markets and technologies are stable and well known.

Profitability analysis depends on the availability of financial data as input to decision on improving operations or focusing on more profitable markets. This is why ERP assembles business and financial functions from all departments and functions in a company. One limitation, however, is that ERP systems do not allow a sensitivity analysis to investigate the impact of managerial choices or technical decisions on profitability or customer retention. Such a capability requires an advanced level of system integration as discussed in the following section.

FOUR STAGES OF SYSTEM INTEGRATION

System integration can be achieved at different levels, which are labeled as follows:

1. Interconnectivity
2. Functional Interoperability
3. Semantic Interoperability
4. Optimization and Innovation

Typically, these levels come sequentially, in the sense that, for example, functional interoperability is not possible without interconnectivity. Similarly, semantic consistency and interoperability is a prerequisite to optimizing the current system or thinking about improved and innovative ones.

INTERCONNECTIVITY

This is the most elementary state of integration. It relies on a telecommunication infrastructure to bring the disparate equipment or applications together so that they could coexist and exchange information through gateways, adaptors, and/or transformers (the term used depends on the discipline involved). A fully meshed configuration, that is, when interconnectivity is taken to the limit, leads to a pervasive computing environment, where every machine is connected to every other machine.

This level of integration can be labeled "loose-integration" because the basic applications, functionalities, and uses of the original equipment or application remain unaffected. To a large extent, the ways in which the business is performed are not modified. A key advantage of advanced telecommunications capacity is to eliminate the transport of the physical storage media. As a reminder, in early EDI systems, messengers would carry magnetic tapes with the data from one location to another to share the necessary data.

FUNCTIONAL INTEROPERABILITY

Interoperability refers to the ability to make one equipment or application work with another directly, without requiring special effort from the end-user. It requires functional and technical compatibility among the protocol interfaces of the network elements, the applications, and the data formats. From a strictly technical viewpoint, the successful exchange of data involves the following components:

- Telecommunication networks
- Protocols for exchanging data
- Format of the messages exchanged
- Security procedures

Functional interoperability implies coordination across organizational lines. The higher the number of interested parties and their dependencies, the stronger is the need to define common interface specifications. Interoperability can be achieved if both sides perform similar functions or if their interfaces are compatible. In that case, all parties have to agree to implement a common profile or interface template, while each may add optional features that should not affect interoperability. This depends on standards either defined by a recognized standardization committee, through market dominance or by regulation. In some circles, this level of interoperability is called "syntactic interoperability" [10], and in Chapter 22, it is called "technical interoperability."

SEMANTIC INTEROPERABILITY

Semantic consistency is achieved when data elements as well as their meanings are shared (semantic unification). All parties could share the same model or, at a minimum, one model could be mapped without ambiguity into the other. For example, there is an equivalence among elements used in the two standards for business-to-business exchanges, X12, and EDIFACT (Electronic Data Interchange for Administration, Commerce, and Transport) despite differences in the coding of the data elements, syntax rules, and security procedures. Without this equivalence, there is the risk that each party would make incorrect assumptions about the other parties leading to semantic interoperability problems.

Standards for semantic consistency are those that define the "what" of the exchange, that is, a shared set of rules to interpret the exchanges and the subsequent actions (the "how" aspects are typically related to the syntax). In this regard, the term "ontology" was borrowed from the realm of metaphysics and epistemology to represent the agreed semantics (i.e., terms and their significance) for a domain of interest. The emphasis at the semantic level is on providing access to data and on minimizing potential errors due to human interpretation through the creation of standards for data definitions and formats. This means that the data elements are uniformly defined and that their significance is consistent from system to system and application to application. For example, the sharing of medical documents requires that the medical vocabularies among the various health-care professions have the same meaning and lead to the same actions. In other words, all parties have to share the same expectation about the effect of the exchange messages. This may be called "pragmatic interoperability" [10]. Chapter 16 discusses how Web technology and legacy enterprise systems could be brought together in a coherent manner to integrate data and applications. Note that Chapter 22 adds an additional level of interoperability at the organizational level.

OPTIMIZATION AND INNOVATION

In this phase, systems integration becomes an enabler for systematic changes in the way technology is used or in the organizations or both. The treatment of information can be optimized through statistical controls and enhanced reporting activities such as improved customer care (retention, collection, etc.), increased capability of fraud detection, the ability to measure and predict returns on investment, to improve the efficiency of day-to-day operations, or the ability to refocus the mix of production in response to changes to the economic configuration.

MODELING AND SYSTEM INTEGRATION

Effective integration of business processes, whether within an enterprise or across enterprises, requires treating similar functions, that is, those that share common properties, using common procedures or rules. This calls for establishing a formal model of the business processes. Modeling covers the processes, the data information models, and the exchange formats and protocols. Formal modeling also captures the implicit and explicit knowledge in the enterprise about these processes (what, how, when, who, where, how much) in a form that can be shared with others and bring out cross-sector commonalities.

Process models should be defined at an abstract level, that is, they should avoid implementation details. This separation increases the flexibility of the design and the implementation. Furthermore, model-driven development facilitates the evaluation of design alternatives and allows the automatic propagation of changes from the requirement to the final implementation. For example, Business Process Management is an approach to model the organization of work within the enterprise as well as with external partners (suppliers, banks and customers, etc.), so that business processes could be investigated using simulations before they are executed.

Approaches for enterprise modeling have been adopted from software engineering. They can be divided into the following categories:

- Descriptive models, such as activity diagrams (Chapter 5) and process maps (Chapter 7)
- Formal models, such as the e3-value methodology (Chapter 12), ARIS (ARchitecture for integrated Information Systems), PIM4SOA (Platform-Independent Model for Service-Oriented Architecture), all discussed in Chapter 14, and UN/CEFACT's Modeling Methodology (Chapters 12 and 22)
- Language models such as BPEL (Business Process Execution Language) also known as WS-BPEL, the Unified Modeling Language (UML), and WSDL (Web Services Description Language) (Chapters 5, 11, 14, and 15)
- Analytical models such as Petri networks and the use of event simulators (Chapter 13)

ISO has standardized several data information models for manufacturing. ISO 10303 or STEP (Standard for the Exchange of Product Model Data) is used to share information among systems and applications for CAD (Computer-Aided Design) and CAM (Computer-Aided Manufacturing) such as technical drawings and product structures and is used in aerospace, automotive, ship building, and construction. Chapter 21 presents ISO 15531, the recent MANDATE (MANufacturing DATa Exchange) standard for information modeling in production systems.

SYSTEM INTEGRATION PROJECTS

System integration projects are typically large, complex, and risky. They have broad ramifications for the organizations involved and sometimes unexpected consequences, both positive and negative. They demand a highly skilled and disciplined project team, a formal methodology to conduct the project and assess progress, and a supportive leadership. As in all large projects, scope creep is lurking at every corner and more often than not, the completion dates have been set arbitrarily, without regard to what can be performed with the resources available (time, personnel, budget). Organizations that are committed to excellence, however, understand that a well-thought-out process for handling integration projects is essential. Some of the components of this process are as follows:

1. Proactive management through effective initial planning as well as contingency planning to take into account the various risks (technological, organizational, project, etc.).
2. Shared accountability and responsibility through multifunctional team work across various organizations (marketing, production, engineering, IT, etc.).

3. Multilevel project sponsorship to ensure that the project is consistent with the overall strategy of the enterprise or enterprises involved and to have all disciplines working together in unison.

Inversely, some of the problems that face integration projects are as follows:

1. Unproven technology or supplier failures.
2. Unrealistic targets in terms of date or cost or scope. Symptoms include the lack of resources for the integration project, uncontrolled changes to the scope, unresolved conflicts among the functional organizations and the project organization, the lack of training of the workforce including end-users, recruitment difficulties, and so on. Another telltale sign is the refusal to adopt statistical quality control to quantify risks, with the result that decisions are made based on subjective criteria as well as market pressures. The root cause is typically the lack of top management support, or worse, their incompetence.
3. Lack of standards and/or exclusive reliance on proprietary interfaces and protocols, which cause a manufacturer lock-in. Alternatively, lack of interoperability of "standard-compliant" implementations may arise from deficiencies in the scope of the standards, ambiguities in the specifications, or flaws in the implementations themselves [11].
4. Lack of quality control, in the sense of specifications defining what is an acceptable performance level, either for the system as a whole or for individual components.
5. Inadequate customer care. The real customer here being the end-user and not the IT department responsible for the integration project. In fact, in many cases, the IT department defines the system's requirements without adequate study of the need of these end-users.
6. Inadequate risk management plan, particularly technology risks. For example, in the process of software customization to fit commercial packages to the business processes of the firm or the administration, the responsibilities are diluted among vendors, particularly in the case of legacy systems, the teams that have defined the requirements and those that are implementing the customization.

Several chapters in this book will expand on these issues. Chapter 10 addresses the way to mitigate risks due to software reliability in enterprise integration projects, while Chapter 24 focuses specifically on managing risks during the project planning process.

ISSUES IN ENTERPRISE/SYSTEM INTEGRATION

Current enterprise (or system) integration plans pose significant challenges because of the nature of the networking technology, the difficulties of standardization, and the security threat to institutions and individuals.

THE NATURE OF THE NETWORKING TECHNOLOGIES

The Internet protocol (IP) is the underlying networking technology in most contemporary systems integration efforts. This is a 30-year-old connectionless protocol designed with no admission control mechanism because it was intended for a trusting environment. As a consequence, network control traffic may under some circumstances occupy a significant segment of the available bandwidth. Further, user and network control traffic compete for the same physical bandwidth. Inopportune or ill-intentioned user packets may be able to bring down a network element (such as a router) and cause distributed denial of service attacks by compromising a sufficient number of hosts to send useless traffic toward a target site. That is, IP-based commercial networks are fundamentally different from other networked services, such as train, airlines, or traditional telephony, where the user payload and the control traffic are separated. In fact, in the public-switched telephone network, common channel signaling was introduced to prevent frauds when user data would mimic network control data to fool charging systems. In a public network, a safe solution would be to identify and authenticate all exchanges with trusted certificates at the expense of additional computational load on the network nodes. Enterprise networks are generally closed so that they can be protected with other means.

There are many aspects to the fundamental insecurity of the IP-based networks due to the confluence of user traffic and network control traffic. For example, the communication with the distributed database that contains the addresses of every site on the Internet—the Domain Name System—is not secure. As a consequence, there are several possible ways for injecting a false IP address to fool a name server to record the fake address as the corresponding entry to a particular site. This would block access to the real Web site by duping people into going to an alternative site and harvest their data [12]. From time to time, a new flaw is discovered [13,14]; but patches only reduce the possibilities of successful attacks without eliminating them. This does not mean that other flaws are not exploited without being revealed to the public.

In addition, the Internet governance remains a problem, because the authority to assign addresses ICANN (Internet Corporation for Assigned Names and Numbers) is not independent in the sense that it is supervised by the U.S. Department of Commerce. This ties the Internet governance more to the political orientation of that Department than to the needs of users or service providers.

Finally, all these integration schemes are based on the assumption of cheap energy for telecommunications and processing. However, by extrapolating the switch and transmission capacity needed for Internet traffic, by the year 2020, it is expected that the average service provider would consume the power output of one nuclear plant [15]. Clearly, new networking and processing technologies as well as more energy-efficient integration architectures are needed to reduce power requirements.

THE DIFFICULTIES OF STANDARDIZATION

Computerization started with isolated systems that did not need to communicate with other systems. This suited the manufacturers as they had captive markets and did not need to worry about competition. This is one reason why standardization of application interfaces lagged behind the standardization of network equipment. The proliferation of proprietary protocols hampers integration efforts. The objective of standardization at the level of a firm or an administration is to reduce this variation to a manageable level. Further, formal ICT (Information and Communication Technologies) standards attempt to meet a multiplicity of needs (network operators, service providers, suppliers, end-users) so that there is an inevitable tension among the different requirements, particularly because of the differences in the time horizons of manufacturers and service providers.

The success of formal standardization requires the correct identification and articulation of the most important issues to be addressed to meet the needs of the various stakeholders: manufacturers, network operators, service providers, end-users, standardization organizations, governments, and so on. Standards needed for successful integration may not deliver their full promise, however, if they are too complex or if they contain too many options and parameters so that partial implementations would end up being incompatible [16].

Presently, there is no corrective market incentive to address the lack of standards quality because of many factors, such as the distributed nature of the standardization management process and the time lag between a standard and its implementation in products and services. In some cases, those who pay the cost of the lack of quality are not those who made the decisions. This means when a formal ICT standard is deficient, the implementers are the ones who pay the cost and not those who have developed the specifications [17].

PRIVACY CONSIDERATIONS

From a marketing perspective, the advantage of integrating customer data in the planning process is to take into account user preferences and purchasing history in production and sales efforts. In that sense, the creation of profiles is a way to improve service offers through targeted marketing. Unfortunately, these profiles are constructed with little consideration to the rights of the individual and some business models rely on exploiting and selling user profiles. In fact, many laws for the protection of privacy do not apply to commercial entities. Also, many governments have invoked moral considerations (e.g., battle against pedophilia) or political arguments (war on drugs or on terror, fight against hooligans or organized crime, etc.) to establish exceptions to the general principles of law with the goal of establishing a global surveillance network of the civilian population worldwide.

The interconnection of different systems coupled with the embedding of processing capacity in appliances, for example, RFID, allows entities to be tracked continuously. This offers possibilities of illicit snooping. An illustration of how such attacks can confound major network providers is the so-called Athens affair, where customers of Vodafone Greece were bugged, including the prime minister of Greece, the mayor of Athens, and at least 100 other high-ranking dignitaries, for at least 6 months in the 2004–2005 time frame [18].

SUMMARY

In recent decades, the rapidly changing business environment has stimulated many integration concepts such as computer-integrated manufacturing, JIT production, and virtual enterprises. Through business process reengineering, several functions can be streamlined across administrative boundaries to include project management, design, manufacturing, or sales support. Systems integration, however, is a progressive process; furthermore, its objectives have changed with the increase of computerization in the society. Facing all these uncertainties and changes, business processes have to be loosely coupled and flexible enough to be easily reconfigurable and to support the collaboration of workers at distributed geographical locations. Many of the issues touched upon in this introduction will be elaborated in the remaining chapters of this handbook.

ACKNOWLEDGMENTS

I would like to thank, in alphabetical order, Professor Anne-Françoise Cutting-Decelle (École centrale de Lille, France), Dr. Tineke M. Egyedi (Delft University of Technology, the Netherlands), Dr. Kai Jakobs (Technical University of Aachen, Germany), and Mr Yasser Sherif (Environics, Egypt) for their comments on earlier drafts of this chapter, which have greatly improved the presentation and its clarity.

REFERENCES

1. Li, M.-S. et al., *Enterprise Interoperability, Research Roadmap*, Final Version (Version 4.0), July 31, 2006, available at ftp://ftp.cordis.europa.eu/pub/ist/docs/directorate_d/ebusiness/ei-roadmap-final_en.pdf
2. Vernadat, F. B., *Enterprise Modeling and Integration: Principles and Applications*, Chapman & Hall, London, 1996, 320.
3. *The Open Group, Definition of SOA*, Version 1.1, available at http://www.opengroup.org/projects/soa/doc.tpl?CALLER=admin_summary.tpl&gdid=10632, June 8, 2006.
4. Erl, T., *Service-Oriented Architecture, A field guide to integrating XML and Web Services*, Prentice Hall PTR, Upper Saddle River, NJ, 2004, 60, 362–364.
5. Manouvier, B. and Ménard, L., *Intégration applicative, EAI, B2B, BPM et SOA*, Hermès/Lavoisier, Paris, 2007, 152.
6. Bonnet, P., Detavernier, J.-M., and Vauquier, D., *Le système d'information durable. La refonte progressive du SI avec SOA*, Hermès/Lavoisier, Paris, 2008, 82–87.
7. Faynberg, I. et al., *The Intelligent Network Standards: Their Applications to Services*, McGraw-Hill, New York, 1997, 2–15.
8. Chesbrough, H., *Open Innovation: The New Imperative for Creating and Profiting from Technologies*, Harvard Business School Press, Boston, 2003.
9. Sherif, M. H. et al., Supply chain management in a virtual enterprise, *Proceedings for the 9th International Conference on Management of Technology (IAMOT 2000)*, February 21–25, Miami, FL, 2000, file name TR 5.1 D.
10. Pokraev, S. et al., Semantic service modeling: Enabling system interoperability, in *Enterprise Interoperability, New Challenges and Approaches*, Doumeingts, G. et al., Eds., Springer-Verlag, London, 2007, 221–230.
11. Egyedi, T. M., An implementation perspective on sources of incompatibility and standards' dynamics, in *The Dynamics of Standards*, Egyedi, T. M. and Blind, K., Eds., Edward Elgar, Cheltenham, UK, 2008, 28–43.

12. Vixie, P., DNS and BIND security issues, *Proceedings of the Fifth USENIX UNIX Security Symposium*, Vol. 5, Salt Lake City, June 1995.
13. Schneider, D., Fresh phish, *IEEE Spectr.*, 45 (10), 35–38, 2008.
14. Davis, J., Collapse, *Wired*, 16 (12), 200–205; 224; 231, 2008.
15. Aoyama, T., A new generation network—Beyond NGN, *Proceedings of the First ITU-T Kaleidoscope Academic Conference, Innovations in NGN, Future Networks and Services*, Geneva, May 12–13, 2008, Geneva, ITU, 3–10.
16. Egyedi, T., Experts on cause of incompatibility between standard-compliant products, in *Enterprise Interoperability, New Challenges and Approaches*, Doumeingts, G. et al., Eds., Springer-Verlag, London, 2007, 552–563.
17. Sherif, M. H., Jakobs, K., and Egyedi, T. M., Standards of quality and quality of standards for telecommunications and information technologies, in *Challenges in the Management of New Technologies*, Hörlesberger, M., El-Nawawi M., and Khalil, T., Eds., World Scientific Publishing Co., Singapore, 2007, 427–447.
18. Prevalakis, V. and Spinellis, D., The Athens affair, *IEEE Spectr.*, 44 (7), 26–33, 2007, available at http://en.wikipedia.org/wiki/Greek_telephone_tapping_case_2004-2005

2 The Dawn of a New Ecosystem of Communications

Roberto Saracco

CONTENTS

This chapter provides a different view of the cosmos of enterprises and the way these can use communications systems. In doing so, I will be exploring the evolution of telecommunications systems in a broad sense, that is, their technology and their business models. Lessons from the evolution of living systems are used to study enterprises in loosely coupled ecosystems. For example, we learn from living systems that differentiation, and not convergence, increases the value of an ecosystem. Charles Darwin claimed [1] that the appearance of more and more variants, first, and species, next, leads to divergence. This divergence is clearly noticeable in ecosystems where the observation period covers millions of years. It is also apparent for shorter observation interval, with faster reproduction cycles, as it is the case for bacteria. So although the convergence of information technologies has been under the spotlight for many years now, the continuous stream of new technologies, new services, and new players seems to indicate that we are in a "divergence*" period. The interplay of market, technologies, and players, however, may give the impression of convergence and this is something I will address later in this chapter. The box on "Technological Darwinism" explains the parallels that can be made between the evolution of species and the evolution of technologies in the market place. In the case of information and communication technologies (ICT), one important enabler for many of these ecosystems is what telecommunications operators call "platforms." The box "From Platforms to Ecosystems" outlines a few of these business ecosystems.

When I talk about enterprises operating within an ecosystem, I mean something different than an enterprise in a value chain. A value chain is governed by explicit agreements among its links, while interactions in an ecosystem are usually not regulated by contracts, but through changes in the environment.

TECHNOLOGICAL DARWINISM

What are the parallels between the Darwinian evolution of species and the evolution of technologies in the market place? The aim of this box is to stimulate thinking about those similarities perhaps to lead to a very productive and disruptive thinking.

The evolution of species occurs through casual mutation mechanisms at the level of genes and at the level of systems that control those genes (still an integral part of the DNA sequence). The mutations that prove to be more efficient in multiplying and/or ensuring offsprings in that particular ecosystem are selected.

Technology evolution occurs through the mechanisms of invention (creativity) in products, in production systems, and in services. In openly competitive environments, the selection happens through market forces. Success attracts more investment to create more variants, an obvious example being the cell phone species, family GSM, that brought the family Iridium close to extinction by blocking its further evolution.

The success of a species is measured in terms of occupation of an ecosystem. The higher the reproduction factor, that is, the quantity of off-springs in a generation divided by the time span of a generation, the likely to see the evolution. The overall success of the species increases as long as the basic characteristics of the ecosystem do not change. Note, however, that the increase in the number of off-springs leads to competition with other species within the ecosystem, with self-regulating mechanisms constraining the quantity of surviving off-springs but not their capacity to create differentiation.

In a similar fashion, the success of a technology in the market leads to an increase in the number of actors (creators and users) and in the investment.

---

* It can also be called "differentiation," see: http://sandhill.com/opinion/editorial.php?id=66&page=1.

This, in turn, accelerates the development of successive generations of that technology. Success, hence, begets success and further innovation as long as the ecosystem characteristics do not change significantly. An obvious example is the already mentioned species "cell phone" and its family "GSM" that has progressively colonized the whole world. Here, the quantity is close to a billion a year (GSM only) with a reproduction time (lifetime of a model) measured in (a few) months.

Every species is part of a primary ecosystem comprising other species that all together form a system in a dynamic equilibrium. The competition among species is a stabilization factor for the ecosystem, and external variations may lead to new stable configurations to the extent the internal dynamics can cope with the external changes.

Every technology is part of an ecosystem comprising technologies used for its production and for its delivery as well as applications using it in a dynamic equilibrium. These technologies form a value chain together with other value chains sharing the same ecosystem whose loose interactions provide the overall stability of the ecosystem. Competition among technologies in the TV ecosystem creates a dynamic equilibrium. The cathode ray tube (CRT); plasma display, liquid crystal display (LCD), and the coming Surface-conduction Electron-emitter Display (SED) and Nano Emissive Display (NED) belong to different value chains, although they share some basic technologies such as Digital Signal Processing (DSP) chips and the same (potential) market target. Their loosely coupled interactions at the technology and (more so) at the market level create the ecosystem. External influences such as the availability of high definition (HD) content, the market preference for thinner displays, may lead to new stable configuration, with the disappearance of the CRT, the dominance of LCD, and plasma displays but as the requirement of higher resolution grows, NED may take the upper hand.

Each species continually creates variants, independent of other species. However, the dominance of a given variant, and hence its evolution, is affected by other species through competition and symbiosis. We say that a species has evolved when one of its variants dominates the other variants (marginalizing them or forcing them to extinction) so that cross-breeding is no longer possible. Blue eyes are a variant that is not considered an evolution since it coexists with brown eyes and does not prevent the interbreeding of people with different eye colors. We say that an ecosystem has evolved when the variant of a species is able to carve out a survival space for itself without leading to the extinction of the parent specie.

Every technology tends to improve linearly through subsequent tunings both at a conceptual level and at the production process level. Beyond a threshold of improvement, the market forces the substitution of other technologies. In practice, the success of one leads to the extinction of others, often in a very short time. This is the case of flat screens replacing the CRTs. In other situations, a technology variant creates a space within the ecosystem to flank existing ones without causing their extinction. This is illustrated by the way mobile communication is eroding the usage of fixed line communication without causing its extinction. This difference is important because in substitution, there is no value creation in the ecosystem: the pleasure of the viewer with better looking screens is compensated by manufacturers having to scrap their CRT production lines. In the second situation, there is an overall creation of value: people are talking and spending more, since they can communicate on the move, even though this may be at the expense of other ecosystems.

Competition among species can occur only within an ecosystem (fish do not compete with cows). If the ecosystem evolves, or if one of its species evolves, competition is no longer applicable; the species that loses ground is not defeated by another but because it is no longer fit to survive in the new ecosystem.

The ecosystem of technology evolutions can be characterized by the business values, the regulatory framework, and the cultural context of the users. The survival of a species through competition is not possible if these elements are part of the structural characteristics of one species but not of another. So an actor (species) that derives its revenues from services to end-users (e.g., telecommunication operators that offer connectivity services) does not compete with another (say Google) whose financial survival depends on other revenue sources by offering free services to these end-users. These two species are in distinct ecosystems and competition does not happen among species belonging to different ecosystems. However, the two ecosystems may be part of a larger ecosystem where the two ecosystems compete. A species, to survive, needs to reposition itself in the context of the winning ecosystem. The same is true when values shift from strict communication to information processing: the challenge to survive has moved from competition within the communication ecosystem to competition between the communication and information-processing ecosystems.

Application of the same technology across a variety of ecosystems (e.g., the same chip ends up in a refrigerator, a car, a digital camera) gives that technology the benefits of the economy of scale. This increases its value across several ecosystems, encouraging the optimization of production processes and accelerating its evolution. Intel has expanded its microprocessors business from the PC ecosystem to all those where computation may be of use. The application of microprocessors in more niches, however, leads to the multiplication of variants and the microchip of the PC is quite different from that in a digital camera or the one processing video signals in a TV or the voice signals for cell phones. Evolution progresses in a very orientated direction and cannot regress. The continuous evolution of a species may lead to a point where it is no longer possible to invert the direction. A grasshopper will never be able to evolve to eventually become a man, nor a man can evolve to eventually become a grasshopper, independently of the time and generations we allow for the evolution process. In fact, any regression would mean stepping back into a condition that is no longer sustainable within that ecosystem and the species would not generate sufficient off-springs to further the evolution.

Industrial systems are a mixture of technology, processes, and markets. They evolve by tuning their capacity the more rapidly and effectively, the more the ecosystem is competitive. The tuning, however, is in the direction of a linear improvement within their ecosystem. If radical changes occur, the industrial system cannot survive through simple improvement strategies: it needs to reinvent itself. This is what happened with the shift from mainframes to departmental computers—the VAX and the rise of Digital Equipment Corporation (DEC)—and to personal computers. In this process, companies like Bull, Honeywell, and later Digital just faded away and disappeared. IBM, to become the leading player in the PC ecosystem (at least for a while, till the rules changed and the PC became a mass market product), detached its engineers to Florida, away from the industrial rules of the mainframe. In fact, IBM did not stop producing mainframes. although they are no longer the main source of revenues, its switch to PC and more recently its metamorphosis to a service company did not happen through a linear evolution, but rather through discontinuous leaps entering and sometimes creating new ecosystems.

A fish is optimized to live in a watery ecosystem and cannot jump into a terrestrial ecosystem. Likewise, moving from a communication ecosystem into the entertainment ecosystem calls for changing the business model. For the industrial system of telecommunications to take a significant role in the entertainment ecosystem, it has to either adopt the rules of the entertainment ecosystem or bring some elements of that ecosystem into the telecommunications one. Whatever strategy is adopted would not be a convergence but an evolution: the entertainment ecosphere could embed communications and interactivity elements (e.g., the live calls from viewers in broadcast TV) or the telecommunications ecosphere could add multimedia elements to offer. For example, telecommunications could become free for users with a business model sustained by advertisement. This would mean changing the rules of the TV world and the taking over of one ecosystem to another. Let us note that the Telecom Italia ecosystem is worth 40 billion euros, the broadcasting is worth 10 billion.

The evolution of species is affected by the availability of energy to sustain the ecosystem and it is always toward an increased efficiency in making use of the available energy. In the evolution of industrial and social ecosystems, the energy efficiency has to be seen in a larger dimension of market economy. Telecommunications networks contribute to the efficiency in an ever growing number of ecosystems. As a consequence, the physical or logical networks that are more energy efficient tend to prevail. For example, the peer-to-peer (P2P) communication provides efficiency in an economic sense and generates friction and reaction that may assume a variety of forms. However, because it has lower (economic) energy requirements, it is bound to prevail.

FROM PLATFORMS TO ECOSYSTEMS

Platforms have pervaded and impacted the last 30 years of technology and service evolution in the Information and Communications Technology (ICT) area. The first example that comes to mind is that of a small company in New Mexico, MITS, back in the 1970s that invented the "bus" to communicate among various PC components (the Altair).

This standardized (and not patented) communications system stimulated the creation of a brand new ecosystem, comprising PC board vendors and the manufacturers of keyboards, disk drives, and memory extensions. This ecosystem expanded further when software platforms—the Disk Operating System (DOS) and the Apple/Mac operating systems—increased the efficiency of the ecosystem. This fuelled the rise of many programming languages with some prevailing over the others (platforms are ideal to stir up competition). At the same time, it stimulated the creation of new programming languages (species) with subsequent competition and new equilibrium. This process is still going on with new programming languages being created. The diffusion of ICT to numerous sectors has stimulated the creation of new platforms as seeds for new ecosystems.

The sector of information distribution has multiple competing distribution channels whose success can be measured with two metrics: the economic value and the volume. Channels are used in different ways by ecosystems with distinct "survival" rules. Within each ecosystem, the metrics allow the study of the prevalence of one species over another. For example, who does prevail when advertisement is attached to content? Is it the content creator, the intermediary assembling various contents into a program, the distributor who manages a single channel, or the one who controls the access? Content may not be, in the future, the key element for an effective advertisement but a mere container, while the direct knowledge of who is accessing the content may represent the new value. This is no longer an ecosystem with well-defined value chains, rather with numerous actors interacting within the ecosystem with mash-up-like models. This can affirm the effectiveness of service exposure through open networks, themselves part of the ecosystem, so that they could negotiate their worth with other members of that same ecosystem. This is a dramatic transformation of the overall business paradigm for network operators.

Which new players would emerge when the value of advertisement moves to the point of access? Could TV manufacturers replace film producers, a hypothesis that today may seem preposterous? Is it possible to imagine a future TV set sold with a bundle of 10,000 movies? Today, it is not feasible because of the way the content rights are managed but why not when the price of memory chips drops would remove the cost barrier?

In the retail sector, the advertisement can move to the point of sale (it is already happening in the United Kingdom) through screens associated with the shelves hosting the mentioned products. In some supermarkets in Germany, advertisements can be activated directly on a 10 in. screen fixed to the shopping cart and selected on the basis of the products the shopper puts into: the cart reads the tags associated to every package in the basket and communicates with the store computer.

Once advertisements are no longer tied to the content but to individual persons or objects, the control and the value get displaced. Also, the concept of value chain, upon which today's publicity is based, will be replaced by mash ups of actors in communication with the end-user by various means leading to the development of numerous business models of which publicity is just one element.

Platforms to support information mobility are also morphing into ecosystems as they move from managing traffic to aggregate and support a variety of players that want to reach the "moving customer." For example, the car navigation system could become an ecosystem-creating platform by offering information provided by local players through a connection established via a nearby cell phone. People on different cars could communicate using any available local network, perhaps in a potentially lengthy sequence of hops. The shift is from a present value—the service I am using right now—to a potential value, the values of all services and information that may be of interest to me even if I am not using them at that particular moment. Because I perceive such a potential value, I become *de facto* a participant in the ecosystem, just like it happens for the Web.

A similar reasoning can be applied to other sectors, such as health care. Here monitoring and communications systems worn by a patient can multiply their value if we move from a focused use (like the Holter-monitoring exam to determine how the heart responds to normal activities and cardiac medications over 24 h) to a much broader usage. The platform attracts and aggregates a plurality of independent actors with service offerings such as the monitoring of chronic diseases, dietary guidelines, personal training and fitness, or the support of social communities enabled by personal communications spaces.

Medications can well be part of this ecosystem, transforming pills from a product to a service, since it becomes possible to monitor the effect and provide consultancy in real time. The transformation of cures is surely moving in this direction.

The examples are truly endless and touch the most diverse fields: they have in common the concept of value creation through a network to create a growing potential value, with social networks becoming the business engine.

INFRASTRUCTURES AND BUSINESS STRUCTURES

Many people consider telecommunications infrastructures as information highways to draw the parallel between wires and roads. However, I think that a more appropriate analogy is with shipping lanes. In sea shipping, tremendous changes have occurred from small vessels to giant container transporters. Today, a single transporter can accommodate up to 10,000 containers and shipping routes have been structured in a variety of networks connecting major nodes. To illustrate this point, a container ship that gets into Hong Kong Harbor carrying 10,000 containers is unloaded and each of these containers is sent individually to other ships to their ultimate destinations while the originating vessel is replenished with other containers. And all this is performed by robots in just 6 h.

Advances in sea shipping have changed the production model and the structure of enterprises to a much bigger extent than the terrestrial infrastructure. While roads have decreased the perception of distance in contiguous geographical areas, sea shipping has shrunk the world. Shipping a T-shirt from Taiwan to Genoa, a 10,000 mile trip, costs 2 cents. This is why production cost in Taiwan can affect workers elsewhere, why an enterprise can design clothes in Treviso in the northeast of Italy, produce them in Taiwan, and sell them all over the world, including the mall in front of their own enterprise headquarters.

Several hundreds of years of value chains (since their conceptualization by Adam Smith) have engrained the idea that making money means to find a niche, to become part of a value chain and process raw materials by adding value, and then passing the product/service to the next link in that chain. Yet, the cells of living organisms do not behave that way; business profit is not their motive. They are basically autonomous systems reacting to local conditions and adapting to them. The business of a living cell or organism is to keep on living by getting sufficient energy from the environment to sustain itself. In living systems, complex food chains involve uncaring players, each focused on its own "business." Furthermore, several living entities may aggregate their efforts as in a herd for better protection, in a pride for more effective hunting, or in a hive, where specialization leads to more sophisticated behavior. In this way, all contributors to the ecosystem can benefit as the ecosystem is enriched. Relationships of these sorts entail lots of communications, information gathering, and processing. But none of these is based on the same model of communications and business that are observed in the traditional telecommunication environment.

Living things are ruled by organized chaos. There is no intelligent design, as we find in telecommunications networks. So we may anticipate that, in the future, when enterprises become part of an ecosystem, what they produce and sell will contribute to the richness of that ecosystem. A product will likely be accompanied by an "electronic butler" throughout its life cycle to assist the user with suggestions for scheduled maintenance, for the availability of new features or special offers. Some of these interactions will originate directly from the producer, who is no longer depending on the distribution chain to reach out to all the end-users of its products. But at some other times, it might be initiated by another enterprise, whose product you just bought, to inform you of the availability of services/devices in your domain that can enhance your experience with the product you just bought. Or a third party might be advising on how to glue together what you already have with something they can offer to get new features. The evolution of technology, the globalization of markets and the efficiency of distribution chains accelerate the creation of new "things" and contribute to the selection of those that fit best a particular economic and cultural environment. Anything you already own becomes part of an ecosystem so that each product or service can multiply its value by integrating within an ecosystem.

The implication is that any business has to distinguish itself from its competitors and, at the same time, to make sure that what it offers fits seamlessly in the environment so that the users can interact with it easily. In other words, enterprises should leverage the technology available to them, including telecommunications, to diversify on the one hand and to conceive products and services that add value to their ecosystem, on the other.

If the world is converging, centralized and uniform management architectures would be better. If, on the contrary, the world is moving toward a multitude of loosely interconnected environments each growing in diversity and overlapping with others in a multidimensional space,* we would be better off by looking at autonomic management strategies.

The comparison between Darwinian evolution of species and technology evolution is consistent with the statistics and nondeterministic laws and phenomena regulating aggregations (or systems) [2] known as Small Worlds. According to the small world concept, a multitude of elements loosely interacting with one another will be able to interconnect and establish an ecosystem in a dynamic equilibrium. The study of these Small Worlds systems can be applied to both the model of Darwinian biological evolution and to the evolution of technology-based product and services. In the case of the Darwinian evolution, the interactions are those of the various species competing for resources in the ecosystem and resulting in an ambient equilibrium. In the business world, the interactions are among the scientific, economic, social, and cultural domains for the contention for basic resources. The box "Small Worlds" presents the similarities between the Darwinian evolution and the small world theory (to whom we can refer for a mathematical interpretation of both Darwinian and technology evolution).

SMALL WORLDS

The theory of small world contributes to the study of complex systems in the area of innovation.

Complex systems can be studied in terms of the interactions among their components. The "shape" of the observed behavior can tell if the phenomena result from a "plan" regulating the interactions, if the interactions are random but present a feedback regulation mechanisms (causal), or if the phenomena do not depend from interactions among the elements of the set.

---

* Multidimensionality is crucial in this discussion. Ecosystems are not overlapping by geographical contiguity or proximity, rather they overlap in the use of resources, in the adoption of different strategies for harvesting resources, and in the impact their growth can have on immaterial aspects such as culture, policies, and concerns. In the past, telephone companies used to protect themselves from contiguous ecosystems, for example, those of other operators in neighboring markets. Now, they have to pay attention to other players such as Google that is playing in a completely different ecosystem but whose "free to the end-user" culture is changing the rules of the game in far distant ecosystems.

In the case of a plan, we have an "ordered system"; in the case of random-ness, we talk about "small worlds." The set of interactions can be plotted into curves having the shape of a power distribution [2]. If the interactions have no influence on the behavior of the overall system, we talk about chaotic systems and the observed behavior can be plotted on curves having a Gaussian shape.

We know that living ecosystems behave according to a power line curve (distribution), even though evolution is steered by interactions among the species, most of the time random interactions, sometime causal, creating feed-back. This is true also if we look at the global evolution of ecosystems and species based on the Darwinian Theory. It seems also to be the case for the technology evolution, at least this is what emerges from a research carried out by the Turin Polytechnic based on the date generated by a study on technology evolution carried out in the European cooperative project FISTERA [3].

This result prompted comparison between Darwinian evolution and tech-nology evolution. Both refer to complex systems with complex interactions, mostly random but each potentially creating feedbacks rippling through the ecosystem that can be analyzed with a statistical approach. Both comply with a set of rules dictating the possible evolution, and strengthening or weakening the effect of interactions.

If we consider a technology such as the display of images using a CRT, we see that in its 50 years' history, the quality of products has improved signifi-cantly. Images used to have an oval shape and it has become perfectly squared, thanks to better control of the electronic beam. Color displays have displaced black and white monitors, and chip technologies, digitalization, and micropro-cessors have sustained this evolution. At the same time, new technologies have appeared in the visualization ecosystem, based on novel approaches, although still making use of those chips that led to the improvement of the display on the cathode tube. These new approaches did not improve image quality but pro-duced thinner screens, a characteristic that has become the reason of choice for the buyer, leading to the progressive disappearance of the CRT.

Besides, in the display ecosystem, the advent of HD has recently become an important factor in steering the evolution. TV evolution, after several turns, took the path of digital signals. This was possible thanks to the availability of low-cost microprocessors capable of compressing over 600 million bits/s into about 15 million/s. Even though the HD is so much more pleasing to see than the normal definition TV, HD is going to flank the normal display for several years before the latter disappears. This is also a good news for the ecosystem value since HD can be offered at a premium price (that would not be possible if it were a mere substitution of the existing one). A significant portion of the content produced by the Majors is in low definition. The competition between standard and high definition TV is regulated by the inertia to replace the TV set that in turns depends on the price of the set and the availability of appealing HD content. Forces pushing toward accelerating or delaying the change-over are by far of economic nature (production and buying) and are further influenced by regulatory policies (subsidy through de-taxation of systems embedding the digital decoder).

We can also simulate the impact deriving from the introduction of new nodes and relations, for example, what happens if the CMOS (complementary metal oxide semiconductor) technology, providing very high-resolution sensors extends from the digital to video cameras. Surely this increases the resolution of content produced by individuals and this in turn may stimulate the demand for higher definition TV sets (4 k, 8 pixel standard, four times the resolution of HDTV) and higher bandwidth for connectivity, thus favoring the growth of fiber at the expense of VDSL. A sufficient number of households connected via optical fibers creates a potential market willing to exploit the 4 k definition TV, thus stimulating their production. The interesting policy question is: is it better to invest in developing 4 k TVs to pull the fiber deployment or in creating the fiber infrastructure that will pull the market of more advanced TV? Small world modeling can help in finding out what is more valuable, the chicken or the egg.

THE MANY FACETS OF CONVERGENCE

From an evolutionary point of view, convergence is nothing but a myth. A myth is something that is true but is presented in a figurative manner; also there is convergence in evolutionary biology, when independent species acquire similar characteristics, even though they evolve in different ecosystems. This myth was created partly by engineers who believe that technology progress can enable any function in any object through a single over-reaching infrastructure, and partly by marketers seeking to expand their portfolios with whatever would allow them to enter new markets and/or increase their value propositions.

It does not require a giant leap of imagination to include in one's portfolio what is already present in somebody else's, such as to embed in the telecommunication portfolio the offer of television (TV) channels. Such an inclusion may bring value to individual actors, but would contribute very little value at a systemic level. Since the end customer is given basically equivalent choices, price becomes the deciding factor: in other words, the overall sector sees a price decline.

Convergence can be further investigated by looking at the following six areas: technologies, infrastructures, processes, services, terminals, and actors (business and players).

CONVERGENCE OF TECHNOLOGIES

Let us start by considering an example of technology convergence with significant impact on products and market, namely the evolution of microchips production. The integrated circuit, now a reality in a multitude of objects, is the result of a production technology that has kept evolving since its invention by Jack Kilby in 1958. Thanks to this evolution from a few hundred transistors packed in a chip we have moved to billions of them. In 2004, researchers at the University of Florida managed to create a production process capable of placing Silicon and Gallium Arsenide in the same chip. Out of this, we got very low cost cell phones that are booming in developing countries for their affordability ($35 for a cell phone) and the growing diffusion of sensors able to communicate via radio.

In 2007, Intel was able to embed in a single chip Indium along with Silicon and Gallium Arsenide and achieve optical-electronics conversion. Nowadays, a single chip will be able to store, compute, and communicate information through wires, fiber, and wireless. Here we may see an example of convergence where one chip would replace three different chips that were needed to process, communicate over a radio link, and over an optical fiber. It should be noted, however, that three production lines converging to produce a single chip leads to an increase in the variety of chips produced. Each of these chips has the same common substrate but is tailored to specific needs and applications, both through a reconfiguration of its internal architecture by multicore software programming and through application software.

The evolution of production processes generates variety, not uniformity, or convergence. Today, we have many more TV models than we had in the past, many more mp3 readers, and many more types of cell phones: The market pushes to implement whatever is possible to explore new market niches, capture new clients, and keep the old ones.

It is true that the availability of EyeFi, a flash memory card with an integrated Wi-Fi communication capability, gives the possibility for transferring photos from digital cameras through a Wi-Fi area. This is an outcome of technology convergence between Gallium Arsenide and Silicon but all flash memory cards have not converged on including this feature. Even if over a long period of time, market forces will make this happen, new cards will add other features to differentiate themselves from their competitors.

The point is that technological evolution pushes continuously toward divergence, leading to ever-new products. Most enterprises today have tremendous flexibility to add new functionalities to their products, but their effectiveness depends on their insertion in an existing ecosystem or their aggregation to form a new ecosystem.

CONVERGENCE OF INFRASTRUCTURES

During the 1980s, integration became the holy grail of telecommunication engineers. The consensus in the telecommunications industry was that digital communications would lead to the integration of all services and the focus was on Integrated Services Digital Network (ISDN). Integration was a slogan, as used and abused as it is convergence today. The idea was that a new technology based on digital communications would have led to the integration of all services.

Things evolved quite differently from the expectations at the time. Rather than the integration of networks and services, we have witnessed tremendous developments in infrastructures, all leveraging on the possibilities offered by the same "digital" technologies. In fact, in the last decades, new networks for mobile communications[*] have

---

[*] Many would claim that Internet is the "thing" but I rather say GSM is the "thing." It is thanks to GSM that we have seen telecommunications reaching any place and really connecting the world. And in the next decade, I bet that the revolution will come from wireless again, bridging atoms and bits and changing the value chains of businesses and enterprises.

been flanking the fixed voice network and have evolved to transport data in addition to voice traffic. The evolution of technology made it possible to use the same resources for any type of traffic, hence again the claim for convergence.

In the last decades of the previous century, packets switching was introduced to avoid dedicating a circuit between the calling and the called parties (or between the data repository and the surfer at his terminal) all throughout the session, even in the absence of any information exchange. Standards such as IP Multimedia Subsystem (IMS) and Session Initiation Protocol (SIP) have been developed to control communications and services.

For access network technology, we could say there is a conceptual convergence on fiber to and inside the home. If we consider the time it will take to implement this "convergence," which is estimated to exceed 5 years in a country like Italy for at least 90% of terminations to be made of fiber, then during this period, intermediate steps will have to be made. Technologies, such as Very High Speed Digital Subscriber Line (VDSL), or radio will appear on the last drop. New solutions may emerge, such as Power Line Communication and mesh networks. Besides, looking at the world scenario, in areas that are scarcely populated and are difficult to reach—at least from an economic point of view—the fiber to the home (FTTH) solution may never be able to displace radio solutions such as the Worldwide Interoperability for Microwave Access (WiMAX), for example, or satellite communication. In other words, there will not be a convergence of infrastructures but a multiplication of what we have today.

Clearly, for services to be successful, all these infrastructures have to interconnect seamlessly in a way as transparent as possible to the end-user. To access any infrastructure, a terminal, possibly in negotiation with the access gateway, would be masking all the intricacies of access to the user. With software-defined radio, a terminal would be able to learn from a variety of radio infrastructures how to access the associated networks in a manner that is completely transparent to the end-user. Mobile terminals already are able to connect transparently to both 2G and 3G wireless networks and some are able to connect to Wi-Fi access points as well. In the coming years, we should expect them to connect to WiMAX access points, to sensors, and to Radio Frequency Identification (RFID). With software-defined radio technology, a terminal would be able to learn from a variety of radio infrastructures how to access the associated networks in a manner that is a completely transparent to the end-user.

The convergence of infrastructures may be a cost-saving measure for an operator, just like an airline company tries to use the same type of aircraft to lower its operating cost. For end-users, however, the real value lies in the transparency of access to the services they require at the lowest possible cost and with the desired quality. Yet, although network operators exert their efforts to converge on a common IP infrastructure, IP is not efficient from the point of view of energy cost per bit. This is why alternatives to IP are being investigated to support communications among sensors, where energy has to be used sparingly (also, Japan has started a program to replace electronic switching with photonic switching to reduce the power consumption). According to HP, by 2016, there will likely be 10 billion devices (cell phones mostly) connected via IP but by that time there will be 1000 billion entities that will be communicating, mostly sensors, and these will not be using IP. Hence a forecast of

10 billion IP users versus 990 billion non-IP users speaks loud in terms of the claims of convergence on IP.

At the enterprise level, we are likely to see a variety of infrastructures (at least one wireline and one or more wireless) within a single premise and possibly more for enterprises spread in many locations. As employees become more mobile and the enterprise boundary expands to include its customers, more and more infrastructures will need to be considered and managed. As business processes integrate several actors to deliver complex services, they will need to be able to "operate" in all these environments.

CONVERGENCE OF PROCESSES

Processes have been considered as an internal affair of an enterprise, not to be shared with outsiders. Actually, efficient processes provide a competitive advantage in terms of cost reduction and time to market, which explains the secrecy of some enterprises or the money charged by consultants to "reveal" best practices. Nevertheless, future management may be asked to support openness, at least as more enterprises participate in ecosystems, where each actor is an autonomous system interacting with the local perceived environment. For example, the growth of Mobile Virtual Network Operators will increase such a sharing of processes at some level.

In the field of entertainment, electronic gaming has exceeded, in terms of revenues, the film industry. Increasingly, the movies produced by the Majors are used to create video games to the point that movies are now made so that they can be easily reused to create videogames, thanks to the technologies of digital rendering. With this technology, actors play independently from the set and from their fellow actors and the various streams are glued digitally during postproduction processing. Actors may also be asked to produce a digitized recording of their movements and their facial expressions that can be used to create avatars that impersonate the actors in video games.

We may, if we like, take this as an example of process convergence, likewise we could say that processes leading to the production of cars are converging. Nevertheless, the business rationale and the ways of using what is becoming possible through the unification of processes are quite diverse.

CONVERGENCE OF SERVICES

Given the unavoidable proliferation of services, knowing the client is crucial. One way to do this is by monitoring usage to create individual profiles for users and keep the experience interesting and engaging. Smart communications among devices and among enterprises in different business areas but participating to the same ecosystem can enable this kind of advanced interactions. This is already happening in the service world in the Internet. A new service springs up taking advantage of the existence of other services and information provided by independent and unknown players. The new service adapts to the existing environment by taking advantage of the opportunities it offers and at the same time enriches and changes the ecosystem leading, unconsciously, to further services and changes. Thus, to increase the overall market value, we need diversification, not convergence. I will be more specific in the box on "From Platforms to Ecosystems."

CONVERGENCE OF TERMINALS

Technology supports the integration of a variety of functions on a single terminal. For example, a terminal may support data, images, and video communications in addition to voice. It may also contain a digital camera, a watch, a Global Positioning System (GPS) receiver and provide an electronic agenda, a calendar, and so on.

The variety of functions that a terminal can perform stimulates our emotions and incites us to buy. This is not convergence, however, because the various functions, whether in the way they are manufactured, marketed, or used, are quite different from each other.

Terminals, however, are a point of convergence of users' attention whenever they use them to access a service. They may induce the user's willingness to try the service. This has been shown recently by the way the iPhone have stimulated data services much more than other types of terminals, even though from a strict functionality point of view all these terminals support the same data services. The message to enterprises is: terminals have to be included in the enterprise strategy.

CONVERGENCE OF ACTORS

With decreasing growth opportunities in their home markets, network operators and service providers have several options: enter into a geographically distant market with growth potential or step into different types of markets. A third strategy is to become efficient in the home market, perhaps through mergers and acquisitions. Telefonica has pursued the first course in South American countries white BT has followed the second route, both with remarkable success.

In approaching new markets, the risks are minimized if the new and existing markets are contiguous, geographically, technologically, or culturally. Significant spare infrastructure capacity encourages businesses to enter in a contiguous market to generate revenues at a marginal cost. This explains why the market of entertainment and information services may look attractive to those that started in the telecommunications sphere and would like to benefit from the changes that go by the name of "convergence," such as IPTV and Digital Video Broadcasting-Handheld (DVB-H), or the incursion of TV cable operators in the telecommunications space, most notably in the United States. With significant investment, current technology allows multiple uses of the same infrastructure to provide a service that, only few years ago, would have necessitated a different infrastructure. However, without service innovation, new entrants are bound to create a price war and squeeze margins. There are several channels for distributing video content and these compete basically on price, with the exception of High Definition Television (HDTV), where the competition is based on the video quality. In looking at this evolution of the telecommunications and TV ecosystems, it is important to note that their business models are quite different. Although the TV world gets most of its revenues from publicity, most revenues in the telecommunications world derive from subscription (or pay as you use). This difference is the key in the examination of how much will the two ecosystems converge.

The broadening of the content offer, made possible by digital TV (or through WebTV or IPTV) is not, per se, sufficient to tip the audience one side or the other. In Italy, digital terrestrial television (DTT) is by far adopted when the reception of on-air broadcast is poor and not to get more channels. Independently of the number of channels, those with the highest audience ratings remain the same. In the future, a network operator may partner with terminals manufacturers like Sony and Nokia rather than siding with the broadcasters.

TECHNOLOGICAL EVOLUTION AND ECOSYSTEMS

That technology evolves is not news. Sometimes it evolves linearly, sometimes by leaps, and sometimes in unexpected ways. Technological evolution as a whole affects business dramatically by changing the rules of the game in a given sector. Some examples are given in the boxes "Electronic Storage Technology Evolution and Looming Disruptions," "Data-Processing Technology Evolution and Looming Disruptions," "Display Technology Evolution: Looming Disruptions," and "Data Capture Technology Evolution: Looming Disruptions."

ELECTRONIC STORAGE TECHNOLOGY EVOLUTION AND LOOMING DISRUPTIONS

Electronic storage is doubling its capacity every 12 months with compact flash and every 24 months with magnetic substrates (hard drive). Even more interesting is that the price is coming down. A 2 GB compact flash cost $3 at the end of 2007; the same price may be expected for an 8 GB in 2010. By that time $50 can buy a 32 GB. The price of storage on a magnetic substrate has gone down to $0.2 per GB at the end of 2007, it may be as low as $0.05 in 2010. By that time, a 5 TB hard drive can cost around $200 and may be found in many homes. That is enough to store all one's life experiences. Storage availability at a few cents per TB is becoming available with the polymer memory, due to appear soon on the market.

The next decade will see a further evolution of storage capacity and continuous price decrease. Already now, however, we can see some implications on networks and enterprise business.

The availability of large storage capacity locally leads to the asynchronous retrieval of data. The transfer of data on the device takes place whenever the device can connect to the network using a low cost, or free, access. Cell phones can be loaded with songs as their batteries are being recharged at the office or at home synchronizing their local storage with the one of the PC. Very little premium download over the wireless network takes place. All information is local. Alternatively, one can see the use of scan disk, compact flash, and polymer memory as a distribution chain alternative to networks.

The impact on the network side is manifold: most of traffic can be transformed from streams to bursts (thus requiring much lower cost); the availability of huge amount of information at the edge of the network stimulates transmission from the edge to the core, hence asymmetrical bandwidth is not adequate; new architectures may provide more efficiency, such as replacing the download of content from a source point with access to a multitude of content repositories situated at the edge of the network (Bit/VidTorrent).

An enterprise can load information on its products on network servers or can give away the information in storage cards associated to the product (information sticks on the product). Given the low cost of storage, one can envision an asynchronous communication with clients based on information provided to the customer at the time of sale. Notice that this information can be further updated through the network or it can be used as a background when providing updates. The crucial part here is the possibility of delivering information along with the product and to use that information on any interaction with the customer. This information can be made accessible to third parties for use in providing additional services.

Information available on million of devices can be analyzed statistically to provide even higher value. Customer care, one of the most critical issues today, can be approached in a completely novel way; it can even become a service not outsourced to another company but hijacked by another company.

DATA-PROCESSING TECHNOLOGY EVOLUTION AND LOOMING DISRUPTIONS

Data processing is progressing in line with the Moore's prediction and is likely to do so at least till 2012.

The next decade will see multicore chips; the Intel Core 80 is expected by 2010 and will provide enough processing power to render HDTV stream in real time. However important, processing speed is not all what counts; other factors will have a larger impact on the business and the overall ecosystems. The first one is the embedding in any single chip of processing, storage (with Silicon), wireless communications (with Gallium Arsenide), and optical communications (with Indium). The latter will give further steam to the deployment of fiber to the home and to intelligent appliances since these will be equipped with chips interfacing directly with the optical fiber. The embedding of wireless, however, will bring on-line any product, any object changing the way enterprises look at their customer. The point of sale will no longer be the interface with the customer. On the contrary it will be the starting point of a binding with the customer through the product. And notice that communications capability would not necessarily require a direct link between that particular product and the Internet: communications may go through another device, be it the media centre or set top box in a home (or through a cell phone).

The key issue is the potential for any product to maintain a link to the producer. Management systems will have to be overhauled for enterprises to be able to interact continuously with their customers through its products.

Another important evolution is the decrease in power consumption. Intel promised in 2005 to slash 100-fold the power consumption of its microprocessor and, as of 2009, a 64-fold decrease has been achieved, which is consistent with the announced roadmap. This achieves the possibility of higher processing capacity with reasonable power consumption, an important factor for hand-held devices. One issue is the storage of the battery and its potential as an explosive device. The other is power dissipation because if the hand-held terminal consumes 100 W, the dissipation of this power transforms it into a red hot brick. The big interest lies in the availability of chips in the submicrowave region, so that sensors could be powered using the environment as the primary power source. There are already road sensors powered by the vibrations produced by cars and trucks. New technologies, such as evanescent waves (that decay exponentially rather than sinusoidally with distance), support the wireless transfer of energy (in the microwatt area).

As a result, we are going to see an explosion in sensors in the environment and in products. This technical evolution provides the basis for smarter products aware of their context and adapting continuously to the changes in environment. This has several implications.

First, software for adaptation needs to be developed. Second, products will need to be maintained so that their capabilities could be evolved remotely. This is, of course, a new service that future enterprises will offer irrespective of the product portfolio. As service providers, their value chain will grow and become more complex to include connectivity; in turn, this will make their products accessible by other enterprises in the same ecosystem, which would require a completely different approach to enterprise management systems.

The subdivision of management systems into "operation" and "business" is no longer tenable today. In the next decade, these two layers will merge (through vertical integration) and, at the same time, will need to open beyond the enterprise boundary. This opening is not the "extranet" where there are clear boundaries and agreements among the parties involved. In the new world, those that will be able to support the growth of an ecosystem around their products (and, in an ecosystem, there is no centralized control) are those that will benefit the most from that market.

DISPLAY TECHNOLOGY EVOLUTION: LOOMING DISRUPTIONS

The conversion of bits into images is fundamental to the creation of value perceivable by humans. Screens are becoming bigger and bigger, at the same time they are increasing their resolution. We have seen the first 4 k screen in the mass market proposed by Sharp in October 2007 (4 k is the resolution used by digital cinema, 4096×2160, with a resolution that is four times the one of HDTV).

Higher resolution can be achieved with a larger screen. Any given technology has a certain limit to the dimension of the pixel; plasma display has bigger pixels than LCD. As an example, it is not possible to have a 4 k resolution on a 20″ LCD screen, since at that point the dimension of the individual pixel would need to be so small that no light is emitted. However, new technologies, such as NED, can shrink the dimension of the pixel to 1/10 of the LCD ones thus paving the way for a very high definition in a normal screen (as an example, 32 Mpixel in a 50″ screen). At this definition, our eyes are no longer able to resolve one pixel from the other and the image becomes indistinguishable from reality. Welcome to the electronic windows of the next decade. Although the presence of large high-resolution screens is relevant for a small subset of enterprises, the displays will be found in any environment and on many products. Products not having a display are likely to be in the vicinity of a display. People will have displays on them most of the time; the little screen of a cell phone comes immediately to mind. Organic Liquid Emission Display (OLED) and NED technologies will transform a small screen into a large window of information. In fact, high resolution on a small screen can be viewed with a magnifying lens to give the impression of looking at a much bigger screen. Obviously, it becomes possible to display a full page of text, something that is unfeasible today on a cell phone screen. Note, however, that from the point of view of the network, the video signal will require much more bandwidth than the one today available. This evolution in terminals (that is also constrained by the energy consumption—the more pixels the more drain on the battery) will not take place before the next decade and the network will not be prepared for such an evolution probably before the effective deployment of Long-Term Evolution (LTE), after 2012. In the first part of the next decade, the higher screen resolution will be put to use in the display of local content.

Screens enable video communications. By far, we associate video screens with TV and what we see to TV program. However, as screens become pervasive and more content can be made available through the network or accessing local storage, we will see a new variety of video. Video will be used to change the perception of an environment or an object; it will be used to communicate with the user of the product. Interactivity will become the usual way to "see" a video.

This new form of "local communication" needs to be mastered by enterprises. Additionally, enterprise will be using screens on their products to communicate with their clients.

DATA CAPTURE TECHNOLOGY EVOLUTION: LOOMING DISRUPTIONS

The next decade will see a tremendous growth of sensors in low-cost and high-cost products, like toys, appliances, cars, and homes. Sensors can fine tune the behavior of any product by adapting it to the changing conditions of the environment.

Sensors with multiple sensing capabilities will provide a more flexible detection of environmental parameters. A variety of powering mechanisms are appearing, from biological ones (sugar powered), for body implants to scavenging environment sources (like using vibration or heat gradients). A third, and fundamental one, is the capability of sensors to communicate through wireless. In parallel, we are seeing two other major areas of evolution: the capability to retrieve information from sensors (a subset of the "sensor" family is all kinds of identification devices, RFID, optical tags, two-dimensional tags, DNA tags, etc.) through cell phones and other hand-held devices; and the capability to analyze data captured by million of sensors to derive higher-level information. Temperature sensors in cell phones, as an example, may be exploited to check the temperature of a population of hundreds of million of people several times a day, thus allowing the identification of anomalies that may herald the beginning of an avian flu epidemic.

These evolutions will impact all ways of life and all production, delivery, and customer care value chains and processes. Enterprises will be able to both micromanage and macromanage their business. Additionally, products may become gateways to sensors' information and can share that information with the environment or via a mediating management system. This possibility creates new business opportunities for an enterprise; this in turn, requires the adoption of new management paradigms and an upgrade of present management systems.

SOA and SDK are the enabling components of this new production, delivery, and cooperative environment. SOA can use both a loosely coupled paradigm (Web service-based) fitting an open environment supporting a variety of loosely interconnected enterprises and a tightly coupled paradigm fitting those services having low-latency requirements. This usually requires explicit agreements and is managed within the enterprise or among enterprises through contractual obligations. The SOA approach supports the new Brokering model that is pivotal in the seeding of an ecosystem. Within the SOA paradigm, other non-SOA paradigms may also exist, such as IP Multimedia Subsystem (IMS), for specific management within the enterprise.

SOA makes possible the offering and access by third parties, enterprises thriving in that ecosystem, in particular, service enablers in the areas of identity management, localization, charging, profiling, presence, messaging, and call control.

A number of major enterprises, such as Telecom Italia, have already adopted these approaches to provide the fabric for other enterprises to develop their offers.

Enterprises, particularly small and medium ones, are exposed to these evolutions in terms of components that they use in their production process and in their products. The availability of cheaper, more powerful components allows them to perform better and improve their portfolio.

Sometimes, however, evolution is not captured internally, rather it is happening beyond the enterprise horizon and as such it seems to be alien to its business. In a world that is getting more and more connected, where distribution chains efficiency is shrinking distances and makes market spaces overlapping, this is often no longer the case. Alien evolutions may bring most threats; they can also be wonderful opportunities to enter new market spaces. For example, the iPod can be seen as a platform that has created an ecosystem exploiting iTunes with a variety of players developing adds-on both software and hardware and new communications paradigms such as the Podcast.

The concept of vertical silos and of walled gardens is disappearing, as illustrated by mash ups (Web applications that combine data from several sources to offer a single tool) as a new form of loose communications and relationships within an ecosystem. New IT architectures open up the internals of the enterprise processes and management systems to the ecosystem through Service Development Kit (SDK), Service-Oriented Architecture (SOA), Web2.0, and so on (see the box "Data Capture Technology Evolution: Looming Disruptions").

Connectivity dramatically increases interactions among systems that used to be separate. A telephone can become a TV since it has (or can have) a display. The TV can be connected to a telephone line providing telephone functions. Telephone and TV may interact. A video call received on a cell phone can be routed so that the video signal can be projected on the larger screen. The telephone terminal and the TV set are aware of each other and can communicate seamlessly to manage services. Yet, the telephone and TV do not converge but coexist in the ever more complex ecosystem of the home environment. The two "species" enter into a symbiotic relationship increasing their value in the eyes of the user.

The concept of an ecosystem in relation to living things and to natural resources is now much better understood in terms of interactions that can be modeled in mathematical terms using the small world theory (see the box "Small Worlds"). At the level of an ecosystem, we rarely speak of convergence and mostly of competition and this can lead to the disappearance of a species or to symbiosis where the interaction between two species increases their respective value (it increases the fitness within the environment and the chance to reproduce successfully). Competition and symbiosis transform the ecosystem. There are evolutions that can lead to an overall increase of value, which are able to generate diversity and to exploit resources better, and there are those that change the balance in the ecosystem by favoring a species. Competition can increase the overall value only if it encourages a more efficient management of resources through a new level of stability, not when one species overwhelms the others. In this case the overall value does not change. This reasoning applies to both bio-ecosystems and economic ecosystems.

Consider, for example, the home ecosystem. In this we can locate species such as "satellite television," "digital terrestrial television," "analogue broadcast television" as well as a video cassette rented from Blockbuster, a DVD packaged with a magazine or bought on-line. To these species, we can now add the "IPTV," thanks to technological evolution and in some cases to new regulations.

Here, as in any other ecosystem, we know that a dynamic equilibrium has to be maintained. If the IPTV, as a new species, succeeds in prevailing over the other species, we can say that the overall value of the ecosystem would not have changed much. The gain of IPTV is at the expense of some other species, but the ecosystem as a whole is not gaining any value and may actually be losing some. An IPTV that offers the same content available through satellite and the same movies available through rental stores is challenging these species but lowers the overall value. In a competitive environment, the shift of value among competing value chains converging on the same user with the same kind of product or service quickly transfers the gain to that end client. Yet, many of the current advertisements for IPTV focus on the savings offered compared with the alternative channels.

On the contrary, let us suppose, for the sake of argument, that IPTV does not compete with the other species in the ecosystem (or that this competition is limited to a sharing of the attention of viewers that may overall increase at the expense of some other ecosystems) but rather that it establishes a symbiotic relation with the other species. In this case, the ecosystem "home entertainment" increases its species variety, and therefore increases its value at the expense of other ecosystems (people enjoy more entertainment at home and go less to see movies at cinema).

What does the symbiosis of the IPTV species with other species mean? The main implication is that what it offers is in harmony with the ecosystem, without encroaching on the vital space of the other species. IPTV would then be a creator of value when it is offered (successfully) at a price that is higher than the sum of its components; otherwise, this clearly leads to a loss of overall value.

Rather than trying to compete with the other "species" in the home entertainment ecosystem, the goal of IPTV should be to provide individual access to content that is not structured as channels like in the other offers. This would establish a symbiotic relationship between the other species in the ecosystem, which are contributing content without facing the danger of being eliminated. More specifically, none of the other species would have such a specific relationship with each individual user. Moreover, flat access to content increases the potential of content distribution by the other species. In other words, the customization per user opens up a new market for products (including advertisement) that was untapped through the other value chains. This opens a totally new perspective for small and medium enterprises that cannot afford today's TV advertisement, given the niche market they serve. The set of potential advertisers is not of interest to the other players; therefore, the success of IPTV in attracting them is not a loss to these other players and the value of the whole ecosystem increases. For enterprises, this means that they would need new capabilities to manage direct advertisement channels to their potential customers.

IPTV would not result in an increase in the number of TV channels; it may even lead to the disappearance of the "channel" concept. Indeed, IPTV would be establishing a new approach to the exploitation of content, based on the single user, a billion channels if you still want to stick to that paradigm, with an electronic program guide that the user creates. It will also be associated with new navigation tools and ways of analyzing the viewer's behavior. IPTV should be seen not only as a "species" that terminates on the TV set, but also as a tool to adapt the quality and the format of the viewing experience depending on end-user's needs.

This interactivity that IPTV can provide is a strong differentiator from the other species in the ecosystem. This interactivity is not confined to the selection of content (zapping); it includes the possibility of interacting with the content and with other species in the form of mash ups, which is likely to increase the value of the whole ecosystem.

CONCLUSIONS

Ecosystems are rising in importance at the level of economic systems. An ecosystem is more than just a set defined by its individual components because they interact in a meaningful way and their interactions characterize the ecosystem as well. Each ecosystem has its own point of dynamic equilibrium that is evolving over time toward a smaller use of energy and higher organization (lower entropy). Survival in ecosystem is derived from lower energy requirements achieved through a higher level of organization.

Enterprises have to open their boundaries to interact, at a business level, with a much larger variety of players, both inside and outside the enterprise boundaries than in the past. The sales and purchasing departments would not be the main interfaces to the external world, rather, in the future, the internals of the enterprise, such as the design and manufacturing sections and other strategic areas, would be its main gateways to the outside. This is quite a revolution. Management of products and services beyond the point-of-sale becomes a crucial enabling factor in the evolution and in differentiating enterprises. This cannot be achieved unless a parallel evolution of internal enterprise processes takes place. Although the internal management can be tied to centralized architecture, thus maximizing efficiency, external management has to rely on loosely coupled interactions. While products and services can (and probably should) be produced within a centralized management architecture, they should embed autonomic systems for their postsale management. And it may pay to have those autonomic systems enabling management from third parties as well.

Enterprises have responded to the need for integration in the 1980s with centralized managing systems and uniform interfaces/applications. In the 1990s, Business Support Systems (BSSs) were the responsibility of business departments while the Operation Support Systems (OSSs) were under the responsibility of the enterprise production area. Convergence, with the resultant shrinking of the value space available to the enterprise, has put pressure on efficiency and resulted in a progressive integration of OSS and BSS within the company.

As the concept of ecosystem comes to the fore, a new approach to management is required to take into account the externalities of the whole ecosystem. However, here the main issue is no longer restricted to efficiency (which remains essential), but the capability to manage what is basically "unmanageable," since not all parts can be under the control of the enterprise. At the same time, as the enterprise feels the need to manage beyond its boundaries, so many other entities belonging to the same ecosystem feel the need to manage what is part of the enterprise.

As a guide, we can use the blueprint of the most awesome evolution, that of the species, as proposed by Darwin 150 years ago (1859) and subsequently refined by modern science. Such a model can help us ask the right questions as to the meaning of evolution in a competitive environment. It is the complexity and variety of the interplaying factors that makes it extremely difficult to think about evolution in mathematical terms; nevertheless an understanding of evolution derived from a broader view that includes the context in which evolution occurs, at the same time modifying the context, may be useful.

Convergence is now an "established" word; it may be important to look at the way the word is being used, asking what it really means and its implications on various aspects of enterprise management. However, as its usage fades away, new words will establish themselves in the language and in the imagination of people. My bet is on ecosystem. I hope this chapter will help the reader take a step in that direction.

REFERENCES

1. Darwin, C., *On the Origin of Species by Means of Natural Selection, or the Preservation of Favoured Races in the Struggle for Life*, Cosimo Classics, New York, reprint of the 1859 edition.
2. Watts, D. J., *Small Worlds: The Dynamics of Networks between Order and Randomness*, Princeton University Press, Princeton, 2003 (Princeton Studies in Complexity).
3. Saracco, R., *Technology Trajectories and Methodology*, Fistera Project, European Community, available at: http://fistera.jrc.es/pages/latest.htm

ADDITIONAL READINGS

1. Dawkins, R., *The Ancestor's Tale: A Pilgrimage to the Dawn of Evolution*, Houghton Mifflin, New York, 2004.
2. Barabasi, A.-L., *Linked: How Everything Is Connected to Everything Else and What It Means*, Perseus Books, Cambridge, MA, 2002.
3. Piancino, M. and Tadei, R., *Analisi degli investimenti ICT: un approccio di teoria dei grafi*, Politecnico di Torino, Torino, Italy, 2004.
4. Iansiti, M. and Levien, R., Strategy as ecology. *Harv. Bus. Rev.*, 69–78, 2004.
5. Moore, J. F., Predators and prey: A new ecology of competition, *Harv. Bus. Rev.*, 71(3), 75–86. 1993.
6. Moore, J. F., Business ecosystems and the view from the firm, *Antitrust Bull.*, 51(1), 31–75, 2007.
7. Nelson, R. R. and Winter, S. G., *An Evolutionary Theory of Economic Change*, Belknap Press, Cambridge, MA, 1982.

Section II

Technologies for Networking, Network Management, and Quality Assurance

3 Fundamentals of Enterprise Networks

Mehmet Ulema

CONTENTS

INTRODUCTION

Networking in general has become mission critical so much so that integrated and efficient use of all networking technologies available in an enterprise is essential in carrying out its mission. This chapter provides the state of the knowledge on various technologies and concepts used in networking, especially from an enterprise perspective. The rest of the chapter is organized into five additional sections as follows:

- Overview—This section starts with a definition of a communications network and its components, and continues with a discussion of the network models and layering concept along with standardization of the protocols and interfaces. It concludes with a brief history of communications networking.
- Types of Communications Networks—This section provides a detailed discussion of various types of communications network used in an enterprise. This includes Local Area Networks (LANs), Metropolitan Area Networks (MANs) and Wide Area Networks (WANs). The Internet and cellular networks are also discussed in this section as two popular and important examples of WANs.
- Communications Layers and Protocols—This section discusses the major protocols used in communications networks. The discussion is structured around the Internet layers, namely: application layer, transport and network layers, data link layer, and physical layer.
- Communications Network Design and Management—This section provides a brief discussion of the design and management of communication networks. The topic of network security is also discussed.
- Future Trends—Finally, the future networking technologies such as pervasive networking, wireless *ad-hoc* networks, and wireless sensor networks (WSNs) are overviewed.

The chapter is written in a tutorial style and therefore can be used by professionals responsible for designing, implementing, and running enterprise networks. The end of the chapter includes a list of sources for additional reading.

OVERVIEW

DEFINITION OF COMMUNICATIONS NETWORKS

A communication network is a collection of elements connected by using transmission facilities to provide end-users with the capability of exchanging messages and information in a variety of formats, for example, voice, data, and video. The elements in this context could be routers, switches, private branch exchanges (PBXs), and multiplexers. [Note that the element is more formally called the *Network Element* (NE), or the *node* in some books.] Transmission links may be twisted wire pairs, co-axial cables, and optical cables, radio links, satellite links, or infrared connections. In addition, communications networks include operations systems to operate, monitor, and manage the network resources. It must be noted here that there are people involved in operations of the networks and services. They make sure that the network operates efficiently and securely and that the services provided to the users meet and exceed the expected level of quality.

Networks can be categorized in many different ways. A well-known categorization scheme is based on the geographical dispersion of its components. If the elements of the network are dispersed in a small area such as a room or a building, the network is called a LAN. Typically, it comprises a group of devices such as personal computers (PCs), workstations, printers, and so on, connected in some fashion. In a campus environment, the network that ties a number of LANs together is typically called the campus network. A larger network spread out in a metropolitan area is called a MAN, which typically connects many LANs, and campus networks at different locations. Finally, we have WANs that cover much larger areas such as a country or the whole world. Although the above discussion about the types of networks is slanted for data transmission and integrated data, voice, and video transmission, similar arguments can be made for voice only networks as well. For example, telephones connected to a PBX in a campus environment can be categorized as a local area telephone network. The types of networks will be discussed in length in the following section.

LAYERING CONCEPT IN COMMUNICATION NETWORKS AND PROTOCOLS

To facilitate the exchange of information, each network element and user equipment must provide a set of comprehensive functions so that they can communicate with each other in an unambiguous way. This set of functions could be rather complex to implement and maintain in one package. Therefore, there is a need to break up this huge undertaking into smaller and more manageable components. This is called the layering model in which each layer contains a group of related communications functions. A communications protocol is then the implementation of certain set of functions in a given layer. (More formally, a protocol is an implementation of a set of unambiguous rules and procedures used in exchanging information via messages among network elements and end-user devices.) This means that there could be one or more protocols at each layer. Furthermore, there could be different implementations of a given set of functions by different vendors and industry groups. In addition to the breakup of a large function into its smaller, more manageable components, the layered approach has a number of other significant benefits. First of all, it makes it easier to develop specialized protocols suitable for a particular layer. This allows companies to excel in their own special expertise areas. Another major benefit is that the layered approach allows mixing and matching of many different protocols. However, as we will discuss later on, to take advantage of this benefit, the specifications of these protocols need to be standardized.

The two most important layering approaches are the Open Systems Interconnection (OSI) model and the Internet model. The OSI model was created by International Organization for Standardization (ISO) in the late 1970s and incorporates seven layers. On the other hand, the Internet model, originally developed under the leadership of Department of Advanced Research Project Agency of the U.S. Department of Defense, has only five layers. Because of the popularity of the Internet, that model has been widely adopted.

The layers of this model are (from top to bottom) as follows:

- Application layer: responsible for interacting with application programs in the end-user equipment.
- Transport layer: responsible for establishing end-to-end connections, delivery of messages, and for breaking messages into smaller "chunks," a.k.a., packets for efficient delivery though the physical transmission media.
- Network layer: responsible for making routing decisions for each packet, typically transmitted independently based on its destination address.
- Data link layer: responsible for providing mechanisms to separate one message from another, making sure that message is transmitted to the next node without errors, and providing mechanisms to share the transmission media, a.k.a., media access control.
- Physical layer: responsible for transmitting bits through the physical link.

With the layered approach, a message generated by an application program is first presented to an appropriate application layer protocol with a specific information about where the message will be delivered. (This is known as the destination address.) The application layer protocol asks an appropriate transport layer protocol to deliver the message to its destination. Message delivery can be either connection-oriented and connectionless.

In connection-oriented delivery, the transport layer protocol establishes a virtual circuit or connection to the destination node by first getting in touch with the destination and making sure that it is available and willing to accept this message. Also, the same protocol breaks the message into smaller segments with routing information in the packet header so that network elements know how to direct the packets to the appropriate physical facilities. Finally, this transport layer protocol then asks an appropriate network layer protocol to send each packet individually to its final

TABLE 3.1

Selected Protocols and Corresponding Communications Layers

Protocols[a]	Internet Layers
HTTP, FTP, SMTP, SNMP, IMAP, POP, X.400, MIME, DNS, DHCP	Application
UDP, TCP, RSVP, RTSP, RTP	Transport
IP, RIP, OSPF, X.25, BGP, ARP	Network
CDMA/CD, CDMA/CA, HDLC, PPP, LAPB, LAPD, Bluetooth, ATM, Frame Relay, WiMax	Data link
Manchester, Unipolar, Bipolar, NRTZ, AM, FM, PM, QAM, PAM, PCM, ADPCM, CAT5, CAT6, T1, E1, T3, E3, SONET, SDH, ISDN BRI, PRI, 802.11 series, Bluetooth, V.22, V.92, DSL, DOCSIS, DWDM, WiMax, TDMA, CDMA, W-CDMA, CDMA2000	Physical

[a] These protocols are presented later in the chapter.

destination based on a route determined by a routing protocol that runs in the background. However, in order for a packet to reach its final destination, it may go through several intermediate network elements. Once the network layer protocol determines the next network element that the packet is to be delivered to, it appends the source and destination addresses to the packet and then requires the services of an appropriate data link layer protocol to transmit the packet to the next node. The data link layer protocol, first, determines the link layer address of the next node, calculates the necessary error control bit sequences, and appends these to the packet it received from the network layer protocol. The last thing to do in this journey is to feed the final version of the packet into the physical layer protocol, which in turns deliver each bit of the packet by applying this physical layer-specific rules in transmitting the bits to the next node.

When the corresponding physical layer protocol in the next node receives the bits, it simply forwards them to the corresponding data link layer protocol for further processing. Then, the protocols at each layer in the destination node, from the bottom to the top layer, remove the headers, and present the remaining part to an upper protocol, until the application layer reconstructs the original message and present it to the application program.

Table 3.1 provides a list of popular standard protocols and their corresponding Internet layers.

STANDARD ORGANIZATIONS

As mentioned briefly above, the layering approach in developing protocols has enormous benefits, but at the same time, the approach creates a problem in that it places a large burden on the industry to standardize these protocols so that different products built by different companies for different platforms (hardware, operating systems, etc.) work properly with each other. The standardization of the protocols and interfaces is especially important for integrated enterprise networking to take advantage of the competitive nature of the business and to drive down the capital and operational expenses. Formal standards are typically developed by industry consortia, professional associations, and government organizations. The following is a list of some of the major standards organizations that play significant roles in the standardization of communications protocols and interfaces:

- ISO—responsible for a wide range of commercial and industrial standards including many information and communication technology-related protocols.
- ITU-T—International Telecommunication Union—Telecommunication Standardisation Sector, formerly known as CCITT International Telegraph and Telephone Consultative Committee; specifies standards for all aspects of worldwide telecommunications.
- ITU-R—ITU Radio Communication Sector (formerly known as CCIR); specifies standards for radio communications systems; responsible for managing the international radio-frequency spectrum.
- IEEE—Institute of Electrical and Electronic Engineers; specifies standards in power and energy, biomedical and healthcare, information technology (IT), telecommunications, transportation, nanotechnology, information assurance, and many more. IEEE 802 project is well known for its Ethernet and Wireless Fidelity (Wi-Fi) standards.
- IETF—Internet Engineering Task Force; specifies standards for the Transmission Control Protocol (TCP)/Internet Protocol (IP) and IP suite.
- 3GPP—Third Generation Partnership Project; specifies standards for a 3G technology based on GSM commonly known as Wideband Code Division Multiple Access (W-CDMA).
- 3GPP2—Third Generation Partnership Project 2; specifies standards for a 3G technology based on IS-95 (CDMA), commonly known as CDMA 2000.
- CableLabs—Cable Television Laboratories; specifies standards for cable and telecommunications networks. Data Over Cable Service Interface Specifications (DOCSIS) is a well-known standard from CableLabs.
- DMTF—Distributed Management Task Force; specifies standards for systems management of IT environments in enterprises.
- OMA—Open Mobile Alliance; specifies standards for network independent application protocols (e.g., instant messaging) to provide interoperable services across operators and mobile terminals.
- TIA—Telecommunications Industry Association; specifies North-American industry standards for a wide variety of telecommunications products including user premises equipment and mobile communications systems such as many 2G cellular network protocols.
- TM Forum; specifies standards on end-to-end service management for Web, telecom, and media networks.
- W3C—World Wide Web Consortium; specifies standards like HyperText Markup Language (HTML) and Extensible Markup Language (XML) for the World Wide Web (WWW or W3).

The above list is by no means complete. Currently there are many other standards fora and organizations working on various aspects of the communications networks.

BRIEF HISTORY OF COMMUNICATION NETWORKS

The evolution of communications networking is tied to the invention of telegraph, telephony, radio, and computers. Initially, the telephone network was used to connect computers to each other and the users to computers via the so-called modems. These low speed (low data rate) telephone lines became quickly insufficient. The next step in the evolution was to use dedicated transmission lines. Furthermore, the use of intermediate components, as in telephone exchanges, were developed along with a new transmission technology called "packet switching" to segment long messages and files into small pieces, called packets, and transmit them or route them to their destinations via switches/routers. ARPANET in the early 1970s and its successor the Internet in the 1980s were the result of these types of efforts. With the PC revolution in the 1980s, it became apparent that PCs need to be connected in some fashion to facilitate PC-to-PC communications, and, as a consequence, LANs and associated equipments, such as bridges and routers, were developed. Also, in the early 1970s, cellular telephony started to provide mainly wireless voice communication. The so-called, anytime, anywhere communication was possible with the widespread acceptance of this technology, which went through several iterations; from analog technology to successive generations of digital technology, for example, 2G and 3G, which also included data and video communications eventually.

TYPES OF COMMUNICATION NETWORKS

In the previous section, networks were discussed based on the geographical dispersion of its components. In this section, we will discuss LANs, MANs, and WANs in more detail. We will then present two special types of WANs, namely the cellular networks and the Internet.

LOCAL AREA NETWORKS

A LAN is used to connect a number of computers and other devices in a small, local, area such as a room, a floor, or a building. A computer in a LAN could be a server, that is, it is permanently assigned a specific task (Web server, e-mail server, file server, or print server) or a client proper, which shares the files, printers, and servers with other client computers in the same LAN. Typically a hub or a switch is used to connect all the servers and clients with network cables. Each node in the LAN must have a Network Interface Card (NIC), which provides the physical layer and data link layer functions. Figure 3.1 shows a typical LAN and its primary components.

Each LAN also has a Network Operating System (NOS), which is distributed among the clients and servers. The NOS in a server handles all network functions, performs data link, network, and application layer functions, and acts as the application software by executing and responding to the requests sent to them by clients. MS Windows Server and Linux Server are two popular examples of a NOS for servers.

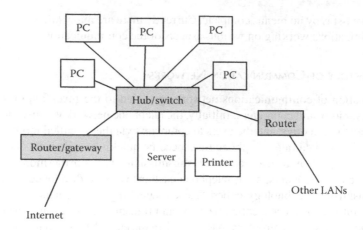

FIGURE 3.1   A LAN and its components.

The NOS in a client computer provides data link and network layer functions and interacts with the application software and the computer's own operating system. The client portion of the NOS software is typically included in the OS software such as Microsoft Windows, Vista, and Linux.

Ethernet, specified in the IEEE 802.3 family of standards, is the most commonly used LAN technology today. There are two different implementation of Ethernet: traditional (or shared) and switched. The shared Ethernet architecture has a bus topology where all messages from any computer flow onto the central cable (bus) and any computer and device connected to this bus receives messages from all other computers, whether the message is intended for it or not. When a frame is received by a computer, the first task is to read the frame's destination address to see if the message is meant for it or not. As discussed in later sections, Ethernet uses a technique, called Carrier Sense Multiple Access with Collision Detection (CSMA/CD), to regulate the sharing of the medium when multiple nodes try to transmit simultaneously. A hub, basically a dumb box containing the bus, is used to connect the computers on the shared Ethernet. Computers are linked into this central hub. If there are more devices to connect than the number of ports available on a hub, then another hub can be connected to the first one in a cascade fashion to double-up capacity.

The *switched Ethernet* implementation uses a *switch*, instead of a hub. A switch is designed to support a small number of computers (16–24) in one LAN. Each computer is connected to the switch via a point-to-point circuit. A switch reads the destination address of the incoming Layer 2 message (a.k.a., frame) and only sends it to the corresponding port (a hub broadcasts frames to all ports). To do this forwarding, the switch relies on a Forwarding Table, which has two columns: a column that contains the Layer 2 [also called Media Access Control (MAC)] addresses and another column containing the corresponding port numbers. The Forwarding Table is populated gradually. The switch starts with an empty Forwarding Table, working like a hub, and it gradually fills it by learning about the nodes that connect to it as follows: when the switch receives a frame from a port, it reads the source MAC address of the frame. If the MAC address is not already in the table, the switch records it in a row that corresponds to the port number on the Forwarding Table. Then, the switch reads the destination MAC address of this frame and checks whether the table already contains it. If the destination MAC address is in the table, the switch determines the corresponding port number from the table and forwards the frame to the computer that is connected to this port. If, however, the table does not include this MAC address, then the switch broadcasts this frame to all ports and waits for the destination computer to respond with an acknowledgment frame. Once the switch receives the response, it enters the source MAC address of this response frame in an appropriate row (i.e., the row that corresponds to the port where the frame came from). By continuing these steps, the switch fills all the entries in the table gradually in a relatively short time. The switched Ethernet is much faster and more reliable than the traditional Ethernet.

The cables connecting various components of a LAN are typically unshielded twisted pair wires categorized based on their quality. For example, Category 3 (Cat 3) and Cat 5 cables are suitable for low-speed Ethernet at 10–100 Mbps (Megabits per second) transmission rates. Faster Ethernets may require the use of fiber optic cables carrying Gbps (Gigabits per second) data rates. By convention, 10Base-T format refers to the Ethernet at 10 Mbps data rate with twisted pair cables. The word "Base" indicate that the transmission is a "base band" in a single channel covering the entire spectrum. A popular Ethernet technology currently commonly used is 100Base-T, which provides 100 Mbps data rate. 1000Base-T (or 1GBase-T) is also popular. More advanced Ethernet technologies typically use fiber optic cables and are referred to as Gigabit Ethernets with *GbE* designation. See the last section of this chapter for more details on the GbE-related trends.

In putting together a LAN, perhaps the most important aspect to watch for is the effective data rate, which is the maximum speed in bits that the hardware layers (i.e., physical and data link layers) can provide. The effective data rate of a LAN has three major components: (i) the nominal data rate that depends on the physical layer properties. For example, the nominal rate for a 100Base-T Ethernet is 10 Mbps; (ii) the error rate of the circuit, which is a critical factor in determining retransmissions, therefore reducing the transmission efficiency; and (iii) the efficiency of data link layer protocol. This is basically the percentage of transmission bandwidth that transports user data, which depends on the number of overhead bits. (The error rate and the protocol efficiency topics will be discussed later in the protocol section of the chapter.) The packet size, which plays an important role in these calculations, depends on the type of the traffic on the LAN. A typical LAN traffic includes a number of small Web application specific (i.e., HyperText Transfer Protocol, HTTP) or the e-mail application-specific (i.e., SMTP, or Simple Mail Transfer Protocol) messages (a.k.a., packets) followed by a large number of larger packets. This results in about 97% efficiency for the Ethernet frames with 33 bytes overhead. To calculate the effective data rate for a whole LAN, we need to consider the efficiency of the media access control. The Ethernet's media access mechanism works well in low-traffic LANs, resulting typically in a 50% capacity utilization. With these numbers, the total effective data rate for a 100Base-T can be determined as follows: 50% capacity × 97% efficiency × 100 Mbps rate = 485 Mbps (shared by all computers on the LAN). With 10 computers in the LAN, each computer's effective data rate would be

485/10 = 48.5 Mbps. The effective rates for switched Ethernets are much higher due to the significant improvements (up to 95%) in capacity utilization since there is no sharing in this architecture. Keep in mind that the switched Ethernet is not affected by the traffic due to the availability of dedicated circuits for each computer.

Once the LAN is set up and operational, there needs to be continuous monitoring and, if necessary, to make changes to improve performance. In this regard, the throughput is an indicator of the performance. The name of the game in this performance improvement business is to identify and eliminate the bottlenecks, which are the components that can not handle all of the incoming traffic. The identification of network bottlenecks is not that difficult. There are mainly two culprits: a server or a circuit. A key indicator to determine whether the server is a bottleneck is the utilization of the server. If a server is overutilized, say over 70%, then it is most likely that this server is the bottleneck. To eliminate this bottleneck situation, the performance of the server needs to be improved by upgrading the hardware (CPU, memory, storage, etc.), software (operating system, applications, etc.), or both. If the server utilization is low, then the bottleneck is the circuit. Improving the circuit capacity, say from 100Base-T to 1000Base-T may do the trick. Keep in mind that there may be other techniques to improve the performance. For example, dividing a LAN into two or more segments, reducing the network demand by scheduling certain applications during off hours, will definitely help to improve the performance of a LAN.

WIRELESS LANs

When the computers on a LAN are connected via unguided media, eliminating the cables, the resulting LAN is called a wireless LAN (wLAN). Even though there are wLAN technologies based on infrared transmission, in this section we focus on the LAN technologies based on the radio transmission, simply because these are the most commonly used wLAN systems today. The IEEE 802.11 series of standards, also referred to as the Wi-Fi technology, dominate the wLAN industry today. Starting with the earliest version 802.11b, these IEEE standards evolved into 802.11a, then 802.11g, and now into the latest 802.11n specifications. (Actually, 802.11a was started long before 802.11b, but was completed after 802.11b became available.) Each new version mainly improved the data rate and security aspects. We should also mention here that there is another wLAN technology called IEEE 802.15 (or commonly called Bluetooth) with limited range and data rates. Bluetooth is sometimes called a Personal Area Network (PAN) technology.

IEEE 802.11b uses many Ethernet technologies and was designed to connect easily to Ethernet. The physical layer specifications are based on the spread spectrum technology where the energy carrying the signal is spread over a rather large band of the frequency spectrum. There are two versions: Direct Sequence Spread Spectrum (DSSS) where each channel and message are distinguished by unique codes, and Frequency Hopping Spread Spectrum (FHSS) where each message is transmitted on a different frequency band (within the allocated pool of bands) that changes dynamically. A wLAN architecture has a simple star topology where the computers

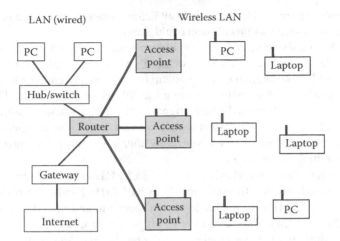

FIGURE 3.2   Major components of a wLAN.

equipped with wireless NICs are connected through an access point (AP). Figure 3.2 depicts the major components of a wLAN.

The AP coordinates the communications among the computers. (Without going further, we should mention that this architecture with an AP is referred to as the *infrastructure mode*. wLAN standards also include an ad-hoc mode where the devices can communicate with each other directly without the help of an AP in the middle.)

All devices using an AP must use the same channel (there are three channels in 802.11b). Several APs may be connected via an Ethernet LAN and users can roam from one AP to another. Usually a set of APs are installed to provide geographical coverage and meet traffic needs. This way NICs can select a less busy channel if its current channel becomes busy because of too many users riding on it. Each NIC, including the ones in the AP, uses antennas to transmit and receive the signals over the air. Omni directional antennas broadcast the signal in all directions, whereas directional antennas project signal only in one direction, providing stronger signals and therefore extending ranges.

IEEE 802.11b uses a scheme to avoid collisions for accessing the medium. This scheme is called CSMA/CA. The letters CA refers to the Collision Avoidance (CA) feature. As we will discuss later in the protocol section, the Ethernet scheme had CD designation referring to Collision Detection. The philosophy in wLANs is to try to avoid collisions as much as possible. To implement this, wLAN uses two complementary MAC methods together: the mandatory Distributed Coordination Function (DCF), a.k.a., Physical Carrier Sense Method and the optional Point Coordination Function (PCF), a.k.a., Virtual Carrier Sense Method.

In DCF, when a node wants to send a message, it first listens to the medium to make sure that an existing transmitting node has finished, then it waits for a period of time before transmission. To transmit, the node sends each frame by using the stop-and-wait Automatic Repeat Request (ARQ), to be discussed later. The ACK/ NAK (Acknowledgment/Negative Acknowledgment) frames are sent a short time after a frame is received. However, the wait before message frames are sent is some-what longer to ensure that no collision could occur.

The PCF actually solves the famous hidden node problem in wireless networks, where two devices may not be able to detect each other's signals, even though both can hear the AP. The solution to this problem is a simple convention where the sending device needs to get a permission from the AP before it transmits. The sending device first sends a Request-To-Send signal to the AP, requesting allocation of a channel in a time period. The AP responds with a Clear-To-Send signal containing the duration that the channel is reserved. Only after it gets this permission, the device starts transmitting its messages.

In the United States, for wLANs, a total of 83.5 MHz between 2.4000 and 2.4835 GHz is allocated for data transmission. This 83.5 MHz bandwidth is divided into three channels, 22 MHz each. Due to spread spectrum and modulation techniques used, the data capacity of the circuit is 11 Mbps. We should keep in mind that this is the upper limit and it drops quickly to lower rates as the device moves away from the AP.

Although the work on the IEEE 802.11a specifications was started much before 802.11b, it was completed after 802.11b was standardized and commercially avail-able. 802.11a operates in the so-called Unlicensed National Informational Infrastruc-ture band, in the 5 GHz frequency range with a total bandwidth of 300 MHz. IEEE 802.11a provides 4–12 channels (20 MHz each) depending on the configuration. Due to the larger bandwidth and more advanced modulation techniques, 802.11a can offer faster data rates, up to 54 Mbps (6, 9, 12, 18, 24, 36, 48, and 54 Mbps depending on the signal strength). However, the range of the 802.11a AP is considerably limited, about 50 m (150 ft). Therefore, it takes more 802.11a APs to cover the same area that can be covered with a single 802.11b AP. Nevertheless, a side benefit of more APs in the same area is that the capacity of the LAN is increased and 802.11a and 802.11b can support more users with higher data rates. Although the packet formats are very similar, the physical layer schemes and frequency bands are quite different. Therefore, 802.11a and 802.11b are not compatible. To solve this interoperability problem, the IEEE created a new set of specification, IEEE 802.11g, which combines the advan-tages of 802.11a and 802.11b. IEEE 802.11g offers data rates up to 54 Mbps in a 2.4-GHz band (as in 802.11b) with longer ranges. 802.11g is backward compatible with 802.11b. This means that 802.11b devices can interoperate with 802.11g APs. We should note here that when an 802.11g AP detects an 802.11b device, all 802.11g devices in the same wLAN downgrades to the 802.11b rates. 802.11g provides three to six channels depending on the configuration. The range is somewhat less than 802.11b. The rate of 54 Mbps can be obtained within 50 m range. IEEE 802.11g has almost the same media access control and error control protocols as 802.11b. Both have a very similar packet layout. For data transmission, 802.11g employs a more advanced modulation technique called Orthogonal Frequency Division Multiplexing (OFDM), which works by splitting the available frequency band into narrower chan-nels, and transmitting simultaneously at different frequencies.

As of this writing, a proposed new version, IEEE 802.11n has been under stan-dardization for the past several years. This new version will add many additional features including Multiple Input Multiple Output (MIMO) to allow the use of multiple antennas simultaneously for both transmission and reception, and to provide more efficient and more reliable communications at even higher data rates (up to 300 Mbps).

IEEE 802.15 (Bluetooth) provides a so-called wireless PAN by connecting a number of devices around a person. These devices may include personnal digital assistants (PDAs), laptops, cellular phones, headphones, mouse, keyboard, and so on. Bluetooth is designed for short range communications (1–100 m) based on low-cost tiny transceivers. A Bluetooth network, referred to as a *piconet*, consists of up to eight simultaneously communicating devices (a piconet can have up to 125 Bluetooth-enabled devices, only eight can be active at the same time). The devices in a piconet can dynamically and in an *ad hoc* fashion form a network by first choosing a *master* device that can control other devices, called *slaves*. The master acts like an AP by selecting frequencies to be used and controlling the access to these frequencies by the slaves. All devices in a piconet share the same frequency range. Bluetooth uses FHSS for media access control. The available frequency range (2.4000–2.4835 MHz) is divided into 79 separate 1-MHz channels. Each packet uses a different channel to transmit. Furthermore, the channel assignment to the packets are highly dynamic (1600 channel changes per second) and is based on a sequence established together by the slave and the master prior to the data transfers. Bluetooth version 1.2 provides a data rate of 1 Mbps, while Bluetooth version 2.0 can provide up to 3 Mbps. Table 3.2 provides a summary of the wLAN technologies discussed above.

It is possible to establish a much larger network by interconnecting many piconets together. The resulting network is called a *scatternet*. Figure 3.3 shows a picture of two piconets forming a scatternet.

The data rate calculations in wLANs are similar to those discussed under the wired LANs section. However, in wLANs, transmission errors play a greater role in the data rate calculations due to the potential interference on the air. Again, as discussed earlier, the errors cause retransmissions, which, in turn, lower the data rates. In terms of the data link protocol efficiency, 802.11b results in about 85% average efficiency, whereas IEEE 802.11a and 802.11g would give us about 75% average efficiency. (These numbers are based on the assumption that a typical 802.11 overhead is about 51 bytes and the average packet length is a mix of short and full length packets.) In determining the MAC efficiency in wLANs, one must also consider the PCF, which introduces more delays. As a result, MAC in wLANs operates with about

TABLE 3.2
wLAN Technologies Standardized by the IEEE

	802.11a	802.11b	802.11g	802.11n	Bluetooth
Maximum data rate (Mbps)	54	11	54	200+	3
Frequency (GHz)	5	2.4	2.4	2.4/5	2.45
Modulation	OFDM	DSSS	OFDM	MIMO	FHSS
Range (ft)	~100	~300	~120	~750	~30

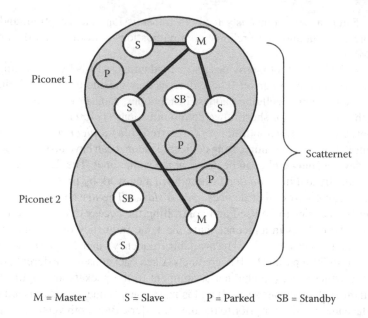

M = Master   S = Slave   P = Parked   SB = Standby

FIGURE 3.3   A Bluetooth scatternet consisting of two piconets.

up to 85–90% of capacity. Based on the above assumptions, the effective data rate for a network based on the 802.11b NICs and APs can be calculated as: 85% efficiency × 85% capacity × 11 Mbps = 9.6 Mbps. Of course this total effective capacity of 9.6 Mbps need to be shared by the number of devices in the network. With 10 devices, each device would get 9.6 Mbps/10 devices = 960 Kbps. For 802.11a and 802.11g, we would get about 34.4 Mbps data rate total.

Putting together, a wLAN requires careful determination of the number of the APS in the network and their placement. The placement of the APs affects the coverage of the area, and the number of APs is important to handle the traffic in the network. A site survey to determine the potential locations of the APs should also include the measurement of potential interference from external sources. Trial and error may be necessary for making sure that the signal strength is acceptable in all areas. Different types of antennas may be used: to cover certain spots, *directional* antennas, instead of *Omni* directional antennas, may be used. About 15% overlap in coverage between APs should be engineered to provide smooth and transparent roaming.

Security is a great concern in wLANS, since the messages are transmitted on the air and can be easily captured and jeopardized. There are a number of measures that wLANs provide to ease this concern. For example, there is a Service Set Identifier, which is required by all computers to include it in every packet they transmit. However, this is transmitted as plain text and can easily be intercepted and captured. Another measure that wLANs use is called the Wired Equivalent Privacy (WEP), which requires users to configure a key manually into the devices (to NIC and AP). In this case, all messages will be encrypted by using this WEP key, which could be between 40 and 128 bits (the longer the key, the harder to break if the algorithm is the same). The Extensible Authentication Protocol is an advanced security feature that requires a login and a password to a server. After the login, the server dynamically creates a different WEP key for each packet transmitted. Wi-Fi Alliance, an industry group providing certification for the 802.11-based equipment, developed a scheme called Wi-Fi Protected Access (WPA) used in the certification process. To take advantage of this enhanced security scheme, a new standard called IEEE 802.11i was designed to provide secured communication of wLANs in a more comprehensive way. IEEE 802.11i is based on the WPA and enhances the WEP in the areas of encryption, authentication, and key management.

CAMPUS NETWORKS

Typically bridges, routers, switches, and gateways are used for connecting LANs together via higher speed circuits, more commonly fiber optical cables. A bridge is a data link layer device connecting similar types of LANs (i.e., the same data link layer protocol). Bridges have lost their place to Layer 2 (data link layer) switches as the latter became cheaper and more powerful. A router operates at the network layer and connects LANs with different data link layer protocols, but with the same network layer protocol. A router processes network layer messages and prepares new data link layer messages for outgoing packets. When a router receives a packet, it reads the destination address of the network layer, chooses the "best" route for the packet (via routing tables), and then sends it out to the next node on the selected route. Gateways also operate at the network layer and connect LANs with different data link layer and different network layer protocols. Figure 3.4 shows a campus network where LANs in different buildings are connected to each other via routers. This way each LAN has its own subnet designation.

The architecture of Figure 3.4 is easier to manage but it tends to impose more delays than bridging due to the Layer 3 processing. An improvement could be to

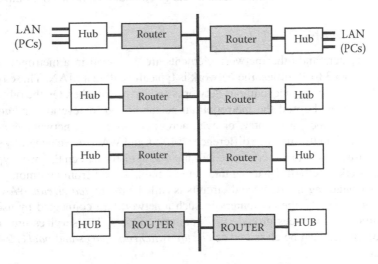

FIGURE 3.4   A campus network with routers connecting its LANs.

connect each hub of the LANs to a switch via a separate circuit (and get rid of all the routers). In this improved configuration, there will be more cables, but less devices to worry about and due to the switched operation, the performance will improve significantly. The down side is that, the use of a single central switch introduces a reliability problem: when the switch fails, the whole network goes down. We could improve the configuration even further by using a higher performance and a more intelligent switch. In this configuration, we can connect all the computers directly to the switch (even eliminating the hubs). This new configuration allows us to create virtual LANs by creating virtual LAN segments via software and assigning computers to them. This way, we can assign any computer to any segment regardless of the location of the computer. This configuration provides a more flexible network management in terms of creating project groups and assigning resources to them. Multiswitch virtual LAN configurations are also possible by using several switches. We should note here that this is a more complex and costly network configuration and it is typically used for larger campus networks.

The LANs and campus networks discussed above are mostly data centric. With additional software and/or hardware changes in the end-user equipment and in the network elements, these networks can transmit voice and video as well. Typically, Voice over IP (VoIP) and multimedia-specific protocols and features that rely on a common network layer protocol, IP, are used to accomplish this. Separately, a PBX (a.k.a., private automatic branch exchange, PABX) can be used to connect all telephones in an enterprise in a campus. With one or more PBXs, a voice only campus network can be deployed. Of course, the PBXs need to be connected via trunk lines to a carrier network in turn to receive and make out-of-campus calls.

With a traditional PBX here, an enterprise need to maintain separate voice and data networks resulting in higher operations and capital expenses for the enterprise. A latest trend in the PBX development is the IP PBXs, which can switch calls between VoIP on local lines. This makes it possible to have a single line to each user for data access, as well as VoIP communications and traditional telephone communications.

MANs AND WANs

If the computers and other network elements are dispersed in a metropolitan area spanning from 3 to 30 miles, the network is typically called a MAN. These types of networks typically connect campus networks and LANs together. On the other hand, if the area spans beyond the metropolitan neighborhood to several hundred miles covering a province, a country, or even across countries, the network is called a WAN. Other than the distance differences, MANs and WANs have generally similar characteristics, so in this section, we will not distinguish between the two. Typically, these networks are built by using dedicated circuits leased from common carriers. A WAN containing the dedicated circuits is called a *dedicated circuit WAN*. However, more typically, the computers in such a network are connected by using the communications services provided by common carriers. The services provided by common carriers can be classified as *circuit-switched services* and *packet-switched services*.

In a *dedicated circuit WAN*, the circuits connecting the locations of an organization are leased from common carriers, which charge a monthly flat fee that depends on the capacity and length of the circuit. The line is dedicated to the customer with the rights of unlimited use of the circuit. The T-Carrier services are the most commonly used dedicated digital circuits in North America. (In Europe and elsewhere, a similar system called E-Carrier service are used.) Commonly used T1 circuits provide 1.544 Mbps data rate (equivalent of 24 voice channels, 64 Kbps data rate). T3 circuits offer 44.376 Mbps data rate (28 T1 lines). For higher data rates, common carriers offer dedicated circuits based on the Synchronous Optical Network (SONET) technology, which is an ANSI standard in the United Sates for optical fiber transmission in Gbps range [similar to ITU-T-based, Synchronous Digital Hierarchy (SDH)]. Hierarchy of data rates in SONET starts with OC-1 (optical carrier level 1) at 51.84 Mbps. Each succeeding SONET hierarchy rate is defined as a multiple of OC-1. For example, OC-3's data rate is 155.52 Mbps, and OC-12's data rate is 622.08 Mbps. Larger networks handling heavy traffic may prefer to use OC-192 providing almost 10 Gbps data rate. There are special equipments, such as Channel Service Unit and Data Service Unit, which need to be installed at the end of each dedicated circuit. Then the customer uses routers and switches to connect its locations together to form a network owned and maintained by the organization itself.

Network designers must determine the best architecture that fits the application at hand, juggling among various factors such as delay, throughput, reliability, and the cost. There are a number of different ways of connecting the locations via dedicated lines. The ring, star, and mesh topologies are the basic dedicated circuit architectures that are used more commonly. Figure 3.5 shows these there basic topologies.

The ring and star architectures are most cost-effective since they result in less dedicated circuits to lease, whereas the mesh architecture is more costly since it requires many more circuits. As for the performance (throughput, delay), the mesh is the best, then the star, and the ring is the worst. From the reliability point of view, again the mesh architecture is the best, and the ring architecture is the worst since the network relies on a central location. To bring the down the cost of a mesh

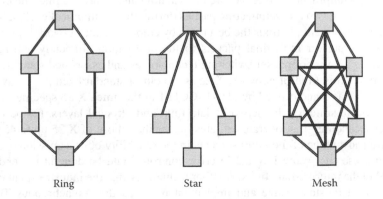

Ring   Star   Mesh

FIGURE 3.5 Three basic architectures for a network of dedicated circuits.

architecture, a partial mesh architecture where only certain pair of nodes are connected directly can be used. In a partial mesh architecture, any node is reachable from any other node (i.e., the nodes that are not directly connected communicate with each other through other nodes).

Enterprises that cannot afford to put together their own dedicated circuit-based network rely on switched services provided by the common carriers. In a switched WAN, end-user equipment are connected via temporary, not dedicated, connections for the duration of the call, or session. Once the session is finished, the connection is no longer available for this end-user and the same connection may be offered to another user. The connection services are offered by common carriers. As discussed earlier, two types of switched services are common: circuit-switched services and packet switched services.

The *circuit-switched services* approach is an old way and perhaps the simplest way to have a WAN. Common carriers offer two types of circuit-switched services: Plain Old Telephone Service (POTS) and Integrated Services Digital Network (ISDN). In POTS, end-user equipments are connected to each other via telephone lines. A computer by using a modem in a location dials the number assigned to a remote computer and the telephone network provides a temporary circuit for this communication. When the session is completed, the circuit is disconnected, and may be allocated to another session. (The circuit is said to be switched to another conversation, or to another session.) The ISDN-based circuit-switched services gives the capability of combined transmission of voice, video, and data over the same digital circuit. ISDN services include the Basic Rate Interface (BRI), which provides 144 Kbps data rate and the Primary Rate Interface (PRI) with 1.5 Mbps data rate. ISDN services require a special modem connected to the end-user equipment. With a wider availability of packet-switched services such as the Internet, circuit-switched services are no longer attractive in WAN applications.

An enterprise wishing to use a *packet-switched service* first leases a short connection from each of its locations to the nearest Point of Presence (POP) of the service provider. An end-user equipment in the enterprise is required to break its message to be transmitted into smaller segments, called packets and attach the address of the destination equipment. Unlike the circuit switching and/or private lines, no circuit is dedicated to the two communicating parties during the communication. The service provider network simply finds the best route by employing the network layer routing protocols to deliver individual packets to the destination efficiently and reliably. There are a number of packet-switching technologies and associated standards used in deploying this kind of network. X.25 is the oldest standardized packet-switched protocol; it was standardized by ITU-T (CCITT at the time). X.25 specifies a three-layer protocol suite for the network, data link, and physical layers. Frame relay is another technology that operates at rates higher than those of X.25 up to 45 Mbps, by taking advantage of the improvements in the reliability of transmission over fiber optic lines so that some Layer 2 in error controls could be done at the endpoints instead of the intermediate links. Another technology that the industry spent considerably effort to standardize and implement is called the Asynchronous Transfer Mode (ATM). A major distinguishing characteristics of the ATM technology is the use of fixed-length packets, 53 byte "cells" instead of variable packet length approach of all other protocols, including the Internet. Small fixed-length cells were believed to facilitate the adoption of ATM for realtime voice transmissions, by avoiding the need for echo cancellers at the access circuits, thereby reducing the cost. The ATM also provides capabilities to enable setting of precise priorities among different types of transmissions (i.e., voice, video, and e-mail). ATM services can be provided at the same rates as SONET: 51.8, 466.5, 622.08 Mbps. With the popularity of the Internet, the ATM-based packet-switched services never became popular because of the large overhead in transmission. The technology is now mainly used in the core infrastructure of major network providers. As alluded to in the above statement, the Internet is the most commonly used packet technology today. Later in this section, the Internet will be discussed in detail.

There are also some packet-switched service offerings based on the *Ethernet/IP Packet Network* technologies, which are based on the Gigabit Ethernet fiber optic networks (bypassing common carrier network). With these services, there is no need to translate LAN protocol (Ethernet/IP) to the protocol used in MAN/WAN services. As the number of services requiring packetized 10-Gbps pipes increases (e.g., video distribution), it is anticipated that within the coming few years there will be a need for a comprehensive network solution to aggregate traffic at rates of $N \times 10$ Gbps. The current consensus is to standardize two such rates: $N = 4$ and $N = 10$. As discussed before, the standardization activities for carrier class Ethernet interfaces are taking place mostly in the ITU-T study group 15. [Remember that the IEEE 802.3 Higher Speed Study Group (HSSG) is focusing on campus and local area specific concerns.] The scope of activities in the ITU-T corresponds unequivocally to a platform innovation: definition of a new transport container for optical transport units (OTU)/optical data units (ODU)—denoted as OTU4/ODU4—for 100-Gbps Ethernet, definition of the characteristics of the interface (e.g., the forward error control scheme), and so on. The two alternative trajectories for the next generation Ethernet networks are summarized in Table 3.3.

In the following subsections, we discuss in more detail two popular examples of a WAN: the Internet and wireless mobile networks.

TABLE 3.3
Alternative Standardization Trajectories for the New Generation of Ethernet Networks

	ITU-T SG 15	IEEE 802.3
Intended rate (Gbps)	100	40/100
Value chain	Carrier networks (e.g., long distances; high reliability)	Server interconnects (e.g., short distances)
Technologies to be standardized	New container for OTU/ODU, new modulation schemes, optical interfaces, network interface controllers, etc.	Extending existing technologies
Characteristics of innovation	Platform	Incremental

The Internet

The Internet is a network of networks; an interconnection of thousands of LANs, campus networks, MANs, and WANs together to form a worldwide area network. Later in the protocol sections of the chapter, we will discuss a number of basic concepts (packet switching, IP/TCP protocols, routing, and addressing, etc.) that are used in the Internet. Here, we discuss its unique architecture, its access technologies, and future of the Internet.

To constitute the Internet, thousands of networks are connected together based on a hierarchical structure. Individual private networks and computers belonging to individual organizations and people are connected to an Internet Service Provider (ISP), and many ISPs are connected to each other via bilateral agreements and connections. Some ISPs are small and local or regional and some are larger and nationwide. National ISPs provide services to their individual customers and sell access to regional ISPs and local ISPs. Regional ISPs, connected with National ISPs, provide services to their customers and sell access to local ISPs. Finally, local ISPs sell access to individual organizations or residential customers. More formally, ISPs are classified into three tiers: Tier 1 ISPs, the largest ones; Tier 2 ISPs, the ones that buy connectivity from Tier 1 ISPs; and Tier 3 ISPs, which buy connectivity from Tier-2 ISPs. Figure 3.6 shows the basic hierarchical architecture of the Internet today. There is a payment-compensation scheme established by the ISPs. ISPs at the same level usually do not charge each other for exchanging messages. This is called *peering.* Higher-level ISPs charge lower-level ones: Tier 1 ISPs charge regional Tier 2 ISPs, which in turn charge Tier 2 ISPs. Of course, Local ISPs charge individual residential and corporate customers for access. Based on this classification, a Tier 1 ISP can reach every other network on the Internet without purchasing connection from any other network. However, a Tier 2 network may do peering with some other networks, but still must purchase connection from a Tier 1 ISP to reach

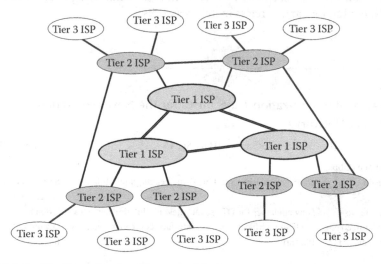

FIGURE 3.6   The hierarchical architecture of the Internet.

some points of the Internet. A Tier 3 ISP must purchase connections from other ISPs to reach the Internet.

As one can observe, there is no one single company in charge of the Internet. However, the Internet Society (ISOC), an open membership professional society with over 175 organizational and 8000 individual members in over 100 countries, provides a platform to develop various industry standards and agreements that are used in the Internet. Among other things such as public policy and education, ISOC is also involved in standards development through its IETF to develop Request For Comments (Internet standards); Internet Engineering Steering Group to manage the standard process; Internet Architecture Board to provide strategic architectural oversight; and Internet Research Task Force to focus on long-term research issues involving the future of the Internet.

To access the Internet, telephone lines via dial-up modems and T1/T3 lines were commonly used until recently. However, today, the so-called broadband access technologies, which include cable modems and Digital Subscriber Line (DSL) modems that provide higher data rates in the Mbps range, are more common. DSL is a technology designed to provide high-speed data transmission over traditional telephone lines. A DSL modem needs to be connected at the customer site to the customer's computer and a corresponding circuit must be part of the central office switch at the phone company's office.

There are several types of DSL technologies: Asymmetric DSL (ADSL) uses a simplex data channel for downstream traffic and a slower full-duplex data channel for upstream traffic (data rates for downstream range between 1.5 and 9 Mbps and for upstream the range is between 16 and 640 Kbps); Very High Speed Digital Subscriber Line (VDSL) is designed for local loops of 1000 ft, ideal for video transmission (data rates over 100 Mbps are offered by the latest VDSL products). As mentioned above, another technology for broadband access to the Internet is based on the coaxial cable that cable TV companies use to bring the TV channels to the residential buildings. A modem, called the *cable modem*, is used to modulate signals coming from the PC so that the transmission can take place on the cable TV wires. In this case, cable TV companies become ISPs.

The most common protocol used by the cable modems is called the Data Over Cable Service Interface Specifications (DOCSIS) produced by CableLabs, an industry forum founded by the cable TV companies. The data rates for the cable modem technology are much higher than those of DSL technology: downstream: 27–55 Mbps; upstream: 2–10 Mbps. The infrastructure is such that the users in a neighborhood share a multipoint circuit (300–1000 customers per cable segment). This means that all messages on a circuit are heard by all computers on that circuit. This also means that the bandwidth is shared among the users in a segment (if a large number of people in the neighborhood use the Internet at the same time, the degradation of the service will be noticeable). To handle the termination of the circuits and provide demodulation, the Cable Modem Termination System (CMTS) is used for the upstream traffic. The CMTS converts data from DOCSIS to the IPs. For the downstream traffic only, a Combiner is used to combine the Internet traffic with the TV video traffic.

In addition to the DSL and cable modems, there are a number of other technologies, some old and some new. We mention, among others, the satellite, wireless fixed access, and wireless mobile access, as some that have been in use. As for the new and upcoming technologies, we should mention the Passive Optical Networking (PON), also called Fiber to the Home (FTTH), already being deployed aggressively by the telephone companies. The PON, using Dense Wavelength Division Multiplexing (DWDM) techniques, can provide enormous data rates for the Internet access and also provides the bandwidth for offering thousands of TV channels (giving phone companies a chance to compete with the cable companies).

Finally, we should mention the Virtual Private Networks (VPNs), which provide the equivalent of a private packet-switched network over the public Internet. VPNs use the so-called tunnels, which run over the Internet so that it appears to the user as a private network. This approach is low-cost, fast, and flexible, but, due to the unpredictability of the Internet traffic, is not reliable.

Wireless WANs

The discussion about the WANs above has considered wireline technologies. As in the LANs, it is possible to have a WAN based on the wireless communications technologies. Wireless wide area networks come in several categories based on the mobility of the user devices and network elements. First of all, there is a category of wireless mobile systems where users can be mobile and they communicate through fixed base stations and through fixed infrastructure. Cellular telephone systems are in this category. The next category is the wireless fixed systems where the users are stationary, base stations are stationary, and the communication is through the air. Early examples of this category are the wireless local loop systems. This is simply the replacement of local loops. The latest example in this category is the Worldwide Interoperability for Microwave Access (WiMAX) initiative (although there are a number of variation of WiMAX standards, some of which can handle mobile users as well). There are a number of other types of wireless networks. For example, wireless networks utilizing satellite communications use different architectures and offer services that are suitable, for example, for large area coverage. In the following, we will focus on the cellular systems.

Although a cellular network is not an enterprise network, almost all employees in today's enterprises have end-user equipment (e.g., cellular phone, smart phones, PDAs, laptops with air cards, etc.) connected to the cellular networks. Therefore, it is important that we provide a brief presentation of this technology here.

Cellular networks are designed such that a large area is divided into a number of smaller cells to achieve coverage and handle traffic in an optimum way. Each cell site has a tower that includes a set of high-power antennas and one transceiver (transmitter and receiver) that can operate on a number of channels (frequency bands) that are licensed from the regulatory agencies. (Channels, with a careful planning, can be reused in nonadjacent cells, providing a capability to serve a large number of users.) The architecture is typically highly hierarchical, although the latest trend is to have a peer-to-per flat structure. The wireless phones can be mobile and were originally designed mainly for voice transmission, but later designs of cellular networks can handle data transmission as well.

Two major capabilities that a cellular network provides for mobile devices are *handoff* (a.k.a., handover) and *roaming*. Handoff is a system capability to handle an on-going call as the user moves from one cell to another without interrupting the existing communication. The roaming capability allows users to move with their cell phones to another city served by another service provider, and still be able to send and receive messages. This depends on the bilateral agreements between the operators, provided that their technologies are compatible. Other major capabilities of a cellular network includes, *registration* of a user when the phone is turned on, *authentication and privacy* to make sure that the user is a good standing one and communications are encrypted to provide privacy, and of course, delivery and reception of customer calls.

The technology in the cellular networking has been through several evolutionary phases. The first generation (1G) cellular systems were analog and voice only, typically operating around 900-MHz frequency range. The digital second generation (2G) systems facilitate the authentication and privacy and provide data service. While Europe and the rest of the world developed and used the digital Global Systems Mobile (GSM) standard-based technology operating in 800 and 1800 MHz, North America came up with several different 2G technologies operating around 1900 MHz: such as IS-95—CDMA-based standard and IS-54 (later IS-136)—Time Division Multiple Access (TDMA)-based standard. (Note that GSM is also based on the TDMA concept.) The U.S. TDMA technology fell out of favor, leaving the CDMA as the only offered technology today. In CDMA, digitized user information is transmitted over a much wider channel (e.g., 1.5 MHz) by attaching unique codes to each bit and employing spread spectrum techniques. On the other hand, in TDMA, the information is transmitted on a specific time slot allocated to that user. 2G technologies supported data transmission up to 64 Kbps first and then via the so-called 2.5G approaches, up to 384 Kbps. (The GPRS and EDGE are the two 2.5G technologies for GSM world, whereas CDMA200 1X is the 2.5G solution for CDMA world.)

To provide higher data rates and enhanced features, third generation (3G) technologies were standardized. 3G networks operating around the 2-GHz range handle a greater number of users, smarter devices that have the power of a small PC, and data including sophisticated Internet access with graphics and video. The GSM camp came up with W-CDMA, and the CDMA camp developed CDMA2000 technologies. Both W-CDMA and CDMA2000 provide more than 2 Mbps data rates. Another major innovation of 3G systems is the change of the infrastructure from a hierarchical architecture to a more flat, peer-to-peer (P2P) architecture in which an IP-based core network with high-speed fiber optics transmission lines supports a variety of 3G components as well as legacy 2G elements. 3G uses packet-switching technology with IP end-to-end. There is much talk about fourth generation (4G) cellular networks. wLANs are overshadowing in popularity 3G-based networks and 4G efforts. This is based on the phenomenon that wLANs are being deployed not only in residential and small offices, but also on a larger scale in enterprises and public areas such as airports, malls, and neighborhoods. Carriers are struggling to take advantage of this by offering public wLAN services and linking them, integrating them with their own infrastructure. In addition, the mobile version of WiMAX is also being considered as a solution for 4G networks.

As far as the enterprises are concerned, the wireless WANs are owned and operated by the common carriers and enterprises and their employees are the users of the services provided by the carriers. These services come in many varieties: different data rates, different frequencies, different technologies, and so on. The end-user equipment, therefore, will also vary, accommodating different technologies and frequencies used in the services. In enterprises today, employees are increasingly mobile and are provided with (for business use) the so-called smart phones that can handle multiple bands of frequencies, multiple technologies, and a variety of services including e-mail, the Internet browsers, and so on. Careful planning for the selection of the appropriate services and end-user equipment with appropriate cost-effective features and strong security measures are essential.

COMMUNICATIONS LAYERS AND PROTOCOLS

In the overview section of this chapter, we discussed briefly the concept of communications layers, the ISO and Internet layering models, and the protocols. We mentioned that each layer is a place holder for a group of closely related communications functions and that a communications protocol is basically the implementation of certain set of functions in a given layer. In this section, we will discuss the functions at each layer and the corresponding protocols in more details; from top to bottom of the protocol stack.

APPLICATION LAYER FUNCTIONS AND PROTOCOLS

The primary purpose of the application layer is to provide a bridge between application programs in the end-user equipment such as a computer and the rest of the communication functions in that computer. Therefore, the application layer protocols are used in general by the end-user equipment. Since there are numerous applications, there will be separate application layer protocol corresponding to each one of the applications. Typical applications that we are familiar with in end-user equipment are the WWW, e-mail, and file transfer protocols. We should also mention that there are a number of emerging applications such as instant messaging, videoconferencing, and so on. In the following, we will discuss the Web and e-mail applications only.

WWW Applications and Related Protocols

The WWW is a way to organize and connect files located on special computer devices called servers, so that they can be accessed remotely over the Internet. The Web application in an end-user device, also called a client, is facilitated typically by an Internet browser, such as Microsoft's Internet Explorer, Firefox, and so on, which allows the users on client devices to access the files on the Web servers. The communications among clients and servers are typically through the HTTP. The address of each file on the server is indicated uniquely via a Uniform Resource Locator (URL), which identifies the server as well as the specific file on that server. For example:

http: //www.manhattan.edu/engineering//index.html

indicates that the server's address is "www.manhattan.edu" and the requested file on that server is "index.html," which is located in a folder called "engineering." The address of the server is based on the domain name mechanism that is administered

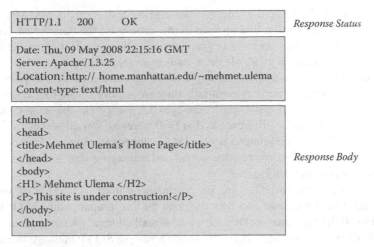

| HTTP/1.1 200 OK | *Response Status* |

Date: Thu, 09 May 2008 22:15:16 GMT
Server: Apache/1.3.25
Location: http:// home.manhattan.edu/~mehmet.ulema
Content-type: text/html

```
<html>
<head>
<title>Mehmet Ulema's Home Page</title>
</head>
<body>
<H1> Mehmet Ulema </H2>
<P>This site is under construction!</P>
</body>
</html>
```

Response Body

FIGURE 3.7 HTTP Response message

by the private companies/organizations that are licensed to do so by the Internet Corporation for Assigning Names and Numbers (ICANN), an industry organization responsible for assigning domain names and Internet addresses. There are a number of domains such as *.com*, *.org*, *.edu*, *.gov*, *.net*, and so on. Once a enterprise registers its unique domain name, it is free to use it as part of the names for its servers. For example, Manhattan College has a domain name called *manhattan.edu* and the Web server has a name called *www.manhattan.edu*.

HTTP has two basic types of messages: HTTP Request and HTTP Response. Typically a client sends an HTTP Request to the servers asking to download a file, and the server response with an HTTP Response message that includes the requested file, which contains the requested information marked up by HTML or XML. The markup language embeds various tags, which are basically instructions to the browser on how the information in the file should be processed and displayed on the client computer. Figure 3.7 shows an example of an HTTP Response message.

E-Mail Applications and Related Protocols

Another popular application, *e-mail*, may also have a two-tier (i.e., client/server) architecture as in the www, or its architecture may include another server in the middle resulting in a three-tier architecture. The combination of a client-based e-mail software (also called user-agent) such as Microsoft *Outlook* or IBM *Lotus Notes*, and an e-mail server (also called mail-transfer agent) is an example of the two-tier e-mail architecture, whereas the so-called Web-based e-mail (e.g., *Hotmail, Gmail, Yahoo! mail*) accessed via the browser on a client machine constitutes a three-tier e-mail architecture.

The primary application layer protocol for the e-mail application is the SMTP. This protocol is used between an e-mail agent originating the message and an e-mail transfer agent forwarding the message to the destination e-mail transfer agent. SMTP is also used between two message-transfer agents as well. The protocol used between the destination mail transfer agent and destination e-mail agent could be the Post

Office Protocol (POP) or the Internet Message Access Protocol (IMAP). Both of these protocols are similar and operate in the same way: the destination user agent simply polls the destination transfer agent periodically to see if there is any message for itself. In the case of POP, all the e-mail messages belonging to this client are downloaded from the e-mail server to the client's computer (with the option to keep the messages on the server, but eventually they are removed from the server). On the other hand, with IMAP all e-mail messages are stored on the server and never removed. Another major difference is that POP stores all e-mail messages sent from the client on the local computer whereas IMAP stores them in the server. We should also mention here that there are other e-mail and messaging standards such as X.400, but their use is somewhat limited.

In a two-tier e-mail architecture, the originating e-mail agent, after the user completes the e-mail message and hits the send button, prepares an SMTP message including all the necessary fields such as the e-mail address, and other fields, as well as the body of the message. Figure 3.8 shows a sample SMTP message header.

When the e-mail transfer agent receives this message, it determines the address of the destination transfer agent and forwards the message to it. The destination transfer agent receives this message and stores it in an appropriate mail box assigned to the destination e-mail agent. When the destination e-mail agent polls its server (via POP or IMAP), it downloads the message to its client machine.

The original SMPT was designed to handle text messages. To handle messages containing graphics and other multimedia features, an extension called Multipurpose Internet Mail Extensions (MIME) was developed. The agent capable of handling MIME translates multimedia format into the text format and use it as a special attachment to permit transmission as part of an SMTP message. Destination e-mail agent software translates the MIME attachment from the text format back into multimedia format. We should note here that there are other protocols handling multimedia formats.

Web-based e-mail is an example of a three-tier e-mail architecture, where the user on a client machine uses a browser first to access the e-mail software (e-mail transfer agent) residing on a Web server first. This e-mail software on the Web server then interacts with the user and the e-mail server (e-mail transfer agent) to facilitate the exchange of message between them (i.e., the client and the e-mail server). So, in this scenario, the client uses the HTTP to interact with the Web server, then the e-mail software in the Web server uses the SMTP to interact with the e-mail server. The rest of the scenario is the same as in the two-tier e-mail architecture discussed above.

The popular Web and e-mail applications provide a good insight into how the application layer functions and protocols interact with the user and the lower layer protocols. There are of course numerous communications applications and therefore many

> *From: Hashem Sherif <hashem_sherif@mac.com>*
> *To: mehmet.ulema@manhattan.edu*
> *Date: Tue, 15 Apr 2008 17:51:46-0400*
> *Subject: Re: Handbook of Enterprise Integration (3rd edition)*

FIGURE 3.8   A sample SMTP message header.

more application layer protocols. For example, a popular and widely used application is the file transfer application. The File Transfer Protocol (FTP) is used to facilitate the file transfer between two clients and between a client and a server. Instant messaging, video streaming, and P2P communications are among other popular applications. P2P applications are based on the concept that every node act as a server and a client. Typically, there is no centralized control for P2P nodes. (In reality, many P2P applications have to resort to a centralized control to help the P2P nodes to share resources. This is sometimes called hybrid P2P. Instant messaging is a good example of a hybrid P2P application.) Initially popular with the individual users, P2P applications are becoming a more accepted way of sharing files and resources even in enterprises due to its cost-effectiveness and its almost unlimited scalability. Currently, there are no accepted open standards in this area, but many proprietary P2P implementations. Some of these are *Napster* and *Gnutella* for file sharing, *AIM (AOL Instant Messenger)* for instant messaging, *Groove* for collaborative computing, *Skype* for VoIP, and *SETI@HOME* for high-speed grid computing.

TRANSPORT LAYER FUNCTIONS AND PROTOCOLS

The main responsibility of the transport layer is to receive the messages from the application layer and prepare them for transmission over the network. To carry out this responsibility, the transport layer provides the following three major functions: (i) linkage to the application layer via an addressing scheme to identify various applications that it serves; (ii) segmentation of large messages into smaller segments for efficient transportation in the network, and reassembly of these segments at the destination to recreate the original message; and (iii) establish an end-to-end virtual connection between the originating machine and the destination machine. The last two functions are necessary when a connection-oriented, reliable delivery is desired. In the connectionless mode, the last two functions are not supported. More on the connectionless versus connection-oriented will be available a little later.

To provide the functions above, a number of protocols have been standardized. Earlier architectures, such as IBM's Systems Network Architecture (SNA), ITU-T's X.25, and Novell's IPX/SPX, had all transport layer protocols. However, due to the popularity of the Internet, the TCP, originally developed in early 1970s for the ARPANET, has become the dominant, most common transport layer protocol in the industry. TCP is a connection oriented reliable protocol. For applications appropriate for connectionless delivery of their messages, User Datagram Protocol (UDP) is used in the Internet. Both TCP and UDP use the IP, a network layer protocol to send their messages to their counterparts in the destination devices. The combination of TCP and IP together with its associated protocols in other layers is typically called the TCP/IP protocol suite.

Port Numbers

A transport layer protocol may serve more than one application layer protocol, and therefore there is a need to identify these application protocols when a message is received from the network layer protocol. This is accomplished by assigning a *port number* to each application layer protocol. As shown in Figures 3.9 and 3.10, both

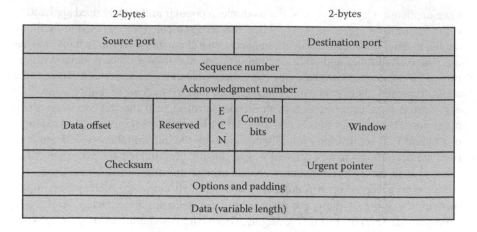

FIGURE 3.9   Format of TCP messages.

TCP and UDP have two fields allocated for this purpose: the first identifies the source port number and the other is for the destination port number. The port numbers for the application protocols in the destination, which is typically a server, are assigned by ICANN. For example, 80 is used for HTTP and 21 is used for SMTP. Table 3.4 shows the port numbers assigned by ICANN for some popular applications. The port numbers for the originating client are generated sequentially by the client's computer.

Segmentation and Reassembly

The second major responsibility of the transport layer is to divide a long message into smaller fragments to be transported on the network from the originating device to the destination device. This function is supported by TCP, but not by UDP. The sizes of the segments are typically determined via the negotiation between the source and destination devices. When a message is segmented, each piece is numbered sequentially within the message so that the transport layer protocol in the destination can put together these pieces in the right order by examining the sequence numbers. The total process is called *segmentation* and *reassembly*. To speed up this complex transport layer function, many implementations offload this function onto the hardware providing data link layer and physical layer functions. This offloading is called Transport Segmentation Offload.

	2-bytes	2-bytes
Source port		Destination port
Length		Checksum
Data (variable length)		

FIGURE 3.10   Format of UDP messages.

TABLE 3.4

Port Numbers (Server Side) for Some Popular Protocols

Ports	Protocols	Applications
21	FTP	File transfer
22	SSH	Secure Shell (remote login)
23	Telnet	Terminal emulation
25	SMTP	E-mail
53	DNS	Domain names
67	BOOTP	IP number Assignment
80	HTTP	Web
110	POP3	E-mail
143	IMAP	E-mail
161	SNMP	Network management
179	BGP	Routing
520	RIP	Routing
547	DHCP	Automatic assignment of IP addresses

Message Delivery

The next and last major responsibility of the transport layer has to do with the delivery of the message to the destination. In message delivery, the transport layer protocols provide two drastically opposite methods for delivery: connection-oriented versus connectionless oriented. In the connection-oriented case, which is used by TCP, the source device first sends a control message to the destination to inquire and make sure that the destination TCP is available and ready to accept the messages.

When the destination responds affirmatively, a *virtual connection* is established between the source and destination devices at the transport layer. During this set-up process, the information about the capabilities of the device such as the maximum data link layer message size are included in the control messages exchanged. This size information will be used in the segmentation process. Only after this exchange has taken place, can the messages be delivered through this virtual connection. In a connection-oriented delivery, after a message has been delivered to the destination, an acknowledgement must be sent back to the originating device to acknowledge that the message was received. There is also a flow control mechanism embedded in this type of delivery to make sure that the destination device is not overwhelmed with more messages than it can process in time.

In a *connectionless delivery*, which is used by the UDP, there is no priory virtual circuit is established. As soon as the transport layer receives the messages from the application layer, it immediately forwards the message to its destination (via the network layer protocol, of course). In this type of delivery, the destination transport layer protocol never acknowledges the receipt of a message. This is why sometimes this type is called a *send-and-pray* method. Therefore, UDP is a relatively small and simple protocol (only 8 bytes containing only four fields).

Which delivery message to be used (thus which protocol, TCP or UDP) depends on the need of the application layer protocol for a reliable underlying delivery mechanism. This is the case for HTTP and SMTP. However, some applications may tolerate errors, therefore a simple delivery without any acknowledgement, flow control, and so on would be sufficient. Voice is one such traffic. We will see later that several commonly used control messages that are usually small, such as Domain Name System (DNS) protocol, Dynamic Host Control Protocol (DHCP), and Simple Network Management Protocol (SNMP) are in this category.

Other Transport Layer Protocols

Although the TCP provides a reliable delivery of the messages end-to-end, some newer applications such as VoIP and streaming multimedia require different availability, reliability, and timeliness values form the transport layer protocols. Delivery of messages within a certain time period may be very important for certain applications so that a smooth output, without interruption, can be obtained by the users. To address these issues, additional transport layer protocols were developed. These types of protocols all rely on the concept of "service classes," where services are ranked based on their requirements. The term quality of service (QoS) is defined for this purpose. For example, the e-mail application is given a lower priority, whereas a VoIP service is given a high priority due to its real-time requirement. Some examples of these kind of transport layer protocols are the Resource Reservation Protocol (RSVP), Real-Time Streaming Protocol (RTSP), and Real-Time Transport Protocol (RTP). They are all used in conjunction with TCP and/or UDP. RSVP is used to set up virtual connections (by reserving resources in the network) for general real-time applications, whereas RTSP is used to set up virtual circuits for real-time multimedia applications to enable controlled delivery of streamed multimedia data. RTP is typically used to transport messages over UDP by simply placing a timestamp on each segment of the message. In the case of VoIP applications, the Session Initiation Protocol (SIP) is used between communicating devices as a signaling protocol for connection establishment, which includes user location detection, session establishment, and session negotiation. Table 3.5 provides a summary of these protocols that ride on top of TPC or UDP.

NETWORK LAYER FUNCTIONS AND PROTOCOLS

The primary function of the network layer is to select the path from the originating device to the destination device based on the network condition and the rules that are established for this selection. This process of path selection and forwarding the packets on this selected path is called *routing*. To be able to route packets, network layer protocols rely on the unique identification of the elements in the network. This aspect is called *addressing*. Therefore, the routing and addressing are the two key responsibilities of a network layer protocol.

Although many network layer protocols have been developed, the IP is the most ubiquitous due to the Internet. IP is relatively simple protocol and provides a mechanism for the network elements to route the packet to the next node in the path to the destination device. The current version of the IP is Version 4, IPv4, which uses 32 bit

TABLE 3.5
Some Transport Layer Related Protocols

Protocol	Typical Use	Typical Application
RTP (Real-Time Transport Protocol)	To transmit time and media information	Real-time audio, video
RTSP (Real-Time Streaming Protocol)	To establish and to control multimedia sessions ("remote control")	Streaming multimedia
RSVP (Resource Reservation Protocol)	To set up virtual connections for general applications	General real time applications
TCP (Transmission Control Protocol)	To deliver messages reliably for general applications	Web, file transfer
UDP (User Datagram Protocol)	To deliver messages for general applications	Network management, voice applications
SIP (Session Initiation Protocol)	To establish connections	IP telephony

addresses. Figure 3.11 shows the format of the IPv4 protocol. A new version of IP, IPv6, with an 128 bit address field was developed to allow a relatively large number of address to be used. Figure 3.12 shows the format of the IPv6. The addressing issue will be discussed in the next few paragraphs. Table 3.6 provides a comparison of some key features for these two versions of the IP.

Addressing Function

As discussed earlier, the URLs are used by the Web applications and HTTP. Similarly, the network layer protocols, such as IP, use network layer addresses, such as IP addresses like *124.65.120.43*. As discussed above, for a network node to forward packets to their destinations, it is necessary that both source and destination computers must have unique addresses. In the Internet, these addresses are known as the IP

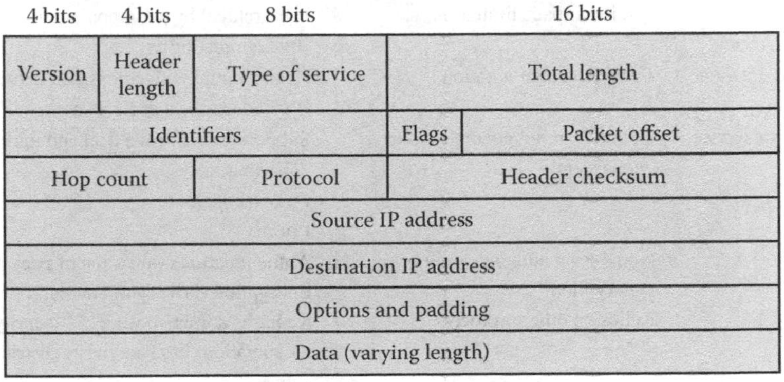

4 bits	4 bits	8 bits	16 bits	
Version	Header length	Type of service	Total length	
Identifiers			Flags	Packet offset
Hop count		Protocol	Header checksum	
Source IP address				
Destination IP address				
Options and padding				
Data (varying length)				

FIGURE 3.11 Format of IPv4 messages.

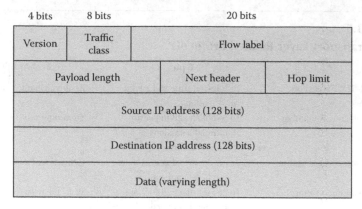

4 bits	8 bits		20 bits		
Version	Traffic class		Flow label		
Payload length			Next header		Hop limit
Source IP address (128 bits)					
Destination IP address (128 bits)					
Data (varying length)					

FIGURE 3.12 Format of IPv6 messages.

addresses or the Internet Addresses. ICANN and numerous private companies/organizations that are authorized by ICANN manage the IP address and domain names. The IP addresses are assigned typically in groups when the domain names are registered. In IPv4, the source and destination IP addresses are indicated in a packet by a 4-byte (32-bit) field each. The IP address example shown above is called the *dotted decimal notation*, where a decimal number corresponding to each byte, rather than

TABLE 3.6
Comparison of IPv4 and IPv6

Feature	IPv4	IPv6
Packet header	Variable size (40+ bytes), complex	Fixed size (32 bytes), simple
Address field	32 bits (4 bytes) resulting in over 10^9 possible addresses	128 bits (16 octets) resulting in over 10^{38} possible addresses
Address allocation	Classfull: network classes A, B, C CIDR: stopgap measure to deal with address space limitation	Hierarchical by registry, provider, subscriber, and subnet Hierarchical by geographic region IPv4 compatibility
Address notation (numeric)	Dotted decimal notation	Hexadecimal with colons and abbreviations IPv4 addresses a special case
Quality of service	Defined but not generally used consistently	Support for real-time data and multimedia distribution Flow labeling Priority
Security	No IP-level authentication or encryption Relies on other protocols	Authentication (validation of packet origin) Encryption (privacy of contents) Requires administration of "security associations" to handle key distribution, etc.

a binary number, is shown for human consumption only. Based on the so called *Classfull Addressing* scheme, ICANN assigns the IP addresses in "classes," varying the size of the address pool, depending on the size of the organization. This is an inefficient and wasteful assignment resulting in a shortage of IP addresses to be assigned for new entrants into the network.

IPv6 uses a 128-bit field (16 bytes) allowing an extremely large number (2^{128}) of IP addresses to be assigned. IPv6 does not use dotted decimal notation, instead it relies on a hexadecimal colon notation to make the addresses more readable. An IPv6 address consists of 32 hexadecimal digits grouped into four and separated by a colon. The following is an example of an IPv6 address:

F45A:B2C4:04C5:0043:ADB0:0000:0039:FFEF.

Once an organization obtains the range of IP addresses, it is now up to this organization to assign specific IP addresses to its computers within its private network. Various techniques including manual, centralized, automated, or a combination of them may be used for this purpose. The most common technique is called *subnetting*. A group of computers on a LAN may be given a group of IP addresses with the same prefix, which is called the subnet address. Subnet addresses make it easier to separate the subnet part of the address from the host part. By applying a corresponding Subnet Mask, a router/gateway can easily determine whether the packets stay in the same subnet or goes outside of the subnet.

The assignment of an IP address to an individual computer can be permanent or temporary. Typically, the computers providing server functions have permanent IP addresses. Also, ISPs assign IP addresses permanently to broadband modems. However, almost all client computers in an enterprise do not have permanent IP addresses. Once a range of IP addresses are allocated to subnet, the assignment of individual IP addresses to individual computers are usually performed dynamically via a server called DHCP server. This eliminates the tedious task of assigning addresses manually to every client computer in the network. When a computer connected to the subnet is turned on, it communicates with a DHCP server requesting an IP address (along with the subnet mask and gateway address). The server, from the existing pool, determines an available IP address and assigns it to this computer. When the computer is turned off, the IP address is returned to the pool and may be assigned to some other computers. There is no guarantee that the same IP will be assigned next time to the same computer.

As discussed above, the application layer protocols typically use application layer addresses involving domain names. But the network layer operates on the IP addresses. Therefore, a mechanism is needed to translate between the domain name-based application layer addresses and the IP addresses. This is called *Address Resolution* and is performed via the DNS. DNS is a set of distributed and hierarchical directories that contain the mappings of the IP addresses to the domain names. ICANN maintains the root DNS directories for the root domains such as .com and .org. Then each individual organization maintains at least one DNS directory for their domains and subdomains. Smaller organizations rely on their ISPs to provide this service. Furthermore, each computer maintains a local directory to keep track of the IP addresses used and the corresponding application layer addresses, so that the next time the user tries to exchange information with an application, the computer can easily determine the corresponding IP address by looking it up in its local directory without polling an external DNS server.

Routing Function

The other major function of the network layer is *routing*, which selects an optimum path between the source and destination computers and forward the packet on this path. To provide this function, each network element builds and maintains a *routing table*, with at least two columns: one lists all the possible destination nodes from this node, and the other indicates the next node to send the packets to for a given destination. This table is constantly updated depending on the status of the network such as congestions, link failures, and so on. So the packet forwarding operation becomes simply a task of determining the address of the next node corresponding to the destination address on the packet, and forwarding the packet to it. The network elements that perform these functions are typically called *routers*. Figure 3.13 illustrates the routing tables for two nodes.

Routing tables may be prepared and maintained manually or dynamically. This could be performed centrally or in a distributed fashion. The more modern techniques employ distributed routing where decisions are made by each node independently and information is exchanged among them to prepare routing tables. Thus the routing tables (at each node) are updated dynamically, based on the information on network conditions exchanged among routers.

There are two major categories of dynamic routing algorithms: distance vector and link state. Distance vector algorithms are based on the use of the least number of hops between the source and destination to decide how to route a packet. This algorithm is used by Routing Information Protocol (RIP).

Link state algorithms are more sophisticated in the sense that they incorporate more factors in their calculations and give more optimum (performance and cost wise) paths because a variety of information types (e.g., number of hops, congestion,

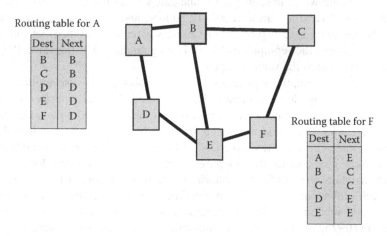

Routing table for A

Dest	Next
B	B
C	B
D	D
E	D
F	D

Routing table for F

Dest	Next
A	E
B	C
C	C
D	E
E	E

FIGURE 3.13 A simple network topology and routing tables for nodes A and F.

speed of circuit) are used to decide how to route a packet. Keep in mind that links state information exchanged periodically by each node to keep every node in the network up to date. This provides more reliable and up to date paths to destinations. However, link state algorithms may be less stable due to their dynamic nature and the many factors involved in building the routing tables. This algorithm is used by the Open Shortest Path First (OSPF) protocol of the Internet. Note that the routing protocol used within a network will be different than the routing protocols used between networks. RIP and OSPF are examples of the routing protocols used inside a network, whereas the Border Gateway Protocol (BGP) is used between two networks.

DATA LINK LAYER FUNCTIONS AND PROTOCOLS

The protocols in the data link layer forward the packet received from a network layer protocol to the identified neighboring network element in a reliable manner. In transmitting the message on the links to its neighboring nodes, a data link layer protocol typically performs the following major functions: (i) MAC to determine when the node begins transmission; (b) error control for detecting and correcting transmission errors; and (c) message delineation for identifying the beginning and the end of a frame.

Numerous data link layer protocols have been developed to implement the above mentioned functions. In this section, we focus on mainly the Ethernet protocol for its dominance in the networking field today. We also discuss High Level Data Link Control (HDLC) since a number of other data link layer protocols such as the Point-to-Point Protocol (PPP), Frame Relay, and so on, use the HDLC as their basis, as will be explained later.

MAC Function

The MAC regulates the access to the medium connecting two or more network elements. For point-to-point circuits, the MAC function may not be that important; however, in a multipoint circuit where a number network elements and user devices share the same medium, the MAC function becomes critical. Ethernet, the most popular LAN protocol, uses a contention-based mechanism to control access to the medium. Each node connected to the medium can transmit its messages whenever the circuit is free. This requires that a node monitors the activities on the circuit to determine whether the circuit is idle. If more than one node starts to transmit at the same time, a collision is said to have occurred. Ethernet uses a *back-off* strategy whenever a collision happens and nodes waits for a random amount of time before attempting to retransmit. This is why Ethernet is also called CSMA/CD.

Protocols like HDLC are typically used on point-to-point circuits and controlling the medium becomes important if a duplex circuit is used. The procedures of the protocol indicate which device will have the control and when.

The data link protocols have their unique addressing scheme, separate from the network layer addresses, to identify individually direct physical links that connect two neighboring nodes. In the case of Ethernet, it is known as the MAC address. A MAC address is a 24-bit field, typically shown as six pairs of hexadecimal digits uniquely assigned in a combination by the IEEE Standard Association (responsible for Ethernet-related protocols) and the manufacturer of the Ethernet cards. The

Address Resolution Protocol (ARP) is used to determine the MAC addresses of the neighboring devices, each of which is connected to the originating device via a physical port. This protocol is used by a node to advertise its IP (via broadcasting) and its MAC addresses. Each node then keeps an address table and updates it according to the ARP messages received. Once the address table is completed, the data link layer checks this table to find out the MAC address that corresponds to the IP address on the packet, and transmits the frame on the link specified by the MAC address.

Error Control Function

The purpose of the error control function of a data link layer protocol is to provide protection during the transmission from interferences that may corrupt the data. Error control functions can be categorized as preventive, detective, and corrective. Note that preventive measures to minimize the occurrence of errors such as shielding the wires and staying away from power lines are outside the scope of data link layer protocols.

There are several error-detection mechanisms employed by different protocols. The most popular error-detection scheme used by almost all current protocols is called the *Cyclic Redundancy Check* (CRC). In this technique, a CRC value is calculated by the sending node and attached to the message. This value is the remainder of a division problem: treating the whole message as an integer value and dividing it by a quotient. Depending on the size of the CRC, this could be a 16-bit value or 32-bit value. Of course, the larger the size, the higher is the probability of catching the errors.

When errors are detected, some actions are needed to recover the corrupted bits. One popular technique, ARQ, uses the retransmission strategy; the receiving node informs the sending node that the transmission was not successful and asks for retransmission of the message. There are a number of variations of the ARQ scheme. There are more sophisticated techniques for correcting errors. For example, the Forward Error Correction technique gives the receiving node the capability to correct incoming faulty messages itself (without retransmission). This requires that considerable overhead information be embedded in the message at the sending port. The extra burden (cost and performance-wise) on both sides is amply justified in certain situations such as radio and satellite transmissions.

Message Delineation and Formatting Function

This major function of the data link layer is to identify the types and formats of messages. Note that, typically, the term "frame" is used, instead of "packet" to refer to a message at the data link layer. The frame delineation and formatting function provides a mechanism for separating frames from each other, defines individual fields of a frame, and identifies a method to determine the length of each frame. In the following discussion, we assume that messages are sent continuously in blocks (i.e., frames) synchronously, as opposed to asynchronous transmission where each character is sent separately.

Some protocols use a flag, a known pattern of bits, at the beginning and at the end of a frame to identify the beginning and the end of the frame. Some other protocols use a synchronization field at the beginning of the frame and a length field that

8 bits	8 bits	8 bits	Variable length	32 bits	8 bits
Flag	Address	Control	Data	FCS	Flag

FIGURE 3.14 Format of HDLC frames.

contains the information about the length of the frame. This way, the receiving node determines the end of the frame by simply counting the bits and stops when the value in the length field is reached. Yet some protocols use both flags and the length fields to provide flexibility in processing of the frame at the receiving node.

The HDLC is a formal standard from ISO. A number of data link layer protocols such as PPP and Frame Relay use a variation of the HDLC. Figure 3.14 shows the format of an HDLC frame.

In HDLC, the length of the frame is variable. Each frame begins and ends with an 8-bit flag, which contains a 0 followed by six 1s and another 0. Using the flags to delineate frames introduces a problem: What if the same pattern shows up in the data field (i.e., as part of the user data)? This problem is solved by using the *bit stuffing* (a.k.a., zero insertion) technique, an extra step in frame processing. The sending node inserts a 0 anytime it detects 11111 (five 1s). When the receiver sees five consecutive 1s, it checks next bit(s): if it begins with a 0, this it simply removes it; if they are 10, this means that the end of frame flag (01111110) is encountered; if they are 11, well, this is impossible, therefore there is an error in transmission.

The most widely used data link layer protocol in LANs today is Ethernet, which was developed jointly by Digital Equipment Corporation (DEC), Intel, and Xerox and is now a formal standard: IEEE 802.3. The Ethernet frame uses a 1-byte beginning flag (10101011), called Starter Delimiter, but no end flag, as shown in Figure 3.15. Bit stuffing is not required in Ethernet, since it uses a length field to determine the end of the frame. Although the length of information field can vary, there is a maximum limit of 1500 bytes, and a minimum limit of 46 bytes, which is required for the proper operation of CSMA/CD.

PHYSICAL LAYER FUNCTIONS AND PROTOCOLS

The major responsibility of the physical layer is to transmit the bit stream from one end of the circuit to the other end as reliably and efficiently as possible. The word circuit here not only applies to the medium such as wires, cables, and air (e.g., microwave, satellite, infrared), but also includes the electronics at each end, as part of the devices that the medium connects to.

1 byte	6 bytes	6 bytes	2 bytes	46–1500 bytes	4 bytes
Starting delimiter	Destination address	Source address	Length	Information field	Frame check sequence

FIGURE 3.15 Format of Ethernet frames.

CHARACTERISTICS OF PHYSICAL MEDIA

Before we discuss various techniques of transmission on physical links, let us quickly review some characteristics and the types of physical media. A circuit could be just the point-to-point type connecting only two network elements, or could be a multi-point type where many network elements are connected through the same circuit. The flow of the transmission on these circuits could be simplex, half duplex, or full duplex indicated that the transmission could be in one direction only, in both directions but one direction at a time, or both directions simultaneously, respectively. The physical media can be grouped into two categories: guided media where transmission flows along a physical guide, and unguided media where there is no physical boundaries (transmission take place in the air). Guided media includes twisted pair wires, coaxial cables, and optical fiber cables, where as wireless media (a.k.a., radiated media) includes radio (microwave, satellite) and infrared communications. Note that the electricity is used in twisted pair wires and coaxial cables, whereas the light created by lasers is used to transmit signals in optical fiber cables. In the unguided category, transmission of electrical (electromagnetic) waves over the air is used in wireless media, whereas "invisible" light waves (frequency below the red light) is used in infrared communications.

Analog versus Digital Transmission

The types of data transmitting on these circuits could be analog or digital. Analog data can take on any value at any time in a wide range of possibilities. (A sound wave and corresponding electrical, continuous, analog waves produced by telephones are good examples of analog data.) Digital data are produced by computers in a binary form as a series of ones and zeros. Similarly, a transmission could be analog or digital. In analog transmissions, the data are transmitted in an analog form (i.e., in a continuous wave format). In digital transmissions, the data are transmitted as square waves (i.e., pulses) with a clear beginning and ending. Typically, telephone circuits at the local loop use analog transmission whereas LAN circuits use digital transmission.

Data need to be converted between analog and digital formats to be transmitted appropriately. To do these, conversion-specific devices are used: a modem (modulator/demodulator) used to convert digital data into analog form that is suitable for sending it over the circuits using analog transmission, whereas a codec (coder/decoder) used to convert analog data into the digital format that is suitable for sending it over the circuits using digital transmission.

Techniques for Transmitting Digital Data over Digital Circuits

At the physical layer, *signaling* (a.k.a., encoding) refers to the representation of bits (0 and 1) in electrical voltages. (Note that the term signaling is also used in telecommunications to refer to an overlay network and related procedures and protocols to setup and disconnect calls.) In digital transmission, signals are sent as a series of "square waves" of either positive or negative voltage corresponding to 0 or 1. Typical values of voltage levels vary between +3/−3 and +24/−24 depending on the circuit. The signaling (encoding) then defines what voltage levels correspond to a bit value of 0 or 1. There are a number of different encoding techniques. We mention only

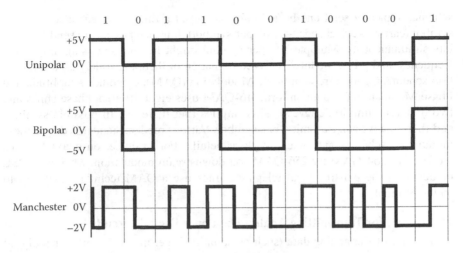

FIGURE 3.16   Three popular channel encoding techniques.

three of them to illustrate the concept: unipolar, bipolar, and Manchester. The unipolar approach uses voltage levels that vary between 0 V and a positive value or between 0 V and some negative value. The bipolar techniques use both positive and negative voltages. A bit transmitted via a bipolar method has a better chance of being interpreted correctly at the destination since the signals are more distinct (more difficult for interference to change the polarity of the current). Figure 3.16 illustrates these techniques.

The *Manchester encoding* used by Ethernet defines a bit by a mid-bit transition of voltage value. As shown in Figure 3.16, a high- to low-voltage transition represents a 0 and a low- to high-mid-bit transition defines a 1. The advantage of the Manchester scheme is that it is less susceptible to having errors go undetected because simply no transition indicates that an error took place. The duration of an interval in which a transition takes place depends on the specifications of the protocol. This time period (i.e., the interval), in turns, defines the *data rate* of the circuit. For example, if the time period is 1/64,000 of a second, then, the data rate will be 64 Kbps (sending a bit every 1/64,000 of a second).

Techniques for Transmitting Digital Data over Analog Circuits

In the case of analog circuits, digital data (0s and 1s) must be modulated into analog format. A well-known example for this case is the use of phone lines to connect PCs to the Internet. A modem is used for this purpose between the computer and the phone line. Modems simply convert the digital data into the analog format. Another modem must be used at the receiver to regenerate the digital data. There are a number of modulation techniques used by the modems: Amplitude Modulation (AM), Frequency Modulation (FM) and Phase Modulation (PM). They are all based on the idea of using an agreed upon so-called carrier wave signal between the sender and the receiver. Each bit is, then, sent, in an interval, by changing one of the characteristics (i.e., amplitude, frequency, or phase) of the carrier. These basic modulation schemes typically send one bit (of information) at a time; 1 bit encoded for each symbol (carrier wave change → 1 bit per symbol). It is also possible to send multiple bits simultaneously. Multiple bits per symbol might be encoded using amplitude, frequency, and phase modulation (or combination of them). A widely used modulation scheme, Quadrature Amplitude Modulation (QAM), combines Amplitude and Phase Modulation (a common form: 16-QAM uses eight different phase shifts and two different amplitude levels). This implies that there are 16 possible symbols and therefore we can transmit 4 bits/symbol. Various modem standards define these modulation schemes and other interface details. For example, on coaxial cables modems use 64-QAM (or 256-QAM) on downstream modulation, whereas ADSL modems on the existing local telephone lines use a QAM technique with up to 15 bits/symbol.

Techniques for Transmitting Analog Data over Digital Circuits

In the case of the analog data (such as sound, image, movies) sent over a digital network, a pair of special devices called codec are used. This is a device that converts the analog signal into a digital format. During this conversion, the analog data is translated into a series of bits before transmission of a digital circuit. This is performed by a technique called Pulse Amplitude Modulation (PAM) involving three steps: measuring the signal by using an agreed upon set of amplitude levels, encoding the signal as a binary data sample, and taking samples of the signal. This creates a rough (digitized) approximation of original signal. The more number of amplitude levels you have and the more samples you take, the better sound quality you get. The wire line telephone network uses 128 levels of amplitudes (resulting in a 7-bit representation) and a music codec may use more than 65,536 levels of amplitudes resulting in a 16-bit representation. The telephone network uses 80,000 samples per second whereas a music player may use about 64,000 and more samples per second.

NETWORK DESIGN AND MANAGEMENT

To put together a network that is a mission critical enabler for the organization, first, the network must be designed with utmost care. The items specified in the design must be acquired or built, then must be deployed after careful installation and testing before to turn it over for service. Finally, the installed network must be managed, administered, and maintained for a long-term continuous useful service to the organization. A brief discussion is provided here for the sake of completeness of the topic in this section. These topics will be discussed in other chapters in the book in greater details.

When designing a network, the starting point is an analysis phase to determine carefully the needs and applications, to estimate traffic and its patterns, and to specify the circuits needed to support the traffic. A cost-effective and high-performance topology of the network needs to be designed to show how the elements of the network are to be connected (ring or star or mesh). While cost-effectiveness and high performance are two general criteria, fault tolerance may be a critical factor as well, especially for certain sensitive applications. Fault-tolerance capabilities built in during the design phase will allow the network to recover from unexpected failures. Alternate routing, backup circuits and processors, backup power, and so on are some of the techniques used for this purpose. The protocols to be used are another technology question that needs to be determined based on the criteria of appropriateness for the user demand and applications. The application architecture should be considered and determined at this point. This refers to whether a client-server or peer-to-peer or two-tier or multitier approach will be taken. When choosing the right technology, the bandwidth required to support the user traffic as well as the requirements on error handling and delays should be considered. In designing the transmission circuits for the network, the use of the existing and cost-effective solutions should be preferred as long as they meet the user needs for a foreseeable future.

Once the design is complete, the next step is to acquire or build the equipment specified in the design blue print. Hardware is typically acquired from network equipment vendors, circuits are typically leased from common carriers, and the software providing various application and management functions are again, preferably, acquired from software vendors. For those rare situations that require specific software, in-house resources or software houses are used to have the proprietary features to be built. Note that this is always costly and time-consuming. Once the equipment are acquired and/or built, they need to be installed and tested. Integration testing is an important part of this process. It is performed to insure that the installed equipment, all together, operate according to the design specifications. Again, this needs to be performed carefully and with great patience since there may be many combinations to be tested.

With the network design and installation complete, the network becomes operational and ready to be used by its users. Network management and operations staff need to be in constant monitoring to make sure that the network operates according to its design specifications (with adequate performance; reliably and securely). Network administrators use various techniques and tools to make sure the network is healthy and operates without any fault. Chapter 7 provides a comprehensive discussion of network and service management. Here we provide a rather brief synopsis for the sake of completeness. Additional components may be connected to the network for this purpose. These are typically known as the Network Management Systems (NMSs) or the Operations Support Systems. They could be general purpose providing a majority of network management functions, or they could be specialized to provide a specific function, such as billing. A specific set of network management protocols such as SNMP are used to exchange network management related information between the network elements and the NMSs. When a fault is detected, it needs to be localized and the root cause determined; the faulty part must be replaced immediately to minimize the service disruption. If performance degradation is detected, appropriate actions such as upgrading the equipment or leasing additional circuits must be taken to keep up with the service level agreements with the users. The topic of security has become critically important in recent days. Network managers must identify potential threats to the network and must prepare comprehensive plans (disaster recovery plans) to deal with when a breach occurs. Network security administrators must have the appropriate methods and tools to detect a malicious act, identify and isolate the parts affected, and immediately restore the service back to its normal state. Also important is to plan and implement protective measures such as firewalls to prevent such malicious acts.

FUTURE TRENDS

Enterprise networking is a fast moving filed. Vendors are racing to be the first on the market, pushing products based on even the draft versions of standard specifications. In such a dynamic environment, it is inevitable that some technologies will flourish while others will fail. This makes it very difficult to predict what the future holds for the networking filed. Having said this, the following sections provide brief discussions on a few interesting new developments in the networking field.

GIGABIT ETHERNET TRENDS

Over the past decade, the Ethernet hierarchy of bit rates was successfully increased from its originals 10 to 100 Mbps, 1 Gbps, and finally to 10 Gbps. The first two extensions could be classified as incremental innovations to increase the access speed to a LAN from desktop and laptop machines. The 10 Gbps Ethernet, in contrast, was of a different nature. Its standardization over twisted-pair cable (known as 10GBASE-T) is on a sophisticated physical layer and required several years of activities. Furthermore, current 10 Gbps Ethernet applications are mostly in WAN and carrier networks. Within enterprises, they are used to interconnect servers in data centers. Their use in a LAN environment to connect workstations has been limited by the capabilities of disk drives to process high data rates. Accordingly, we can view 10 Gbps Ethernet as a platform innovation suitable to two distinct value chains: carrier networks and high-speed server interconnections.

The standardization activities for enterprise networking are taking place mostly in the IEEE 802.3 HSSG. The IEEE 802.3 is positioning the activity as an incremental innovation intended to extend the longevity of existing 10 Gbps designs to 40 Gbps and beyond. The intent is to reduce development risks through technology reuse. This would ensure backward compatibility as well by using the same frame format, same MAC layer, and same physical layer.

NEXT GENERATION INTERNET

There have been a number of projects directed to develop the technologies that will be part of the next generation of the Internet. Internet2, Large Scale Networking (LSN), China's Next Generation Internet (CNGI), and CA*net are some of the efforts in this regard. These projects all have some backbone networks that have been used as the test bed for experimenting with new ideas and new technologies. Some of the common features include the use of IPv6, a backbone in multiples of 100 Gbps data rates, efficient multimedia transmission with adequate QoS parameter values, and tools and protocols to facilitate new applications such as videoconferencing.

Internet2 is a consortium that includes major U.S. universities, corporations, government agencies and laboratories, and international organizations. Internet2 activities focus on advanced network applications such as remote access to unique scientific instruments, new network capabilities such as IPv6, middleware, and high-performance networks linking member institutions. Internet2's network has a common overlaid infrastructure that includes several logical networks including an "Advanced IP" network, a "Dynamic Circuit" network, and a "Core optical" network.

The LSN project of the U.S. government deals with the research in new networking technologies and services to ensure that the next generation of the Internet will be scalable, trustworthy, and flexible. Among the primary topics addressed in this project are network security; new architectures that include optical, mobile wireless, and IP components; and advanced network components that include grid networking.

The purpose of CNGI project is to promote China's status in the Internet technology. A key aspect of CNGI is the immediate adoption of IPv6 to solve the IPv4's address shortage problem. China showcased CNGI at the 2008 Summer Olympics in broadcasting the events, monitoring the facilities, and controlling the operations. CNGI connects many universities, research institutes, and companies in numerous cities in China.

CA*net is a Canadian approach to the next generation Internet, directed by CANARIE, Canada's Advanced Research Agency. CANARIE Network links universities, schools, government labs, and other private organizations.

4G CELLULAR NETWORKS

As discussed in the cellular networks section, 4G refers to a new type of wide area wireless systems that will provide more bandwidth and will use packet switching based on the IP. While 3G networks are being enhanced incrementally through initiatives such as High Speed Data Packet Access (HSDPA) and High Speed Uplink Packet Access (HSUPA), 4G networks are expected to provide even higher data rates by using more advanced technologies such as MIMO and Orthogonal Frequency Division Multiplexing (OFDM). Two leading candidates for 4G networks are the Long Term Evolution (LTE) being developed by 3GPP and IEEE 802.16 (a.k.a. WiMAX).

LTE is following EDGE, W-CDMA, and HSDPA on the GSM path. On the downlink, LTE uses OFDM, which can provide higher data rates in larger spectrum bands: up to 326 Mbps on downlink and up to 86 Mbps on uplink with 20-MHz bandwidth. There are already a number of trials going on as of this writing and a number of announcements made about the planned deployment of the LTE-based 4G networks. LTE assumes an IP-based network architecture and the voice communications is supported in the packet domain.

The WiMAX refers to a series of IEEE 802.16 wireless MAN standards. (WiMAX is actually the name of an industry forum that supports the certification of compliance to IEEE 802.16 standards.) WiMAX is based on the OFDMA and IP technologies. The carrier-class 802.16 supports full QoS, bandwidth-on-demand, voice, data, and video. IEEE 802.16 is an evolving standard. The current version of the IEEE Standards 802.16 is IEEE 802.16-2004, as amended by IEEE 802.16e and IEEE 802.16f and by Corrigendum 1. The mobile enhancements in 802.16e are specified for licensed bands below 6 GHz. Sprint Nextel in the United States announced in 2007 that they plan to deploy a nationwide 4G network based on the WiMAX technology.

WIRELESS AD HOC NETWORKS AND WSNS

With fundamentally different architectures and services, wireless *ad-hoc* networks and WSNs are positioned to be the enablers for ubiquitous computing and communications. These new networks will be autonomously formed and will include large numbers of nodes (PDAs, laptops, sensors, etc.) with varying functionalities and power levels. A WSN usually consists of a large quantity of low-cost, low-power radio devices dedicated to certain functions such as collecting various environmental data and sending them to processing nodes. In essence, a WSN is an intelligent information service infrastructure that provides context-aware information and knowledge services, which are developed by detecting, storing, processing, and integrating situational and environmental information gathered from sensor nodes attached to/embedded into to almost everything, even the human body. In a way, WSNs connect the physical world to computer networks by deploying hundreds to thousands of sensor nodes. A WSN consists of tiny tags, tiny sensors, networks, and tiny memories, and tiny central processors that process the information gathered from the sensors. This is made possible by the advances in integrated circuit technology, manufacturing of more powerful yet inexpensive sensors, radios, and processors, and mass production of sophisticated systems. The applications for WSN are in both civilian and military fields. Civilian applications include environment and habitat monitoring, health care, home automation, and intelligent transport systems. These networks will perform significant functions during natural disasters where preexisting infrastructure may be destroyed. Another significant area that WSNs are expected to be useful is the so-called smart spaces and smart office applications, which may have significant impact on enterprise networking.

BIBLIOGRAPHY

Andrews, J.G. et al. *Fundamentals of WiMAX: Understanding Broadband Wireless Networking*, Prentice Hall, Upper Saddle River, NJ, 2007.

Bekkers, R. *Mobile Telecommunications Standards*, Artech House, Norwood, MA, 2001.

Bulusu, B. and Jha, S. *Wireless Sensor Networks*, Artech House, Norwood, MA, 2005.

Ciciora, W.S. et al. *Modern Cable Television Technology*, 2nd edn, Morgan Kaufmann, San Francisco, CA, 2004.

Comer, D.E. *Hands-On Networking with Internet Technologies*, 2nd edn, Prentice Hall, Upper Saddle River, NJ, 2005.

Comer, D.E. *Internetworking with TCP/IP: Principles, Protocols and Architecture*, 5th edn, Prentice Hall, Upper Saddle River, NJ, 2006.

Davie, B.C. and Peterson, L.L. *Computer Networks: A Systems Approach*, 4th edn, Morgan Kaufmann Publishers, San Francisco, 2007.

Egyedi, T.M. and Sherif, M.H. *Standards' Dynamics through an Innovation Lens: Next Generation Ethernet Networks*, Proceedings of the First ITU-T Kaleidoscope Academic Conference, Geneva, Switzerland, May 12–13, 2008, pp. 127–134.

Fitzgerald, J. and Dennis, A. *Data Communications and Networking*, 9th edn, John Wiley & Sons, New York, 2007,

Forouzan, B.A. *TCP/IP Protocol Suite*, 2nd edn, McGraw-Hill, New York, 2003.

Forouzan, B.A. *Local Area Networks*, McGraw-Hill, New York, 2003.

Forouzan, B.A. *Data Communications and Networking*, 3rd edn, McGraw-Hill, New York, 2004.

Gast, M. *802.11 Wireless Networks: The Definitive Guide*, 2nd edn, O'Reilly Media, Sebastopol, CA 2005.

Glisic, S.G. *Advanced Wireless Networks: 4G Technologies*, John Wiley & Sons, New York, 2006.

Goldsmith, A. *Wireless Communications*, Cambridge University Press, New York, 2004.

Goodman, D.J. *Wireless Personal Communications Systems*, Addison Wesley, Reading, MA, 1997.

Holzmann, G.J. *Design and Validation of Computer Protocols*, Prentice Hall, Upper Saddle River, NJ, 1991.

Huitema, C. *Routing in the Internet*, 2nd edn, Prentice Hall, Upper Saddle River, NJ, 2000.

Huurdeman, A.A. *The Worldwide History of Telecommunications*, John Wiley & Sons, Hoboken, NJ, 2003.

Jacobs, K. *Information Technology Standards and Standardization*, Idea Group Publishing, Hershey, PA, 2000.

Karl, H. and Willig, A. *Protocols and Architectures for Wireless Sensor Networks*, John Wiley & Sons, New York, 2006.

Kurose, J.F. and Ross, K.W. *Computer Networking: A Top-down Approach Featuring the Internet*, Addison Wesley, Reading, MA, 2005.

Lee, W.C.Y. *Mobile Cellular Telecommunications*, 2nd edn, McGraw-Hill, New York, 1995.

Lin, Y.B. and Chlamtac, I. *Wireless and Mobile Network Architectures*, John Wiley & Sons, New York, 2001.

Matthews, J. *Computer Networking: Internet Protocols in Action*, John Wiley & Sons, New York, 2005.

Moy, J.T. *OSPF: Anatomy of an Internet Routing Protocol*, Addison-Wesley, Reading, MA, 1998.

Mukherjee, M. *Optical WDM Networks*, Springer, New York, 2006.

Panwar, S. et al. *TCP/IP Essentials: A Lab-Based Approach*, Cambridge University Press, New York, 2004.

Perkins, C.E. *Ad Hoc Networking*, Addison-Wesley, Reading, MA, 2001.

Rappaport, T.S. *Wireless Communications: Principles & Practice*, Prentice Hall, Upper Saddle River, NJ, 2002.

Schwartz, M. *Telecommunications Networks: Protocols, Modeling and Analysis*, Addison-Wesley, Reading, MA, 1987.

Sherif, M.H. *Managing Projects in Telecommunication Services*, John Wiley & Sons, New York, 2006.

Tanenbaum, A.S. *Computer Networks*, 4th edn, Prentice Hall, Upper Saddle River, NJ, 2003.

Zhang, Y., Luo, J., and Hu, H. *Wireless Mesh Networking: Architectures, Protocols and Standards*, Auerbach Publications, Boca Raton, FL, 2006.

4 Next Generation Networks in Enterprises

Koichi Asatani

CONTENTS

INTRODUCTION

This chapter describes the concepts and architecture of the Next Generation Networks (NGN) and its implementation in a commercial offer by Nippon Telegraph and Telephone Corporation (NTT). Enterprise applications of NGN of voice and Internet services are attractive from the viewpoints of service flexibility and cost-effectiveness and the capability of integrating third-party applications with high dependability and high security.

CLASSICAL VERSUS NEW TELECOMMUNICATION PRINCIPLES

Public Switched Telephone Networks (PSTN) went into service more than 100 years ago. Their main mandate was to provide stable and reliable nation-wide telephone service to the public.

Traditional telecommunication networks followed the so-called "network principle," that is, the network operator is responsible for all aspects of the service including user terminals. In most countries, telephone terminals were used as the property of the network providers that rented them to their subscribers. The PSTN supplies electric power to the users' telephone sets. The network generates its own electric power for supplying the user terminals, so that subscribers could continue to enjoy their service even when the commercial electric power fails, a useful feature in an emergency.

In the Internet, on the contrary, end-hosts or user terminals are responsible for all, except the simple transport capability provided by IP network. The role of IP network is limited to the simple end-to-end packet transport, that is, to provide packet reachability. The IP network is designed as a simple transport platform independent from end-host controls; these end-hosts are responsible for information delivery end-to-end. This principle is called by names such as the "stupid network" or "best effort network." The principle is also called the "end-to-end principle" [1]. In this chapter, we use the shortened term "end principle." In the same vein, the telecommunication principle can also be labeled as the "stupid terminal," because terminals have very limited access functions and rely on the network infrastructure for control. We can also call the telecommunication principle as the "network principle," whereas the Internet principle is the "end principle," given that the end-hosts perform all the functions except that of packet transport.

Operation under the network principle allows the design and management of reliability and dependability, since the terminals as well as network elements are under the responsibility of a single entity, the network provider. Service enhancements and evolutions are generally performed network-wide. As a consequence, the market is mostly monopolistic and stable; service enhancement and evolution are performed in a conservative manner.

With the end principle, in contrast, application enhancements and evolutions can be easily achieved without affecting the network infrastructure. Network transparency is therefore required as much as possible, that is, no modification and differentiation of the packets by the network. In practice, complete network transparency is not desirable, because it prevents the differential treatment of packets, including the identification of harmful viruses or attacks, which is detrimental to security. In addition, early users of the Internet were computer experts at universities and industrial institutes. These expert users were assumed to behave properly following unwritten rules, that is, a network etiquette or "netiquette." With the commercialization of the Internet in 1990, less-expert users in residences and in commercial firms could access the network equally. This increased the security risks because when users misbehave, intentionally or unintentionally, the Internet operation could be affected. Therefore, to ensure continuous operation, the desire for transparency is conditionally violated, by introducing counter measures such as firewall proxies and security software.

This evolution parallels changes to the network principle when users could own their own terminal after terminal liberalization. This meant that terminals could be maintained independently from the network so that function enhancements and evolutions did not have to depend on the network evolution.

Another force that is imposing the modification of the end principle is users' demands for quality of service (QoS) guarantees for applications, such as IP telephony and video streaming, by adopting RSVP (Resource Reservation Protocol, RFC2205) or DiffServ (Differentiated Service, RFC2474, and RFC2475) in the network.

Designs based on the network principle can guarantee the QoS. But with the adoption of Asymmetric Digital Subscriber Line (ADSL) on access lines, the throughput provided to the user terminal depends on external conditions, such as the number of active users accessing the same cable, and the distance between the end-office and the user terminal. The maximum throughput is achieved under limited conditions. Thus, ADSL access can only provide a best-effort type of throughput.

As mentioned earlier, to protect against intentional and/or unintentional attacks, the network transparency called by the end principle is restricted. Another restrictions is due to network address translation (NAT). This is brought about because the total capacity of the IPv4 address space is limited, and therefore the local IP addresses in enterprise networks must then be mapped to and from the global IP address space.

In summary, both the network and the end principles are two idealistic positions that should be merged in a new combination offering the best of each. The convergence of the principles of telecommunication and of the Internet is illustrated in Figure 4.1 [2].

TELECOM NETWORKS AND INTERNET CONVERGENCE (OR FUSION) TOWARD NGN

Telecom networks and the Internet were evolving independently until early 1990s, when World Wide Web (WWW) applications triggered the rapid growth of Internet penetration.

Thanks to the development in broadband access technology, such as cable, ADSL and FTTH (Fiber to the Home), Internet could provide real-time and streaming type of applications such as IP telephony and IPTV.

Telecommunication networks are connection-oriented. They support QoS guaranteed, reliable, and dependable services. The charging principle in telecom services is basically usage-based. The Internet is connectionless and provides best-effort type

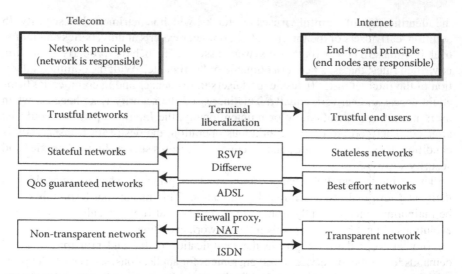

FIGURE 4.1 Principles and convergence of telecommunications and the Internet (ADSL, Asymmetric Digital Subscriber Line; Diffserve, Differentiated service; NAT, Network address translation; RSVP, Resource reservation protocol).

of applications, that is, no QoS guarantee. The charging principle in Internet services is, in general, fixed charging or flat rate.

With broadband access and high-speed packet processing, connectionless networks can support real-time and streaming types of broadband applications as well as nonreal-time packet mode.

The evolutions of applications and network technology for telecom and Internet are shown in Figure 4.2 [3]. The analog telephone network evolved to Integrated Services Digital Network (ISDN) after network and terminal digitalization. ISDN

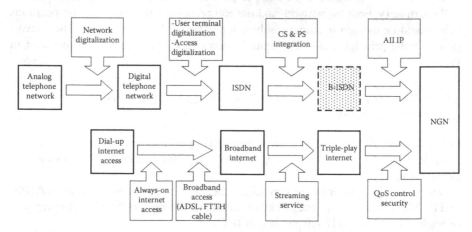

FIGURE 4.2 The evolution from PSTN/Internet to NGN (ADSL, Asymmetric Digital Subscriber Line; FTTH, Fiber to the Home; ISDN, Integrated Services Digital Network; QoS, Quality of Service).

was expected to evolve to Broadband ISDN (B-ISDN). Asynchronous Transfer Mode (ATM) was intended as a core transport technology for B-ISDN, but it is used today only in some core ISDN and digital cellular networks. ATM cell transfer service was introduced for enterprises in Japan. But B-ISDN was not commercially introduced, which is indicated by the dotted line box in Figure 4.2, whereas others in the solid line boxes were put into for commercial services.

Today, many traditional telecom services and the corresponding Internet services are almost equivalent from the users' point of view, with the obvious exception of broadband services.

ADVANTAGES OF NGN

NGN are designed to be capable of QoS management and controls like in traditional telecommunication networks and to support economical, versatile multimedia applications like those on the current Internet. NGN also provides fixed-mobile convergence (FMC) with generalized mobility, and horizontal and vertical roaming as well as improved security.

The "horizontal" handover roaming is the capability of moving among mobile networks of the same technology, for example, from a GSM network to another GSM network, across the boundary of two operators' networks or countries. On the other hand, the handover between two networks using different technologies is called "vertical" roaming, for example, or from/to any cellular network to/from any Wireless Local Area Network (LAN). FMC enables free roaming between fixed and mobile network access.

NGN security is based on the security provided by registration and authentication of user terminals when they request calls. Only registered and authenticated users are allowed access to protect against fake and anonymous communications like spam e-mails that are congesting the current Internet. In specific applications and services, security functions are required in application servers and user terminals.

The advantages of NGN from view points of network operators are as follows:

1. Cost-effective networks by adopting IP technology as a core transport technology. Having a single core technology enables flexible and efficient network operation, which leads to cost-effective network and service operation.
2. PSTN emulation/simulation service because telephone service remains a basic pillar application, even while it is expected that the importance of broadband will grow in time.
3. More competitive presence in market places globally by enabling FMC and by providing the so-called triple services, that is, telephone, Internet access, and TV broadcast services.

The advantages of NGN from view points of users are as follows:

1. More versatile mobility and nomadicity than with the existing cellular phone service. More generalized handover roaming is supported, between

fixed and mobile access points, roaming among domestic and international cellular networks, and between any type of wireless access including cellular networks and WLANs. It enables communications from/to anywhere, at anytime.

2. The triple play services of telephone, Internet access, and TV broadcast services. In addition, through a single FMC network access arrangement, users can also enjoy broadband and ubiquitous services. Ubiquitous services provide relevant content and information delivery to users wherever they are, by using ubiquitous technologies, such as radio-frequency identification (RFID). NGN provides networking and interconnection of such devices in appliances such as refrigerators, television sets, vehicles, garage doors for remote sensing and controlling, and so on.

NGN EVOLUTION

Evolution in core network technologies typically requires a long transition period. The transition from the current telecommunication networks to the NGN may require many years for completion. Thus, the NGN specifications are developed by adopting a release-wise approach of three steps, called the "Three Release Approaches." These approaches are shown in Figure 4.3. The timeframes for Releases 1 and 2 are 2008 and 2009, respectively. The timeframe for Release 3 is still under discussion.

NGN RELEASE 1

The list of services available in NGN Release 1 is given in Table 4.1. They include all existing telecommunication and Internet services such as multimedia services, PSTN/ISDN, emulation/simulation services, Internet access, and public interests.

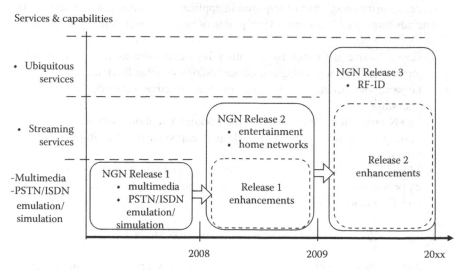

FIGURE 4.3   Release approach to NGN standardization.

TABLE 4.1
Service Capabilities of NGN Release 1

Service Type	Outline
Multimedia service	Real-time conversational voice services (interworking with PSTN and cellular networks)
	Real-time text
	Presence and general notification services
	Messaging service
	Push to talk
	Point-to-point interactive multimedia services (video telephony)
	Collaborative interactive communication services
	Content delivery services
	Push-based services
	Broadcast/multicast services
	Hosted and transit services for enterprises (e.g., IP Centrex)
	Information services (e.g., highway monitoring)
	VPN services
	3GPP Release 6 and 3GPP2 Release A OSA-based services
PSTN/ISDN emulation	Same or better PSTN/ISDN service
PSTN/ISDN simulation	PSTN/ISDN like service
Internet access	Legacy Internet Access
Other services	VPN
	Data retrieval (e.g., tele-software)
	Data communications (e.g., file transfer, Web browsing) online applications (e.g., online marketing, e-commerce)
	Sensor network service
	Remote control/tele-action (e.g., home application control, telemetry, alarming)
	OTN (Over-the-Network) device management
Public interests	Lawful interception
	Malicious communication identification
	Emergency telecommunication
	User identifier presentation and privacy
	Network or service provider selection
	Support of users with disabilities
	Number portability
	Service unbundling
	Unsolicited bulk telecommunications protection

Public interests are concerned with social infrastructural services, such as lawful interception, malicious calling identification, emergency calls, and so on.

NGN RELEASE 2

NGN Release 2 adds streamlining services including entertainment services, such as multicast streaming services, and seamless connection with home networks. Further enhancement of NGN Release 1 services is also supported.

NGN RELEASE 3

NGN Release 3 introduces ubiquitous services using ubiquitous devices, such as RFID, in addition to further enhancement of services introduced in NGN Releases 1 and 2.

From an enterprise application point of view, VPNs, IP Centrex and wide area Ethernet are implemented based on NGN Release 1 services. Enterprise applications supported by Releases 2 and 3 are to be studied based on the requirements to Releases 2 and 3.

NGN ARCHITECTURE

The IP technology is adopted as the NGN core transport technology. To facilitate QoS management in NGN, IP packet transport- and service-related functions are clearly separated.

A group of transport-related functions is named *transport stratum*, and a group of the service-related function is named *service stratum*. The terminology "stratum" is adopted in order to avoid any confusion with the "layers" defined in the Open Systems Interconnection (OSI) model. Transport layer functions are limited to the OSI lower layer functions. But, the transport stratum could include OSI higher layer functions in heterogeneous network environments. The NGN architecture is shown in Figure 4.4 [4,5].

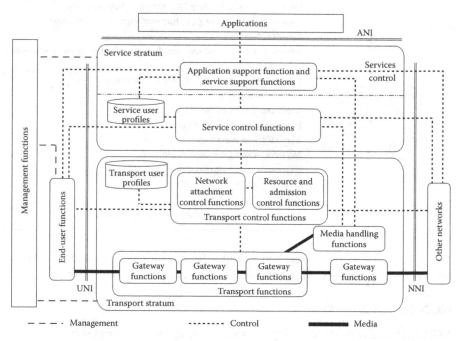

FIGURE 4.4   Overview of NGN architecture. (From Fig.7.1/ITU-T Rec.Y.2012 and Fig.1/ ITU-T Rec. Y.2401/M.3060. With permission.)

NGN TRANSPORT STRATUM

The NGN transport stratum provides the functions to transfer data designated as *transport functions*, and the functions to control and manage transport resources associated with the data transport designated as *transport control functions*. The transport control functions refer to the user-related information on user access such as registration/authentication information and available bandwidth. Such user-related information is called transport user profile. The NGN transport stratum consists of single- or multiple-layer networks [6]. Multilayer network means a combination of multiple single-layer networks; two single-layer networks have a client and server relationship. One single-layer network is a client to another single-layer network. Examples of single-layer networks are IP network, Ethernet, and Synchronous Digital Hierarchy (SDH) networks. The IP packet can be transmitted on Ethernet and the Ethernet can be a client to an SDH network. This kind of layered structure can be repeatedly, or recursively, adopted for providing a single service under NGN environments.

Transport Control Functions

The transport control functions include the Resource and Admission Control Function (RACF) and the Network Attachment Control Function (NACF). The RACF manages transport elements and achieves admission controls depending on the resource usage. The NGN QoS management and control are dealt with by RACF, whereas the NACF manages terminal authentication and address assignment.

Transport Functions

The transport functions include access and core transport functions. The access transport functions include access node gateway, access packet transport, and edge node functions. The access node gateway provides connections between a user terminal and access packet transport function elements. The edge node function is to manage the admission/rejection of IP packets from an access network or from another adjacent non-NGN network. The core transport functions include access border gateway functions, core packet transport functions, gateway functions to non-NGN entities, and media handling functions.

Access border functions provide interconnection with the access network. The core transport functions manage IP packet routing and transmission to a destination terminal. The gateway functions provide interworking capabilities with user terminals and other networks such as PSTN and other networks including other NGNs.

Media handling functions provide media resource processing for service provision, such as the generation of tone signals and transcoding. These functions are specific to media resource handling in the transport stratum. The examples are voice announcement, voice guidance, and voice bridging.

Transport User Profile

The transport user profile is the user's information and other control data in the transport stratum, such as QoS profile, the Proxy Call Session Control Functional Entity (P-CSC-FE) address, and Home GateWay Configuration Functional Entity (HGWC-FE) home gateway address related to the transport stratum.

The P-CSC-FE acts as the primary contact point to the user terminal for session-based services. Its address is discovered by terminals using such mechanisms as static provisioning and NACF. Typical functions of the P-CSC-FE are forwarding session control requests related to registration to an appropriate Interrogating Call Session Control Functional Entity (I-CSC-FE), forwarding session control requests from the terminal to the Serving Call Session Control Functional Entity(S-CSC-FE), and forwarding session requests or responses to the terminal. The I-CSC-FE and S-CSC-FE are described below.

SERVICE STRATUM

The NGN service stratum provides functions to transfer service-related data and the functions to control and manage service resources and network services enabling user services and applications. The NGN service stratum is concerned with applications and services. Services, in this context, are operated between any peer node devices and systems in any configuration, not necessarily between end-user terminals. Applications are served by services as clients to services. Services are related to voice, data, or video applications, arranged individually, or in some integrated manners in the case of multimedia applications.

Service User Profile

The service user profiles are stored in databases that contain users' authentication, authorization, service subscription information, location, presence, and charging.

Service Control Function

The service control functions include resource control, registration, authentication, and authorization functions at the service level in Figure 4.4. They can also include functions for controlling media resources, that is, specialized resources and gateways for service signaling. The service control functions accommodate service user profiles.

Application Support and Service Support Functions

The "application support functions and service support functions" shown in Figure 4.4 include functions such as registration, authentication, and authorization functions for the applications. They also include the gateway functions to other packet networks. All these functions are available to the "applications" and "end-user" functional groups in Figure 4.4.

The application support functions and service support functions work in conjunction with the service control functions to provide end-users and applications with the NGN services they request, with registration, authentication, and authorization at these two levels.

NGN INTERFACES

Fundamental NGN interfaces are defined as User-to-Network Interface (UNI), Network-to-Network Interface (NNI), and Application Server-to-Network Interface (ANI). The UNI is the interface between the terminal equipment and an NGN network termination, where the access protocols apply. The terminal equipment also includes user premises networks such as LANs and home networks.

The NNI is the interface between two peer core networks, or interface between core and access networks. The ANI is the interface between the NGN service stratum and application servers, for example, servers for IP Centrex service and video conferencing.

One of the most important requirements to NGN is to provide technical specifications that can be applied worldwide, irrespective of the regulatory regime. Thus, the access to a network and access to a service are independent. Users can choose any access to any of competitive networks and to any of competitive service providers.

To accelerate NGN penetration, the UNI—the demarcation point between the NGN and user terminals—is defined to accommodate existing protocols. Thus, NGN provides the integrated access of all existing communication media including voice, video, text, and multimedia data. As a consequence, roaming between fixed and mobile network access should be supported.

Ubiquitous commutations by using ubiquitous communication devices such as RFID will also be supported. Currently, networked RFID applications are used in many areas such as logistics, manufacturing, and retailing as dedicated private networks. NGN will provide capabilities such as global VPNs to support global enterprise applications.

NGN AND INTELLIGENT NETWORKS

The separation of transport stratum and service stratum is similar to the concept of separation of transport functions and service control functions in intelligent networks (IN).

IN were developed for quick provisioning of supplementary services in telephone networks by separating basic transport functions and service control functions. Intelligent networks deploy the common channel signaling network for signaling transport between switching systems. Switching controls are achieved by the service control point (SCP). Each switching system is dedicated to the basic switching functionality as a service switching point (SSP) under the control of a common SCP. The basic configuration of the IN is shown in Figure 4.5.

The separation of the two functional groups enables quick and easy service creation and service provisioning by adding/modifying service software to the SCP, which is shared among all SSPs. This was not the case in traditional telephone network where a new service deployment would require changes to all related switching systems.

The toll-free dial service, for example, requires translation of the dialed number to/from the regular subscriber telephone number as a service control function at SCP. The simple addition of that translation function to SCP enables a new toll-free dial service on a nation-wide basis.

IMS-BASED NGN CONFIGURATION

The NGN is implemented using the IP Multimedia Subsystem (IMS) that the 3GPP (3rd Generation Partnership Project) has developed for multimedia communication

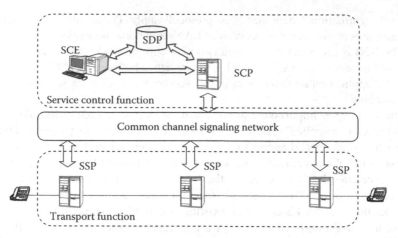

FIGURE 4.5   Basic configuration of IN (SCE, Service Creation Environment; SCP, service control point; SDP, service data point; SSP, service switching point).

with the third generation cellular technology [7,8]. The IMS-based NGN deploys IMS accommodating NGN architecture and requirements such as FMC. An example of IMS-based NGN configuration is shown in Figure 4.6.

The IMS core consists of three types of SIP (Session Initiation Protocol, RFC3261) servers at the service stratum to carry out the following functions: CSCF (Call Session Control Function), S-CSCF (Serving-Call Session Control Function), I-CSCF

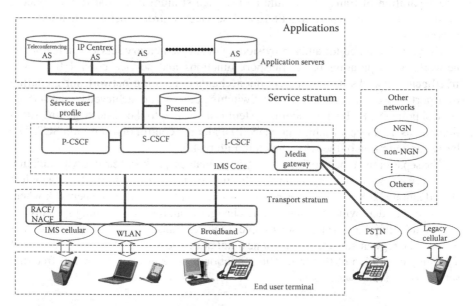

FIGURE 4.6   Example of an IMS-based NGN configuration (CSCF, Call Session Control Function; I-CSCF, Interrogating-CSCF; IMS, IP Multimedia Subsystems; P-CSCF, Proxy-CSCF; PSTN, Public Switched Telephone Network; RACF, Resource and Admission Function; S-CSCF, Serving-CSCF).

(Interrogating-Call Session Control Function), and P-CSCF (Proxy-Call Session Control Function).

The S-CSCF SIP server is the primary server providing user authentication and relaying messages to application servers. The I-CSCF SIP server receives SIP registration messages from the P-CSCF SIP server and reroute the massages to the appropriate S-CSCF SIP server. Finally, the P-CSCF SIP server is the primary server, which directly contacts user terminals.

IP telephony for business users or IP Centrex is expected to replace the traditional Centrex and provide wider flexibility with the help of Internet integration capability. IP Centrex services are provided by an IP Centrex server, as shown in Figure 4.6. Legacy cellular phones without IMS capability are connected to IMS through legacy mobile-switching center and media gateway. For IP Centrex service, cooperative operation is necessary among IP Centrex server, user service profiles controls, and transport user profiles.

NGN MANAGEMENT

NGN is essentially about delivering new services that are available at any place, any time, and on any device, through any customer-chosen access mechanism.

The goal of the NGN management framework is to increase customer satisfaction with a significant reduction in operating costs. The NGN management (NGNM) provides management functions for NGN resources and services. It offers communications between the management plane and the NGN resources or services and other management planes. NGNM also provides end-users with access to management information, and end-user-initiated business processes.

The management functional areas of NGNM are as follows: (1) fault management, (2) configuration management, (3) accounting management, (4) performance management, and (5) security management. The aim of NGNM is to facilitate the effective interconnection between various types of Operations Systems (OSs) and/or NGN resources for the exchange of management information through standardized interfaces, protocols, and messages. The architecture accommodates existing OSs, telecommunications networks, and equipment, which are installed by network operators and service providers. Thus, NGNM is not defining a new OS dedicated to NGN management. It provides mediation functions to form NGN OS with the use of existing OSs, and possible new OSs if defined. Management objectives for NGN include minimizing mediation work between different network technologies, management reaction times to network events.

NGN MANAGEMENT FUNCTION BLOCKS

A management function is the smallest part of a business process (or management service), as perceived by the user of the process (or service). A management function block is the smallest deployable unit of management functionality. The management function blocks are shown in Figure 4.7.

The Service Management Function (SMF) relates to the management of the service life cycle, including the contractual aspects of service-level agreements, the

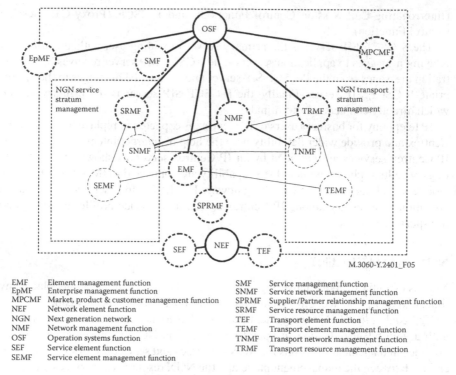

M.3060-Y.2401_F05

EMF	Element management function	SMF	Service management function
EpMF	Enterprise management function	SNMF	Service network management function
MPCMF	Market, product & customer management function	SPRMF	Supplier/Partner relationship management function
NEF	Network element function	SRMF	Service resource management function
NGN	Next generation network	TEF	Transport element function
NMF	Network management function	TEMF	Transport element management function
OSF	Operation systems function	TNMF	Transport network management function
SEF	Service element function	TRMF	Transport resource management function
SEMF	Service element management function		

FIGURE 4.7 NGN management functional blocks. (Reproduced from Fig.5/ ITU-T M.3060/ Y.2401. With permission.)

association between customers and service profiles, and the service profiles and provisioning of network resources for activation of the service.

The Service Resource Management Function manages the logical service infrastructure management and the service capabilities (e.g., presence, location and nomadism) from a users' perspective, the subscriber data, and the user profile database.

The Transport Resource Management Function is responsible for the realization of the requested connectivity. This includes mapping of SMF requirements into network service profiles and the management of network resources, for example, admission control configuration and QoS mechanisms.

The Network Management Function (NMF) controls all network elements and coordinates among them on a network-wide basis. It supervises the provision, cessation or modification of network capabilities as well as their maintenance. The Service Network Management Function and the Transport Network Management Function are the parts of the NMF located in the Service stratum and in the Transport stratum, respectively.

The Element Management Function is responsible for the control and coordination of a subset of network elements. This includes the collection and maintenance of statistical and other data about the elements status and performance.

The Service Element Function and the Transport Element Function are responsible for the management information for the Service and Transport strata, respectively.

Additional management function blocks are associated with internal and external communications. The Supplier/Partner Relationship Management Function handles the communication with members of the supply chain or with partners for the purpose of importing external transport or service resources for use by the enterprise. The Market, Product, & Customer Management Function is devoted to the creation, management, and maintenance of the offers from the service provider. Finally, the Enterprise Management Function is the block associated with disaster recovery, security and fraud management, quality management, and IT planning and architecture, all at the enterprise level.

RELATIONSHIP TO SERVICE-ORIENTED ARCHITECTURE

One of the architectural principles behind the management architecture for NGN is the Service-Oriented Architecture (SOA). SOA is a software architecture of services, policies, practices, and frameworks in which components can be reused and repurposed rapidly in order to achieve shared and new functionality. This enables rapid and economical implementation in response to new requirements, thus ensuring that services respond to perceived user needs.

The SOA uses the object-oriented principle of encapsulation in which entities are accessible only through interfaces and where those entities are connected by well-defined interface agreements or contracts.

Major goals of the SOA are to enable fast adaptation to changing business needs, and cost reduction in the integration of new services, as well as in the maintenance of existing services.

The SOA provides open and agile business solutions that can be rapidly extended or changed on demand. This will enable NGN management to support the rapid creation of new NGN services and changes in NGN technology.

The main principles of SOA are as follows [9]:

1. The reusable services, location independent, and loosely coupled
2. The server and client relationship between services, that is, any service as a client or a server with respect to another service
3. The "find-bind-execute" paradigm for the communication between services
4. The independent interface of a service from the service's implementation.

The "find, bind and execute" paradigm enables the any service provider/consumer (agency) can reuse any other agency's services. First, an agency can *find* any published service component in the service registry, which is shared by all agencies. Then the agency *binds* other agency's services and *executes* the message and data exchange as a bound service.

NGN IMPLEMENTATION AT NTT

NTT started its commercial NGN services, at the end of March of 2008. This section describes the NGN services, and UNI protocols associated with this offer.

NGN Services

The NGN services supported by NTT's NGN based on Release 1 as of end of March 2008 are summarized in Table 4.2 [10–12].

The *Optical Broadband service* is called "FLET's Hikari Next." The term comes from the combination of "F," "let's IP service," "optical (Hikari)," and "next." The "F" stands for "Friendly and flexible." The translation of the service brand name is "Let's enjoy friendly and flexible next generation optical IP services."

The *Optical Broadband service* provides secure Internet access service but with the best-effort type of QoS. NGN telephony service called *Optical Telephony service—Hikari Denwa* in Japanese—provides QoS-guaranteed interactive voice communications with the same QoS level as the plain old telephone service POTS and with 7 kHz bandwidth for higher voice quality. IP video telephony provides the same voice QoS associated with video capability.

VPN service called *FLET's VPN Gate service* currently supports only the best-effort type of QoS. VPN with guaranteed QoS is to be provided in 2009. Content delivery service provides video program unicast and multicast distribution with QoS guaranteed and best-effort type of QoS. Ethernet over NGN called *FLET's Ether Wide service* provides a wide area Ethernet service like WAN, whose configuration is shown in Figure 4.8.

TABLE 4.2
NTT's NGN Services

Service		Content
Optical Broadband service (FLET's Hikari Next service)		Service for residential users (single family house)
		Service for residential users (apartment house)
		Service for business users
Optical Telephony service (Hikari Denwa and Hikari Denwa office type)	QoS guaranteed	Hikari Telephony (standard QoS, high QoS: 7 kHz)
		Business Telephony (to be provided)
		Video Telephony
VPN service (FLET's VPN gate service)	QoS guaranteed / Best effort	VPN (center-to-end, CUG) to be provided
		VPN (center-to-end, CUG)
Content delivery service (FLET's Cast service)	QoS guaranteed / Best effort	Unicast
		Multicast
		Unicast
		Multicast
Ethernet over NGN (Business Ether Wide service)		Ethernet

CUG, Closed User Group.

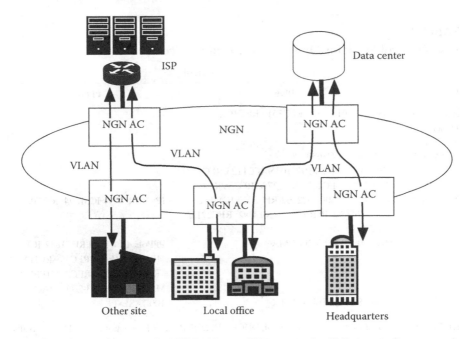

FIGURE 4.8 Configuration for NGN wide area Ethernet service (AC, Access Concentrator).

Enterprise-oriented services are VPN, Ethernet over NGN, Hikari broadband service, and NGN telephony for business users.

UNI FOR OPTICAL BROADBAND SERVICE: FLET'S HIKARI NEXT SERVICE

The UNI for Hikari Broadband Service is shown in Table 4.3. It provides two modes of services. One is using Point-to-Point over Ethernet (PPPoE) for IPv4 Internet access, and the other is IPv6 access. Communication set-up and communication release processes for PPPoE IPv4 access are shown in Figures 4.9 and 4.10.

UNI FOR VPN: FLET'S VPN GATE SERVICE

The UNI for VPN protocol stack is shown in Table 4.4. NGN does not support the Class D and Class E IP addresses as defined in RFC1700, and supports private IP address as defined in RFC1918. NGN also supports global IP address, which is given by the general Internet addressing rule.

Remote Authentication Dial In User Service (RADIUS, RFC2865, RFC2866) is used for authentication and accounting. Terminals should be equipped with RADIUS server functions and communicate with NGN as RADIUS clients. Users can use two RADIUS servers: a primary server and a backup that is used when the primary fails.

TABLE 4.3
UNI Protocol Stack for Optical Broadband Service

Layer	Protocol	
	IPv6	PPPoE
Application Presentation Session	DHPCv6: RFC3315/RFC3513/RFC3646	
Transport	DHCPv6: RFC3633 DNS RRFC1034/RFC1035/RFC1123/RFC2181/ RFC2308/RFC2671/RFC2782/RFC3596	
Network	IPv6: RFC2460/RFC2462/RFC3513 ICMPv6: RFC4443 NDP: RFC2461 MLDv2: RFC2711/ RFC3810	IPv4: RFC791 ICMPv4: RFC79
Data link	MAC: IEEE802.3-2005 MAC	PPPoE: RFC1332,RFC1877(ICPC)/ RFC1334(PAP)/RFC1994(CHAP)/ RFC1661(PPP)/RFC2516(PPPoE) MAC: IEEE 802.3-2005 MAC
Physical	100BASE-TX, 10BASE-TX	100BASE-TX

DHCP, Dynamic Host Configuration Protocol; DHCP-PD, DHCP Prefix Delegation; DNS, Domain Name System; IP, Internet Protocol; ICMP, Internet Control Message Protocol; MLD, Multicast Listener Discovery; NDP, Neighbor Discovery Protocol; PPPoE, Point-to-Point Protocol over Ethernet.

UNI FOR NGN TELEPHONY SERVICE:OPTICAL TELEPHONY SERVICE (HIKARI DENWA)

NGN telephony is a QoS-guaranteed service. The difference between NGN telephony and the existing IP telephony over Internet, or Internet telephony, is that NGN telephony has an additional stage for the terminal registration and authentication before call set-up, which makes NGN telephony secure. NGN IP telephony uses only SIP as a call control protocol. In general, Internet telephony adopts several options, such as SIP, ITU-T H.323 [13], and H.248/MEGACO [14,15].

After the terminal registration and authentication, the terminal sends a call request using SIP [16]. NGN will establish the connection provided that network resources are available and the called party is not engaged. The session will end when either the calling party or called party sends a release request packet.

The UNI protocol for NGN telephony is shown in Table 4.5. Session set-up is carried out by Session Control Protocols using SIP and SDP (Session Description Protocol) over User Datagram Protocol (UDP). Media (voice and video) communication is handled by Real-time Transport Protocol (RTP), G.722 [17], H.264 [18] over UDP, and RTCP (RTP Control Protocol) over TCP (Transmission Control Protocol). HTTP (HyperText Transfer Protocol) is also supported, for integrated voice and data and other services.

NGN telephony terminals are required to support some supplementary services such as calling party number identification and call waiting.

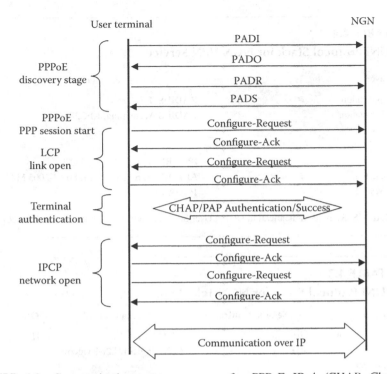

FIGURE 4.9 Communication set-up sequence for PPPoE IPv4 (CHAP, Challenge-Handshake Authentication Protocol; IPCP, Internet Protocol Control Protocol; LCP, Link Control Protocol; PADI, PPPoE Active Discovery Initiation; PADO, PPPoE Active Discovery Offer; PADR, PPPoE Active Discovery Request; PADS, PPPoE Active Discovery Session-Confirmation; PAP, Password Authentication Protocol; PPPoE, Point-to-Point Protocol over Ethernet).

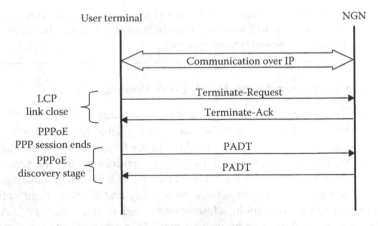

FIGURE 4.10 Communication release sequence for PPPoE IPv4 (CHAP, Challenge-Handshake Authentication Protocol; IPCP, Internet Protocol Control Protocol; LCP, Link Control Protocol; PAP, Password Authentication Protocol; PADT, PPPoE Active Discovery Terminate; PPPoE, Point-to-Point Protocol over Ethernet).

TABLE 4.4
UNI Protocol Stack for NGN VPN Service

Layer	Protocol
Application	RADIUS: RFC2865
Presentation	RADIUS Accounting: RFC2866
Session	
Transport	
Network	IPv4: RFC791 ICMPv4: RFC79
Data link	ARP: RFC826 MAC: IEEE 802.3-2005 MAC
Physical	100BASE-TX

RADIUS, Remote Authentication Dial In User Service; ARP: Address Resolution Protocol.

TABLE 4.5
UNI Protocol Stack for NGN Telephony

Layer	Session Control	Media Control	Others
Application	SIP	RTP RTCP	HTTP
	SDP	G.722 (voice) H.264(video)	
Presentation			
Session			
Transport	UDP	UDP/TCP	
Network	IPv4/ICMPv4	IPv6/ICMPv6	
Data Link	ARP		
	IEE802.3-2005 MAC		
Physical	100Base-TX/10BaseTx		

ARP, Address Resolution Protocol; HTTP, HyperText Transfer Protocol; RTCP, RTP Control Protocol; RTP, Real-Time Transport Protocol SDP, Session Description Protocol; SIP, Session Initiation Protocol.

UNI FOR ETHERNET OVER NGN: FLET'S ETHER WIDE SERVICE

Access to the wide area Ethernet service can be achieved at 10 Mbps, 100 Mbps, and 1 Gbps. A dual access is also available for highly reliable services. Under normal operating conditions, packets are discarded if they are forwarded to the backup access line. When the primary access line fails, network control switches the access to the backup. The UNI protocol stack for Ethernet over NGN is shown in Table 4.6.

This service also provides in-service monitoring and alerting as an option, by using Ethernet OAM (operation, administration and maintenance) [19]. Alerting information is notified to users by using e-mail. Monitored objects for alerting are shown in Table 4.7.

As an option, Ethernet over NGN can support QoS control, by prioritizing packets by assigning a ToS (Type of Service), a CoS (Class of Service), or a VID (Virtual

TABLE 4.6
UNI Protocol Stack for NGN Ethernet

Layer	Protocol
Application	
Presentation	
Session	
Transport	
Network	
Data link	IEE802.3-2005 MAC
Physical	IEEE 802.3-2005 10BASE-TX, 100BASE-TX, 1000BASE-SX, 1000BASE-LX

TABLE 4.7
NGN Ethernet Managed Objects

Exchange Type	Monitoring Function		Managed Information
Ping command	Ping monitoring	Reply to ICMP echo	
SNMP message	Interface monitoring	Polling	Change in link status
		Trap	Change in object maintenance entity
	Interface performance	Statistics	Numbers of total sending and receiving packets/numbers of errored packets/ numbers of discarded packets/traffic volume/number of unicast packets/ number of nonunicast packets
	Server performance	Statistics	CPU usage. memory usage/HDD usage
Status codes	Service monitoring	Response time	Response to HTTP/HTTPS/FTP/DNS/ IMAP4/POP3
	Service response	Response	Response to HTTP/HTTPS/FTP/DNS/ IMAP4/POP3

LAN Identifier). ToS is defined as in IPv4. CoS is a 3-bit code in the Priority Code Point of VLAN tag defined in IEEE802.2p. VID is 12-bit VLAN identifier in the VLAN tag defined in IEEE802.1Q. In this case, terminals subscribing to this service should be able to manage assigning priority.

CONCLUSIONS

NGN is expected to be a service and application platform for any type of communications and information delivery including ubiquitous communications. Europe, North America, and Asian regions should collaborate in establishing unique and single global standards to cope with the very demanding, rapidly growing, and changing environments. It is the challenge for players including traditional common carriers, new, but not new now, common carriers, and new players such as application providers. Unique and single global standards of NGN are essential for the success of NGN.

REFERENCES

1. Saltzer, J. H., Reed, D. P., and. Clark, D. D., End-to-end arguments in system design, *ACM Trans. Comput. Syst.* 2(4), 277–288, 1984.
2. Asatani, K., *Introduction to Information Networks—Fundamentals of Telecom & Internet Convergence, QoS, VoIP and NGN*, Ch.12, Corona Publishing Co., Tokyo, 2007 (in Japanese).
3. Asatani, K., *Introduction to Information Networks—Fundamentals of Telecom & Internet Convergence, QoS, VoIP and NGN*, Ch.1, Corona Publishing Co., Tokyo, 2007 (in Japanese).
4. ITU-T Recommendation Y.2012, Functional Requirements and Architecture of the NGN Release 1, Geneva, September 2006, available at http://www.itu.int/publications.
5. ITU-T Recommendation.Y.2401/M.3060, Principles for the Management of the Next Generation Networks, Geneva, March 2006, available at http://www.itu.int/publications.
6. ITU-T Recommendation Y.2011, General Principles and General Reference Model for Next Generation Network, Geneva, October 2004, available at http://www.itu.int/publications.
7. Camarillo, G. and García-Martín, M.-A., *The 3G IP Multimedia Subsystem (IMS): Merging the Internet and the Cellular Worlds*, 2nd edn., Ch. 3, John Wiley & Sons, New York, 2006.
8. ITU-T Recommendation Y.2021, IMS for Next Generation Networks, September 2006, available at http://www.itu.int/publications
9. Mahmoud, Q. H., Service-Oriented Architecture (SOA) and Web Services: The Road to Enterprise Application Integration (EAI), April 2005, available at http://java.sun.com/developer/technicalArticles/WebServices/soa, last accessed June 29, 2009.
10. NTT EAST, Interface for IP network service (data communications) on Next Generation Network v.1, NTT EAST Technical reference, 2007 (in Japanese), available at www.ntt-east.co.jp/tekigou/shiryou/index.html.
11. NTT EAST, Interface for IP network service (voice communications) on Next Generation Network v.1, NTT EAST Technical reference, 2007 (in Japanese), available at www.ntt-east.co.jp/tekigou/shiryou/index.html.
12. NTT EAST, Interface for IP network service (LAN type communications) on Next Generation Network v.1, NTT EAST Technical reference, 2007 (in Japanese), available at www.ntt-east.co.jp/tekigou/shiryou/index.html.
13. ITU-T Recommendation H.323, Packet-based multimedia communications systems, June 2006, available at http://www.itu.int/publications.
14. ITU-T Recommendations H.248.1, Gateway control protocol, Version 3, September 2005, available at http://www.itu.int/publications.
15. IETF RFC3525, Gateway control protocol Version 1, June 2003, avilable at http://www.ictf.org/rfc/rfc3525.txt.
16. Sinnreich, H. and Johnston, A. B., *Internet Communications Using SIP: Delivering VoIP and Multimedia Services with Session Initiation Protocol*, 2nd edn., Ch. 11, John Wiley & Sons, New York, 2006.
17. ITU-T Recommendation G.722, 7 kHz audio-coding within 64 kbit/s, November 1988, available at http://www.itu.int/publications.
18. ITU-T Recommendation H.264, Advanced video coding for generic audiovisual services, November 2007, available at http://www.itu.int/publications.
19. ITU-T Recommendation Y.1731, OAM functions and mechanisms for Ethernet based networks, February 2008, available at http://www.itu.int/publications.

5 Mobile Middleware in Enterprise Systems

*Dario Bruneo, Antonio Puliafito,
Marco Scarpa, and Angelo Zaia*

CONTENTS

INTRODUCTION

In recent years, mobile computing has become the new frontier of communication processes with the effects of several changes on the design and provision of distributed services, thus producing new business scenarios. Enterprise systems integration, a key process to enable interoperability among applications and to allow resource decentralization, has to take into account, from now on, mobility aspects. Mobility introduces significant challenges to enterprise system integration, by extending the interoperability concept and by promoting new forms of collaboration. Portable devices are able to access miscellaneous services or to provide location-dependent data anyway, anytime, and anywhere, thanks to the connectivity powered by the modern network technologies. Mobile computing scenarios call for a careful management of issues such as context awareness, mobility management, seamless connectivity, and so on.

Traditional middleware solutions cannot adequately deal with these issues. Conceived on the idea of a static context, such middleware systems hide low-level network details from applications. Instead, in mobile environments, the context is extremely dynamic and cannot be managed by *a priori* assumptions. Then, to connect applications with several mobile devices and systems it is mandatory to extend the middleware concept by introducing mobile facilities. Mobile middleware solutions [1] overcome mobility issues thanks to reconfiguration techniques able to react to the changes in the operating context, and powerful mechanisms to propagate such changes until the application level, that is, where it is possible to take the right decisions.

In this chapter, in order to highlight the issues related to the mobile middleware design, we will show some typical mobile business scenarios, focusing on the main aspects that have to be taken into account. We will then give some basic concepts of mobile middleware solutions, analyzing in detail all the technological aspects. In particular, critical aspects related to the adoption of such paradigm in enterprise systems integration, such as security, will be discussed. Finally, a real case study will be discussed presenting the WhereX® middleware.

MOBILE BUSINESS SCENARIOS

The interest of companies for cooperation-oriented software solutions has grown over time, driven by the needs of operating in the market. For a medium/large scale company, the use of an information system is no longer limited to the use of a single software package, possibly closely related to the activity field of the company itself—i.e., computer-aided design (CAD) for an industrial design company, data base for an import/export company, bookkeeping system for a hotel, and so on—but increasingly requires the use of different software that help in the automation of production activity.

As an example, consider a hotel, a relatively simple enterprise, where the reservation of a room is done through the following many different phases (as depicted in Figure 5.1):

1. An inquiry arrives from a potential guest about the availability of an accommodation with particular characteristics
2. If the room is available, return the estimated cost of the room to the inquirer
3. Formal acknowledgment of the room estimate
4. Reservation of the room by the hotel staff
5. Preparation and maintenance of the room during the arranged period
6. Payment and billing when the customer leaves

All these activities require the use of the following "enterprise applications:"

- E-mail (phone and fax could be used as well): activities 1, 2, and 3
- Electronic calendar or organizer: activities 2 and 5
- Booking system: activities 2 and 4
- Human resource management system: activity 5
- Invoicing system: activity 6

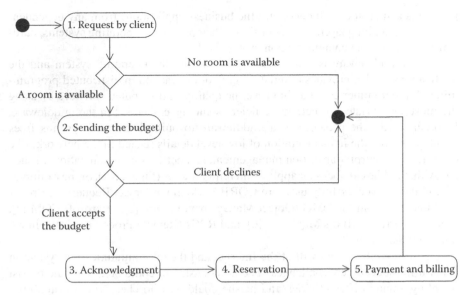

FIGURE 5.1   Activity diagram of a hotel reservation.

All these activities have a high degree of interdependence. This can be considered a typical example of "enterprise software." Enterprise software, already the largest software market segment, has rapidly grown over the last few years and will continue to explode as companies keep on improving communication and integrating applications.

Of course, the motivation towards the use of multiple software packages is mainly due to the need of improving productivity and internal efficiency such that the enterprise is able to quickly answer to market requirements and easily meets its changes. Following this trend, enterprises acquired new technologies simply by adding new tools to the preexisting ones without an in-depth reorganization of their operational procedures. The final result is the creation of a heterogeneous environment where *islands of technology* live together. To better meet the needs of companies, it is necessary to provide more complex software tools with the aim of integrating software applications together.

As the hotel example shows, the growth of the Internet has played an important role in the evolution of the enterprises; the ease of exchanging information and sharing data has opened the way to new cost-effective services, allowing to connect employers and/or customers worldwide, to directly communicate with costumers, to link suppliers and partners, and to access the enterprise's own data all over the world in a seamless and effective way.

Nevertheless, managing all the islands of technology becomes very complex or even impossible if an adequate integration has to be met. The better solution to easily deal with the integration is to provide the developers with software to *glue* all the "islands" together. This is the role of a *middleware*.

A middleware can be defined as "an enabling layer of software that resides between the business application and the networked layer of heterogeneous (diverse) platforms and protocols. It decouples the business applications from any dependencies on the plumbing layer, which consists of heterogeneous operating systems, hardware platforms, and communication protocols" [2].

Thus, a middleware is a software layer between the operating system and the applications, which provides a higher degree of abstraction in distributed programming. A programmer can thus improve the quality of distributed software by using the most appropriate, correct, and efficient solutions embedded in the middleware. In other words, the presence of a middleware to build distributed systems frees developers from the implementation of low-level details related to the network, like concurrency control, transaction management, and network communication, in such a way that he/she can focus on application requirements (Figure 5.2). Some examples of middleware successfully used are CORBA (Common Object Requesting Broker Architecture) from the OMG (Object Management Group) [3], Microsoft COM [4], Sun Java RMI [5], IBM's MQSeries [6], and RPCs (Remote Procedure Calls) introduced by Sun in 1980s.

That is not all! The growth of the Internet and the telecommunication system in general introduced new challenges. The hotel customer could be a nomadic tourist traveling among different cities and he/she could have to check room availability during his/her travel and, in some cases, to book it.

More generally, enterprises have to take into account two main changes in the environment where they operate. The market is becoming more and more *virtual* and employees would like to access enterprises services wherever they are, particularly because workers are becoming more and more mobile.

Decreasing costs of mobile communications drive the development of today's enterprises, offering the opportunity to provide new added-value services. Mobility

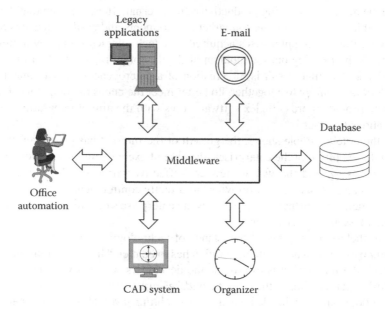

FIGURE 5.2 Software integration through middleware.

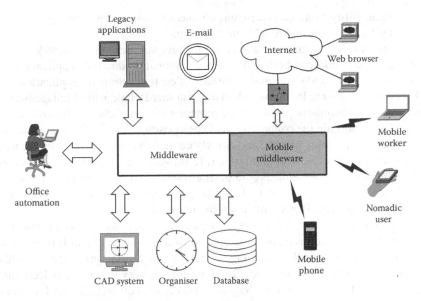

FIGURE 5.3 Software integration through mobile middleware.

can also help in increasing productivity of the sales force because they can reach their customers more easily and quickly.

The middleware has to consequently be able to adapt to such changes and provide the necessary features to promptly face these new challenges. The concept of *mobile middleware* is a natural extension of the basic middleware functionalities to deal with the mobile Internet (Figure 5.3).

As explained in the following sections, a mobile middleware extends a "traditional" middleware with services and protocols such that enterprise software developers can easily provide access to applications and data to mobile devices. The existence of such middleware improves the software development process in terms of security, reliability, and development speed.

ENTERPRISE MOBILITY REQUIREMENTS

The Gartner Group foresees that by 2012, 50% of traveling workers will use mobile devices instead of notebooks; therefore a typical business scenario very likely will involve thousands of mobile devices [7].

Mobile devices are heterogeneous in terms of capabilities and operating platforms. Some of the more popular are as follows:

- Microsoft Windows Mobile OS
- Symbian OS from Symbian Foundation
- Apple iPhone platform
- Android from the Open Handset Alliance

Each of these platforms adopts different solutions with regards to software development, applications and OS maintenance, and data synchronization. Therefore, managing mobility in an enterprise environment requires that some specific issues be tackled by a flexible and reliable middleware.

Transparent device management is the first requirement that a mobile business application has to address, both in the case of personal productivity applications such as e-mail, calendar, and so on, and in the case of custom enterprise applications, such as Enterprise Resource Planning (ERP) or Customer Relationship Management. For this reason, IT administrators have to be provided with a unique administration panel to set up and maintain the configuration of enterprise-related applications, regardless of the specific operating system, and quickly enough to promptly react to infrastructure or service changes. Mobile middleware provides the underlying technologies, such as common application programming interfaces (APIs) or services, to send reconfiguration messages and to translate platform-agnostic commands, like an e-mail server address change, into a set-up operation.

Deploying and maintaining mobile applications that address enterprise needs adds another set of requirements regarding software updates. IT administrators wish to have a quasi-real-time delivery of the updates to all the enterprise devices, without any involvement from the user side. Delays could be very expensive indeed, due to security-related issues, such as bug corrections or vulnerability and functional patches untimely delivered. Due to its proved flexibility, the Web seems to be adequate to solve such issues, allowing each mobile device to directly access enterprise applications without any further superstructure. Unfortunately, the Web has some limitations relevant to the mobile business scenario, such as disconnects and data or events dissemination. For example, consider a salesman registering on his personal data assistant a purchase order: he wishes to send it immediately to his enterprise, but due to connection unavailability, he has to defer such transmission to the future. The Web itself does not permit such kind of disconnected operation, but a well-designed mobile middleware could automatically allow order data, temporarily stored on the device, to be synchronized with the enterprise server, once the connection is active again. Projects like Google Gears are focused on this challenge, although they are still in their infancy. On the other hand, when the salesman places an order, the sales supervisor must receive an alert on his mobile device. Such push operations are not allowed by the currently available Web technology and mobile users have to explicitly refresh their browsers to retrieve new data. On the contrary, mobile middleware pushes data or events through message-based communications.

Security-related issues have to be adequately considered in general and specifically in a mobile environment, where data are transferred from the enterprise to the mobile device, and vice versa. Information stored on the mobile device, in fact, has to be considered as a critical corporate asset, and its loss or fraudulent access has to be promptly prevented. In order to address such issues, mobile middleware has to provide security mechanisms for data retrieving, gathering, and synchronization, powerful enough for IT managers and easy to implement for developers. Using authentication mechanisms, in conjunction with channel or message encryption techniques, the middleware layer allows developers to create intrinsically secure applications without additional efforts.

Performance-related requirements are extremely important in some business scenarios, where delays and losses due to mobility have to be kept to a minimum.

The functional requirements described so far need to be analyzed in conjunction with the related architectural and developmental aspects of a typical enterprise system. As described in other chapters of this handbook, enterprise systems are shifting from a chaotically organized group (technology islands) of monolithic applications to an ecosystem of services organized according to a service-oriented architecture (SOA) and coordinated by a business process management (BPM) engine. The SOA vision of an enterprise system assumes an asynchronous interaction of loosely coupled reusable services to replace the tightly integrated monolithic architecture of legacy systems. Such architecture is, in brief, constituted by

- Providers and services aggregators
- Brokers, to act as services yellow pages
- Consumers

Providers publish their services (Web service) and register their availability on the Universal Description, Discovery, and Integration (UDDI) registry. Web services are described using the Web Service Description Language (WSDL), which defines exposed methods and input/output data and formats. Consumers can access the services referenced by brokers through the Simple Object Access Protocol (SOAP), the Extensible Messaging and Presence Protocol (XMPP) [8], or the REpresentational State Transfer (REST) protocol [9]. XMPP is a secure, decentralized, and flexible communication protocol based on the publish–subscribe paradigm while REST is a style of software architecture for distributed hypermedia systems such as the World Wide Web.

In order to compose services as a business process, a BPM engine executes activities described through the Business Process Execution Language (BPEL). Each of the mentioned protocols and languages are open standards and can be effectively used to extend enterprise services to mobile devices.

The adopted strategy to extend enterprise applications to mobile users is to make the mobile devices part of the SOA architecture through a mobile middleware layer. The middleware resides both on the server side and on the client side and its functionalities can be accessed through API and/or Web service requests. The middleware layer has to satisfy all the previous requirements, thus allowing management, monitoring, and secure data retrieving, gathering, and synchronization. In order to integrate the enterprise, SOA architecture with heterogeneous mobile devices, open standards for protocols, and data formats should be used. All of the above-mentioned operating platforms allow the use of the Extensible Markup Language (XML) that, in conjunction with HTTP or XMPP as the communication channel, represents the foundations of each protocol and data representation method of modern applications. From a software engineering point of view, we have many development frameworks that can be used to program mobile devices and the choice depends on the specific operating platform. Microsoft Windows Mobile OS, thanks to the .NET Framework, supports XML and Web Services. Java 2 Micro Edition (J2ME) devices, such as Symbian OS or Windows Mobile OS, can access the enterprise SOA through kSOAP, which is a J2ME-based SOAP parser, and the JSR 172, which provides a standard set of XML and SOAP APIs. The Android SDK (software development kit) allows the development of applications based on the Java programming language. Instead of J2ME, Android devices use the Dalvik virtual machine, which relies on the Linux kernel. Nowadays, however, many Web services are REST compliant, meaning that the query is encoded in a regular HTTP request and the results come back in a simple XML format. In that way, Android devices can be part of an enterprise SOA. The same REST compliant approach can be used for the iPhone devices, due to the lack of a specific SOAP API.

MOBILE MIDDLEWARE: CONCEPTS AND TECHNOLOGIES

Protocols and operational problems should be transparent to users accessing distributed (e.g., Internet-based) services. Typically, they would run an application and expect results from it, without being aware of all the operations involved. However, a connection must be established; a negotiation about the most appropriate communication parameters and other complex activities should be performed. All of these activities are not known to most network users. In a distributed system environment, developers must attend to all details related to the communication (addressing, error handling, data representation, etc.). This is due to the fact that developers use the low-level abstraction provided by the network operating system. To free developers from the expensive and time-consuming activity of resolving all the problems related to the network management, more abstraction must be introduced through a *middleware* layer.

Mobile access to distributed applications and services raises many new issues related to wireless technologies (limited bandwidth, signal loss), to portable devices (limited computational resources, power consumption), and to user mobility (hand-off, location management). In fact, several disconnections can occur either voluntarily (i.e., related to power saving policies) or suddenly (i.e., due to the signal loss). Wireless technologies differ greatly in terms of performances and reliability: portable devices have a high degree of heterogeneity, and several services have to adapt their features to the real position of the user. This is why new and enhanced features have to be duly taken into consideration, thus resulting in the so-called *mobile middleware*.

Context transparency makes the development of complex applications easier, but it does not allow for decisions about the environments at the service level where applications run [10]. Then, it is mandatory to implement reconfiguration techniques able to react to the changes in the operating context, and powerful mechanisms to propagate such changes upto the application level, that is, where it is possible to take the right decisions.

Several aspects have to be managed by mobile middleware [including but not limited to service discovery, QoS (quality of service) management, service tailoring, load balancing, power management, handoff management], thus calling for new design strategies [11,12] that can be classified into three main groups: context management, connection management, and resource management. Table 5.1 summarizes the main aspects to be taken care of with regard to such management issues.

TABLE 5.1
Mobile Middleware Management Issues

Context management	Metadata definition
	Binding techniques
	Computational reflection
	Location awareness
Connection management	Asynchronous communication
	Data synchronization and replication
	Handoff management
	Session management
Resource management	Load management
	Location management
	Modular design
	Delegation

CONTEXT MANAGEMENT

Mobile computing applications need to adapt to changes in the context to overcome the issues related to high-level service provisioning. To enable applications to adapt to such context evolutions, parameter reconfiguration at provision time is necessary [13,14]. Mobile middleware systems cannot hide the context at the upper layers, but instead must both represent it and announce changes until the service layer is reached. It is at this layer, in fact, that decisions can be made about the most powerful way to react to context changes. Clearly, such decisions can be taken only by knowing the service typology and not on the basis of low-level information. Then it is necessary to implement middleware systems, reaching a trade-off between transparency and awareness [15].

One of the main design aspects of a context-aware middleware is related to the study of a representation of the operating context to capture its features and to make them available to the upper layers. Such representation has to be flexible and powerful in order to allow applications to easily react at provision time to the frequently context evolutions. A common technique adopted for the context representation is the definition of metadata; in particular, profiles and policies are metadata that describe, with a high level of abstraction, context features and actions to carry out in the case of its evolution. These metadata, represented by a meta-language (e.g., XML [16]), have to be separated from the implementation details to facilitate the management of operations. Suitable binding techniques have to be implemented to enable applications to change their execution at runtime according to the envisaged policies. Such requirements make *computational reflection*, introduced in Ref. [17], an attractive technique for a mobile middleware design. This is the ability of a software system to monitor its computation and to change, if necessary, its execution. These two phases, monitoring and adapting, are generally called introspection and interception.

Some context aware middleware, based on the concept of reflection, can be found in the literature; see, for example, Refs. [18,19]. One of the context features that has raised a lot of interest in recent years is location management [20]. Location-aware middleware provides services according to the user's position by tracking the user's movements; this has been developed for applications such as e-health [21], e-learning [22], and cultural heritage [23].

CONNECTION MANAGEMENT

User mobility, intermittent signals, and resource management policies give rise to frequent disconnections and reconnections of mobile devices. Such behavior, not found in traditionally distributed systems, makes synchronous communication unsuitable, because the sender and receiver are not connected simultaneously during the communication. As a consequence, mobile middleware has to provide asynchronous communications so that tasks could be carried out, notwithstanding the intermittent link between sender and receiver. To this end, solutions to decouple the sender and the receiver are required. Decoupled middleware systems have to manage the issues related to the data synchronization by implementing data replication techniques.

A common solution is the use of tuple space systems to provide shared memory areas where both the sender and the receiver can input their data in an asynchronous way [24]. Once a message has been sent (that is after a *write* operation), the sender can continue his/her tasks without waiting for the receiver to carry out the *read*.

In such a way, a mobile user can make a query, disconnect from the network, and, once reconnected, retrieve the results. Examples of tuple spaces-based middleware are Tspaces [25] and JavaSpaces [26].

Another technique adopted is the use of data subsets downloaded in the mobile device in order to create a local representation of the information scattered in the wired network; mobile users can conduct offline transactions using these local data subsets and the actual operations can be accomplished once the user switches to online [27,28]. For example, these subsets can be adopted in an e-commerce scenario so that users could download part of the product list and create, offline, a local shopping cart with the selected products. Once the connection is set up, the system has to retrieve the local shopping cart and carry out the order.

The drawback of these solutions in data synchronization is the need to use advanced techniques for the synchronization of the data; in the previous scenario we have to deal, for example, with the issues related to price updates between the local product list and the official one, or we have to take into account the problems related to product availability. The system should be able to disseminate these updates and do an effective comparison between data, verifying the correctness of the transactions. Such operations highly depend on the manner the data are structured.

Another issue related to connection management is the provision of services based on the concept of session (e.g., the multimedia streaming). A temporary disconnection or the change of an address could cause session loss and the end of the service provisioning.

Such issues can be solved by adopting proxies to decouple client and server and to hide these disconnections to the service layer [29,30]. Proxies have to interact with the specific protocol involved in service provisioning; then their development is strictly related to the particular typology of the service that we want to use.

Robust protection of the data transfer is provided by solutions such as Simple Authentication and Security Layer (SASL) [31] and Transport Layer Security (TLS) [32]. TLS is a cryptographic protocol that enables secure communications over the Internet cloud. SASL can be used in conjunction with TLS in order to make available robust authentication mechanisms to applications. Protocols like XMPP and HTTP may be successfully adopted in developing mobile middleware for a SOA environment.

RESOURCE MANAGEMENT

The design of mobile middleware and the management of the discussed techniques are strictly related to the hardware resources to be used for their execution, which are usually really scarce. This introduces another constraint on the design of such systems: mobile middleware has to be lightweight [33]. A mobile middleware, then, on the one hand, has to implement techniques able to guarantee better usage of the available resources by reducing, for example, wireless transmissions and by adapting service typology to the real features of the client devices. On the other hand, a mobile middleware has to be designed in an efficient way in order to avoid overloading the device itself.

First of all, we have to take into account the use of the sensors needed for the accomplishment of the middleware goals; a right context representation, in fact, foresees the use of several sensors (for example of position) for the collection of the data that have to be monitored, in order to manage the context evolutions. The use of sensors must to be restricted as much as possible because such components are very onerous in terms of resource consumption. For example, if location management is needed, triangulation techniques could be implemented rather than using Global Positioning System (GPS) modules on the mobile devices [34].

A second aspect is related to the computational load of the middleware. In addition to low memory usage, a mobile middleware has to reduce the amount of data processing within the limits of the computing resources of the mobile devices. To this end, it is important to design highly modular middleware systems capable of activating only modules that are absolutely necessary for the required operations (deactivating the superfluous ones at runtime) [13]. The remaining parts of the whole system (for example to the wired infrastructure) are relegated to operations that require a high computational load, such as multimedia service tailoring [30].

THE WHEREX MIDDLEWARE

The goal of this section is to present a mobile middleware being used in enterprise systems, named *WhereX* and produced by Inquadro, a spin-off company of the University of Messina. WhereX is the middleware provided with *WhereBox*, an integrated hardware and software product designed for the management of infra-structures for automatic identification based on the modern Radio Frequency Identification (RFID) technology, sensor networks, GPS, Bluetooth and Wi-Fi. WhereX introduces significant perspectives to enterprise system integration, by extending the interoperability concept and by promoting new forms of collaboration and a careful management of issues such as context awareness, mobility management, and seamless connectivity.

WhereX is based on a J2EE (Java 2 Platform, Enterprise Edition) architecture, is integrated with Oracle Application Server 10 g, and can adapt its behavior according to the customer's needs and allows the following:

- Simultaneous management of many objects and readers, even with different technologies (active RFIDs, HF and UHF passive RFIDs, semi-passive RFIDs, ZigBee, Sensor Network, etc.), as shown in Figure 5.4
- Management of many sensors placed on wide surfaces, not covered by previous infrastructures
- High scalability to meet the requirements of modern and dynamic companies
- On- and offline interfacing with mobile devices

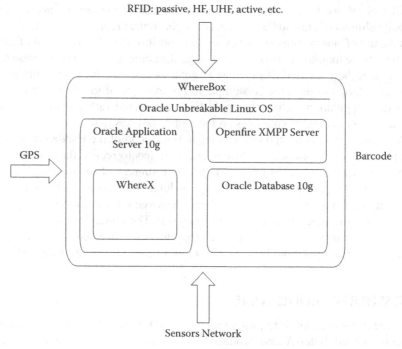

FIGURE 5.4 Technological choices in WhereBox/WhereX.

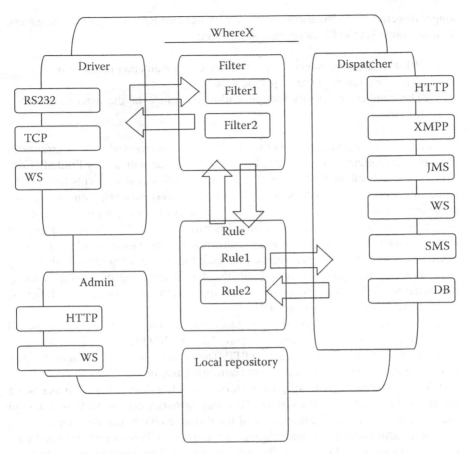

FIGURE 5.5   WhereX architecture.

The core of WhereBox—that is, the WhereX middleware—was created using the state-of-the-art technologies of communication architectures and infrastructures, with the final goal of offering a solution compliant to Web services and capable of providing multichannel communications.

Figure 5.5 shows the architecture of the WhereX middleware and depicts the main components, that is, the drivers, filters, rules, dispatcher, repository, and the administration console.

To allow a simple and effective integration of enterprise systems, WhereX offers all the basic functionalities to collect data from different sources (sensors), managing many readers connected through the most widely used interfaces (RS232 and Ethernet). It can also collect the data coming from the readers that work offline and that send the information collected later through a subsequent synchronization.

WhereX implements data-filtering operations to remove the redundant information arriving from the different readers (such as the continuous reading of the same piece of information). For instance, it is sometimes sufficient to detect only the time instant when an event occurs for the first time and the time instant when it is no longer detected, thus discarding all the detections made between these two moments. WhereX provides the filters necessary to detect:

- Whether a sensor enters or exits the range of the antenna-reader system
- Whether a sensor enters a specific area
- The number of sensors present within the range of the antenna-reader system

The filters provided can be applied both to each device and to logic groups of devices. Customized filters can also be easily developed with a very limited effort. Filters can be combined into rules that allow the origination of events for specific situations. This feature enables WhereX to assure safety processes, and to manage situations where an object must or must not be in a specific area, or groups of specific objects are in a specific area, and so on. This way, alerts, VoIP call forwarding, and e-mails can be managed. Thus, the user can create the most suitable rules for his/her needs, without rebooting WhereBox and facilitating the integration with legacy systems of an enterprise. More specifically, data dispatching consists of sending reconstructed information to the different applications interacting with WhereX, through the processes mentioned above.

The most recent communication protocols, which allow WhereX to be integrated in enterprise systems, as shown in Figure 5.5, are XMPP, VoIP, Short Message Service, Java Message Service, and HTTP. They can be used simultaneously, thus providing a powerful multichannel communication feature.

WhereBox is also able to keep the history of the data detected, as well as storing the set-up information of the system. This way, statistics can be made on the data even at a later time, and the movement of the different objects can be traced.

System administration is made through a user-friendly Web interface created with the most innovative technology available on the market. This enables administrators to add and remove devices, filters, rules, and dispatchers—and of course to configure the parameters of the system itself, to view the state of the system, and to extract reports even from remote stations (intranet and/or Internet), without being in the place where WhereBox was installed. The administration interface also contains a graphic module that enables a virtual reconstruction of the context where the administrator works, by loading maps and by placing the objects and the devices managed by WhereBox appropriately in the maps. This virtual representation makes the localization and tracking of objects easier and allows the selection of areas where some rules can be fixed.

COMMERCIAL APPLICATIONS

WhereX has already been successfully used to provide mobility features in enterprise systems. Examples of commercial applications fully developed on top of the WhereX middleware are the following:

WhereDoc®: an application for the identification, tracing, and management of paper archives. This developed solution, which can be customized according to the user's needs, uses a mixed strategy, by combining the "virtual life" of the electronic document with real life, through the use of RFID technology. It makes wide use of multichannel communication features, events management, and mobility.

WhereArt®: a software that replaces tourist guides both in parks and museums and in cities. It uses the potential of RFID, GPS, Bluetooth, and ZigBee technologies, but the main advantage of the system is that it is not strictly linked to a specific technology, but can simultaneously use all of them. It also offers powerful graphical features to optimally distribute information toward mobile users.

WhereObj®: an application for asset management that makes extensive use of RFID technology and sensor networks. Special attention is paid to the usability of the system and to the possibility of integrating it with the procedures and the systems used by the customer. This application is used in wide and dynamic realities, where the management of assets is a complex work, with long processes and management times. If this management is partly automated, data accuracy and cost savings can be improved.

Such applications are clear examples of the great potentialities of the WhereX middleware, which allows the programmer to focus on the specific problem to be solved, taking care of all the aspects related to the integration with legacy systems and enterprise systems in general, providing very powerful features to manage user and components mobility, and thus reducing the time-to-market of the final solution, as well as its quality and performance.

SUMMARY

This chapter presented the role of the widespread diffusion of mobile computing in the design of emerging enterprise systems. Starting from an analysis of the new business scenarios offered by mobile connectivity, we thoroughly investigated the requirements (such as context and location awareness, security, data integrity, etc.) on mobile facilities in enterprise applications. Mobile middleware allows a powerful integration of different and distributed business components by reaching a trade-off between transparency and awareness and by providing the mobility support from the early stages of the design phase.

Technological aspects related to mobile middleware implementation have been presented by analyzing the state-of-the-art and by highlighting the adjustments that have to be carried out in order to realize an effective enterprise system integration.

Finally, a real case study has been proposed introducing the WhereX middleware with the final goal of illustrating a real solution that extends the interoperability concept and promotes new forms of collaboration.

REFERENCES

1. Bruneo, D., Scarpa, M., and Puliafito, A., Mobile middleware: Definition and motivations, in *The Handbook of Mobile Middleware*, Bellavista, P. and Corradi, A., Eds, Auerbach, Boca Raton, 2007, 145–167.

2. Kanoc, T., Mobile middleware: The next frontier in enterprise application integration, White paper, Nettech Systems Inc., Princeston, NJ, 1999.

3. Pope, A., *The Corba Reference Guide: Understanding the Common Object Request Broker Architecture*, Addison-Wesley, Boston, MA, 1998.

4. Box, D., *Essential COM*, Addison-Wesley Longman Edition, Boston, MA, 1998.

5. Java Soft, Java Remote Method Invocation Specification, Revision 1.5, JDK 1.2 edition, Sun Microsystems, Inc. October 1992.

6. Gilman, L. and Schreiber, R., *Distributed Computing with IBM MQSeries*, John Wiley & Sons, 1996.

7. Gartner, Highlights Key Predictions for IT Organisations and Users in 2008 and Beyond, available at http://gartner.com/it/page.jsp?id=593207

8. XMPP Standard Foundation, available at http://www.xmpp.org

9. Pautasso, C., Zimmermann, O., and Leymann, F., RESTful web services vs. big web services: Making the right architectural decision, *Proceedings of the 17th International World Wide Web Conference* (WWW2008), Beijing, China, 2008.

10. Chan, A. and Chuang, S., MobiPADS: A reflective middleware for context-aware mobile computing, *IEEE Trans. Softw. Eng.*, 29(12),1072–1085, 2003.

11. Eliassen, F. et al., Next generation middleware: Requirements, architecture and prototypes, *Proceedings of the 7th IEEE Workshop on Future Trends of Distributed Computing Systems*, 1999, 60–65, 1999.

12. Mascolo, C., Capra, L., and Emmerich, W., Middleware for mobile computing (A servers), in *Advanced Lectures in Networking, Networking 2002 Tutorial*, LNCS 2497, Gregori, E., Anastasi, G., and Basagni, S., Eds, Springer-Verlag, Berlin, 2002, 20–58.

13. Bellavista, P. et al., Context-aware middleware for resource management in the wireless Internet, *IEEE Trans. Softw. Eng.*, 29(12), 1086–1099, 2003.

14. Capra, L., Emmerich, W., and Mascolo, C., CARISMA: Context-aware reflective middleware system for mobile applications, *IEEE Trans. Softw. Eng.*, 29(10), 929–945, 2003.

15. Capra, L., Emmerich, W., and Mascolo, C., Middleware for mobile computing: Awareness vs. transparency, *Proceedings of the 8th Workshop Hot Topics in Operating Systems*, IEEE CS Press, Los Alamitos, CA, 2001, 164–169.

16. Extensible Markup Language (XML), available at http://www.w3.org/XML

17. Smith, B., Reflection and semantics in LISP, *Proceedings of the 11th Annual ACM Symposium on Principles of Programming Languages*, Salt Lake City, Utah, 1984, 23–35.

18. The OpenORB Project, available at http://openorb.sourceforge.net

19. Ledoux, T., OpenCorba: A reflective open brocker, in *Meta-Level Architectures and Reflection*, LNCS, Vol. 1616, Cointe, P., Ed., Springer-Verlag, Berlin, 1999, 197–214.

20. Hazas, M., Scott, J., and Krumm, J., Location-aware computing comes of age, *IEEE Comput.*, 37(2):95–97, 2004.

21. Rodriguez, M. D. et al., Location-aware access to hospital information and services, *IEEE Trans. Inform. Technol. Biomed.*, 8(4), 448–455, 2004.

22. Griswold, W. G. et al., ActiveCampus: Experiments in community-oriented ubiquitous computing, *IEEE Comput.*, 37(10), 73–81, 2004.

23. Krosche, J., Baldzer, J., and Boll, S, MobiDENK—Mobile multimedia in monument conservation, *IEEE Multimedia*, 11(2), 72–77, April–June 2004.

24. Nitzberg, B. and Lo, V., Distributed shared memory: A survey of issues and algorithms, *IEEE Comput.*, 24(8), 52–60, 1991.

25. Wyckoff, P. et al., TSpaces, *IBM Syst. J.*, 37(3), 454–474, 1998.

26. Freeman, E., Hupfer, S., and Arnold, K, *JavaSpaces: Principles, Patterns, and Practice*, Addison-Wesley, Essex, UK, 1999.

27. Mascolo, C. et al., Xmiddle: A data-sharing middleware for mobile computing, *Wireless Pers. Comm.: An Int. J.*, 21(1), 77–103, April 2002.

28. Satyanarayanan, M. et al., Coda: A highly available file system for a distributed workstation environment, *IEEE Trans. Comput.*, 39(4), 447–459, 1990.

29. Bellavista, P., Corradi, A., and Stefanelli, C., Mobile agent middleware for mobile computing, *IEEE Comput.*, 34(2), 73–81, 2001.

30. Bruneo, D. et al., VoD services for mobile wireless devices, *Proceedings of the 8th IEEE Symposium on Computers and Communications (ISCC'2003)*, Antalya, Turkey, 2003, 602–207.

31. Melnikov, A. and Zeilenga, K., Simple Authentication and Security Layer (SASL), RFC, June 2006, available at http://tools.ietf.org/html/rfc4422

32. Dierks, T. and Rescorla, E., The Transport Layer Security (TLS) Protocol Version 1.2, August 2008, available at http://tools.ietf.org/html/rfc5246

33. Yu, Y., Krishnamachari, B., and Prasanna, V.K., Issues in designing middleware for wireless sensor networks, *IEEE Netw.*, 18(1), 15–21, 2004.

34. Hightower, J. and Borriello, G., Location systems for ubiquitous computing, *IEEE Comput.*, 34(8), 57–66, 2001.

6 Secure Wireless Access to Services in Enterprise Networks

*Paolo Bellavista, Antonio Corradi,
and Alessandra Toninelli*

CONTENTS

INTRODUCTION

Modern enterprise networks offer a wide variety of wireless connectivity to their recognized users, thereby enabling them to work in geographically distributed offices, including the premises of their business partners. In practical terms, this often requires the integration of heterogeneous wireless access solutions, heterogeneous security mechanisms, and a decentralized autonomous management of security. For instance, IT workers in multinational companies usually move between different, possibly geographically distributed, departments of the same company, or sometimes visit the offices of a collaborating company with well-established business relationships. All these networks have Wi-Fi (Wireless Fidelity) access points with different implementations, as well as enterprise-level Bluetooth or WiMAX (Worldwide Interoperability for Microwave Access) base stations from different vendors. Furthermore, the security policies for each subnetwork are usually adopted independently of the others taking into account the constraints and requirements of only one administrative environment. Thus, security management is performed autonomously in each locality. This integrated scenario poses novel and challenging security issues. In addition to the well-known low-layer vulnerabilities due to the nature of wireless access, the additional challenges include the secure discovery and access to enterprise resources and services. In other words, the design assumptions of traditional enterprise networks, where users were assumed to be mostly sedentary, will have to be re-examined. The main thesis of this chapter is that novel approaches to secure wireless access to services must take into account the operational and environmental context in the personalization of security/service provisioning over enterprise networks. A review of security in enterprise wireless networks, with a specific focus on secure discovery and secure access control, would give a guide to the advantages and disadvantages of each solution in practical situations. It also reveals the open challenges that remain to be solved in order to make these solutions ready for the industrial market and for their wide-scale exploitation.

PROBLEM DEFINITION

The secure discovery and secure access to enterprise resources/services are two largely unexplored aspects of security in wireless enterprise networks. First, personalized discovery is a central activity when clients are not fully aware of their execution environment, as it is usual in mobility-enabled scenarios. Securing discovery permits a personalized visibility of resources/services depending on the user's privileges, preferences, and session state. In addition, access control in dynamic environments brings to the fore novel security issues that are not encountered when the lack of frequent mobility allows simplifying assumptions. In fact, in mobile environments, it is impossible to assume resource stability and unrealistic to ask the users to have full knowledge of the networking environment where they are working.

To better outline the peculiar characteristics of wireless enterprise scenarios with a practical example of common deployment scenario, let us consider the case of a team of business consultants visiting a client company. Typically a team of consultants, whose membership might vary over time, visits or resides for a period of time at the client company to gather the necessary information or to train the employees and managers of the client company. In our example, depicted in Figure 6.1, the visiting consultants might need to access services residing on their enterprise network via the wireless network provided by the hosting company. In addition, the consultants may wish to connect to the client company network to access local resources/services, such as spreadsheets and documents, in order to accomplish their business tasks and objectives, and to interoperate with the client company managers. Note that useful resources might also be hosted on the portable devices used by the managers of the client company, such as informal work schedules or technical specification details that, being under development, have not been published as official enterprise documents yet.

While the consultant team is visiting the client, some of its members may decide to set up an informal meeting with a group of managers to discuss some specific issues, such as the re-design of the actual department organization. To promote knowledge transfer and cooperation among the consultants and the client company managers, it is important to facilitate the easy exchange of documents hosted on the participants' laptops, useful to the meeting purpose. Access to each other's documents should not, however, compromise security. In particular, resources that are not relevant for the meeting and/or have a confidential nature should be protected against unauthorized access. In addition, once the meeting is terminated, and particularly after the consultant team has left the company building, the managers who took part in the meeting might wish to prevent access to the previously shared documents.

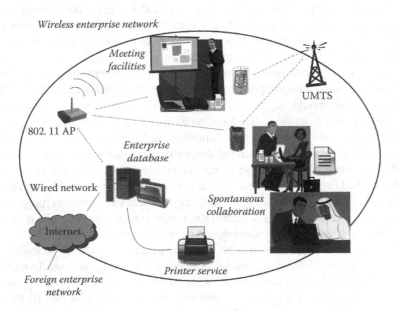

FIGURE 6.1   Scenario of wireless enterprise networking.

CONTEXT-AWARE PERSONALIZED SERVICES OVER ENTERPRISE WIRELESS NETWORKS

In highly dynamic and mobility-enabled computing environments, users can connect to different points of attachment and wireless portable devices. They can also roam and expect to maintain connectivity and service sessions. For example, a user might be connected with his/her smart phone via GPRS (General Packet Radio Service) while outdoor, and wish to attach to the IEEE 802.11 enterprise wireless network once indoor. Disconnections of users/devices are rather common operating modes that can occur either, voluntarily, to reduce connection costs and to save battery power, or accidentally due to the abrupt loss of wireless connectivity, for example, because the user enters a no-coverage area. The result is that dependability issues and the automatic management of temporary disconnections should be treated as central and crucial functions of any support solution. In addition, mobile computing environments tend to be open and exhibit a high degree of heterogeneity of both access devices, for example, screen size/resolution, computing power, memory, operating system, supported software, and networking technologies, such as, IEEE 802.11b/g, Bluetooth, GSM, GPRS, and UMTS (Universal Mobile Telecommunications System).

As already stated, the main thesis of this chapter is that *context*-based approaches can offer suitable novel guidelines to support the above environments. Context is a complex concept that has several definitions [1,2]; here, it is considered to be any information that can characterize the state or the activity of an entity as well as the environment where that entity operates. More specifically, it can be the full set of metadata describing the current execution session, including the user's preferences, characteristics and roles, as well as the service profiles and security policies. In fact, the high degree of variability and heterogeneity of the targeted deployment environments makes service management a very complex task. Supporting and personalizing services require novel methodologies and tools to specify which management actions should be taken based on contextual information [3,4]. For instance, consider the case of an enterprise user visiting a client company where he/she would be provided with services, such as a printing facility or a virtual tour of the building. Mobile enterprise users should be enabled to dynamically search and retrieve location-dependent resources/services that could be of interest and supported them in carrying their tasks in the current context. Simultaneously, the scope of their visibility is to be restricted to avoid unintentional disclosure of sensitive business information. Finally, they should be able to act as service providers in addition to being service clients, by making resources and/or functions hosted on their devices available to other allowed users. Given the high dynamicity of these environments, proper access control solutions are required to permit the secure interaction of mobile users wishing to interact by reciprocally sharing and exchanging resources.

The increasing complexity of network management and application logic in context-aware systems raises the demand for adequate support solutions. In particular, several kinds of functionality for the support of wireless enterprise applications need to be provided at development and execution times, including: (i) the interaction and/or integration of possibly heterogeneous systems (such as networks and resource management systems); (ii) the abstraction of underlying facility details so to hide network, operating system, and programming language heterogeneity; and (iii) the implementation of these abstractions in transparent application programming interfaces.

A *middleware*-level approach starts to be widely recognized as a suitable solution to offer a set of flexible and reusable support services that facilitate the design, deployment, and execution of a distributed application by implementing the above-mentioned features. In particular, middleware solutions for wireless enterprise networks should be context-dependent and support at least two functions: (i) to securely discover only resources/services of interest for requesting users and (ii) to securely access resources/services, even hosted on portable devices, in open and dynamic wireless environments. Conventional middleware was designed for static contexts and tend to hide low-level network details. In contrast, because the context of enterprise wireless networks is extremely dynamic, the corresponding middleware solutions should allow the adaptation of mobile computing applications to frequent changes in the execution environment and consequently frequent modifications in the applicable context [5].

Thus, the middleware should meet the following requirements:

1. It should collect and represent context information, such as user location, application execution conditions and device status, at a high level of abstraction, and propagate this information up to the application level.
2. It should provide means to specify and enforce context-dependent adaptation strategies for running applications, transparently from the point of view of the application logic (thus requiring no modifications). For instance, a service providing a virtual tour of a building should adapt the data to be visualized to the characteristics of client device display, ranging from a laptop to a smart phone.

Context-aware behaviors should be expressed at a high level of abstraction by separating context-dependent decisions from the specific application logic and its implementation [1,6,7]. This *separation of concerns* is essential to reduce the complexity of service development and management in highly dynamic environments and to favor rapid prototyping, run-time configuration, and maintenance of application components. This is pushing toward the proposal of novel middleware supports to assist service developers/managers/providers [4,6–8].

One primary mechanism to fulfill the above goals is through the exploitation of metadata. Metadata can describe both the structure/meaning of the resources composing a system and the management operations to perform when given conditions apply, expressed at a high level of abstraction [9]. Middleware solutions based on metadata for representing both context and adaptation of service behavior can provide a high level of abstraction and a clear separation between service management and application logic.

Among the different possible types of metadata, *profiles* and *policies* are particularly suited to build context-aware middleware solutions. Profiles represent characteristics, capabilities, and requirements of system components, such as users, devices, and services. Policies express the choices for ruling the system behavior, in terms of the actions subjects that can or must perform on resources [10]. Profiles and policies are maintained completely separated from the details of system implementation and are expressed at a high level of abstraction, usually in terms of a declarative specification language, thus ensuring the *separation of concerns* between context-aware application management and the implementation of the application logic.

The design-time and run-time effectiveness of metadata adoption, that is, respectively, the suitability to accelerate/simplify the development process and the lightweight efficient exploitation of metadata to tailor service provisioning dynamically, depend on the characteristics of both the chosen specification language and the middleware support infrastructure. Recent literature in the field suggests that *semantic technologies* represent a valid option for metadata specification and management [3,4,11]. Semantic technologies consist in a set of languages and frameworks for expressive knowledge representation and reasoning. The powerful representation capabilities of semantic languages can model complex context information and dynamically extend defined context models with additional concepts and properties. As a key feature, semantic languages allow the formal specification of context models whose underlying semantics is unambiguously defined, thus facilitating the dynamic exchange of context knowledge among interacting entities, even those that do not statically know each other, without loss of meaning. Let us suppose, for example, that a user is looking for a printing service within a client company wireless network. It might happen that there exists a printing service, whose name is unknown to the interested user. In this case, it is crucial for successful discovery that the user is enabled to express his/her desired service functionality based on the meaning of his/her query rather than on a particular keyword. Semantic technologies also allow automated reasoning to infer additional and/or more complex knowledge from available context data. The ability to reason over context knowledge can be successfully exploited to build middleware solutions capable of recognizing context and taking appropriate management decisions based on it. In addition, the adoption of semantic languages for metadata specification simplifies metadata reuse in open wide-scale deployment scenarios and facilitates the analysis of potential conflicts and inconsistencies.

SERVICE DISCOVERY

As already stated, effective service discovery in dynamic enterprise network environments is a complex task. It has to take into account user and device mobility, changes in service availability, variations of user roles within mutual interactions, and heterogeneity of security mechanisms and access terminals.

For example, in a new environment, such as when visiting the client company, the consultants are not likely to be (completely) aware of the company service deployment infrastructure, but they would need to only find and access some specific services of interest, such as a printing service or a browsing service to access useful enterprise documents and spreadsheets. Similarly, providers need to advertise their services to clients whose technical capabilities and interaction situations are not known precisely beforehand. Searching for a service based on keywords or classification patterns, for example, XML tags, might lead to imprecise requests that cannot capture all relevant services and/or retrieve services not intended by the original search. Another complication is that the same subject may switch among roles from a user to a service provider and vice versa. Wireless enterprise service discovery is further complicated by the impossibility to foresee all the possible interactions that may take place among users and services and the environmental situations in which these interactions take place.

Moreover, the search and retrieval of business resources by external users, such as the consultant team members, may raise critical security issues on the client company network infrastructure. Several security requirements need to be guaranteed, such as authentication of both users and services, communication privacy, and service integrity, while keeping the company service infrastructure manageable for enterprise system/security administrators and usable for enterprise users. A crucial aspect is represented by the need to control visibility of resources not only at the time the consultants try to access services, but also before they can actually find and retrieve them. Preventing unauthorized users not only to access, but also to view more services than the ones strictly needed to perform their tasks would avoid the unintentional exposure of sensitive business information.

Significant research efforts have been addressed toward the design and development of conceptual frameworks and support systems for service discovery, not only in mobile ubiquitous environments, but also in enterprise wireless networks. The following sections aim to provide an overview of related work in service discovery and access control for enterprise and mobile environments by providing common classification criteria.

DISCOVERY FUNCTIONS AND CHARACTERISTICS

Service discovery solutions differ in many different aspects of both design and implementation, ranging from low-level mechanisms and protocols, such as service announcement and lookup, service naming, and service registration/deregistration, to higher level functionalities, such as service description and selection [12]. Additional features have been progressively considered, especially due to the growing diffusion of ubiquitous environments, in particular, the support for security [13] and for context-awareness [12].

Service Core Functions

The core basic discovery functions are service registration, announcement, and lookup. Discovery solutions designed for traditional distributed environments typically rely on the presence of a directory, which stores information about registered services, such as their name, description, and invocation endpoint. The directory can be either centralized, such as in the case of Jini (http://www.jini.org), and the service location protocol (SLP) (http://www.openslp.org), or distributed, such as in Superstring [14] and PrudentExposure [12], to balance computational load across different nodes and avoid bottlenecks. Discovery solutions targeted at more dynamic network environments such as MANET (Mobile Ad-hoc NETworks), adopt a completely distributed approach, that is, without a directory. In this case, either the services advertise their presence via periodical broadcast/multicast (push-based approach) or the clients broadcast/multicast service requests to which services might reply, thus signaling their presence (pull-based approach). To the former case belongs, for example, DEAPspace [15], to the latter Bluetooth service discovery protocol (SDP) (http://www.bluetooth.org/), while most solutions support both search and advertisement, for example, Intentional Naming System [16], Jini, SLP, and Universal Plug and Play (UPnP) (http://www.upnp.org). The SLP framework supports both directory-based and directory-less infrastructure models.

Discovery Scope

Conventional discovery solutions have been designed for traditional enterprise/ home environments and mobile computing scenarios [12]. The underlying assumption shared by these traditional discovery solutions is that services can still operate in dynamic heterogeneous environments provided that the network has well-defined boundaries that remain under the management of the enterprise system administrators. Therefore, most existing discovery solutions implicitly define the boundaries of the service discovery searching space (discovery scope), albeit with different approaches:

- One class of solutions, such as INS and Bonjour (http://www.developer. apple.com/networking/bonjour/), considers administrative domains as the implicit discovery scope. Clients can search only within the collection of services under the control and responsibility of their same administrator.
- Another class adopts a network topology-based approach to fix the search boundaries. The implicit assumption is that clients and services in the same discovery scope belong to one administrative domain. This means that the set of services currently accessible by the user corresponds to those residing on nodes connected within the same network. In particular, solutions like for instance UPnP use the client/service Local Area Networks (LAN) environment as the default discovery scope, whereas DEAPspace and Bluetooth SDP choose a single-hop in the wireless network as the search range.
- Approaches based on peer-to-peer (P2P) technology, such as the JXTA protocol suite (https://jxta.dev.java.net/), allow peers to federate in groups that do not necessarily corresponds to either low-level networks or administrative domains, and to dynamically join/leave those groups. The grouping mechanism allows each peer to only view those services that are hosted by other peers within the same group.
- Other less-conventional and more recent discovery proposals, such as Ninja SDS, SLP, and Jini, slightly extend the previous approaches with search services so that users could specify either their roles or their physical locations to refine the discovery scope. However, the offered security is unsuitable for enterprise wireless scenarios because different nearby users would have the same views of available services, regardless of other high-level attributes.

Naming

Existing discovery solutions also differ in the way they support service naming and description:

- Most solutions (UPnP, Bonjour, Jini, SLP, and Bluetooth SDP) provide a template-based approach that defines the scheme for names and attributes.
- A few proposals, such as INS and Ninja SDS, specify the format for service description only, without further support for attribute definition.
- Some solutions, such as JXTA, adopt a more portable approach by providing XML-based templates for service description and query.
- Other discovery solutions, for example, DEAPspace and PrudentExposure, do not provide any facility for naming and description.

SERVICE RETRIEVAL AND SELECTION

Most methods have the same approach to service retrieval: clients perform their searches by specifying service name and attributes, possibly expressed according to the naming template supported by the specific discovery solution. Service selection is then performed based on the exact syntactic match of names/attributes in the discovery scope.

WEB SERVICES AND SEMANTIC SOLUTIONS

Implementations following the Service Oriented Architecture (SOA) require new support infrastructures to search, retrieve, and access distributed services. In particular, these infrastructures should support two conceptually distinct functionalities, namely: service discovery and service delivery.

Among other SOA implementations, Web services represent a notable example of interoperable service description standard that is being widely adopted in enterprise settings. Web services are described by means of XML-based formats, for example, the Web Service Description Language (WSDL) (http://w3.org/TR/wsdl/), and retrieved based on keywords and fixed taxonomies, such as in the case of the Universal Description, Discovery and Integration (UDDI) protocol and its mechanisms for dynamically discovering and invoking Web services (http://uddi.xml.org). Although Web service technologies represent a significant and successful effort of standardization and cross-organizational interoperability, it must be noted that WSDL descriptions are mainly input/output-based and provide little support for expressing service functions at a high level of abstraction. In addition, the lack of semantic support in Web services protocols causes service discovery to be imprecise if the user does not have a syntactically defined description of the service features.

Given the above weaknesses, novel discovery solutions are starting to emerge that exploit semantic technologies so that discovery results could be based on the semantic matching of service request and offer. Semantic languages permit the formal representation of properties describing services, devices, and users, at a high level of abstraction and with explicit semantics, thus enabling automated reasoning about this representation. Among other languages, the Resource Description Framework (RDF) and Web Ontology Language (OWL) have been standardized by the W3C consortium (http://www.w3.org/sw/). In particular, OWL Description Logics (OWL-DL) is currently the most widely adopted ontology language, as it provides a viable trade-off between expressivity and existing reasoning support provided by inference engines (see e.g., http://clarkparsia.com).

In recent years, several research proposals have emerged that adopt semantic techniques for advanced service matchmaking and discovery. The Matchmaker Project at Carnegie Mellon University (CMU) represents the first significant example of semantic technology applied to service matching and introduced the base-matching categories between service offer and request that have been extensively adopted by subsequent research work in the field: exact, with self-explicating meaning, subsumes and plug-in, which refer, respectively, to the case when the offer is more/less generic than the request [17]. Several solutions for semantic matchmaking have been then proposed, such as the semantically enhanced UDDI registry in Ref. [18], the matching algorithm for automatic service binding in Ref. [19], and MobiONT, a semantic discovery solution specific for tiny devices [20]. Other relevant pieces of work have extended the CMU Matchmaker base categories with similarity-based relations between services [21], additional logic-based relations [22], or potential/partial match relations [23]. In addition, they implemented appropriate algorithms to compute and give ranking scores to compatibility and/or similarity between services.

Several languages for service description have also been proposed, such as OWL-S (http://www.w3.org/Submission/OWL-S/), Web Service Modeling Ontology (WSMO) [24], and Meteor-S [25], to model both service interface, mainly input/output arguments, and service process workflow. We note that, similar to the case of Web services, these languages and the associated matchmaking algorithms are generally more focused on input/output description than on user-defined service capabilities. In addition, it is currently not clear whether these proposals will finally converge into a standard language for semantic service description.

The other emerging research guideline concerns the exploitation of context information to perform personalized adaptive discovery. This design trend has been developing within a more general frame of reference in the research on mobile pervasive environments, namely a novel approach to mobile middleware based on context-awareness [3–6,8]. Some interesting proposals are starting to emerge along this promising research direction: the importance of taking context into account in service discovery is recognized, for example, in Refs. [26,27] where context-related attributes, such as service location and load, are introduced as discovery query parameters to refine service selection. The Middleware for Intelligent Discovery of context-Aware Services (MIDAS) framework supports user-centric discovery by providing mobile users with service views, that is, set of accessible services, that are personalized based on user current context. To achieve such context-awareness, MIDAS relies on a semantic metadata representing the properties of interacting entities, and it exploits automated reasoning to match user requests against service offers [28].

SECURITY ASPECTS

Despite the significant number of existing solutions for service discovery, both in traditional and wireless environments, only few have been designed with security as a design principle. In particular, in mobile and pervasive computing environments, security is considered after the system has been developed, such as in the case of access control frameworks, or is included as an additional feature to existing service discovery systems. In the latter case, security support often tends to be insufficient, or sometimes even useless, mainly due to the fact that the system has not been originally designed to address security requirements [13]. Some research works take the perspective of applying traditional security features for distributed environments, such as authentication, privacy, and integrity, to more dynamic wireless enterprise scenarios [29]. However, this approach fails to capture the essential challenges facing traditional security models due to the novel wireless enterprise environments. In fact, security is important not only during service delivery, but also during discovery, mainly in terms of access control and mutual user-service authentication [13]. Another important factor regards the secure registration/deregistration of services, although it must be noted that this requirement is less stringent when discovery is on a distributed basis, that is, without relying on centralized directory.

Very few discovery solutions have implemented security mechanisms. In particular, only SLP, Ninja SDS, and Splendor [12] support secure registration of services. Privacy of both users and services is addressed by Ninja SDS (services only), Prudent-Exposure, and Splendor (for both services and users). Secure delivery is supported by most solutions in terms of service authentication, confidentiality, and integrity.

Some solutions also implement access control to services by supporting authorization mechanisms, such as capability lists (Ninja SDS), access control lists (ACLs)-Ninja SDS and UPnP, digital certificates (UPnP and PrudentExposure), and privilege levels (Splendor). Quite surprisingly, the same systems generally tend to neglect access control during service search and selection, by implicitly assuming that service discovery is not a security-sensitive action *per se*. On the contrary, other solutions developed for enterprise environments are starting to consider potential security issues in resource/service discovery [30].

SUMMARY

The major limitations of the presented approaches are that they focus on each aspect separately, without providing integrated support for both context awareness and semantic technologies, and typically addressing security as an additional feature rather than an essential design requirement. In general, there are several proposals concerning advanced matchmaking, although discovery frameworks providing personalized results are relatively few and tend to focus more on the issue of collecting user queries/preferences rather than on exploiting (implicit) context information. In addition, as suggested in Ref. [13], it is often the case that the analysis of security requirements is separately performed from the general analysis of target application, environment, and use case, thus leading to generic and/or not effective security solutions for service discovery. Table 6.1 summarizes the comparison of the major

TABLE 6.1
Comparison of the Major Service Discovery Solutions

	Service Registration, Announcement and Lookup	Discovery Scope	Service Naming	Service Selection and Retrieval	Security Services
Jini	Centralized directory; client search and service advertisement	Network (LAN) + user location	Service template	Syntactic matching (attributes/keywords)	Authentication, authorization, integrity
SLP	Centralized directory; client search and service advertisement	Network (LAN) + administrative domain	Service template	Syntactic matching (attributes/keywords)	Secure service registration
Superstring	Distributed directory	Network	Query template + preferences	Syntactic matching + context attributes	None
PrudentExposure	Distributed directory	Administrative domain	No naming facility	Syntactic matching (attributes/keywords)	Authentication, authorization, integrity, confidentiality, privacy
Splendor	Directory + proxy; client search and directory advertisement	Administrative domain	No naming facility	Syntactic matching (attributes/keywords)	Authentication, authorization, integrity, confidentiality, privacy
DEAPspace	Service advertisement (push)	Single-hop wireless network	No naming facility	Syntactic matching (hierarchical descriptions)	None
Bluetooth SDP	Client search (pull)	Single-hop wireless network	Service template	Syntactic matching (attributes/keywords)	Authorization, confidentiality
INS	Client search and service advertisement	Administrative domain	Service format (no attribute schema)	Syntactic matching (hierarchical attributes)	None

UPnP	Client search and service advertisement	Network (LAN)	Service template	Syntactic matching (attributes/keywords)	Authentication, authorization, privacy, integrity
Bonjour	Client search	Administrative domain	Service template	Syntactic matching (attributes/keywords)	None
JXTA	Client search	Combined network (p2p) + administrative domain (peer federation)	XML-based service template	Syntactic matching (attributes/keywords)	Java security
Ninja SDS	Distributed directory; client search and service advertisement	Network (LAN) + administrative domain (user role) + context (location)	XML support (no attribute schema)	Syntactic matching (attributes/keywords)	Authentication, authorization, integrity, confidentiality, privacy
UDDI	Directory	Administrative domain	Service template	Syntactic matching (attributes/keywords)	None
CMU Matchmaker and followings	N/A	N/A	Service template	Semantic matching	N/A
Enhanced UDDI registry [18]	Directory	Administrative domain	Service template	Semantic matching	N/A
MobiONT [20]	N/A	N/A	Service template	Semantic matching	None
OWL-S, WSMO, Meteor-S	N/A	N/A	N/A	Semantic matching	N/A
Jini extension with context attributes [27]	Centralized directory; client search and service advertisement (Jini)	Network + user location (Jini) + context	Service template (Jini-based)	Syntactic matching (Jini) + context attributes	Authentication, authorization, integrity (Jini)
MIDAS	Directory; client search	Context-based	Service template	Semantic matching + context-awareness	Security features in S-MIDAS

service discovery solutions. For the readers' convenience, the examined solutions are presented in their order of appearance throughout the section. Let us note that, since CMU Matchmaker, OWL-S, and MobiONT are examples of frameworks for service browsing and/or matchmaking (rather than discovery support systems), most categories reported in the table do not apply to them. Their contribution is, however, significant for the crucial issue of service retrieval/selection.

ACCESS CONTROL

The issue of controlling access to distributed resources within various organizational settings, such as hospitals, educational institutions, and companies, has been extensively studied [31]. The following sections describe well-known access control solutions for enterprise settings, as well as more recent and emerging approaches.

ACCESS CONTROL IN ENTERPRISE SETTINGS

Several methods to access control, the most widely known being capability lists, ACL, and Role-Based Access Control (RBAC) [32], have been designed to regulate access to shared resources. RBAC basically assigns access permissions to roles instead of assigning them directly to users, and allows users to cover different roles. By introducing a level of indirection between access privileges and user identity, it brings increased flexibility and efficiency in access control management, mainly due to the recombination of roles that may apply to several users, and vice versa. RBAC can be combined with public key infrastructures to achieve secure sharing of Web services [33].

Campbell [34] dealt with user authentication issues when accessing different enterprise services: instead of performing multiple logons, he proposed to associate user authentication credentials with low-level network identifiers, such as the MAC (Media Access Control) address, to allow access to different services, while maintaining control over user activity by means of logging. Chieu et al. [30] presented a solution for secure search of private business documents that relies on XML annotations: the proposed search engine incorporates XML-encoded security annotations into the document search index used to retrieve links from enterprise documents, thus restricting user search results to links pointing to user-accessible documents. Although this approach is limited to document links, it clearly recognizes the need to avoid the unintentional exposure of sensitive business information during resource/service discovery. All these solutions represent interesting efforts but they often tend to extend and apply traditional approaches, without rethinking security models.

ACCESS CONTROL POLICIES

A promising approach to access control management in novel dynamic environments is represented by policies. Policies have been widely recognized as a suitable means to express choices in security management and, particularly, in access control [10]. Policy-based systems generally distinguish two different kinds of policies [10]. *Authorization policies* specify the actions that subjects are allowed to perform on resources depending on various types of conditions, for example, subject identity and resource state. *Obligation policies* define the actions subjects must perform on resources when specified conditions occur. Over the last decade, policies have been applied to automate network administration tasks, such as configuration, security, recovery, or quality of service. In particular, authorization policies have been widely adopted, especially within the academic research community, to define, manage, and enforce access control strategies in distributed environments.

It is worth noting that, in enterprise settings, possible conflicts might arise between access control policies defined at the corporate level and user-defined access control policies, such as the one described at the beginning of the chapter. Different solutions to policy conflict resolution have been proposed, such as the definition of an adequate priority among policies establishing policy application order. Policy conflict resolution being out of the scope of this chapter, we refer the reader to relevant literature in the field, such as Ref. [10].

Semantic technologies, which permit to represent and reason about policies and application domains, increase the flexibility of policy specification and expressiveness in policy evaluation. Well-known policy frameworks, such as KAoS and Rei [35], have adopted a high-level abstraction in the specification of security policies using ontology-based and rule-based policy languages. In particular, KAoS uses OWL as the basis for representing and reasoning about policies within Web services, grid computing, and multiagent system platforms [36]. Context information is represented by means of semantic techniques and used to constrain the applicability of policies. Rei adopts OWL-Lite to specify policies and can reason over any domain knowledge expressed in either RDF or OWL [37]. KAoS and Rei represent intermediate approaches between two opposite approaches to policy specification. *Ontology-based policies* describe contexts and associated policies at a high level of abstraction, in a form that allows their classification and comparison. This helps detecting conflicts among various policies before they are actually enforced, thus granting interoperability among entities belonging to different domains that adopt different policies. On the other side, rule-based approaches rely on the features of logic programming languages, for example, Prolog, to enable evaluation and reasoning about concrete context and policy instances. This allows the definition of policies based on variables, which simplifies policy specification and provides greater expressivity. For example, by using variables, one can define the concept of "co-location" by stating that X and Y are co-located if they are both located in the same place Z. A KAoS policy is a list of rules expressed as OWL properties of the policy and a context represented in terms of ontologies, used to restrict policy applicability. Though represented in OWL-Lite, Rei still allows the definition of variables that are used as placeholders as in Prolog.

CONTEXT-BASED ACCESS CONTROL

The specification of adequate access control policies in mobile enterprise settings requires tackling several challenges. Recall, for instance, the example of spontaneous meeting described at the beginning of the chapter. In this situation, the complete list of participants may not be known in advance or may be modified just before the meeting starts or even during a meeting, thus making it infeasible to define access control policies based on requestor's identity. Even the RBAC approach seems cumbersome in cross-organizational situations, since role definitions and hierarchies might vary across organizational boundaries. Therefore, recent research aims at a more general and comprehensive approach to access control that exploits not only identity/role information but also additional contextual information, such as location, time, and ongoing activities. In particular, it may be advantageous for each participant to define access control policies for his/her managed resources according to the current resource context. For instance, in an informal meeting, access should be granted to those who are currently located in the same room where the resource owner is located, if they actually participate in the activity/project relating to the meeting, as long as the current time corresponds to the time scheduled for the meeting.

The integration of access control with the multifaceted context concept has the following two main characteristics:

- First, it is an example of an active access control model [38]. Active security models are aware of the context associated with an ongoing activity, which distinguishes it from the passive concept of permission.
- Second, the exploitation of context as a mechanism for grouping policies and for evaluating applicable ones can simplify access control management by encouraging policy specification reuse and by facilitating policy update/ revocation.

In traditional access control solutions, the tight coupling of the identities/roles of principals with their permissions and with the operating conditions requires security administrators to foresee all execution environments where each principal is likely to operate. In a context-centric access control approach, instead of managing principals and their permissions individually, administrators can benefit from the simple definition of the set of permitted actions for each context: when a principal operates in a specific context, the evaluation process of his/her permissions in that context is triggered.

The idea of adapting access control policies to changing context recently emerged in a first few research activities, such as the Proteus access control framework [39]. In this framework, a context-aware policy model allows dynamic adaptation of access control policies to variations in context. The importance of taking context into account for securing pervasive applications is also evident in the work of Covington et al. [41] where contexts are represented through a new type of role, called *environment role*. Environment roles capture the relevant conditions used for restricting and regulating user privileges. Permissions are assigned both to (traditional and environmental) roles and role-activation/deactivation mechanisms.

By focusing on access control in spontaneous coalitions in pervasive environments, Liscano and Wang [42] proposed a delegation-based approach, where users participating to a communication session can delegate a set of their permissions to a temporary session role and enable access to each other's resources. In particular, one endpoint user assigns the session role to the entities he/she is willing to communicate with. Contextual information is used to define the conditions for the assignment to take place, thus limiting the applicability scope of this process. Only a limited set of contextual information can be specified and there is no support for semantic representation of the session role and delegation context constraints. In addition, security problems may arise whenever the entity delegated to play the session role leaves the communication session. In fact, unless the user explicitly states he/she is leaving the session, there is no way for the framework to be aware that the session role must be revoked.

Finally, the most recent trend in access control policy definition for highly dynamic wireless environments is the integration of context awareness with semantic technologies. Relevant examples include the Proteus framework, which relies on a combined ontology/rule-based approach to policy and context representation/reasoning, and the policy model presented in Ref. [40], where contexts and policies are defined by adopting an OWL-based representation, and OWL inference rules are exploited to derive relationships among contexts. Let us note that a semantic-based approach allows the description of contexts and associated policies at a high level of abstraction, in a form that enables their classification and comparison. This feature is essential, for instance, in order to detect conflicts between policies before they are actually enforced. In addition, semantic techniques can provide the reasoning features needed to deduce new information from existing knowledge. This ability may be exploited by the policy framework when faced with unexpected situations to react in a context-dependent and appropriate way.

A PRACTICAL EXAMPLE OF EMERGING SOLUTION GUIDELINES: THE S-MIDAS FRAMEWORK

Secure-MIDAS (S-MIDAS) is our original proposal of secure discovery and access control, which exploits semantic-based context descriptions for collaborative services in wireless enterprise networks. S-MIDAS extends the work presented in Ref. [28] with support for access control during service discovery. In particular, as shown in Figure 6.2, S-MIDAS provides mobile enterprise users with personalized views on available services according to their professional interests, device capabilities, and supported security features. Thus, it is a useful tool for enterprises to protect sensitive business information by limiting the visibility of resources/services to only authorized users. The S-MIDAS key feature is its context-aware approach to the modeling of both service profiles and access control policies. In particular, S-MIDAS relies on context-aware mobile proxies acting on the fixed network on behalf of (and locally to) mobile users: proxies can follow users' movements across different wireless networks by dynamically migrating over the wired network. In addition, S-MIDAS adopts semantic-based context/policy descriptions to provide expressive representation and reasoning over service capabilities and access control policies. Here, we rapidly present the primary characteristics of the S-MIDAS framework as a practical exemplification of the emerging trend for novel enterprise middleware based on semantic technologies, context awareness, and the design/implementation guideline of mobile proxy exploitation.

THE S-MIDAS METADATA MODEL

The S-MIDAS discovery identifies users, devices, and services as the key entities. Services are "black boxes" encapsulating physical/logical resources and providing

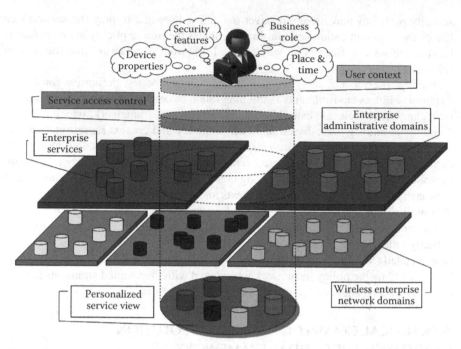

FIGURE 6.2   S-MIDAS personalized service view based on user context and service access control.

the functions to operate on them. Users are the principals that can provide/request services via possibly heterogeneous devices. To support secure and context-aware discovery, S-MIDAS adopts semantic-based metadata: profiles for properties and characteristics of involved entities, and policies to specify conditions to access services not only during service delivery, but also during discovery. Profiles have a modular structure including different parts, each one grouping metadata with a common logical meaning and comprising static or dynamic data. In particular, profiles include three common key parts for context-aware semantic discovery: identification, requirements, and capabilities (other profile parts, such as binding metadata [28], are out of the central scope of this chapter). The identification part provides information to name users/devices/services and to identify their location, together with security-related authentication credentials, such as security certificates. Capabilities define S-MIDAS entity abilities: user capabilities include native languages, enterprise roles, and implemented security features, such as support for encryption mechanisms; device capabilities represent technical characteristics, supported functions, and resource state, such as Bluetooth connectivity, secure socket layer support, and battery level; service capabilities describe provided functions and how they are achieved, for example, supported interfaces, communication protocols, and security mechanisms. Finally, the requirements part describes entity desiderata: user requirements express interests/preferences and user-specified conditions to respect during discovery, including security mechanisms such as encryption to support confidentiality and integrity; device requirements specify technical conditions that must hold for the device to properly access services; service requirements describe conditions that clients should satisfy.

A particular kind of service requirement is represented by access control policies, which define the conditions under which a service can be included in the service view of a user based on his/her context. Based on our previous work [43], we associate a context with each resource to be controlled, which represents all and only those conditions enabling access to that resource. Access control policies define for each context how to operate on the associated resources. In particular, entities can perform only those actions that are associated with the contexts currently in effect, that is, the contexts whose defining conditions match the operating conditions of the requesting entity, requested resource, and current environment. Recalling the example described at the beginning of this chapter, each company manager could define a policy for his/ her resources stating that access is granted to those who are currently located in the same room where the resource owner is located, if they actually participate in the activity/project relating to the meeting, as long as current time corresponds to the time scheduled for the meeting. As long as the consultants make this context active by participating to the meeting, they would automatically view the needed resources stored on the managers' portable devices. People who do not take part in the meeting cannot even see those resources in their service view, thus preserving confidentiality and protecting possibly sensitive business information. Let us note that the definition of such a context-aware policy might be fully compatible with existing corporate policies, by appropriately setting priorities among policies.

We adopt a semantic-based approach to metadata specification. In particular, both profiles and policies are represented as ontologies. As for profiles, we have defined a base capability ontology, which has been extended with different application-specific ontologies based on the UNSPSC (United Nations Standard Products and Services Code Standard) taxonomy, such as the Management and Business Professionals and Administrative Services (http://unspsc.org/). We have also defined a base context and policy ontology to express access control policies, and extended it with an ontology specific to the spontaneous collaboration scenario; all our ontologies* are modeled in OWL-DL.

In this section, we provide a brief overview of the S-MIDAS middleware architecture. A more extensive description, together with detailed implementation insights, is in Refs. [28,43]. S-MIDAS provides various middleware services organized into two different logical sets. The discovery management set provides the needed functionalities to support service discovery and selection based on user context information and access control requirements. In particular, it includes graphic tools for the specification, modification, checking for correctness, parsing, and installation of profiles and policies. In addition, S-MIDAS supports the creation of user contexts at the beginning of a discovery session, the monitoring of changes in both created user contexts, for example, in user profiles, and in relevant external environment conditions, for example, the addition of new services in other user contexts. Moreover, it is in charge of support management functions such as the notification of changes to

---

* Our ontologies and additional implementation details are freely available at: http://www.lia.deis.unibo. it/research/MIDAS; http://www.lia.deis.unibo.it/research/Proteus

interested entities and the associated updates of involved user contexts. Based on these functions, S-MIDAS provides mobile users with advanced discovery functions to determine personalized service views based on the semantic matching between user/device/service requirements and capabilities, and automatically updates these views when relevant changes occur in the considered user context.

The configuration management set provides the needed facilities to allow each portable device to have S-MIDAS discovery facilities configured and properly executing, either on-board or on the proxy node. In particular, the main support element is the user proxy (UP), an application-independent middleware component that represents a portable device on the fixed network. S-MIDAS associates one UP with each portable device. UP covers various management roles, including retrieving the profiles of its companion user/device and coordinating with discovery management services during a discovery session. In addition, based on the device profile, UP decides where to allocate the various discovery management services, either completely/partially on board of its companion device, or executing on the fixed network, or remotely on other trusted mobile devices. In the case of rich devices, UP runs management functions and instantiates all discovery management services on-board. Having completely on-board discovery facilities allows to better preserve user privacy since requirements/capabilities and personalized service views are locally stored. In addition, on-board reasoning may be useful in case the user's device experiences frequent disconnections or poor bandwidth connectivity. On the contrary, in the case of resource-constrained devices, UP behavior is a trade-off between technical device characteristics and privacy needs. In particular, UP decides whether to perform its management operations on-board or remotely, and which discovery management services to instantiate on the portable device, based on profile data such as CPU, memory size, and battery level.

LESSONS LEARNED, EMERGING TRENDS, AND CONCLUSIVE REMARKS

As shown in the previous sections of this chapter, securing access to resources and services is a complex management issue that requires novel approaches to discovery and security paradigms suitable for the emerging wireless enterprise scenarios. Until now, several discovery solutions have been proposed and adopted in enterprise settings. Only few of them have addressed security from the very beginning of their design process. In other cases, security requirements are defined by simply extending traditional security aspects, for example, authentication, authorization, and privacy, to the case of dynamic wireless environments, without taking into account the specific characteristics of wireless enterprise applications. Both approaches tend to have limited effectiveness because of the overhead in terms of manual management of security support systems and because of incomplete and/or inadequate analysis of the security requirements in service discovery and access. The loss of control in enterprise service visibility might lead to the unintentional disclosure of sensitive business information, thus compromising enterprise security.

Another common characteristic of mostly adopted discovery solutions is that they are usually built from scratch by redesigning and reimplementing *ad hoc* low-level mechanisms, such as communication protocols and interaction modes between service provider and user nodes. As a result, most current discovery supports are generally not interoperable, which raises relevant integration issues for cross-enterprise organizations wishing to interconnect and access each other's services. Web services represent a notable effort toward the interoperation of independently developed services by providing common standards for service description, discovery, and invocation. With this approach, novel solutions for discovery and access to business services can be designed by separating low-level details from high-level facilities, such as service description, matching, and selection, and mapping onto existing low-level mechanisms and protocols.

EMERGING TRENDS

In wireless enterprise networks, novel solutions for secure and user-centric discovery are essential to provide personalized retrieval of resources/services to clients who are not fully aware of their execution environment. The most manifestly emerging trend to support context awareness and to perform resource/service management accordingly is the adoption of *middleware solutions based on metadata*. Metadata are exploited for representing both context and adaptation of service behavior at a high level of abstraction, with a clean separation between service management and application logic. They can describe both the structure/meaning of the resources composing a system and the specification of management operations expressed at a high level of abstraction. Providing support for context-awareness requires the middleware to collect and flexibly represent context information, and propagate its visibility up to the application level. In addition, emerging middleware solutions should provide powerful means to specify and enforce context-dependent adaptation strategies, without interfering with or modifying the application logic.

Of course, context-aware middleware should be deployed on heterogeneous devices operating under various conditions, such as different user needs and application requirements, device connectivity abilities, and computational capabilities, as well as changing environment conditions. Thus, a crucial issue relates to the deployment of middleware components on board of resource-constrained mobile devices. A related emerging design guideline is to dynamically extend the Internet infrastructure with proxies acting on behalf of (possibly disconnected) limited devices [7,44]. Proxies can handle several complex management tasks, transparently to client devices, by hiding network heterogeneity and by managing network dynamicity. For instance, several middleware solutions exploit context-aware proxies to retrieve metadata associated with their companion user/device and to coordinate with discovery and access control management services.

In addition, a crucial emerging issue for the achievement of context awareness is the ability of middleware to properly describe and interpret context information. The semantics of those descriptions must be unambiguously defined and standardized to allow interoperability with minimal human intervention. Therefore, the other primary trend is the adoption of *semantically-rich representations* for metadata definition. Numerous research efforts have been spent over the past decade toward the design and development of metadata-driven middleware solutions for service management based on semantic technologies. Recent results show that semantic technologies effectively increase metadata expressiveness, facilitate flexibility and adaptation to different operating conditions, and favor interoperability between different middleware support systems.

OPEN RESEARCH CHALLENGES

Several open issues, however, need to be addressed to pave the way toward the wide-scale exploitation of novel context-aware semantic middleware in enterprise scenarios. First, metadata currently lack well-assessed specification guidelines and standard models. Despite some important standardization efforts regarding service profiles (e.g., with the WSDL specification) and device profiles (such as the Composite Capabilities Preference Profiles standard of W3C, www.w3.org/Mobile/CCPP/), a recognized standard for user profiles is still needed, and profiles are currently defined based on specific application requirements. Policy specification is even more problematic since very different proposals exist, ranging from rule-based to ontology-based models.

Further research is also needed to take advantage fully of the integration of context-awareness and semantic technologies. An adequate trade-off is needed between the complexity overhead introduced by semantic technologies and the advantages of secure efficient discovery. Semantic technologies must be reliable before context-aware middleware solutions can be adopted for wireless enterprise networks. This means, for example, that a semantic-based matching process between service offers and requests should terminate in a reasonable and predictable time, and that an ontology base should be semantically consistent and should not include or infer incorrect knowledge. The need to ensure semantic reliability makes the design of context metadata and context processing tools a challenging task. From our experience, we suggest that a viable trade-off between semantic metadata expressivity and management issues might be reached by carefully limiting the complexity of adopted semantic models. Initial research efforts in semantic-based models for enterprise service applications demonstrate the growing industrial interest for Semantic Web technologies [45].

Finally, the deployment of middleware solutions for context-aware service access and discovery should solve the issues of portability over resource-constrained mobile terminals, such as smart phones and personal digital assistants. Despite various solutions for specific applications have been proposed and implemented, to the best of our knowledge there is neither a generic framework nor an agreed methodology for semantic support configuration. We have suggested a possible approach to overcome these limitations, that is, the exploitation of mobile proxies acting over the fixed network on behalf of portable devices. Some preliminary studies have also been conducted to evaluate the efficiency and portability of semantic support services, such as performance measurements on loading/reasoning over huge ontology bases [46]. However, further research is needed to make a reliable assessment about the feasibility of deploying semantic support facilities in an effective and scalable way over large-scale enterprise wireless networks.

REFERENCES

1. Dey, A.K., Understanding and using context. *Pers. Ubiquit. Comput.*, 5(1), 4–7, 2001.
2. Strang, T. and Linnhoff-Popien, C., A context modeling survey, *Proceedings of the Workshop on Advanced Context Modelling, Reasoning and Management As Part of UbiComp 2004*, Tokyo, Japan, 34–41, 2004.
3. Masuoka, R., Parsia, B., and Labrou, Y., Task computing—The Semantic Web meets pervasive computing, *Proceedings of the Second International Semantic Web Conference (ISWC 2003)*, Fensel, D., Sycara, K., and Mylopoulos, J., Eds, Lecture Notes in Computer Science, Vol. 2870, Springer, Sanibel Island, FL, 866–881, 2003.
4. Chen, H. et al., Intelligent agents meet the Semantic Web in smart spaces, *IEEE Internet Comput.*, 8(6), 69–79, 2004.
5. Bellavista, P. and Corradi, A., *The Handbook of Mobile Middleware*, Auerbach, Boca Raton, FL, 2006.
6. Capra, L., Emmerich, W., and Mascolo, C., Carisma: Context–aware reflective middleware system for mobile applications, *IEEE Trans. Softw. Eng.*, 29(10), 929–945, 2003.
7. Bellavista, P. et al., Context-aware middleware for resource management in the wireless internet, *IEEE Trans. Softw. Eng.*, 29(12), 1086–1099, 2003.
8. Ranganathan, A. and Campbell, R.H., A middleware for context–aware agents in ubiquitous computing environments, *Proceedings of the ACM/IFIP/USENIX International Middleware Conference 2003*, Lecture Notes in Computer Science, Vol. 2672, Springer, Rio de Janeiro, Brazil, 143–161, 2003.
9. Nissen, H.W. et al., Managing multiple requirements perspectives with metamodels, *IEEE Softw.*, 3(2), 37–48, 1996.
10. Sloman, M. and Lupu, E., Security and management policy specification, *IEEE Netw.*, 16(2), 10–19, 2002.
11. Lassila, O., Web metadata: A matter of semantics, *IEEE Internet Comput.*, 2(4), 30–37, 1998.
12. Zhu, F., Mutka, M., and Ni, L.M., A private, secure, and user-centric information exposure model for service discovery protocol, *IEEE Trans. Mobile Comput.*, 5(4), 418–429, 2006.
13. Cotroneo, D., Graziano, A., and Russo, S., Security requirements in service oriented architectures for ubiquitous computing. *Proceedings of the 2nd Workshop on Middleware for Pervasive and Ad-Hoc Computing*, Vol. 77, ACM International Conference Proceeding Series, New York, NY, 172–177, 2004.
14. Robinson, R. and Indulska, J., A context-sensitive service discovery protocol for mobile computing environments, *Proceedings of the 11th International Conference on Mobile Business*, IEEE Press, Sydney, 565–572, 2005.
15. Nidd, M., Service discovery in DEAPspace, *IEEE Wireless Commun.*, 8(4), 39–45, 2001.
16. Adjie-Winoto, W. et al., The design and implementation of an intentional naming system, in *Proceedings of the 17th ACM Symposium on Operating Systems Principles (SOSP '99)*, Kotz, D. and Wilkes, J., Eds, ACM, Kiawah Island, SC, 186–201, 1999.
17. Paolucci, M. et al., Semantic matching of Web Services capabilities, in *Proceedings of the First International Semantic Web Conference*, Sardinia, Italy, Horrocks, I. and Hendler, J., Eds, Lecture Notes in Computer Science, Vol. 2342, Springer-Verlag, Berlin/Heidelberg, 333–347, 2002.
18. Miles, S. et al., Personalised Grid service discovery, *IEEE Proc. Softw.: Special. Issue Perform. Eng.*, 150(4), 252–256, 2003.
19. Klein, M. and Konig-Ries, B., Combining query and preference—An approach to fully automatize dynamic service binding, *Proceedings of the International Conference on*

Web Services, San Diego, CA, IEEE Computer Society, Piscataway, NJ, 788–791, 2004.

20. Wagner, M. et al., Towards semantic-based service discovery on tiny mobile devices, *Proceedings of the Workshop on Semantic Web Technology for Mobile and Ubiquitous Applications*, Hiroshima, Japan, 2004. http://www.informatik.uni-ulm.de/ki/Liebig/papers/iswc2004_ws_mobiONT.pdf.

21. Klusch, M., Fries, B., and Sycara, K., Automated semantic web service discovery with OWLS-MX, *Proceedings of 5th International Conference on Autonomous Agents and Multi-Agent Systems (AAMAS)*, Hakodate, Japan, ACM Press, 2005.

22. Li, L. and Horrocks, I., A software framework for matchmaking based on semantic web technology, *Proceedings of the Twelfth International World Wide Web Conference (WWW 2003)*, Budapest, Hungary, ACM, 331–339, 2003.

23. Donini, F., Di Noia, T., and Di Sciascio, E., Extending semantic–based matchmaking via concept abduction and contraction, in *Proceedings of the 14th International Conference on Engineering Knowledge in the Age of the Semantic Web (EKAW 2004)*, Motta, E. et al., Eds, Whittlebury Hall, Lecture Notes on Artificial Intelligence, Vol. 3257, Springer, Berlin, 307–320, 2004.

24. Roman, D. et al., Web service modeling ontology, *Appl. Ontol.*, 1(1), 77–106, 2005, IOS Press.

25. Verma, K. et al., METEOR-S WSDI: A scalable infrastructure of registries for semantic publication and discovery of Web Services, *J. Inform. Technol. Manage., Special Issue on Universal Global Integration*, 6(1), 17–39, 2005.

26. Capra, L., Zachariadis, S., and Mascolo, C., Q-CAD: QoS and context aware discovery framework for adaptive mobile systems, *Proceedings of the International Conference on Pervasive Services (ICPS)*, Santorini, Greece, IEEE Press, 453–456, 2005.

27. Lee, C. and Helal, S., Context attributes: An approach to enable context-awareness for service discovery, *Proceedings of the Int. Symposium on Applications and the Internet (SAINT)*, Orlando, FL, IEEE Computer Society Press, 22–30, 2003.

28. Bellavista, P. et al., Context-aware semantic discovery for next generation mobile systems. *IEEE Commun. Magaz, Special Issue on Advances in Service Platform Technologies*, 44(9), 62–71, 2006.

29. Casole, M. and Cheng, Y., Secure access to corporate resources in a multi-access perspective: needs, problems, and solutions, *Proceedings of the 5th European Conference on Personal Mobile Communications*, Glasgow, IEEE Press, 482–489, 2003.

30. Chieu, T.C., Nguyen, T., and Zeng, L., Secure search of private documents in an enterprise management system, in *Proceedings of the IEEE International Conference on e-Business Engineering*, S. C. Cheung, et al., Eds, Hong Kong, China, IEEE Computer Society Press, 105–112, 2007.

31. LeVeque, V., *Information Security: A Strategic Approach*, Wiley-IEEE Computer Society Press, Hoboken, NJ, 2006.

32. Sandhu, R. et al., Role based access control models, *IEEE Comput.*, 29(2), 38–47, 1996.

33. Furst, G., Schmidt, T., and Wippel, G., Managing access in extended enterprise network, *IEEE Internet Comput*, 6(5), 67–74, 2002.

34. Campbell, T.R., Self-authorization: a methodology for secured network access in a distributed paradigm, *Proceedings of the IEEE Southeast Conference*, Fort Lauderdale, FL, IEEE Press, 372–377, 2005.

35. Tonti, G. et al., Semantic Web languages for policy representation and reasoning: A comparison of KAoS, Rei, and Ponder, in *Proceedings of the Second International Semantic Web Conference (ISWC 2003)*, Fensel, D., Sycara, K., and Mylopoulos, J., Eds, Lecture Notes in Computer Science, Vol. 2870, Springer, Sanibel Island, FL, 419–437, 2003.

36. Uszok, A. et al., KAoS policy management for semantic web services, *IEEE Intell. Syst.*, 19(4), 32–41, 2004.
37. Kagal, L., Finin T., and Joshi, A., A policy language for pervasive computing environment, *Proceedngs of the IEEE Fourth International Workshop on Policy (Policy 2003)*, Lake Como, Italy, IEEE Computer Society, Los Alamitos, CA, 63–74, 2003.
38. Georgiadis, C.K. et al., Flexible team–based access control using contexts, in *Proceedings of the 6th ACM Symposium on Access Control Models and Technologies (SACMAT 2001)*, ACM, Chantilly, VA, 21–27, 2001.
39. Toninelli, A. et al., A semantic context-aware access control framework for secure collaborations in pervasive computing environments, in *Proceedings of the Fifth International Semantic Web Conference (ISWC)*, Cruz., I. et al., Eds, Athens, GA, Lecture Notes in Computer Science, Vol. 4273, Springer-Verlag, Berlin/Heidelberg, 473–486, 2006.
40. Ko, H.J. et al., A semantic context-aware access control in pervasive environments, *Proceedings of ICCSA 2006*, Lecture Notes in Computer Science, Vol. 3981, Springer, Glasgow, 165–174, 2006.
41. Covington, M.J. et al., Securing context-aware applications using environmental roles, *Proceedings of the 6th ACM Symposium on Access Control Models and Technologies (SACMAT 2001)*, ACM, Chantilly, VA, 10–20, 2001.
42. Liscano, R. and Wang, K., A SIP-based architecture model for contextual coalition access control for ubiquitous computing, in *Proceedings of the Second Annual Conference on Mobile and Ubiquitous Systems (MobiQuitous'05)*, Singh, S., Bonnet, P., Joshi, A., and Masuoka, R., Eds, IEEE Computer Society, Los Alamitos, CA, 384–392, 2005.
43. Toninelli, A., Corradi, A., and Montanari, R., Semantic-based discovery to support mobile context-aware service access. *Comput. Commun. J., Special Issue on Mobility Management and Wireless Access*, 31(5), 935–949, 2008.
44. Karmouch, A., Ed., Special section on mobile agents, *IEEE Commun. Magaz.*, 36(7), 1998.
45. Feigenbaum, L. et al., The semantic web in action, *Scientific American*, 297, 90–97, Dec. 2007.
46. Wang, S. et al., Rapid benchmarking for semantic web knowledge base systems. *Proceedings of the International Semantic Web Conference (ISWC 2005)*, Lecture Notes in Computer Science, Vol. 3729, Springer, Galway, Ireland, 758–772, 2005.

7 An Introduction to Network and Service Management

Raouf Boutaba and Jin Xiao

CONTENTS

OVERVIEW

This chapter is organized as follows. First, we give an introduction to network and service management and a brief overview of the prominent network and service management architectures and research trends in the past. The evolution of the networks and services from a management point of view is presented. We then present three current ongoing network and service management frameworks, namely the Next Generation Networks (NGN) initiative, the Next Generation Operation Support Systems (NGOSS) framework, and the Information Technology Information Library (ITIL) initiative. The NGN and NGOSS originate from the telecommunication management sector and the ITIL originates from the Internet management sector. The Web service management and service oriented architecture are discussed. Next, we introduce the concept of self-management and some of the challenges it poses. The conclusion summarizes the main points discussed. Due to the variety and longevity of networks and the extensive research on service management, this chapter can only provide a glimpse of the area by highlighting the most relevant topics to the subject. For additional information, the readers may find the historical perspective on network management [1] useful as well our previous writings on telecommunication network management [2] and self-managing networks and systems [3].

NETWORK MANAGEMENT

The traditional service offerings in telecommunication were few and primarily oriented toward voice communication, which tended to be well defined and relatively homogenous. In contrast, the simple and best-effort delivery paradigm of the Internet has resulted in the lack of formalization in its past service management practices with no effective mechanism for service quality assurance. Today, with the integration of telecommunication and the Internet, the proliferation of digital multimedia, Web services, social networking concepts, and virtual organizations, the future service spectrum is as diverse as it is complex. In this chapter, we present an overview of the network and service management of telecommunication networks and the Internet, management concepts, historical perspectives, current activities, and insights into the future of service management.

In the late 1980s, with increased computer communications, the International Telegraph and Telephone Consultative Committee—now the International Telecommunication Union–Telecommunication Standardisation Sector (ITU-T) and the International Organization for Standardization (ISO)—jointly published a set of network and system management standards under the X.700 series [4–7]. This has since been known as the Open Systems Interconnection (OSI) Reference Model for network and service management. A number of concepts introduced in the OSI Reference Model are fundamental to the development and structuring of network and service management to date, in particular, the following definition of network management: "A network management system is an application. Its aim is to analyze, control and manage network and service infrastructure in order to ensure its configuration correctness, robustness, performance quality and security."

Two types of entities are defined in the management scope: the managed objects and the manager. The managed objects are the network resources and end-systems being managed, while the manager is responsible for all of the management activities. The managed objects generally have an information view pertaining to their management information and management capacities. For example, a router could have processing speed, buffer size, and number of input/output interfaces as part of its management information, as well as the set of configurable parameters as part of its management capacity. This gives rise to the dual view of a managed object in terms of what is functionally present and what is manageable. Considering the diverse set of resources and devices present in networks and systems today, it is immediately apparent that some sort of common information model (CIM) is necessary to present such information in a consistent manner. This is well understood even outside the telecommunication sector, as evident in the prominent management information base (MIB) [8] standardized through the Internet Engineering Task Force (IETF), whose principle interest lies in the operation and management of the Internet.

From a functional perspective, the OSI reference model defines five functional areas of management: configuration, fault, performance, accounting, and security (FCAPS).

Configuration management is concerned with resource configuration such as network path setup, resource provisioning, device configuration, and so on. In telecommunication networks, configuration may also include user terminal configuration, user profiling, and service personalization.

Fault management deals with fault detection, identification, isolation, recovery, path protection, and so on. The immediate cause and effect relationship between fault and service disruption makes the fault management a highly regarded area of research. With the increasing distributedness of systems and resources, as well as the growing size and complexity of the networks, it is extremely difficult to identify network faults and to address them efficiently.

Performance management is concerned with the quality of service delivery of network services, the monitoring of traffic, traffic control techniques, and resource management. With the introduction of telecommunication services in Internet Protocol (IP) networks and the desire to support multimedia services spanning across both wireless and wired networks, the need for an effective performance management has increased significantly.

Accounting management focuses on the charging and accounting of user traffics. This area of management has not been a major focus of network management research. However, works on pricing and charging in networks directly impact the way accounting management could be performed. Furthermore, as more and more application service providers and usage-based premium services (e.g., real-time broadcasting) are being made available as part of the telecommunication service offering, effective accounting management becomes a necessity.

Security management is about aspects such as integrity of traffic, authentication of parties, authorization, security auditing, access control, and so on. Although security management is an important area of network management, it has received less attention compared with the other areas in the past. This can be attributed to the fact that the traditional telecommunication network was a tightly managed private network separate from the packet-switched Internet. With the convergence of communication infrastructures, and the increased severity of security attacks on networks and services, security management has become the main management problem to be addressed nowadays.

TELECOMMUNICATION MANAGEMENT NETWORK

In implementing the OSI Reference Model, the Telecommunication Management Network (TMN) [9] framework was perhaps the most influential and prominent architecture. It adopted a layered view of management in the same spirit as the layered network protocol stack. Each layer builds on the functions of the layer below it and is considered an abstraction of the lower layer.

In TMN, four management layers are defined as follows:

- *Element management*: is concerned with the management of individual or a collection of network components (e.g., a switch, a link, etc.). It also mediates data between the network element and the network manager. It is device and technology-specific.
- *Network management*: provides an end-to-end network view of the managed resources and devices. It is device neutral.
- *Service management*: is concerned with service orders and is translation into the establishment of a circuit. It includes contacts with customers and service providers, service order fulfillment, quality of service assurances, billing information, and troubleshooting.
- *Business management*: is concerned with the area of business and human resource planning. It is focused on the services as a whole and a company's financial concerns.

Figure 7.1 presents a combined model of telecommunication network management according to the TMN and OSI models [2]. This layered management view has

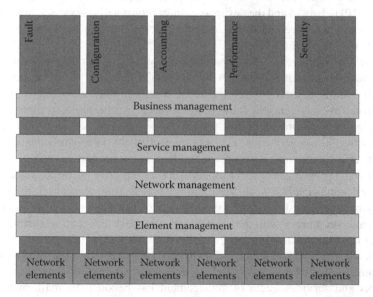

FIGURE 7.1   Telecommunication management network overview.

become prevalent in structuring management system development and research. However, as the networking infrastructures and functions continue to evolve, some problems have emerged, especially regarding the service management layer. In particular, the definition of services and their scope has changed drastically. The traditional telecommunication services consisted mainly of telephony features and their supporting business processes, such as installation, call set-up, session management, customer care, billing, and so on. In contrast, the types of services today are far more diverse and often include generic software applications and processes. They encompass a wide range of applications and features: text messaging, Web services, wired and wireless voice communications, video on demand, location-dependent services, and so on. It is becoming increasingly difficult to maintain a uniform management view of these diverse services in a single layer (e.g., the service management concerns of a telephone call are quite different from that of a Web application). Furthermore, the TMN model lacks the explicit representation of the customers. With the growing service differentiation and customization, there is an increasing need for the formal representation and structuring of customer-oriented processes in the management framework.

SERVICE MANAGEMENT

In a generic sense, we consider that: *a service is a process or functionality (or set of) that is offered by a service provider to the customer based on a common agreement of service quality and price.* The important aspects of a service with respect to management are: the service specification, a Service Level Agreement (SLA), and a service life cycle model. The service specification is service provider-oriented; it details the function of the service, its service access point (or interface), capacities, expected input, and expected output. The SLA is customer-oriented: it contains a general service description as it relates to the customer, the servicing terms, technical quality guarantees in the form of Service Level Specifications, and monetary clauses.

The service life cycle describes the various stages of a service, from design to de-installation. It is particularly relevant in the context of Internet services because of their transient and dynamic nature compared with network components: a service could be created and accessed at the request of a user and quickly torn down thereafter or the features or characteristic of a service could change during run-time due to changes in the environment or user requirements.

The general service life cycle is depicted in Figure 7.2. It comprises the following phases: design, negotiation, provisioning, usage, and de-installation. The *design phase* is concerned with the design and implementation of a service; the *negotiation phase* deals with the contract between the service provider and the user, including agreements on service quality; the *provisioning phase* deals with service configuration and resource reservation. The *usage phase* comprises operation and change. Change covers modifications to the existing service because of changes in network conditions or user requirements and may induce a renegotiation of the service contract or even the redesign of the service itself. The *de-installation* deals with service termination and service contract fulfillment.

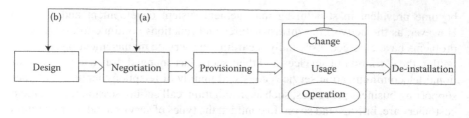

FIGURE 7.2   The service life cycle.

NETWORK AND SERVICE MANAGEMENT ARCHITECTURES

In this section, we first present a number of influential network and service management architectures, including Simple Network Management Protocol (SNMP), Telecommunication Information Networking Architecture (TINA), Web-Based Enterprise Management (WBEM), and policy-based management. Then, we summarize the research on network and service management and its implications for the topic at hand. The topics are ordered in an approximate chronological order.

SIMPLE NETWORK MANAGEMENT PROTOCOL

SNMP [10] was adopted by IETF in 1988 for IP network management. This is a very simple protocol that works over of the User Datagram Protocol without any guarantees. From an architecture view point, SNMP assumes simple manager and agent relationships, whereby the manager does the management processing and decision making while the agent supplies the managed information.

The SNMP MIB [11,12] is derived from ASN.1 (Abstract Syntax Notation) [13]. ASN.1 defines data presentation, syntax, transmission, and encoding/decoding. In this case, resources are represented as objects containing a set of data variables, mostly scalar. An SNMP MIB is a collection of such managed objects. The definition of objects is standardized across resources of the same type; however, proprietary extensions to these objects are also common. The values of variables are typically set by the agent on behalf of the manager.

The SNMP communication protocol has four simple commands: get, getNext, set, and trap. Managers use the get and getNext commands to retrieve specified variable values from the SNMP MIB at the agent side. The set command is used for setting variable values. The trap command allows for agents to send notifications to the manager unsolicited. Because the manager has to send a separate get command per variable to be retrieved, SNMP can be very inefficient when operating over managed objects with large variable tables. A common performance improvement for SNMP is to have the manager perform get operations only at sparsely spaced time intervals and have the agent "trap" the manager with any variable value update. The SNMPv2 fixed this problem by adding the getBulk command to allow the retrieval of entire list of variables (usually a complete table) with a single command. The latest version of SNMPv3 further augments the SNMP protocol with additional security features. To date, SNMP has been one of the most popular management protocols for network management, especially for IP networks.

TELECOMMUNICATION INFORMATION NETWORKING ARCHITECTURE

The TINA Consortium (TINA-C) was formed in 1993 to establish the TINA architecture [14] for telecommunication networks as a realization of the TMN reference model. TINA is a conceptual model that captures many essential aspects of the telecommunication operations: resources, networks, software, services, and participants. However, the business process is not part of the TINA model.

The TINA effort is strongly influenced by concepts of distributed processing environment of the time, most notably CORBA (Common Object Request Broker Architecture). Thus, TINA views all software and applications as consisting of distributed processing objects and the distributed processing environment is an integral part of the TINA architecture.

The overall architecture can be viewed as a computing layering and a management layering. The computing layering is ordered bottom up as hardware, operating systems, distributed processing environment, and applications; the management layering borrows from the TMN and is ordered bottom-up as element, resource (corresponds to the element management and network management layers of TMN), and service. Functional separation is applied in TINA to the management and service domains to allow for better modularity and focus of concerns. Management separation follows the TMN functional areas while service separations divide service functions among participants of a service. For example, a point-to-point communication service can have participants taking the roles of consumer, network provider, and service provider. The service access and set-up is the responsibility of the service provider while the service transport is the responsibility of the network provider.

From an architectural point of view, four subarchitectures are defined: computing architecture, network architecture, management architecture, and service architecture. The management architecture is further divided into computing management, which is the management of generic software components and distributed processing environment, and telecommunication management, as prescribed in their element, resource, and service management layering.

The service architecture [15] is perhaps the most influential part of the TINA model. Its session, access, and management concepts established a basis for service management. TINA defines a session as a temporal period during which activities are carried out to achieve a goal. The types of sessions are service session, user session, communication session, and access session. Service session represents an activation of the service; user session represents user(s) interaction with a service; communication session represents the connections associated with a service; and access session represents the user(s) attachment to the service. The access concept differentiates the user from the terminal, where the terminal is a collection of hardware and software component from which the user accesses a service. Session management includes create, activate, modify, suspend, resume, and complete a session relationship.

TINA-C is no longer active. The last TINA deliverable was released in 1999. Despite some research activities on TINA in the past, very little industry realizations of TINA have seen the light of day, mainly due to the complexity of its implementation and maintenance. However, some ongoing initiatives within the framework of NGN have many of the service and session concepts in TINA.

WEB-BASED ENTERPRISE MANAGEMENT

The WBEM initiative was launched in 1996 by Microsoft, Intel, BMC software, Compaq, and Cisco systems. It was soon adopted by the Distributed Management Task Force. WBEM allows for transparent and location-independent access to managed objects with a simple client side architecture (Figure 7.3).

The CIM [16] is central to WBEM. All object classes and interfaces are specified with CIM schema and their format defined with the Managed Object Format (MOF) of CIM. CIM is a set of schemas for defining classes, properties, associations, and methods. It is an object-oriented and extensible information model. It has three levels of schemas: core schema, common schema, and extensions schema. Core schema defines top-level classes and associations. Common schema defines series of domain-specific but platform neutral class specifications for devices, systems, applications, databases, and networks. The common schema extends from the core schema. The extension schema is used for defining platform- or vendor-specific extensions of the common schema. Associations in CIM are much richer than extensions and inheritance relations, other association such as component, dependency, contains, and so on are also specified. Thus, it is possible to represent the complex and diverse relationships of networks, software components, applications and systems, and business organizations in today's enterprise and networking landscape.

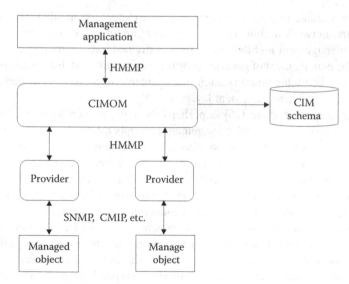

FIGURE 7.3   The WBEM architecture.

The CIM Object Manager (CIMOM) serves as the mediator between management applications and providers. It interacts with both the manager and provider side with the same protocol, the HyperMedia Management Protocol (HMMP) [17]. HMMP is an encoding protocol over other transport protocols, most commonly over Transmission Control Protocol (TCP)/IP. It provides access to the objects and classes constructed from the CIM model. The encoding format also follows MOF. HMMP supports diverse range of operations for object and class manipulations in CIM, such as class and instance creation, update, retrieval, and deletion. As a consequence, it is possible to construct nested CIMOMs (i.e., a manager of a set of managed objects could be treated as managed object by another manager at higher level). The management application does not have to be directly aware of the CIMOM, instead the application interacts with a "namespace" (an abstract representation of the object) that a CIMOM has provided. Several providers and CIMOMs may contribute to the definition of the same namespace. Static objects could be provided by the CIMOM directly. All other object manipulations are performed with the help of providers. The HMMP has security features such as access control on managed objects, and authentication and authorization of the CIMOM.

To date, the CIM model is at version 2.5 and many existing managed entities are standardized and specified in the model. With the creation of CIM–Extensible Markup Language (XML) [18] in 1999, the CIM MOF and HMMP have been superseded. HTTP is recommended as the transport protocol and XML–CIM defines the messages.

The WBEM architecture, more specifically the CIMOM and HMMP, is not widely deployed. In contrast, CIM, due to its extensibility and standardization, remains a favored information model in systems management.

POLICY-BASED MANAGEMENT

Policy-based management describes a whole series of management concepts and designs that administer and manage networks and service infrastructures through the specification, distribution and enforcement of policies. Policies are rules consisting of condition and action pairs specifying what to do and when to do it. It is an effective way of creating and executing management intelligence in networks. A policy can have diverse levels ranging from device-specific configuration rules to network control policies to business goals.

There is no single standardized framework for policy-based management. However, the IETF has been in the forefront of standardization for policy-based management protocols and information models, most notably the IETF Policy Decision Point (PDP)–Policy Enforcement Point (PEP) concept of the Common Open Policy Standard (COPS) protocol [19] (Figure 7.4). Both PDP and PEP are generic designs. The PDP–PEP construct is essentially a client server model in which PDP accepts policy requests from PEPs located on network elements and responds with policy decisions. A PDP has a persistent connection to a policy repository. Whenever a PEP sends a policy request or state information to a PDP, the information is kept for future decision associations, until being explicitly removed by the PEP. A PDP may also make decisions in reaction to some external event without being solicited by a

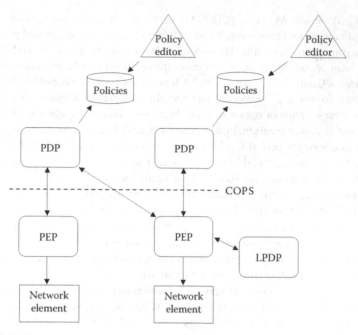

FIGURE 7.4 Overview of the PDP–PEP policy-based management.

PEP. The Local PDP (LPDP) is an optional component capable of making local decisions. A PEP may defer decision making to the LPDP in the absence of a PDP, perhaps due to a network fault, or when the decision is local. In actual implementation, a mechanism must be included so that the PDPs and PEPs could ensure the policies being exchanged are consistent in structure and type.

The policies are defined using a Policy Information Base. The IETF has standardized the Policy Core Information Model (PCIM) [20] for policy specification and formatting. PCIM is an object-oriented model based on an extension of CIM. Its definition of policy classes and associations is generic and follows CIM schema for objects and associations. The initial application of PCIM is on QoS policies (for DiffServ and IntServ) and on IPSec. The core classes `PolicyGroup`, `PolicyRule`, and `PolicyTimePeriodCondition` are considered the foundation classes for representing and communicating policy information. `PolicyGroup` is used to define a set of related policies, such as configuration, error and event reporting, installation, security, and so on. Specific classes derived from `PolicyCondition` and `PolicyAction` can be used to capture application-specific policy definitions. Vendor specific extensions can be derived from `VendorPolicyCondition` and `VendorPolicyAction`. There is also a `PolicyRepository` core class for specifying format for storing and accessing policies.

The concept of roles was introduced in PCIM to ease policy design and implementation. A role specifies a set of policies common to a particular entity. Managed resources can be assigned multiple roles thereby forming a role-combination. Hence each managed resource could have customized policies through the description of their unique role combinations while the policies associated with a role are universally applicable across resources with that role. More recently, the QoS Policy Information Model [21] has been derived from PCIM for specifying and representing policies that administer, manage, and control access to network QoS resources.

The COPS protocol has thus far been the most popular policy-based management protocol with its application in existing product such as the HP *OpenView PolicyXpert*.

SUMMARY OF RESEARCH ACTIVITIES

Despite the lack of common consensus in network and service management among the operators today, many advances have been made in network and service management research over the past decades. As early as 1991, work on management by delegation [22] showed that the one central manager and many agents approach of management suffer from two significant problems. First, the central manager is often overloaded with management requests from the agents and agent state collection operations. Second, the amount of work a manager does in order to satisfy the agents may be tedious and could result in an extremely inefficient design. By using delegation agents, some managerial tasks could be offloaded to these secondary managers specialized in dealing with a subnetwork or a specific function of the management. The concept of management delegation is now prevalent in management systems and the work has inspired many distributed management concepts and architectures and existing management protocols such as SNMPv2.

Advances in agent technology in the late 1990s in the field of artificial intelligence prompted the network and service management research community to explore its application in management system design [23–26]. Three directions are explored: code on demand, remote evaluation, and mobile agent. *Code on demand* allows the transportation of code at run-time from server to client and has the execution carried out remotely on the client. *Remote evaluation* is related to code on demand. Rather than sending the entire code from server to client. The server sends a set of code fragments (or groups of commands) that relies on local code fragments or programs to execute. In this way, it is possible to construct generic code logic at the server side and have its device specific execution at the client side. *Mobile agents* are autonomous and intelligent agents that could roam among the network components and perform execution on site. It is also envisioned for groups of mobile agents to coordinate among themselves and exchange information. Compared with the code on demand and remote evaluation, mobile agents are much more powerful, as execution states could be maintained by the agents from different sites and correlated. However, a mobile agent is also far more complex in structure and costly to support, requiring dedicated execution environment, migration mechanisms, large code size to transport, and poses security concerns. Other design considerations include security, resource management, identification, agent control, data management, and so on. The extra software and resource overhead and additional design issues that mobile agent technology brought to network management often overshadowed its benefits. In the end, few works on mobile agents have been embraced and realized by the industry.

Another trend that has come to pass is active networks. With increased processing power and programmability of the network hardware, the network research community sought after a new type of distributed management paradigm that can effectively distribute the management intelligence into the networks [27–29]. As a result, active networks were conceived as a fully distributed and highly programmable management and control infrastructure that builds right into the network itself. The main idea is to turn each network element into a distributed processing environment, and have the network packets not only carry user data but also management and control programs. Thus, the active packet could be executed within the network using the same communication infrastructure and protocol as data packets. Some early applications of this concept included proposals on traffic shaping, packet filtering, and user-controlled routing. Management applications based on active networks tended to be more elaborate and complex. However, the industry has been reluctant to embrace the concept of active networks. The fact that programmable network elements could be exposed to the applications and be used for general purpose code execution was controversial. In the end, the main weakness of the concept of active networks lies in the false assumption that networks are open systems programmable and manageable by entities outside the network operator's administration.

Looking back over the years, we see a definitive change in the philosophy of management system design: moving from centralized and stand-alone management systems to more decentralized and embedded designs where management intelligence is distributed into the networks. For enterprise networks, the plethora of divergent networks, devices, systems, and applications depict a similar landscape, especially when considering the rapid growth in the size and complexity of today's enterprises that often span over multiple continents. In fact, the importance of management is even more critical and essential to the efficient and successful operation of business enterprises, whose management cost comprises a large portion of their capital expenditure. The same distributed and autonomous vision that motivated much of the network and service management research is applicable in the enterprise environment as well.

SERVICE AND BUSINESS MANAGEMENT FRAMEWORKS

In this section, we present a number of current initiatives aimed at providing a structured and integrated view of management, encompassing network, service, and business operations. Three frameworks are detailed, the NGN, the Next Generation Operational Support Systems (NGOSS), and the ITIL. As explained earlier, NGN and NGOSS originate from the telecommunication sector while the ITIL has its roots in the IT service sector.

NEXT GENERATION NETWORKS

With the convergence of telecommunication networks and IP networks, the ITU-T has already begun the process of creating a new standardized network and service model for NGN [30,31]. The primary aim of this initiative is to create a manageable packet-based network capable of providing telecommunication services and using QoS-enabled transport technologies. The NGN model has a strong focus on services. To address the issues of mobility and network heterogeneity, a technology neutral transport layer is proposed that also support generalized mobility. Figure 7.5 illustrates the NGN model.

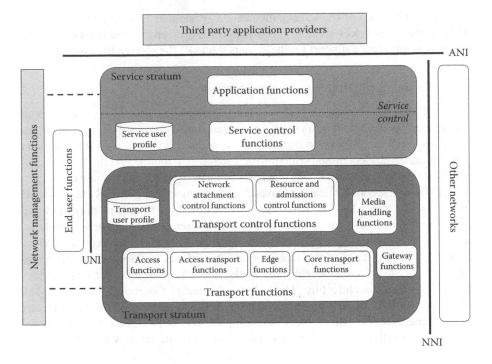

FIGURE 7.5 Overview of the NGN model.

The NGN network model consists of a transport stratum and a service stratum. The transport stratum is IP-based, with additional access functions to interwork with different access technologies and transport QoS controls. The service stratum supports both session-based and nonsession-based services; functions such as session control, subscribe/notify, instant message exchange, presence information, user profiling, and application plug-in APIs are also included. The service stratum provides Public-Switched Telephone Network (PSTN) capabilities and interworking through PSTN/ISDN (Integrated Services Digital Network) emulation. Management functions are distributed within both stratums; however, the specific on management components and models are yet to be specified. User control to NGN networks is facilitated both at the transport and the service stratums through User-to-Network Interfaces; application interaction with the service stratum is facilitated through Application-to-Network Interfaces; interworking with other networks is facilitated through Network-to-Network Interfaces. Compared with the traditional TCP/IP-layered model, the addition of a service stratum allows for a much stronger service-oriented control and management from the provider side. The type of services the NGN network model is aimed at supporting are session-based services the such as IP telephony and video conferencing, nonsession-based services such as video streaming, and PSTN functions (through software emulation). Additional considerations are made for multimedia support within the network through IP Multimedia Subsystem (IMS) consisting of core network functional entities and interfaces that can be used by network service providers to offer SIP-based services to subscribers. Much of the call session intelligence of the telecommunication services is to be supported through IMS. However, services are not explicitly modeled and represented in NGN and thus there is no structured support for the various stages of the service life cycle.

Next Generation Operation Support Systems

The NGOSS [32] is an ongoing effort in the Telecommunication Management Forum (TMF) to provide a new framework for the design and development of telecommunication business and service management systems. Compared with the traditional OSS systems of telecommunication, which are largely founded on the TMN model, the NGOSS system places strong emphasis on the integration of business and service processes in telecommunication management systems. The NGOSS effort is composed of four interrelated activities: design of technology neutral platform architecture, business process model specification, definition of a shared data model, and creation of compliance programs. The Technology Neutral Architecture (TNA) is a new NGOSS service platform that integrates traditional "OSS silos" (i.e., independent OSS systems for different parts of the telecommunication network) under a single distributed architecture. The Enhanced Telecom Operations Map (eTOM) is the new NGOSS business process model that seeks to replace the old TMN layered management model. The map defines multiple levels of processes with each below level further refines and realizes the level above. Figure 7.6 shows the top process

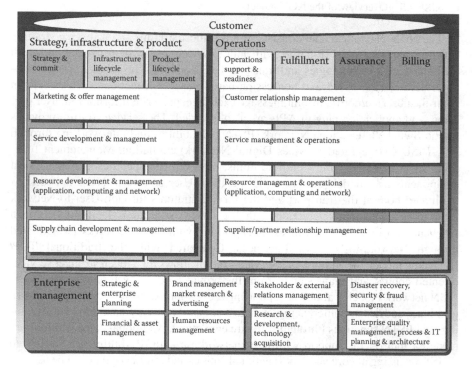

FIGURE 7.6   eTOM top-level process map.

level, which gives a general view of the NGOSS organization and management areas. It includes fulfillment, assurance, billing, and operations support and readiness as the top-level processes and each is broken down into level two subprocesses. The lower levels consist of activities in support of each subprocess. Four functional areas are defined spanning across these processes. A Shared Information and Data (SID) model captures the business and system entity definitions, relations, and management abstractions. It is defined with the Unified Modeling Language (UML), a standard language for architectural specification in software development. A Compliance Program consists of a NGOSS system testing strategy and a suite of test cases for validating NGOSS systems. An implementation of NGOSS is being developed under the TM Forum program OSS/J: the OSS through Java initiative. The goal is to deliver standards-based NGOSS interfaces implementations and design guidelines for the development of component-based OSS.

In comparison with NGN, NGOSS has a much stronger focus on the service and business processes in telecommunication, including many nontechnical aspects such as customer relation management, marketing, and so on. In some sense, NGN and NGOSS are complimentary in that both are telecommunication service- and business-oriented: NGN focuses primarily on the integration of the IP in the telecommunication infrastructure, operations, and service offers while the scope of NGOSS is the service and business support at the operational level. Both NGN and NGOSS do not consider the management of service life cycles. This is because telecommunication services tend to be manually designed, their deployment are preplanned, and the services have long lifetime, which makes automated service life-cycle management less crucial than in the IT sector. However, with the merging trend of IT and telecommunication sectors, NGOSS has introduced Telecom Application Map [33] to specifically address this issue.

IT INFRASTRUCTURE LIBRARY

The ITIL [34] is a collection of international best practices for IT service management. Its primary purpose is to provide service support and service delivery guidelines for IT business. *Service support* addresses issues that arise in service operations and maintenance, such as the role of a service helpdesk in effective incident management and in managing customer problem reports. *Service delivery* relates to service provisioning and maintenance to meet business requirements. Important service factors being considered are as follows: Change Management for impact assessment and scheduling of service change; Release Management for coordination, control, and physical introduction of different service versions such as incremental application upgrades; Configuration Management for ensuring service component information, relationships, and documentations are comprehensive and accurate; Availability Management to ascertain component reliability and recovery procedures; Capacity Management for efficient resource and infrastructure usage; and Financial Management for effective business budgeting and accounting. It is apparent that although ITIL is deeply rooted in the IT industry and is largely software service oriented, it shares much of the same management concerns as the TMF management areas, such as configuration, fault, and performance.

In 2005, ITIL v3 formally introduced the ITIL service life-cycle guidelines. It includes explicit support for three service life-cycle stages: service design, service transition, and service operation. Service design deals with the creation or change of services and service management processes. Service transition deals with the validation of services utility (a measure of a service's performance, similar to what QoS is to networks except much broader and more general) and to guide their transiting into service operation. Service operation deals with providing the services effectively and efficiently. This roughly corresponds to the general service life-cycle stages depicted in Figure 7.2. Service transition encompasses service negotiation and provisioning. Continual service improvement maps to the service change stage, and deals with service adjustment to satisfy changing business needs. Furthermore, an overarching service strategy provides the general service guidelines and how a service should be designed, configured, and operated. Compared with NGOSS and NGN, ITIL views services as a set of software components that are dynamically designed and deployed and then evolves to suit the changing business needs of IT industry.

Note that both NGOSS and ITIL deal with service and business management from a very general and comprehensive viewpoint. Contrary to the network management architectures discussed earlier, there are little architectural specifications or tools to support the actual implementation of the service and business management systems.

WEB SERVICES MANAGEMENT AND SERVICE-ORIENTED ARCHITECTURE

The increasing presence of Web services as the leading technology for distributed applications and services has given rise to a new service design paradigm: the Service-Oriented Architecture (SOA) approach which is based on loosely coupled Web service components with clear defined interfaces, functionalities, and access behavior. This is similar to the idea of having standard interfaces in telecommunication to interconnect equipment from different vendors. SOA is a computing model that strives for the creation of software or applications based on a set of independent service components that are loosely coupled. The only obligation among these components is to provide a set of promised service features through defined service interfaces (this is a more strict definition, as the service interfaces could potentially be discovered dynamically as well). In this sense, Web service composition (the interconnection of Web services to form a single application) could be viewed as an example of the SOA model. With the proliferation of Web Services, service customization will be strongly influenced by models of distributed component.

The concept of a Web service is underpinned by a set of XML-based technologies. It allows for data representation, access and processing, standardized interface definition, and access through the Web Service Definition Language (WSDL) and a Uniform Resource Identifier, customizable information transport and object invocation/access through the Simple Object Access Protocol (SOAP), and open service specification and discovery through Universal Definition, Discovery and Integration (UDDI). This poses questions on how to utilize Web service as a management technology for networks and services and how to manage Web services effectively? In

2004, the Organization for the Advancement of Structured Information Standards (OASIS) released a set of standards for Web Service Distributed Management (WSDM) [35]. Some of the WSDM design goals include unified management through Web services irrespective of how manageable resources are organized and composed and what information is modeled by the resource, and whether a Web service could be composed with others and under what preconditions.

WSDM consists of two standard sets, Management Using Web Services (MUWS) [36,37] and Management of Web Services (MOWS) [38] that address the previous two questions, respectively. In this section, we first present the framework of WSDM and its two subtopics. Then, we introduce the Web service orchestration and choreography tools that are essential to facilitate the automation of Web service composition, components configuration, and runtime behavior.

WEB SERVICE DISTRIBUTED MANAGEMENT

WSDM defines a framework to access and receive management information from manageable resources with Web services. Using a standardized set of XML specifications and Web service technology, the WSDM framework is an attempt to bridge resource heterogeneity and to integrate existing management products. In essence, the WSDM framework proposes to wrap all manageable resources and management software with Web service-based interfaces. In the WSDM context, the term manageable resource covers network resources, end-user devices, software components, and Web services. These manageable resources can be accessed through Web service endpoint references. In addition, manageable resources must support one or more standardized manageability capabilities, such as identity, description, state, configuration, advertisement, and so on.

MUWS defines the representation of and the access to the manageability interfaces of Web services. A *manageability interface* is a Web service-based management interface to a Web service. MUWS provides a set of basic and interoperable manageability specifications for management system design. It defines manageability capabilities as a composable set of properties, operations, events, metadata, and so on, which support management functions. A set of standard manageable resource definitions are described in order to achieve integration between WSDM management systems and non-Web service-managed resources, for example, SNMP agents. Some capabilities defined in the base model represent generic management information such as resource metrics, configuration parameters, characteristics of the manageability interfaces, operational status, properties, and so on. Furthermore, relationships among resources and management components are described with a Web service data representation such that it is possible to query about these relationships at run-time. MUWS also provides some support for manageable resource discovery and advertisement through advertisement, relationships, and registration events. Management messages and events are defined through the WSDM Event Format, organized as an event reporter, event source, and situation data. The advertisement event allows a newly created resource to advertise its manageability (i.e., a publish/subscribe mechanism). The relationships event allows the discovery of relationships among manageable resources. The registration event allows a manageable resource to expose its manageability via some registries (i.e., a lookup mechanism).

MOWS is an extension and application of MUWS by specifying how Web services could be managed within the WSDM framework. More specifically, MOWS defines the following set of manageability capabilities for managing Web services:

- Identity: a unique MUWS capability identifier for the Web service.
- Identification: a reference for the Web service being managed.
- Metrics: a set of MOWS basic metrics such as `NumberOfRequests`, `NumberOfFailedRequests`, `ServiceTime`, `MaxResponseTime`, and so on.
- Operational state: the MOWS operational status of the Web service being either UP (Busy or idle) or DOWN (stopped, crashed, or saturated).
- Operational status: A MUWS equivalent of the MOWS operational states, except in more generic terms: available, unavailable, and partially available.
- Request processing state: it defines a request state diagram and provides mechanisms to define events to be sent when request processing states change.

Thus MOWS and MUWS are complimentary in WSDM, in that one specifies how management should be structured and management information modeled, while the other specifies how management functions and information could be accessed and understood.

Much of the WSDM framework is focused on representing and managing software components. Although this is a fairly narrow view of service management, it occupies a much needed niche in today's network and service management spectrum.

WEB SERVICE ORCHESTRATION AND CHOREOGRAPHY

A formal methodology to specify the interactions among components and run-time behavior is needed to support SOA. In traditional software engineering practices, entity-relation diagrams and sequential diagrams describe the interactions among various software blocks and participants; similarly, operational state diagrams are used to track the operational status of the software. SOA promotes component-based interactions and run-time compositions, which are far more dynamic and unpredictable than traditional distributed software design. For instance, the individual components of a Web service could have been developed by different service providers, independently and at different times, and maybe even with different design requirements. Thus, it is indeed a challenge to know what components could interwork, how, and with what configurations.

Web service, as a technology that favors SOA design, can provide a set of mechanisms to address the issues discussed. In particular, there are two promising technologies: Web service orchestration and Web service choreography. Web service orchestration is concerned with the business protocols of the Web services as they interact to fulfill the business logic. It describes how these services collectively perform a business execution. For example, the actions a recipient Web service will executed in response to a service request. Thus, Web services orchestration provides a map for the interaction of the services at the message level (i.e., their order of execution, the timing of message exchanges among the Web services, etc.), and defines the ownership of the processes by the service providers (i.e., which process belongs to which service provider). Web services choreography details how each party of an interaction behaves in terms of the sequence of messages exchanged among the participants. Hence choreography is more collaborative in the sense that the overall message exchange is the combined interplay of each mutual participant.

The Business Process Execution Language for Web Services (BPEL4WS) [39] is a standard for describing Web service orchestration. It was proposed by Microsoft, IBM, Siebel Systems, BEA, and SAP to OASIS, which adopted it as a standard way for describing control logics and Web service process coordination using WSDL. Primitives in BPEL4WS include sequential and parallel activities, conditional looping, dynamic branching, and so on, commonly supported by process flow languages. Dynamic branching is a form of conditional branching in that the direction of process flow is guided by the particular run-time state of a process (i.e., the branching process). A partner is a participant in the business protocol whose role is clearly defined by a BPEL4WS role specification. The concept of "partner" is therefore essential in BPEL4WS because of its business execution-oriented view point.

Web Service Choreography Interface (WSCI) [40] is an extension of WSDL to implement Web service choreography. It was initially proposed by Sun Microsystems, SAP, BEA, and Intalio to the W3C (World Wide Web Consortium). WSCI specifies the stream of WSDL messages that the Web services exchange and does not describe any component behavior. WSCI uses tags to differentiate various activities. The tag <action> denotes a request or response message, with each <action> specifying the operation involved and the role played by the participant described with WSDL. The <call> tag is used to invoke external services. The <all> tag indicates that the associated messages must all be performed but in any order. Similar to BPEL4WS primitives, all of these activities could be sequential, parallel executions, or conditional loops. The dynamic branching primitive from BPEL4WS is not present in WSCI because it is dependent on the state of the component which is outside the scope of WSCI.

A short comparison between Web service orchestration and choreography is given in Ref. [41], which also highlighted the need for both in Web service operations.

SELF-MANAGEMENT

With the rising complexity, scale and management cost of networks and services today, service and application providers are actively seeking solutions to reduce the overhead of service operations and maintenance. The current held belief among the network and service research community is that the ultimate solution to the management problem lies in automation; in another word, to create self-managed networks and services that is intelligent enough to be autonomous.

The concept of self-management has thus gained much attention in research and industry development in the past years. This was particularly highlighted by IBM researchers in 2003 [42], who coined the term "autonomic computing" and defined it as: "a distributed system where a set of software/network components that can regulate and manage themselves in areas of configuration, fault, performance and security to achieve some common user defined objectives." The word "autonomic" originates from the autonomic nervous system that acts as the primary conduit of self-regulation and control in humans. Four self-managing properties of autonomic computing are defined as follows:

- *Self-configuration.* The entities (networks and systems) can automate system configuration following high level specifications, and can self-organize into desirable structures and/or patterns.
- *Self-optimization.* The entities constantly seek improvement to their performance and efficiency, and are able to adapt to changing environment without direct human input.
- *Self-healing.* The entities can automatically detect, diagnose, and recover from faults as the result of internal errors or external inconsistencies.
- *Self-protection.* The entities can automatically defend against malicious attacks or isolate the attackers to prevent system-wide failures.

Although the autonomic computing concept was first proposed for distributed systems and software components, it is equally relevant to self-managed networks and services, especially given the rise of Web services and SOA designs. In an autonomic environment, each service or network component is expected to take inputs from the external environment, to apply analysis and reasoning logic, to generate the corresponding actions, and to execute them. This monitoring, reasoning, and action loop is carried out today with individual tools with multiple operational views, requiring significant input from a human administrator. Manual operation is the source of the majority of the service operational cost and is error prone. Self-management would ultimately eliminate some of these challenges or at least reduce their impact on the service cost and therefore the cost of business operations. This constitutes a departure from traditional management system design because the manager is being automated, rather than merely focusing on effective operation of the managed objects. Accordingly, new challenges arise that self-managing systems must take into account. Here, we discuss some of these challenges that researchers have just started to examine and understand in the context of self-management designs:

- The creation of self-managing network must follow a rigorous engineering approach to ensure the validity, consistency, and correctness of the system from its development, deployment, to operation and removal. This process must be firmly established in order to ensure that the resulting system is reliable and robust to faults, changes in the environment, attacks, and so on. In addition, there must be independent validation and benchmarking methodologies and mechanisms in place that not only can evaluate the performance of autonomic systems in general, but also can provide safeguard against unforeseeable errors. To date, these methodologies and mechanisms are not in place.
- Monitoring is of paramount importance to self-managing networks. Because of the sense-learn/plan-execute interaction pattern that an autonomic component exhibits, the component must be able to determine what, when, and

where to monitor. The monitoring data may be diverse in content and context, and the monitoring parameters are likely to be subject to frequent changes. It is not clear how such a process should be structured in a distributed and efficient manner. What overhead the monitoring activities place on the networks? And to what granularity, in time and in volume, should the monitoring activities be bounded by?

- Knowledge of the environment, the systems, and even self-awareness is critical to autonomic reasoning, analysis, and decision making. The knowledge an autonomic system is required to gather and formulate far exceeds the level of data representation and interpretation capability of today's network management applications and distributed systems. We must be able to represent a wide range of knowledge such as the environment, various processes, services and objects, the autonomic component, the states the system could take on, the interactions a component could have, the properties the system and components are associated with, the features/services the system or component provides, and so on. Some of these representations exist today (e.g., Web service descriptions, CIM models, MIBs, etc.) but in diverse and unrelated sources. The problem is further complicated by the wide range of context such knowledge could be taken from. We need a common information representation to take into account the varied semantics and interpretations that different knowledge sources could have even on the same topic.

- Interactions among autonomic components or even autonomic systems pose another challenge. How do they coordinate to achieve system wide objectives? How do they negotiate services and requirements? How can the overall system behavior be determined from the interactions of individual components? These are but some of the important problems that requires well formulated solutions.

- System stability, robustness, resilience, and correctness are some of the key properties of self-managing networks. Not all of them are well understood or easily analyzable, especially in the self-management context. For example, how does localized reasoning based on limited information lead to stable global behavior? How does one avoid global inconsistencies and undesirable system behaviors in autonomic systems?

- In a dynamic environment, processes must undergo constant change to adapt to the new environment and maintain optimality. The concept of homeostasis [43], which is central to the adaptation to the environment of biological systems, is prevalent in the concept of self-managing networks and services as well. The need for constant adaptation poses new challenges: as the autonomic system evolves overtime in response to changes in the environment, how to ensure validity and consistency? What effect does this adaptation have on the stability of the system? And how to effectively handle transitions?

- Self-managing networks exhibit many negative traits: the lack of conformity among autonomic components, the complexity of the autonomic systems, the constant evolution of the network environment, and the implicit designs and architectural assumptions the designers are prone to make. All of these factors make interoperability among components and systems difficult.

For interested readers, a more comprehensive treatment of the subject could be found in Ref. [3]. Although the ultimate goal of self-management may well be unreachable in the near future, it helps the community in re-evaluating the established foundations of management system designs and re-thinks the management philosophy.

ENTERPRISE INTEGRATION: A MANAGEMENT POINT OF VIEW

The evolution of the Web technologies and its integration with the telecommunication infrastructure within enterprises has had a pronounced effect on the network and service management processes, not only in terms of management scale and complexity, but also in terms of the service environment and business model. It is increasingly difficult to manage a rapidly growing set of services and their associated security with stand-alone and human-reliant management applications. At the same time, application-level virtual networking concepts, such as overlay networks and peer-to-peer networks, and the integration of wireless and wired services are posing additional challenges. Enterprise networks today consist of a mixture of networks and virtual networks, whose management are far more involved than the management of network resources and components. Centralized management solutions are ill-suited for the situation and it is highly unlikely that a unified set of management functionalities would emerge in the short- or mid-term future. Current trends on self-managing systems and large distributed management designs may bring some relief, however.

From the management point of view, the service-driven nature of future enterprise networks has significant ramifications in the design of the management infrastructures. First, the functional areas of the network management (i.e., fault, configuration, performance, security and accounting) must be extended to the service layer. Secondly, with the focus shifting from networks to services, service assurance and customer support are the essential aspects of management. For instance, the configuration of a service must also consider its usability to the users; the changes made at run-time must account for their impact on user perception. Thirdly, services mostly consist of software applications and processes, are more short-lived, and less reliable than network elements. They lack the location dependence property prevalent to most of the network elements. Finally, the dynamics of services require much stronger run-time management support, as the capability or features of a service may very well change due to changes in the network environment, user requirements, and so on.

The implication of user diversity is that management functions may vary greatly with the type of interactions. For example, a low capability edge device would expect the management system to exhibit high autonomy and have a few specialized functions; a novice user might expect a rich management feature set to interact with, but only at a very abstract service level, leaving the system to figure out the management implementations; while a network expert might want the management system to expose details at the network component and resource level and have limited control over them. Hence, the management system for the future enterprise networks must be intelligent with high degrees of autonomy, but appear simplistic and customizable to the users. Furthermore, there exists a discrepancy between the user and network views of a service. Taking the end-to-end connection example, the user view of the connection topology will be composed of a set of services (i.e., clouds of interconnected physical networks and virtual networks) while the actual end-to-end physical connectivity may be quite different. Network managers will have little control over the formation of such topologies, for example, in peer-to-peer sessions.

The administration and management of the enterprise networks today is characterized by isolation and segregation. Each network domain and each service block has it own management tools and its own sets of policies and controls. Their integration in a unified architecture necessitates rethinking and reengineering of network and service management designs.

These are requirements of a new management design that must be taken into account of and have invalidated some of the existing design assumptions. For example, it is reasonable to assume that the probability of simultaneous multinode network failure is very low. However, in the case of services, it is common that a failure of a single software component would trigger a multicomponent cascaded failure. The degree of customization that will be common in the future Internet also means that they will have specific management requirements, and they may even change during the lifetime of a service. Consequently, it favors management designs that are dynamic and customizable.

CONCLUSION

The dominance of Web service concepts is affecting the design of systems that manage networks and services. This chapter provided an introductory guide to the challenging area of research and development. The business model of future enterprise or public networks will differ significantly from that of today. The diversity of new networked devices, the various means of communication and social networking, and the emergence of Web service applications all poses new challenges to today's enterprise networks. As we have discussed, self-managing network and system design may offer an eventual solution to the problem but the road to there is still full of unresolved issues and problems that we have just begin to understand and explore. Innovation and efficient design in network and service management will be pivotal in supporting the enterprise networks of today and tomorrow.

REFERENCES

1. Pavlou, G. On the evolution of management approaches, frameworks and protocols: A historical perspective, *J. Netw. Syst. Manage. (JNSM)*, 15(4), 425–445, 2007.
2. Boutaba, R. and Xiao, J., Telecommunication network management, in *Encyclopedia on Life Support Systems*, UNESCO-EOLSS, Eloss Publishers Co. Ltd., available online at http://www.eolss.net, 2007.
3. Boutaba, R. and Xiao, J., Self-managing networks, in *Cognitive Networks: Towards Self-Aware Networks*, Mahmoud, Q. Ed., John Wiley & Sons, Chichester, 2007, Ch. 4.
4. X.701, Information technology—Open system interconnection—System management overview, CCITT, Geneva, Switzerland, 1989.
5. X.710, Common management information service definition for CCITT applications, CCITT, Geneva, Switzerland, 1991.

6. X.711, Information technology—Open system interconnection—Common management information protocol specification—Part 1: Specification, 2nd edn, CCITT, Geneva, Switzerland, 1991.

7. X.720, Information Technology—Open System Interconnection—Structure of management information: Management information model, CCITT, Geneva, Switzerland, 1992.

8. RFC 1212, Concise MIB definition, IETF, 1991, available at http://www.ietf.org.

9. M.3010, Principles for a telecommunications management network (TMN), CCITT, Geneva, Switzerland, 1996.

10. RFC 1157, A Simple Network Management Protocol (SNMP), IETF, 1990, available at http://www.ietf.org.

11. RFC 1212, Concise MIB definition, IETF, 1991, available at http://www.ietf.org.

12. RFC 1213, Management information base for network management of TCP/IP-based Internets: MIB-II, IETF, 1991, available at http://www.ietf.org.

13. X.208, Abstract Syntax Notation Number 1 (ASN.1), CCITT, Geneva, Switzerland, 1988.

14. TINA, Principles of TINA, TINA-C, 1995, available at http://www.tinac.com/about/principles_of_tinac.htm, last accessed July 14, 2009.

15. Kristiansen, L. et al., TINA service architecture, v5.0, TINA-C, 1997, available at http://www.tinac.com/specifications/documents/sa50-main.pdf, last accessed July 14, 2009.

16. CIM, Common Information Model, DMTF, 1997, available at http://www.dmtof.org/standards/cim, last accessed July 13, 2009.

17. HMMP, HyperMedia Management Protocol, DMTF draft-hmmp-opns-05, 1997.

18. CIM-XML, Specification for the Representation of CIM in XML, v2.0, DMTF, 1999, available at http://www.dmtf.org/standards/documents/WBEM/CIM_XML_Mapping20.html, last accessed July 14, 2009.

19. RFC 2748, The COPS (common open policy service) protocol, IETF, 2000, available at http://www.ietf.org.

20. RFC 3060, Policy Core Information Model—version 1 specification, IETF, 2001, available at http://www.ietf.org.

21. RFC 3644, Policy quality of service (QoS) information model, IETF, 2003, available at http://www.ietf.org.

22. Yemini, Y., Goldszmidt, G., and Yemini, S., Network management by delegation, *Proceedings of 2nd International Symposium on Integrated Network Management (IM)*, Washington, DC, USA, 1991.

23. Goldszmidt, G. and Yemini, Y., Delegated agents for network management, *IEEE Commun. Magaz.*, 36(3), 66–70, 1998.

24. Boudaoud, K. et al., Network security management with intelligent agents, *IFIP/IEEE Network Operations and Management Symposium (NOMS)*, 579–592, Honolulu, USA, 2000.

25. Bohoris, C., Pavlou, G., and Cruickshank, H., Using mobile agents for network performance management, *IFIP/IEEE Network Operations and Management Symposium (NOMS)*, 637–652, Honolulu, USA, 2000.

26. Papavassiliou, S. et al., Mobile agent-based approach for efficient network management and resource allocation: Framework and applications, *IEEE J. Selected Areas Commun.*, 20(4), 858–872, 2002.

27. Raz, D. and Shavitt, Y., Active networks for efficient distributed network management, *IEEE Commun. Magaz.*, 38(3), 138–143, 2000.

28. Kawamura, R. and Stadler, R., A middleware architecture for active distributed management of IP networks, *IFIP/IEEE Network Operations and Management Symposium (NOMS)*, 291–304, Honolulu, USA, 2000.

29. Silva, S., Yemini, Y., and Florissi, D., The NetScript active network system, *IEEE J. Selected Areas Commun.*, 19(3), 538–551, 2001.

30. Y.2001, General overview of NGN, ITU-T, Geneva, Switzerland, 2004.
31. Y.2011, General principles and general reference model for Next Generation Network, ITU-T, Geneva, Switzerland, 2004.
32. Telecommunication Forum, Next Generation Operation Support Systems (NGOSS), TM Forum, available at http://www.tmforum.org/TechnicalPrograms/NGOSS/1911/Home.html, last accessed July 13, 2009.
33. Telecommunication Forum, Telecom Application Map (TAM), TM Forum, available at http://www.tmforum.org/BusinessSolutions/TelecomApplications/2322/Home.html
34. ITIL, IT Infrastructure Library, available at http://www.itil-officialsite.com/home/home.asp, last accessed July 13, 2009.
35. WSDM, Web Service Distributed Management (WSDM), v1.1, OASIS Standard, 2006, available at http://www.oasis-open.org/committees/tc_home.php?wg_abbrev=wsdm.
36. MUWS, Web Services Distributed Management: Management Using Web Services (MUWS 1.1) Part 1, OASIS Standard, 2006, available at http://docs.oasis-open.org/wsdm/wsdm-muws1-1.1-spec-os-01.htm, last accessed July 13, 2009.
37. MUWS, Web Services Distributed Management: Management Using Web Services (MUWS 1.1) Part 2, OASIS Standard, 2006, available at http://docs.oasis-open.org/wsdm/wsdm-muws2-1.1-spec-os-01.htm, last accessed July 13, 2009.
38. MOWS, Web service distributed management: Management Of Web Services (WSDM-MOWS), v1.1, OASIS Standard, August 1, 2002, 2006, available at http://docs.oasis-open.org/wsdm/wsdm-mows-1.1-spec-os-01.htm, last accessed July 14, 2009.
39. IBM, Business Process Execution Language for Web Services v1.1, August 8, 2002, available at http://www.ibm.com/developerworks/library/specification/ws-bpel, last accessed July 13, 2009.
40. W3C, Web Service Choreography Interface (WSCI) v1.0, available at http://www.w3.org/TR/wsci, last accessed July 13, 2009.
41. Peltz, C. Web service orchestration and choreography, *IEEE Comput.*, 36(10), 46–52, 2003.
42. Kephart, J. and Chess, D., The Vision of autonomic computing, *IEEE Comput.*, 36(1), 41–50, 2003.
43. Herrmann, K., Muhl, G., and Geihs, K., Self management: The solution to complexity or just another problem?, *IEEE Distrib. Syst. Online*, 6(1), 2005, available at http://doi.ieeecomputersociety.org/10.1109/MDSO.2005.3.

8 Monitoring Quality of Service in Enterprise Multicast Networks

Ehab Al-Shaer

CONTENTS

INTRODUCTION

The rapid growth of multicast services in IP networks has shown the limitations of traditional network management tools in monitoring the quality of multicast delivery. Because of the peculiar characteristics of multicast routing trees and the potential of message implosion problem, service delivery in multicast networks is more complex than in traditional unicast networks [1,2]. Monitoring networks is important to observe and maintain the quality of service (QoS) as specified in the Service Level Agreement. Efficient monitoring tools are necessary to observe the health of the multicast delivery trees, to report faults and performance problems, such as high latency or packet loss in the delivery path, unreachable members, and abnormal disconnections, due to routing misconfigurations or bugs in the protocol implementation [3]. Thus, the deployment of multicast services requires easy-to-use and easy-to-integrate management tools that are based on a widely used network management protocol, such as Simple Network Management Protocol (SNMP) [4].

In this chapter, we will first review the exiting monitoring tools for IP multicast. Then, we will describe a framework for multicast network reachability monitoring, called SMRM. SMRM utilizes SNMP and the standard structure of management information (SMI) [5] and is based on the dynamic MIB technology [6–8] to ensure a highly extensible management framework. The SMRM framework enables SNMP agents to generate multicast streams with various traffic parameters (such as rate, packet size, and distribution) and monitor the network latency, jitter, and packet loss from source to destination. It provides scalable monitoring via using multicast communication between managers and agents, avoiding the packet implosion problem [9]. The SMRM sessions are dynamically created and configured from a central Web-based management station (called SMRM manager). Network Operations Center (NOC) personnel can use the SMRM framework to generate directed multicast traffic and collect real-time reports about the reachability and the quality of the multicast delivery at any point or segment in enterprise networks.

Unlike many other tools, SMRM provides a scalable, extensible, and easy-to-use monitoring framework for monitoring multicast based on SNMP standard. Thus, it is easy to add new multicast management tasks or tests to the SMRM framework.

OVERVIEW OF EXISTING MULTICAST MONITORING TOOLS

IP MULTICAST

IP multicast is the Internet standard for delivering packets to a group of receivers. It is widely used for multimedia application such as video conferences, video on demand, and collaborative applications such as whiteboard and document sharing. IP multicast provides one-to-many communication over an IP infrastructure. The multicast packets sent from a single source to a multicast group (using a class D address) will be replicated by multicast routers whenever necessary and delivered over multicast forwarding trees to all joining receivers. For example, if some receivers join group 239.9.9.9, the network will set up a multicast forwarding tree to deliver the traffic sent to this address to all receivers listening to this address. IP multicast can scale to a large number of receivers because it does not require any prior knowledge of the receivers, and joining and leaving group can be performed dynamically and autonomously. The protocol used by receivers to join a group is called the Internet Group Management Protocol (IGMP) [10] and the protocol to construct the multicast forwarding trees is the Protocol Independent Multicast (PIM) [11,12]. Monitoring of IP multicasting is a complex task because it is an unreliable transport service using User Datagram Protocol (UDP), so the network does not report any transport problems to the multicast parties (senders and receivers). For example, the sender is unaware when the receivers do not receive their multicast packets status. Similarly, the receivers are unaware whether the multicast packets that are destined to them have been lost or their group is just inactive.

Conferencing applications, whether audio or video, require multicasting to provide multipoint communication to a group of participants. In these applications, the QoS is usually evaluated with three metrics: loss, delay, and jitter. The reachability problem can results from high packet loss. Monitoring the reachability allows troubleshooting of network problems, such as when users are unable to access remote network services or when they experience considerable degradation (e.g., high latency or packet loss). Thus, efficient monitoring is needed to constantly diagnose and recover IP multicast problems in real-time [13].

MULTICAST MONITORING-RELATED WORK

Traditionally, *ping* and *traceroute* programs are used to test and diagnose reachability problems in unicast networks. However, these tools cannot be used for multicast and many ideas, experiments, and tools were especially developed to compensate for this gap [14]. However, only few proposed multicast monitoring solutions that are scalable, easy-to-use, and easy-to-deploy. In this survey, we classify the related work into the following two categories: monitoring tools and monitoring frameworks.

Multicast Monitoring Tools

One of the very useful tools in this category is *mtrace*, which discovers the routers in the reverse multicast path from a given receiver to the source of a multicast group [15]. It was developed to substitute for traceroute in IP multicast environments and to describe the discovered path with simple statistics such as packet loss and delay. Mtrace requires a special support in the network routers to collect this information and does not scale well with large groups, which limits its deployment. Other tools, such as *Sdr-monitor* [16,17], *MHealth* [18], and *RTPmon* [19], observe the global reachability of the Session Directory (SDR) and Real-Time Transport Protocol RTP multicast messages to group members by collecting feedback from multicast receivers. *Mrinfo* shows some traffic details of a multicast router, such as active multicast tunnels and interfaces. Other similar tools are presented in Ref. [20].

Many of these tools suffer from the following limitations: (1) they cannot be easily extended to monitor other aspects of interest in multicast networks such as reachability and performance problem; (2) they either require a special support in the network (*mtrace*) or are restricted to RTP or SDR applications (*Mhealth* and *sdr-monitor*); and (3) they do not scale with large multicast groups due to the reply explosion problem.

The *mcping* tool [21] is used to verify multicast availability between a multicast receiver in the local site and a remote multicast sender. *Mcping* uses active probing; a positive response indicates that the local receiver can successfully join and receive multicast data from the remote host. The *mcroute* tool [21] is a multicast route discovery tool analogous to the unicast *traceroute* utility. It uses the underlying PIM-Join mechanism to propagate the query request and the underlying multicast packet forwarding mechanism for query response propagation. In this way, *mcrout* can safely use the result of a successful query as the proof of multicast reachability between the end points. The *mcrout* tool is an improvement over *mtrace* because it gives a more accurate representation of the connectivity between the sender and the receiver. Nevertheless, the deployment of any of *mcping* and *mcrout* require extensions to the current protocols/infrastructure.

Multicast Monitoring Frameworks

These systems tend to offer a broader solution for multicast monitoring. The *Mmon* application in HP *Openview* was the first attempt to provide a complete framework for multicast management. It provides an automatic discovery of tree topology and multicast-capable routers, a query service to investigate the status of multicast routers, paths, and traffic information through a graphical user interface (GUI). This tool allows operators to identify and isolate faults as they occur in the network. *Mmon* uses the SNMP to gather the information from various MIBs of multicast management and routing protocols, such as IGMP MIB, PIM MIB, and IPMROUTE MIB. The main limitations of the *Mmon* approach are: (1) it is not scalable due to SNMP unicast communication [9]; (2) it lacks the active monitoring capability to allow the injection and monitoring of multicast traffic at any selected points in the network for fault diagnoses and isolation, (3) it does not support inter-domain multicast management.

Other approaches use proprietary protocols (instead of SNMP) to address the previous limitations. The Multicast Reachability Monitor (MRM) [22,23] was the first framework to introduce a new protocol for multicast reachability monitoring. MRM uses active monitoring; a multicast traffic is originated by a delegated sender—called test sender (TS)—to multicast receivers—called test receivers (TRs)—which continuously collect statistics and send status reports to the manager. Although MRM is a step forward toward efficient multicast monitoring, its deployment was limited because it uses a proprietary protocol and special agents. Also, in the absence of clock synchronization between the sender and receivers [23], it is not clear how the delay and jitter would be calculated. In addition, MRM framework lacks real-time traffic analysis and the ability to upload management scripts into the monitoring agents dynamically.

Another tool, the Hierarchical Passive Multicast Monitor (HPMM) uses a proprietary protocol for fault detection and isolation in multicast networks [24]. Unlike MRM, HPMM use passive monitoring agents that communicate with each other using unicast. The HPMM agents are organized in a hierarchy according to their locations from the multicast sender. Monitoring reports are collected and correlated in a hierarchical fashion to provide large-scale monitoring.

The idea of hierarchical monitoring and filtering was also used in the HiFi system [25,26]. However, HPMM is different because it sets up a hierarchy of agents overlaying the actual multicast tree. The main limitation of this approach is that it requires the deployment of new HPMM agents in routers and network domains. Another limitation is the use of passive monitoring for fault isolation. Although passive monitoring is less intrusive, active monitoring is helpful for detecting and isolating network problems. Accordingly, HPMM is strictly a fault management tool and does not assist in monitoring other network parameters such as delay and jitter. In addition, the use of unicast for agent communication increases the overhead for maintaining the monitoring hierarchy significantly [27].

MRMON [28] is an SNMP-based tool that exploits the widely used management infrastructure of SNMP agents; as a consequence, it requires no changes in the network elements. However, it uses a passive approach, which restricts it to monitoring. In contrast, SMRM is active [13] and can track delay and jitter.

SMRM ARCHITECTURE

SMRM consists of three main SNMP entities: (1) the SMRM manager that defines multicast reachability test configurations, and the role of the SNMP agents, as senders or receivers, during the test; (2) the SMRM senders' agents that originate multicast streams according to the session profile defined by the manager; and (3) the SMRM receivers' agents that sink the multicast streams for traffic monitoring and analysis. The senders' and receivers' agents are called SMRM testers. This is illustrated in Figure 8.1.

In a typical SMRM session, the NOC administrators use the SMRM manager to define the SMRM *traffic* and *session* parameters (described in the framework implementation). When the session is activated, the SMRM manager configures the SMRM testers by setting the proper MIB objects in the agents to define the parameters of the SMRM session configuration profile, such as packet length and data rate, and the agents' role (senders or receivers). Based on the configuration profiles, the SMRM manager can start sending a multicast traffic from one or more SMRM senders to a group of SMRM receivers in the network. With the extended SNMP framework described below, the SMRM senders generate multicast streams directed to a specific multicast group as specified in the session profile, while the SMRM receivers can join the same multicast group. The SMRM receivers monitor and process multicast packets as they are received and analyze the traffic to extract the reachability information (packet loss, latency, and jitter). They use special MIB objects for storing the monitoring information and can store the header information

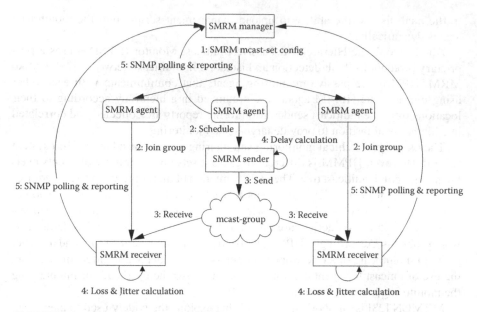

FIGURE 8.1   The architecture of SMRM.

of the received packets to be retrieved by the manager for subsequent analysis. Thus, the receivers perform real-time analysis, which is useful particularly when real-time monitoring is required and the monitoring agent has enough bandwidth and processing power.

We can summarize the SMRM operations in the following four steps:

1. *Create and load the SMRM session*: In this step, the network manager creates a new SMRM profile and defines the session and traffic parameters.
2. *Identify the network segments to be tested*: Then the network manager determines the network segments and testing/monitoring by specifying which SNMP agents (network nodes) should act as SMRM senders and SMRM receivers.
3. *Activate the SMRM session*: By activating the SMRM session, the manager will transfer the configuration information to the appropriate SMRM agents to inform them of the session configurations.
4. *View monitoring information*: The manager program retrieves, on-demand, the monitoring information from the receivers and plots the results in the management console. The frequency of the monitoring information retrieval is a configurable parameter.

The manager may create a number of SMRM sessions simultaneously. SMRM testers use unique session IDs to distinguish different SMRM sessions. To prevent different managers from using the same session ID, the manager's IP address is used as a prefix.

SMRM OPERATION

By integrating the SMRM functionality into SNMP, NOC, personnel can test and monitor any portion of the network for fault detection and diagnoses using the SNMP agents that are available in most network nodes today. In this section, we describe SMRM design and its integration into SNMP entities (agents and manager).

This integration is performed in two steps:

- Integrating multicasting into SNMP so that the SNMP agents become multicast-capable and
- Integrating reachability monitoring into SNMP.

The following sections describe both steps.

INTEGRATING MULTICASTING WITH SNMP

Although SNMP is specified over UDP [4], it only uses the unicast transport service for communication. However, supporting multicast group communication among agents and managers is important to provide scalable network management services that can handle a large number of managed objects and agents [9]. Using IP multicasting reduces the latency and the number of messages significantly in the network management system. Furthermore, making SNMP agents understand multicasting is a basic requirement for an efficient management of multicast networks. For these reasons, a practical approach is to incorporate IP multicasting in the SNMP framework with minimal code changes [9]. This allows managers to re-configure the agents' group membership so that communication is established on-demand. The manager sets the group configuration information such as multicast IP address and port using Set requests in a new MIB group called Multicast Information Group or mcastInfoMIB in SNMP agents. The mcastInfoMIB group is divided into the following two classes of objects (Figure 8.2):

1. *Group Management Objects* that hold the address information such as the agentGroupIPAddr and agentGroupPort objects to store the multicast IP address and port number, respectively, which agents use to join the multicast group. This class also contains the managerGroupIPAddr and managerGroupPort objects that hold the IP address and port number of the manager multicast group, respectively, so that the agent could use them for replying to a multicast request. If the managerGroupIPAddr or managerGroupPort are unspecified (i.e., NULL), then the agent uses the unicast IP address of the requesting manager to reply.
2. *Group Communication Objects* that hold information about the communication parameters. It contains the groupTTL object that specifies the Time-to-live (TTL) in the IP header of multicast packets, and the mcast-Timer object that indicates whether the agent must use a randomized timer before sending the reply to avoid reply explosions at the manager [29]. Timer randomization is used to offer a scalable agent–manager communication.

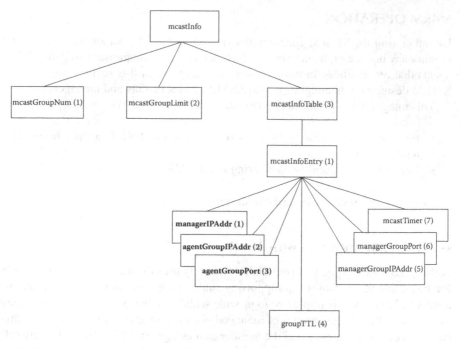

FIGURE 8.2   The `mcastInfoMIB` group for multicast SNMP (the bold entries represent the key index and the primary keys of the MIB tables).

The manager configures the group communication by setting the multicast information in the `mcastInfo` objects of the agent. The manager sends this request as a unicast message to every agent involved in the group communication. Consequently, the agent reacts by updating the `mcastInfo` object in the MIB and joining the specified multicast group. On the other hand, the agent leaves the multicast group specified by `agentGroupIPAddr` if the manager changes this address to 0.0.0.0. After leaving a multicast group, the agent also deletes the corresponding entry in the `mcastInfo` table.

INTEGRATING REACHABILITY MONITORING INTO SNMP

We describe now the SMRM architecture and techniques for supporting multicast reachability monitoring based on SNMP. The presented techniques enable SNMP entities to perform reachability monitoring in unicast as well as multicast networks. However, we focus on multicast reachability because multicast services are more difficult to manage due to the lack of appropriate monitoring tools.

In our framework, the SMRM testers can reside in any network device or end host running a standard SNMP agent (`snmpd`) extended with the following MIBs: Schedule MIB (`schedMIB` [6]), Multicast MIB (`mcastInfoMIB` [9]), and the Multicast Reachability Monitoring MIB (`smrmMIB`), which are described in this section. In the following section, we also describe the SMRM MIB objects and how SNMP entities use these MIBs to perform multicast reachability monitoring tasks.

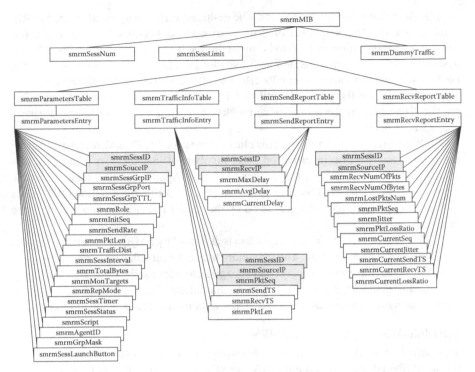

FIGURE 8.3 The smrmMIB group (the shaded entries are indices or key values for particular tables).

Figure 8.3 shows the structure of the SMRM MIB, with the shaded entries indicating the indices or key values for particular tables.

Multicast Reachability Monitoring MIB

The smrmMIB is a new MIB used to store SMRM configurations, such as the session and traffic parameters used by the SMRM testers to create and monitor sessions. The smrmSessNum and smrmSessLimit groups indicate the number of active SMRM sessions and the maximum number of allowed SMRM sessions, respectively. In addition, there are four classes of objects supported in the smrmMIB group as described below.

SMRM parameters objects. This class is used by SMRM testers (senders or receivers) to store the SMRM configurations sent by the manager (Figure 8.3). This class consists of two types of configuration objects: *session objects* and *traffic objects*. Among the session objects are smrmSessGrpIP and smrmSessGrpPort for storing the multicast IP address and port number, respectively (the SMRM receivers use them to join and monitor the multicast groups whereas the SMRM senders use them to deliver the multicast stream). The SMRM senders use the following traffic objects: smrmSendRate, smrmTraffDist, smrmPktLen, and smrmSessInterval, which define the average multicast sending rate, the traffic distribution, the multicast packet length, and when to stop sending, respectively.

SMRM traffic information objects. The multicast traffic originated by the SMRM senders is actually a sequence of Set-request packets, each contains the following object identifiers (OIDs) to be set in the agent smrmMIB: smrmSessID for a session ID, smrmSourceIP for the sender IP address, smrmPktSeq for the packet sequence number, smrmPktSenderTS for the sender timestamp, and smrmPktLen for the packet length (see Figure 8.3). To make the Setrequest packet size equal to the value in smrmPktLen, a dummy OID (smrmDummy-Traffic) is used.

SMRM receive report objects. This class is also used by SMRM receivers to store the target monitoring information, the number of packet lost (smrmLost-PktsNum), and the traffic jitter (smrmJitter). Agents use this class if on-line monitoring is selected. In this case, the agent uses the traffic information OID values in the multicast Set requests generated by the sender to continuously calculate the monitoring targets.

SMRM sender report objects. This class is also used by SMRM senders to store the delay monitoring information. The maximum transmission delay (smrmMaxDelay), and the average transmission delay (smrmAvgDelay) are used for on-line monitoring. The variable smrmCurrentDelay stores the intermediate delay values for calculating a smoothed average as described in this section on the calculation of targets.

Schedule-MIB Application in SMRM

The Schedule-MIB [6] allows the scheduling of simple SNMP Set operations on the local SNMP agent in a regular basis or at specific future points in time, in conjunction with the Script-MIB that controls the launch of short-time scripts at regular intervals or the start and termination of scripts at scheduled intervals. Using the schedule-MIB, the manager can schedule an SMRM test session in the following three different ways:

1. Periodic execution, in which case the SMRM senders will periodically trigger the SMRM script that sends *Set* requests to a specified multicast group.
2. One-shot execution, in which case the SMRM sender triggers the SMRM script once.
3. Calendar-based execution, in which case the SMRM script will be launched at a specified time and date. The smrmSessLaunchButton in smrmMIB is the script-trigger object that schedMIB sets to launch smrmScript.

The schedMIB functionality can be integrated in SMRM managers or the senders. However, we choose to integrate schedMIB in the SMRM senders for scalability purposes, because the session manager may become a bottleneck if it participates in too many SMRM sessions.

SMRM MONITORING TARGET CALCULATION

After showing how SMRM can be used to initiate test traffic and record statistics, this section describes the calculation process of packet loss, delay, and jitter as performed by the agents during on-line monitoring mode.

Packet Loss Calculation

When an SMRM agent receives a multicast *Set* request, it increments the value of smrmRecvNumOfPkts and updates smrmCurrentSeq with the new sequence number, if it exceeds the current sequence number. Then, the value of smrmLost-PktsNum is set to smrmCurrentSeq-smrmRecvNumOfPkts and the loss ratio, smrmPktLossRatio, is calculated as smrmLostPktsNum/smrmCurrent Seq. The manager retrieves and plots the *accumulative loss* ratio in a graph interface frequency and based on a polling interval. The *polling interval* parameter determines the frequently at which the manager should do the polling. This parameter controls the trade-off between information freshness and monitoring intrusiveness. The manager updates the loss ratio graph only if the smrmRecvNumOfPkts or smrmCurrentRecvTS objects have been incremented in the TR since the last retrieval. Otherwise, if no packet is received during this polling period, a special flag is marked in the graph to indicate that this receiver path is currently *unreachable*. The minimum polling time of the manager is 1 s, which is significantly larger than the minimum packet inter-arrival time.

To calculate the loss ratio for each individual polling, the manager must set smrmLostPktsNum and smrmRecvNumOfPkts in the agents' MIB to zero every time the loss ratio information is retrieved. Similarly, if smrmRecvNumOfPkts remains unchanged (zero), the graph will indicate that the network is unreachable.

Delay Calculation

There are two alternative methods to measure the delay from the sender to the receivers in the multicast delivery tree. The first technique is by using time stamps. This is an accurate and simple technique but it requires synchronizing the sender and receiver clocks using Network Time Protocol (NTP) or any other such protocol. However, this solution is not feasible if network nodes do not support NTP. Therefore, we propose the "ping-pong" technique that uses schedMIB and the MIB scripts to make the sender and the receivers send ping-pong SNMP *Set* requests to each other.

Simply, schedMIB of the SMRM sender sends a multicast *Set* request that includes the sender timestamp as an OID to receivers to set smrmCurrentSendTS variable in their MIBs. This consequently triggers a receiver MIB script, which sends back to sender a unicast Set request that includes the original sender timestamp, smrmCurrentSendTS, and sequence number, smrmCurrentSeq (the sequence number is used to identify out of order messages). When the SMRM sender receives the *Set* request from a receiver, it calculates the current round trip time (M) by subtracting the sender timestamp, included in the message, from the current time in the sender, as follows:

$$M = CurrentTime \boxtimes smrmSenderTS.$$

M is then used to calculate the smoothed RTT average (L), as follows [30]:

$$L = \boxtimes \times L + (1 \boxtimes \boxtimes) \times M,$$

where M is the measured round trip time (RTT) and ⊠ is a smoothing factor between 0 and 1 (recommended value is 0.9). However, because the returning path of the Set request to the sender may not be the same as the outgoing multicast path in the ping-pong scenario, the calculated delay ($\frac{1}{2} \times L$) may not be as accurate as in the NTP technique. The user, however, has the option to use the NTP technique if network elements support it. In addition, a simple extension to the current SMRM implementation would allow the sender to measure the unicast delay (in a *traceroute*-like technique) to each receiver in advance and then subtracting it from the multicast RTT value.

Jitter Calculation

The inter-arrival jitter (J) is defined to be the mean deviation (smoothed absolute value) of the difference D in packet spacing at the receiver compared with the sender for a pair of packets. The traffic that the sender sends to measure the delay is also used by agents. We use the RTP jitter calculation described in Ref. [31]. Therefore, assuming S_i as the sender timestamp from the Set request (or packet) i and R_i as the time of arrival in timestamp units of that same Set request i, then for the two requests i and j, D may be expressed as:

$$D(i, j) = (R_j ⊠ R_i) ⊠ (S_j ⊠ S_i) = (R_j ⊠ S_j) ⊠ (R_i ⊠ S_i).$$

SMRM receivers calculate the inter-arrival jitter continuously as each set request i is received from a source using the difference D for that packet and the previous packet ($i ⊠ 1$) in the order of arrival (not necessarily in sequence) and according to the following formula:

$$J_i = J_{i⊠1} = \frac{|D(i ⊠ 1, i)| ⊠ J_{i⊠1}}{16}.$$

This algorithm is the optimal first-order estimator and the gain parameter 1/16 gives a good noise reduction ratio while maintaining a reasonable rate of convergence [31]. A sample implementation is also shown in Ref. [31].

SMRM MANAGER–AGENT INTERACTION

The SMRM framework uses the SNMP *Get*, *GetBulk*, and *Set* operations to communicate with SMRM testers and retrieve monitoring results. SMRM managers play a central role in deploying an SMRM test session. Figure 8.4 shows the basic interaction between a manager and two SMRM agents: one sender and one receiver (we use one receiver to simplify our illustrative example; multiple receivers would be used in the same manner). The manager starts by configuring in the sender `smrmMIB` the session parameters such as `smrmRole`, `smrmRate`, `smrmPktLen`, and then the `mcastInfoMIB` of the receivers by setting `agentGroupIP` and `agentGroup-Port` of the SMRM receivers. As a result, the receivers can join the specified multicast group. Up to that point, the manager has used unicast to communicate with agents. Next, the manager sends a multicast Set request to configure the objects in the `smrmParametersTable` such as `smrmSessID`, `smrmRole`, `smrmSessGrpIP`, `smrmSessGrpPort`, `smrmRepMode` of all the session receivers. Immediately,

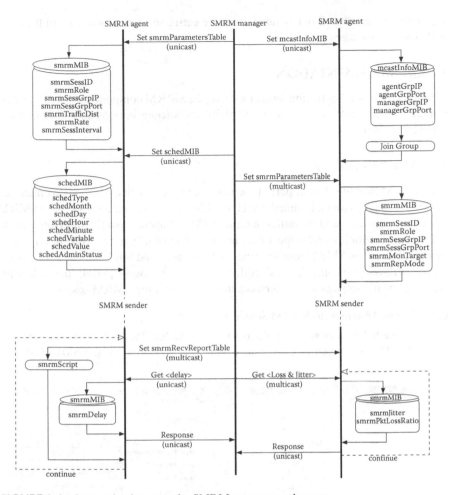

FIGURE 8.4   Interaction between the SMRM manager and agents.

they start monitoring the multicast test packets sent by the SMRM sender in the same session. The manager also configures the `schedMIB` objects such as `schedValue`, `schedContextName`, and `schedVariable` of the SMRM sender to schedule the execution of the SMRM traffic generator script, `smrmScript`. Thus far, the SMRM testers (sender and receivers) are ready to initiate the SMRM test traffic and collect the monitoring information.

When the manager activates the SMRM session, `schedMIB` sends a Set request to trigger the traffic generator script at the specified starting time. The traffic generator script in the sender originates a multicast stream of Set requests to the multicast group `smrmSessGrpIP/smrmSessGrpPort` that the SMRM receivers monitor to calculate real-time loss, delay, and the jitter. At the same time, the manager sends multicast Get/GetBulk requests periodically to retrieve the monitoring results (`smrmPktLossRatio` and `smrmJitter`) from SMRM receivers and `smrmAvgDelay` from the senders, and then plot the monitoring graphs. If the manager sets `smrmSessID` to 0 in any table, then the entire session information in the table is deleted by the agent.

SMRM IMPLEMENTATION

This section describes the implementation of the SMRM components: user interface, manager, and agents (testers). It also explains the various options and parameters of SMRM sessions.

SMRM USER INTERFACE

The SMRM user interface is part of the manager functionality. The SMRM interface has the following two main functions: (1) enabling users to create one or more SMRM monitoring sessions and to configure remote SMRM agents; and (2) allowing users to collect and to monitor and inspect the multicast reachability in real-time or on a post-mortem basis. The SMRM user interface is Java-based and is integrated in the SNMP manager developed using AdventNet development framework [32]. In the following, we describe the steps and the interfaces used for launching SMRM sessions.

Creating or Loading an SMRM Session

When a reachability monitoring test is to be conducted, the NOC manager creates a new SMRM session using the interface in Figure 8.5 to define the SMRM agents'

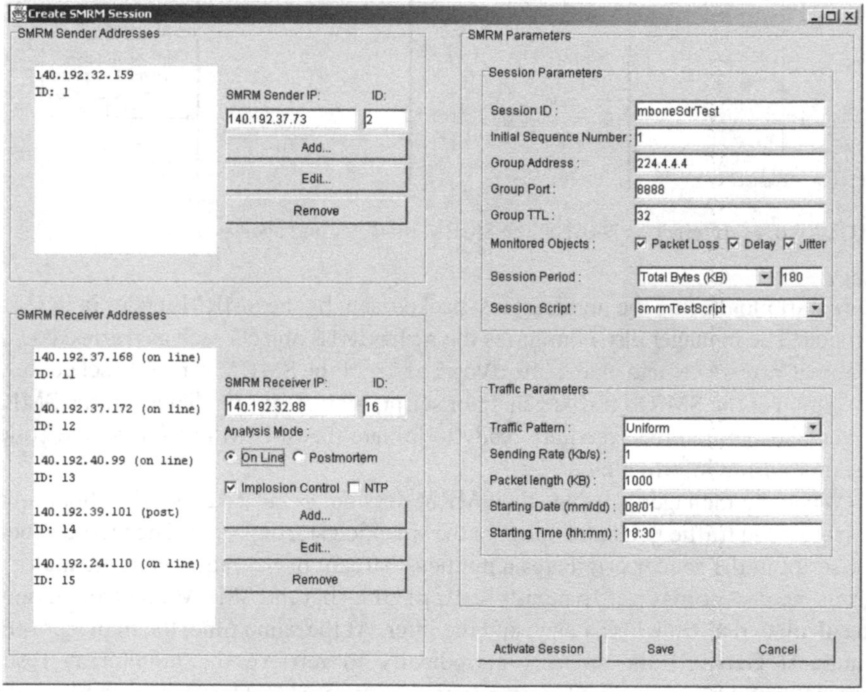

FIGURE 8.5   SMRM create interface.

configurations. A manager can initiate multiple SMRM monitoring sessions simultaneously on the same network. For each SMRM session, users must configure the Session, Traffic, and Agents parameters shown in Figure 8.5 as follows:

- *Session parameters*—Users have to define the multicast group to be monitored using *Group Address* and *Group Port* in the create session interface. The *Session Period* defines the length of the testing session in seconds (*Time Interval*) or in number of bytes (*Total Bytes*) as shown in Figure 8.5. The SMRM testers provide information about three *monitoring objects*: packet loss, latency, and jitter, which are major attributes for determining the QoS for multicast networks. An SMRM session must be assigned a unique name in the (*Session ID*) parameter. The SMRM receivers use the <smrmSessID, smrmSourceIP, smrmPktSeq> tuple included in the Set requests to uniquely identify multicast traffic generated by different senders in SMRM sessions.
- *Traffic parameters configuration*—This configuration section is to shape the outgoing multicast traffic according to specific parameters such as the *sending rate, packet length, traffic distribution* (e.g., uniform, Poisson, Pareto), and when to start sending this traffic (*Starting Time* and *Starting Date*).
- *Agents configuration*—We assume that the NOC personnel intending to use SMRM knows the topology or at least the end-point nodes of the network under test. This is important to determine the network segments under test/ monitoring. Users can specify this by listing the IP addresses of the sender(s) and the receivers in the SMRM session. The SMRM receivers can be configured either to use the on-line monitoring capability or the *postmortem* analysis in an SMRM sessions. This feature is important to accommodate a wide range of monitoring requirements and network environments. The user can enable packet explosion control to prevent flooding the manager by the sheer number of replies. The user can also select the NTP option to enable delay calculations based on the sending/receiving timestamp. Otherwise, the ping-pong technique is used to measure the delay.

When the SMRM session configuration is completed, the manager can initiate a session by activating it (*Activate Session* in Figure 8.5). This causes the manager to contact and configure the SNMP/SMRM agents of the IP addresses in this session.

SMRM View Session

The SMRM view interface (Figure 8.6) allows managers to retrieve and present the monitoring results of various SMRM sessions from different agents in graphical form. Each graph area is used to plot one of the monitoring targets (packet loss, delay, or jitter) for a specific tree path defined by the *Session ID, Sender IP*, and a group of *Selected Receivers*. Once the session ID is selected, the interface shows the associated senders and receivers. The sender IP address is needed to distinguish among senders because many may participate in the same session. The loss ratio, delay, and jitter charts show the total percentage of packet loss, average delay, and average jitter, respectively, after each polling interval.

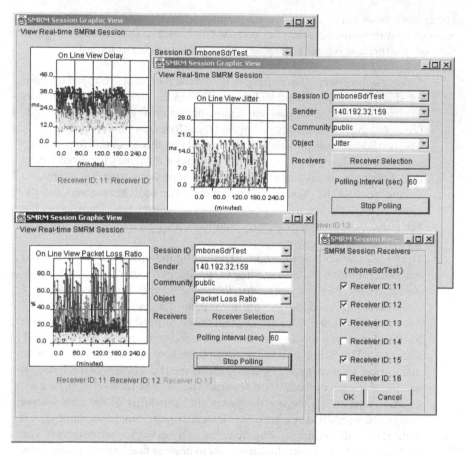

FIGURE 8.6   SMRM view interface.

SMRM MIB Browser

The SMRM user interface provides a standard MIB browser to view the MIB objects values of the various SMRM Testers. This function is useful for debugging and verification purposes. Figure 8.6 also shows the delay and jitter of the same receivers in real-time.

SMRM IMPLEMENTATION

We first extended the standard MIB II [5] module to include the mcastInfo and smrmMIB group under enterprises group [7]. We used: (1) the Net-SNMP agent package 4.2 (previously known as UCD-snmp) from the University of California at Davis (http://www.net-snmp.org) as a development platform for the framework; (2) the implementation of schedMIB [6]; and (3) the Perl 5 SNMP module supported by the Swiss Academic and Research Network [33]. We use the Perl 5 SNMP package to create the script (smrmScript) launched by the schedule MIB.

There are three steps to implement SMRM agents and manager, which are as follows:

1. Incorporate the multicast functionality and `mcastInfoMIB` in the SNMP agent and manager
2. Integrate the SMRM-specific MIBs, i.e., `schedMIB` and `smrmMIB`
3. Integrate the SMRM management GUI

The SMRM manager is a JAVA-based program developed using AdventNet SNMP API Release 3.2 package [32]. It also incorporates the multicast functionality and the SMRM-specific MIBs. The SMRM manager is developed based on SNMPv1.

PERFORMANCE EVALUATION

The SMRM implementation was used and tested in the DePaul University Intranets network, which connect five different campuses around the Chicago metropolitan area. It is a multicast-capable network. The minimum and maximum geographical distances between campuses are 8 and 33 miles, respectively. We also used 100 Mbps switched Ethernet LANs and Sun Ultra 10 with Solaris 8 as end systems. The main goal of these experiments was to compare SMRM performance and overhead with other path monitoring tools such as *traceroute*, and *ping* and sending UDP messages to echo port (port number 7).

We compare the effect of the hop counts on the *traceroute* and ping-pong techniques in SMRM. Although *traceroute* uses unicast and ping-pong uses multicast, we use the same network path (sender–receiver pair) to compare the RTT. Figure 8.7 shows that when the hop count is relatively high, such as in a WAN environment,

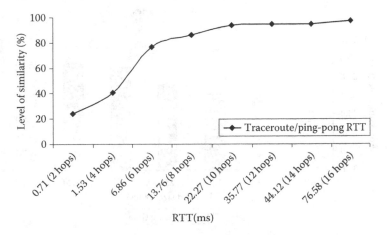

FIGURE 8.7 Comparing the round trip time (RTT) of *traceroute* and ping-pong. Note that 100% similarity means that the RTT for *traceroute* and for ping-pong are the same.

the ping-pong RTT value is typically close to that of *traceroute*. However, in a LAN, where the RTT is small, the ping-pong encounters more delay (2 msec) compared with *traceroute*, due to the SNMP packet encoding/decoding and parsing overhead [34] and the packetization process. We found this overhead constant (1 ms) in both the receiver and sender side. So if this value is determined for a specific platform, then it can be subtracted from the estimated delay. On the other hand, when SMRM is used in an enterprise (or WAN) environment, this overhead is shown to be negligible.

Figure 8.8a illustrates that the impact of payload size on the RTT for ping-pong and *traceroute* are almost the same. Also, the RTT is larger with ping-pong than with UDP echo when large payload sizes are used. This is because the UDP echo writes back the payload; however, ping-pong sends back only the timestamp. In other words, this shows that the payload size has no significant delay overhead in ping-pong comparing with other traditional tools. Similarly, Figure 8.8b shows that the overhead increase of the agent processing time due to packet encoding and MIB access is very

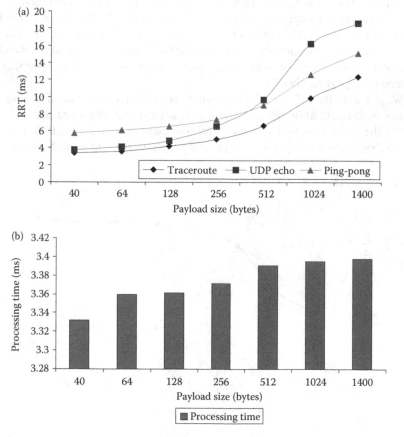

FIGURE 8.8   (a) Impact of the payload on the RTT. (b) Impact of the payload on the processing time of SMRM agents.

small: 1.8% when the payload size increases from 40 to 1400 bytes. By comparing both figures, we conclude that the main source of the overhead is the system call primitives (send and receive) and not the agent processing of the requests.

SCALABILITY

Scalability is an important character of SMRM that can be used in multicast monitoring tools. Scalable monitoring means that the manager can communicate with the agents with minimum latency and that agents can avoid the report implosion when reporting back their status.

SMRM is scalable with respect to the number of agents, sessions, and groups because the SMRM agents incorporate multicasting through mcastInfoMIB, which allows managers to configure a group of agents using a single multicast *Set* request. Similarly, managers can request monitoring results from a group of agents by sending a single multicast *Get* or *GetBulk* request. Simulation experiments were conducted based on the formalization given to compare the scalability of different network management architectures, in particular, synchronous centralized (i.e., requests and replies are sent and received sequentially), asynchronous centralized (i.e., requests and replies are interleaved), hierarchical, or multicast-based [9]. Figure 8.9a and b illustrates the effect of multicast-based network management architectures on latency. The response time of management operations is reduced by several orders of magnitude with multicast monitoring compared to hierarchical and centralized systems for both low and high RTT values. It is also that the advantage of multicast-based management increases as RTT increases (such as in a WAN environment) or the number of managed objects increases.

MANAGER PACKET IMPLOSION CONTROL

SMRM agents avoid reply implosion by using randomized timers as discussed in Ref. [9]. Each agent waits for a random time interval* before sending its reply. This random pause is enough to disperse the interleaved responses from the agents and alleviate the report implosion in the manager network.

Sender Implosion Control

One form of packet implosion occurs when agents send *Set* requests simultaneously to the SMRM sender during the ping-pong process. The SMRM framework provides two ways to avoid the sender implosion.

In the first, the manager divides the receivers' group into subgroups and uses a group mask to block replies from some subgroups. The group mask is a compressed binary string that is matched against the AgentID (typically the IP address of the machine) to figure out if the agent should send the reply or not. The other technique is by using a randomized timer before sending Set request to the sender similar to the manager implosion control. However, in this case, receivers have to add a "waiting time" offset to the sender timestamp (*smrmSendTS*) in the Set request sent to the

---

* This time interval is bounded based on the group size [5].

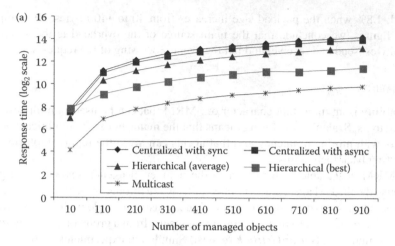

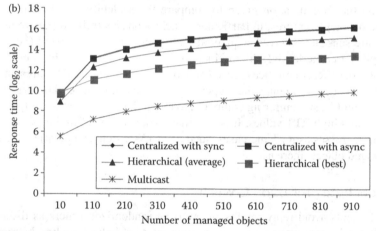

FIGURE 8.9 Response time for centralized vs. hierarchical vs. multicast monitoring architectures: (a) RTT = 8 ms; (b) RTT = 38 ms.

sender. The second technique is more suitable when monitoring very large-scale groups as group masking becomes less efficient.

PRACTICAL CONSIDERATIONS

FLEXIBILITY

The SMRM framework offers a highly flexible management service throughout the following features:

- It allows the user to deploy session testers (multicast senders and receivers) at any point in the network as long as an SNMP agent with SMRM-specific MIBs exists.

- It allows users to select the characteristics of the generated traffic such as rate, packet length, and traffic distribution. NOC personnel can configure different senders per group, different monitoring targets for different receivers (i.e., some receivers monitor delay and others monitor packet loss in the same session), and also agents can participate as senders in one SMRM session and receivers in another SMRM session simultaneously.
- It allows for sending Set-request reliably as described in Ref. [9].
- It provides on-line and postmortem monitoring analysis to suit different network environments.

MINIMUM INTRUSIVENESS

The following are the main design features that minimize the monitoring intrusiveness in SMRM:

- The polling interval enables users to reduce the information retrieval traffic on the network.
- The SMRM postmortem monitoring is important to minimize the processing overhead on agents.
- Using *Set/Get* multicast requests eliminate unnecessary traffic caused by the unicast requests.
- Furthermore, SMRM testers require minimal administration overhead from the NOC personnel because no special agent structure is required as is case with other hierarchical monitoring schemes [24].

EASE OF USE AND DEPLOYMENT

The successful deployment of a multicast monitoring tool depends on the simplicity of integrating this tool into the existing legacy network management systems. The SMRM framework is made easy-to-integrate with SNMP agents, SNMP being the most widely used protocol for network management today. Furthermore, the SMRM deployment is completely manager-centric, which enables configuring (e.g., rate, packet length, distribution) and controlling (e.g., when to start and stop) the SMRM agents easily and dynamically from a central Web-based interface. In addition, the SMRM manager GUI is intuitive and easy-to-use.

EXTENSIBILITY

SMRM is extensible due to the extensibility of SNMP framework (i.e., adding new MIBs). New management scripts can be incorporated into smrmMIB without having to change or to re-compile the agent code. They can also control the execution schedule of these scripts at run-time via schedMIB.

SECURITY

Security is an important issue in network application, especially for network management systems. Messages between network manager and agents should be authenticated and encrypted to prevent malicious attacks. The SMRM framework can leverage the security features developed in SNMPv3 [35] such as authentication, encryption, and view-based access control MIBs. The current implementation of SMRM uses SNMPv1 but using SNMPv3 is still work-in-progress.

SUMMARY

Multicast is an important network service that provides scalable group communication on the Internet. With the constant evolution of multicast routing, multicasting becomes more widely deployed but more complex as well. Multicast monitoring is necessary not only for debugging and fault detection, but also for measuring the quality of multicast reachability to the group members.

This chapter gave an overview of multicast monitoring tools and then presented a new framework (called SMRM) for multicast reachability monitoring. SMRM monitors the essential QoS parameter including packet loss, delay, and jitter of the multicast traffic injected between arbitrary points in the networks. SMRM is a monitoring framework that utilizes the existing SNMP infrastructure and requires minor extensions of SNMP agents. SMRM features includes scalability to a large number of groups and agents, extensibility via dynamic MIB scripts, which allow developers to deploy their own multicast management scripts, providing on-line and postmortem monitoring analysis, allowing for the selection of traffic characteristics, leveraging the SNMPv3 security framework, and minimizing operational overhead.

REFERENCES

1. Almeroth, K., The evolution of multicast: From the MBone to inter-domain multicast to Internet2 deployment, *IEEE Netw.*, 14(1), 10–20, 2000.
2. Deering, S. E. and Cheriton, D., Multicast routing in internet works and extended LANs, *ACM Trans. Comput. Syst.*, 8(2), 85–110, 1990.
3. Diot, C. et al., Deployment issues for the IP multicast service and architecture, *IEEE Netw.*, 14(1), 78–88, 2000.
4. Case, J. et al., Simple Network Management Protocol, RFC1157, IETF, May 1990.
5. Rose, M. and McCloghrie, K., Structure and Identification of Management Information for TCP/IP-based Internets, RFC 1155, IETF, May 1990.
6. Levi, D. and Schoenwaelder, J., Definitions of Managed Objects for Scheduling Management Operations, RFC 2591, IETF, May 1999.
7. Rose, M. and McCloghrie, K., Concise MIB Definitions, RFC 1212, IETF, March 1991.
8. Schoenwaelder, J. and Quittek, J., Script MIB Extensibility Protocol Version 1.0, RFC 2593, IETF, May 1999.
9. Al-Shaer, E. and Tang, Y., Toward integrating IP multicasting in Internet network management protocols. *J. Comput. Commun. Rev.*, 24(5), 473–485, 2000.
10. Cain, B. et al., Internet Group Management Protocol Version 3, RFC 3376, October 2002.
11. Adams, A., Nicholas J., and Siadak, W., Protocol Independent Multicast—Dense Mode (PIM-DM): Protocol Specification, RFC 4601, January 2005.
12. Fenner, B. et al., Protocol Independent Multicast—Sparse Mode (PIM-SM): Protocol Specification, RFC 4601, August 2006.

13. Al-Shaer, E. and Tang, Y., QoS path monitoring for multicast networks, *J. Netw. Syst. Manage.*, 10(3), 357–381, 2002.
14. Almeroth, K. C. and Saac, K., Monitoring IP multicast in the Internet: Recent advances and existing challenges, *IEEE Commun. Mag.*, 43(10), 85–91, 2005.
15. Asaeda, H. et al., Mtrace Version 2: Traceroute Facility for IP Multicast, Internet Draft, November 3, 2008, available at http://www.ietf.org/internet-drafts/draft-ietf-mboned-mtrace-v2-02.txt
16. Handley, M., *Sdr: Session Directory Tool*, Technical Report, University College London, March 1995.
17. Saac, K. and Almeroth, K. C., Application layer reachability monitoring for IP multicast, *Comput. Netw. J.*, 48(2), 195–213, 2005.
18. Makofske, D. and Almeroth, K., MHealth: A real-time graphical multicast monitoring tool for the MBone, *Workshop on Network and Operating System Support for Digital Audio and Video* (NOSSDAV 99), Basking Ridge, NJ, USA, 1999, available at http://www.nossdav.org/1999/papers/53-1441030863.pdf
19. Bacher, D., Swan, A., and Rowe. L., rtpmon: A third-party RTCP monitor, *Proceedings of the Fourth ACM International Conference (ACM Multimedia '96)*, Boston, MA, 1996, ACM, New York, NY, 1997, 437–438.
20. Almeroth, K., Managing IP multicast traffic: A first look at the issues, tools and challenges, White Paper, *3rd Annual IP Multicast Initiative Summit*, San Jose, CA, February 1999, available at http://www.ipmulticast.com/events/summit99/whitepaper.htm
21. Namburi, P., Saac, K., and Almeroth, K. C., Practical utilities for monitoring multicast service availability, *Comput. Commun.*, 29(10), 1675–1686, 2006.
22. Saraç, K. and. Almeroth, K. C., Supporting multicast deployment efforts: A survey of tools for multicast monitoring, *J. High Speed Network.*, 9(3/4), 191–211, 2000.
23. Almeroth, K., Saraç, K., and Wei, L., Supporting multicast management using the Multicast Reachability Monitor (MRM) protocol, *Technical Report in Computer Science*, TR2000-26, University of California, Santa Barbara, 2000, available at http://www.cs.ucsb.edu/research/tech_reports/reports/2000-26.ps
24. Walz, J. and Levine, B., A hierarchical multicast monitoring scheme, *Proceedings of the 2nd International Workshop on Networked Group Communication*, Palo Alto, CA, ACM, New York, 2000, 105–116.
25. Al-Shaer, E., Active management framework for distributed multimedia systems, *J Netw. Syst. Manage.*, 8(1), 49–72, 2000.
26. Al-Shaer, E., Abdel-Wahab, H., and Maly, K., HiFi: A new monitoring architecture for distributed system management, *Proceedings of the International Distributed Computing Systems (ICDCS'99)*, Austin, TX, 1999, 171–178.
27. Al-Shaer, E., A dynamic group management framework for large-scale distributed event monitoring, *Proceedings of the 2001 IEEE/IFIP International Symposium on Integrated Network Management (IM'2001)*, Seattle, WA, May 14–18, 2001, IEEE, NY, 361–374.
28. Al-Shaer, E. and Tang, Y., MRMON: Remote multicast monitoring, *IEEE/IFIP Network Operations and Management Symposium (NOMS 2004)*, Vol. 1, 2004, 585–598.
29. Floyd, S. et al., A reliable multicast framework for lightweight sessions and application level framing, *IEEE/ACM Trans. Network.*, 5(6), 784–803, 1997.
30. Jacobson, V., Congestion avoidance and control, *Comput. Commun. Rev.*, 18(4), 314–329, 1988.
31. Schulzrinne, H. et al., RTP: A Transport Protocol for Real-Time Applications, IETF, July 2001.
32. AdventNet API for SNMP Development, available at http://www.adventnet.com/products/snmp/index.html

33. Perl 5.005 SNMP Package., Swiss academic and research network (switch), Author, Simon Leinen, available at http://www.switch.ch/misc/leinen/snmp/perl
34. Steedman, D., *Abstract Syntax Notation One (ASN.1): The Tutorial and Reference*, Technology Appraisals, Twickenham, UK, 1993.
35. Harrington, D., Presuhn, R., and Wijnen, B., An Architecture for Describing SNMP Management Frameworks, RFC 2271, IETF, January 1998.

9 Platforms for Enterprise Servers

Binnur Kurt and Zehra Cataltepe

CONTENTS

INTRODUCTION

In this chapter, we introduce enterprise applications and enterprise server platforms. We give details on JavaBeans, Java EE (Java Platform, Enterprise Edition) Enterprise Server Platform, and Java EE Application Programming Interfaces (APIs).

Enterprise applications are designed to solve business problems in a highly distributed and complex environment. They share two basic features. First, they are multiuser applications accessible from anywhere on the network. They are also distributed applications. This means that the solution to a specific problem is divided into several pieces, each of which may live on different machines and work independently of the others. A piece is also called a layer or a tier. Thus, enterprise applications are multilayered applications. This layered architecture simplifies development, deployment, and maintenance.

Consider, for example, a banking application where a customer can access his/her account and transfer money to another account of his/her own or someone else's through the Internet. Even this relatively simple operation requires that several pieces of software work together to make the operation atomic, secure, multithreaded, and persistent. The first issue is that of transaction management. A transaction is a sequence of operations that typically deal with information exchange and related work. A transaction is called *atomic* if, when all operations succeed, their effect is permanent or if any single operation in the transaction fails, then it has no effect. Consider the case when money is to be transferred from one account to the other; if one step in the sequence of operations that constitute the transaction fails then the state of the application state should be rolled back to the previous state. Transaction management makes the money transfer transaction atomic to guarantee that the operation is performed as all-or-nothing. *Security* in an enterprise application is enforced through authentication and authorization. Authentication means that only the allowed users should be able to access the application. Authorization means that authenticated users can execute the permissible operations without any problems. Since enterprise applications are multiuser applications, several users may execute the methods that implement the business logic simultaneously. *Multi-threading* enables concurrent execution of the same methods in a scalable way. Account information should be persistent after consecutive and concurrent operations such as deposits and withdrawals over the same account. *Persistence* guarantees that the changes made by consecutive or concurrent user accesses are consistently reflected on the account.

The end-user of an enterprise application could be a human being using a Web browser to send requests through HTTP (HyperText Transfer Protocol) and retrieve responses usually in HTML (HyperText Markup Language) format, or it could be another enterprise application connected to the Internet that sends requests and receives responses in Extensible Markup Language (XML) format. Returning to the banking example, in either case, the application should be designed to be atomic, secure, persistent, and multithreaded. This is not a simple task and the design involves several analyses, architectural, and design decisions related to the application logic and functionality.

APPLICATION SERVERS

Application servers take the responsibility of the problems of atomicity, security, persistence, and multithreading defined above, so that the application coding will focus on the business logic. Application servers provide the solution as a service that the software developer accesses using an API. Application server may contain and manage many enterprise applications. The application server guarantees that the enterprise applications running on it are isolated from each other, so that if one fails this does not affect the operations of the others.

Application servers usually support component-based services and this leads to a *component-based programming model*. Each software project comes with its own time, budget, and human resource constraints. Yet, when a software developer needs to write code to solve a specific problem, there is a big chance that someone else would have solved the same problem before. Component-based software development promotes reusability to alleviate the constraints of time budgets and human resources, without reducing the quality of the software produced. So enterprise applications would be comprised of components with APIs expressing contracts between the various components and application servers. Components access the component-based services using a set of APIs that encapsulate the corresponding service so that any component could work on any application server.

An enterprise application is comprised of components in this layered architectural model. Developers can switch between application servers without having to change the code with the help of the contracts. Thus, component-based programming is similar to object-oriented programming, in the sense that both a component and an object do a specific task; the difference is that a component can exist independently of an application.

ENTERPRISE SERVER PLATFORMS

An Enterprise Server Platform is a development, deployment, and application platform for business solutions. It is a development platform because it presents interfaces (APIs) to solve common and recurring problems that arise as the enterprise conducts its business transactions such as persistence, security, and so on. It is a deployment platform because a developer can pack the application and deliver it to the executing platform, which is the application server. It is an application platform because it manages the life cycle of the application components.

The Java platform is available in three different editions: Java EE (Enterprise Edition), Java SE (Standard Edition), and Java ME (Mobile Edition). Java SE is used to develop console or graphical user interface (GUI) applications. Java ME is used to develop applications running on mobile devices. Java EE is used to develop the enterprise applications covered in this chapter.

Java EE* (Java Platform, Enterprise Edition, http://java.sun.com/javaee) [1,2] is an enterprise server platform, which is a set of enabling technologies in the form of

---

* J2EE acronym is used for versions earlier than Java EE 5.

APIs that significantly reduces the cost and complexity of developing, deploying, and managing multitier applications. Java EE itself is neither a framework to develop enterprise applications nor a running software. It only defines a set of APIs between the components and the services such as persistence, security, and transaction. These APIs are managed by the Java Community Process (JCP, http://www.jcp.org) established in 1998. Each API follows a formal process to become a final Java Specification Request (JSR). The JSR is a formal document that describes proposed specification and technologies to be added to the Java platform. Formal public reviews of JSRs are conducted by community members and the public before the JSR becomes final and is voted on by the JCP Executive Committee. A final JSR provides a reference implementation which is a free implementation of the technology in the form of a source code and a Technology Compatibility Kit to verify the API specification. JCP 2.6 is actually defined by a JSR and has its own document called JSR 215.

Each API in Java EE has its own specification JSR accessible from the JCP Web site. The open nature of the community enables application developers to write their code without worrying about which application server they use. Thus, they can use one application server in development phase and switch to another in production, if performance, scalability, or other issues arise. This also encourages competition among vendors. The most popular application servers today are the open source projects *Glassfish* (http://www.glassfish.org) and Apache *Geronimo* (http://geronimo. apache.org), and the commercial offers from RedHat, *JBoss* (http://www.jboss.com), Oracle *Application Server* (http://www.oracle.com/appserver), and IBM's *WebSphere Application Server* (http://www-306.ibm.com/software/webservers/appserv/was). A list of Java EE compatible application servers is available at http://java.sun.com/javaee/ overview/compatibility.jsp.

JAVA COMPONENT MODELS

There are two component models in Java technology: JavaBeans™.* [3] and Enterprise JavaBeans (EJB) [4,5]. Both component models support reusability. JavaBeans are used to develop components that are usually used for desktop applications (although nonvisual JavaBeans may sometimes be used on the server side also). EJBs differ from JavaBeans in a number of ways. They are used in enterprise applications on the server side. The life cycle of EJB components is managed by application servers, that is, they are created and destroyed according to demands of clients by the application servers. EJBs implement the business logic in the multitiered architecture.

In the following section, we go through JavaBeans and provide an example. The next section gives details on Java EE APIs and EJB.

JavaBeans

As software projects grow in size, it is much more desirable to use well-tested components from previous projects. JavaBeans is a Java technology that enables

---

* Java, JavaBeans, and related terms are all copyrighted by Sun Microsystems, Inc.

component-based and reusable software development. A JavaBean is a software component that does a specific task and is isolated enough to be reused in any other project. Since it is based on Java Technology, it is also platform-independent.

The Sun JavaBeans tutorial (http://java.sun.com/docs/books/tutorial/javabeans) describes a JavaBean as "a portable, platform-independent component model written in the Java programming language and can be visually manipulated using builder tools." The JavaBeans API enables users to create "re-useable, platform-independent components." Components can be put together (nested, linked) in order to produce more complex components. For example, buttons are components and they can be linked through some events to produce a calculator. The calculator component can also be used in a spreadsheet application. Unlike software libraries, such as Java Database Connectivity (JDBC) for database connectivity or Swing for GUI, which come up packaged in a class library to be manipulated by a programmer, beans are designed to serve domain experts.

JavaBeans are designed as either visual or nonvisual components. They do not need to be inherited from a specific class. When a bean class is inherited from javax.swing.JComponent, it becomes a visual component. Visual components are mostly used in desktop GUI applications. Non-visual JavaBeans are used on both desktop and server side applications. A spell-checker bean could be used in a desktop application, and a credit card transaction-processing bean could be used on a server side application.

JavaBeans are designed with methods and properties that can be manipulated by component builder tools. Component builder tools (or application builders), such as NetBeans, can be used to develop and manipulate beans visually. They allow modifications on properties of components and they can also be used to hook them up and define events they respond to. On the other hand, GUI builders only allow for visual construction of GUI items. Some Integrated Development Environments (IDEs), such as *JBuilder 2008* (http://www.codegear.com/product/jbuilder) and *Eclipse*, come with both components and GUI builders.

JavaBean Class

A JavaBean class should satisfy the following conditions:

- All attributes should be private.
- The properties, which are private attributes that need to be accessed from outside, should have getter and setter methods.
- There should be a default constructor.
- The class should implement the Serializable interface, which enables saving the class information in nonvolatile storage and thus helps with object persistence.

There are basic properties of a JavaBean that enable its use as an independent software component that can be combined with other components in order to achieve a programming goal. The properties are as follows: *Property Control, Persistence,*

Event Handling, Customization, and *Introspection.* We now cover each of these properties in detail. At the end of this section, we provide a full JavaBean example to illustrate them.

Property Control

Certain properties of a bean may need to be read and updated for customization and programming uses. Just like any other Java class, property control is achieved through getter and setter methods. The setter and getters should follow a naming convention such as `getPropertyName/setPropertyName`. This naming convention allows bean aware applications to access the properties.

Persistence

Persistence allows the customized state of a bean to be saved and reloaded later. For a bean to continue its existence way it was at the last instantiation of the application, it needs to store itself in the nonvolatile storage. Since components may be nested together, a standard mechanism of serialization needs to be used. Persistence of a JavaBean in binary format can be achieved through Java object serialization (`Serializable` interface) using `ObjectInputStream` and `ObjectOutputStream`. Two classes in the JavaBeans package, `java.beans.XMLEncoder` and `java.beans.XMLDecoder`, enable representation of the JavaBean object also in textual XML document format.

Event Handling

Events let components take actions based on state changes of other components. By signaling events, a component lets other components know of a change. Through the use of event listeners, a component is able to know when to take appropriate action in case an event happens.

Customization

Customizers allow a bean to change its appearance and behavior to meet the demands of an application. For example, there might be customizers to change the text in a label. Customizer classes are usually kept separate from the bean. When an application does not need customization, customization routines do not need to complicate the bean.

Introspection

Introspection allows a builder tool to analyze how a bean works. Just as in customization, classes required for introspection are usually kept in a `BeanInfo` interface. The corresponding `BeanInfo` interface for a JavaBean class is usually part of the same package and has the same name as the bean appended with "BeanInfo." This class should extend `java.beans.SimpleBeanInfo` class and override any methods that are required to be returned explicitly. When extending `SimpleBeanInfo`, a programmer would only need to provide the methods he wants to override; on the other hand, implementation of `BeanInfo` interface requires all methods to be overridden.

A JavaBean Example

Now we give a simple visual JavaBean example. In this example, information about a person, his name, last name, phone number, and e-mail are collected through Java Swing components (JTextField). Figure 9.1 depicts the Netbeans IDE showing the design view of the component. Netbeans allows automated design of the component, its contents, and `actionsPerformed` method. Listings 9.1 displays the source code for the PersonBean class (`PersonBean.java`). In this listing, some of the text that was automatically inserted into the code by NetBeans was removed for the clarity of the presentation. Listing 9.2 provides a BeanInfo class for the sample bean, that is, PersonBean.

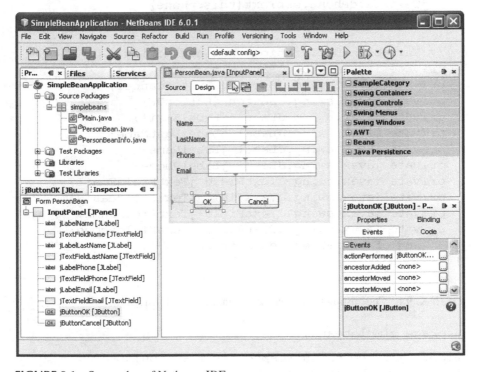

FIGURE 9.1   Screenshot of Netbeans IDE.

```
public class PersonBean implements Serializable {
  private String name, lastName, e-mail, phone ;

  // <editor-fold defaultstate="collapsed" desc=
  "Generated Code">
  private void initComponents() {

  ...

  }// </editor-fold>
```

```
  private void jButtonOKActionPerformed(java.awt.event.
   ActionEvent evt) {
     this.name= jTextFieldName.getText();
     this.lastName= jTextFieldLastName.getText();
     this.phone= jTextFieldPhone.getText();
     this.e-mail= jTextFieldEmail.getText();
}

  private void jButtonCancelActionPerformed(java.awt.
   event.ActionEvent evt) {
     jTextFieldName.setText(this.name);
     jTextFieldLastName.setText(this.lastName);
     jTextFieldPhone.setText(this.phone);
     jTextFieldEmail.setText(this.e-mail);
  }
  // Variables declaration - do not modify
  private javax.swing.JPanel InputPanel;
  private javax.swing.JButton jButtonCancel;
  private javax.swing.JButton jButtonOK;
  private javax.swing.JLabel jLabelEmail;
  private javax.swing.JLabel jLabelLastName;
  private javax.swing.JLabel jLabelName;
  private javax.swing.JLabel jLabelPhone;
  private javax.swing.JTextField jTextFieldEmail;
  private javax.swing.JTextField jTextFieldLastName;
  private javax.swing.JTextField jTextFieldName;
  private javax.swing.JTextField jTextFieldPhone;
  // End of variables declaration
}
```

LISTING 9.1   Code listing for sample JavaBean, `PersonBean.java`.

```
package simplebeans;

import java.beans.IntrospectionException;
import java.beans.PropertyDescriptor;
import java.beans.SimpleBeanInfo;

public class PersonBeanInfo extends SimpleBeanInfo {

  public PropertyDescriptor[] getPropertyDescriptors() {
      PropertyDescriptor[] pd = new PropertyDescriptor[4];
       try {
      pd[0] = new PropertyDescriptor("name", PersonBean.
      class);
      pd[1] = new PropertyDescriptor("lastName",
      PersonBean.class);
```

```
      pd[2] = new PropertyDescriptor("phone",
        PersonBean.class);
      pd[3] = new PropertyDescriptor("e-mail",
        PersonBean.class);
    }
    catch (IntrospectionException ex) {
    }
    return pd;
  }

  public int getDefaultPropertyIndex() {
    return 0;
  }
}
```

LISTING 9.2 Code listing for BeanInfo, `PersonBeanInfo.java`.

JAVA EE APIs

Java EE is an enterprise server platform. The platform presents several important services to the enterprise components in the form of APIs. The services are provided by containers called *Web container* and EJBs container (Figure 9.2). A Web container holds Web components, Servlets, and Java Server Pages (JSP). A Servlet is a Java class inherited from the `HttpServlet` class with two frequently used methods, `doPost()` and `doGet()`. These methods are called by the Web container triggered by an http request that the Web user sends by filling an HTML form and clicking the submit button. Web container calls the `doPost()` method if the `post` method is defined in HTML form element and it calls the `doGet()` method if the `get` method is defined. JSP is an HTML file with Java codes inside `<script>` element. Pages in JSP are converted into Servlet classes and compiled at runtime once when the JSP page is called for the first time. EJB container holds one or more of the following EJB components: session beans, message-driven beans, and so on. Java EE compliant

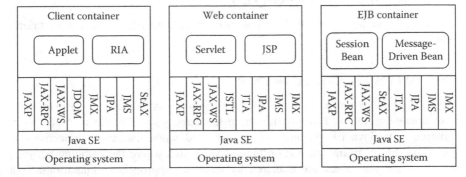

FIGURE 9.2 Java EE services provided by the containers.

application servers usually have both Web and EJB containers. Client container is usually a Web browser that renders documents coded in HTML format to the user. User interface is generally coded using HTML form presenting very simple user interface compared with desktop applications. There are two other alternative technologies. One is older and called Java Applet. A Java Applet is a special Java SE GUI application that could be run by Web browsers. Java Applets are heavy-weight applications because they implement some business logic of the enterprise application. On the other side, developers can design more complex user interfaces. The other solution, called Rich Internet Application (RIA), is a Web application with a user interface experience similar to the one procured by desktop applications. There are several tools available to help developers design and code RIAs: Ajax Frameworks, Adobe Flash, JavaFX, Mozilla's Prism, Google's Gear, and Microsoft Silverlight.

ENTERPRISE PLATFORM SERVICES

Enterprise platform services can be grouped into four categories:

- API-based services: These services are accessed by programs using APIs defined in JSRs. Examples of API-based services are naming service, messaging service, and connector.
- Descriptive services: These services including persistence, transaction, and security are declared in a deployment file (e.g., Web.xml, persistence.xml). With Java EE 5, by means of special annotations, developers can use the descriptive services without writing code.
- Container-based services: Container-based services, such as component life-cycle management, pooling, remote method invocation (RMI), and threading are automatically provided by the container.
- Vendor-specific services: These services depend on the vendor of the application server being used. An example of vendor-specific services is clustering, which provides load balancing and scalability. If vendor-specific services are used in the application, it may not be possible to deploy it to another application server supplied by another vendor.

API-BASED SERVICES IN JAVA EE 5

The most frequently used API-based services in the Java EE 5 platform are briefly explained below.

JDBC API FOR DATABASE CONNECTIVITY

This API provides a vendor-neutral way for applications to execute relational database operations in the Java-programming language with SQL (Structured Query Language). In Java EE 5, entity beans are used when database connectivity is necessary. Entity beans are just ordinary Java classes where the mapping between the class and the tables are declared by inserting appropriate annotations. Java Persistence API, explained below, is used to keep the entity objects persistent.

Java Naming and Directory Interface API for Locating Remote Components

This API is used for vendor-neutral access to directory services, such as NIS+ (Network Information Service Plus), LDAP (Lightweight Directory Access Protocol), and Microsoft's Active Directory. Java EE applications also make use of the Java Naming and Directory Interface (JNDI) API to locate components and services using a central lookup service:

```
Context c = new InitialContext();
Object o = c.lookup("java:comp/env/BankManagerLookup");
```

If the client and destination component reside in the same application server, instead of JNDI lookup, the dependency injection mechanism is used by inserting the @Resource annotation:

```
@Resource private javax.ejb.SessionContext context;
 public void myMethod() {
    BankManager bankManager = (BankManager)
        context.lookup("java:comp/env/BankManagerLookup");
}
```

RMI over Internet Inter-Object Request Broker Protocol

Communication between clients and EJBs are through RMI over the Internet Inter-Object Request Broker Protocol (IIOP). This is a CORBA (Common Object Request Broker Architecture) compliant RMI strategy. The strength of this strategy over Java RMI schemes is that it is independent of programming languages, so not all clients of a particular enterprise application need to be written in the Java programming language.

JavaMail API and JavaBeans Activation Framework API

These APIs provide a platform- and protocol-independent way to build mail and messaging applications. The JavaMail API is available as an optional package for use with Java SE platform and is also included in the Java EE platform. The package contains classes for reading, composing, and sending electronic messages. JavaMail API requires the JavaBeans Activation Framework (JAF). The framework adds support for typing arbitrary piece of data and instantiate an appropriate bean to perform the operation.

Java EE Connector Architecture

Java EE Connector Architecture (JCA) is a Java-based technology solution for connecting application servers and Enterprise Information Systems as part of Enterprise Application Integration solutions. While JDBC is specifically used to connect Java EE applications to databases, JCA is a more generic architecture for connection to legacy systems. This API allows the provision of integration modules, called resource adapters, for legacy systems in a way that is independent of the application server vendor. JCA is developed under the JCP as JSR 112 (JCA 1.5). The Java EE Connector API is used by Java EE tool developers and system integrators to create resource adapters.

JAVA MESSAGE SERVICE API

The Java Message Service (JMS) is an API for reliable asynchronous communication between applications in a distributed computing environment. The JMS supports both message queuing and publish-subscribe styles of messaging. A JMS provider is the entity that implements JMS for a messaging product. With Release 1.4 of the J2EE platform, the JMS provider may be integrated with the application server using the JCA.

JAVA TRANSACTION API

The Java Transaction API (JTA) enables developers to initiate and monitor distributed transactions. Java Transaction Service (JTS) specifies the implementation of a transaction manager, which supports JTA 1.0. Although JTS is quite complex, JTA makes the use of JTS simple. The code in Listing 9.3 is a typical transaction management code used in Java EE applications. UserTransaction resource is defined using dependency injection inside EJB class. Transaction operations are then called between **begin**() and **end**() calls. If any transaction operation fails, the code jumps into the catch block where the transaction rolls back to the beginning by the **rollback**() call.

```
import javax.ejb.*;
import javax.annotation.*;
import javax.transaction.*;

@Stateful
@TransactionManagement(BEAN)
public class ExampleBean implements ExampleSession {
  @Resource UserTransaction ut;
  public void service() {
    try {
      ut.begin(); // Transaction starts
      // .. transaction operations
      ut.commit(); // Transaction finishes
    }
    catch (Exception e) {
    // if transaction fails, roll back to the beginning
      ut.rollback();
    }
  }
}
```

LISTING 9.3 Code listing for transaction management example.

Java Authentication and Authorization Service

The Java Authentication and Authorization Service (JAAS) is a set of packages that enables services to authenticate and enforce access controls upon users. It implements a Java version of the standard Pluggable Authentication Module (PAM) framework and supports user-based authorization. PAM can be used to integrate login services with various key exchange technologies, such as RSA and Kerberos. In the Java EE platform, JAAS might be used to integrate an application server with an external security infrastructure.

Java API for XML Processing

This API provides access to XML parsers. The parsers themselves might be vendor-specific, but as long as they implement the Java API for XML Processing (JAXP) interfaces, vendor distinctions should be invisible to the application programmer. The JAXP enables applications to parse and transform XML documents independent of a particular XML parser implementation. It provides basic functionality for reading, manipulating, and generating XML documents. The standard defined in JSR 206 enables the integration of any XML-compliant parser with a Java application. Switching from a particular XML parser to another one does affect the application code.

Web Services Integration APIs

These services include Simple Object Access Protocol (SOAP) for the Java application, SOAP with Attachments API for Java™ (SAAJ), Java API for XML Registries (JAXR), and Java API for XML Web Services (JAX-WS). Together these services will allow Java EE software applications to respond to, and to initiate XML-based Remote Procedure Call and messaging operations, which provides a full Web services platform.

Java Management Extensions

This API exposes the internal operation of the application server and its components for control and monitoring vendor-neutral management tools. Java Management Extensions (JMX) technology provides the tools for building distributed, Web-based, modular and dynamic solutions for managing and monitoring devices, applications, and service-driven networks. JMX is suitable for adapting legacy systems, implementing new management and monitoring solutions, and plugging into those of the future.

The Java Persistence API

The Java Persistence API [6] defines a mapping between relational data and Java objects and enables applications to keep the state of these objects persistent in a relational database management system. The mapping is simply defined by using several annotations. In the following example (Listing 9.4), a mapping between a single table and a class is given. It is possible to map more than one table to a class.

```java
import java.io.Serializable;
import javax.persistence.*;

@Entity @Table(name = "PERSON")
public class Person implements Serializable {
 @Id @Column(name = "SSN") private String ssn;
 @Column(name = "NAME") private String name;
 @Column(name = "AGE") private int age;
 @Column(name = "SALARY") private double salary;

 protected Person() { }
 public MyEntity(String ssn, String name,int age,double
  salary)
 {
  this.ssn = ssn;
  this.name = name;
  this.age = age;
  this.salary = salary;
 }

  public int getSSN() { return ssn; }
  public String getName() { return name; }
  public void setName(String name) { this.name = name; }
  public String getAge() { return age; }
  public void setAge(int age) { this.age = age; }
  public double getSalary() { return salary; }
  public void setSalary(double salary) { this.salary =
    salary;
 }
}
```

LISTING 9.4   Code listing for sample entity class `Person.java`.

EntityManager is used to control the persistence context in an application. EntityManager is obtained using dependence injection in managed classes:

```java
@PersistenceContext private EntityManager em;
```

The following code shows several examples on persistence operations. Persistence-related method calls are shown in bold.

```java
String ssn = "481-51-62342";
Person person = em.find(Person.class, ssn); // retrieve
record
```

```
person.setAge(36);
em.persist(person); // updates record

person.setName("John Locke");
em.remove(person); // deletes record
```

CONCLUSIONS

In this chapter, we provided properties and components that make up enterprise server platforms. JavaBeans and Java EE APIs were treated in detail with the help of Java code examples. It should be kept in mind that Java EE is an evolving platform, therefore the reader should refer to the Java Web site (http://java.sun.com) and Java developers' network (http://developers.sun.com/) for the latest available standards and APIs.

REFERENCES AND FURTHER READING

1. Jendrock, E. et al., *Java EE 5 Tutorial*, 3rd edn., Prentice Hall, Santa Clara, CA, 2006.
2. Heffelfinger, D., *Java EE 5 Development using GlassFish Application Server*, Packt Publishing, Birmingham, UK, 2007.
3. Englander, R., *Developing Java Beans*, O'Reilly, Sebastopol, CA, 1997.
4. Burke, B. *Enterprise JavaBeans 3.0*, O'Reilly, Sebastopol, CA, 2006.
5. Panda, D., Rahman, R., and Lane, D., *EJB 3 in Action*, Manning Publications, Greenwich, CT, 2007.
6. Keith, M. and Schincariol, M., *Pro EJB 3: Java Persistence API*, Apress, New York, 2006.

10 Software Reliability and Risk Management

Xuemei Zhang

CONTENTS

INTRODUCTION

Enterprise integration, like other software development and deployment projects, suffers chronically from cost overruns, schedule delays, unmet customer needs, and buggy systems. Frequently, this is a result of failing to address appropriately the uncertainties associated with complex, software-intensive systems. Better risk management depends on more structured and systematic ways for handling these uncertainties, particularly as they relate to the developers, to the customers and to the end-users. For all three categories of stakeholders, risk management entails assessing what can go wrong to estimate the likelihood of failures, to understand the severity of the impact, and to devise coping strategies. In the case of enterprise integration systems, the questions to answer are: is the system designed to be fault-tolerant? What is the likelihood that end-users would encounter service-affecting failures? How quickly can the failures be detected and fixed? Finally, what is the expected average downtime, annually and per incident?

Software risk management can be defined as "an attempt to formalize risk oriented correlates of success into a readily applicable set of principles and practices" [1]. The goals are to identify the risk items and the probability of their occurrence, to analyze their consequences, and then to mitigate corresponding potential losses. Software risk management is typically studied and documented in a general project management context [2–13]. These studies, however, focus on general project-management risks such as schedule and timing risks, personnel management risks, resource usage risk, and so on. Risks associated with software reliability do not seem to receive much specific attention, even though this is critical for enterprise integration projects: it is the guarantee that the necessary messages will be delivered across all services with minimum risks in terms of delay, security, integrity, and so on.

It is understood that software reliability risk management should be carried out through the entire development and integration cycle. In this chapter, we concentrate on software risk management and reliability improvement during the software development and integration cycle. In contrast with methods that rely in expert opinions, the distinctive feature of our treatment is that it takes advantage of quantitative metrics and methods to obtain more objective evaluations throughout the software lifecycle.

The chapter is organized as follows. First, we discus metrics and methods for risk management in the requirements specification phase. Next, we consider architecture-based software reliability models and how to connect the early evaluation of system architecture during the design with risk management. More importantly, the architecture-based models establish a framework for continuous metrics-driven reliability and risk management through the other development phases. The next section concerns risk management during coding. Metrics collected during software development provide the statistics for evaluation activities such as fault-proneness analysis, reliability/quality assessment, and so on. Established software reliability metrics such as defect rate and residual defects and the concepts of software reliability growth and field reliability prediction are introduced. Testing is the last stage where the project team can find and fix defects before the product is shipped. This section discusses how to collect test data such that they can be used in the validation process and how to feed these measurements back to improve the architecture-based reliability models. We also show how to benefit from field data described by the field-failure rate, outage rate, outage durations, and so on, to improve the complete framework of reliability and risk management. We conclude by a summary of the best practices in each development phase to ensure software reliability and risk management on a continuous basis.

RISK MANAGEMENT IN THE REQUIREMENTS PHASE

The goal of software risk analysis and management during the requirements phase is to identify those risky requirements that can lead to the loss of any feature of the software system. The following two metrics are considered: (1) the probability of problematic requirements that could cause malfunctions (*failures*) and (2) the impact (*severity*) of the failure. Many risk-assessment methods use the product of these two metrics to rank risk priorities. Architecture design languages (ADLs) can be used to describe the software architecture and its control flow and then to identify the risky requirements.

Additionally, changes in the scope of the project may bring negative effects on the product reliability by adding uncertainties to the development processes. We present methods to characterize the risks introduced by requirement changes.

RISK ASSESSMENT IN THE REQUIREMENTS PHASE

Traditional risk assessments in the requirement phase rely on expert opinion to identify failure modes for each requirement and to estimate the impact of these failure modes. Techniques combining graphical and analytical models to represent the system control flow are used to reduce the dependency on domain experts. These techniques are known as ADLs. Examples of ADL are the Unified Modeling

Language (UML) and the Colored Petri-Net (CPN). Requirement risk assessment using these methods can be summarized into the following steps:

1. Represent software requirements with control flow models such as UML, CPN, or any other similar methods.
2. Estimate the failure probability based on the complexity of the requirements and use scenarios. Complexity metrics are discussed in this section, which include a basic complexity metric and complexity metrics that take software execution issues into account.
3. Analyze the severity of the failures based on their consequences, which are determined by degree of injuries or system damages. Typical methods include failure mode and effects analysis (FMEA) [14] and function failure analysis (FFA) [15]. Severity levels are defined and numeric indices for each level are used to quantify the severity levels.
4. Combine the two risk metrics—complexity and severity—and calculate the risk levels for each requirement.
5. Rank the requirements according to their risk levels and identify high-risk components.

In the following subsections, examples of using these methods are discussed in details.

The UML Method

The UML is a general-purpose modeling language that uses a graphical notation to create an abstract model of a system, referred to as an UML model. It is a standard visual specification language for object modeling [16,17]. The steps to implement this method in requirement risk assessment are as follows [16]:

1. First, the requirements are mapped to UML sequence diagrams. A sequence diagram shows how processes operate one with another and in what order (e.g., a call flow in telecommunications applications). For each sequence diagram, control flow graph of the *scenario* is constructed from the sequence diagrams. Possible failure situations (known as *failure modes*) are identified on the control flow graph in the form of nodes and arcs with the nodes representing different states of components and the arcs representing the flow of control.
2. For each scenario, the risk of each failure mode is measured by the product of the complexity and severity associated that failure mode. The severity of the failures is assessed using FFA [15]. The complexity of the scenario for the failure mode is measured by the product of McCabe's cyclomatic complexity (MCC) [18] and the number of messages. MCC measures the number of linearly independent paths through a program:

$$\text{MCC} = E \boxtimes N + X, \tag{10.1}$$

TABLE 10.1

Risk Scores for Requirements

		Failure Modes				
Requirement	Scenario	FM1	FM2	FM3	FM4	FM5
R1	S1	0.11	0.37	0.47		
R2	S2	0.15	0.28	0.57		
R3	S3			0.01	0.23	0.33

where E is the number of edges in the graph of the control flow in the program, N is the number of nodes or decision points in the graph, and X is the number of connected components. In programming terms, edges are the decision points of the code. The exits are the explicit return statements. Normally, there is one explicit return per function call and no explicit return for subroutines. In the UML case, there are two connected components and hence $X = 2$.

3. Based on FMEA and FFA, severity is assessed into four categories: minor, marginal, critical, and catastrophic, which corresponds to four severity indices: 0.25, 0.50, 0.75, and 0.90, respectively [14,17]. The product of severity and complexity is used as a risk indicator to rank the requirements.

4. The risk of the scenario is then the summation of the risk measures across all failure modes. The process is repeated for each failure mode and for each scenario. The results are put in tabular form so that risk factors could be compared across requirements; see Table 10.1. Next, the requirements are ranked according to their risk scores to identify those with high risk.

The CPN Method

Similar to the UML method, the CPN method also estimates the complexity of the requirements and the severity of failure modes, using the CPN notation [15,19]. A Petri-Net is a modeling language that represents the structure of a distributed system as a directed bipartite graph with annotations. As such, a Petri-Net has place nodes, transition nodes, and directed arcs connecting place nodes with transitions. CPNs combine the strengths of ordinary Petri nets with the strengths of a high-level programming language. Petri nets provide the primitives for process interaction, while the programming language provides the primitives for the definition of data types and the manipulations of data values.

There are several advantages with using CPN models (as compared with other ADLs):

- The flexibility of the CPN notation to express the control flow greatly reduces the effort to design alternative specifications and to explore their behavior under specification changes.

- CPN allows the modeling of the concurrency, synchronization, and resource sharing in a system.
- CPN provides rich mathematical platforms and objective-oriented design architecture that support rich performance analysis and analysis automation.
- CPN allows complicated complexity measurements such as the dynamic and concurrent measures of system complexity.

Like in the case of the UML method, complexity and severity are used as risk indicators. Severity of the requirements are modeled and estimated by FMEA and FFA. There are four severity levels and four severity indices, which is very similar to the UML method. The complexity estimated from the MCC method, is regarded as a "static complexity," and two more complexity metrics are introduced. They are referred to as "dynamic complexity" and "concurrence complexity" [15].

Dynamic Complexity

Dynamic complexity is a measure of complexity for the subset of the code that is actually executed when the system is performing a given function. Dynamic complexity is measured by the dynamic functional complexity and the dynamic operational complexity. For the former, the execution profile for a given functionality is the proportion of time, say, p_k, spent in each component during which that function was expressed. The latter can be estimated as the fraction of the flow graph that was activated, say, c_k. Both parameters can be estimated via simulation. Both p_k and c_k can be calculated from simulation results. The dynamic complexity is then the product of the dynamic functional complexity and operational complexity.

Concurrence Complexity

Concurrent processes are frequently used in real-time environments. The degree of concurrence can be measured from simulation, then incorporated into the complexity measure.

For the CPN method, the complexity is assessed by calculating the product of the three complexity metrics. The product of complexity and severity, named as *heuristic risk factors* (HrFs) [15], is computed for each requirement as

$$HrF_k = cpx_k \cdot svrty_k, \quad 0 < cpx_k \leq 1, 0 \leq svrty_k \leq 1, \qquad (10.2)$$

where cpx_k is the complexity metric for the kth requirement and $svrty_k$ represents the severity metric for the kth requirement.

The HrFs are calculated at four levels each corresponding to one complexity: static, dynamic functional, dynamic operational, and concurrence complexity. Based on these risk metrics, the requirements are ranked and high-risk requirements can be identified so that appropriate actions could be considered.

RISKS ASSOCIATED WITH REQUIREMENT CHANGES

Another issue that arises is that the changes to the scope of the requirements. In a series of papers, Schneidewind [20] discussed how to assign risk factors to these changes using, for instance, the number of changes, their size, that is, the number of lines of code affected by the change and their complexity. Some of these factors are intuitively related to software reliability and maintainability and most of them can be estimated during the requirement phase. But not all of them are significant predictors of software reliability and maintainability risks.

Schneidewind identified 19 risk factors including metrics reflecting complexity, size, criticality of change, locality of change, performance, and personnel resources. Using categorical data analysis and based on the data from the Space shuttle flight project, he found that four factors are statistically significant, that seven are not significant and eight are inconclusive. The four significant factors are as follows: (1) the number of modifications or iterations on the proposed change; (2) the number of lines of code affected by the change; (3) the number of possible conflicts among requirements; and (4) the amount of memory space required to implement the change [20].

Schneidewind further studied the relationship between failure reports and requirement change requests by testing the hypothesis that the probability of failure reports due to requirement changes will increase nonlinearly with the risk factors [21]. In this study, the dependent variables were the number of possible conflicts among requirements and the amount of memory space, and the independent variable was the predicted probability of failure reports. A logistic regression method was used to link the dependent and independent variables, and a logit function was used to describe the risk-prediction probability (failure reports) as a function of the risk factors. The study provided a means to evaluate the possibilities of predicting risk on the basis of the risk factors and of determining threshold values for the risk factors to alarm the potential risks using a logit model. Different projects may define different risks (like failure reports in this example) and different risk factors (such as the number of possible conflicts among requirements and the amount of memory space here). These investigations show that the logistic regression method can be applied to correlate the specific risks and risk factors for specific projects and to predict the risk probability for specific risk factors.

RISK MANAGEMENT IN THE ARCHITECTURE DESIGN PHASE

During the architecture design phase, hardware platforms and software structures are selected and critical decisions are explored to determine the system hierarchy and dependability. Hence this is a critical phase to assess whether system reliability goals (including availability goals for real-time applications) can be met, to understand potential reliability related risks if there are deviations, and to identify cost-effective investments to close reliability gaps if any.

Availability is a critical aspect of reliability for real-time applications. It is defined as "the ability of a unit to be in a state ready to perform a required function at a given instant in time or for any period within a given time interval, assuming that the external resources, if required, are provided" [22]. Thus availability is just a probability (expressed in percentage). Practically, availability considers two factors: how often does the system fail, and how quickly can the system be restored to service following that failure.

Once the system architecture is finalized, it would be very costly to make major changes to the design. It would be highly desirable to set up models to evaluate reliability and risk evaluation early in the development cycle. As a consequence, there is a need to establish in that phase a framework for reliability and risk evaluation and management that can be carried out through the development and integration phases. The architecture-based models would incorporate updates derived during the development phase and from test data when they become available later in the life cycle. Moreover, this framework should include field data collected after the product has been deployed to validate the models and to calibrate modeling parameters. Should there be a gap between the field observations in terms of reliability and availability and the baseline requirements, sensitivity analyses based on these models would assist in identifying cost-effective ways for improving software reliability and mitigating risks.

The following section discusses how to construct these architecture-based models and how to use them in reliability and risk management.

QUANTITATIVE ARCHITECTURE-BASED RELIABILITY MODELS

Markov models represent the random behavior of systems that vary discretely or continuously with respect to time and space. The Markovian approach is bottom-up and allows thorough analyses of complex systems subsystem and components using stochastic-modeling techniques and tools that can be applied to computer and general engineering applications [23]. The foundation for Markov modeling is the state transition diagram (or state diagram, for short) that describes the possible states of the system, the events that cause it to transition from one state to another, and the rates at which these transitions occur.

In the case of reliability and risk analysis, Markov models use states to represent different failure conditions at any given instant [24]. In this approach, the system can be further divided into subsystems and modules. The states in the Markov models represent the operational conditions for a module or a subsystem, for example, normal operation, certain failures, and failure detection and recovery. The transitions between the states represent the probabilities of failures and failure detections and recoveries. The time-dependent or steady-state probabilities can be calculated. Summing up the time spent in the down states yields the downtime for the subsystem and/or modules, from which the system-level downtime can be estimated.

There are several advantages in using the Markov models of software reliability. First, different architecture options (e.g., simplex vs. duplex designs) can be compared with respect to fault recovery strategies (e.g., process restart attempts, process switch-over attempts, and manual failover attempts) to evaluate reliability/risk and costs trade-offs. Secondly, the models allows the consideration of imperfect recoveries (unsuccessful restart and failover attempts) and imperfect failure detections, so manual intervention will be needed. Such a model also supports sensitivity analyses. For example, the benefits of additional failure detection and recovery features can be evaluated by introducing extra states in the models. Similarly, the impact on reliability of higher or lower failure rates and/or faster or slower fault detection and recoveries can be compared and contrasted. With such a probabilistic structure, a sensitivity analysis can be conducting to evaluate the impact of potential design features in improving the overall availability.

The following sections illustrate the architecture-based modeling approach in the case of a software system for a real-time application product. This example explains the modeling methodology and its practical usefulness in exploring the reliability risks of various architectural features to estimate.

DESIGN OF A RELIABLE REAL-TIME SYSTEM

A typical requirement for the expected annual downtime for many real-time systems is 5.256 min/year (i.e., 99.999% availability), that is the expected downtime for the system is no greater than 5.256 min/year. This overall availability requirement can then be broken down and allocated to subsystems based on the architecture and the capability of the subsystems. This is often known as reliability-budgeting activities. To simplify the illustration here, let us assume 99.999% is a requirement for the subsystem understudy. Different architectures result in different availability levels and they also have different implications on time-to-market risk and development cost as well. Markov models for three alternative software designs are developed below, followed by a sensitivity analysis showing how to use the architecture-based models to achieve better feature planning and reliability and risk assessment.

Simplex Architecture: No Restart Capability

The first software design considered was a simplex (no redundancy) design with no enhanced reliability features. In this design, the software executes in a simplex mode on a single server. A software module, MonSW, is continually executing software failure-detection diagnostics, and upon detection of a failure it initiates a reboot of the entire system. When a software failure escapes system detection, the system reboot is preceded by a manual detection interval.

Figure 10.1 depicts the various states that the software system could be in at any given time. State 0 denotes the working state. A transition to state 1 occurs if the software fails and MonSW detects the failure. In Figure 10.1, λ_1 denotes the failure rate of the controller application software and c is called the coverage factor, which is the probability that MonSW is able to detect the failure. Once in state 1, the system is rebooted after which it returns to state 0. The rate at which the system can reboot is also shown in Figure 10.1 as λ_R.

If the software fails in a manner that escapes MonSW, the system transitions from states 0 to 2 where it waits for a manual detection (that occurs with rate λ_d) to occur which takes the system to state 1. The rate at which MonSW fails is λ. State 3 corresponds to a self-reported failure of MonSW (It is assumed that the fraction of self-reported failures is c). With probability r_m, a manual recovery of MonSW will succeed in taking the system back to state 0. If the manual recovery does not succeed, then the system transitions to state 1 where a reboot takes the system back to state 0. If MonSW fails silently (state 4), a subsequent failure of the system software will necessarily be silent, which is shown by the transition to state 2.

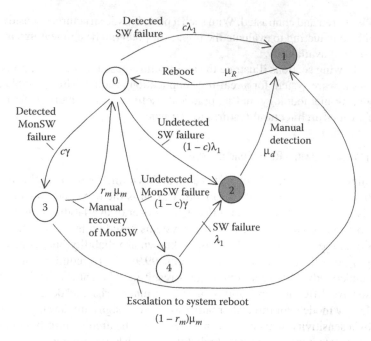

FIGURE 10.1 Simplex with no restart software design.

States 1 and 2 in Figure 10.1 correspond to downtime states. Using standard balance equation techniques, it is easy to show that the steady-state occupancy probabilities for states 1 and 2 are

$$P_1 = [\boxtimes_1 + (1 \boxtimes cr_m)\boxtimes]P_0/\boxtimes_R \quad \text{and} \quad P_2 = (1 \boxtimes c)(\boxtimes_1 + \boxtimes)/\boxtimes_d, \tag{10.3}$$

where

$$P_0 = \left[1 + \frac{\lambda_1 + (1 - cr_m)g}{m_R} + \frac{(1 - c)(\lambda_1 + g)}{m_d} + \frac{cg}{m_m} + \frac{(1 - c)g}{\lambda_1} \right]^{-1} \tag{10.4}$$

The software contribution to the expected annual downtime (minutes) is $D = (P_1 + P_2) \times 525{,}600$ with 525,600 min/year. In the early design phase, historical data and early estimations of software metrics (size, complexity, reuse, and maturity) are typically used to estimate the input parameters [24]. Assume that the values for the model parameters shown in Table 10.2 are the outcomes. The corresponding downtime for this set of parameters values is 26.4 min/year, or in other words, the availability of 99.9949%.

The input parameters can be updated once data on the specific project/release becomes available. This is the reason why this kind of models can be used to establish a reliability and risk-assessment framework. The recovery parameters are

TABLE 10.2
Baseline Parameters for Simplex, No Restart Architecture

Parameter	Symbol	Value
Application software failure rate (failures/year)	λ	2
Coverage factor	c	0.95
MonSW failure rate (failures/year)	λ	0.1
MonSW recovery probability	r_m	0.9
MonSW recovery duration (min)	$1/\mu_m$	30
Controller reboot time (min)	$1/\mu_R$	10
Manual detection time (min)	$1/\mu_d$	60

typically easier to measure while the software failure rate λ_1 (aside from MonSW) and the coverage factor c can be updated from testing data and field outage data.

Simplex Architecture: With Restart Capability

A more sophisticated software design implements a capability to locally restart software processes that incur a failure. Not all software processes can be restarted (e.g., the operating system is not typically restartable) and not all restartable software processes can be restarted in every failure case. But the restart feature does reduce the failure recovery time for a significant fraction of the failures, since the restart attempt duration is usually much shorter than the reboot duration.

Figure 10.2 expands Figure 10.1 to include the process restart feature and should be fairly self-explanatory in light of the detailed description of Figure 10.1. The main difference is that there are now two software failure rates λ_1 and λ_2 to distinguish between software that is not restartable and software that is restartable. The portion of the figure pertaining to MonSW has also been modified to account for the fact that MonSW is restartable. Parameters are introduced to represent the fraction of restart attempts that succeed and the fraction of failed restart attempts that are automatically detected by the system.

Once again, balance equation techniques could be used to solve for the steady-state probabilities of the downtime states 1, 2, and 5, and a formula for the expected annual downtime of the system software could be obtained. The details of the solution are omitted here. Table 10.3 contains the additional parameters in the model that can be estimated with reasonable certainty. For the purpose of this illustration, assume that half of the application software can be designed so that it is restartable. This means $\lambda_1 = \lambda_2 = 1$ failure/year. The annual downtime corresponding to this design is then 17.9 min/year with an availability of 99.9966%. The downtime saving from the no-restart design to restartable design is a significant 8.45 min/year.

Active-Standby Architecture with Restart and Failover Capability

The ultimate in the progression of increasing sophistication is a redundant active-standby software design. Note that this architecture also enhances the

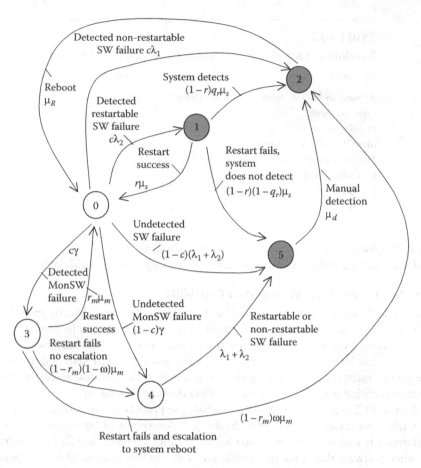

FIGURE 10.2 Simplex with restart software design.

TABLE 10.3

Additional Parameters for Simplex with Restart Architecture

Parameter	Symbol	Value
Restartable software failure rate (failures/year)	λ_1	1
Nonrestartable software failure rate (failures/year)	λ_2	1
Restart success probability	r	0.9
Restart duration (s)	$1/\mu_s$	1
Failed restart detection probability	q_r	0.99
Fraction of failed MonSW restarts that automatically escalate to reboot	w	0.99

availability of the hardware design. (In reality, hardware availability would see a more significant improvement [as compared to software availability] when the design changes from simplex to duplex, because the hardware replacement takes a much longer time than software reboot.) This design allows the recovery from failed nonrestartable software processes, or failed restart attempts for restartable software processes, by activating shadow processes for each software process on a standby unit. Process activation on the redundant controller is referred to as a "failover." During a failover, all of the processes on the standby controller are activated, thereby idling the previously active controller so that it can be rebooted without affecting service.

Figure 10.3 shows a state diagram for the active-standby architecture. Two guiding principles are used to prevent state explosion and keep the size of the state diagram manageable. First, detected failures on the standby side were neglected since their relatively fast recoveries makes the probability of an overlapping failure on the active side is small. Second, consecutive silent failures (e.g., a silent failure on the standby side followed by a silent failure on the active side) are neglected since the probability of these types of simultaneous failures is very small.

The detailed solutions for the steady-state probabilities of the down states shown in Figure 10.3 are omitted. Table 10.4 defines and gives values for the additional parameters of the model that can be estimated with reasonable certainty. As before, let us assume that half of the system software is restartable. The downtime corresponding to the design in Figure 10.3 is 8.1 min/year with an availability of 99.9985%. The downtime saving is 9.8 min/year from the restartable design or a total of 18.2 min/year from the original simplex design.

By combining Figure 10.3 with the cost associated with achieving various feasibility points for the software failure rate and the coverage factor, a cost-effective software design that meets the availability target can be selected. It would remain to ensure that the software, as it progresses through the coding and test phases of the development cycle, actually meets the failure rate/reliability target. To ensure this compliance, the software reliability growth models (SRGMs) discussed later in the chapter can be utilized for testing the data analysis. In addition, the coverage factor value would need to be verified based on the observed fraction of software failures during the test period that were (or should have been, except for a bug that was subsequently removed) detected by system diagnostics.

Table 10.5 summarizes the downtime and availability levels for the three design options. It is shown that the architecture-based models are useful to evaluate the reliability capabilities and identify associated risks for each. Figure 10.4 shows the feasible regions to achieve 99.999% availability for the three designs. Sensitivity analysis discussed in the next section is useful to identify the steps that could take to achieve 99.999% for the three designs.

SENSITIVITY ANALYSIS AND RISK ASSESSMENT

This section describes how to use architecture-based Markov models to compare different design options. Once a software design has been selected, an important input to the architecture team is to identify the most cost-efficient features to achieve

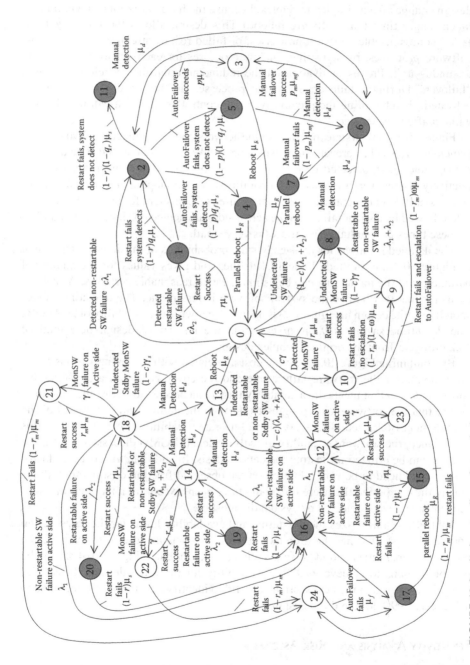

FIGURE 10.3 Active-standby software design.

TABLE 10.4
Additional Parameters for Active-Standby Architecture

Parameter	Symbol	Value
Failover success probability	p	0.9
Failover duration (s)	$1/\mu_f$	10
Failed failover detection probability	q_f	0.99
Manual failover success probability	p_m	0.8
Manual failover duration (min)	$1/\mu_{mf}$	10
Standby-side nonrestartable software failure rate (failures/year)	λ_{1s}	0.1
Standby-side restartable software failure rate (failures/year)	λ_{2s}	0.1
Standby-side MonSW failure rate (failures/year)	λ_s	0.1

TABLE 10.5
Downtime and Availability Summary

Design Option	Downtime (min/year)	Availability (%)
Simplex with no restart	26.4	99.9949
Simplex with restart	17.9	99.9966
Duplex with failover	8.1	99.9985

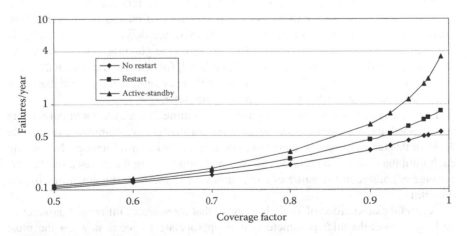

FIGURE 10.4 Five-9s feasibility regions for alternative architectures.

higher availability or mitigate a reliability risk. Sensitivity analysis addresses this question by identifying the most influential reliability parameters in the architecture-based models.

Theoretically, by examining the formula for system downtime, one could identify influential parameters. However, there are two difficulties in practice with this approach. First, the function is quite complex for all but the simplest systems. It would be difficult to undertake a graphical analysis of the downtime function since it depends on many input parameters. The analysis of derivatives (as in Refs. [25,26]) is not that simple since it is the global behavior (i.e., the behavior over the entire domain of the function) of the derivatives that is of interest, not merely their value at a particular point in the domain of the function.

A practical approach for sensitivity analysis is proposed here. This approach starts from the initial nominal values of the parameters in the Markov model, and vary them one at a time to achieve the same amount of downtime savings, say 5%. Once the change percentage for each input parameter is calculated, they can be ranked in an increasing order, that is, the one with the smallest percentage comes first, followed by the second smallest change, so that the less influential parameters, as determined above, come last.

As a practical matter, one usually looks for an increase in the system downtime because some parameters may be too close to the limit of perfection, (especially in well-designed systems) to decrease the downtime by an additional 5%. Typically, some parameters cannot change enough to increase the downtime by 5%. In this case, the limit may be something like a 600% increase in value for those parameters that increase the downtime by 5%, and a 1% decrease in value for those that would increase the downtime likewise 1%. In other words, if a six-fold increase in the parameter value increases the downtime by <5%, this parameter will be excluded from consideration. Likewise, if a parameter decreases to 1% of its default value without augmenting the downtime by 5%, one shall quit and mark the parameter as noninfluential. These limits are arbitrary—other limits could be reasonably used, but have been found to be satisfactory.

Next detailed analyses of the more influential parameters can be conducted to reveal greater details of the impact of the parameter and related features. For this, charts can be created to show the range of the expected downtime given the likely range of the input parameters. This helps determine the potential gain in downtime for a change in that particular parameter. This is helpful because the system developers may be able to change the value of one parameter significantly more than they can a different, potentially more influential, parameter.

For the example shown in the Figure 10.3, assume that all the input parameters are selected and the nominal values of these parameters are summarized in Table 10.6. In this table, the parameters are ranked in the order of influence—by varying each until the downtime increases by 5%, and then ranking them based on the percentage of change in the value of each parameter to increase the downtime by 5% downtime.

A careful examination of Table 10.6 shows that there are 12 influential parameters and eight noninfluential parameters. It is appropriate to focus now on the most

TABLE 10.6
Model Parameters and Nominal Values

Parameter	Values	% Change to Increase 5% Downtime
Coverage, c	0.9	−0.32
Failover success probability, p	0.9	−4
Silent failure detection duration, $1/\lambda_d$	1 h	−7
Failure rate of nonrestartable software, λ_2	1.0 failures/year	9
Failure rate of restartable failure rate, λ_1	1.0 failures/year	12
Software reboot duration, $1/\lambda_r$	10 min	−26
Restart success probability, r	0.9	−27
Manual failover duration, $1/\lambda_{mf}$	10 min	−29
Failover success probability, p_m	0.9	−52
Escalation probability, w	0.99	−72
Failover duration, $1/\lambda_f$	10 s	−72
MonSW failure rate, λ	0.1 failures/year	125
Prob. of detecting restart failure, q_r	0.9	NA
Prob. of detecting failover failure, q_m	0.99	NA
Standby nonrestartable software failure rate, λ_{2s}	0.1 failures/year	NA
Standby restartable failure rate, λ_{1s}	0.1 failures/year	NA
Standby MonSW failure rate, λ_{3s}	0.1 failures/year	NA
Restart duration, $1/\lambda_s$	1 s	NA
MonSW restart duration, $1/\lambda_m$	1 s	NA
MonSW restart success probability, r_m	0.9	NA

influential parameters, for example, parameters that changed 20% or less to create a 5% downtime change. Of the 12 influential parameters, there are seven that had to change more than 20% to change the downtime by 5% (and hence they are not the most influential ones). This definition results in five parameters to consider. For each of the five influential parameters, more detailed analysis can be done to study the relationship of the downtime and the individual parameters.

The next step is to investigate the features in the development and integration plans and to use these model and analyses to guide the feature planning. For instance, it is shown that software fault coverage is an influential parameter for software reliability. If the fault coverage for the current product is still relatively low, then investment in features that would increase fault coverage would be appropriate. Examples of fault coverage improvement methods are as follows:

1. Add process monitoring capability to all software processes
2. Add heartbeats between subsystems to allow additional layer of healthiness monitoring
3. Add data auditing to the software to find data inconsistencies

4. Test only feature that adds numerous robustness tests
5. Design a system-wide exception hierarchy for software exceptions

One good way to visually assess these features is to build a mapping table that links the features to the five parameters that are candidate for improvement. Quantitative estimates of the impacts of these features on fault coverage can be input into the Markov models to understand the potential benefits and/or risks.

In contrast to reliability growth due to the introduction of reliability improving features, other new features might have a negative impact on reliability. For example, new code could potentially inject additional software faults, which may offset some of the improvement from better fault coverage discussed earlier. Hence, a better risk management strategy is to balance the negative impacts with reliability improving features. Architecture-based models and sensitivity analysis are useful modeling and analysis tools that provide quantitative reliability evaluation and features prioritization for a better risk management.

Additionally, reliability growth is best achieved by a process of continuous improvement through the product development life cycle and across a number of releases. The reliability growth targets are planned out in a reliability roadmap. In each release, reliability and risk management activities are carried out to ensure the reliability growth meets the release target or estimates the gaps. Architecture-based reliability modeling is the heart of this continuous reliability improvement and risk management process. This is how it works:

1. During the requirements phase, initial modeling helps both feasibility assessment of reliability targets and budgeting which allocates the downtime requirements to subsystems.
2. During the architecture phase, architecture-based models assist in the selection of design options and in feature planning from a reliability risk perspective.
3. In the coding and testing phases, metrics estimates from the software and verification/validation processes are integrated into the architecture-based model to update the reliability evaluation and identify risks and improvement areas.

In summary, the architecture-based reliability and risk modeling has a critical role to play, it:

1. Provides a quantitative approach to evaluate reliability/availability for different architectural designs
2. Highlights the most influential reliability features for achieving high availability target in a cost-efficient way (with sensitivity analysis)
3. Lays a strong foundation for a quantitative framework for reliability and risk management throughout the development cycle

In the next section, we will discuss metrics and methods used in risk assessment in the coding phase, which can also be incorporated into the architecture models.

SOFTWARE RELIABILITY AND RISK MANAGEMENT DURING THE CODING PHASE

In the coding phase, more measurements about software and software development process become available. This is why the coding phase and testing phase have enjoyed greater success in using software metrics as software quality/risk predictors. The goal of software quality and risk management during coding phase is to use software metrics to predict software quality, to identify risky or fault-prone components and to assist other project risk-management activities such as predicting development efforts (resources), time/schedule to release (or release readiness), and so on.

Here, we will focus on discussions of using these metrics for software reliability-related risk management, where efforts have been spent to find answers to the following questions:

1. How to predict the number of defects from the size and complexity metrics?
2. How to identify fault-prone modules using more sophisticated metrics?
3. How to evaluate quality of development processes and to identify software reliability and software risks?

Historically, a wide range of prediction models have been proposed and applied to address these three questions and other related ones. This section gives a brief review of these metrics and methods used to identify fault-prone modules and estimate reliability-related software risks. The number of defects in the code is a well-recognized indicator for predicting software quality, development efforts (resources), delivery schedule, and so on. Code size and complexity are two basic and widely used metrics in defect prediction. The following section discusses defect prediction models based on code size and complexity. Other more sophisticated metrics are discussed and a multivariate approach is shown for fault-proneness analysis using these metrics. Last, models and methods of evaluating software development processes and predicting risks are discussed.

DEFECT-PREDICTION MODEL USING SIZE AND COMPLEXITY

Code size and code complexity are two essential metrics to predict the development effort, fault-proneness analysis, and other risk management activities during coding phase. For example, it is widely accepted that software size and complexity are closely related with the number of defects in the code. Regression methods have been widely used to find the relationship of defects (D) and size and complexity. The earliest model was proposed by Akiyama [27], that the total number of defects, D, can be predicted by the size of the software in the line of code (LOC):

$$D = 4.86 + 0.018 \text{ LOC}. \qquad (10.5)$$

Halstead [28] defined several size/complexity metrics based on the number of operators and operands and a language-dependent volume metric, V, and he proposed an equation to predict the number of defects in a program:

$$D = \frac{V}{3000},$$ (10.6)

where 3000 represents the mean number of mental discriminations between decisions made by the programmers. Akiyama's method is the regression analysis based on the data and Halstead's method based on the psychological theory, that is, each decision made by the programmer can potentially result in some kind of error and hence a software defect. The input metrics are summarized as follows:

$n1$ = the number of distinct operators
$n2$ = the number of distinct operands
$N1$ = the total number of operators
$N2$ = the total number of operands

Five Halstead measures can be derived from these metrics:

Program length: $N = N1 + N2$
Program vocabulary: $n = n1 + n2$
Volume: $V = N \times (\log_2 n)$ (10.7)
Difficulty: $D = (n1/2) \times (N2/n2)$
Effort: $E = D \times V$

Lipow [29] further proposed the defect-prediction method using a software size, that is, line of executable code, L:

$$\frac{D}{L} = A_0 + A_1 \ln L + A_2 \ln^2 L,$$ (10.8)

where each of the A_i is dependent on the average number of usages of operators and operands per LOC for a particular language. For instance, $A_0 = 0.0047$, $A_1 = 0.0023$, and $A_2 = 0.000043$, for FORTRAN and $A_0 = 0.0012$, $A_1 = 0.0001$, and $A_2 = 0.000002$, for an assembly language.

Albrecht and Gaffney [30] used Lipow's data to reduce Equation 10.8 by arguing that the relationship between D and L was not language dependent:

$$D = 4.2 + 0.0015(L)^{4/3}.$$ (10.9)

This early research addressed the defect prediction from the one of most available metrics, code size, with straightforward means. However, it is realized that size-based metrics alone are poor defect predictors. This triggered the search of more discriminating complexity metrics. MCC (Equation 10.1) has been widely used in many studies.

A simpler method of computing the MCC is given by Equation 10.1, that is,

$$MCC = E \boxtimes N + X.$$

Here, decision points can be conditional statements. Each decision point normally has two paths. For a program with multiple exits (return statements), the definition is instead:

$$MCC = E \boxtimes N + X + R, \qquad (10.10)$$

where R is the number of return statements (equivalently, terminal nodes).

MCC is also useful in determining the testability of a program. Testability measures how easy/difficult it is to test a piece of code. Often, the higher the MCC value, the more difficult and risky the program is to test and maintain. Some standard values of MCC are shown in Table 10.7 [16].

Kitchenham et al. [31] examined the relationship between the changes experienced by two subsystems and a number of metrics including McCabe's complexity metric and Halstead's metrics. Two different regression equations were obtained:

$$C = 0.042 \text{ MCI} \boxtimes 0.075 \ N + 0.00001 \text{ HE} \qquad (10.11)$$

$$C = 0.25 \text{ MCI} \boxtimes 0.53 \text{ DI} + 0.09 \text{ MCC} \qquad (10.12)$$

where C is the number of changes, DI the number of static data elements accessed by a module, HE the Halstead's effort metric, MCI the machine code instructions, and N the operator and operand totals.

For the first subsystem [31], the number of changes C was found to be reasonably dependent on MCI, N, and HE. For the second subsystem, C can be partially explained by the MCC, along with the MCIs and DIs. This example shows that there does not seem to be a general formula to estimate software risks (the number of changes in this case) or at least estimating software risks with one metric or two might not be sufficient.

Besides using the size/complexity of software code to estimate software risks, the approach known as Albrecht's function points (FPs) received significant attention. FP is a standard metric for the relative size and complexity of a software system, originally developed by Alan Albrecht of IBM in the late 1970s [32]. It is believed that FPs are a better size metric than LOC; they are language independent and they get round the lack of uniformity problem. Defect density defined based on FPs can be found and empirical studies are the basis for predictive models using FPs. For

---

TABLE 10.7
Standard Values of McCabe's Cyclomatic Complexity

Cyclomatic Complexity	Risk Complexity
1–10	A simple program, without much risk
11–20	More complex, moderate risk
21–50	Complex, high risk
51+	Untestable, very high risk

TABLE 10.8
Defects per Life-Cycle Phase
Prediction Using Testing Metrics

Defect Origins	Defects per FP
Requirement	1.00
Design	1.25
Coding	1.75
Documentation	0.60
Bad fixes	0.4
Total	5.00

FP = Function Point

example, Table 10.8 reports the results of a benchmarking study on defect density based on large amounts of data from different commercial sources [33].

These software size and complexity are used to predict development efforts, number of defects, and other measures that can be used to predict software quality and risks in the early days of software development and risk management. As software and development methods evolve, more software metrics and more sophisticated methods are required to estimate software quality and risks. The next section discusses how to combine more metrics using multivariate approach, and how to predict fault-proneness with the combined metrics.

IDENTIFICATION OF FAULT-PRONE MODULE USING MULTIVARIATE APPROACH

Historically, size and complexity are two basic software metrics widely used in defect prediction. However, it is found that size and complexity metrics only become inadequate to describe the attributes of modern software. Additional metrics that describe attributes of software product and software development process are also used in software risk assessment. This section discusses these metrics and shows risk-assessment approaches that involve these metrics.

Product Metrics for Software

Some product metrics include software size, call graph, control flow, and statement metrics [34], which are defined as follows:

- *Software size metrics*: the number of NCLOC (noncomment lines of code), TLOC (total lines of code), total comments, total code character counts, and total comment character counts.
- *Call graph metrics*: the number of distinct procedure calls to others, number of second, and following calls to others.
- *Control flow graph metrics*: the number of nonconditional arcs, number of loop constructs, and number of knots. A knot in a control flow graph is where arcs across due to a violation of structured programming principles.

- *Statement metrics*: the number of control statements, number of executable statements, number of global variables, total span of variables, and maximum span of variables.
- *Object-oriented metrics*: with the development of object-oriented programming, specific object-oriented metrics are defined and studied [35,36]: the number of classes declared, number of base class inherited, number of uniquely named base classes inherited, total number of members declared, number of members declared public, number of uniquely named members, number of members declared private, number of methods declared, number of virtual methods, number of overloaded operators, and number of uniquely named overload operators.

Software Fault-Proneness

One of the activities during the coding phase is to identify fault-prone software modules. Statistical approaches such as regression analysis and factor analysis [37–45] have been used to predict software defects and to identify fault-prone modules based on these metrics. Since many software metrics are highly correlated, it is often desired to transform these metrics to variables that are not correlated and thus improve the robustness of the classification models. Principle component analysis is a technique to transform the original data-software metrics into orthogonal principal component variables, known as domain metrics. Then a multivariate modeling technique called discriminate analysis can be used to assign software module to one of two or more groups, for example, fault-prone vs. nonfault-prone groups. The assignment is carried out according to a rule that minimizes the overall probability of misclassification. For example, in Ref. [40], the following original software metrics are reported for three builds of total 261 modules for a real-time military application:

N_STMTS = number of statements
N_COM = number of comments
TOT_OPND = total operands
DIFF_OPND = different operands
TOT_OPTR = total operators
DIFF_OPTR = different operators
MCC = McCabe's complexity metrics
MAX_LVLS = maximum nesting levels
MAX_DEG = maximum degree of node
N_OUT = number of exits
N_STRUC = number of control structures
N_SEQ = number of sequential nodes
N_JUMPS = number of jumps
MAX_NODES = maximum number of nodes in a control structure
MAX_STMTS = maximum number of statements in a control structure
DRCT_CALLS = direct calls

These metrics are further transformed into five domain metrics based on principle component analysis. Each domain metric is a function of the original metrics and the five domain metrics contain a cumulative of 90.5% of variances from the original metrics, that is, significant information from the original metrics.

The discriminate analysis relates the independent variables—the domain metrics from the principal analysis to the dependent variable—group membership (fault-prone or nonfault-prone) by a discriminate function. Modules can then be assigned to either group by minimizing the probability of misclassification.

Statistical analysis techniques have been applied to correlate software quality and reliability metrics (such as the number of residual defect, defect find and fix rate, defect density, software failure rate) to these metrics. Beside regression analysis and discriminate classification, other techniques are also used, such as neural networks, factor analysis, principle component analysis, clustering analysis, and so on. Also used, but to a lesser degree, are canonical correlation analysis, nonparametric approach, and so on [37–45].

EVALUATING DEVELOPMENT PROCESS FOR RISK MANAGEMENT

It is believed that the quality of the development process can be a good indicator of software quality. A development team that follows a healthy and structured process typically produces software with less defects. This section discusses some well-known methods for verifying the health of the development processes. From these methods, unhealthy patterns of the processes can be used to identify the risky areas that are lack of quality. Software metrics such as fault density, fault introduction, and fault-removal rates can be tracked in each development phase. Well-documented data can be used to support the reliability and risk prediction in subsequent releases.

Orthogonal Defect Classification

Orthogonal Defect Classification (ODC) was invented by IBM Research [46] to provide an in-process measurement by extracting the key information from the defects pointing to the part of the process that needs attention. ODC defines a set of orthogonal classes, which can be mapped over the space of development or verification. ODC highlights inconsistent or abnormal trends of software and development process, which can then be used in risk identification and management. One of the pitfalls with the ODC method is that it is subject to the usual problems of human errors such as confusion, misclassification, and so on.

Capability Maturity Model Integration

The most popular model for software process is the five-level Capability Maturity Model® Integration (CMMI) from the Software Engineering Institute (SEI). Table 10.9 shows the quality targets for each CMMI level as hypothesized in Refs. [47,48].

However, there is no evidence that higher CMMI-level companies always deliver products with lower residual defects compared with companies with a lower CMMI level. Clearly, the strict 1–5 level ranking, as prescribed by the SEI–CMMI is too coarse to be used directly for defect prediction. But the CMMI model promotes structures for the development process improvement and therefore is definitely worthy following.

TABLE 10.9
Relationship between CMMI Levels and Delivered Defects (per KLOC)

SEI CMM Levels	Defect Potentials	Removal Efficiency (%)	Delivered Defects
1	5	85	0.75
2	4	89	0.44
3	3	91	0.27
4	2	93	0.14
5	1	95	0.05

Fault Propagation Model

The fault propagation model shown in Figure 10.5 provides a framework to track defect introduction, defect removal, and residual defect by software development phases. Such benchmark data can then be used to project defect finding and fixing rates for similar products.

The basic assumption here is that the new project is similar to the existing ones both in terms of the development team's skill levels and processes they follow. This approach also requires large and well-tracked historical data.

SOFTWARE RELIABILITY AND RISK MANAGEMENT DURING THE TESTING PHASE

In the testing phase, most of the software modules are available or integrated, and failure and recovery measurements can be taken from executing the software. Compared with the coding phase, the emphasis of risk management in the testing phase is on understanding whether most of the defected are detected and to verity whether found defects are removed, and hence the reliability growth is achieved. In

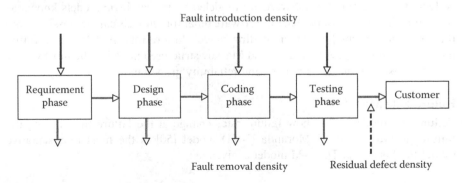

FIGURE 10.5 Fault propagation model.

the reliability and risk assessment during this phase, the following questions can be addressed:

1. How many residual defects are expected at any point in time during testing?
2. Is the software ready to be released? What is the predicted initial field failure rate?
3. How much more time/effort is needed to "ensure" targeted software reliability and stability?

In general, there are two perspectives for testing phase reliability and risk management, they are: (1) the developer perspective, and (2) the integration team's perspective. The former case reflects a "white box" situation where the testing is performed by the development team whose goal is to find and fix the last bug; while the latter represents a "black box" situation where the testing is performed by the integration teams whose goal is to verify deployability of the software. For risk management purposes, the developers need to ensure that the number of residual defects and the software failure rates are both lower than a predefined thresholds (which can be determined by historical data and/or reliability requirements from the budgeting analysis); the integration team, on the other hand, needs to verify whether the software is acceptable for deployment, what blocks the deployment, and whether the potential loss that could be incurred after deployment of the software is less than if the release is delayed to perform additional testing.

In both cases, answering the questions above involves careful collection of testing data and quantitative analyses of the data. For the developers' perspective, metrics such as the number of residual defects and predicted software failure rates need to be estimated. And for the integration perspective, the degree of readiness or deployability needs to be assessed. This section discusses the models and methods used to estimate these metrics and to assess software deployability.

SOFTWARE RELIABILITY MODELS

Since the failure occurrences and the fault removals are probabilistic events, data collected from testing the software are modeled by probabilistic models known as software reliability models. General software reliability models can be classified into the following groups [49]: error seeding model, failure rate models, curve fitting models, reliability growth models, and Markov structured models. The most widely used models are failure rate models and reliability growth models.

Failure Rate Models

Failure rate models study how failure rates change at the failure time during the failure intervals. Jelinski–Moranda (J–M) model [50] is the most representative model for this group. The J–M model is given by:

$$\boxtimes(t_i) = \boxtimes[(N \boxtimes (i \boxtimes 1)], \quad i = 1, 2, \ldots, N, \tag{10.13}$$

where $\lambda(t_i)$ is the failure rate at time t_i; ϕ a proportional constant, the contribution of any one fault makes the overall code; N the number of initial faults in the program; and t_i the time when the ith failure occurs.

The J–M model assumed that the error detection rate is proportional to the number of residual errors. This is a common assumption that most of the other SRGMs were based on. In the J–M model, though, the number of residual errors decreases exponentially. Later SRGMs relax such assumptions. Also, they consider the ensemble of products and give an average property.

Another way to look at this is that the J–M model focuses on the failure rate of a particular product [51]. In Ref. [51], the authors proposed a "product-centric" model that represents the time series of the defects as a series of step functions and the failure intensity (defect discovery rate) is given by:

$$\lambda(t) = [N - n(t)]B, \tag{10.14}$$

where N is a finite number of defects; B the mean of exponential distribution that describes the interdiscovery time; $n(t)$ the expected number of defects $n(t) = m$ that satisfies

$$\frac{1}{B} \sum_{j=0}^{m-1} \frac{1}{N-j} \le t \le \frac{1}{B} \sum_{j=0}^{m} \frac{1}{N-j}, \quad \text{for } m = 0, 1, N;$$

and $\lambda(t)$ the failure intensity.

The parameters in the product-centric model are interrelated with the process model, for example, the Musa basic model. That is, $E(N) = v_0$ and $E(B) = \lambda_0/v_0$.

Also a failure rate model that follows the S-curve of reliability/fault discovery is available in Ref. [52]:

$$\lambda(t) = [N - n(t)] \frac{\mathrm{d}^2 n(t)}{1 + \mathrm{d}n(t)} + f, \tag{10.15}$$

where $\lambda^2 n(t)/1 + \lambda n(t)$ is the functional form of a Gamma distribution with a shape factor of 2 that add S-shape to account for "speed up" of the discovery rate. The rest of the notations are the same as those in the product-centric model.

Software Reliability Growth Models

The most widely used class of SRGMs models the software debugging process as a stochastic process and hence they are "process-oriented" models. For example, the most popular group of SRGMs assumes that the fault discovery process follows a non-homogenous Poisson process (NHPP), that is, the mean of the Poisson process is not a constant, but a function of time. In this chapter, the term "fault" is used to mean a bug in the software and the term "failure" to mean the realization by a user of a fault.

Let $N(t)$ denotes the cumulative number of software failures at time t. The counting process $\{N(t), t \le 0\}$ is said to be a nonhomogeneous Poisson process with intensity function $\boxtimes(t)$, $t \le 0$, if $N(t)$ follows a Poisson distribution with mean value function (MVF) $m(t)$, that is,

$$\Pr\{N(t) = k\} = \frac{[m(t)]^k}{k!} e^{-m(t)}, \quad k = 0, 1, 2, \quad , \tag{10.16}$$

where $m(t) = E[N(t)]$ is the expected number of cumulative failures, which is also known as the MVF. Software reliability $R(x/t)$ is defined as the probability that a software failure does not occur in $(t, t + x)$, given that the last failure occurred at testing time $t (t \le 0, x < 0)$. That is,

$$R(x/t) = e^{\boxtimes[m(t+x)\boxtimes m(t)]}. \tag{10.17}$$

For special cases, when $t = 0$ then $R(x/0) = e^{\boxtimes m(x)}$ and $t = \infty$ then $R(x/\infty) = 1$.

NHPP models assume that the failure intensity is proportional to the residual fault content. A general class of NHPP SRGMs can be obtained by solving the following differential equation:

$$\mathsf{I}(t) = \frac{dm(t)}{dt} = b(t)[(a(t) - m(t)]. \tag{10.18}$$

The general solution of the differential equation 10.18 is given in Refs. [53,54]:

$$m(t) = e^{-B(t)} \left[m_0 + \int_{t_0}^t a(t)b(t)e^{B(t)} \, dt \right], \tag{10.19}$$

where $B(t) = \int_0^t b(\boxtimes) \, d\boxtimes$ and $m(t_0) = m_0$ is the marginal condition of Equation 10.19 with t_0 representing the starting time of the debugging process.

The simplest NHPP proposed by Goel and Okumoto (GO) [55] has a MVF as follows:

$$m(t) = a(1 \boxtimes e^{\boxtimes bt}). \tag{10.20}$$

The GO model is one of the earliest but widely used model with $a(t) = a$ and $b(t) = b$. A constant $a(t)$ estimates the total number of inherent defects. A constant $b(t)$ implies that the failure intensity function ($\boxtimes(t)$) is proportional to the number of remaining faults. Here, a denotes the expected number of faults in the software at $t = 0$ and b represents the average failure rate of an individual fault. The GO model remains popular today [24,56,57].

John Musa [58] proposed a similar model with emphasis on failures and failure process, which is known as the Musa Basic Model:

$$m(t) = n_0 \left[1 - e^{-\frac{\boxtimes_0}{n_0} t} \right], \tag{10.21}$$

where $\boxtimes(t)$ is the expected number of failures at time t, v_0 the total number of failures; and $\boxtimes_0$ the initial failure rate at time $t = 0$.

Many existing NHPP models can be considered as a special case of the general model in Equation 10.19. They have different MVFs based on different assumptions of the total fault function, $a(t)$, and the defect detection function, $b(t)$. An increasing $a(t)$ function implies an increasing total number of faults (note that this includes those already detected and removed and those inserted during the debugging process) and reflects imperfect debugging. A time-dependent $b(t)$ implies an increasing fault-detection rate, which could be either attributed to a learning curve phenomenon [59,60], or to software process fluctuations [61], or a combination of both. This group of models with time-dependent fault-detection function is also referred to as "S-shaped" model since the fault-detection function captures the delay at the beginning due to learning.

In summary, according to the patterns of their MVFs, the NHPP models are typically classified as: (1) the concave models and (2) the S-shaped models. The concave model depicts the defect debugging process naturally, that is, the defects found cumulates as testing process continues and the cumulative number of defects grows at a slower slop and eventually approaches the asymptote as the software behave stably. The S-shaped curve, on the other hand, indicates a slower defect-detection rate at the beginning of the debugging process. Then the detected defects cumulate at a steeper slope as testing continues and eventually the cumulative defect curve approaches asymptote. Appropriate models are selected based on the pattern of their MVFs and the model that gives the best fit is determined. Table 10.10 summarizes some widely used NHPP SRGMs and their MVFs.

References [66–81] documented more detailed information about software reliability models, such as imperfect debugging, fault introduction while removing existing faults, fault detection and fault-removal processes, and so on.

The most important application of SRGMs from the developer perspective is to analyze the stability of the software under testing and to predict the initial field failure rate of software and the number of the residual (unknown) defects as it exits a test interval. Software risks can be assessed from these metrics. Using SRGMs to dictate how much additional test time is required to "ensure" the failure rate is below a specified threshold and the number of residual defects are less than a target level when it is released is less common. This failure rate and additional testing information are provided to the product teams to support the "when to stop testing" decision. Additional factors such as the availability of testing resources and the timing of product market windows play into the decision as to what is an acceptable release date.

In addition to qualitative estimating software failure rates and the number of residual defects, SRGM offers a quantitative, easy-to-understand comparison of releases by overlaying multiple releases onto a single chart, for example, consider Figure 10.6. The diamonds give the fitted SRGM curve for the first major release of a particular product; the squares give the fitted curve of the second major release. Even though the second release was tested more than the first release, the testers clearly had to work harder to find fewer stability-impacting defects; this suggests a significant software reliability growth from the first release to the second release.

TABLE 10.10
Summary of the NHPP Software Reliability Models

Model Name	Model Type	MVF ($m(t)$)	Comments
GO [55]	Concave	$m(t) = a(1 - e^{-bt})$ $a(t) = a$ $b(t) = b$	Also called exponential model or Musa Basic Model [58]
Delayed S-shaped [62]	S-shaped	$m(t) = a(1 - (1 + bt)e^{-bt})$	Modification of G–O model to make it S-shaped
Inflection S-shaped SRGM [63]	Concave	$m(t) = \dfrac{a(1 - e^{-bt})}{1 + \beta e^{-bt}}$ $a(t) = a$ $b(t) = \dfrac{b}{1 + \beta e^{-bt}}$	Solves a technical condition with the G–O model. Becomes the same as G–O if $\beta = 0$
Yamada exponential [64]	Concave	$m(t) = a(1 - e^{-r\alpha(1 - e^{-\beta t})})$ $a(t) = a$ $b(t) = r\alpha\beta\, e^{-\beta t}$	Attempt to account for testing-effort
Yamada Rayleigh [64]	S-shaped	$m(t) = a(1 - e^{-r\alpha(1 - e^{-\beta t^2/2})})$ $a(t) = a$ $b(t) = r\alpha\beta t\, e^{-\beta t^2/2}$	Attempt to account for testing-effort (learning effect)
Yamada imperfect debugging model (1) [60]	S-shaped	$m(t) = \dfrac{ab}{\alpha + b}(e^{\alpha t} - e^{-bt})$ $a(t) = a\, e^{\alpha t}$ $b(t) = b$	Assume exponential fault content function and constant fault-detection rate
Yamada imperfect debugging model (2) [60]	S-shaped	$m(t) = a[1 - e^{-bt}]\left[1 - \dfrac{\alpha}{b}\right] + \alpha at$ $a(t) = a(1 + \alpha t)$ $b(t) = b$	Assume constant introduction rate α and the fault-detection rate
Pham–Zhang model [54]	S-shaped and concave	$m(t) = \dfrac{1}{(1 + \beta e^{-bt})}[(c + a)(1 - e^{-bt})]$ $\quad - \dfrac{ab}{b - \alpha}(e^{-\alpha t} - e^{-bt})]$ $a(t) = c + a(1 - e^{-\alpha t})$ $b(t) = \dfrac{b}{1 + \beta e^{-bt}}$	Assume introduction rate is exponential function of the testing time, and the fault-detection rate is nondecreasing with an inflexion S-shaped model. This model has the flexibility to fit most data sets, but it is better used in cases with more data points (due to more model parameters)
Product-centric model [61]	Concave	$\lambda(t) = [N - n(t)]B,$ $\dfrac{1}{B}\displaystyle\sum_{j=0}^{m-1}\dfrac{1}{N - j} \le t \le \dfrac{1}{B}\displaystyle\sum_{j=0}^{m}\dfrac{1}{N - j}$	Represents the time series of the defects as a series of step functions
Integrated model [52]	S-shaped	$\lambda(t) = [N - n(t)]\dfrac{d^2 n(t)}{1 + dn(t)} + f$	Based on product-centric model with modifications borrowed from Yamada S-shaped model [60]

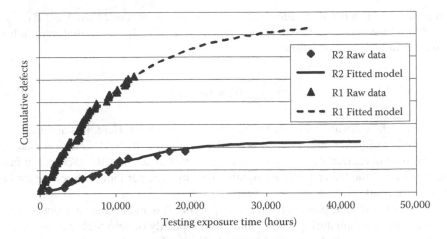

FIGURE 10.6   Software reliability growth for two releases R1 and R2.

System Test Phase Risk Assessment

As explained earlier, the risk assessment and management during the testing phase centers around the following areas:

1. Is the expected number of residual defects lower than the threshold? Is the predicted initial field failure rate lower than the threshold? The threshold is typically determined from historical data, standards, and reliability requirements derived from architecture based models and budgeting activities.
2. If the software is not yet ready to be released, how much more testing is needed to meet the exit criteria? What is the risk mitigation plan? This often includes activities such as increasing testing time, modifying testing plans, and so on.
3. Can the customer reliability requirements be met? This can often be carried out by estimating software failure rate (from SRGMs) and other fault coverage and failure recovery metrics from the testing data, and feeding the new estimates back to the architecture-based models to update the availability prediction.
4. What are the problematic features and blocking issues? Rank the software modules according to their failure rates and number of residual defects and identify the high-risk software modules and features. It is often found that a big portion of the software defects are condensed in a limited number of features/modules. The blocking modules and features typically deserve more attention.

Predicting Software Failure Rate and Residual Defects

Assume the GO model is selected to analyze the testing data, and the number of residual defects and the average failure rate of a fault are combined by the end of the testing interval. The number of residual defects is $\hat{\bar{a}}(T) = \hat{a}(\infty) \boxtimes \hat{m}(T) = \hat{a} \boxtimes \hat{a}(1 \boxtimes e^{\boxtimes \hat{b} T}) = \hat{a} \, e^{\boxtimes \hat{b} T}$ and the average failure rate of a fault is $\hat{b}$ [24,57,82]. The initial field failure rate can be predicted as follows:

$$\hat{l}_{\text{ini.field}}(t) = \left(\hat{a}(T)\right) \hat{\bar{b}}, \tag{10.22}$$

where t is the software exposure time in the field operation. Here, it is assumed that the number of total initial faults in the software during the field operation matches the number of residual defects from the testing environment and the average per fault failure rate of the field operations equals to the average per fault failure rate during testing interval.

Actually, the first practical issue on applying this method is that the average failure rate of a fault during testing interval is typically (much) higher than average failure rate of a fault during field interval. This is due to the mismatch of the test environment and the field environment, which can be explained by the following reasons:

1. During the testing phase, testers intentionally try to break the software and find the defects. In this sense, software testing is more aggressive and hence yields a much higher defect detection rate.
2. In the field, the users are using the software for their functionalities, and hence the field operation is much less aggressive.
3. Most of the software defects are detected and removed at the end of the testing interval and the remaining defects are significantly less to trigger failures in the field.

Therefore, calibration factors are proposed to adjust the average per fault failure rate from testing data to prediction field failure rates [24,57,65,82]. Equation 10.22 can be adjusted as:

$$\hat{l}_{\text{ini.field}}(t) = \hat{\bar{a}}(T) \frac{\hat{b}}{K}, \tag{10.23}$$

where K is the calibration factor.

For products with earlier releases in the field, the calibration factor is best estimated by comparing the observed failure rate during the testing of the previous release(s) against the field failure rate for that same release [24,52,60]. To assess whether adjustments are necessary, a likelihood ratio test can be carried out to verify whether the calibration factor between the test and field failure rates is unity [65]. For the first release of a product, a calibration factor can be borrowed from similar products, or a sensitivity analysis can be carried out to produce the upper and lower bounds of failure rates.

The second practical issue in the field failure rate prediction is noninstantaneous defect-removal time. Most SRGMs focus on defect detection and they assume fault removal is instantaneous and software reliability growth can be achieved after software defects are detected. In practice, it takes a significant amount of time to remove defects, in particular to remove the defects detected during the field operation. The fault-removal time is considered by incorporating the mean time to remove a fault into the SRGM [57].

The third practical issue is deferral of defect fixes. In real applications, not all detected defects are fixed before the software is released. Fixes of some defects might be deferred to the next release for various reasons, for example, some defects will be removed as part of a new feature introduction, and so on.

The following equation is proposed to incorporate the three realistic issues into prediction of the initial field failure rate:

$$\hat{\lambda}_{field}(t) = (\hat{a}(T)) \cdot \left[\hat{q} \cdot \frac{\hat{b}}{K} + (1 - q)\frac{\hat{b}}{K} e^{-\frac{\hat{b}/K}{(1+nm\hat{b}/K)}t} \right] \qquad (10.24)$$

where T is the system test exposure time; a the expected number of initial faults in the software at the beginning of test interval; for some NHPP models, $a(t)$ is reduced to a constant a; $\bar{a}(T)$ the expected number of residual faults in software at the end of system test; q the percentage of the defects that are fixed before deployment; $(1 - q)$ the percentage of the defects whose fixes are deferred; b the average failure rate of a fault in the test environment; K the calibration factor that relates the average failure rate of a fault in a test environment to the average failure rate of a fault in a field environment; n the number of systems that will be deployed in the field; m the average fault-removal time; and ^ denotes maximum likelihood estimate.

So the first term in Equation 10.24 corresponds to a constant failure rate and the second term of the growth failure rate assuming that defects detected during the field will be fixed with an average fault-removal time of m.

So far, we discussed about how to obtain the point estimates of the two metrics— the number of initial defects and the initial field failure rate. The variances and the confidence intervals (upper and lower bounds) of the point estimates can also be calculated [59,67]. Also, the estimation of parameter and calibration factors for other SRGMs can be carried out with similar approaches; Refs. [24,57,65,82] documented the theoretic developments and real-world examples of these approaches.

SRGMs can be carried out to the software modules if enough data are collected on the specific modules (usually the major ones). Or the overall software failure rate can be factored into component failure rates, which can be often inputs to the availability model to update software reliability prediction and risk assessment.

Assessing Deployability

In this section, we explain how software readiness can be estimated from a system's integrator. References [51,52,84] defined a metric called "deployability" and compared the likelihood of the product-centric model with that of the Poisson model with a constant mean when using both models to fit the same set of testing data.

In Ref. [51] for example, m defects were defected during the system test, the likelihood of the Poisson model with a constant mean is given by:

$$\ln L_0(t_1, t_2, \ldots, t_m) = m\ln(l) - l\,t. \tag{10.25}$$

The likelihood of the product-centric model is given by:

$$\ln L_1(t_1, t_2, \ldots, t_m) = n(t)\ln B + \sum_{j=0}^{n(t)-1}\ln(N - j) - B\sum_{i=1}^{n(t)} t_i - [N - n(t)]Bt. \tag{10.26}$$

The deployability is defined as the logarithm of the ratio of the likelihood function of the product-centric model to the likelihood function of the Poisson model:

$$g_m = \frac{L_1(t_1, \ldots, t_m)}{L_0(t_1, \ldots, t_m)}. \tag{10.27}$$

If $\boxtimes_m < 20$ or $\ln\boxtimes_m < 3$, the product is deployable, since the time series of the defect data has departed the linear phase [51].

If the software lacks the adequate level of stability and deployability, recovery plans need to be considered and put into place, such testing plans might need to be revisited, unstable areas need to be exposed to longer testing hours or more combinations of stress/performance configurations, and so on.

FIELD DATA FOR SOFTWARE RELIABILITY AND RISK MANAGEMENT

Field data analysis is critical to understand the reliability of the software since no matter how closely developers try to mimic the field operation environment in their labs, there are always problems associated with the mismatch of the two environments. There are typically two phases of the field operation: controlled introduction (CI) and massive field operation in the users' networks. This section discusses software reliability and risk management activities for both phases.

CONTROLLED INTRODUCTION

CI refers to an early phase of software field deployment in which the software product is deployed in a carefully chosen number of sites at a limited time [83]. Since the CI environment is actually very close to the field operation environment, it often uncovers defects that may be slipped through developers' system test, for example, defects due to repeated operation, defects due to interactions among multiple units, defects associated with high transaction/traffic loads, and so on.

The analysis of the CI data helps determine whether the software is ready to massive deployment. Sherif et al. [84] presented a risk assessment procedure for CI that consists of two steps: (1) estimate the total defects and software failure rates (prior failure rate based on Bayesian terminology) from system test data and calculate the deployability; and (2) analyze the data collected from the CI phase and calculate the failure rate (posterior failure rate) based on the prior failure rate and the CI data to confirm the prior belief that the product is ready to be deployed.

A loss function is proposed to estimate the expected gain from continuing the CI phase for a certain amount of time. The loss function, L, is defined in terms of the field failure rate estimated from system test data and the data collected from CI [84]:

$$L(\lambda ,\text{CIdata}) = d \int_{\lambda_U}^{\infty} 10^4 (\lambda - \lambda_U)\, \text{posterior}(\lambda /\text{CIdata})\, d\lambda, \tag{10.28}$$

where λ is the initial field failure rate predicted from system test data; x the number of failures during T time units of CI execution; and λ_U the failure rate threshold.

The expected gain from continuing the CI phase for Δt time units is [84]:

$$E[G(\Delta t, \lambda, \text{CIdata})] = L(\lambda, \text{data}) - L\{\lambda, [\text{data} + E(\text{data}/\Delta t)]\}, \tag{10.29}$$

where $E(\text{data}/\Delta t)$ represents the expected data after Δt given the current field failure rate of λ. Sherif et al. [84] showed some examples of using this method to analyze the CI data and correlated with the system test data analysis.

This section illustrated some methods and procedures to verify software readiness for general deployment into real networks. A Bayesian approach is used to correlate the data from the system test and the data from CI phase, which overcomes the lack of well-defined operational profiles and technology complexities. The results can be interpreted to determine whether the product can be safely deployed.

Massive Field Operation

After the software is released to the customers, software system suppliers and their customers generally keep maintenance records—often called trouble tickets—for all manual emergency and nonemergency recoveries, and often at least some automatic recoveries. Records often capture the details such as: date and time of outage event, outage extent, such as number of impacted subscribers or percentage of capacity lost, outage duration, typically resolved to minutes or seconds, and so on. Another piece of useful information is the deployment information, such as how many systems/software copied are deployed and the time they are installed and put to service. The deployment data and the outage data can provide a lot of useful insights on software/system failure rates, outage duration, availability, and so on.

Analyzing these trouble tickets typically reveals the actual field reliability and performance of the software and highlights areas for reliability and risk management improvement, which is a good feedback to the development of the next release or product generic. This section explains how to analyze the customer outage data to estimate important software reliability and risk metrics. Moreover, a close-loop software reliability and risk management framework needs to be established to achieve continuous improvement of reliability and risk management.

METRICS ESTIMATED FROM FIELD OUTAGE DATA

This sections discuss the key reliability and risk metrics that can be estimate from field data.

Exposure Time

Exposure time of systems in-service is measured in system-years. Operationally, one typically calculates this on a monthly basis by summing across the number of elements in-service in a particular month time with the number of days in that month. If this is combined with software releases to perform an outage analysis on software releases, information such as "installed date" and "service start date" and "uninstalled date" need to be verified and implemented into the exposure time calculations.

Outage Rates

Outage rates are not prorated by capacity loss, and they are estimated by the ratios of number of outage occurrences over the exposure time—system-years.

One should separately compute hardware, software, and procedural outage rates. Optionally, one can compute outage rates for secondary categories (e.g., the functionality of the software). If the data size is large enough, one can estimate software outage rates on the software module level (or at least for the modules that are highly service-impacting).

It is often insightful to compare outage rates for hardware, software, and procedural causes; what percent of outages are coming from each category? Comparing the outage rates across software modules (hardware components) is helpful in identifying the highly risky software modules and hardware components. Tracking the outage rates on a regular time basis is critical in learning the trend of software reliability and verifying software maturity and potential risk.

Outage Duration

Outage durations typically have large variance due to difference in failure modes and detection and recovery situations. Rather than averaging the brief, typical events with the extraordinary cases, it is recommended using the more robust median value of manually recovered outage duration. In contrast, the mean value (average) of manually recovered outage durations is often rather pessimistic because some portion of the long duration outages may have been deliberately parked and resolved on a nonemergency basis. Outage duration distribution should be studied to learn more details of the outage recovery patterns. Outage durations can be tracked on a periodic base to verify the trend of outage detection and recovery capabilities. This can help to identify risks in software fault detection and recovery area. Are the current fault-detection mechanisms sufficient in detecting and reporting failures? Can failures be isolated and diagnosed quickly and accurately? Are the current recovery mechanisms sufficient in delivering fast remedies when failures occur?

Availability

The availability can be derived from dividing prorated outage durations by the total in-service time; mathematically, this is given by:

$$A_k = 1 - \frac{\sum_k \sum_i T_{ki} \cdot P_{ki}}{\sum_j S_j}, \qquad (10.30)$$

where A_k represents the availability for the kth category. The categories can be hardware, software, procedural, and so on. T_{ki} represents the ith outage duration in the kth category, P_{ki} represents the percentage of capacity loss for the ith outage in the kth category and S_j is the service time for the jth system.

The annualized downtime is generally the easiest availability-related number to work with because it is easy to understand, budget, and consider "what-if" scenarios with. One should estimate annualized downtime for different outage categories separately, as well as overall product-attributable downtime. Like the outage rates, the availabilities should be tracked on a regular time basis for trend analysis and risk management.

Coverage Factor

Estimating coverage factor from the field data is limited by the fact that typically detected and automatically recovered failures are either not recorded or not clearly indicated. Zhang et al. [84] proposed a method to estimate coverage factor by categorizing the outages according to their impact. Instead of describing the system failures as detected and undetected failures, the authors considered critical and major failures that are not outage-inducing and failures that are outage-inducing. A high-level three-node Markov model describes the state diagram for this way of system failure description. Since the system availability and other parameters (except the coverage factor) can be estimated from the field data (including the overall system downtime), one can obtain an estimate for the coverage factor by solving the Markov model to match the equivalent downtime estimated from the field data. The solution to this Markov model estimates the lower bound for the system-level coverage factor. This provides more realistic means to verify whether the system has sufficient fault-detection capabilities.

BUILDING RELIABILITY ROADMAPS AND RISK MITIGATION PLAN

If the reliability evaluation shows that the product's or system's availability does not meet expectations, a reliability roadmap should be drawn so that the gap could be closed. Key elements of a reliability roadmap are as follows:

1. Explicitly specifies the "ultimate" quantitative system reliability/availability goal(s) and definition (e.g., product-attributable total plus prorated partial service availability for one or more specific system configurations).

2. Availability estimate of current release and previous releases when applicable.
3. Per-release availability targets: actual reliability growth often follows an exponential curve. Setting release-by-release targets provides a measurable way to drive software reliability improvement.
4. Enumerate specific reliability-improving features: features that improve fault coverage, lower failure rates and shorten failure detection and recovery times should be planned at least for some releases. Natural software growth is typically not enough to drive reliability improvement and mitigate risks.
5. Quantify both planned availability-improving features and other product features in reliability evaluation and prediction. Recognizing that complex, new features often initially increase failure rates and may slow failure detection and recovery and the expected reliability growth that occurs as defects are found, debugged, and removed from the product.
6. Per-release availability budgets to plausibly close the gap between current release performance and specific availability goal in target release.

As field data for additional releases become available, failure rates and other reliability parameters are recalibrated, predictions for future releases are recalculated, and business leaders decide if any changes in to the reliability roadmap are appropriate.

SUMMARY

This section summarizes the strategies for applying software reliability and risk management techniques presented in the earlier sections of this chapter. Figure 10.7 illustrates the software reliability and risk management activities during the development life cycle.

The major development-phase activities are reviewed below.

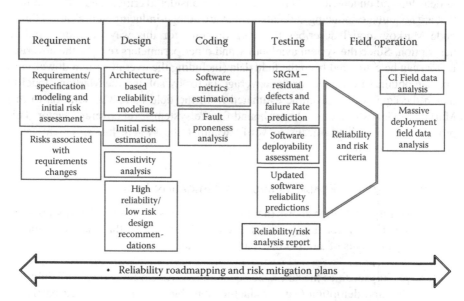

FIGURE 10.7   Overview of reliability risk management activities in product life cycle.

REQUIREMENT PHASE ACTIVITIES

Requirement/specification modeling. Model and analyze software specifications and requirements using graphical tools/models, and estimate risks from quantifying the potential probabilities failures/conflicts (failure) and their impacts (severity). Requirement changes shall be analyzed to identify risk factors.

Establish reliability/availability requirements. If setting clear requirements based on reliability modeling and budgeting and improves their traceability and testability.

DESIGN PHASE ACTIVITIES

Architecture-based reliability models. Mathematical models should be developed to both assure that the architectural reliability techniques chosen are sufficient to meet the reliability requirements and that the quantitative system performance characteristics like switchover and recovery times, failure rates, and coverage factors are taken into account. Architecture-based models also establish a framework to incorporate updated information from a later development phase to update the reliability prediction and risk assessment.

Initial risk estimation. Based on the reliability/availability models, identify risk items and estimate risks; that is, are the reliability requirements achievable based on the underlying designs? What are potential factors that might cause reliability risks? Are the high level reliability and risk plans for coding and testing phases established? Are they targeted to address the potential risks?

Sensitivity analysis. Sensitivity analyses rank the parameters according to their impacts on reliability/availability, and hence identify the most cost-effective ways to achieve high reliability/availability. Sensitivity analysis also helps prioritize features and plan the improvement across multiple releases.

High reliability/low-risk recommendations. At the end of the design phase, recommendations that improve reliability and lower risks should be provided to the development team.

CODING PHASE ACTIVITIES

Software metrics estimation. Software metrics such as software size, complexity, and defect density are estimated. They can be used to estimate software failure rates and quantify reliability risks such as the number of potential defects and other schedule and effort-related defects, and so on.

Fault-proneness analysis. Software metrics such as flow metrics, statement metrics, and language-specific metrics can be used to perform fault-proneness analysis via statistical methods, such as multivariate analysis, principle component analysis, factor analysis, and so on. Fault-prone modules are identified, and detailed verification methods, such as code inspections and tests, can be planned to reduce risks.

Evaluate development processes. The healthiness of the development process can be a good indicator of software reliability and risks. Methods such as ODC, CMMI, and fault propagation model are well-known methods for development process evaluation and risk management.

TESTING PHASE ACTIVITIES

In the testing phase, SRGMs should be performed to estimate number of residual defects and software failure rates.

Software readiness assessment. SRGM and deployability-assessment methods should be used to assess whether software stability is achieved and hence software is ready to be released. Are there any abnormal and risky patterns in terms of the number of residual defects and failure rates? Does the deployability indicate the time series of the defect data has departed from the linear phase? Should additional testing be done to verify certain areas/modules?

Software reliability prediction. Software recovery times and fault coverage should be estimated from the testing data and results. These metrics and the software failure rate estimated using SRGM should be fed back to the architecture-based model to update software reliability predictions from which reliability risk should be assessed. Can the updated software reliability (including availability) meet the reliability requirements?

Reliability and risk analysis report. It is recommended that reliability and risk analysis reports are documented for further evaluations and future improvements.

FIELD OPERATION PHASE ACTIVITIES

Controlled introduction. Data shall be collected from the CI phase and they should be analyzed to correlate with the failure rates and the number of residual defects estimated from the system test data. The results should be interpreted to determine whether the correlation confirms the prior belief that the product can be safely deployed. The data can also support the estimation of the expected gain if the CI phase is to be carried out for a certain amount of time.

Massive field operation. Field data are collected and analyzed to estimate field outage rates, outage duration, and reliability/availability. The field data analysis should be compared and correlated with pre-release predictions and updated to establish the close-loop evaluation framework. The field data analysis should also contribute to the reliability roadmap and risk mitigation plans for future improvement.

Reliability roadmapping and risk mitigation plan. If there is a gap between actual field performance and requirements, then a release-by-release roadmap of reliability/availability-improving feature and testing investments can be constructed and executed.

REFERENCES

1. Ropponen, J. and K. Lyytinen, Components of software development risk: How to address them? A project manager survey, *IEEE Trans. Softw. Eng.*, 26(2), 98–112, 2000.
2. Barki, H., Rivard, S., and Talbot, J., Toward an assessment of software development risk, *J. Manage Inform. Syst.*, 10(2), 203–225,1993.
3. Boehm, B.W., Improving software productivity, *IEEE Comput.*, 20(9), 43–57, 1987.
4. Boehm, B.W., Software risk management: principles and practices, *IEEE Softw.*, 8(1), 32–41, 1991.

5. Beynon-Davis, P., Information systems "failure" and risk assessment: The case of London ambulance service computer aided despatch system, *Proceedings of the Third European Conference on Information Systems*, Athens, Greece, 1153–1170, 1995.
6. Charette, R.N., *Software Engineering Risk Analysis and Management*, Intertext Publications, McGraw-Hill Book Co., New York, 1999, Chap. 6.
7. Fairley, R., Risk management for software projects, *IEEE Softw.*, 11(3), 57–67, 1994.
8. Griffith, M., and Newman, Eds., M., *J. Inform. Technol.*, 12(4), 1996, special issue on software development risk management.
9. Karolak, D.W., *Software Engineering and Risk Management*, IEEE Computer Science Press, Los Alamitos, CA, 1996, Chaps. 4 and 6.
10. Keil, M. et al., Against All Odds: A New Framework for Identifying and Managing Software Project Risks, *Comm. ACM*, 41(11), 77–83, 1998.
11. Lyytinen, K., Mathiassen, L., and Popponen, J., A framework for software risk management, *J. Inform. Technol.*, 11(4), 275–285, 1996.
12. Willcocks, L., and Margetts, H., Risk assessment and information systems, *Eur. J. Inform. Syst.*, 3(2), 127–138, 1994.
13. Chittister, C. and Haimes, Y.Y., Risk associated with software development: A holistic framework for assessment and management, *IEEE Trans.Syst., Man, Cybern.*, 23(3), 710–723, 1993.
14. FMECA website, http://www.fmeca.com
15. Ammar, H.H., Nikzadeh, T., and Dugan, J.B., Risk assessment of software-system specifications, *IEEE Trans. Reliab.*, 50(2),171–183, 2001.
16. Palmer, J.D. and Evans, R.P., Software risk management: requirements-based risk metrics, *Proceedings of the 1994 IEEE International Conference on System, Man, and Cybernetics*, San Antanio, TX, Vol. 1, 836–841, 1994.
17. Appukkutty, K., Ammar, H.H., and Postajanova, K.G., Software requirement risk assessment using UML, *Proceeding of the 3rd ACS/IEEE International Conference on Computer Systems and Applications*, Cario, Egypt, 112, 2005.
18. McCabe, T.A., Complexity measure, *IEEE Trans. Softw. Eng.*, 2(4), 308–320, 1976.
19. Design with CPN, available at http://www.daimi.au.dk/designCPN/
20. Schneidewind, N. F., Investigation of the risk to software reliability and maintainability of requirements changes, *Proceedings of the. IEEE International Conference on Software Maintenance*, Florence, Italy, 127–136, 2001.
21. Schneidewind, N. F., Predicting risk as a function of risk factors, *Proceedings of the 29th Annual IEEE/NASA Software Engineering Workshop*, Washington, DC, 131–141, 2005.
22. *TL9000's Quality Measurement Systems Handbook*, v4.0, available at http://aww.usa.alcatel.com/dept/quality/tl9000/books/measurements.pdf
23. Trivedi, K., *Probability and Statistics with Reliability, Queueing, and Computer Science Applications*, 2nd edn., John Wiley & Sons, New York, 2001, Chap. 8.
24. Jeske, D.R. and Zhang, X., Some successful approaches to software reliability modeling in industry, *J. Syst. Softw.*, 74(1), 85–99, 2005.
25. Wang, W., Architecture-based software reliability modeling, Ph.D. thesis in Computer Science Department, University at Albany, State University of New York, 2002.
26. Gokhale, S. et al., Reliability prediction and sensitivity analysis based on software architecture, *Proceedings of the 13th International Symposium on Software Reliability Engineering*, Annapolis, MD, 64–75, 2002.
27. Akiyama, F., An example of software system debugging, *Proceedings of the International Federation of Information Processing Societies Congress*, Ljubljana, Yugoslavia, Vol. 71, 353–379, 1976.
28. Halstead, M.H., *Elements of Software Science*, Elsevier, New York, 1975.
29. Lipow, M., Number of faults per line of code, *IEEE Trans. Softw. Eng.*, 8(4), 437–439, 1982.

30. Albrecht, A.J. and Gaffney, J.E., Software function, source lines of code, and development effort prediction: a software science validation, *IEEE Trans. Softw. Eng.*, 10(4), 639–648, 1983.
31. Kitchenham, B.A., Pickard, L.M., and Linkman, S.J., An evaluation of some design metrics, *Softw. Eng. J.*, 5(1), 50–58, 1990.
32. International Function Point Users Group (IFPUG), available at http://www.ifpug.org, last accessed on July 11, 2009.
33. Jones, C., *Applied Software Measurements*, McGraw Hill, New York, 1991, Chaps. 3 and 6.
34. Khoshgoftaar, T.M. et al., Classification-tree models of software–quality over multiple releases, *IEEE Trans. Reliab.*, 49(1), 4–11, 2000.
35. Szabo, R. and Koshgoftaar, T., An assessment of software quality in a C++ environment, *Proceedings of the 9th International Symposium on Software Reliability Engineering*, Padeborn, Germany, 240–249, 1998.
36. Briand, L.C. et al., Predicting fault-prone classes with design measures in object-oriented systems, *Proceedings of the 9th International Symposium on Software Reliability Engineering*, Padeborn, Germany, 344–353, 1998.
37. Khoshgoftaar, T. and Munson, J.C., Predicting software development errors using complexity metrics, *IEEE J. Select. Areas Comm.*, 8(2), 253–261, 1990.
38. Munson, J.C. and Koshgoftaar, T., Detection of fault-prone programming, *IEEE Trans. Softw. Eng.*, 18(5), 24–33,1992.
39. Khoshgoftaar, T. et al., Predictive modeling techniques of software quality from software measures, *IEEE Trans. Softw. Eng.*, 18(11), 979–987, 1992.
40. Khoshgoftaar, T. et al., Detection of Faultprone software modules during a spiral life cycle, *Proceedings of the International Conference on Software Maintenance*, Monterey, CA, 69–76, 1996.
41. Khoshgoftaar, T. et al., Early quality prediction: A case study in telecommunications, *IEEE Softw.*, 13(1), 65–71, 1996.
42. Gao, K. and Khoshgoftaar, T., A comprehensive empirical study of count models for software fault prediction, *IEEE Trans. Reliab.*, 56(2), 223–236, 2007.
43. Neumann, D.E., An enhanced neural network technique for software risk analysis, *IEEE Trans. Softw. Eng.*, 28(9), 904–912, 2002.
44. Ohlsson, N. and Alberg, H., Predicting fault-prone software modules in telephone switches, *IEEE Trans. Softw. Eng.*, 22(12), 886–894, 1996.
45. Zhong, S., Khoshgoftaar, T.M., and Seliya, N., Analyzing software measurement data with clustering techniques, *IEEE Intell. Syst. Appl.*, 19(2), 20–27, 2004.
46. The ODC Method, available at http://www.research.ibm.com/softeng/ODC/ODC.HTM
47. Jones, C., The pragmatics of software process improvements, *Softw. Eng. Technical Council Newslett.*, *Technical Council Softw. Eng.*, IEEE Computer Society, 14(2), 1996.
48. CMMI, available at http://www.sei.cmu.edu/str/descriptions/cyclomatic_body.html
49. Pham, H., *Software Reliability*, Springer, Singapore, 2000, Chaps. 4 and 5.
50. Jelinski, Z. and Moranda, P.B., Software reliability research, in *Statistical Computer Performance Evaluation*, Freiberger, W., Ed., Acadamic Press, New York, 465–484, 1972.
51. Sherif, M. H., Hoeflin, D., and Recchia, M., Reliability assessment of network elements using black box testing, *Proceedings of the 7th IEEE Symposium on Computers and Communications ISCC2002*, Taormina-Giardini Naxos, Italy, 1015–1120, 2002.
52. Hoeflin, D. and Sherif, M.H., An integrated defect tracking model for product deployment in telecom services, *Proceedings of the 10th IEEE Symposium on Computers and Communications ISCC2005*, Cartagena, Murcia, Spain, 927–932, 2005.
53. Pham, H., Nordmann, L., and Zhang, X., A general imperfect software debugging model with s-shaped fault detection rate, *IEEE Trans. Reliab.*, 48(2), 169–175, 1999.

54. Pham, H. and Zhang, X., An NHPP software reliability model and its comparison, *Int. J. Reliab., Quality Safety Eng.*, 4(3), 269–282, 1997.

55. Goel, A.L. and Okumoto, K., Time-dependent fault detection rate model for software and other performance measures, *IEEE Trans. Reliab.*, 28(3), 206–211, 1979.

56. Wood, A., Predicting software reliability, *IEEE Comput. Magaz.*, 29(11), 69–77, 1996.

57. Zhang, X., Jeske, D.R., and Pham, H., Calibrating software reliability models when the test environment does not match the user environment, *Appl. Stochastic Models Bus. Indus.*, 18(1), 87–99, 2002.

58. Musa, J.D., *Software Reliability Engineering*, McGraw-Hill Book Company, New York, 1988, Chaps. 4 and 5.

59. Ohba, M., Inflexion S-shaped software reliability growth models, in *Stochastic Models in Reliability Theory*, Osaki, S. and Hatoyama, Y., Eds., Springer-Verlag, Berlin, 144–162, 1984.

60. Yamada, S., Tokuno, K., and Osaki, S., Imperfect debugging models with fault introduction rate for software reliability assessment, *Int. J. Syst. Sci.*, 23(12), 2241–2252, 1992.

61. Rivers, A.T. and Vouk M.A., Resource-constrained non-operational testing of software, *Proceedings of the 9th International Symposium on Software Reliability Engineering*, Paderborn, Germany, 154–163, 1998.

62. Yamada, S., Ohba, M., and Osaki, S., S-shaped reliability growth modeling for software error detection, *IEEE Trans. Reliab.*, 32(5), 475–484, 1983.

63. Hossain, S.A. and Dahiya, R.C., Estimating the parameters of a non-homogeneous Poisson process model for software reliability, *IEEE Trans. Reliab.*, 42(4), 604–612, 1993.

64. Yamada, S., Ohtera, H., and Narihisa, H., Software reliability growth models with testing effort, *IEEE Trans. Reliab.*, 35(1), 19–23, 1986.

65. Jeske, D., Zhang, X., and Pham, L., Adjusting software failure rates that are estimated from test data, *IEEE Trans. Reliab.*, 54(1), 107–114, 2005.

66. Pham, H. and Pham, M., *Software Reliability Models for Critical Applications*, Report EG&G-2663, Idaho National Engineering Laboratory, 1991.

67. Xie, M. and Zhao, M., The Schneidewind software reliability model revisited, *Proceedings of the Third International Symposium on Software Reliability Engineering*, Research Triangle Park, NC, 184–193, 1992.

68. Schneidewind, N.F., An integrated failure detection and fault correction model, in *Proceedings of the International Conference on Software Maintenance*, Montreal, Quebec, 238–241, 2002.

69. Pham, H., *Software Reliability Assessment: Imperfect Debugging and Multiple Failure Types in Software Development*, Report EG&G-RAAM-10737, Idaho National Engineering Laboratory, 1993.

70. Littlewood, B. et al., Modeling the effects of combining diverse software fault detection techniques, *IEEE Trans. Softw. Eng.*, 26(12), 1157–1167, 2000.

71. Wu, Y.P. et al., Modeling and analysis of software fault detection and correction process by considering time dependency, *IEEE Trans. Reliab.*, 56(4), 629–642, 2007.

72. Huang, C.-Y. et al., Software reliability growth models incorporating fault dependency with various debugging time lags, *Proceedings. of the 28th Annual International Computer Software and Applications Conference*, COMPSAC, Hong Kong, Vol. 1, 186–191, 2004.

73. Gokhale, S.S., Lyu, M.R. and Trivedi, K.S., Software reliability analysis incorporating fault detection and debugging activities, *Proceedings of the Ninth International Symposium on Software Reliability Engineering*, 202–211, 1998.

74. Levendel, Y., Software quality and reliability prediction: a time–dependent model with controllable testing coverage and repair intensity, *Proceedings of the Fourth Israel Conference on Computer Systems and Software Engineering*, Herzlia, Israel, 175–181, 1989.

75. Malaiya, Y.K. et al., The relationship between test coverage and reliability, *Proceedings of 5th International Symposium on Software Reliability Engineering*, Montercy, CA, 186–195, 1994.
76. Malaiya, Y.K. et al., Software reliability growth with test coverage, *IEEE Trans. Reliab. Eng.*, 51(4), 420–426, 2002.
77. Lyu, M.R. et al., An empirical study on testing and fault tolerance for software reliability engineering, *Proceedings of the 14th International Symposium on Software Reliability Engineering*, Denver, CO, 119–130, 2003.
78. Gokhale, S.S. and Mullen, R.E., From test count to code coverage using the lognormal failure rate, *Proceedings 15th International Symposium on Software Reliability Engineering*, Rennes/Saint-Malo, France, 295–305, 2004.
79. Cai, X. and Luy, M. R., Software reliability modeling with test coverage: Experimentation and measurement with a fault-tolerant software project, *Proceedings of the 18th IEEE International Symposium on Software Reliability Engineering*, Trollhätton, Sweden, 17–26, 2007.
80. Xie, M., *Software Reliability Engineering*, World Scientific, Singapore, 1991, Chap. 4.
81. Lyu, M.R. (Ed.), *Handbook of Software Reliability Engineering*, IEEE Computer Society Press, Los Alamitos, CA, 1996, Chap. 3.
82. Zhang, X. and Pham, H., Field failure rate prediction before deployment, *J. Syst. Softw.*, 79(3), 291–300, 2006.
83. Zhang, X., Sharma, M., and Franklin, P., Evaluating system reliability from the customer perspective to improve availability predictions, *Proceedings of the Reliability Availability Maintainability Symposium*, Alexandria, VA, 126–132, 2005.
84. Sherif, M.H., Hoeflin, D., and Recchia, M. Risk management for new service introduction in telecommunications networks, *Proceedings of the 8th IEEE Symposium on Computers and Communications ISCC2003*, June 30–July 3, Kemer-Antalya, Turkey, 597–601, 2003.

Section III

Software and Service Architectures

11 Software Architectures for Enterprise Applications

Yurdaer Doganata, Lev Kozakov, and Mirko Jahn

CONTENTS

INTRODUCTION

The subject of software architectures for enterprise applications touches upon many different areas of software engineering. The complete coverage of all aspects requires several volumes rather than several sections. Nevertheless, our aim is to give the reader enough information and familiarity on various perspectives of the topic. As the title of the chapter suggests, we will try to explore software architectures within the context of enterprise applications.

SOFTWARE ARCHITECTURE AND COMPETITIVENESS

Information technology (IT)-based solutions, increasingly seen as strategic competitive assets, are a critical part of companies' efforts to remain competitive. Faster and reliable information sharing among application systems is helping organizations accomplish their strategic objectives. Yet, today, many mission-critical business processes are stretched across mainframe, mid-range, and distributed environments.

The legacy applications introduce many problems: applications that do not work together; too much data and not enough information; incompatible and incorrect data; excessive maintenance costs; and so on. An additional complication is that most legacy applications have been patched and modified over and over to fix errors and respond to changing requirements. Many established firms are faced with the necessity of modernizing their applications reduce maintenance overheads and improve the quality and responsiveness of their information systems.

Migration strategies face several key challenges:

*   How to preserve the business logic of these applications and their valuable data?

- How to maintain scalability, reliability, transactional integrity, and other quality of service (QoS) attributes in a new environment?
- How to ensure that migrated applications continue to meet performance requirements?
- How to achieve predictable, cost-effective results and ensure low risk project?

Enterprise application modernization solutions have to be flexible enough to work in any IT environment, yet rigorous and disciplined enough to produce consistent results. Common modernization strategy may include the following activities:

- Reverse engineering of existing applications and databases to document and model the existing application architecture
- Defining and modeling business information and data requirements
- Defining and modeling business functional requirements
- Comparing application architecture models with requirements and performing gap analysis
- Choosing appropriate integration methods for the enterprise applications

In an environment where business solutions are independently produced and marketed by different vendors, IT departments of companies are challenged not only to deploy the right solutions for the business, but also to make them interoperable with the existing ones. Organizations have historically integrated applications in an *ad hoc* manner to address specific integration requirements as they have arisen over time. The most common solution tried over the years has been to develop interfaces between the applications. But as the number of interfaces grew, the result was additional maintenance problems. In an enterprise, multiple application architectures need to include the business solutions that do not even conform to the same architectural standards. Therefore, it is critical that software architectures for enterprise applications can support various forms of heterogeneity within the enterprise. In order to achieve this, IT organizations provide a technical blue print, which is a high-level logical and physical representations of the IT infrastructure. This blue print constitutes the software architecture of the enterprise.

Today, enterprises need a long-term vision and a plan for the evolution of their IT infrastructure. The plan would define how long legacy applications should be supported, how they should be retired and how newly released solutions will be integrated with the legacy system. This requires understanding of the architectural styles of various software solutions, the circumstances under which they operate, their architectural specifications, limitations as well as benefits, and their integration points with other applications and platforms.

This chapter is about understanding various software architectural styles and their evolution in enterprise application development. We will start with a brief discussion on what software architecture is and define the concepts of enterprise architecture and applications. We then review a number of common software architectural styles, particularly those that are extensively used in current enterprise application development. Service-oriented computing is also overviewed as a new cross-discipline focusing on enabling IT technology to perform business processes more efficiently and effectively. We touch upon some IT trends and enterprise application modernization strategies and solutions. The final section is dedicated to the overview of the infrastructure and middleware for enterprise software integration.

WHAT IS SOFTWARE ARCHITECTURE?

Although there is no one single accepted definition, we define software architecture as a structure that consists of software components, their externally visible properties and relations [1,2]. An architecture is an abstraction of the way these components interacts with each other and with the external world that excludes the implementation details of the components. It provides a common framework to communicate the requirements and to elicit discussions among the stakeholders so that concerns can be articulated, problems defined and solutions negotiated at the appropriate moment of the development cycle [3].

In large IT organizations, there is a need for high-level specifications of information systems to control the ever-growing complexity and support the heterogeneity of software systems. This is the main motivation behind developing and updating software architectures for an enterprise. In designing an enterprise system, software architects evaluate existing design patterns for their suitability as a solution within a particular context. Design patterns provide for a rich set of predefined element types, their interconnections and relations to be used as input for a detailed software design [1]. Design elements are combined in a principled and proven way through the guidance of design patterns to enable reusability and ease the process of designing software systems. Architectural styles can also be viewed as design patterns with a broader scope [4]. Architectural styles use various useful design patterns to solve specific domain problems whereas patterns focus on solving smaller, more specific problems within a given style. Architectural styles also provide for a framework within which design patterns work.

There is a rich source of information in the literature about common software architecture styles [3]. A number of software architectural styles have been documented and widely used to provide proven and repeatable software solutions. We will list some of the styles that are commonly used in designing the information systems for enterprises.

EVOLUTION OF SOFTWARE APPLICATION DEVELOPMENT

The use of computers for business applications expanded rapidly starting from late 1950s [5]. In early 1960s, major hardware manufacturers provided software libraries to be used to develop applications for their specific hardware. Computer programmers did not have many alternatives other than using the libraries provided by the hardware vendor. In the first stages of evolution of software applications, programmers created applications that are self-contained. These monolithic code pieces were tightly coupled to a specific hardware and achieved a specific functionality. There was almost no reusability and basic functions had to be rewritten every time a new application was created. It was not possible to port applications to a hardware that it was not originally created for. Until the mid-1970s, software had to be custom-developed for each customer and the market for using off-the-shelf software had not been developed yet. Data were managed within the application without utilizing or managing databases. Each application was responsible for storing and retrieving data. In many cases, a complete redevelopment was necessary for the same functionality when porting to another computer system is needed. Hence, application development was very inefficient and costly. A good summary of early systems architectures can be found in [2].

In the later stages of application development, operating systems separated the responsibility of managing hardware-specific functions from the applications. Applications started to include hardware-specific functionality by using the interfaces provided by the operating systems. Operating systems provide a set of functions needed and used by applications to link and control and synchronize the computer hardware. Without an operating system, application programmers had to develop drivers for peripheral devices like printers and card-readers. Introduction of operating systems greatly reduced the complexity and increased efficiency as the specific features of the computer hardware were hidden from the applications by the operating system. The same application could be run in different computing machines as long as the drivers for the new hardware devices were installed into the operating system.

The need for consistent data across interfaces and for the separation of the user interface from application logic arose with the increased use of software applications for business solutions. Database management systems (DBMSs) were introduced to manage enterprise data in a cost-effective and efficient manner. A DBMS is a complex set of software programs that controls the organization, storage, modification, and retrieval of information from a database, which is an entity or a resource external to the application. With the introduction of relational databases, it became possible to quickly and efficiently search and find the information. Efficient data access, transaction processing, recovery, backup, and security functions are provided by DBMSs, which are invoked through the programming interface available to the applications.

To separate user-interface functionality from the application layer, more elaborate user interfaces were necessary. Graphical User Interfaces (GUIs) introduced a very effective means of interaction with computers through the manipulation of visual indicators or special graphical elements instead of using text menus or typing commands.

The separation of user interface and database management from application development enabled application programmers to focus on the business logic only. At the same time, different roles were created for the people who work in the IT organization, with each role requiring different skills and knowledge.

SOFTWARE ARCHITECTURAL STYLES

Architectural styles are used to categorize characteristics of systems that share common structural and semantic properties. Each style provides an abstraction for the components of the architecture and their interaction patterns [4,6,7]. It is possible to view common characteristics from many different perspectives. There are attempts to categorize styles from the viewpoints of process, data, and connection or the network [8,9]. The view points, however, are often application-specific [10]; therefore, a good architect is expected to select a pattern that best fits the requirements of the system to be built.

As enterprise applications become more complex and difficult to manage, modularity emerges as an important and desirable system property. Modularity facilitates the reuse of system components by maintaining the independence of individual components from the overall system. With distributed computing, many architectural styles support modularity by sharing the work among independently run processes. In contrast, in monolithic applications there is no modularity; a single-tiered software application combines user interface and data access in a single program running on one platform. As defined in the European Initiative ICCI (Innovation co-ordination, transfer and deployment through networked Co-operation in the Construction Industry—IST-2001-33022) [11], a monolithic application operates independently from other applications, performing every step of the process needed to complete the entire business function. It does not share any logic or data across system or organizational boundaries.

As a result of an evolutionary process, styles are sometimes disjoint, sometimes overlapping and this evolutionary development has not been studied. Below is a brief overview of some common software architectural styles.

PIPES AND FILTERS

This simple architecture style consists of a number of filters arranged in a pipeline that process a data stream. A filter is the basic component of a system that processes the data stream before passing it to other filters. Each filter transforms the data that it receives from another filter in the same pipe. The pipe connects the filters and passes the data from one filter to another. Pipes and filters are often used in multitasking operating systems, such as Unix, where the output of one program is linked to the input of others by pipes.

Pipes and filters are used when many data transformations take place. Most systems implementing pipes use pipe buffers. Buffers allow the source process to provide more data than the destination process is able to receive. Proper configuration of filter buffers is important to avoid performance problems, even deadlocks in some cases. The following references may help to get more details about this architectural style [12,13]. Figure 11.1 depicts a simple pipe-and-filter schema where data are generated at the source, carried through the pipe, transformed by the filters, and finally consumed by the sink.

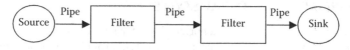

FIGURE 11.1   Pipe and filter.

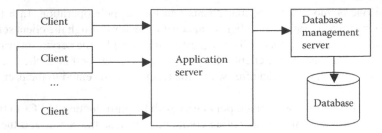

FIGURE 11.2   Tiered architecture.

TIERED COMPUTING

Tiered computing is an architectural that is extensively used to ease the complexity of enterprise information systems because each tier is only aware of its adjacent tiers and can only communicate with its immediate adjacent tiers. In a three-tiered architecture style, the functionality of the application is distributed across three independent systems. Tier 1 consists of client components that run on local workstations; tier 2 is that of the application servers where business processes and application logic are executed on remote servers; and tier 3 is a set of databases and information systems. In a typical second tier, the application logic describes the functions or algorithms to execute business processes that exchange information between a database and a user interface. As illustrated in Figure 11.2, the client components of the first tier, through a user interface or a browser, give the user access to the application server of the second tier in a secure and intuitive manner. For example, a client application provides a form for a customer to place an order. Once the form is filled and submitted, the client components submit this form to the second-tier application server, where the order is processed and tasks related to billing and shipping are performed. Note that multiple client components can access the application layer simultaneously.

The third tier, the data access tier, enables access to the databases where business entities reside. In the previous example, once the order is placed, the application logic layer that resides in the application server checks and updates the databases, and informs the customers with the availability of the product, and so on. Separation of the second and the third tiers reduces the load on the third tier and supports a more effective connection management improving performance. All the client interactions with the third-tier must go through the second tier.

The clear separation of business logic, business transactions, and user interface and data access also increases manageability and flexibility of the enterprise applications. In such an environment, one tier can be replaced or updated without disturbing other tiers provided that the specific interface definitions are followed. This is the main advantage of tiered computing style.

CLIENT/SERVER

Client/server software architectures are sometimes called a two-tier architecture because they comprise two distinct element types, a client and a server. Servers provide one or more services that clients can use in their operation. In a typical client/server configuration, the client connects to a server through the client software and sends a request to a server. The request is processed by the server software and a response is sent back to the client. This process may repeat itself until client receives all the necessary information after which the results are presented to the user by the client software.

This architectural style gained popularity with the introduction of PCs in the late 1980s. It is also a form of distributing computing because the server and the client may run on different machines communicating over a network so the roles and responsibilities are distributed, thereby ensuring modularity and ease of maintenance. With the increase in the number of client requests to servers, performance bottlenecks may appear due to server overload. The architecture is also vulnerable to network congestion.

LAYERED IMPLEMENTATION

The layered architectural style is based on a single type of system element or layer that represents a particular functionality of a network. The network, as a whole, is represented by stacking layers, with the most abstract on top and least in the bottom. The Open Systems Interconnection reference model (OSI Reference Model or OSI Model) for communications protocols is such a case; it has seven layers, each providing specific services or functions to the layer above it and relying on the services of protocols of the layer below.

A tier can be implemented by using a layered architecture style where complexity of low-level details, such as operating system-specific functions, are hidden from the top layers, which are reserved for business- or organizational-level details. Figure 11.3 depicts the layered architecture for the Internet protocol stack.

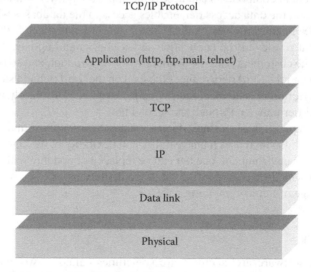

FIGURE 11.3   Layered architecture for the Internet protocol stack.

PEER-TO-PEER

This architectural style comprises a single-type system element, called peer, capable of connecting directly to the other peers in the network. The participants in a peer-to-peer (P2P) networking connect to each other in an ad hoc fashion without going through a central server as shown in Figure 11.4. This style does not have the notion of distinct clients or servers, and each node or peer can act as a client and a server simultaneously. Such connections are useful for multimedia content or file sharing, telephony and media streaming.

From the architecture point of view, a pure P2P network consists of peer nodes that simultaneously function as both "clients" and "servers" to the other nodes on the network. P2P applications may allow a group of computer users with the same networking software direct access to files on each others' hard drives.

P2P systems are resilient to single-point failures since there are multiple paths between two peers in the network. They are inherently scalable, as more users are added to the system, the demand increases but the capacity increases as well. However, there is no guarantee of service availability or of quality because of service dependency on the number of active peers.

The basic P2P technology has been used in Usenet (1979) and in FidoNet (1985)—two very successful and completely decentralized networks of peers.

EVENT-DRIVEN STYLE

This architectural style is based on designing and building software components—called events—to generate, detect, consume, and react to changes in the state of a system. An event-driven system consists of event producers that publish events, event managers that distribute these events to subscribers or event consumers. Each event triggers the exchange of messages among independent software modules through an

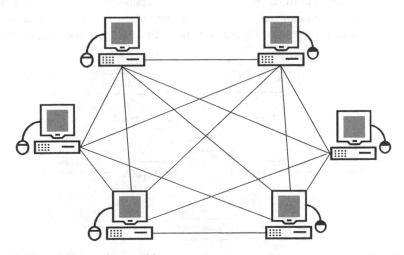

FIGURE 11.4 P2P-based networking.

event manager. This is a middleware component with an event-processing engine that is responsible for matching messages to subscribed programs to notify them of the occurrence of relevant events [14,15].

There are two main types of events, message events and control events. Message events carry the information to be consumed, while control events are used to update the status of the subscribers at the event manager.

Event-driven architectures are used to send a message to multiple destinations efficiently. Since they are modular, new business components can be easily built from existing components and software maintenance is facilitated. However, the lack of standards makes it difficult to integrate products from different vendors. Also, scarce expertise in designing complex event-processing applications and lack of common development and integration tools constitute additional disadvantages of this architectural style.

PUBLISH/SUBSCRIBE

Publish/Subscribe is a variant of event-driven systems developed mainly for asynchronous messaging. In this style, the publisher is one element type and the subscriber is the other. Some Publish/Subscribe systems implement a third element type called broker that is responsible for managing subscriptions and filtering. Others eliminate the brokerage functions by distributing its functions among the subscribers and publishers.

Published messages are classified into subjects independent of the subscribers that could consume this information. Subscribers register their interest and are notified when the publishers update or create registered information. The process of receiving relevant information by the subscribers is called filtering.

Many messaging systems run by message-oriented middleware (MOM) support the Publish/Subscribe architecture, for example, Java Message Service (JMS).

Publish/Subscribe systems have better scalability than client/server architectures because publishers and subscribers can operate independently. The drawback is that delivery cannot be guaranteed; in most cases, the publisher stops the delivery after several unsuccessful attempts. Figure 11.5 shows that two publishers are publishing

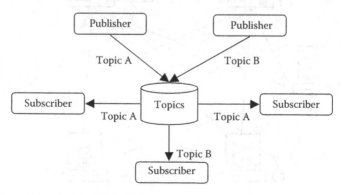

FIGURE 11.5 Publish/Subscribe architecture.

on two different topics, Topic A and Topic B. Some subscribers are registered to receive information about Topic A and some others are on Topic B.

ASYNCHRONOUS DATA REPLICATION

Asynchronous data replication architectures can be considered as a variation of the Publish/Subscribe style. This style addresses the need to replicate and synchronize the information in the primary enterprise data store. Partial or full replication may be needed for different reasons, such as to improve performance, to synchronize the data maintained by different vendors, to maintain the data from different applications, and so on.

The three elements of this style are: the primary store that contains the enterprise information; the replicator that detects the changes in the primary stores and performs synchronization with the third element, the replica data store. The delay to update the replicated-site databases depends on the type of business application and user requirements.

SYNCHRONOUS DATA REPLICATION

In synchronous data replication, data replication takes place as soon as the source data is changed, provided that all hardware components and networks in the replication system are available [16]. A transaction is applied only if all the interconnected sites agree. Synchronous data replication is appropriate for applications that require immediate data synchronization.

DISTRIBUTION TREE

Distribution tree is another variant of the Publish/Subscribe style where the system element are arranged as a tree. This is the preferred style for multicast solutions and push-client products. There are three system elements: publisher, distributor, and consumers as shown in Figure 11.6. The publisher is the root of the tree, distributors are the intermediate nodes, and consumers form the leaves of the tree. The content created and posted by the publisher is distributed by the distributors to the consumers. Multicast-capable routers create distribution trees for the path that IP multicast traffic takes all receivers.

Distribution tree styles have the advantage of scalability, since the size of the tree can be increased easily by adding new distributors and consumers. Cashing and high update frequency requirements when the tree size gets larger may become disadvantageous because the data that are pushed to the consumers are replicated at every node and the processing time increases with increases in the update frequency.

BLACKBOARD SYSTEMS

The Blackboard architectural styles [17] consists of three components: specialist software models to provide specific expertise or knowledge for the application, a shared repository or a dynamic library called "blackboard" that contains partial

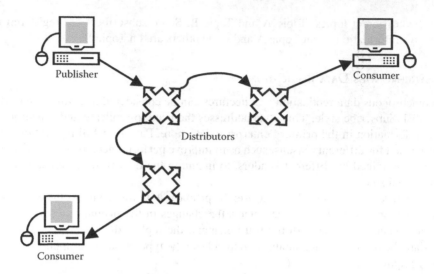

FIGURE 11.6   Distribution tree.

solutions or information provided by specific expert models or knowledge resources, and a control mechanism to control the integration task. Blackboard was originally designed in artificial intelligent systems to handle uncertainty in problem definitions. Examples of early implementation include Hearsay II speech recognition system [18] and the mission control system for RADARSAT-1 [19].

TUPLE SPACE

Tuple spaces are a form of blackboard architectural systems. This style is used mainly in distributed computing systems to enable sharing data on a client/server system. The clients are the producers and the consumers of data. Servers are used to implement the shared object space where the data is shared. Hence, the clients create and consume the information in a tuple space implemented as a server, which is a storage area or a shared memory that clients can access. Clients can reference any tuple regardless of where it is stored without requiring a physically shared memory.

The tuples are also accessed by association to their content types, without the need for knowing their physical addresses. Various implementations of tuple spaces can be found in SmallTalk, Java, Phython, Ruby, Lisp, Prolog, and others. When a process produces data to be shared by other processes, it posts the data in the tuple space and the consumer processes retrieves the data that match certain simple search patterns. In this style, consumers and the producers of data do not interact with each other. Hence, tuple spaces support loosely coupled systems. This style is derived from the Linda research system developed at Yale University [20].

DISTRIBUTED COMPUTING ARCHITECTURE STYLE

Distributed computing is a method of computer processing, in which different parts of an application run simultaneously on two or more computers that are communicating with each other over a network. Also, different sections of an application can run in different environments (different operational systems, hardware components, etc.). Recent years have seen the increased adoption of distributed computing platforms in all IT areas. This trend can be attributed to several factors such as the significant performance improvements in the networking hardware and recent advances in the software architecture and integration technologies. Economical and business factors also played important roles in the advancement of distributed computing such as the ever-growing cost of IT system ownership and the increasing demand for greater information sharing among enterprise application systems. In short, distributed systems help organizations accomplish their key strategic objectives for cost control.

Distributed computing is distinct from computer networking or fragmented computing where silos of applications run in their own isolated environments. The World Wide Web is an example of a computer network, but not of a distributed computing platform.

Over the last 20 years, numerous technologies and standards had been developed in the area of distributed computing. One of the major efforts of 1990s was the Distributed Computing Environment, which supplies a framework and a tool kit for developing distributed applications. The framework includes a Remote Procedure Call mechanism as well as a number of other network-based services and protocols. More recent technologies include Remote Method Invocation (RMI) or .NET Remoting (see, for instance [21]).

The general goal of a distributed computing system is to connect users and resources in a transparent, open, and scalable way to achieve significantly more fault-tolerant and more powerful arrangement than just the combinations of stand-alone computer systems. The following are brief descriptions of the main qualities provided by a distributed computing system:

- *Transparency.* Transparency means that after any change in a distributed computing system, such as adding new components, the system continues to adhere, as much as possible, to all previous external interfaces while transparently changing its internal behavior. The purpose is to shield all users, whether humans or programs, from changes in the internals of the system.
- *Openness.* Openness of a distributed computing system means that each subsystem is continually open to interaction with other systems. In general, an open scalable system has an advantage over a perfectly closed and self-contained system. Open distributed systems are required to meet the following properties:
  - Once something is published in an open system, it cannot be taken back.
  - There is no central arbiter in an open system; different subsystems may include heterogeneous, overlapping, and possibly conflicting information.
  - Different subsystems within an open system can come up and go down asynchronously, so the time to complete an operation cannot be bounded in advance.
- *Scalability.* Scalability of a distributed computer system is its ability to either accommodate growing volumes of work in a graceful manner, or to be readily enlarged when resources are added to the system.

GRID COMPUTING

Grid computing [22] is, perhaps, the most popular term today in the area of distributed computing. At the heart of grid computing is the concept that applications and resources are connected through a pervasive network grid, analogous to the electrical power grid that is accessible everywhere and sharable by everyone. Thus, grid computing is a special type of parallel computing.

Grid computing platforms extend traditional computer in the following aspects:

- Massive scaling and higher throughput, by grouping hardware and software components effectively to achieve greater performance and scalability.
- Inherent resilience and availability, thanks to the use of multiple, replicated components within a grid.
- Mutability (ability to evolve) and flexibility that result in greater efficiency and agility.
- Service orientation. Grid computing is focused on managing applications and services, rather than the individual resources within the network grid. This mandates a functional, rather than component-centric, approach to the management of networked applications and resources.

Functionally, we can distinguish several types of grids as follows:

- Computational grids, which focus primarily on computationally intensive operations
- Data grids or the controlled sharing and management of large amounts of distributed data
- Equipment grids, which are used to remotely control the equipment and to analyze the data produced

ENTERPRISE GRID COMPUTING

Enterprise grid computing [22] is a grid that is controlled and managed by a single business to meet a specific set of business goals. The extent of an enterprise grid is defined in terms of organizational responsibility and not in terms of geography or asset ownership. Thus, an enterprise grid may span multiple locations or IT centers and even include applications or services that run on behalf of other organizations, such as in an outsourced environment.

CLOUD COMPUTING

Cloud computing [23] refers to a paradigm where computing resources, such as storage, software, and services are made available independently and accessed remotely by network connections. The term "cloud" means a public network, such as the Internet. Grid computing is a technology approach to manage a cloud. Specifically, a computer grid and a cloud are synonymous whereas a data grid and a cloud can be different.

The architecture behind cloud computing is a network of interconnected "cloud servers" running in parallel. Cloud computing can be seen as the unification of grid and utility computing under a new paradigm where customers are allowed to use the services, bandwidth, processing power, and storage as they need. They are billed based on the resources utilized. A front-end interface allows users to select services from a catalog. This request gets passed to the system management, which finds the correct resources, and then calls the provisioning services to assign existing resources in the cloud or to request additional resources to meet the request.

ENTERPRISE APPLICATIONS

Enterprise applications are software applications developed to manage the business operations, assets, and resources of an enterprise. Their development process integrates the work of at least four groups: namely, application programmers focusing on coding the business logic for the solution of a particular business problem; database managers building data models to structure and manage data storage, access, security, and consistency; GUI developers responsible for the design and development of widgets to ease human computer interaction and finally; and application integrators for integrating existing applications and available technologies with the new applications.

In principle, there is no difference between enterprise applications and regular software applications other than the specific business purpose they are developed for. As the nature of business goals and processes vary, software solutions delivered for specific business problems vary as well. As a consequence, the number and the variety of applications delivered for each solution increase the complexity of managing the overall IT system. While having an automated solution to business problems increases effectiveness and efficiency and reduces cost, managing the complexity of the automation solution is a new business problem that companies have to deal with. A high-level blueprint of a standard application template for a company can reduce that complexity. In response to this need, the design characteristics, limitations, interfaces, and rules of developing enterprise applications have been documented. This high-level description, the blueprint, of how an application should be developed to satisfy the business goals is known as *Enterprise Application Architecture*. This architecture defines an organizing structure for software application elements and the resources, their relationships and roles in an organization.

Enterprise applications are usually developed independent of each other and each of these applications manages their own data in their specific database system. This leads to data heterogeneity and inefficiency because the same data elements are stored multiple times in different databases. This creates the problem of managing the same logical data object stored in multiple data stores. Differences in data structures as well as in semantics are also possible. One of the challenges facing enterprises today is the task of integrating all these applications within the organization, even though they may use different operating systems and employ a variety of database solutions. Simplistic approaches soon become unmanageable as the number of applications to be integrated increases. Enterprise application integration (EAI) is the task of making independently developed applications that may also be geographically dispersed and may run on multiple platforms work together in unison with the goal of unrestricted sharing of data and business processes [24].

In order to accomplish this goal, middleware vendors provide solutions to transform, transport, and route the data among various enterprise applications. As stated in Ref. [25], EAI faces significant more management challenges than technical challenges and its implementation is time-consuming and needs substantial resources, particularly in upfront design. Among the software applications for managing company assets and resources, the most commonly used are Enterprise Resource Planning (ERP), Customer Relationship Management (CRM), Supply Chain Management (SCM), Business Intelligence Applications, and Human Resource (HR) Applications.

ERP [26] is, probably, the most general class of enterprise software that attempts to integrate all departments and functions across a company. ERP incorporates many different families of more specific enterprise applications.

CRM solutions [27] focus on strategies, processes, people, and technologies used by companies to successfully attract and retain customers for maximizing profitability, revenue, and customer satisfaction.

Enterprise Content Management solutions [28] provide technologies, tools, and methods used to capture, manage, store, preserve, and deliver content (document, voice and video recordings, etc.) related to organizational processes across an enterprise.

SCM solutions [29] focus on the process of planning, implementing, and controlling the operations of the supply chain, which includes the flow of materials, information, and finances as they move in a process from supplier to manufacturer, to wholesaler, to retailer, and to consumer.

HR Management solutions [30] provide a coherent approach to the recruitment and management of people working in organizations.

MANAGEMENT OF COMPLEXITY IN ENTERPRISE APPLICATIONS

One common characteristic of enterprise applications is the challenges in creating and maintaining them. The aim of this section is to point out the main features associated to the complexity of enterprise applications. The focus is not on the technical aspects of protocols, languages, or functional logic, but rather on eight conceptual domains that are applicable on a wider area of applications. Figure 11.7 illustrates

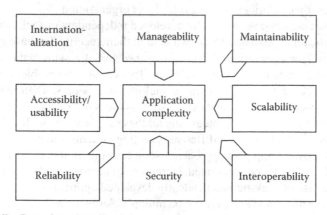

FIGURE 11.7 Domains of application complexity.

these eight domains of manageability, maintainability, scalability, interoperability, security, reliability, accessibility/usability, and internationalization.

Manageability

Enterprise software systems are confronted by ever-changing requirements and environments and should be able to adapt to these changes dynamically. As a consequence, better solutions have the following features:

- A high degree of adaptability and extendibility of the whole system built into the design
- Support for mass deployment
- Support for business-driven configuration scenarios
- A configurable security management system based on users, roles, and access control lists with distinct and configurable privileges
- Tracing capability for user actions

Another aspect of application complexity is the ability to manage software components that constitute the application. The average lifetime of applications [31] is shrinking due to the increasingly competitive market. Incorporating updates to provide these features over time becomes an obstacle for managing software components. The problem is not new, but became increasingly important with the growing number of two-tier applications at the end of the 1990s. The applications that are often built as rich clients and capable of directly accessing backend databases are prime candidates for version conflicts and data integrity frauds, if the software update is not planed and enforced perfectly. All clients have to be updated before they attempt to interact with a new version of the backend system. If this is not possible, a proper mitigation solution has to be deployed. Such a solution may sound promising upfront, but can become very difficult to manage over time. Releasing a mitigation solution for every version deployed soon becomes a maintenance nightmare and may actually hinder future development, because every iteration of the software has to be aware of all previous combinations. The root cause of the problem is that client software has to keep track of the changes to remain up-to-date. The advantage of three-tier applications is that only the application deployed on the server needs to be updated, which is one reason for the success of typical three-tier Web applications.

Different versions, however, are not the only problem, software updates implicate code-change in the runtime environment, which can consequently affects the availability of the running application, because the code could not always be replaced during run-time. Legacy systems often need a reboot after major system updates. Depending on the usage scenario, these downtimes have to be minimized and made transparent to the user. This is one of the main reasons behind new concepts like the OSGi (Open Service Gateway initiative) that supports hot deployment with 24 × 7 availability (24 h/day and 7 days/week).

Maintainability

Given the inevitability of change, software components must be designed to support modification and extension over their lifetime. Maintainability enables utilization of software components over time. Developers use well-known software engineering techniques to achieve this goal. In addition to producing well-written documents for the source code and for the software itself, the design and the appropriate naming are crucial. Patterns like the ones described by the so-called "Gang of Four" (Gamma, Helm, Johnson, and Vlissides) with their well-known book *Design Patterns: Elements of Reusable Object-Oriented Software* [32] and many after them, have helped to develop a common language and encourage the use of best practices, and simpler, more intuitive ways of understanding and maintaining applications.

Scalability

Enterprise applications are long-term investments and are meant to adapt to changing business needs. One of these needs is the capability to scale according to usage requirement. Scalability, in contrast to maintainability, does not imply an actual change of the features of certain software, but rather addresses the need to sustain a running and most importantly usable system in terms of growing user numbers and traffic.

There are two major different techniques to achieve scalability: vertical scaling and horizontal scaling [33]. With vertical scaling, an existing system is basically extended or updated to increase the capacity of existing hardware or software adding more processing power or, for instance, data storage. In contrast, horizontal scaling involves adding multiple entities of hardware and software together to act as one single logical unit. Vertical scaling is possible for most applications, whereas horizontal scaling may not always be possible or efficient enough. Mixtures of these two approaches are often referred to as diagonal scaling.

Which of the aforementioned scaling technique eventually is best for an application depends on many different factors, such as the programming language, architecture [34], deployed protocols, message size and frequency, requirements on the deployment environment, throughput [35], responsiveness, availability or the total cost of ownership [36]. As an example, consider a two-tier application with an old mainframe-based database. Porting the database to another hardware system, changing the entire database, or enhancing the existing database with clustering capabilities would be very expensive. In this case, vertical scaling is a better choice because it is less invasive than the horizontal approach and does not impose any internal changes on the application. In case of a typical three-tier application with a Web front-end and an application server and a database in the back, horizontal scaling is more flexible. New nodes of the Web front-end can be added dynamically as soon as the load increases, thus providing the flexibility by allocating resources dynamically where needed.

Interoperability

The ability of disparate applications working together is considered one of the most important characteristics of an Enterprise Application Architecture. Companies typically integrate business solutions from different software vendors. Starting from e-mail clients to intranet portals, customer relationship management systems, finance management systems, supply chain management software, and many more one can think of. Furthermore, companies are experiencing continuous changes (takeovers, mergers or restructures, and even splits). All this and the fact that the lifetime of software is limited [37] forces IT departments to go through a transition phase in order to adapt to these changes. Software has to be built in a way to accommodate these inevitable changes and ensure interoperability with other applications.

Current software designs aim to address interoperability by providing flexible and extendable solutions. Monolithic software solutions and legacy applications were connected via proprietary communication protocols. This approach makes the enterprise depend on the solutions produced by a single vendor. Standardization organizations are responding to the demand for open and flexible specifications. Many IT companies including IBM, Microsoft, Sun Microsystems, and BEA are now providing a whole arsenal of software based on standards interfaces with the ultimate goal of making independently developed systems work together seamlessly.

Security

Compared to the last decade, security plays an increasing role in current enterprises. Attackers are now no longer a minority seeking publicity or just trying to boost their ego. Hacking has become an industry, aiming equally at individuals and companies. Renting or selling of botnets [38], industrial espionage, or paid denial of service attacks to hurt market competitors have become industrialized. As a consequence, companies have to dedicate special resources to protect themselves from this growing threat. Mistakes done in this area often not only cause direct financial losses, but can also have dramatic impact on the reputation and the value and trust of the company, especially for companies handling sensitive personal data, such as insurance, financial, and medical companies. Even the partial loss of sensitive data can put such companies out of business as soon as the customers are loosing their trust. This is one reason why in the current Basel II Accord [39] of the Bank of International Settlements, the security concept of a company is evaluated to assign a risk level and ultimately affect the credit ranking.

An enterprise faces three different kinds of threats:

- Attacks against personal and customer related data like medical records
- Attacks against company goods like confidential contracts, licenses, or detailed business objectives
- Attacks to abuse the company infrastructure in order to run illegal businesses like file sharing with pirate copies for instance

In order to protect the business, the IT systems have to be up-to-date. Besides well-known mechanisms such as virus scanners, firewalls, and demilitarized zones, modern software architectures contain their own security layers. In Java for instance, a SecurityManager [40] enforces policies to limit the rights a distinct part of the source code. If an attacker manages to exploit a certain part of the code, he/she only obtains the minimal subset of rights the code was granted in order to fulfill its tasks. This helps to minimize the impact of vulnerabilities.

In spite of all the efforts, data breaches are bound to happen [41]. Depending on the domain a company is working in, they may be even obliged to comply with rules and regulations and may face noncompliance charges for not following the regulations such as the Payment Card Industry Data Security Standard [42], Visa

Member rules [43], or the Health Insurance Portability and Accountability Act [44]. Hence, companies must adopt solutions to protect their data and provide forensic evidence of attacks that can be used in courtrooms. To minimize the risks, a plan has to be developed to detect security breaches by monitoring IT systems for unusual behavior. The system must respond to such anomalies. Once a breach has been detected, a previously established response plan has to be invoked to handle the incident appropriately. The response plan has to be comprehensive and should not only cover what steps to take in order to fix the security gap, but also define whom to notify, how to gather forensic evidence, and how to handle them in order to be valid in court.

Reliability

Enterprise grade software is not only supposed to provide certain functionality, at least equally important is the reliability of the system. Reliability is defined as the ability to perform and maintain distinct functionalities within predefined parameters for a specified period of time. The importance of this nonfunctional requirement may vary drastically depending on the usage scenario. An intranet portal will most likely have different availability requirements than a stock-trading portal during business hours.

Reliability can be differentiated into a data-centric part and a service-centric part. Data-centric reliability concerns the data the application is working with. Service-centric reliability focuses on the guaranteed availability of services. In online shopping, credit card validation is a vital service for the business, whereas a service to verify zip codes for the order address has a noticeable lower priority. A service to provide currency exchange rates have to be as accurate as possible and its data reliability is essential.

Service reliability is characterized by the number, date, time, and time span of scheduled downtimes, what is or what is not considered *force majeure*, and how much latency is acceptable.

Some of the questions to be asked before the actual software are developed or chosen concern its tolerance to failure, to latency, and the fallback plans if a failure occurs.

Accessibility/Usability

In his best selling book *Don't Make Me Think*, Steve Krug [45] described why certain design standards and methodologies are beneficial. While well-designed and ergonomic software is better accepted by users, the usability in general has a lot to do with acquired habits. How can we decide if the Microsoft Windows GUI or the GUI from Apple Macintosh is better? Objectively it is not possible to tell right away, because we are familiar with the systems that we currently use and we are biased toward them. In addition, external factors can play an important role as well. To get certain governmental contracts, a distinct level of accessibility is required to be met. There are standards to evaluate and measure the accessibility and the usability for different user groups, as defined in Section 508 of the Rehabilitation Act [46] or the Web Content Accessibility Guidelines [47] from the World Wide Web Consortium (W3C). However, rules, regulations, and laws change from region to region, which makes it almost impossible to find one standard for all situations. In short, while accessibility and usability are critical for the acceptance of applications, which standards apply depend on the context.

Internationalization

Globalization plays an important role and many software companies try to be present in international markets with their products. Internationalization may seem straightforward, but the effects of errors can be catastrophic. Despite its obvious experience, Microsoft [48] made several costly mistakes in this area. In one particular incident, eight pixels out of 800,000 were, accidentally colored with the wrong shade of green, which seemed to indicate that the disputed Kashmiri territory did not belong to India. This resulted in banning every Windows 95 version immediately from the Indian market and making 200,000 copies worthless over night. Another incident offended Spanish speaking women when they were asked during software set-up to select their gender between "not specified," "male," and "bitch." As this example shows, it is important to pay attention to the details of translations and to differences in cultural perspectives, traditions, and religions. Another kind of internationalization problem is the technical one. The program must be capable to handle different code pages and character sets and time zones. Although the programming language Java for instance internally uses Unicode, the application still has to be aware of this capability to work as expected [49].

PATTERNS FOR EAI

In this section, we will overview some of the most common integration patterns. In [24], more than 60 integration patterns are organized into four integration styles: file transfer, shared database, remote procedure invocation, and messaging. Most are categorized under messaging, which provides solution for many integration problems.

Based on the way applications are connected, integration patterns can be grouped into point-to-point integration and hub-and-spoke integration [2]. In the first approach, the applications are directly connected, while in the second message exchanges go through a third party before being delivered to final destination. Both point-to-point and spoke–hub can be realized by using some of the patterns described in Ref. [24].

POINT-TO-POINT INTEGRATION

Point-to-point integration is the simplest way to integrate independently developed application silos and do not require significant upfront investment. As shown in Figure 11.8, each application is connected directly and explicitly to others. To link each application to another directly, an interface needs to be developed. This style may work well if the number of applications to be integrated is not large and there is no intention to scale out. Otherwise, it may quickly become unmanageable as the number of applications silos increase: if there are N applications to be integrated then the number of interfaces to be developed becomes $N \times N$, that is, the number of interfaces to be developed grows in the order of N^2.

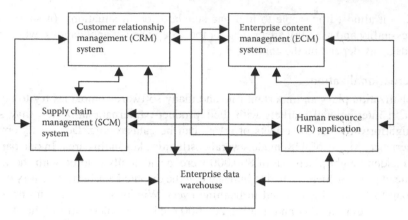

FIGURE 11.8   Point-to-point integration.

Another problem with point-to-point integration is the inability to respond to changes quickly. This is because the interfaces are hard-wired to the application pairs and changes within the enterprise information infrastructure may require re-wiring the interfaces.

MESSAGE-ORIENTED INTEGRATION

In message-oriented integration solutions, the applications communicate with each other by sending and receiving messages through a middleware that manages the message queue associated with each application. Integration of two applications is by sending and receiving messages to the appropriate queue and the middleware ensures that the messages are delivered. However, point-to-point aspect of the integration is not eliminated, since applications are required to specify the recipients of the messages.

SPOKE–HUB INTEGRATION

Spoke–hub integration eliminates the need to encode the address of the recipient. A centralized enterprise application middleware routes messages to their destinations based on the content and the format of the message. All applications are connected to the central integration hub like the spokes on a bicycle wheel. For this reason, this integration style is called spoke–hub integration. Figure 11.9 shows how various enterprise applications are integrated by using the spoke–hub integration technique. The concept is effectively used in many industries, such as transportation and telecommunication.

Spoke–hub integration reduces the number of connections from $O(n^2)$ to $O(n)$, $O(\ )$ indicating the order of. This means that only as many interfaces as the number of applications needs to be developed. In practice, a centralized integration hub provides a place for the adapters and it is the responsibility of the application developer

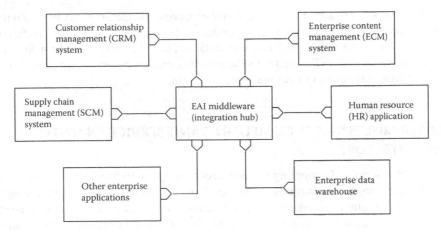

FIGURE 11.9   Spoke–hub integration.

to provide an adapter for each hub they connect to. Without standardization of adapters, this requires some development and testing resources.

The spoke–hub integration is effectively implemented by a message broker software that translates messages from one protocol to another, making sure that the data structures are compatible. Message brokers allow the rules of communication between applications to be defined outside the applications, so that application developers do not need to worry about designing adaptors for every other application. When a message is received, the message broker runs the rule over the received message, transforms the data if needed, and inserts it into the appropriate queue. The rules are defined in a declarative way based on the communication protocols used by the applications. The message broker uses these rules to identify the message queues where the messages should be relayed. Figure 11.10 shows the integration of various enterprise applications by using a message broker architecture.

Publish/Subscribe software architecture style can be used to implement message brokers. Accordingly, applications publish their messages that are then relayed to the receiving applications that subscribe to them.

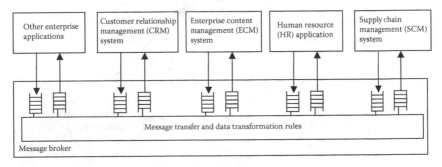

FIGURE 11.10   Architecture of the message broker.

The major drawback of the message broker approach is the difficulty in managing and configuring the rules when the dependencies between applications are complex. Also, because message-based communications are inherently asynchronous, the solution may not be well suited for synchronous communication requirements, such as real-time computing or near-real-time computing.

ENTERPRISE SERVICES COMPUTING AND SERVICE-ORIENTED ARCHITECTURE

Enterprise Services Computing is a new cross-discipline to bridge the gap between the IT technologies and business processes. Enterprise software architecture design, development, and deployment are significantly influenced by this new discipline. The ultimate goal is to increase the flexibility of business processes by creating connections among these business services that run as disparate applications and reusing existing IT investments [50]. This is accomplished through the Service-Oriented Architecture (SOA) where business tasks are considered services available over a network. These services are specified independently of underlying implementation and can be combined and reused to create new business applications. Enterprise applications expose their various functions through services. Business tasks, such as receiving loan applications, define the context of services. Within SOA, services are independently evolving logical units that conform to a set of principles and interfaces [51].

There are mainly three roles in SOA as shown in Figure 11.11: service providers, service requestors, and a service registry that stores the description of services available through service providers. The service providers publish their services to the service registry, which is used to look up and find a desired service by the service requestor.

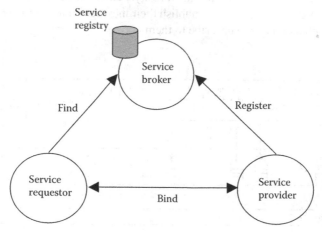

FIGURE 11.11   Different roles in SOA.

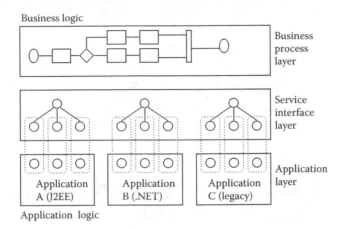

Business logic

Application logic

FIGURE 11.12 Separation of business logic from application logic in SOA.

The SOA concept allows the separation of business logic from application logic as seen in Figure 11.12. The business logic captures the operational requirements in terms of the business tasks captured as services. The application logic, on the other hand, implements the business tasks and is deployed in its proprietary environment. The encapsulation of individual application logic into services is also the responsibility of the application layer. The services that are encapsulated by individual applications are then mapped onto the business logic through service interface layer. The readers are referred to Ref. [51] for further details.

SOA AND WEB SERVICES

Web Services, as defined by the W3C, comprise a software system that supports machine to machine interactions expressed in the Extensible Markup Language (XML) format and exchanged through the Hypertext Transfer Protocol (HTTP) as Simple Object Access Protocol (SOAP) messages. The core specifications that define Web services include: SOAP as an XML-based communication protocol over HTTP; Web Services Description Language (WSDL) as an XML-based language for describing Web Services and how to access them; and Universal Description, Discovery and Integration (UDDI) as a directory service where business can register and search for Web Services.

As shown in Figure 11.13, the service provider and service requestor exchange messages encapsulated in XML using SOAP for transport. Service providers describe their services using WSDL and publish them with UDDI, and service requestors find and download these WSDL-based service descriptors.

A WSDL document consists of description of actions, known as operations, to be performed by the service; input and output messages to be received and sent by this service; and the physical address, port, or endpoint, at which the service can be accessed and an XML Schema Definition schema to formalize the structure of

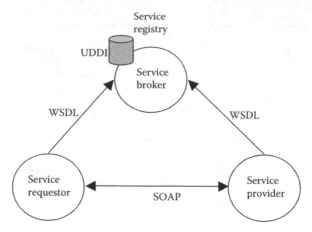

FIGURE 11.13   Architecture of Web services.

incoming and outgoing messages. Each service uses a SOAP node—a physical implementation of the SOAP communication server—to exchange SOAP messages.

The Enterprise Service Bus (ESB) is a connectivity infrastructure for integrating applications and services. It is used at the center of SOA to route messages among services, to perform protocol conversions when needed, to handle events, and to monitor the quality of service. In a sense, the ESB is an enterprise middleware for automating the underlying services. Figure 11.14 illustrates how applications, data, and services are integrated via an ESB.

The concept of service-oriented computing enables individual Web services to work together coherently. Business processes that automate the business tasks can be realized by combining services. Application composition is performed through a logic that involves only with the interaction of underlying services. The behavior of the composite application is captured by a description called *workflow*. Application integration middleware, such as the ESB, connects the services through standardized services interfaces.

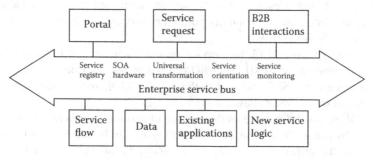

FIGURE 11.14   The Enterprise Service Bus.

ORCHESTRATION AND CHOREOGRAPHY

Orchestration and choreography constitute a significant part of the Business Process Management (BPM) discipline. BPM covers the design, modeling, execution, monitoring, and optimization of business processes [2,52–54]. While both concepts imply coordination and control of Web services to work together coherently, BPM experts distinguish between them. The primary difference is about having a central control. Orchestration implies a control of the information flows and the service interactions among remote systems. It introduces an abstracted workflow logic that simplifies integration so that different processes within an organization can be connected through a standardized and service-based approach. A choreography, in contrast, specifies the collaboration rules and protocols among the participants to ensure their interoperability, that is, it represents the agreements among services from different organizations work together to realize a business solution. The notion of choreography implies that there is no single point of control, much like dancers, even while the members of a distributed system follow a global scenario.

The Business Process Execution Language (BPEL) specifies an executable process where the sequence of the message exchanges is controlled by the orchestration designer, in a fashion analogous to a conductor of a musical group. It facilitates automation of the integration process both within the enterprise and across enterprises. It has been used by many EAI middleware products to integrate various legacy environments. In short, orchestration is the key to a successful application composition by linking various applications running on disparate computing platforms.

CURRENT TRENDS IN ENTERPRISE SOFTWARE SYSTEMS

Recent years have shown significant changes in the structure of enterprise software systems and their integration strategies. Among the main driving forces for these changes are the growing adoption of the Internet, the greater focus on the costs associated with managing IT systems and the increasing role of the IT in the overall business process. There have also been noticeable changes at the infrastructure and hardware levels. Specifically, the computational equipment that once was used to serve individual department needs has become an enterprise-wide commodity, while organizations are evolving toward consolidated data management centers. Similar processes are taking place at the software architecture level, where increasing consolidation has lead to the service-based integration of business applications with multiple services deployed on the same infrastructure, which reduces the relevance of hardware boundaries.

Some of the IT trends that impact the enterprise software architecture and integration are: Software as a Service (Saas), virtualization, and on-demand computing.

SaaS is a software distribution model in which applications are hosted by a vendor or service provider and made available to customers over a network, typically the Internet [55]. For Saas to be operational, the SOA must be adopted so that enterprise solutions could be composed through the integration of services and on-demand service provisioning could be possible.

Virtualization is the process of presenting a logical grouping or subset of computing resources so that they can be accessed in ways that give benefits over the original configuration [56]. Virtualization implies the "commoditization" of computing resources, including operating systems and that on-demand usage of resource is enabled. It is accomplished by creating an abstraction layer between physical hardware and operating systems. This way physical boundaries are removed.

Finally, *on-demand computing* or utility computing is an enterprise model in which computing resources are made available to the user as needed [56]. This solution depends on open standards for the integration of enterprise software but increases the security risks. Enterprise-level security requires eliminating potential risks introduced by open-source software. Service provisioning is based on service-level agreements, which means that performance measures should be established and tracked.

It should be noted that SOA-based enterprise applications are often proposed to modernize enterprise applications [57]. SOA is a component model that is based on exposing application functions as services that can be invoked by external parties. SOA approach relies on using the Enterprise Services Bus to establish a mechanism for routing messages between service consumers and providers. SOA approach enables loose-coupling between service requestors and providers by allowing substitution of one service implementation with another, with no effect to the consumers of that service. There are always risks associated with changes to an enterprise IT infrastructure. The risks of modernization are reduced with the phased approach of the SOA-based EAI.

INFRASTRUCTURE AND MIDDLEWARE FOR ENTERPRISE SOFTWARE INTEGRATION

APPLICATION SERVERS

Application servers are perhaps the most critical element of almost every networked computing platform in today's IT market. By definition, an application server [58] is a software engine that delivers business applications to networked clients. In a three-tier architecture [59], application servers usually run at both the presentation tier and the business logic tier as described when tiered architecture styles were discussed above, providing a platform for deploying and running applications that access enterprise data bases, perform business operations, and present results to their clients through the network. Although application servers typically use the same HTTP as Web servers or HTTP servers, they should be distinguished from them. Web servers typically provide static content, such as HTML (HyperText Markup Language) pages, while application servers use server-side dynamic content and frequently are integrated with database engines. In many practical usages, an application server works with a Web server that forwards client requests to the application server and sends the fetched Web pages back to the client. Such a combination of an application server and a Web server is denoted as a *Web application server.*

Application servers run on many platforms and bundle middleware that enables applications to communicate with other applications and back-end services, such as DBMSs. In today's IT market, the term application server often refers to a Java 2 Platform, Enterprise Edition (J2EE or JEE) application server [60], which will be discussed further. Among the most popular JEE application servers are both the industrial leaders, such as IBM *WebSphere Application Server* [61] and BEA (now Oracle) *WebLogic Server* [62], and open source Apache *Tomcat* [63] and *Geronimo* [64], *JBoss* [65]. Microsoft's contribution to application servers is the *.NET Framework* [66], a part of Microsoft Windows operating system, which manages the deployment and execution of applications written specifically for the framework.

MESSAGE-ORIENTED MIDDLEWARE

An important aspect of the application integration architecture is the ability of applications running on heterogeneous platforms to communicate with each other. One of the best-known infrastructures for inter-application communications is Message-Oriented Middleware (MOM) [67]. Communication is thus formally defined messages, as opposed to a request/response model. In general, messaging is an asynchronous method of passing information between applications. MOM often involves message queues and message brokers. Message queues provide temporary storage when the destination application is not available (busy or not connected). Data sent by one application can be stored in a queue and then forwarded to the receiving application when it becomes available to process it. Queuing frees the communicating parties from establishing connections with one another and other complexities of communicating directly. A message broker is a software that adds routing intelligence and data conversion capabilities to translate messages from the formal messaging protocol of the sender to the formal messaging protocol of the receiver. For instance, a rule engine analyzes the messages to determine which application should receive them, and a formatting engine converts the data into the structure required by the receiving application.

The Java EE platform provides the standard messaging API called JMS [68], which is implemented by most MOM vendors, such as the industrial leader IBM *WebSphere MQ* [69] or open source Apache *ActiveMQ* [70], and aims to hide the particular MOM API implementations. The JMS is defined by a specification developed under the Java Community Process (JCP) as JSR 914.

Perhaps, the most comprehensive discussion of architectural aspects of message-based enterprise integration solutions can be found in Ref. [71]. This reference provides a consistent vocabulary and visual notation framework to describe large-scale message-based integration solutions across many technologies. It also explores in detail the advantages and limitations of asynchronous messaging architectures.

ALTERNATIVE ARCHITECTURAL PLATFORMS

In principle, enterprise applications can be built on many different technologies. However, looking into current real-life examples, it is evident that a rather small set of platforms are used to build the majority of enterprise applications. The current job market with its job offers provides a good indicator. According to the statistics published by indeed.com, the majority of job offers are made for .NET Framework (including C#) and J2EE/Java developers. Hence, we can safely assume that most enterprise applications actually rely on either of the two aforementioned technologies. Regardless of the difference in platforms, the fundamental concepts apply for both platforms. Here we will briefly describe the J2EE platform and introduce the basic concepts of .NET, to provide a conceptual foundation for further considerations.

J2EE is an application development platform for building robust enterprise systems in the Java programming language. The J2EE Platform extends the Standard Edition (J2SE or JSE) of Java by adding functionality for deploying fault-tolerant, distributed, multi-tier Java software, based largely on modular components running on application servers. J2EE is designed to support applications that implement enterprise services for customers, employees, suppliers, partners, and others who make demands on or contributions to the enterprise. Such applications are inherently complex, potentially accessing data from a variety of sources and distributing applications to a variety of clients. To provide support for a wide variety of enterprise applications, J2EE platform includes numerous Java APIs and tools including RMI, Enterprise JavaBeans, JavaServer Pages and Servlets, JMS, Java Database Connectivity, Web Services, XML, and others, which are the building blocks for enterprise application development. J2EE is defined by its specification. As with other JCP specifications, J2EE specifications were developed by the members of JCP, an open and participative process to develop and revise Java technologies. Providers of Sun-certified J2EE software products must agree to certain conformance requirements in order to declare their products as J2EE compliant on which clients can rely on when choosing between different vendors, which makes the market more transparent. The variety of J2EE certified software products include application servers, such as IBM *WebSphere*, BEA *WebLogic*, or Apache *Geronimo OpenSource Server*, for instance. The proven portability, security, and developer productivity they provide forms the fundamental of the application-programming model. For more details on J2EE, the readers are referred to Refs. [72,73].

As the successor of the former Windows Software Developer Kit, the .NET Framework introduced a completely new and entirely object-oriented programming approach. The core of .NET is the Common Language Runtime (CLR), virtual machine. Like Java, this intermediate abstraction enables the development of platform-agnostic applications. Although Microsoft only supports Windows derivates like the open source .NET implementation. Mono [74] demonstrates the portability by supporting platforms like Linux, Mac OS X, and Solaris. The CLR integration architecture is illustrated in Figure 11.15. All supported languages like C#, VB.NET, or J#.NET, for instance, are compiled into an intermediate language (IL). Thus, developers are no longer forced into a certain programming language, but can choose from one of the many provided for the .NET platform [75], which is very compelling. With such a freedom of programming language, developers trained in a certain language do not need to be trained in an other language and can be productive right away.

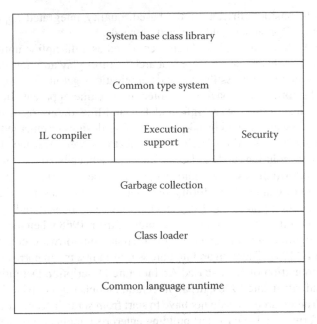

FIGURE 11.15   CLR integration architecture.

Thanks to the IL, .NET was able to introduce many convenient and security enhancing features, such as Memory Management, Life Time/Cycle support, Garbage Collection, a class loading mechanism, and Reflection similar to Java, which ASP or other Windows-based development environments were lacking before. The great advantage .NET provides compared with Java is the superior component support with assemblies that facilitates development and its many reusable components such as the system base class library, Web Forms, Windows Forms, the XML support library, or the Web Service support.

On top of .NET, Microsoft provides the BizTalk [76] Server, an enterprise ready integration framework. It supports all recent software architectures, like message-driven, service-oriented, or tier-based architectures, for instance; BizTalk positions itself as a direct J2EE competitor. The question, which of the two technologies is better or suits a certain scenario best, is highly dependant on the requirements and cannot be answered in a general manner. A deeper understanding of both technologies is needed in order to make reasonable business decisions. From the .NET perspective, Microsoft's knowledge base [77] of articles are providing a wealth of information. For those who prefer written and compiled reading materials, Microsoft Press [78] offers many titles covering these grounds.

CONCLUDING REMARKS

Enterprise application modernization is a gradual, logical, repeatable process that transitions an enterprise IT system from poorly integrated set of substandard applications to business-driven, model-based, quality integrated applications that exactly meet enterprise data and information needs.

Software Architecture had not been recognized as a discipline until early 1990s at which time people began to accept that architectures play an important role in the success of product design. As the software applications get more complex, the need for a more disciplined approach to architecture became apparent. In the past, the architectural descriptions were informal box-and-line diagrams without distinct properties. They were created by adopting previous designs or emerged as a result of trials and many errors. Many architectural features were learned the hard way. Domain-specific solutions and hard experiences have been passed from one architect to the others informally as a tacit knowledge. Over the last 20 years, however, there have been a lot of changes. The formal representations that describe the interactions between system components and subsystems were documented and system properties were identified. This is a significant evolution from 1968 when the first reference to software architecture was given in a conference on software engineering organized by NATO [79]. The term architecture was used in a much narrower sense then. After the introduction of XML-based Architecture Description Definition Language (ADDL) standards in late 1990s, the architectural models started to be shared broadly and reused. Today, architects do not have to start from scratch. There are many architectural platforms available to start building enterprise applications such as J2EE or .NET. Architectural standards, open source software, architecture description languages, and tools are influencing the way architects think and work.

While it is difficult to predict the future, it is expected that pressures to reduce time-to-market will make system integration more prominent than software development. In house developments are costly and time-consuming. Companies increasingly find acquiring external solutions more cost-effective. In-house developments are mostly focusing on creating "glue" among various software solutions. That is why there is a big thrust behind Web services and SOA-based solutions. There are several trends that are being watched by the industry for their potential to impact the future of software architectures. One of them is the growing complexity of software applications driven by bigger and more pervasive application environments. Another one is about the infrastructure. Internet is more reliable. Wireless connections are more ubiquitous. Processing speed is faster. Limitations of computing power and infrastructure over software development are diminishing. Computing resources are accessible to all behind the "cloud" and maintenance is not a concern. A new concept of software delivery, so-called SaaS, is emerging where applications are hosted as a service provided to customers across the Internet. Amazon's Elastic Compute Cloud Web service and Amazon's Simple Storage Service are the examples to this new concept. Combining SaaS applications into companies SOA will be important tasks for IT departments. Network-centric computing as opposed to PC-centric computing trend will provide a much broader set of services that a PC can provide. Another trend is the increasing user mobility. This will impose a different kind of challenges on the software architectures since the requirements of pervasive devices for computing resource are different. In addition, the need for dynamic software updates will impose new architectural challenges. Yet another major trend is the emerging social networks and knowledge-based communities. Productivity is seen to be increasing with wikis, blogs, and other social software. Enterprises will look into possible ways of leveraging the power of social networks within the company.

One thing we can be sure about is the growing complexity of the information content. Enterprise architects have to deal with an abundance of e-mails, instant messages, unstructured documents, and so on, and put them in context. Enterprise software will need to analyze data, and extract information relevant to business. Internet brings an unprecedented growth in data that are waiting to be mined. No matter in which direction technology moves, how much standards improve, and how often we reuse off-the-shelf technologies, there will always be a need for innovation and imagination. The ability to recognize the needs of user communities and address those needs with innovative solutions will shape the future.

REFERENCES

1. Bass, L., Clements, P., and Kazman, R., *Software Architecture in Practice*, 2nd edn., Addison-Wesley, Boston, 2003, pp. 21–24.
2. Weske, M., *Business Process Management*, Springer, Berlin, 2007, Chapter 2.
3. Rozanski, N. and Woods, E., *Software Systems Architecture*, Addison-Wesley, NJ, 2005, Chaps. 2 and 11.
4. Monroe, R. T. et al., Architecture styles, design patterns, and objects, *IEEE Softw.*, 14(1), 43–52, 1997.
5. The Software Industry in the 50s: http://www.softwarehistory.org/history/d_50s.html, last visited July 12, 2009.
6. Di Nitto, E. and Rosenblum, D., Exploiting ADLs to specify architectural styles induced by middleware infrastructures, *Proceedings of the 1999 International Conference on Software Engineering*, Los Angeles, May 16–22, 1999, pp. 13–22.
7. Shaw, M., Toward higher-level abstractions for software systems, *Data Knowl. Eng.*, 5(2), 119–128, 1990.
8. Fielding, R. T., *Software Architectural Styles for Network-based Applications*, University of California, Irvine, CA, URL: http://www.ics.uci.edu/~taylor/ics280e/Fielding%20 arch_survey.pdf, July 15, 1999, last visited July 12, 2009.
9. Perry, D. E. and Wolf, A. L., Foundations for the study of software architecture, *ACM SIGSOFT Softw. Eng. Notes*, 17(4), 40–52, 1992.
10. Kerth, N. L. and Cunningham, W., Using patterns to improve our architectural vision, *IEEE Software*, 14(1), 53–59, 1997.
11. ICCI (Innovation co-ordination, transfer and deployment through networked Co-operation in the Construction Industry), European project IST 2001-33022, 2001/09-2004/02, available at http://cic.vtt.fi/projects/icci/public.html, last accessed July 12, 2009.
12. Pipe-And-Filter, available at http://www.dossier-andreas.net/software_architecture/ pipe_and_filter.html, last visited July 12, 2009.
13. March, D. L., IT533—Software architectures—Class 3—Pipe-and-Filter-Style, available at http://www4.desales.edu/~dlm1/it533/class03/pipe.html, last visited July 12, 2009.
14. Sliwa, C., Event-driven architecture poised for wide adoption, *Computerworld*, Los Angeles, available at http://www.computerworld.com/s/article/81133/Event_driven_ architecture_poised_for_wide_adoption?TaxonomyId=063, last accessed July 12, 2009.
15. Event Driven Architecture, *Wikipedia, The Free Encyclopedia*, http://en.wikipedia.org/ wiki/Event_Driven_Architecture, last visited July 12, 2009.
16. IBM Informix Dynamic Server v10 Information Center, available at http://publib. boulder.ibm.com/infocenter/idshelp/v10/index.jsp?topic=/com.ibm.erep.doc/erep34. htm, last accessed July 12, 2009.

17. Hayes-Roth, B., A blackboard architecture for control, *Artif. Intell.*, 26(2), 251–321, 1985.
18. Lee, D. E. et al., The Hearsay-II Speech-Understanding System: Integrating knowledge to resolve uncertainty, *Comput. Surveys*, 12(2), 213–253, 1980.
19. Corkil, D. D., Countdown to Success: Dynamic objects, GBB, and RADARSAT-1, *Commun. ACM*, 40(5), 48–58, 1997.
20. Gelernter, D., Generative communication in Linda, *ACM Trans. Program. Lang. Syst.*, 7(1), 80–112, 1985.
21. NET Remoting Overview, available at http://msdn2.microsoft.com/en-us/library/kwdt6w2k(VS.71).aspx, last visited July 12, 2009.
22. Foster, I., What Is the Grid? A Three Point Checklist, Argonne National Laboratory & University of Chicago, URL: http://www-fp.mcs.anl.gov/~foster/Articles/WhatIsThe Grid.pdf, last visited July 12, 2009.
23. Strong, P., Enterprise grid computing, *ACM Queue*, 3(6), 50–59, 2005, http://www.acmqueue.com/modules.php?name=Content&pa=showpage&pid=324&page=5, last accessed July 12, 2009.
24. Hohpe, G. and Woolf, B., *Enterprise Integration Patterns*, Addison-Wesley, Boston, 2004, Chap. 1.
25. AIIM International, Enterprise Applications: Adoption of E-Business and Document Technologies, 2000–2001 Worldwide, Gartner/AIIM International, Silver Spring, MD, April 2001, available at http://www.techstreet.com.
26. Enterprise Resource Planning, *Wikipedia, The Free Encyclopedia*, available at http://en.wikipedia.org/wiki/Enterprise_resource_planning, last accessed July 12, 2009.
27. Customer Relationship Management, *Wikipedia, The Free Encyclopedia*, available at http://en.wikipedia.org/wiki/Customer_relationship_management, last accessed July 12, 2009.
28. Enterprise Content Management, *Wikipedia, The Free Encyclopedia*, http://en.wikipedia.org/wiki/Enterprise_content_management, last accessed July 12, 2009.
29. Supply Chain Management, *Wikipedia, The Free Encyclopedia*, available at http://en.wikipedia.org/wiki/Supply_chain_management, last accessed July 12, 2009.
30. Human Resource Management, *Wikipedia, The Free Encyclopedia*, available at http://en.wikipedia.org/wiki/Human_resource_management, last accessed July 12, 2009.
31. Wiederhold, G., What is Your Software Worth? *Comm. of the ACM*, 49(9), 65–75, 2006.
32. Gamma, E. et al., *Design Patterns: Elements of Reusable Object-Oriented Software*, Addison-Wesley, New York, 2005, Chaps. 3, 4, and 5.
33. What is vertical scalability?—A definition from Whatis.com: http://searchcio.techtarget.com/sDefinition/0,,sid182_gci928995,00.html, June 5, 2007, last accessed July 12, 2009.
34. Sun Java Communications Suite 5 Deployment Planning Guide, available at http://docs.sun.com/app/docs/doc/819-4439/acrih?a=view, last visited July 12, 2009.
35. Capacity Planning Example, available at http://e-docs.bea.com/wli/docs92/capplanguide/example.html, last visited July 12, 2009.
36. Atwood, T., Cost and scalability in vertical and horizontal architectures. Implications for database and application layer deployments—Technical White Paper, available at http://www.sun.com/servers/wp/docs/cost_scalability.pdf, September 2004, last accessed July 12, 2009.
37. Scacchi, W., Understanding open source software evolution, Institute for Software Research, University of California, October 2004, http://www.ics.uci.edu/~wscacchi/Papers/New/Understanding-OSS-Evolution.pdf, last accessed July 12, 2009.
38. Clark, C. et al., *Infosecurity 2008—Threat analysis*, Syngress, Burlington, 2007, p. 26.
39. About the Basel Committee, available at http://www.bis.org/bcbs/index.htm, last visited July 12, 2009.

40. Java Platform Standard Edition 6 Java doc, available at http://java.sun.com/javase/6/docs/api/index.html?java/lang/SecurityManager.html, last visited July 12, 2009.
41. Schwartz, M., Data breach kit: Five steps to help you survive the inevitable, June 19, 2007, available at http://esj.com/articles/2007/06/19/data-breach-kit-five-steps-to-help-you-survive-the-inevitable.aspx, last accessed July 12, 2009.
42. PCI Security Standards Council, available at https://www.pcisecuritystandards.org, last visited July 12, 2009.
43. Rules for Visa Merchants—Card Acceptance and Chargeback Management Guidelines, available at http://usa.visa.com/download/merchants/rules_for_visa_merchants.pdf, last visited July 12, 2009.
44. HIPAA, available at http://www.hipaa.org/, last visited July, 12, 2009.
45. Krug, S., *Don't Make me Think: A Common Sense Approach to Web Usability*, New Riders, Berkley, 2000, pp. 35–90.
46. Electronic & Information Technology (Section 508) Homepage, available at http://www.access-board.gov/508.htm, last visited July 12, 2009.
47. Web Content Accessibility Guidelines 1.0, available at http://www.w3.org/TR/WCAG10, last accessed July 12, 2009.
48. How eight pixels cost Microsoft millions—CNET News.com, http://www.news.com/How%20eight%20pixels%20cost%20Microsoft%20millions/2100-1014_3-5316664.html, last accessed July 12, 2009.
49. Scherer, M., A brief introduction to code pages and Unicode. IBM Unicode Technology Group, http://www.ibm.com/developerworks/library/codepages.html, last modified March 1, 2000.
50. Carter, S., *The New Language of Business: SOA and Web 2.0*, Pearson Education, IBM Press, Indianapolis, IN, 2007, Chapters 4–8.
51. Erl, T., *Service-Oriented Architecture: Concepts, Technology, and Design*, Prentice Hall PTR, Upper Saddle River, 2005.
52. Becker, J., Kugeler, M., and Rosemann, M. (Eds.), *Process Management*, Springer, Berlin, Germany, August 2003, Chaps. 1–10.
53. Burlton, R., *Business Process Management: Profiting From Process*, Sams Publishing, Indianapolis, IN, May 2001, Chaps. 3 and 5–16.
54. Chang, J. F., *Business Process Management Systems*, Auerbach Publications, Boca Raton, FL, September 2005, Chaps. 1–3.
55. What Is Software as a Service?—A definition from Whatis.com, http://searchcrm.techtarget.com/sDefinition/0,,sid11_gci1170781,00.html, last accessed July 12, 2009.
56. What Is On-Demand Computing?—A definition from Whatis.com. http://searchdatacenter.techtarget.com/sDefinition/0,,sid80_gci903730,00.html, last accessed July 12, 2009.
57. Papkov, A., Develop a migration strategy from a legacy enterprise IT infrastructure to an SOA-based enterprise architecture, available at http://www.ibm.com/developerworks/webservices/library/ws-migrate2soa/, April 29, 2005, last visited July 12, 2009.
58. Application server, *Wikipedia, The Free Encyclopedia*, available at http://en.wikipedia.org/wiki/Application_server, last visited July 12, 2009.
59. Multitier architecture, *Wikipedia, The Free Encyclopedia*, available at http://en.wikipedia.org/wiki/Multitier_architecture, last visited July 12, 2009.
60. Java EE at a Glance, available at http://java.sun.com/javaee/, last visited July 12, 2009.
61. IBM—WebSphere Application Server–Software, available at http://www.ibm.com/software/webservers/appserv/was/, last visited July 12, 2009.
62. Oracle Fusion Middleware IIg, available at www.oracle.com/appserver/index.html, last visited July 12, 2009.
63. Apache Tomcat, available at http://tomcat.apache.org/, last visited July 12, 2009.
64. Apache Geronimo, available at http://geronimo.apache.org/, last visited July 12, 2009.

65. JBoss.com—JBoss Enterprise Middleware, available at http://www.jboss.org/products/index, last visited July 12, 2009.

66. .NET Framework Developer Center, available at http://msdn2.microsoft.com/en-us/netframework/default.aspx, last visited July 12, 2009.

67. Message-oriented middleware, *Wikipedia, The Free Encyclopedia*, available at http://en.wikipedia.org/wiki/Message_Oriented_Middleware, last visited July 12, 2009.

68. Java Message Service Tutorial, http://java.sun.com/products/jms/tutorial/, last visited July 12, 2009.

69. IBM—WebSphere MQ—Software, available at http://www-01.ibm.com/software/integration/wmq/, last visited July 12, 2009.

70. Apache ActiveMQ, available at http://activemq.apache.org, last visited July 12, 2009.

71. Hohpe, G. and Woolf, B., *Enterprise Integration Patterns: Designing, Building, and Deploying Messaging Solutions*, Addison-Wesley, New York, 2004.

72. Bodoff, S., *The J2EE Tutorial*, Addison-Wesley, New York, 2004.

73. Haugland, S., Cade, M., and Orapallo, A., *J2EE 1.4: The Big Picture*, Prentice Hall, Upper Saddle River, NJ, 2004, Chaps. 1–19.

74. Mono Project Homepage. http://www.mono-project.com, last visited July 12, 2009.

75. dotnetpowered Language List: A list of languages targeting the .NET Framework provided by dotnetpowered.com, available at http://dotnetpowered.com/languages.aspx, last visited July 12, 2009.

76. Microsoft BizTalk Server: Home, available at http://www.microsoft.com/biztalk/default.mspx, last visited July 12, 2009.

77. Microsoft Help and Support, available at http://support.microsoft.com, last visited March 24, 2008.

78. Microsoft Press Homepage, available at http://www.microsoft.com/mspress/, published March 13, 2008.

79. Naur, P. and Randell, B. (Eds.), Software Engineering: Report of a conference sponsored by the NATO Science Committee, Garmisch, Germany, October 7–11, 1968, Brussels, Scientific Affairs Division, NATO, 1969.

12 Service-Oriented Enterprise Modeling and Analysis

Christian Huemer, Philipp Liegl, Rainer Schuster, Marco Zapletal, and Birgit Hofreiter

CONTENTS

MOTIVATION

This chapter concentrates on the modeling and analysis of enterprises that collaborate in a service-oriented world. According to the idea of model-driven development, modeling of service-oriented enterprises collaborating in a networked configuration must address three different layers. The first layer is concerned with business models that describe the exchange of economic values among the business partners. An appropriate methodology on this level of abstraction is e3-value [1,2]. The second layer addresses the inter-organizational business processes among business partners. The third layer addresses the businesses processes executed at each partner's side, that is, what each partner implements locally to contribute to the business collaboration.

A business process in a peer-to-peer collaboration is called a choreography. Accordingly, a choreography describes the flow of interactions between business partners to interlink their individual processes. We distinguish a global choreography from a local choreography. A global choreography defines the peer-to-peer process from the perspective of a neutral observer, whereas a local choreography describes it from the perspective of a participant. For example, a global choreography may specify that "the buyer sends a quote request to the seller, and the seller sends a quote in return to the seller." The related local choreography that the buyer defines is "I send a quote request and I receive a quote in return," whereas the seller defines in its local choreography that "I receive a quote request and, subsequently, I send a quote in return."

The UN/CEFACT Modeling Methodology (UMM) of the United Nations Centre for Trade Facilitation and Electronic Business (UN/CEFACT) [3] customizes the Unified Modeling Language (UML) in order to model inter-organizational business processes between two partners from an observer's perspective. Thus, UMM models describe bilateral global choreographies.

Once two business partners have agreed on a global choreography, the next step is to derive a local choreography for each partner. A local choreography includes those tasks that are carried out, most likely by a software system, at each partner's side to contribute to the collaboration. Therefore, the local choreography should be machine-processable. The most popular language for describing local business processes in a service-oriented environment is the Web Services Business Process Execution Language (WS-BPEL) [4,5].

By deriving the local BPEL processes from the agreed UMM model, we ensure that the local processes are complementary, that is, the flow among the activities is the same, but the activities are inverse to each other. This inverse nature of the local choreographies is best understood by looking again at the request for quote example we used before. The buyer sends the request for quote and receives the quote. Inversely, the seller receives the request for quote and sends the quote.

In the following sections, we describe the e3-value methodology for business models followed by a discussion of UMM and its use in modeling the global choreography of inter-organizational processes. Furthermore, we explain the derivation of a local choreography described by BPEL. This results in a straight-through approach starting from business models, leading to business process models and eventually to machine-interpretable process specifications. The approach is illustrated with the example of a *letter of credit* scenario.

E3-VALUE METHODOLOGY

The e3-value methodology has been developed to model a value Web of actors who create, exchange, and consume things of economic value such as money, physical goods, services, or capabilities [1]. It is a methodology for modeling and designing business models for business networks borrowing from concepts in requirements engineering and conceptual modeling (including a graphical notation). E3-value is based on the principle of economic reciprocity between two sides of an economic exchange, for example, if a seller delivers goods to a buyer, he/she receives money in return.

The e3-value methodology has its own graphical notation introduced by Gordijn and Akkermans [1] and Gordijn [2]. The notation elements are shown in Figure 12.1. We explain the notation by means of a simple example depicted in Figure 12.2.

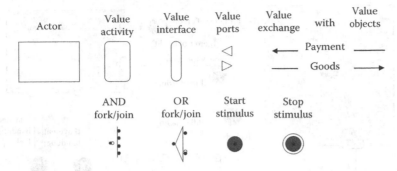

FIGURE 12.1   E3-value notation elements.

Actors (A) are independent economic entities that strive for profitability (in case of an enterprise) or maximizing their economic utility (in case of an end-consumer). Actors signal their willingness to provide or to request value objects through *value interfaces* with *value ports* (B). The rationale of value ports is to hide an actor's internal processes and focus exclusively on the external connections to its business partners (i.e., actors) and other components. Two value ports are connected to conduct a *value exchange* (C) of a *value object* (D). A value object may be either material, such as physical goods, products, or money, or immaterial, such as services, capabilities, or experience, that is valuable to one or more actors of the business network.

There are two kinds of ports on a *value interface* (E): in-ports to receive value objects and out-ports to provide value objects. Usually a value interface includes at least one of each kind. The presence of both represents the concept of economic reciprocity and shows the *value objects* that are exchanged.

In order to satisfy a particular consumer's need, many value exchanges may have to take place among different actors. For this purpose, use case maps [7] connect value interfaces that, in combination, satisfy a consumer's need. A scenario path (F) is indicated by a dotted line and starts at a *start stimulus* (G) and ends with a *stop stimulus* (H). AND and OR forks are used to model parallel and alternative paths. Please note that, in our simple example of Figure 12.2, the scenario path does not connect value interfaces due to its simplicity. However, a combination of different value interfaces on the same scenario path is later on demonstrated in the more complex example of Figure 12.3.

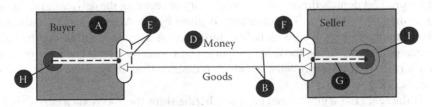

FIGURE 12.2   Simple e3-value example.

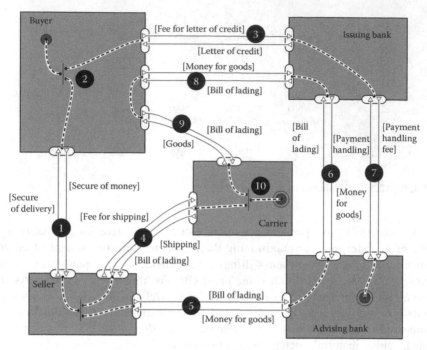

FIGURE 12.3   E3-value model "letter of credit."

It is important to stress that e3-value does not specify any sequential order. This means that there is no order between the *value exchanges* within a *value interface*, nor is there any order between the *value exchanges* of *value interfaces* connected by *scenario paths*. This is a significant difference between e3-value representing a business (value) modeling methodology and business process modeling approaches [6].

We demonstrate the concepts of e3-value by the means of the *letter of credit* scenario depicted in Figure 12.3. The letter of credit is a common business scenario in international trade transactions. The main purpose of the letter of credit is to secure the interests of both the *seller* and the *buyer*. The seller's economic value is to ensure that the buyer is able to pay the goods he/she is delivering whereas the buyer's economic value is ensuring to get the goods he/she is paying for. The value exchange (1) in Figure 12.3 depicts this economic reciprocity of securing the delivery in exchange to securing the payment. This insurance is given by the AND-fork in (2) indicating that if the buyer wants a good, he/she must request a letter of credit via the value exchange (3) *AND* doing the value exchange (1) (a good for a fee). The letter of credit is a service of the *issuing bank* by which it ensures that, if the seller ships a good, then he/she gets paid.

If the seller has a guaranteed payment, he/she ships the goods via a *carrier* in (4). In order to get the *bill of lading* (which has a significant economic value similar to the money for the seller*) he/she pays a fee for the shipping. Via the value exchange in (5), the seller trades the bill of lading in exchange for money. Furthermore, the bill of lading is transferred via the issuing bank to the buyer—value exchanges (6) and (8). In return for the bill of lading (9), the carrier delivers the ordered good to the buyer. The AND-join in (10) manages, that the bill of lading should also be obtained by the carrier, once the good has been delivered. For the services granted, the issuing bank pays a handling fee to the advising bank as shown in the value exchange (7).

BUSINESS PROCESS MODELING WITH UMM

After having successfully created the business value model, the next logical step is the definition of a business process model. In the field of enterprise integration, the business process modeler first focuses on the inter-organizational business process as it represents the global choreography accepted by all participating business partners. As mentioned earlier, a global choreography describes a business process from a neutral perspective, whereas a local choreography describes a process from a business partner's perspective. Hence, the global choreography is used to derive the local choreography.

UN/CEFACT MODELING METHODOLOGY

We now focus on UMM for modeling inter-organizational business processes [3]. An inter-organizational business process is an organized group of related activities carried out by multiple organizations to accomplish a common business. UMM is developed and maintained by the UN/CEFACT. The UMM is based on UML and customizes the UML to the specific needs of inter-organizational business process modeling [8]. Thereby, the UMM specifies new elements beyond those specified by the UML meta-model. These new elements, or stereotypes, are derived from existing UML modeling elements.

Figure 12.4 shows an example of a UMM model describing the letter of credit use case between an issuing bank and an advising bank. As denoted by (A) in this figure, a UMM model is split up into three distinctive and self-contained views: *business requirements view* (bRequirementsV), *business choreography view* (bChoreographyV), and *business information view* (bInformationV). The terms in brackets denote the used stereotypes. Due to space limitations, only the most important views are shown in detail on the right-hand side of Figure 12.4.

BUSINESS REQUIREMENTS VIEW

The business requirements view identifies the relevant processes within the participating business partner's enterprises that are possible candidates for the integration

---

* The bill of lading is a legal document between the shipper of a particular good and the carrier detailing the type, quantity and destination of the good being carried. The bill of lading also serves as a receipt of shipment when the good is delivered to the predetermined destination. This document must accompany the shipped goods and must be signed by representatives of the carrier, shipper, and receiver.

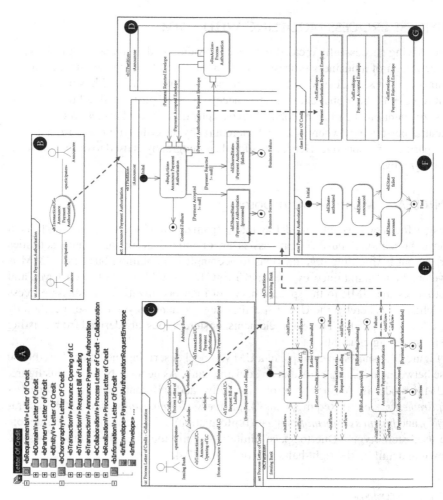

FIGURE 12.4 UMM descriptions of the processes for "letter of credit."

into an inter-organizational business process. As shown in (A) in Figure 12.4, the business requirements view consists of three subviews: *business domain view* (bDomainV), *business partner view* (bPartnerV), and *business entity view* (bEntityV), which are defined as follows.

- The business domain view is used to classify the existing business processes on each partner's side according to predefined schemes such as the Common Business Process Catalogue [9] or the ISO Open-edi model [10].
- The business partner view described the identities of the different parties participating in the inter-organizational process. Both views are not shown in detail since they provide no additional value for the overall understanding of the UMM.
- The business entity view shows each *business entity* in the transaction process between two partners (e.g., a `paymentauthorization`). Each business entity has a lifecycle described using state diagrams. Diagram (F) in Figure 12.4 shows the life cycle for the `paymentauthorization` business entity.

BUSINESS CHOREOGRAPHY VIEW

The modeler uses the requirements captured in the artifacts of the business requirements view in order to further detail the identified processes in the so-called business choreography view. A business choreography view has three different subviews: a *business transaction view* (bTransactionV), a *business collaboration view* (bCollaborationV), and a *business realization view* (bRealizationV). Due to space limitations, the *business realization view*, which reuses the same collaboration between different sets of business partners, is not further elaborated in this chapter.

Each business transaction has a dedicated business transaction view. As shown in (B) in Figure 12.4, the modeler first captures the participants of a *business transaction* using the concept of a *business transaction use case* (bTransactionUC) and *authorized roles* (`announcer` and `announcee`, i.e., the one who receives the announcement).

A business transaction use case is further refined using the activity diagram of a business transaction (D). The purpose of a *business transaction* is to align the business information system of the collaborating business partners. The synchronization can be unidirectional or bidirectional. In an unidirectional transaction, the initiator of the business transaction informs the responding partner about an already irreversible state change that the responder has to accept, for example, a notification about the arrival of goods. It follows, that responding in such a scenario is not required. In a bidirectional transaction, the initiating partner sets a business entity to an interim state and the responding partner decides about its final state.

A business transaction consists of two *business transaction partitions*—one for the *requesting business action* (ReqAction) and the other for the *responding business action* (ResAction). Each partition is assigned to exactly one authorized role. It must be one of the roles assigned to the corresponding business transaction use case in (B). On the left-hand side of (D) in Figure 12.4, the `announcer` is shown and on the

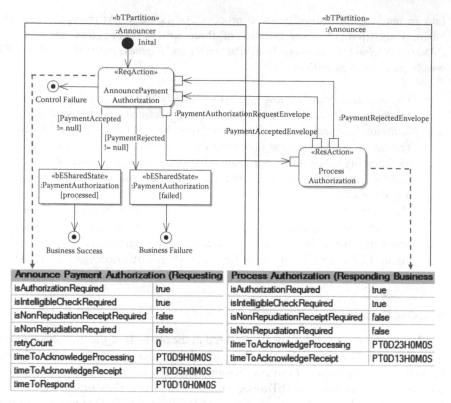

FIGURE 12.5   A UMM business transaction and its tagged values.

right-hand side the `announcee`. The `announcer` announces the *payment autho-rization* by sending a `paymentauthorizationrequestenvelope` to the `announcee`. After evaluating the request the `announcee` either replies with a `pay-ment acceptedenvelope` or a `payment rejectedenvelope`. Depending on the type of result, the `announcee` is sending to the `announcer` the *business entity* `payment authorization` changes to a different state—either `processed` or `failed`. It is important to note that each of these states reflects one of the business entity states previously defined in the business entity lifecycle (F).

Of particular importance for the later derivation of deployment artifacts (e.g., BPEL and Web Services Description Language [WSDL]) from a UMM model are the so-called tagged values. As shown in Figure 12.5, the *requesting business action* and the *responding business action* have a set of tagged values coordinating the so-called business signals. The detailed meaning of these business signals will be discussed later in the section covering the derivation of the WSDL files.

In complex scenarios such as in the case of a `letterofcredit`, business col-laborations chain a sequence of business transactions together. First a business col-laboration use case (bCollaborationUC) is defined together with the participating *authorized roles*. As shown in (E) in Figure 12.4, the *authorized roles*, `issuing bank` and `advising bank`, are participating in the *business collaboration* process letter of credit. The dependency between *business transactions* and a *business collaboration* is denoted by the *include* dependencies in (C). The *business collaboration* process letter of credit thereby consists of three *business transactions*: announce opening of letter of credit, request bill of lading, and announce payment authorization.

The *business collaboration use case* is further refined using the concept of a *business collaboration* as shown in (E). A business collaboration defines the exact execution order of the different business transactions associated with it. In (E), the overall *business collaboration* process letter of credit between the issuing bank and the advising bank is split up into three different *business transactions*. Please note the dependency between the last *business transaction* announce payment authorization in (E) and its refining *business transaction* diagram in (D). The two results of the *business transaction* in (D) (payment authorization in state processed or failed) directly map to the *business collaboration*. In case the *business transaction* fails, the *business collaboration* also fails. This is denoted on the lower side of the *business collaboration* in (E) using the two guard conditions leading to the final states success and failure.

BUSINESS INFORMATION VIEW

The last and final view of UMM is the business information view (bInformationV). This view is used to unambiguously define the business document information exchanged in a business transaction. For example, the transaction announce payment authorization outlined in (D) is associated with three business documents: namely, payment authorization request envelope, payment accepted envelope, and payment rejected envelope. In order to set the exchanged document type, the outgoing pin of the *requesting action* and the outgoing pins of the *responding actions* are classified using the *information envelopes* (InfEnvelope) as defined in the *business information view* (G). In UML, pins are used to denote instances of incoming and outgoing information. The *information envelope* thereby serves as the root element in a business document hierarchy. Any additional business document data is attached to an *information envelope* using associations. The UMM specification does not specifically mandate a particular way to describe business documents. However, a modeler is strongly encouraged to use UPCC (UN/CEFACT UML Profile for Core Components) [11–13] for document modeling, since it allows for a seamless integration into a UMM model.

TRANSFORMATION TO WS-BPEL

UMM models capture business collaborations in a graphical representation readily understandable by humans. They provide the foundation for deriving process specifications that implement a partner's business service interface. In this section, we briefly describe the mapping of a UMM model to the relevant standards of the Web services stack—the WSDL [14] and the WS-BPEL [4]. UMM artifacts of the *business transaction view* (e.g., a *business transaction*) follow strict rules enabling the definition of generic transformation rules to BPEL.

In the following, we outline the code generation by our example business transaction announce payment authorization. Instead of showing formal transformation rules, we describe the mapping by means of the resulting code, since this greatly facilitates understanding.

Generating the business service interface usually starts with an identification of the services that each partner must offer. Each partner must provide services for receiving business documents and services for receiving business signals. In the first step, we concentrate on the former. In a one-way business transaction, only the responder must provide a service for receiving documents, since there is only an information flow from the transaction's initiator to the responder. In a two-way business transaction, business documents are communicated in both directions. Hence, the initiator of the transaction has to offer a service for receiving the response business document as well. A two-way business transaction is implemented by two asynchronous service calls for exchanging the business documents. This solution is favored instead of using just a single synchronous call in order to avoid blocking in long-running business transactions.

Let us consider the *business transaction* announce payment authorization of our UMM example model in Figure 12.4 conducted between the issuing bank and the advising bank. The service interface of the advising bank must be capable of receiving a payment authorization request envelope, whereas the issuing bank must offer services for picking up a payment acceptance envelope and a payment rejection envelope. As said before, besides receiving business documents, each partner must provide services for receiving business signals. In UMM, business signals acknowledge the successful receipt and/or processing of a prior received business document. The exchange of exceptions for reporting errors on the same topic is required as well but due to space limitations not detailed any further. In a UMM business transaction, business signals are specified for each message exchange using the quality of service parameters *time to acknowledge receipt* and *time to acknowledge processing* (*cf*, Figure 12.5). The former is communicated after a received business document passed schema validation, grammar validation, and finally sequence validation in the context of the process. The latter is sent after the business document passed checks against additional business rules and is handed over to the processing business application. Accordingly, the interface of a business partner must offer two additional service operations: one for receiving *acknowledgements of receipt* and one for *receiving acknowledgements of processing*. The following listings (Listings 12.1 and 12.2) show stubs of WSDL port types describing the service interfaces of the issuing bank and the advising bank, respectively.

In order to map the flow of a UMM model to the Web Services stack, we employ WS-BPEL to describe the choreography of service interactions. UMM captures the global choreography of a business collaboration—this means it specifies a neutral perspective for all business partners. It specifies the single version of truth on which the business partners agree to interact with each other. BPEL, however, describes a local choreography by defining the partner-specific view of a business process. Thus, the BPEL process of the issuing bank is not the same as the one of the advising bank, but both processes must be complementary to each other. In other

```
<portType name="IssuingBk-PT">
 <operation name="receivePaymentAcceptanceEnvelope">
 <input message="tns:PaymentAcceptanceEnvelope" />
 </operation>
 <operation name="receivePaymentRejectionEnvelope">
 <input message="tns:PaymentRejectionEnvelope" />
 </operation>
 <operation name="receiveAckReceipt">
 <input message="tns:receiveAckReceipt" />
 </operation>
 <operation name="receiveAckProcessing">
 <input message="tns:receiveAckProcessing" />
 </operation>
</portType>
```

LISTING 12.1   Port types of the issuing bank.

words, whenever someone sends something the other one has to receive something. By deriving partner-specific BPEL processes from the global UMM choreography, it is ensured that the resulting local choreographies are in fact complementary. The local choreographies serve as blueprints to check if the local implementations are compliant with the agreed flow.

BPEL describes a business process as a flow of interactions between Web services. The relationship between two interacting services is captured by the concept of a *partner link type*. It describes two interacting services by their role in the business process and the port types they have to provide. Considering our example, the partner link type shown in the following listing binds the services of the issuing bank and the advising bank together. Consequently, the party that acts as the issuing bank has to provide the services of the listing in Listing 12.1, whereas the services in Listing 12.2 correspond to the interface of the advising bank.

In the following, we elaborate the mapping of a UMM business transaction to BPEL code. We outline the mapping by means of the resulting BPEL code for the advising bank (Listing 12.3) of the example *business transaction* announce

```
<portType name="AdvisingBk-PT">
 <operation name="receivePaymentAuthorizationRequestEnvelope">
 <input message="tns:PaymentAuthorizationRequestEnvelope" />
 </operation>
 <operation name="receiveAckReceipt">
 <input message="tns:receiveAckReceipt" />
 </operation>
 <operation name="receiveAckProcessing">
 <input message="tns:receiveAckProcessing" />
 </operation>
</portType>
```

LISTING 12.2   Port type of the advising bank.

```
1.  <process>

2.  <partnerLinks>
3.  <partnerLink name="Issuing-Advising" partnerLinkType="Issuing-
    Advising-PLT" myRole="Advising-Bk" partnerRole="Issuing-Bk"/>
    </partnerLinks>

4.  <variables>
5.  <variable name="PaymentAuthorizationRequestEnvelope" ... />
6.  <variable name="AckReceipt" .../>
7.  ...
8.  </variables>

9.  <sequence>
10. <receive partnerLink="Issuing-Advising" portType="AdvisingBk-PT"
    operation="receivePaymentAuthorizationRequestEnvelope"
    variable="PaymentAuthorizationRequestEnvelope" />
11. <sequence>
12. <invoke partnerLink="Issuing-Advising" portType="IssuingBk-PT"
      operation="receiveAckReceipt" variable="AckReceipt"/>
13.   <invoke partnerLink="Issuing-Advising" portType="IssuingBk-PT"
      operation="receiveAckProcessing" variable="AckProcessing"/>
14. </sequence>
15. <if>
16.   <condition>isPaymentAuthorizationRequestAccepted()</condition>
17.   <invoke partnerLink="Issuing-Advising" portType="IssuingBk-PT"
      operation="receivePaymentAcceptanceEnvelope"
      inputVariable="PaymentAcceptanceEnvelope" />
18.   <else>
19.   <invoke partnerLink="Issuing-Advising" portType="IssuingBk-PT"
      operation="receivePaymentRejectionEnvelope"
      inputVariable="PaymentRejectionEnvelope" />
20.   </else>
21. </if>
22. <pick>
23.   <onMessage partnerLink="Issuing-Advising" portType="AdvisingBk-PT"
      operation="receiveAckReceipt" variable="AckReceipt">
24.   <empty />
25.   </onMessage>
26.   <onAlarm>
27.   <for>PT6H</for>
28.   </onAlarm>
29. </pick>
30. <pick>
31.   <onMessage partnerLink="Issuing-Advising" portType="AdvisingBk-PT"
      operation="receiveAckProcessing" variable="AckProcessing">
32.   <empty />
33.   </onMessage>
34.   <onAlarm>
35.   <for>PT6H</for>
36.   </onAlarm>
37. </pick>
38. </sequence>
39. </process>
```

LISTING 12.3   BPEL code for the advising bank in the business transaction announce payment authorization of Figure 12.5.

payment authorization (Figure 12.5). One should note that the code frag-
ment is simplified by removing namespaces, name attributes for activities, and so on,
in order to enhance readability. The derived BPEL code describes the local choreography of the advising bank—that is, the responder in the business transaction.
The local choreography captures the observable and required behavior for interacting in the business transaction. It does not reveal internal implementation details
how the advising bank binds its private processes for participating in the
business collaboration.

The example code starts with a *partner link* defining the role of the owner of the
BPEL process and the role of the collaborating partner (starting with line 2 in Listing
12.3). Since we show the responder's part of the business transaction, the owner
of the process is the advising bank and the partner role is taken up by the
issuing bank.

The *partner link* element is followed by the *variables* section. Each exchanged
information in a UMM transaction, no matter if it is a business document or a business signal, is mapped to a *variable* in BPEL. Lines 5 and 6 exemplify the definitions of the business document payment authorization request envelope
and of an *acknowledgement of receipt* business signal. We omit to list all the other
variable definitions.

The control flow of the advising bank's local choreography starts with line
10. Corresponding to the example in Figure 12.4, the first activity of the advising
bank is to receive the payment authorization request envelope. This
is denoted by the *receive* activity in line 10. Reception is confirmed with an *acknowledgement of receipt* (line 12). Similarly, the *invoke* activity in line 13 results in
sending an *acknowledgement of processing*, to confirm that the document is being
processed.

The *if* element starting with line 15 specifies that advising bank can in this
step either accept or reject the payment authorization—either by sending a payment
acceptance envelope (line 17) or a payment rejection envelope (line
19). The decision about acceptance of the payment is internal to the advising bank.
The condition in line 16 is an opaque function accessing the internal decision.

Subsequently, the advising bank expects an *acknowledgement of receipt* of
the issuing bank, which confirms the receipt of either of the two response documents. The advising bank waits for an amount of time specified by the tagged
value *time to acknowledge receipt* for the *acknowledgement of receipt* of the responding business action process authorization. The fact that the advising bank
awaits the document within a certain timeframe is denoted by the *pick* element in
line 22. Within the *onMessage* element, the *acknowledgement of receipt* message
specifies the message type that the advising bank is expecting in this step. The
onAlarm element holds the maximum time the advising bank can wait for the
acknowledgement before declaring an error. In this example, this wait time corresponds to 13 h. Upon receipt of the acknowledgement within the maximum allowed
time interval, the control flow moves to the next message exchange. In case the
acknowledgement does not arrive, a time-out exception is sent and the business
transaction is re-started. The code related to the exception handling is not shown in
Listing 12.3.

Both *acknowledgement of processing* and *acknowledgement of receipt* are handled in a similar way. Hence, we use a similar *pick* construct for picking up the *acknowledgement of processing* starting with line 30. In this case, the maximum time frame corresponds to 23 h (see the example business transaction in Figure 12.5). After the receipt of the *acknowledgement of processing*, the choreography of the example *business transaction* announce payment authorization ends successfully.

UMM business transactions follow always the same pattern. Thus, each UMM business transaction may be transformed to BPEL following the procedures outlined above. Mapping a whole business collaboration protocol requires the transformation of the business transactions of which it is composed and the control flow between the different business transactions. To ensure a well-defined mapping from business collaboration protocols to BPEL, not all the flow concepts of UML activity diagrams are allowed. A mapping is guaranteed, if the business collaboration protocol is limited to the following basic control flow patterns [15]: sequence, parallel split, synchronization, exclusive choice, multiple choice, and simple merge. In this case, the BPEL process can be created by basic activities and by the structured activities sequence, switch and flow.

CONCLUSION

In this chapter, we discussed a three-layered approach for modeling the business goals and processes of business partners that collaborate in a service-oriented environment. On the top layer—the business model layer—we introduced the e3-value methodology to analyze the value proposition of each partner in the network. The e3-value methodology was exemplified by the means of the letter of credit business scenario, which requires the collaboration between buyer, seller, carrier, issuing bank, and advising bank. On the middle layer—dealing with the inter-organizational business process—we focused on the UMM. It is used to define bilateral and global choreographies between two business partners. We continued the letter of credit example and presented the resulting choreography between issuing bank and the advising bank. On the bottom-layer—concentrating on the local processes of each partner—we discussed how BPEL is able to model both a local choreography as well as an orchestration. Thereby, an orchestration specifies an executable business processes internal to an enterprise. A local choreography is a subset of an orchestration comprising only those process steps required for interacting with the orchestrated business process. We demonstrated a transformation from the global UMM choreography to the local BPEL choreography by means of the local process of the advising bank in the letter of credit scenario.

REFERENCES

1. Gordijn, J. and Akkermans, H. Value based requirements engineering: Exploring innovative e-commerce ideas, *Require. Eng. J.*, 8(2), 114–134, 2003.
2. Gordijn, J., Value-based requirements engineering; Exploring innovative e-commerce, PhD dissertation, Vrije Universiteit, The Netherlands, 2002, available at http://e3value.few.vu.nl/docs/bibtex/pdf/GordijnVBRE2002.pdf, last accessed on July 26, 2009.

3. UN/CEFACT TMG, UN/CEFACT's Modeling Methodology (UMM), UMM Meta Model—Foundation Module Candidate for 2.0, draft for implementation verification, United Nations Centre for Trade Facilitation and Electronic Business, Geneva, Switzerland, 30 January 2009, available at http://www.untmg.org/wp-content/uploads/2009/01/specification_umm_foundation_module_v20_implementationdraft_20090130.pdf, last accessed on July 26, 2009.

4. OASIS, *Web Services Business Process Execution Language (WS-BPEL)*, Version 2.0, Billerica, MA, 2007, available at http://docs.oasis_open.org/wsbpee/2.0/wsbpel-v2.0.html, last accessed on July 26, 2009.

5. Juric, M., *Business Process Execution Language for Web Services: BPEL and BPEL4WS*, 2nd edn., Packt Publishing, Birmingham, UK, 2006.

6. Gordijn, J. and Akkermans, H. Designing and evaluating e-business models, *IEEE Intell. Syst.*, 16(4), 11–17, 2001.

7. Buhr, R. J. A. Use case maps as architectural entities for complex systems, *IEEE Trans. Softw. Eng.*, 24(12), 1131–1155, 1998.

8. Zapletal, M., Liegl, P., and Schuster R., Eds., *UN/CEFACT's Modeling Methodology (UMM) 1.0—A Guide to UMM and the UMM Add-In*, VDM Verlag Dr. Müller, Saarbrüken, 2008.

9. UN/CEFACT, *Common Business Process Catalog*, Version 1.0, 30 September 2005, available at http://www.uncefactforum.org/TBG/TBG14/TBG14%20Documents/cbpc-technical-specification-v1_0-300905-11.pdf, last accessed on July 26, 2009.

10. ISO 14662, *Open-edi Reference Model*, Geneva, Switzerland, 2004, available at http://www.iso.org, last accessed on July 26, 2009.

11. UN/CEFACT, Core Components Technical Specification—Part 8 of the ebXML Framework, United Nations Centre For Trade Facilitation and Electronic Business, Version 2.01, Geneva, Switzerland, 2003, available at http://www.unece.org/cefact/ebxml/CCTS_V2-01_Final.pdf, last accessed on July 26, 2009.

12. UN/CEFACT, Core Components Technical Specification 3.0 draft, United Nations Centre for Trade Facilitation and Electronic Business, Geneva, Switzerland, 12 December 2008, available at http://www.unece.org/cefact/forum_grps/tmg/CCTS-SecondIteration-ODP6.pdf, last accessed on July 26, 2009.

13. UN/CEFACT, UPCC—UML Profile for Core Components (VPCC), Version 1.0, Final Specification, Geneva, Switzerland, 16 January 2008, available at http://www.unece.org/cefact/codesfortrade/UPCC_UML-CoreComponents.pdf, last accessed on July 26, 2009.

14. W3C, *Web Services Description Language (WSDL)*, Version 1.1, W3C, MIT, Cambridge, MA, 2001, available at http://www.w3.org/TR/wsdl, last accessed on July 26, 2009.

15. van der Aalst, W. M. P. et al., Workflow patterns, *Distrib. Parallel Databases*, 14(1), 5–51, 2003.

16. Weigand, H. et al., Value object analysis and the transformation from value model to process model, in *Enterprise Interoperability, New Challenges and Approaches*, Doumeingts, G. et al., Eds., Springer-Verlag, London, 2007, 55–65.

13 Granting Flexibility to Business Process Management

Dario Bottazzi and Rebecca Montanari

CONTENTS

INTRODUCTION

The dynamic nature of the business environment today requires flexibility so that enterprises may revise their structure and reorganize their workflows rapidly [1]. Process-oriented approaches are emerging as a way to optimize business processes and rationalize interactions among enterprise departments to make way for changes in work practices and arrangements [1–3].

323

Process-oriented enterprise management is not a trivial activity and raises several challenging problems. Despite the efforts spent on business process management (BPM) solutions [4], over 50% of process reengineering projects do not meet their expected goals [3]. This high failure rate can be attributed to the complexity and the dynamic nature of business processes and the high degree of interdependence among the services and resources integrated within the same processes. As a result, it is very difficult to foresee and quantify the full impact of radical proposals for change and to compare alternative designs. The consequence is that the reengineering of business processes is typically implemented without full appreciation of its implications on the cost, timeliness, and frequency of reworks.

Business intelligence (BI) and business activity monitoring (BAM) solutions can improve the management of existing business processes but offer limited help in the evaluation and assessment of different re-design proposals. What is needed is a systematic way for comparing process design options through simulation of the alternative business processes. First, we describe the BPM cycle and the state-of-the art in business process simulation. Next, we present the main requirements that business process simulators should meet and introduce our PROSIT business process simulator. The solution implements the main standards of BPM and supports the rapid prototyping of business processes, service designs and resource allocation schemes within enterprises. We describe its model, architecture, and implementation algorithm. The chapter concludes with remarks on future research directions.

CURRENT PRACTICES IN BUSINESS PROCESS SIMULATION

The large majority of quantifiable approaches for BAM and BI tend to focus on business process monitoring and postexecution analysis. Available technologies cannot predict whether the proposed processes would ever meet management's requirements and expectations; simulations are the main way to mitigate the risks of ending up with unsatisfactory outcomes [5–7].

The early attempts in business process simulation adopted general-purpose discrete event simulators. More recently, process-oriented solutions have been considered but these solutions are often stand-alone applications that do not readily integrate with existing BPM products. In addition, available simulators tend to group business processes as well as the business context (i.e., the enterprise services and resources) within the same simulation model, thus concealing several relevant aspects such as the dependencies and interactions among the enterprise services and resources. In addition, the notations used in the simulation models are often quite complex and must be translated manually to other languages before they could be implemented.

The above considerations underline the need for models that separate the business process from the simulation context. Accordingly, the business process model would represent the sequence of steps to be executed, whereas the simulation context covers the set of enterprise services and resources involved in the process. Implementing simulated services and resources in terms of executable code would permit fine-grained modeling of the interactions among processes and enterprise services and resources. It would open the possibility of simulating business processes that can be readily enacted in production environments. Finally, a further relevant guideline is compliance to the main standards of the BPM field, for example, Workflow Management Coalition (WfMC) standards and the XML Process Description Language (XPDL) [8]. Standard compliance allows process simulation to run over the enterprise BPM infrastructure with a few (if any) changes. In addition, the compliance of the simulation results with conventional audit trails from BPM engines can facilitate their analysis through well-known BI tools and techniques.

BPM Cycle

The BPM research field provides a rich set of tools, techniques, and methodologies to model, implement, maintain, and analyze enterprise business processes. There is a wide consensus that BPM can be modeled as a cyclic activity composed of four iterative steps (Figure 13.1): process design, system configuration, process enactment, and process diagnosis [4]. During *process design*, designers model a business process by taking into account various aspects including enterprise organization/re-organization and control and data flows. Because process design often requires an in-depth reconsideration of the enterprise structure and organization, process designers need the collaboration of the various departments and functional units of the enterprise.

System configuration is the phase where all services and resources available within the organization are integrated into the enterprise information system according to the technical requirements and constraints, for example, security, system reliability, and so forth. Sometimes the configuration phase requires the development of *ad hoc* services to address specific problems. More frequently, system configuration calls only for the integration of existing legacy services and applications.

The *process enactment* phase is where the process is actually implemented and run. In the *process diagnosis* phase, the alignment between the enacted business processes and the goals set by the enterprise management is evaluated. To conduct this evaluation, BPM solutions (often) integrate data mining software to identify possible design inefficiencies in the implemented services or redundancies in process execution. The diagnosis phase is typically based on audit trails that BPM solutions generate during process execution. The information learned during the diagnosis phase provides a suitable basis for design improvements, thus fostering further iterations of the BPM cycle.

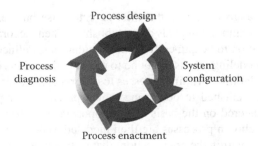

FIGURE 13.1 Model of the BPM cycle.

Despite its popularity, the above model has several limitations. In particular, adjustments to process design can take place only late in the cycle, which is particularly onerous in highly dynamic environments characterized by frequent changes. In fact, process diagnosis depends on the availability of large data sets of audit trails to identify possible design deficiencies from the implemented processes.

The above considerations suggest that the evaluation of business process reengineering efforts should take place in the process design and system configuration phases using simulations. However, process designers often underestimate this task and <10% of processes reengineering initiatives are supported by simulations [9]. On the contrary, over 80% of reengineering projects rely on graphical tools, such as static flow charts, to promote a shared understanding among the stakeholders of what is involved, even though that these tools do not provide quantifiable measures for the analysis. As for the evaluation of alternatives, some reengineering projects have adopted spreadsheet-like solutions for analytical evaluations and comparison of the design options, even though they cannot account for the dynamic and the stochastic nature of enterprise business processes and cannot consider critical but rare events. This is why simulation appears as a viable and cost-effective way to make informed decisions. It allows the estimation of the important parameters that may not be directly available, perhaps because the necessary information was not collected by the organization [5].

METHODOLOGY FOR BUSINESS PROCESS SIMULATION

Business process simulation can be considered from the point of methodology and technology. The methodology perspective considers the best practices to organize work and to minimize the risk of failures in business process re-design. The technology perspective focuses on technical requirements of business process simulation solutions.

Business process simulation methodologies comprise several distinctive steps: preliminary process analysis, process modeling and testing, and results analysis [3,10]. Although these steps are sequential, they are usually executed iteratively and incrementally until they produce a suitable outcome, perhaps after several iterations.

PRELIMINARY ANALYSIS

The preliminary analysis targets the existing enterprise business processes. First, precise process reengineering goals are established. Then, according to these goals, the set of information to be gained from the simulation is defined. For example, the objective of the modeling efforts might be to evaluate the effects of downsizing or of allocating particular tasks within processes to different employees. Then, simulation boundaries are established to determine which processes, or parts of a process, should be reengineered on the basis of the importance of these processes or their inefficiency. The chosen processes are then modeled to define the current structure and work practices within the organization, that is, to define the *status quo* precisely so as to be the benchmark for comparison. Key performance indicators (KPIs) are then defined to quantify the performance of the business processes and the degree of their alignment with management goals [11].

MODELING AND TESTING

Business process modeling and testing are provided in the following steps. The starting point is process redesign, either by implementing iterative incremental changes to the organization or by proposing a radically new structure. Reengineered processes KPIs are then compared with those of the *status quo*; should they be judged satisfactory, the model-testing phase could follow. Model testing requires experimentation with several models through verification and validation techniques. If no significant problems are discovered during a thorough testing of the simulation model, an extensive phase of model experimentation can begin. Process model experimentation relies on simulations of business process execution, provided that the experiment is as simple as possible and that enough alternatives are included to cover a wide range of organizational units and to allow sound statistical analysis.

OUTPUT ANALYSIS

Output analysis is the final step of business process simulation to define changes or improvements to be brought on the *status quo*. Output results obtained during experimentation should be analyzed using standard statistical techniques. Statistics, such as, for example, the average time to complete the execution of a business process, can be used to determine whether there are significant differences between the key model output variables of different experiments.

TECHNICAL REQUIREMENTS

Simulating business processes is a challenging task; yet, despite the relative immaturity of the field, there is a consensus on the main requirements of business process simulation tools. This common view is summarized as follows:

- Use of graphical notations to promote a common understanding among all functional entities involved in the process reengineering. The notation should be simple enough for those that are not expert in process reengineering to understand. In addition, notation should be formally defined to avoid misinterpretations.
- Simulation to cover a range of processes from strategic, up to financial, production, and logistic processes. As a consequence, the degree of details needed in the model would vary according to the process to be simulated.
- Modeling and simulation of all parameters of interest to evaluate the process KPIs before actual process enactment [12–14]. Parameters of interest depend on the context and application and may range from the time needed to complete activities and business processes to the cost associated to resource access.

- Integration of the simulation support with existing BPM solutions. Simulation solutions should be used both during process design to optimize processes and at run-time to foresee properties and outcomes that currently running processes are likely to exhibit in the future.
- Stochastic representation of business processes [14,15] to improve understanding of the average properties of business processes and to identify critical situations. Some of the stochastic processes represent the time to complete an activity, for example, process completion time or down-time, and so forth, which may lead to significant variations in process outcomes.
- Capability of addressing different scenarios [16,17] to model potential critical situations. Scenario set-up should be simple to permit experimentation by modifying the instantiation patterns, availability of resources or variability in the time needed to complete process activities execution, and so forth.
- Storage for the results for retrieval, distribution, and input to analysis [12,14].
- Report of the results by composing documents for distribution to interested parties.

BUSINESS PROCESS SIMULATION

Early simulation solutions were based on general-purpose discrete event simulators, whereas current trends suggest consideration of process-oriented simulations using Petri networks. Finally, event-driven process chains (EPCs)-based solutions have been gaining more attention in recent years.

GENERAL PURPOSE DISCRETE EVENT SIMULATION

General purpose discrete event simulators model business processes and track the parameters of interest by considering the stochastic properties of the processes and are still adopted in several business process simulation solutions [18,19].

The main drawback of this approach is its complexity because the simulation models are described with executable code, which prevents their understanding by the noninitiated. The inherent complexity of process representation makes simulation results expensive, particularly, because errors in the simulation code logic are often difficult to detect and fix. It is also very difficult to provide customized models that would fit the needs of each category of interested parties. As a consequence, designers have to build different simulation models of the same process, each producing a different view of the results, without a guarantee of consistency of these views.

Finally, the integration of general purpose discrete event simulators with an existing BPM environment is a nontrivial task, given that such an environment was never designed with business process simulation in mind and that legacy systems do not offer standardized interfaces.

PETRI NETWORK-BASED SIMULATION SUPPORT SOLUTIONS

Petri networks avoid some of the problems associated with general-purpose discrete event simulators [20,21]. They are well suited to model workflow execution and provide designers with a formally specified modeling notation and the capability of automatic verification of process models. However, business process simulations require extensions to the basic Petri Networks model in the form of temporal Petri networks (Petri-Net and Colored Petri-Net), to represent resource handling and timing aspects.

Petri-Net formalism appears to be more difficult to understand than informal modeling languages [22]. In fact, some model constructs can only be established indirectly, so that some parts of the model may be unintelligible to the business process owners.

In Petri-Net-based solutions, the simulation model encapsulates the business process as well as the set of services and resources the process requires. In other words, the same formalism is used to represent different aspects of process management, making it difficult to separate elements associated with the business process from those related to an enterprise service/resource. This complicates the simulation models and hinders their comprehension by people unfamiliar with Petri-Net formalism. Furthermore, because the process and its context are included in the same simulation model, reengineering efforts based on Petri-Net solutions call for a manual translation of the description of the reengineered processes to the formalism of the enterprise BPM solution, an operation that is costly and error-prone. Finally, Petri-Net can provide limited support for business process evaluation.

SIMULATION WITH EPCs

EPCs [23] are very popular for semi-formal process documentation and for representations of the flow control aspects of business processes. The lack of precise semantics makes them unsuitable to business process modeling without modifications [23]. In addition, EPC solutions cannot explicitly represent several process designs, for example, state-based workflow patterns, and they are not capable of handling multiple instantiation of the same business process.

Scheer has demonstrated the feasibility of an EPC-based approach for process modeling and simulation purposes [24]. This has stimulated research activity to overcome existing limitations and to specify a precise semantics for EPC to make the technique suitable for business process simulation [25].

RETHINKING PROCESS SIMULATION

To overcome the limitations affecting currently available simulation solutions, two main characteristics are needed: the separation of concerns between the business process and context simulation models, and the compliance with the major standards of the BPM field.

The *separation of concerns* between business processes and their context simulation models makes dependencies more explicit, so that the complex interactions between business processes and enterprise services and resources can be highlighted. In addition, the separation of concerns allows the simulation of services and resources that constitute the process context as executable software components with the same interfaces as their real-life counterparts. Depending on the level of simulation details, these software components may either show a purely stochastic behavior or may implement the same logic and behave as their real counterparts. Finally, rapid prototyping is possible because enterprise services/resources are simulated using executable code. For example, it may be possible to investigate the tolerance of a new service implementation to load surcharges for different operating situations.

Conformance to standards. BPM standards simplify the design and development of process models through the use of standard process modeling languages that run over standard-compliant solutions with minor (or even with no) modifications. In addition, standard compliance ensures that the simulation results are readily accessible by conventional BPM solutions. Finally, the process simulation solution can be integrated with the enterprise BPM infrastructure.

With the above considerations in mind, we now turn to PROSIT, a novel business process simulation support that we have developed.

PROSIT SIMULATION TOOL

PROSIT is a simulation tool to support the modeling and simulation of the execution of business processes. PROSIT decouples the process logic of simulated business processes from the logic of simulated services and resources that are supposed to be available within the organization. PROSIT therefore can simulate the interactions between process participants and the set of available services and resources within the organization.

PROSIT uses the XPDL language to model business processes. In addition, PROSIT implements all of the five interfaces specified in the WfMC Workflow API. In particular, WfMC Interface 1 is used to set up the business process model to be simulated, whereas Interfaces 2 and 3 are used to enable the interactions among the simulated processes and simulated services and resources. With Interface 4, PROSIT can set up the initial simulation state, thus enabling what-if analysis. Finally, Interface 5 is used to store within a centralized database the information related to the different simulation steps executed by the various instances of the simulated process. Because, PROSIT is WfMC-compliant, it can be integrated with enterprise BPM solutions.

The PROSIT Model

The process dynamics in PROSIT are represented by a sequence of simulated and logically correlated events that occur during the simulation interval. Each event in PROSIT, such as the execution of an activity or the creation of a new process instance, takes place at a specified time and causes a variation in the process state. The simulation time in PROSIT allows the chronological ordering of simulated events. When PROSIT has completed the simulation of all events scheduled at a given simulated time, it updates its simulation time and starts simulating events accordingly.

Business processes in PROSIT are depicted as oriented graphs that establish the execution order of process activities, as well as the synchronization policies required to accomplish a determined piece of work. A business process consists of a number of business process instances executing at the same time and accessing the same set of simulated services and resources. The time to accomplish an activity may be constant or may vary according to the Poisson or Erlang stochastic processes. Simulated process instances can be created at regular time intervals, or according to different stochastic models or on the basis of historical records obtained from the enterprise BPM system. Each simulated process instance is characterized by several pieces of information, including its unique process instance identifier and the process creation time.

A process activity represents a single step in the workflow to be executed. Typically, it concerns the coordination of the process with the service and resource of its simulation context. The duration of an activity is the time needed for it to complete. Each activity is associated with several types of information: the representation of all preconditions to enable its execution, the set of actions to be executed, and its duration. The activity preconditions represent the logical conditions for the PROSIT simulator to start the execution of the activity. An activity precondition typically represents the availability of a specific service or resource needed for the execution of the process. These actions form the set of operations to be executed on a specific set of services and resources. Finally, the duration of an activity is the time needed for the activity to complete.

Business process variables can be defined in PROSIT with an extended scope to cover all instances executing the same business process. The scope of a variable can also be restricted to a single process instance. The value of process and instance variables can be accessed and modified by the different process activities and may affect the decision of the next process activity to execute, that is, process variable can guide process routing decisions.

A key concept in PROSIT is the simulation state. This is the set of all previously executed activities (including their identifiers, time of execution and completion, and so forth), along with the set of values that instance variables have assumed over the time. PROSIT also defines the state of a process as the set of states assumed by all currently running and previously simulated instances. The state of the process is recorded and successively made available to interested users.

THE **PROSIT** SIMULATOR ARCHITECTURE

The PROSIT simulator has a layered architecture and is implemented on top of the Java Virtual Machine as shown in Figure 13.2.

The *Simulator Graphical User Interface* (SGUI) is the interface through which users to define processes, to load and set up different software modules representing the set of services and resources, to control the simulation execution, and to display simulated events processed by the different simulmd process instances. The SGUI is built on top of JAWE [26], an open-source, XPDL-compliant graphical modeling tool.

The *Process Model Loader* (PML) is used to load the XPDL-compliant process models to be simulated and to extend their representation by including all needed information for simulation management. Loaded models are filtered to delete possible dependencies to services and resources deployed in the enterprise information infrastructure. The filtering phase is followed by the model extension phase, where simulation parameters are included in the process model, such as process instantiation patterns and binding between process model to simulated services and resources

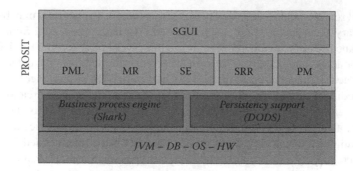

Legend
SGUI: Simulator Graphical User Interface
PML: Process Model Loader
MR: Model Repository
SE: Simulation Engine
SRR: Simulation Results Repository
PM: Participants Manager

FIGURE 13.2   Architecture of the PROSIT simulator.

composing the simulation context. Finally, the process model is persistently stored in the *Model Repository* (MR).

The MR stores the process models to be simulated in a dedicated database. The process models are loaded from the PML and can be retrieved and executed by the *Simulation Engine* (SE). The MR is implemented on top of the Data Object Design Studio persistence framework [27], to avoid any link to a specific database technology, thereby alleviating problems of database incompatibilities that may occur in large organizations.

The SE is in charge of the actual execution of the simulation of the processes and of organizing the interactions between services and resources composing the simulation context. The SE comprises a *Simulation Manager* (SM) and a *Simulation Worker* (SW). The SM obtains the model of processes to be simulated from the MR and creates new instances of the simulated process instances and controls their execution. The SM maintains the simulation clock and generates and maintains the list of events that are to be simulated; it also associates events with the different process activities. The SW extends the *Enhidra Shark* BPM engine [28] and, in turn, is in charge of interpreting the XPDL-based representation of the process to be simulated and of controlling its execution. The SW guides the flow of the instances of the simulated process that are executing a specified process model, schedules the different actions and handles the various variables of simulated process and process instance. In addition, the SE also implements WfMC-compliant Workflow API that permit process instances to coordinate with simulated participants, as well as with the set of simulated services and resources composing the simulation context. SW also coordinates with *Simulation Results Repository* (SRR) that, in turn, stores the simulation results, for example, the set of simulated actions, the value of variable, and so forth.

The SRR is in charge of storing all simulation results. The information includes, for example, the executed activity unique identifier, the simulated process instance identifier, the time the activity was started and has completed, and so forth. In addition, for each simulated process and process instance, the SRR stores the sequence of values that the process and process instance variables have assumed during the time. The SRR implements the WfMC Interface 5 to allow access and analysis of the collected simulation and data through conventional BI tools.

Finally, the *Participants Manager* (PM) set-ups and binds the simulated models to simulated enterprise services and resources. In particular, the PM obtains the name of a simulation script from SGUI and it is in charge of controlling its execution. These simulation scripts can be implemented in different languages including Java, Python, Ruby, and TCL/TK [29–32]. The PM assumes that each simulated service and resource exposes the same interface as its real counterpart in the enterprise information infrastructure. The PM also enables simulation scripts to access simulated processes and process instances variable and to modify their current value. The PM allows both stateless and stateful simulation scripts to enable fine-grained simulation enterprise services and resources.

IMPLEMENTATION ALGORITHM

Simulation with PROSIT requires suitable configuration phases. During the monitoring and configuration phases, designers model the business processes to be simulated, along with the set of services and resources composing process context. In addition, several simulation parameters, such as, duration of process activities, and process instantiation models, are defined.

Whenever a simulation starts, the simulation clock is reset; the PM instantiates and binds all software components that represent the simulated services and resources of the process context to the SW. Next, the SE launches the simulation and the SW coordinates with the PR access to the simulated process model. The SM generates and schedules simulation events according to the simulation parameters entered through the SGUI and delivers them to the SW (e.g., the creation of new process instances).

Process instances begin by executing the business process simulation model one activity at a time, provided that the SW has determined that the associated condition is verified. Activities are scheduled according to their duration, and their execution typically requires SW to access the simulated services and resources. Following the execution of an activity, the SW coordinates with the SRR to store all changes in the process status. In particular, the process and process instance variables values, as well as activity execution beginning and completion times are stored in a central database. These data are available for business process evaluation.

CONCLUDING REMARKS AND OPEN RESEARCH QUESTIONS

BPM requires frequent revisions of the enterprise structure and organization of work. However, the impact of these changes should be carefully evaluated in terms of their effectiveness before actual implementation. Business process simulation can reduce the risk of enacting processes with inefficient or unsatisfactory designs. Despite the widespread interest, available solutions can only partially address the challenging problems raised by business process reengineering.

This chapter presented PROSIT, a process-oriented simulator, designed to facilitate the evaluation of process design options. The simulator decouples process and context simulation models and follows workflow standards. Its main advantage is that the business process simulation models can be readily enacted within the framework of the enterprise BPM infrastructure. In addition, our approach takes into account complex coordination that may occur between processes and enterprise services and resources. Finally, PROSIT facilitates the analysis of simulation results, because they are represented according to standard formats, and can be accessed and processed by conventional BI tools.

Even though this solution is an important step for business process simulation, it does not cover the case of partnerships between different companies. Available business processes simulators are designed for intra-enterprise scenarios, so that it is possible to assume agreement on reengineering goals. On the contrary, in inter-enterprise scenarios, the collaborating parties may have distinct or even contradictory objectives. In addition, the needed information may be proprietary and unavailable to process designers.

We are currently extending PROSIT to overcome these limitations through a fully distributed simulation environment where each partner can simulate all the business process of interest without requiring full visibility of partners' processes.

ACKNOWLEDGMENTS

This work was supported by the MIUR FIRB TOCAI and by the CNR Strategic Project IS-MANET.

REFERENCES

1. Grover, V. and Kettinger, W. J., *Business Process Change*, Idea Group Publishing, Hershey, PA, 1998.
2. Davenport, T. H., *Process Innovation: Reengineering Work through Information Technology*, Harvard Business School Press, Boston, MA, 1993.
3. Hammer, M. and Champy, J., *Reengineering the Corporation: A Manifesto for Business Revolution*, Harper Collins, New York, 2001.
4. van der Aalst, W. M. P., Business process management demystified: A tutorial on models, systems and standards for workflow management, in *Lectures on Concurrency and Petri Nets*, Lecture Notes in Computer Science 3098, Springer-Verlag, Berlin/Heidelberg, 2004, 1–65.
5. Tumay, K., Business Process Simulation, *Proceedings of the 27th Winter Simulation Conference (WSC 95)*, ACM Press, Arlington, VA, 1995, 55–60.
6. Barber, K. D. et al., Business-process modelling and simulation for manufacturing management: A practical way forward, *Business Process Manage. J.*, 9 (4), 527–542, 2003.
7. Greasley, A., Using business-process simulation within a business process re-engineering approach, *Business Process Manage. J.*, 9 (4), 408–420, 2003.
8. Workflow Management Coalition (WfMC), XML Process Definition Language (XPDL), Standard Specifications, Doc. No. WFMC-TC1025-Oct-10-08-A (Final XPDL 2.1

Specification) 2008, available at http://www.wfmc.org/index.php?option=com_docman&task=doc_details&Itemid=72&gid=32, last accessed July 8, 2009.

9. Gladwin, B. and Tumay, K., Modelling business processes with simulation tools, *Proceedings of the 26th Winter Simulation Conference* (WSC 94), ACM Press, Washington DC, December 1994, 114–121.

10. Furey, T. R., A Six-step Guide to Process Reengineering, *Planning Rev.*, 21 (2), 20–23, 1993.

11. Parmenter, D., *Key Performance Indicators: Developing, Implementing, and Using Winning KPIs*, John Wiley & Sons, Hoboken, NJ, 2007.

12. Bradley, P. J. et al., Business Process Reengineering (BPR)—A study of the software tools currently available, *Comput. Industry*, 25 (3), 309–330, 1995.

13. Reijers, H., Design and control of workflow processes: business process management for the service industry, Lecture Notes in Computer Science 2617, Springer-Verlag, Berlin, 2003.

14. Law, A. M. and Kelton, W. D., *Simulation Modeling and Analysis*, McGraw-Hill, New York, 2000.

15. Paul, R. J., Giaglis, G. M., and Hlupic, V., Simulation of business processes, *Am. Behav. Sci.*, 42 (10), 1551–1576, 1999.

16. Kelton, W. D., Analysis of output data, *Proceedings of the 26th Winter Simulation Conference* (WSC 94), ACM Press, San Diego, CA, December, 1994, 62–68.

17. Laguna, M. and Marklund, J., *Business Process Modeling, Simulation, and Design*, Pearson Prentice Hall, Upper Saddle River, NJ, 2005.

18. Page, B. and Neufeld, E., Extending an object oriented Discrete Event Simulation Framework in Java for Habour Logistics, in *Proceedings of the 5th International Workshop on Habour, Maritime & Multimodal Logistics Modelling and Simulation (HMS 2003)*, Riga, Latvia, September 2003, 79–85.

19. Kelton, W. D., Sadowski, R. P., and Sturrock, D. T., *Simulation with Arena*, McGraw-Hill, New York, 2004.

20. Get-Process Income Simulator, available at http://www.get-process.com/en/process simulator.php

21. Verbeek, H. M. W. et. al., Protos 7.0: Simulation made accessible, *Proceedings of the 26th International Conference on Application and Theory of Petri Nets (ICATPN 2005)*, Lecture Notes in Computer Science 3536, Springer-Verlag, Berlin/Heidelberg, 2005, 465–474.

22. Sarshar, K. and Loos, P., Comparing the control-flow of EPC and Petri Net from the end-user perspective, *Proceedings of the 3rd International Conference on Business Process Management (BPM2005)*, Lecture Notes in Computer Science 3649, Springer-Verlag, Nancy, France, September 2005, 434–439.

23. van der Aalst, W. M. P., Desel, J., and Kindler, E., On the semantics of EPCs: A vicious circle, *Proceedings of the 1st GI-Workshop on Business Process Management with Event-Driven Process Chains (EPK 2002)*, Trier, Germany, November 2002, 71–79.

24. Scheer, A. W., *ARIS: Business Process Frameworks*, Springer-Verlag, Berlin, 1998.

25. Kindler, E., On the semantics of EPCs: Resolving the Vicious Circle, *Proceedings of the 2nd International Conference on Business Process Management (BPM 2004)*, Lecture Notes in Computer Science 3080, Springer-Verlag, Potsdam, Germany, June 2004, 82–97.

26. Enhydra JAWE, Web site: jawe.enhydra.org

27. Enhydra DODS, Web site: dods.enhydra.org

28. Enhydra Shark, Web site: shark.enhydra.org

29. Java Language, Web site: java.sun.com

30. Python Language, Web site: www.python.org

31. Ruby Language, Web site: www.ruby-lang.org

32. TCL/TK Language, Web site: www.tcl.tk

14 Architectures for Cross-Enterprise Business Integration

Jörg P. Müller, Stephan Roser, and Bernhard Bauer

CONTENTS

INTRODUCTION

Today, many companies are organized in global networks and outsource activities that can be performed quicker, more effectively, or at lower cost by others [1]. Their competitiveness depends heavily on support systems that can keep up with constantly evolving business relationships and cross-organizational value chains. This requires methodologies, methods, software architectures, and infrastructures to support changes defined at a strategic level and propagate them down to the working levels in terms of business processes and associated information and communication technology (ICT) systems. One way to achieve this is by integrating the ICT systems within an enterprise and across networked enterprises.

The main objective of most integration initiatives is to achieve a new level of interoperability while minimizing the impact on existing ICT environments. According to Erl [2], this means the following:

- Avoiding the creation of a fragmented environment through the introduction of business logic that resides outside of established application boundaries
- Avoiding tightly bound integration channels between applications that are easily broken if either application is modified
- Minimizing redevelopment of applications affected by the integration

A discipline that plays a key role in this task is Enterprise Application Integration (EAI) [3]. The goal of EAI is to make sure that all corporate applications and application systems work together transparently to cover all business activities as if they were designed as one system from the start. Yet, today's EAI have limited robustness because changes in one part of the system are likely to have undesirable impact in other parts, they also have a high implementation and maintenance cost, and lack principled end-to-end methodologies and methods to deal with the challenge of cross-enterprise business integration. In fact, EAI solutions face, like the organizations themselves, the challenge of adapting quickly in response to changing requirements.

An essential means to making EAI solutions more robust, less costly, and more adaptive, is to foster and increase the reusability of proven architecture patterns [3] and technologies.

In Chapter 15, the authors consider traditional EAI as an *ex post* integration technology, whereas they regard the standardized service-oriented architecture (SOA)/Web Services technology stack an *ex ante* integration technology. We take a broader view of EAI and believe that with Model-Driven Software Development (MDSD) methods and SOA principles, EAI can be planned and performed *ex ante* rather than after the fact. In our view, SOA is foremost a distributed software architecture that can be used for a flexible and adaptive integration with enhancements such as MDSD and patterns that consider semantics and business functions.

A prerequisite for the seamless integration of cross-organizational business processes (CBPs), whether within the enterprise applications or across enterprises, is to embed EAI into a principled end-to-end overall development approach, taking all levels of abstraction of cross-enterprise collaboration into account. MDSD (see, e.g., [4][6]) is such an approach, consistent with the shift from program-based implementations toward model-driven implementation. MDSD, as a particular case of the new trend in software design of model-driven engineering (MDE) [4], provides techniques to realize and automate the propagation of changes at business level to the technical level.

The structure of this chapter is as follows. We first survey the state of the art in business integration architecture from a service-oriented perspective. Next, we outline the pillars and key architectural components of a model-driven EAI approach, and develop a taxonomy of cross-enterprise EAI approaches. In the following section, by detailing on the different levels of this taxonomy, we develop an MDSD solution that can be used as a reference and basis to realize EAI systems for concrete businesses. In particular, we identify and characterize three generic service-oriented EAI topologies within this model-driven approach, with a focus on the platform-independent IT level. The chapter ends with conclusions and an outlook to future research challenges.

SERVICE ORIENTATION AND BUSINESS INTEGRATION

While we refer to Chapters 11 and 15 for a comprehensive overview of the state-of-the-art in the area of SOA, we shall discuss some important related work that investigates requirements and approaches for using SOA in the context of EAI, before we cover the related work on MDSD.

Service orientation is based on the concept of service, defined "as a well-defined, self-contained function that does not depend on the context or state of other services" [7]. SOA is an architecture paradigm for IT systems where functions are separated into distinct, loosely coupled units or *services* [8], accessible over a network in order that they can be combined and reused in the development of business applications [9]. The concept of services can be the basis for platform-independent models (PIMs); thus, service orientation can be used to make EAI more effective and adaptive, to provide flexible integration of IT applications and functions. Further down in this section, we introduce categories of service-oriented integration approaches and describe how they can be used to realize a model-driven EAI. Before doing so, however, we briefly survey MDSD.

MODEL-DRIVEN ENGINEERING

Software engineering is currently witnessing a paradigm shift from programming-based implementation toward model-driven implementation. This carries important consequences on the way information systems are built and maintained [4]. MDE raises the level of abstraction at which developers create and evolve software [6,10] by treating models as first class artifacts that can be used for representation as well as code generation. This reduces the complexity of software artifacts by separating concerns and aspects of a system [5]. Thus MDE shifts the focus of software development away from the technology toward the problem to be resolved. Largely automated model transformations refine (semi-)automatically abstract models to more concrete models or simply describe mappings between models of the same level of abstraction. In particular, transformation engines and generators are used to generate code and other target domain artifacts with input from both modeling experts and domain experts [11]. MDE is an approach to bridge the semantic gap between domain-specific concepts of applications and programming technologies used to implement them [12]. It provides a technical basis for automation and reuse in terms of generation techniques like model transformation and code generation as well as reusable assets like infrastructures, components, templates, and transformations. Two prominent representatives of MDE are the Object Management Group (OMG)'s Model-Driven Architecture® (MDA) and the software factory initiative from Microsoft.

In MDE, models and model transformations, which can also be treated as models, embody critical solutions and insights to enterprise challenges and hence are seen as assets for an organization [13]. Assets are artifacts that provide solutions to problems, should be reusable in, and customizable to various contexts. Similarly, in MDSD, architectural and technology patterns are encoded in model transformations, enabling a partial automation and synchronization of modifications (e.g., resulting from process or structure evolutions) across modeling levels, as well as the possibility to extensively reuse assets.

MDSD can be used to provide end-to-end support for the realization of business processes, from the business level (users' view) down to deployed applications (ICT view) on specific platforms via well-defined, largely automated model transformations and refinements. MDSD treats models as primary development artifacts, uses models to raise the level of abstraction at which developers create and evolve software [8], and reduces the complexity of the software artifacts by separating concerns and aspects of a system under development [5].

TOPOLOGIES FOR CROSS-ENTERPRISE EAI

In the following, we introduce three categories of integration solutions on the basis of their topology, as previously described in the literature, see, for example, [2,14]. Our model-driven approach, however, is not restricted to these categories and be extended to new or other classifications. Figure 14.1 depicts the three integration solution topologies.

In a *fully decentralized (peer-to-peer, P2P)* topology, services (in the sense of self-contained functions) of the participating organizations implicitly establish the collaborative process through direct message exchange. Examples are *P2P* networks or multiagent systems. Changes in the business protocol would result in changing one or more peers. Furthermore, the interface and external behavior of the peers are directly exposed to the collaboration space and therefore are directly accessible by entities outside enterprise boundaries.

In a *hierarchical topology*, a controller service defines the steps necessary to achieve the overall goal and maps these steps to services provided by the contributing organizations. Messages exchanged among the services of the collaborating organizations through a central broker component. Typically, a broker realizes a controller service to act as a global observer process that coordinates the partners

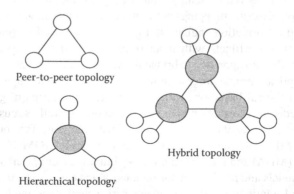

Peer-to-peer topology

Hybrid topology

Hierarchical topology

FIGURE 14.1   Integration topologies.

and makes decisions on the basis of data used in the collaboration. Changes to the protocol's messages and semantics would affect only the broker process. Since the broker is not necessarily owned by one of the participating partners, organizations may hide their elementary services from their collaborators. However, they have to reveal them to the broker.

In many cases, a mixture of hierarchical and the fully decentralized topology, that is, a *hybrid topology*, is used to realize complex multipartner collaborations [14]. Elements of the fully decentralized topology are introduced in the hierarchical topology and the controller service is distributed among several controller processes jointly providing the broker functionality. Each participating organization provides one controller service that orchestrates and encapsulates that organization's services. Messages that cross organizational boundaries go through the controller services.

In our experience, these three general topology patterns are general enough to model the EAI architectures or topologies normally occurring in practice (e.g., tree structures), either by variation or combination of these topologies.

TAXONOMY OF CROSS-ENTERPRISE EAI

The topologies depicted in Figure 14.1 are generic in a sense that they do not yet relate to specific IT platforms and technologies. In this section, we present a model-driven taxonomy of different EAI approaches. This taxonomy, illustrated in Figure 14.2,

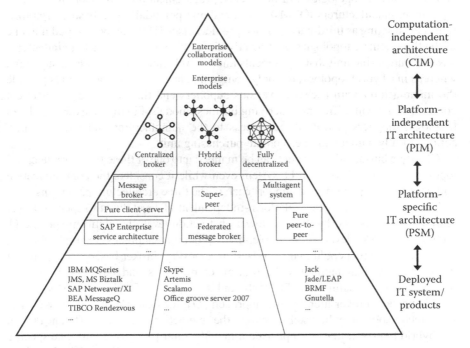

FIGURE 14.2 Classification of architectural approaches according to the model abstractions of MDA.

helps us organize the various topologies in a hierarchy according to the abstractions of the model-driven development. As such, the taxonomy provides a guideline for the structure of the remainder of this chapter.

The top-most level of the pyramid is the Computation-Independent IT Architecture level, also referred to as the Computation-Independent Model (CIM) level, following the MDA terminology. It contains business-level architectures and models of enterprises and their collaborations. There are many available methodologies at this level such as the ARchitecture for integrated Information Systems (ARIS) House of Business Engineering, the Zachman Framework, PERA (Purdue Enterprise Reference Architecture), GRAI (Graphs with Results and Actions Inter-related), CIMOSA (Computer-Integrated Manufacturing Open Systems Architecture), or GERAM (Generalized Enterprise Reference Architecture and Methodology) [15]. At the CIM level, we can represent an enterprise collaboration architecture as a set of enterprise models covering different aspects of the participating enterprises, such as organization, data, services, functions, and process flow plus a conceptual (non-IT-oriented) description of collaboration use cases between the enterprises, such as supply chain relationships. More explanations are available later.

The second level of our taxonomy deals with Platform-Independent IT Architectures, abbreviated as PIM as per the MDA conventions, and which excludes the implementation details. In the context of this section, the architectures of interest follow the service-oriented paradigm without being tied down to a specific target platform.

Architectural decisions made at this level account for different communication and coordination topologies. For instance, a procurement process involving original equipment manufacturers (OEMs), suppliers, and potentially purchasing organizations (POs) acting as third-party service providers (see [16]) may be mapped into one of the three generic topologies. In a strictly hierarchical topology, each manufacturer has one purchasing unit that implements and controls interactions with its suppliers, whereas in a hybrid topology, not only competing, but also cooperating POs provide the manufacturer with access to various suppliers and their products, at different conditions and with different underlying business models. Finally, in a decentralized topology, suppliers provide direct access to the manufacturer and manage interactions locally without an intermediate purchasing unit.

Clearly, a business-level model can be mapped into one of these three architectural topologies using a PIM of an IT system even while it considers the communication and coordination patterns that support each of the three architecture paradigms.

The step from conceptual, platform-independent IT level down to specific target platforms is supported by the next lower abstraction level, the platform-specific IT architecture (PSM) level. For example, in the procurement process example above, a hierarchical solution could manifest itself as a message broker-based architecture at the central PO that facilitates the routing of messages and business documents between the manufacturer, the PO itself, and the suppliers. On the other hand, a federated message broker architecture approach [17], for example, based on Web services technology, may be used to realize the interactions between different POs in the hybrid topology, that is, to provide a manufacturer partnering with one specific PO access to products available at one supplier only via a different PO. Finally, a structured *P2P* topology, such as described in Ref. [18], may provide a distributed collaboration space, where OEMs can postrequests, identify potential suppliers, and pursue collaborations without a dedicated central element.

The lowest level describes how platform-specific models (PSMs) are mapped into actual deployed IT systems using dedicated platforms and products. For instance, in the hierarchical case, our central PO could host an SAP Netweaver-based application system using the SAP XI (eXchange Infrastructure) to facilitate the routing of messages and business documents between the OEMs, the PO itself, and the suppliers. In the second case, an IBM Websphere message broker-based federation of Enterprise Service Buses [19] may be used to implement the heterogeneous, federated message broker topology. Finally, a full decentralized information and collaboration space may be built up using the P2P business resource management framework [20] based on distributed hash table lookup protocols such as Chord [17].

METHODOLOGICAL ISSUES IN APPLICATION INTEGRATION WITH MDSD

In EAI systems, similarly structured solutions can be considered as members of the same software systems family (SSF) when they "... share enough common properties to be built from a common set of assets" [21]. This is the case for service-oriented EAI systems. Their shared functionalities are in services that form the common set of assets of the SSF. Other Functionalities that cannot be composed from this common set of assets, whether because they are new or are obtained from other ICT systems, are then encapsulated as services and then integrated.

MDSD provides means to realize SSFs. It can be used to realize software product lines (SPLs), where each SPL consists of an SSF [22] whose members share some common functions in addition to having their specific functionalities [23].

MDSD, by itself, does not provide the methods and concepts to build SPLs and model-driven solutions. Such issues can be addressed by SPL engineering techniques [24], which distinguish two phases: building the MDSD solutions, called *domain engineering*, and applying the MDSD solution for EAI development called *application engineering*.

Domain engineering, which consists of domain analysis, domain scoping, and variability analysis, is used to obtain appropriate modeling languages for the CIM level. Reference implementations of the EAI solutions are used to factor out commonalities and variable aspects of the EAI solutions. These commonalities become part of the reusable components, such as transformations, generation templates, or frameworks. Transformations and templates consist of common code that is configured through the content of the models they are applied to. The model content is used to bind the variables of the transformations and templates to concrete values during transformation execution, that is, the execution of templates is triggered by the model content. The languages used to model EAI systems provide means to represent the variable parts of the EAI solutions. Variability is further realized through the choice of certain transformations and generators.

At application engineering time, the MDSD solution is applied. Using the four-level approach presented in Figure 14.2, this means application modeling and specification at the CIM level, the appropriate CIM to PIM transformations and the application of model transformations and generators from PIM to PSM and further on to code level, takes place. After mapping of high- to lower-level models, the next step is to manually refine the generated models (PIM and PSM) by further narrowing down the variables in the solution.

MDSD solutions also allow the PIM-level model to be directly mapped to a textual representation ("code") without an explicit PSM layer. For instance, a transformation to the Web Services Business Process Execution Language (WS-BPEL) could provide either the WS-BPEL text files as an output (model-to-text transformation), or a model representing the WS-BPEL process description (model-to-model transformation). In the following, we will not distinguish between these two possibilities and use the term PIM-to-PSM to denote either.

REALIZATION OF EAI WITH MODEL-DRIVEN ENGINEERING

We now present an MDSD solution that can be used as a basis to realize EAI systems for concrete businesses. We describe and discuss our reference MDSD solution for EAI, its application, and provide insights in the decisions when building the solution.

Our MDSD solution for EAI follows the methodology depicted in Figure 14.2. In this approach, coarse-grained high-level models are transformed and manually refined to more fine-grained lower-level models. When enough information is available, the ICT system is generated. This top-down approach works extremely well when changes in the business model precede the development of the ICT system. Yet, it may be necessary to consider bottom-up development as well, for example, to take into account legacy systems. Bottom-up design can be supported in one of two ways. The first option is to encapsulate the legacy systems by enlisting the domain engineer to describe their services and add them to the MDSD solution as reusable components or modeling elements in the domain-specific modeling language. The other possibility is for the application engineer to model the legacy systems in PIMs, as in classical reverse engineering (also called architecture-driven modernization (ADM) [25]).

Another relevant scenario concerns the evolution of ICT systems and platforms. This affects the MDSD solution since transformations, frameworks, infrastructure, and so on may have to be modified or added at domain engineering time. Roser and Bauer [26] described an approach to cope with the evolution of models and model transformations. Further, existing models of systems may have to be adjusted at application engineering time.

In practice, one will mostly find and apply hybrid methodologies that combine top-down and bottom-up development aspects. In the following, we will focus on the top-down development aspects to describe the application of an MDSD-based EAI solution. In such a solution, one can find horizontal and vertical transformations. *Horizontal transformations* represent information via different model types at the same abstraction level. They improve the interoperability and exchange of models among the various enterprise modeling formats. *Vertical transformations* implement mappings for higher- to lower-level models, typically mapping one element in the higher-level model into several elements in the lower-level model.

Changes to one model in the model-driven development framework (Figure 14.2) often percolate to other models and to other abstraction levels than where the change originated. To support the change management and ensure the consistency of models throughout this process with a minimum of human intervention, model transformations should be specified in a bidirectional way whenever possible. Unidirectional model transformations could impose restrictions on changes or adjustments of existing solutions. Unfortunately, for some vertical transformations (e.g., CIM to PIM, PIM to PSM), this may be inevitable because bidirectional transformations may require considerable effort that cannot be expended in practice.

COMPUTATION-INDEPENDENT MODEL

At the computation-independent level (CIM), our MDSD approach considers two main variability aspects of application development. First, enterprise business processes are represented using a modeling language like ARIS [27]. The modeler can define new processes and functionality on the basis of existing systems, services, and (sub-) processes provided by the MDSD solution. Figure 14.3 provides an example of a cross-organizational strategic sourcing business process modeled with ARIS. The participants of this process are: an OEM whose goal is the sourcing of an engineering service from a supplier (SU) and the PO that ensure the procurement.

The process starts with the OEM issuing a Statement of Requirements (SOR) to one or more suppliers via the PO. Suppliers generate offers, offers are collected and checked by the PO, and then sent to the OEM for evaluation. The example process ends with a selection of a supplier by the PO based on feedback by the OEM. To obtain good-quality models, which can be used for transformation to and refinement at PIM level, it is necessary to provide and enforce appropriate modeling guidelines. Modeling guidelines also support the modeler at business level in formulating his/her solution.

Second, it is crucial to consider further influence factors and constraints in our MDSD solution at CIM. The realization of EAI is not only influenced by the ICT systems to be integrated, but in addition by internal and external influence factors (also called contingencies [28]) of the enterprises. Examples are vertical standardization in the enterprise business segment, legislation and regulation, market

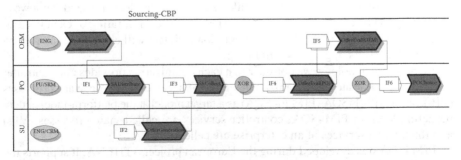

FIGURE 14.3   Example of a model at the CIM level.

structure, and topologies (e.g., "star" vs. "net"), domain-specific distribution of data, rights, control, and so on. Other internal factors include competition for access to the departmental ICT and of the integrated ICT systems. Modeling at the CIM requires evaluating the importance of these factors, even through the modeling languages currently available do not yet support the inclusion of such constraints in CIMs. Accordingly, these constraints and additional factors need to be captured in separate decision models, where the constraints are decomposed in a decision tree with factors and subfactors. There is still demand for further research about how to represent this information in "enterprise network models" in order to increase automation and quality in ICT systems development.

CIM TO PIM

In the next step, the integration architect has to select an appropriate integration solution architecture and a set of model transformations to implement the architectural topology. This can be carried out via a multicriteria decision model as described in Ref. [29]. Basically, the integration architect compares and evaluates the possible coordination and integration topologies on the basis of desired properties like modifiability, interoperability, or data security for various scenarios [30]. The rating criteria depend on the contigencies of the enterprises involved and the integration scenarios.

In our example, one OEM and a few big first-tier suppliers form a virtual enterprise by establishing a temporary association of independent companies, suppliers, and customers. They are linked by information technology to share costs, skills, and access to each other's markets. In one scenario, we assume that half of the cross-organization business processes are supported by legacy proprietary applications and that these applications would be replaced within the next 5 years.

The integration architect compares the integration topologies in terms of their support of future changes in the organizations' services. In the fully decentralized topology, services need to know the identity of any service that would replace a service they communicated with and adjust the syntax or semantics of the message exchanges accordingly. In the hierarchical topology, changes have to be made only in the controller service. In the hybrid topology, such changes are further restricted to the local controller service of the organization where the new service is introduced. Since in our scenario half of the applications are proprietary, the hybrid architecture would have the highest ranking and the fully decentralized the lowest. The rating can be extended to other scenarios and the overall rating of each integration topology is calculated [29]. The integration architect will choose the integration solution that has the highest overall rating.

In the hybrid topology, we consider that each organization provides one controller service to orchestrate the organization's internal services, called private processes (PPs). We use PIM4SOA (PIM for SOA) as a target model at the platform-independent modeling level. In PIM4SOA, controller services are called view processes (VPs) and the internal services of an enterprise are called PPs.

PIM4SOA was developed during the European project ATHENA. It supports the smooth transformation of business process models into Web Service environments

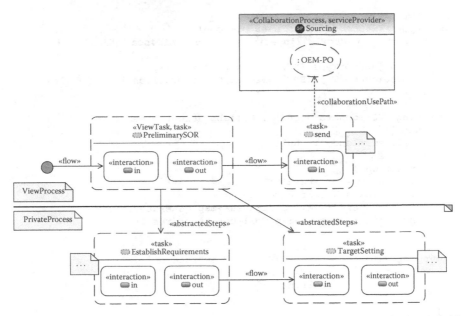

FIGURE 14.4 PIM4SOA model generated for the sourcing CBP of the hybrid architecture.

and composition standards, like BPEL (see [31] for more details). Its metamodel supports platform-independent modeling through generic constructs, such as collaborations and service providers.

Figure 14.4 depicts a Unified Modeling Language (UML) visualization of the PIM4SOA model generated by applying a model transformation to the "Sourcing CBP" in the CIM for the hybrid architecture shown in Figure 14.3. The VP integrates and combines the services offered by the OEM's ICT system. For example, the OEM realizes the task *Preliminary SOR* through the *Establish Requirements* and *Target Setting* services. The model comprises further integration code like sending messages to collaborating partners. For example, the OEM sends a message, which is part of the Sourcing collaboration, to the PO.

To implement model-to-model transformations like our CIM-to-PIM transformation, a variety of transformation approaches exist [32]. The OMG's model transformation standard Queries/Views/Transformations (QVT) [33] supports declarative (QVT Relations) and imperative (QVT Operational Mappings) transformation approaches. Declarative transformation approaches are best applied to specify simple transformations and relations between source and target model elements, while imperative approaches lend themselves for implementing complex transformations that involve detailed model analysis [34]. Since our CIM-to-PIM transformation requires more detailed source model analysis to generate the target model, an iterative approach to implement the model transformation is appropriate. Listing 14.1 depicts an excerpt of the CIM-to-PIM transformation formulated with QVT

```
modeltype ARIS "strict" cimModel ;
modeltype PIM4SOA "strict" uses pimModel ;
transformation CIMtoPIM (in aris:ARIS , out pim4soa: PIM4SOA) {
  main () {
    aris.objectsOfType(EPC)->map generateCBP();
    aris.objectsOfType(EPC)->map mapCollaborations();
    ...
  }
  mapping EPC::generateCBP() : CollaborationProcess {
    when {
      self.swimlanes <> null;
    }
    population {
      result.type = 'ABSTRACT';
      result.name = self.name;
      result.views = self.swimlanes->map generateVP();
      self.controledges->map Collaborations(result);
    }
  }
  mapping Swimlane::generateVP() : ViewProcess {
    population {
      result.name = self.name;
    }
  }
  mapping ControlFlowEdge::mapCollaborations(in
cbp:CollaborationProcess) : Collaboration {
    init {
      result = cbp;
    }
    population {
      if self.source.swimlane = self.target.swimlane
      then result.collaborations = self->object(e) Collaboration {
        ...
      }
      else ...
      endif;
      ...
    }
  }
}
```

LISTING 14.1   Sample ARIS to PIM4SOA model transformation.

Operational Mappings. The rules describe the procedure to transform the structural part of the CBP description into service-oriented models. The notation uses a pseudo-metamodel of ARIS and the PIM4SOA metamodel. More details can be found in Ref. [35].

PIM to PSM

The selection of a particular integration topology at the platform-independent level reduces the number of possible realizations or PSMs. For instance, a hybrid topology could be realized through a *super-peer approa*ch or by using federated message brokers. A super-peer a *P2P* network is an architecture with two types of nodes:

normal peers or super peers, which are dedicated nodes with specific capabilities. A federated broker consists of several workflow orchestration engines working together.

In our example scenario, we choose to realize a federated broker architecture. The PIM-to-PSM transformation maps the processes and the services onto WS-BPEL [36] and Web Services Description Language (WSDL) [37] descriptions.

A *template* is used for the generation of the WSDL code. A template consists of the target text containing slices of metacode to access information from the source and to perform code selection and iterative expansion. Templates are close to the structure of the code to be generated and are perfectly suitable to iterative development as they can be easily derived from examples. Hence, templates are a good choice for the generation of WSDL code or other complex invocation patterns that can occur in workflow languages and platforms (see Ref. [38]).

When generating the BPEL code, however, the code generation depends also on the control flow of the modeled processes. In our application scenario, the generated BPEL code has a specific sequence of processing steps depending on the control flow of the described process. This sequence is produced through complex graph transformation algorithms and with the invocation of the generation templates in a specific order (see [38]). Because a purely template-based generation of the BPEL code is hard to maintain and to extend, it is beneficial to combine template-based and visitor-based code generations [32,38].

In the following we have look at our "Sourcing" process to illustrate the BPEL code generation for the example model shown in Figure 14.4. Basically, a visitor mechanism traverses the process flow of the process at the platform-independent level (a more detailed description of the applied workflow code generation framework can be found in [38]). For each node in the PIM the visitor invokes the templates that generate the respective BPEL code. For the PIM process depicted in Figure 14.4, it works as follows:

- The visitor starts by traversing the VP at the start node. When the visitor enters the action "*PreliminarySOR,*" it calls the respective templates for entering a model element of the type «*ViewTasks*» (cf. Listing 14.2 depicts some sample generation templates specified using the openArchitectureWare [oAW] framework [39]). The information (the variable parts) reused from the PIM is italicized. Code interpreted by the oAW framework is contained in 'double-brackets' («,»). An attribute is evaluated for the current model element (for which the template is applied). For example, «*name*» for the model element of the type «*ViewTask*» in Figure 14.4 is evaluated to "*PreliminarySOR.*" One can use these properties to navigate through the model, for example, «*collaborationUsePath. collaboration.name*».
- Next, the visitor processes the tasks as a view task abstract from «*abstractedSteps*» and calls the generation templates for «*task*».
- Finally, the visitor processes the «*send*»-message to another integration process (which may run on another workflow engine of the federated integration solution).

```
«DEFINE EnterViewProcess FOR PIM4SOA::ViewTask»
  <scope name=' «name» '>
«ENDDEFINE»

«DEFINE ExitViewProcess FOR PIM4SOA::ViewTask»
  </scope>
«ENDDEFINE»

«DEFINE SendTask FOR PIM4SOA::Task»
  <reply name=' «name» ' partnerLink='
«collaborationUsePath.collaboration.name» ' operation=' «...» ' />
«ENDDEFINE»
```

LISTING 14.2   Sample oAW templates.

Listing 14.3 shows the integration code that a BPEL engine generates using the templates of Listing 14.2 (the templates for «*task*» are omitted in the listing). The examples are kept simple for the sake of understandability; in real-world applications, the transformations can be much more complicated (e.g., in the AgilPro project [40], about 80 lines of BPEL code need to be generated for a single task [38]).

CONCLUSIONS AND FUTURE OUTLOOK

In this chapter, we have presented how a combination of service orientation and model-driven engineering can be applied in the area of EAI. This approach provides a structured way for cross-enterprise applications and automates the propagation of changes in business requirements to the design and realization of IT systems.

In process-driven enterprises, enterprise applications need to be developed, managed, and integrated in the context of the business processes that these applications support. Therefore, EAI activities aim to align, harmonize, and coordinate the business processes of co-operating enterprises. Business process-level integration has been accomplished through a variety of point-to-point integration models, most commonly facilitated by broker and orchestration components.

```
<process name='OEM_Sourcing' ...>
  <scope name='PreliminarySOR'>
    <invoke name='EstablichRequriements' partnerLink='OEM_internalLink'
operation='...' />

    <invoke name='TargetSetting' partnerLink='OEM_internalLink'
operation='...' />

  </scope>

  <reply name='send' partnerLink='OEM-PO' operation='...' />
</process>
```

LISTING 14.3   BPEL code generated using the template in Listing 14.2.

In recent years, a new generation of EAI solutions has been developed under the service-oriented paradigm, which lends itself to the development of highly adaptable solutions and to the reuse of existing applications. This is because service-oriented integration adopts the concept of service to establish a PIM that can be used with various integration architectures. As a consequence, in a service-oriented world, sets of services can be assembled and reused to quickly adapt to new business needs. However, service-orientation does not provide an integration solution by itself.

Even though the example realization used BPEL and WDSL, the approach works for other standards in the service-oriented area. The applicability of this approach has been shown in several projects like AgilPro [40] or the European Project ATHENA.

Supporting EAI for service-oriented systems and the enactment of CBPs with MDSD poses a number of challenges. One of these challenges is the development of software architecture coordination patterns that can be applied for the integration of cross-organizational systems and the coordination of the relevant business processes. Another challenge in this context is the automatic derivation ICT system models that are based on the coordination patterns from higher-level CBP descriptions. One of the remaining challenges that this approach would have to meet is to ensure the interoperability of the different systems, possibly by extending it using ontological concepts (see Refs. [40,42,43]).

Four important issues are still open in the field of model-driven engineering. First, MDE introduces additional costs to the development process, since metamodels and model transformations first have to be developed. They only pay off when they can be applied several times. For example, they can automate recurring tasks or encode patterns that can be reused in different projects.

Second, models and model transformation have to track the evolution of standards, applications, and metamodels. Possible approaches have been presented [44–46], including the use of Semantic Web technologies [26,47].

A third point of discussion is the number of abstraction levels that are applied in MDE solutions. More abstraction levels provide more possibilities for customization (and more difficulties in uncovering errors) and also have to be accompanied with model transformations between the different abstraction levels. The "model-driven light" idea (see e.g., [48]) using one consolidated metamodel for more than one abstraction layer supports different views for each abstraction layer, for example, by using event-driven process chains, Business Process Modeling Notation, or any other process modeling standards, may simplify MDE and reduces the number of model transformations.

Fourth, the reusability of application is another topic of discussion. The ADM of the OMG [25] supports the bottom-up approach, thus complementing MDE. Reuse of models and model transformations in the design are also interesting aspects. Here again Semantic Web technologies can help.

So far, the focus of most research on MDSD has been on the computer-supported coordinated management of models at the levels of business process, IT architecture, and IT platform. Models of the strategic vision of the enterprise vision such as the Balanced Scorecard [13] need to be incorporated systematically in an MDSD context. The scope of consideration has to be extended from the business processes to the enterprise strategy and enterprise goals, and—taking the reverse view—knowledge about long-term strategic objectives of enterprises and groups of enterprises ultimately have to be made available and be used more effectively in order to shape and optimize architectures of cross-enterprise business integration.

REFERENCES

1. Snow, C.C., Miles, R.E., and Coleman, H.J., Managing 21st century network organizations, *Organ. Dyn.*, 20 (3), 5–20, 1992.
2. Erl, T., *Service-Oriented Architecture: A Field Guide to Integrating XML and Web Services*, Prentice Hall, Upper Saddle River, NJ, 2004.
3. Fowler, M., *Patterns of Enterprise Application Integration*, Addison Wesley Professional, Indianapolis, IN, 2002.
4. Bézivin, J., On the unification power of models, *Softw. Syst. Model.*, 4 (2), 171–188, 2005.
5. Hailpern, B. and Tarr, P., Model-driven development: The good, the bad, and the ugly, *IBM Syst. J.*, 45 (3), 451–461, 2006.
6. Stahl, T. and Völter, M., *Model-Driven Software Development: Technology, Engineering, Management*, John Wiley & Sons, Chichester, England, 2006.
7. Alex, B. and Ritsko, J., Preface to service-oriented architecture, *IBM Syst. J.*, 44 (4), 651–652, 2005.
8. Bell, M., *Introduction to Service-Oriented Modeling, Service-Oriented Modeling: Service Analysis, Design, and Architecture*, John Wiley & Sons, Hoboken, NJ, 2008.
9. Erl, T., *Service-Oriented Architecture: Concepts, Technology, and Design*, Prentice Hall, Upper Saddle River, NJ, 2005.
10. Greenfield, J. et al., *Software Factories: Assembling Applications with Patterns, Models, Frameworks, and Tools*, Wiley Publishing Inc., Indianapolis, IN, 2004.
11. Schmidt, D.C, Guest editor's introduction: Model-driven engineering, *Computer*, 39 (2), 25–31, 2006.
12. Booch, G. et al., An MDA manifesto, *MDA J.*, May, 2–9, 2004.
13. Kaplan, R.S. and Norton, D.P., The balanced scorecard—Measures that drive performance, *Harv. Bus. Rev.*, January–February, 71–80, 1992.
14. Leymann, F., Roller, D., and Schmidt, M.T., Web services and business process management, *IBM Syst. J.*, 41 (2), 198–211, 2002.
15. Bernus, P., Nemes, L., and Schmidt, G., Eds, *Handbook on Enterprise Architecture*, Springer-Verlag, Berlin, 2003.
16. Stäber, F. et al., Interoperability challenges and solutions in Automotive Collaborative Product Development, in *Enterprise Interoperability II: New Challenges and Approaches (I-ESA'07)*, Gonçalves, R.J. et al., Eds, Springer-Verlag, London, 2007, 709–720.
17. Stoica, I. et al., A scalable peer-to-peer lookup service for Internet applications, in *Proceedings of the ACM SIGCOMM'01 Conference*, San Diego, CA, 2001. Also, *IEEE/ACM Trans. Netw.*, 11 (1), 17–32, 2003.
18. Stäber, F. and Müller, J.P., Evaluating peer-to-peer for loosely coupled business collaboration: A case study, in *Proceedings of 5th International Conference on Business Process Management (BPM'07)*, Alonso, G., Dadam, P., and Rosemann, M., Eds, Lecture Notes in Computer Science, vol. 4714, Springer-Verlag, Berlin, 2007, 141–148.
19. IBM Corp. IBM Websphere Message Broker, available at http://www-01.ibm.com/software/integration/wbimessagebroker/, last accessed July 13, 2009.
20. Friese, T. et al., A Robust business resource management framework based on a peer-to-peer infrastructure, *Proceedings 7th International IEEE Conference on E-Commerce Technology*, Munich, Germany, 2005, 215–222.

21. Czarnecki, K. and Eisenecker, U., *Generative Programming: Methods, Tools, and Applications*, Addison-Wesley Professional, Indianapolis, IN, 2000.
22. Parnas, D., Designing software for ease of extension and contraction, *IEEE Trans. Softw. Eng.*, 5 (2), 128–138, 1979.
23. Clements, P. and Northrop, L., *Software Product Lines: Practices and Patterns*, Addison-Wesley Professional, Indianapolis, IN, 2001.
24. van der Linden, F.J., Schmid, K., and Rommes, E., *Software Product Lines in Action: The Best Industrial Practice in Product Line Engineering*, Springer-Verlag, New York, 2007.
25. OMG. White paper: Architecture-driven modernization—Transforming the enterprise, available at http://www.omg.org/docs/admtf/07-12-01, December 2007, last accessed July 14, 2009.
26. Roser, S. and Bauer, B., Automatic generation and evolution of model transformations using ontology engineering space, *J. Data Semant.*, 11, 32–64, 2008.
27. Scheer, A.W., *ARIS—Vom Geschäftsprozess zum Anwendungssystem*, 3rd Edn, Springer-Verlag, Berlin, 1998.
28. Donaldson, L., *The Contingency Theory of Organizations*, SAGE Publications Inc., Thousand Oaks, CA, 2001.
29. Roser, S., Designing and enacting cross-organizational business processes: A model-driven, ontology-based approach, PhD thesis, University of Augsburg, 2008.
30. Bass, L., Clements, P., and Kazman, R., *Software Architecture in Practice*, Addison-Wesley, Indianapolis, IN, 2003.
31. Benguria, G. et al., A platform independent model for service oriented architectures, in *Enterprise Interoperability: New Challenges and Approaches*, Doumeingts, G. et al., Eds, Springer-Verlag, London, 2007, 23–34.
32. Czarnecki, K. and Helsen, S., Feature-based survey of model transformation approaches, *IBM Syst. J.*, 45 (3), 621–645, 2006.
33. OMG, Meta Object Facility (MOF) 2.0 Query/View/Transformation Specification— Final Adopted Specification, July 2007, available at http://www.omg.org/docs/ptc/07-07-07.pdf, last accessed July 13, 2009.
34. Gardner, T. et al., A review of OMG MOF 2.0 Query/Views/Transformations submissions and recommendations towards the final Standard, *Proceedings of 1st MetaModeling for MDA Workshop*, York, England, 2003, 178–197, available at http://www.zurich.ibm.com/csc/bit/bpia.html or http://www.omg.org/docs/ad/03-08-02.pdf, last accessed July 13, 2009.
35. Bauer, B., Müller, J.P., and Roser, S., A decentralized broker architecture for collaborative business process modeling and enactment, in *Enterprise Interoperability—New Challenges and Approaches*, Doumeingts, G. et al., Eds, Springer-Verlag, London, 2007, 115–125.
36. OASIS, Web Services Business Process Execution Language Version 2.0, April 2007, available at http://docs.oasis-open.org/wsbpel/2.0/wsbpel-v2.0.pdf, last accessed July 13, 2009.
37. W3C, Web Services Description Language (WSDL) 1.1, available at http://www.w3.org/TR/wsdl, March 2001.
38. Roser, S., Lautenbacher, F., and Bauer, B., Generation of Workflow Code from DSMs. In *Proceedings of 7th OOPSLA Workshop on Domain-Specific Modeling*, Montreal, Canada, Sprinkle, J., Gray, J., Rossi, M., and Tolvanen, J.P., Eds, 7th OOPSLA Workshop on Domain-Specific Modeling, Number 38 in Computer Science and Information System Reports, University of Jyväskylä, 2007.
39. oAW, openArchitectureWare (oAW), available at http://www.openarchitectureware.org
40. AgilPro, AgiPro project: Agile Business Processes with Service Enabled Applications, Munich, Germany, available at http://e-mundo.de/en/agilpro.html, last accessed July 13, 2009.

41. Elvesæter, B. et al., Towards an interoperability framework for model-driven development of software systems, in *Interoperability of Enterprise Software and Applications, Proceedings of the 1st International Conference on Interoperability of Enterprise Systems and Architecture (Interop-ESA'2005)*, Konstantas, D. et al., Eds, Springer, London, 2005, 409–423.

42. IDEAS, Interoperability Developments for Enterprise Application and Software Roadmaps, available at http://www.istworld.org/ProjectDetails.aspx?ProjectId=7707af8839 92432e8d6a963a5aedc8ac, last accessed July 14, 2009.

43. Missikoff, M., Schiappelli, F., and Taglino, F., A controlled language for semantic annotation and interoperability in e-business applications, *Proceedings of the 2nd International Semantic Web Conference (ISWC2003)*, Sanibel, FL, 2003, available at http://ftp. informatik.rwth-aachen.de/Publications/CEUR-WS/Vol-82

44. Didonet Del Fabro, M. et al., Model-driven tool interoperability: An application in bug tracking, in *5th International Conference on Ontologies, DataBases, and Applications of Semantics (ODBASE'06)*, vol. 4275, Lecture Notes in Computer Science, Meersman, R. et al., Eds, Springer-Verlag, Berlin, 2006, 863–881.

45. Didonet Del Fabro, M. and Valduriez, P., Semi-automatic model integration using matching transformations and weaving models, *Proceedings of the 2007 ACM Symposium on Applied computing (SAC)—Model Transformation Track*, Seoul, Korea, 2007, 963–970.

46. Wimmer, M. et al., Towards model transformation generation by-example, *Proceedings of the 40th Annual Hawaii International Conference on System Sciences (HICSS-40)*, Big Island, HI, 2007, 285b, available at http://doi.ieeecomputersociety.org/10.110g/ HICSS/2007.572.

47. Kappel, G. et al., Lifting metamodels to ontologies: A step to the semantic integration of modeling languages, in *Proceedings of the ACM/IEEE 9th International Conference on Model Driven Engineering Languages and Systems (MoDELS/UML)*, Lecture Notes in Computer Science, vol. 4199, Nierstrasz, O. et al., Eds, Springer, Berlin/Heidelberg, 2006, 528–542, available at http://www.bioinf.jku.at/publications/ifs/2006/1006.pdf.

48. Roser, S., Lautenbacher, F., and Bauer, B., MDSD light for ERP, *Proceedings of the 23rd Annual ACM Symposium on Applied Computing, Track on Enterprise Information Systems—EIS*, Fortaliza, Ceara, Brazil, 2008, 1042–1047.

49. Stiefel, P. et al., Realizing dynamic product collaboration processes in a model-driven framework: Case study and lessons learnt, *Proc. of 14th International Conference of Concurrent Engineering*, Lisbon, Portugal, 2008. Available at http://www.itaide.org/ projects/408/ICE%202008/Enterprise%20Interoperability/122%20-%20303%20 ICE%202008_Stiefel_Mueller_20080211_submit.pdf, last accessed July 14, 2009.

15 Enterprise Application Integration and Service-Oriented Architecture Integration Scenarios

Bettina Fricke and Klaus Turowski

CONTENTS

INTRODUCTION

Enterprises are forced to adapt their business processes to a constantly changing environment due to globalization, scarcity of resources, and decreased customer loyalty. Strategies to retain competitiveness may include acquisitions, reorganization, product innovation, or collaboration with international business partners to gain access to foreign markets and resources. Although the adaptation of business processes is primarily an organizational task, IT systems are required to implement this change. Consequently, application systems have to be connected, reconfigured, replaced, integrated, or extended to re-arrange their business functionalities and to automate the execution of newly defined business processes. However, changes made to existing application interfaces and business logic are very time-consuming and costly. Automation requires coordination of all involved applications and exactly matching interfaces for information exchange. Additionally, complexity of coordination increases with the number of technologies at hand, business tasks, and related organizational units. Therefore, a flexible but also maintainable application infrastructure is needed to cope with the variability and complexity of changing business scenarios. With an integrated view on organizational and technological aspects, the relevant information can be generated and shared across the enterprise.

Enterprise Application Integration (EAI) and the Service-Oriented Architecture (SOA) provide architectural concepts to design an integrated IT infrastructure in order to support business activities in a competitive environment, in terms of flexibility, interoperability, and manageability. The aim of this chapter is to describe and compare both approaches as well as their suitability for different integration scenarios. The description of EAI and SOA starts with a brief introduction to basic interoperability concepts. Then, both approaches with their characteristics and their respective interoperability strategies are described. Subsequently, the potential benefits of integrated architectures like flexibility and manageability are discussed in more detail. Examples of integration scenarios are given that show the possible application areas of EAI and the SOA.

ESTABLISHING INTEROPERABILITY: INTEGRATION VS. STANDARDIZATION

Interoperability is the *ability to combine and share information across system and organizational boundaries* [1,2]. It increases the efficiency of an application infrastructure as it facilitates automation of business tasks and establishes a basis for the development of new functionality. For example, real-time data analysis or automated e-commerce processes require highly integrated application environments to complete business tasks that depend on different application systems processing data in a coordinated way. This coordination is based upon the communication of interoperable application systems during business process execution. As depicted in Figure 15.1, communication can be regarded as an information exchange across the following three layers: transfer, content, and interaction [1].

- The transfer layer refers to the communication infrastructure used to exchange data between applications. A communication infrastructure may implement multiple channels with different communication models. These models can be described using several properties, for example, delivery (direct/indirect), trigger (event/schedule), response (asynchronous/synchronous), or activation style (push/pull).
- The content layer describes the representation of messages that are used for information exchange, that is, specification of message format, structure,

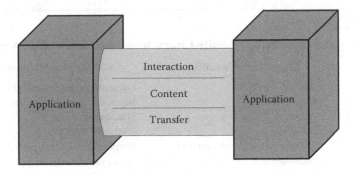

FIGURE 15.1 Cross-application communication.

and semantics. Messages may contain documents (e.g., a purchase order), events (e.g., an error signal), or commands for remote procedure invocation (e.g., print command).

• The interaction layer specifies reactions to received messages. Therefore, message exchange sequences can be described using conversation rules that define reliable transactions between applications. Based on these transactions, a cross-application business process can be designed and executed.

Cross-application or even inter-organizational information exchanges must be interoperable at these three levels. However, application systems are often designed and implemented by independent software vendors or organizations. Since there are many alternatives for interpreting real-world concepts, modeling data, or implementing relevant objects and functions, interoperability between resulting application systems cannot be expected. In order to communicate and automatically process the received information, there has to be a minimum degree of compatibility among business object definitions, data representations, and terminology. Typically, several heterogeneity problems have to be solved before independently developed systems can be interconnected. Generally, there are two main strategies to address heterogeneity problems: *integration* and *standardization*.

Integration means that the differences between existing software parts that are basically compatible can be bridged using suitable extra software. The role of application integration is therefore the mediation between heterogeneous concepts and technologies with the help of the so-called *middleware* functionality. Middleware is a specific software that addresses interoperability of several technical aspects like network, platform, database, object, presentation, and messaging. This masks technical details when cross-application workflows and integrated information systems have to be designed. Depending on the extent of coverage, middleware solutions for integrating functionality range from simple messaging systems to fully featured integration platforms.

The other strategy to achieve interoperability is the use of standards. A standard is a specification that provides a reference framework for the development of software systems or the provision of services [3]. If the communication partners apply a standard specification consistently, it becomes a common technological language.

TABLE 15.1

Comparison of the Interoperability Characteristics of EAI and SOA Solutions

	EAI (*Ex Post* Integration)	SOA (*Ex Ante* Standardization)
Interaction	Hub topology	Orchestration language (BPEL)
	Message routers	Interaction styles (remote procedure call,
	Process definition languages	document)
Data	No standard	XML-based syntax
	Transformators for different data	Interface description standard (WSDL)
	definition schemas	No semantic standard
Transfer	No standard	Messaging standard (SOAP)
	Different channels	Internet protocol stack
	Different adapters	

Standards exist for different implementation aspects at the three mentioned communication levels (e.g., data transport, security, data format, etc.). In principle, every new application that adheres to the chosen set of standards can now be easily connected to the communication system. This cross-application communication through the use of common standards depends on the adoption of, and compliance with, the specification. But even with only partly implemented standards, the variability of possible integration solutions and the complexity of the heterogeneity problem are reduced.

The integration approach with its mediation techniques establishes interoperability *ex post*, that is, after the external interfaces of the application system have already been implemented. Standardization, in contrast, requires the use of standards *ex ante*, that is, during implementation of application system interfaces. Table 15.1 compares the characteristics of the *ex post* integration approach followed by EAI and the *ex ante* standardization approach of the SOA with respect to achieving interoperability. These characteristics are further discussed in the following sections.

ENTERPRISE APPLICATION INTEGRATION

The concept of EAI was introduced in the mid 1990s to overcome heterogeneity problems in enterprise-wide information systems. Previously, independent application systems with incompatible interfaces had to be connected through a middleware to mediate among different communication styles and data representations. Middleware technology, however, addresses the only technical aspects without providing a holistic view of the cross-application business processes to be executed. EAI extends the pure technological approach of middleware with an architectural concept and a methodology for *ex post* integration of business applications. In doing so, it does not give any guidelines for the design of compatible applications but defines an infrastructure for establishing interoperability between heterogeneous systems.

EAI solutions are characterized by a centralized integration architecture based on the so-called *hub-and-spoke* topology, that is, applications are connected to the integration platform only rather than to each other [4]. This reduces the amount of interfaces needed for communication compared with a point-to-point communication between each of the application systems. Instead of a maximum of $n(n-1)$ interfaces in a point-to-point integration architecture (each connection includes two interfaces— one per communication direction), a central hub reduces the number of interfaces to $2n$. When adding a new application to the infrastructure, only one connection to the hub has to be established instead of one connection to each existing application.

The EAI integration platform includes a variety of middleware technologies and makes use of some recurring integration concepts to support interoperability of applications: *channels*, *adapters*, *transformators*, and *message routers* [4,5]:

- Channels represent specific communication models for transport and delivery of messages between applications that are implemented using communication protocols. They form the basis of the communication infrastructure.
- Adapters establish connections between channels and applications since they are able to access an application's programming interface and extract or insert relevant data.
- Transformators convert data regarding format and structure and therefore allow mediating between two data schemas. To achieve this, data contained in messages can be filtered, enriched, split, aggregated, or replaced.
- Message routers are able to pass data to different applications according to certain conditions and also to temporary store data. Chaining of single message routers can provide a basis for process support.

Figure 15.2 shows how these integration concepts work together. Adapters extract data from applications using *application programming interfaces* or database connectors and send them via communication channels to the central hub (1). There, adapters load the received data into the integration platform. Often, messaging systems are used for transport, so that data are packed as payloads in messages and delivered to the message receiver via the central hub. At the hub, messages are checked and assigned to a particular integration procedure depending on criteria like the sending application and the message type. According to the integration procedure, messages are transformed to the required data format (2) and routed to a dedicated communication channel (3). Using this, channel messages are finally delivered to a target application (4).

In real-world integration scenarios, there are concrete implementations of the mentioned integration concepts, for example, there are several possible communication channels implementing different transport protocols like the HTTP (Hypertext Transfer Protocol) or the SMTP (Simple Mail Transfer Protocol). These implementations of integration concepts can be called *integration artifacts* since they represent pieces of an integration software. These artifacts can be reused in different scenarios and stored independently from a particular procedure within the EAI solution. Integration platforms store these artifacts in a so-called *repository* (e.g., the Integration Repository of the SAP Exchange Infrastructure).

Sophisticated EAI solutions extend these message transformation and routing capabilities by handling process models. These solutions are positioned as *business*

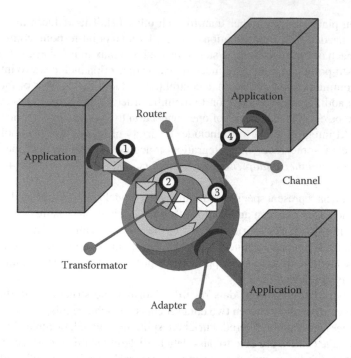

FIGURE 15.2 EAI platform and integration concepts.

process management systems that model and execute cross-application workflows. Modeling is performed with the help of process definition languages using a dedicated designer module within an EAI solution [4]. It is possible to model workflows that may contain multiple message exchange sequences and integration steps. Such workflows therefore do not terminate after the first message exchange. To execute this kind of process models, a *process manager* is used. The integration methodology consists of the following three consecutive phases to implement an application integration scenario:

- In the design phase, process models are defined and stored in a repository along with data schemas, mappings, and adapter implementations. At this stage, process models are called *abstract process models*, because they are not bound yet to a specific application.
- In the configuration phase, abstract process models are tailored to a specific cross-application workflow. Application functionality is bound to single process steps of the central process model and business rules are specified to automate message routing decisions.
- In the execution phase, process instances are executed based on the previous configuration. During the execution, process instances are monitored in order to detect run-time errors and to collect data for analysis and reporting purposes.

An EAI solution provides an overall view on processes implemented by several applications, because they are now logically tied to central process definitions that are often graphically modeled. However, EAI solutions integrate application systems that may have not been designed for being orchestrated by cross-application process models. Sometimes applications provide more functionalities that what is necessary for a specific process, and sometimes missing interfaces hinder the access to relevant procedures.

SERVICE-ORIENTED ARCHITECTURE

Process support at the business level requires an execution logic with the granularity of business tasks to represent actual business processes rather than the technical processing steps. Consequently, the application logic should be split into modules, each of which encapsulates all the functionalities and data needed to execute a distinct business task. This set of functionality is then called a *service* and is provided through a defined interface. SOAs rely on this concept of self-contained services that can be reused and combined based on interface descriptions. Service orientation requires a paradigm shift in application design to include the identification of services in the form of functional components and to consider a communication infrastructure for the distributed services.

For service identification, there must be a modularization strategy to encapsulate the relevant functionalities. On the one hand, services have to be comprehensive with regard to a business task; on the other hand they should not be too specific or tightly coupled with other services in order to be reusable in different business processes. Therefore, services are derived by grouping coherent business functions into components, such that inter-component communication for data access is minimized. To address these communication requirements, the software industry has agreed on a minimum of common XML-based standards, the so-called *Web Service standards* for messaging (Simple Object Access Protocol, SOAP), service description (Web Services Description Language, WSDL), and service discovery (Universal Description, Discovery and Integration). Their use increases interoperability on a technical level and improves significantly the practicability of the distributed service concept.

The encapsulation of business functionality into business task-level services and the message-based communication among services leads to a loosely coupled application system that can be reconfigured easily to address different business processes. The following key elements of an SOA (see also Figure 15.3) make use of the described modularization and standardization [6,7]:

- *Services.* Services are self-contained and consist of an implementation and an interface. The interface contains a description of the service operations provided and the activation information. The implementation is hidden and can only be activated through the service interface. Since the interface description and the message exchange between services are both standardized, different technology platforms or languages can be used for implementation (e.g., a Java-based service can interact with a .NET-based service).

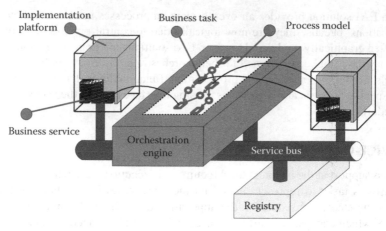

FIGURE 15.3   Elements of a SOA.

- *Service bus.* Web Service standards provide an XML-based implementation framework for service interfaces and the messaging infrastructure, the so-called *service bus.* Each service interface that adheres to these standards can be discovered and activated in a Web Service environment. Besides service discovery and activation, the service bus provides mechanisms to manage quality of service and security constraints locally.
- *Orchestration engine.* Business logic in a SOA is composed by an orchestration engine that executes services according to process models. Process execution is built on Web Service standards and introduces additional XML-based protocols like the Business Process Execution Language (BPEL) to define the control flow among services. Abstract process models can be designed and linked to specific services.
- *Registry.* Interface descriptions are published in a registry so that services can be located and activated by service consumers, that is, other services or user interfaces that interact with a service through messages. Interface descriptions contain information about the designated application domain, quality parameters, or usage constraints. A service consumer can then assess the provided functionality and possible dependencies.

Since the orchestration engine has access to the registry, dynamic discovery and binding of services is possible. However, the search for compatible services can be very complex and is only feasible if comprehensive service descriptions are available. Additionally, the service infrastructure does not provide a general semantic interoperability because it does not define an enterprise data model. Also, services do not rely on a shared database by adherence to the paradigm of loose coupling. Nonetheless, reconfiguration based on known and compatible service interfaces can easily be accomplished using the SOA infrastructure.

Business and IT people typically have a different view of processes and therefore also a different understanding and expectations of the SOA approach. SOA projects are often technology-driven and therefore do not address the business needs or do not address the right abstraction level. However, in the SOA approach, a service is a shared concept because the definition of a service at a technical level should correspond to a service at a business level. This tight linkage offers the chance for a business–IT alignment by an architecture where services are used as building blocks for business process models [8].

COST–BENEFIT COMPARISON OF EAI AND SOA

Although EAI and SOA can both enhance interoperability of an application infrastructure, they require significant initial investments in IT and in personnel. Their respective benefit is reflected in long-term cost savings and increased the quality and flexibility of processes. These benefits can only be achieved if integration projects are carefully planned and supported by business units and top management. It is important to assess the costs and possible benefits of both approaches in order to set the right expectations in implementation projects.

INTEGRATION COSTS

A starting point for the analysis of integration costs is the observation that the degree of *automation* of interfaces is the main driver for cost-efficiency in integrated architectures [1]. Automation is primarily dependent on the extent and degree of interoperability among application systems. Although EAI provides mediation techniques and a centralized platform in order to establish interoperability, SOA uses basic interface description and messaging standards. In the case of EAI, a high degree of automation can be achieved if the provided mediation techniques allow the definition of all the structural and semantic mappings needed to overcome the given heterogeneity problems, so that no further manual interaction is necessary. Automation within a standardized environment like the SOA is dependent on the widespread adherence to standards used in a given integration scenario.

The costs with regard to an integrated application infrastructure reflect the effort of planning, implementing, and operating an integration solution, for example, a particular EAI software package. These costs, derived from the transaction cost theory, can be related to the following three integration phases [1]:

- *Formation phase.* The costs are due to the analysis and implementation of an integration solution. They include the cost of establishing the requirements and examining the heterogeneity problems. Implementation includes either the development or the acquisition of a software product and the respective startup costs.
- *Execution phase.* Execution of an integration solution involves data processing and operating costs. Processing costs include efforts for monitoring and manual intervention if there are unexpected errors or when processes are not fully automated processes. Operating costs refer to infrastructure services, such as application hosting, whether internally or through external providers.

- *Evaluation phase.* Costs in this phase arise from error correction and for the adaptation of the integration solution, for example, for recurring configuration tasks. Additionally, there are opportunity costs from missing or inaccurate information due to incomplete integration.

It is possible to derive measures for each cost type to determine the integration costs for a particular integration scenario, for example, coverage and error rate of automated matching or resources needed for error correction [9].

The same cost structure used to evaluate integration solutions is suitable for assessing the efforts for implementing standards, that is, the standardization costs. Compared with an EAI solution, in a standardized approach like the SOA, the burden of resolving integration problems and ensuring error-free automation is shared across the whole industry. Standardization reduces costs in the execution and evaluation phases since, in a standardized environment, an error-free automation can be expected. On the other side, the correct and complete implementation of standards requires more effort in the formation phase. One reason for this is that a standard is generic and needs to be tailored to the particular instance under consideration. Another reason is that the full benefits of a standard solution depend on its wide adoption; therefore, standard selection requires a thorough analysis of technical- and business-related considerations. This analysis may include a comprehensive process analysis and evaluation of different standards.

Another driver for cost-efficiency is the reuse of existing implementations to save the costs of requirements analysis and software development. In case of the SOA, services can be reused in different implementations. They represent black-box components that are recombined based on their interface descriptions. Reuse within EAI solutions follows predominantly a white box approach where stored artifacts can be adjusted before they are used in another process definition.

INTEGRATION BENEFITS

Integration solutions do not only have to establish interoperability in a cost-efficient way, but also have to adapt to different integration scenarios quickly and cope with the growing complexity. The following characteristics of integrated systems address these requirements and increase the value of an IT infrastructure. Thus, they can be considered as benefits of an integrated architecture:

- *Flexibility.* This is the ability of an IT infrastructure to adapt to changing requirements from a business as well as a technical perspective. Flexibility on a business level refers to the variability of supported business processes. On technical level, it describes the ability to cope with different technologies and formats.
- *Manageability.* This is the ease with which an IT infrastructure can be managed or controlled. This includes several aspects of application life-cycle management (e.g., configuration, deployment, maintenance, and monitoring) and also transparency and quality of implemented business processes [10].

Flexibility

Flexibility is one of the key requirements in a changing business environment. This means that the application infrastructure implementing the business process must support every change on the organizational level. This may require the adaptation, reconfiguration, or the development of a new functionality as well as the introduction of new technologies. An integration solution is flexible when adaptation to a new scenario can take place very fast and at short notice. However, this adaptation has to be performed with reasonable costs and quality. Typically, flexibility requires a quite high effort in the formation phase when respective architectures have to be designed. Hence, there is often a trade-off between cost-efficiency and flexibility.

Generally, the degree of flexibility of integration solutions can be described using different adaptation levels [1]. Hard coded processes are completely defined at design time and therefore do not provide any flexibility. Manually adaptable integration solutions support functional changes during configuration time. This is achieved by parameterization or composition of application components. The next flexibility step is the automated adaptation during configuration time with automatic parameterization, for example, with the help of templates. Finally, dynamic adaptation during run-time allows immediate reaction to external inputs. Another approach to measure flexibility is the scope of standard usage and the compliance with respective specifications [11]. If standards are implemented, switching to another application or business partner that uses the same set of standards is relatively easy. In environments where no exclusive standard exists, the resulting flexibility increases with the number of concurrent standards for a single integration aspect (e.g., data format, transport protocol, security). Additionally, the implementations have to comply with the standard specifications so that the switch-over to another application can be performed seamlessly. Therefore, the use of standards combines the two mechanisms of unification and reuse to enhance flexibility.

The described criteria can be used for the evaluation of flexibility in EAI solutions and SOA. Although, there are some approaches for (semi-)automatic adaptation within EAI platforms (e.g., templates and wizards), most commercial integration solutions support mainly manual adaptation during configuration time. Also, EAI solutions may implement certain standards, for example, data formats, as further alternatives for a specific integration aspect. As mentioned above, already implemented standards and artifacts like adapters or mappings between data formats can be stored and reused in other integration scenarios. Consequently, EAI solutions offer a high degree of flexibility regarding the connection of new application systems to the centralized platform, especially if there are various technologies and standard implementations available. However, this is often a technical flexibility rather than a flexibility with regard to business requirements.

The SOA provides flexibility with the help of loose coupling and autonomy. These characteristics facilitate the reconfiguration of services since they reduce dependencies among them. Message-based and asynchronous communications allow the deferral of the execution of a specific application logic. Additionally, service autonomy requires that any information needed for service execution is contained within the service or can be received through message exchanges. Therefore, different service consumers can activate services. This increases the flexibility considerably because services can be used in scenarios they were not originally designed for. On a technical level, adding of new services is again very easy because of the messaging and interface standards.

Manageability

With the added flexibility, the complexity of an application infrastructure increases. This means that the number and types of applications and the architectural connections do not allow an overview of all application interrelationships and of the role of every application [10]. Manageability is needed to reduce such complexity. This can be achieved with the help of tools and mechanisms for modeling and monitoring of implemented processes and software components. The presence of an EAI solution has a positive effect on the manageability of an IT infrastructure because it consolidates and simplifies architectural connections. Additionally, process-enabled EAI platforms provide tools for modeling and for monitoring the implemented processes. This is often called *business activity monitoring* because it gathers information about process instances that can help to overview and control cross-application processes. In this way, it reduces the overall complexity and leads to more control over networked application systems.

Although the large number of architectural elements of an SOA increases its complexity, a standardized communication infrastructure and a common interface description model can attenuate these negative effects. Additionally, reuse of already implemented services is possible and new functionality can be added easily. This reduces uncertainty that comes along with the change or new implementation of application code and protects previous IT investments. In fact, in combination with a comprehensive service registry including all relevant software contracts and appropriate management tools, this allows increased control and a better view of the IT architecture. Table 15.2 summarizes the characteristics of EAI and the SOA with respect to flexibility and manageability.

TABLE 15.2
Flexibility and Manageability Characteristics of EAI and SOA

	EAI	SOA
Flexibility	Configuration support	Modularization/reuse on business level
	Centralized platform	Loose coupling and autonomy
	Reuse of integration artifacts	Standardized communication infrastructure
	Adaptation techniques	
Manageability	Centralized platform	Standardized communication infrastructure
	Tools for modeling and	Common interface description model
	monitoring	Reuse

INTEGRATION SCENARIOS

Several integration scenarios for EAI and the SOA make use of the provided interoperability, flexibility, and manageability of the resulting application infrastructures. Scenarios that call for coupling and consolidation of existing IT infrastructures range from the support of best-of-breed approaches and backend automation of Web-based e-commerce applications to mergers and acquisitions, and the integration of legacy systems [7,12]. Scenarios that benefit from reuse and reconfiguration of business logic can be found, for example, in business-to-business (B2B) processes that integrate customers and suppliers and in multichannel applications where channel-specific application front ends with a different process logic or user interface are encapsulated and connected to the invariant services of the functional core [7]. In the following, the possible application of EAI and the SOA in the areas of legacy system integration and B2B integration will be described more in detail.

Legacy Systems

One of the main drivers for integration is to reduce the time-to-market of a new functionality. Often, this new functionality relies on existing data or has to be accessed through an existing interface provided by older application systems. Frequently, these so-called legacy systems must be maintained over a certain period of time because their immediate modernization would be time-consuming and costly or even not possible. In such a case, an integration-based on mediation is often the only practicable solution.

Legacy systems represent critical application systems that may put obstacles to future business goals. These obstacles include complex and tightly coupled internal structures, limited openness to other systems, poor documentation, and nontransparent transaction states [12,13]. Since a complete redesign of a legacy system is a challenging and time-consuming task, only a stepwise modernization is feasible. With this approach, the functionality of a legacy system is analyzed and split into system fragments that can either be reused in new business processes or be replaced by newly developed components. Reuse is then based on adapters for the legacy system's interfaces to overcome structural and semantic heterogeneity. Therefore, adaptation is regarded to be the key technique for aligning new business process requirements and legacy system functionality [12]. Only fragments where mediation is not possible, that is, where there is no sufficient matching potential, are candidates for replacement, white-box modification, or retirement.

The alignment with new business processes as a main goal of an IT architecture and also of the modernization of legacy systems requires a flexible architectural reconfiguration at the business level. As discussed above, this can be achieved with the composition of services. In the long run, the integration of legacy systems, starting with the adaptation and integration of functionality, leads to a transformation from a tightly coupled control and execution logic to a SOA with distributed and loosely coupled components that are centrally orchestrated. Once this architecture is adapted syntactically and semantically to the new functionality, it would be possible to build wrappers that expose the functionality according to Web Service standards [14].

B2B PROCESSES

In a B2B environment, business relationships are constantly changing as partners redefine their strategies and suppliers are replaced. In addition, the exchange of information across system and organizational boundaries link independently developed and operated application systems. Besides the basic definition of common data interchange formats and interaction patterns, many other coordination aspects have to be considered, for example, security of communication and consistency of data. Since there is no central coordination instance to impose a particular communication behavior for all B2B partners, integration and coordination has to be accomplished separately for every business relationship. This calls for a flexible IT infrastructure that can be manageable across organizational interfaces.

There are several service-oriented approaches for B2B processes that make use of the reusability of services, that is, implementations of certain B2B standards, and the flexibility to reconfigure cross-organizational information exchanges. For example, Vanderhaeghen, et al. [10] discuss how both flexibility and manageability can be realized in inter-organizational business processes. They stated that an organization in a B2B environment acts more or less like a black-box and therefore the functionality that it provides cannot be overlooked by the business partners. However, deeper knowledge about the encapsulated business processes is needed for manageability and continuous improvement. This can only be achieved by a certain degree of process transparency.

Therefore, we propose a mixed strategy of service orientation for the interoperability and flexibility of inter-organizational process chains and process-orientation, for example, with the help of process modeling techniques of EAI solutions, for better planning and continuous improvement. In a top-down approach, large services at the inter-organizational level are split into smaller services to constitute *process modules*. At the level of these process modules, business processes that integrate inter-organizational and internal process steps can be designed. For each process module, there exists a detailed process description containing performance indicators and access rights. Depending on their access rights, business partners can control the information flow and monitor the process execution. Using this information, the inter-organizational business process can be better adjusted and improved while the flexibility that comes with the service-oriented approach is preserved.

CONCLUSIONS

EAI was introduced at a time when stand-alone applications dominated business computing and point-to-point connections were the means to exchange data between applications. EAI solutions integrate various application systems with the help of a centralized architecture, their support for many different communication technologies, and tools for mediation and process execution. The EAI approach therefore provides a methodology, an architecture, and the technology to establish interoperability between heterogeneous applications and to manage cross-application business processes. The benefit of EAI regarding flexibility and cost-efficiency increases with the number of implemented interfaces because of the positive effects of the hub topology, that is, comparatively fewer interfaces and potentially more technological options for reuse. However, EAI has been a predominantly technical approach so that its impact at the business level was limited.

Nowadays, the SOA is discussed as an enhanced integration concept. Business logic is split into distributed services and communication among services is based on a standardized communication infrastructure. This has positive effects on interoperability and flexibility of an IT infrastructure, and has the potential to improve the integration of processes at the business level. Therefore, the SOA is suitable for business–IT alignment and a variety of integration scenarios, especially for those that benefit from service reuse and process reconfiguration. Considering its potential benefits, the SOA approach is very promising provided that large parts of the IT architecture are transformed for these benefits to be realized.

In summary, both concepts for integrated architectures are able to increase the interoperability and flexibility of application infrastructures, but they have a different focus and scope as shown by the comparative analysis of their integration characteristics and the different integration scenarios. The provided examples in the application areas of legacy system integration and B2B integration show that it is also possible to combine the two approaches within one integration strategy.

REFERENCES

1. Fricke, B., *Flexible B2B-Integrationsarchitekturen*. Eul-Verlag, Lohmar, Köln, 2008, Chaps. 2 and 3.
2. Institute of Electrical and Electronics Engineers. *IEEE Standard Computer Dictionary: A Compilation of IEEE Standard Computer Glossaries*. New York, 1990.
3. International Organization for Standardization, General information on ISO. Available at http://www.iso.org/iso/support/faqs/faqs_general_information_on_iso.htm.
4. Bussler, C., *B2B Integration*. Springer, Berlin, 2003, Chaps. 1 and 2.
5. Hohpe, G. and Woolf, B., *Enterprise Integration Patterns*. Addison-Wesley, Boston, 2004, Chap. 3.
6. Erl, T., *Service-Oriented Architecture: Concepts, Technology, and Design*. Prentice Hall, Upper Saddle River, NJ, 2005, Chap. 8.
7. Krafzig, D., Banke, K., and Slama, D., *Enterprise SOA—Service-Oriented Architecture Best Practices*. Prentice Hall, Upper Saddle River, NJ, 2005, Chaps. 4, 7, and 10.
8. Chen, H.-M., Towards service engineering: Service orientation and business-IT alignment. *Proceedings of the 41st Hawaii International Conference on System Sciences*, Waikoloa, Big Island, HI, 2008, 1.
9. Bazijanec, B., Gausmann, O., and Turowski, K., Parsing effort in a B2B integration scenario—An industrial case study, in *Enterprise Interoperability II. New Challenges and Approaches*, Goncalves, R. J. et al., Eds. Springer, London, 2007, 783.
10. Vanderhaeghen, D. et al., Service- and process-matching—An approach towards interoperability design and implementation of Business networks, in *Enterprise Interoperability—New Challenges and Approaches*, Doumeingts, G. et al., Eds., Springer, Berlin, 2007, 189–198.

11. Stelzer, D., Fischer, D., and Nirsberger, N., A framework for assessing inter-organizational integration of business information systems, *Int. J. Interoper. Bus. Inform. Syst.*, 2(2), 9, 2006.
12. van den Heuvel, J.-W., To adapt or not to adapt, that is the question: towards a framework to analyze scenarios for aligning legacy and business components, in *Enterprise Interoperability—New Challenges and Approaches*, Doumeingts, G. et al., Eds., Springer, Berlin, 2007, 45–54.
13. Rabon, J., Using SOA, EAI, and BPM to re-engineer legacy applications to J2EE. JavaOne, 2008. Available at http://developers.sun.com/learning/javaoneonline/2008/pdf/TS-5534.pdf?cid=925517.
14. Lawrence, C., Adapting legacy systems for SOA. Available at http://www.ibm.com/developerworks/webservices/library/ws-soa-adaptleg.

Section IV

Enterprise Applications

16 Integrating the Web and Enterprise Systems

Chang-Yang Lin

CONTENTS

INTRODUCTION

The growth of the World Wide Web, the Web in short, for electronic business has been phenomenal since graphical user interface (GUI)-based browsers became available in the middle of 1990s. The Web has evolved from the original concept of being a static poster for existing content to a delivery platform for enterprise applications, business-to-business (B2B)/business-to-consumer (B2C) e-commerce, and electronic publishing and interactive collaboration. Increasingly Web applications by way of B2B/B2C are being incorporated within the Web 2.0 to provide users with more seamless integration across enterprise-wide systems in order to advance customer and partner connection and to encourage participation. A report by a McKinsey global survey conducted in 2007 found that more than 75% of organizations are already investing in Web 2.0 [1].

Almost all of these Web applications or Web site usages involve interaction with some forms of data ranging from structured (e.g., relational databases, legacy data, or flat files) to semi-structured (e.g., XML-based data) and unstructured (e.g., e-mails, static Web pages, documents, and user-generated data in reviews, blogs, etc.). Fueling this data complexity are personal productivity applications and proprietary applications that operate on a regular basis. As more and more organizations are committed to Web applications to deliver their core business functions, the issues of making applications "Web-enabled" and integrating a variety of data in support of Web applications naturally arise.

This chapter explores the various issues related to the integration of enterprise-wide systems in the context of the Web. After a short background on the Web, the likely Web-based architecture is presented. Web limitations are examined and the resulting business questions or challenges are raised. Three types of Web applications are explained to reflect the relevance of data and application integration. Approaches for integrating the Web and enterprise systems into a coherent manner are described from two separate but related processes: data integration and application integration. Finally, solutions that address the challenges are suggested. The planning and strategic issues useful in preparing for Web-based enterprise systems are offered.

WEB-BASED ARCHITECTURES

The World Wide Web is a way of organizing information in small chunks, called pages, that can be displayed page by page through electronic links. A Web-based system is basically structured into a three-tiered architecture, with the browser providing the user-interface, the Web server processing business services, and a

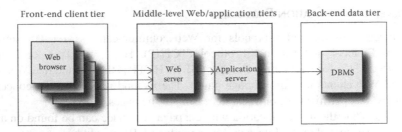

FIGURE 16.1   Four-tier Web-based architecture.

database storing the data. For a Web-based system that involves access to dynamic content or back-end databases, adding an application server between the Web server and the database will make a four-tier configuration, an effective and scalable solution. Under the four-tiered architecture, the Web server is used to retrieve and deliver Web pages and the application server to provide business logic through any number of protocols. Figure 16.1 illustrates the high-level four-tiered architecture of a Web-based system.

A Web client acts as a front-end browser for requesting and receiving service from the servers. Popular Web browsers include Microsoft's Internet Explorer, Mozilla's Firefox, Opera Software's Opera, and Apple's Safari. These browsers are equipped with GUIs to make Internet navigation relatively easy.

A Web server is the back-end distributing system that processes and manages requests for service from the clients. A Web server also supports such interfaces as Common Gateway Interface (CGI), Java Server Page (JSP), Hypertext Preprocessor (PHP), and ASP.net to handle static and dynamic data. Two leading Web servers are Apache and Microsoft's Internet Information Server.

An application server provides the business logic in the form of data and method calls for application programs. The logic is mostly built into a component API (Application Programming Interface), such as the EJB (Enterprise JavaBeans) component found on J2EE (Java 2 Platform, Enterprise Edition). J2EE and .NET Framework are two latest versions of application servers for Web applications. The application server can be evaluated in terms of such factors as reusability, scalability, manageability, performance, and integration.

A database server provides database services mainly to application servers. Database management systems (DBMSs) frequently provide database server functionality. Popular DBMSs are all relational, including IBM's DB2, Oracle's Database, Microsoft's Structured Query Language (SQL) Server, and the open sources mySQL by Sun Microsystems.

STANDARD PROTOCOLS FOR THE WEB

The Web as the fundamental platform for integration depends on open standards, the most important being Internet communication protocols, Extensible Markup Language (XML), and Hypertext Markup Language (HTML).

INTERNET COMMUNICATION PROTOCOLS

The three main Internet protocols for Web communications are: Transmission Control Protocol and Internet Protocol (TCP/IP), Hypertext Transfer Protocol (HTTP), and Uniform Resource Locator (URL). HTTP is the method that Web servers and Web clients use to exchange pages. The method is built on the concept of hypertext that permits the nonlinear accessing of the pages.

URLs define the unique location where a page or service can be found on a host computer connected to the Internet. An example of URL would be

http://www.internetworldstats.com/stats.htm

This URL begins with the letters "http" to indicate the protocol of format exchange and that the last portion of the address (i.e., stats.htm) is an HTML page. The section after "://," in this case, "www" stands for the host computer name and "internetworldstats. com" stands for the domain name. As the technology of the Web evolves, URLs have become more complex, in particular, in the case where content is retrieved from a back-end database.

XML: AN OPEN DOCUMENT STANDARD

XML is an open standard for structured documents and data on the Web. XML permits authors to create XML-based markup languages for describing any type of data that support data interchange. One example is FpML (Financial Products Markup Language) that became a standard in B2B for a range of financial services from electronic trading and confirmations to portfolio specification for risk analysis in the over-the counter derivatives market.

XML-based technologies such as XML Schema, XSL (Extensible Stylesheet Language), WSDL (Web Services Description Language), and SOAP (Simple Object Access Protocol) are all open standards that can be used for B2B integration with heterogeneous systems.

HTML PUBLISHING TOOLS

HTML is an open platform markup language to define Web pages. This language uses a standard set of tags for formatting and displaying hypertext document. The Extensible Hypertext Markup Language (XHTML) is an XML-simplified and XML-compatible version of HTML; therefore it can be easily integrated into XML-based applications. XHTML requires an exact syntax due to the increasing demand for small devices [e.g., personal digital assistants (PDAs) and mobile phones] that cannot accommodate regular browsers such as Internet Explorer.

Creating an XHTML page involves primarily the process of tagging documents; XHTML encoding can be performed by inserting the tags in a hypertext file. Although word processors and other text editors can be used to create Web pages from scratch, tools specifically designed to develop Web pages are available to make working with XHTML tags easier. Examples of two leading publishing tools are Adobe Dreamweaver and Microsoft FrontPage.

Whereas creating static pages using these publishing tools requires no specific skills, rich and interactive pages will require extensive knowledge and skills to integrate hyperlinks, multimedia, and embedded objects. Object-oriented programming skills will also be required for the development of Web applications that involve the access of back-end databases.

WEB LIMITATIONS AND CHALLENGES

The Web has the potential of facilitating electronic business transactions, information inquiries, and collaborative decision support. Nevertheless, from a business perspective, four fundamental questions as described below create some challenges with which an innovative organization must deal to stay competitive.

IS THE WEB SUITABLE FOR MISSION-CRITICAL BUSINESS APPLICATIONS?

The Web in its original concept is "stateless" rather than "state full" and is used to provide "static" rather than "dynamic" information. On the other hand, modern mission-critical applications must maintain "state" information and require interaction with back-end databases. To overcome this limitation, Web scripting tools and programming techniques are used to maintain continuous user sessions on the Web. To date, many organizations' mission-critical business processes are being supported by either legacy systems or packaged applications such as Enterprise Resource Planning (ERP), Supply Chain Management (SCM), and Customer Relationship Management (CRM). Making these enterprise applications Web-enabled to support core business processes is increasingly becoming one of the most important goals for the organizations.

IS THE WEB DATA STRUCTURE ADEQUATE TO SUPPORT INFORMATION REPORTING AND QUERY RESPONSES?

The Web employs a hypertext data structure with hypertext pages defined using HTML. HTML, however, has no descriptive markup features to provide the meaning of pages. In other words, the Web data is unstructured and has minimal metadata. Text documents, marketing materials, and objects may be fitted into these pages. Search engines can find the most relevant Web content but the results are still presented as unstructured ones that must be read individually. As for the traditional record-based business data, they are not suitable for storage in pages, mainly because business data, if stored in pages, are not easily accessible and manageable on a record-by-record basis. Consequently, user-controlled queries cannot be easily formulated are the key business information and knowledge cannot be automatically derived from hypertext databases.

CAN ENTERPRISE DATA OR LEGACY DATA BE AVAILABLE ON THE WEB?

To date, enterprise data—mostly transaction oriented—are stored mainly in mainframe computers. The problem is that many of these legacy systems predate modern data exchange standards or interfaces for integration. That is the reason why enterprise data are mostly inaccessible from the Web. Getting the new Web applications to access and update these legacy enterprise data becomes a challenge for organizations.

CAN THE WEB BE LEVERAGED FOR AUTOMATIC QUERIES?

The issue here is to make the Web a fundamental enterprise repository for structured, semi-structured, and unstructured data to automatically query, browse, or search for data and enable Web applications. Data integration has been successful for some enterprise systems. Such successful integration is partially due to the fact that enterprise systems rely on structured data stored in relational databases, which are relatively easy to integrate. In contrast, the Web encompasses a wide range of data from the unstructured HTML pages, e-mails, images, audio, and video, to the semi-structured XML-based documents and the fully structured XML data that are not compatible with relational databases. These Web data have not been integrated into enterprise systems' databases. The problem with a focus on relational databases only is that it excludes valuable information and knowledge that resides in the form of Web content. Leveraging the Web as an enterprise repository to automatically query, browse, or search for all of the data will be a very complex task.

WEB APPLICATIONS

Technically, scripting technologies and new programming techniques are used to overcome some of the Web limitations and, thus, to enable the development of dynamic and data-intensive Web applications. An increasing number of corporations are now turning to the Web as a delivery mechanism for a wide range of applications. These applications include core business functions, intranets, extranets, and collaboration and communications. It has been reported that 42% of the organizations were providing Web access to enterprise applications for internal and external users [2].

This section describes three types of Web applications: electronic commerce (e-commerce) applications that are designed to interact with customers, suppliers, and other business partners; intranets and portals for internal users; and Web 2.0 applications that focus on collaboration and communications.

E-COMMERCE APPLICATIONS

Some of the most popular forms of Web applications are e-commerce Web sites, which are designed specifically to allow authorized customers, partners, and suppliers to access certain business applications. These e-commerce Web sites are used to market a company, sell its products and services, provide and distribute information, and link users into its business processes. Some—like Internet retail banking and certain online business applications—are B2C applications that facilitate electronic transactions and communications between a business seller and individual customers. Others—like SCM systems and e-procurement sites—are B2B applications that facilitate transactions and communications between two or more participated businesses. U.S. Census Bureau figures show that, in 2005, B2B transactions accounted for 92% of total e-commerce and B2C sales accounted only for 4.1% [3].

INTRANETS

An intranet or a portal is designed for the internal communications of an organization. It has been reported that intranets or portals are the most widely deployed of all Web applications.

Portals are used to publish a variety of information in multimedia. Some information may be drawn from enterprise applications. The employee directory is the most used feature on all intranets. Some portals allow employees to update their data online, and the result is that such collaborative authoring intranets are much more informative and current than a typical "static" intranet. Examples of applications on intranets are given as follows:

- Web-based internal e-mail systems
- Project planning, monitoring, and reporting
- Forums for brainstorming, collaborations, or problem solving
- Delivering marketing materials, training materials, or software products
- Sales and customer portals—on-line customer information queries
- On-line human resource queries on employee benefits, company policies, employee and telephone directories, job listings, and training and education workshops

WEB 2.0 APPLICATIONS

Web 2.0 involves a new way of thinking and a set of techniques that leverage the Web as a participative medium with greater collaboration among users, enterprises, and content providers. The Web 2.0 applications enable organizations to improve Web site usability by adding functionality, generating and sharing content in real-time, and facilitating user participation and many-to-many communications. Web 2.0 technologies include Ajax, RSS feeds, and mash-ups. Ajax, for example, uses XHTML and CSS (Cascading Style Sheet) for content presentation, DOM (Document Object Model) for dynamic display and interaction, XML and XSLT (Extensible Stylesheet Language Transformation) for data interchange and manipulation, and JavaScript for integrating all other components. Wikis, blogs, podcasts, online forums, message boards, and social networking Web sites are all typical Web 2.0 models.

Web 2.0 is increasingly being incorporated into corporate Web sites or portals to provide business users with more seamless integration across enterprises in order to communicate with customers and partners and to encourage collaboration. A manager can now, for example, retrieve sales data from a variety of internal and external sources, create a portal for data sharing, and then contact other members online for a group analysis of data over the portal. Web 2.0 has been used for communicating with customers and business partners, and helping manage knowledge internally. Blogs and podcasts are generally focused outside the organization to support sales and marketing efforts.

DATA INTEGRATION WITH THE WEB

The process of integrating the Web and enterprise systems can be approached from two directions. The first involves integrating enterprise data, Web content, and other unstructured data into a virtual data repository for data retrieval, data storage, and data modification, and for enabling Web applications. The other involves building a link to make existing applications Web-enabled and capable of accessing back-end databases. Regardless of which approach is used, the goal remains the same; that is, making corporate data and the various business applications accessible through Web browsers. The use of Web browsers eliminates concerns about heterogeneous hardware and various operating systems over the Web platform.

This section describes the process of data integration and identifies the tools that support the integration. The data integration process includes three development activities: migrating enterprise data to relational data, migrating Web content and other unstructured data to XML data, and unifying XML and relational data.

MIGRATING ENTERPRISE DATA TO RELATIONAL DATA

The majority of enterprise data, which are typically scattered among multiple enterprise applications, come from heterogeneous data sources such as relational databases, hierarchical databases, and flat files. Of these data sources, relational databases are more effective in supporting e-business processes due to their superior accessibility and scalability. For example, relational databases can speed up the process of loading the data into targeted databases and applications inside the organization or packaging the data into files or documents for exchange with other organizations. Thus, migrating nonrelational enterprise data into relational databases will be an important step toward a virtual data repository. The methods for migrating to relational databases have been widely discussed in the literature, including data conversion, data replication, data propagation, database gateway, and reverse-engineering and re-engineering [4–6].

MIGRATING UNSTRUCTURED DATA TO XML DATA

While enterprise data are mostly structured, Web content in HTML is exclusively unstructured. Company Web sites, e-commerce sites, blogs, discussion forums, and personal home pages all contain mainly HTML data and few XML data. Nevertheless, any software that exchanges data with other applications, whether those applications are internal or external to the organization, may eventually use XML as a data format, due to its descriptivity, flexibility, and readability. As XML is becoming the *de facto* standard for retrieving and exchanging data, it is important to convert HTML content and other unstructured data into XML data. Several steps can be taken toward an XML-based database:

- *HTML-to-XML conversion.* Web content or documents that will be used for data exchange should be structured in XML. In the past, conversion from

HTML to XML was a complex, time-consuming process. To date, HTML-to-XML conversion tools such as Altova's StyleVision HTML Importer allow developers convert existing HTML content into XML, separating it into a stylesheet containing the page layout, and an XML file containing the page data.

- *HTML-to-XHTML conversion.* HTML pages that are not data-related may be converted into XHTML pages. XHTML itself is an XML application, and therefore XHTML pages will be able to interface with other XML-based applications.
- *Direct conversion to XML.* The approach here is to upload the key enterprise data using the ETL (extract, transform, and load) process and then convert them into XML data [7]. This will certainly give users speedy query responses regarding critical business information.

UNIFYING XML AND RELATIONAL DATA

Unifying XML and relational data involves mapping DTD (Document Type Definition) or W3C (World Wide Web Consortium) XML Schema, which describe the structure of the XML data, into and from relational tables and fields. The intrinsic differences in XML data and relational databases make data unification a challenging task.

To be effective, the mapping tools should provide such important features as mapping definitions, tools to support mapping operations, and the ability to integrate XML processors for query, selection, and transform the XML views obtained from relational data [8]. Although current technologies are not mature enough to support a seamless integration, several products (e.g., Altova's XMLSpy and Progress Software's Stylus Studios Enterprise XML Suite) have been used to facilitate the mapping process automata. Specifically, XMLSpy allows the developers to connect to a relational database, generate an XML Schema based on a relational database, import and export data based on database structures, and generate relational database structures from XML Schemas. Most of the leading relational database management system vendors have enhanced their data management features with an additional component to support for structured XML and relational data co-existence.

APPLICATION INTEGRATION WITH THE WEB

Application integration with the Web may be approached from two directions: augmenting XHTML programs and Web-enabling enterprise applications. Both approaches involve building a link either to make XHMTL pages capable of interacting with back-end databases or to make enterprise applications Web-enabled.

AUGMENTING XHTML PROGRAMS

The static XHTML programs can be enhanced and augmented to include a data-access subprogram for interaction with back-end databases. This subprogram may contain SQL statements and procedure codes, called scripts, which can be developed using server-side scripting technologies such as PHP, ASP.net, JSP, or Perl.

Server-side scripting works by embedding scripts that provide the business logic separate from the XHTML pages that define page layout. It also provides features for connecting to, querying and updating databases via standard database-access middleware such as JDBC (Java Database Connectivity), ODBC (Open Data Base Connectivity), or OLEDB (Object Linking and Embedding Data Base).

WEB-ENABLING ENTERPRISE APPLICATIONS

Making enterprise applications Web-enabled is often based on wrapping. Wrapping consists of surrounding the legacy enterprise system from the Web with a software layer that hides the complexity of both systems. Two wrapping approaches are as follows:

- Establishing a bridge to link Web applications and enterprise systems
- Embedding XHTML forms into enterprise programs

The first approach is to establish a bridge linking Web applications and legacy systems that run today's enterprises. A tremendous effort must be devoted to the development of a translator or a driver that facilitates interaction in the forms of XML or XHTML (that can be understood by Web applications) and messages (that can be understood by enterprise applications). For instance, the Sombers Group's Evolve and its underlying middleware—Netware by Vertex Interactive—provide such a driver that integrates Web applications and enterprise applications.

Another interesting application is to use the XML adapter to act as the data exchange center between corporate enterprise systems and external organizations. The XML adapter communicates with enterprise systems such as ERP and legacy applications, and it also interoperates with external organizations by exchanging XML documents.

The second approach is to augment enterprise programs by embedding Web forms to capture input transaction data from Web clients. The input data are then fed into enterprise programs for processing. For example, Visual Object COBOL uses CGI to link Web forms to COBOL programs and therefore let COBOL programs take input from Web forms.

Besides the above two approaches, packaged applications can be Web-enabled with the implementation of Web components. For instance, SAP Enterprise Portal and SAP Exchange Infrastructure can be incorporated into packaged applications to drive the intranets and extranets for employees, customers, and partners. In addition, SAP NetWeaver may be used to integrate SAP modules and legacy systems.

STRATEGY AND PLANNING

While scripting technologies and new programming techniques are being used to overcome most Web limitations, the challenges raised by these limitations will need a strategy to deal with them. The following provide some suggestions that address these challenges for Web-based enterprise systems:

- *How do corporations attract potential customers via the Web?* They can build a presence on the Web, and then expand and enhance their Web sites.
- *How do corporations make enterprise data accessible via the Web to enhance service effectiveness for employees, customers, and partners?* They can move enterprise data into an XML format, use Web technology to connect legacy data, and develop enterprise portals and B2B gateways.
- *How do corporations deal with the tremendous Web content that contains key business information and knowledge?* They can structure Web content into an XML database and represent more Web content in data warehouses to enrich enterprise applications and processes.
- *What strategies will corporations need to develop to remain competitive?* They can integrate data and applications into a coherent enterprise-wide Web-based system. All or part of this new system may be developed internally with information systems (IS) staff or outsourced from outside organizations. In either case, a corporation must include education and training as part of the transition strategy to address uncertainty and to cope with staff growth.

Facing these challenges and thus effectively deploying Web-based enterprise systems requires planning. The following expand on the previous suggestions for better planning.

MAINTAINING A STRONG PRESENCE ON THE WEB

Corporations should position themselves on the Web by building and maintaining up-to-date Web sites. As competitors' presences on the Web increase, one way to guarantee failure in the face of the above challenges is to adopt a "wait on it" approach.

EXPANDING AND ENHANCING THE WEB SITE FUNCTIONALITY

Simply providing static information and marketing materials is insufficient to attract potential users to visit the organization's Web sites repeatedly. Corporations need to think of new ways to both enhance and expand corporate Web sites. These may include the following:

1. Personalizing the Web site to deliver relevant content according to each user's particular interests.
2. Embracing Web 2.0 to advance customer and partner connections, to facilitate participation, and to improve knowledge sharing and collaboration.
3. Coding Web pages in XHTML to deliver content for not only desktops and laptops clients, but also wireless clients such as mobile phones, PDAs, and pagers.

4. Making key enterprise data accessible via Web browsers. Enterprise data always serve as the foundation from which information can be derived. Both predesigned and *ad hoc* queries on key enterprise data must be considered to reflect friendliness and flexibility.

STRUCTURING WEB CONTENT AS AN XML DATABASE

Bringing structure to Web content will enable automation for the extraction of information and data exchange across enterprise with ease. One choice is to convert unstructured Web content to XML, an open data standard. For B2B data exchanges, corporations must comply with the latest XML-based standards in order to maintain their competitive edge.

The integrated XML data often contain some hidden business-critical knowledge. Corporations must also leverage the Web as a virtual repository by unifying XML data and relational databases to enrich enterprise applications and enable data-intensive Web applications.

BUILDING INTRANETS, EXTRANETS, AND WEB APPLICATIONS

How the Web should be used to deploy various applications within a corporation and to external corporations must be planned. The applications that support core business processes and that involve communication, information sharing, and information distribution should all be planned and built first. These applications may include enterprise portals, B2B e-commerce, and Web 2.0 applications.

PREPARING FOR ELECTRONIC COMMERCE

As Web technologies continue to mature, solutions designed to prevent security breaches, stateless transactions, and performance concerns have been proposed [9]. Thus, corporations must plan for electronic commerce by integrating enterprise data and Web content into a virtual data repository for data-intensive Web applications and by moving existing applications into a Web-based architecture. This may include reengineering and creating data-intensive Web applications, building the linkages between enterprise applications and the Web, Web-enabling packaged applications, linking the enterprise data to the Web, converting Web content to XML, and unifying XML and relational data.

Corporations should identify and plan projects for electronic commerce. Information reporting or inquiry projects such as customer portals and sales portals may be built first, because linking SQL databases to the Web will be easier to do. Upload of key enterprise data to the Web will also be necessary for fast inquiry response.

Building the linkage between existing enterprise applications and the Web can be performed next. The proven tools and techniques necessary for building such linkages should be evaluated and selected. Creating dynamic or data-intensive Web applications with server-side scripting tools can be performed as well. Depending on the specific needs of the individual corporations, applications to be built are ranked.

An XML-based database to store Web content, business document, and other unstructured data should be gradually implemented. Enterprise data and business document that will be exchanged with external organizations in B2B must be converted into XML-based industry standards.

Planning a Make-or-Buy Strategy

All of the above projects toward the enterprise-wide Web-based system will have to be evaluated and prioritized in terms of the make-or-buy decisions depending on the individual corporations and the complexity of the projects themselves. A make-or-buy plan must be developed to identify the most efficient and cost-effective manner for facilitating the integration projects. The plan will establish a preference for the various projects on a least-cost basis, subject to the make-or-buy criteria consistent with business objectives. The plan will also include a cost/benefit analysis to assess the costs and benefits of both "make" and "buy" options.

For instance, converting databases to XML is considered a complex project; it requires in-depth knowledge of data structures, and custom developing it will be both expensive and time consuming. As a result, corporations may elect to purchase software packages or outsource conversion programming to a third party rather than custom develop their own solutions with in-house IS staff. Small and midsized businesses often find "buy" or "outsourcing" a viable alternative because very few firms can afford to employ enough of the highly skilled IS developers to perform the integration. The new systems once completed can be hosted internally; alternatively, they can also be placed in a hosted third party service provider.

In addition to cost, corporations may also approach make-or-buy from a strategic perspective. One often cited factor on which the solutions are based is core competency. It has been suggested that core activities should stay in-house, while nonstrategic subsystems can be outsourced.

Education and Training

Special attention should be given to the training needs of both developers and business users for the new Web-based enterprise systems whether they are internally built or purchased. Corporations might have to spend a large investment in education, including in-house or vendor-led training programs. The training costs must be detailed and well documented as part of the process in the make-or-buy decisions.

Developers and other project team members will have to be sent to training classes so that they can learn the use of the specific integration tools, Web programming, or packaged software. Developers must also learn how to configure the purchased software, and write interfaces and queries. Business users must learn how to perform business processes in new ways to take advantage of the new system's capabilities.

Overall, developers and business users should understand how the Internet and the Web can be accessed, used to gather information, and implemented to enable collaboration and create business opportunities. Business users are required to have a higher level of training to deal with faceless, paperless, nonphysical interactive transaction and information inquiry. The users who are responsible for publishing must learn authoring tools to create pages. Developers must learn the development tools to build and reengineer data-intensive applications on the Web. Developers mastering the tools, including Web-scripting technologies, XML, J2EE, Java, and Ajax will be essential for a successful Web-enabled transformation.

CONCLUSION

Web technologies or capabilities are extensive and growing more complex and sophisticated at a rapid rate. To keep abreast of such advancements, systems developers must consider factors such as transfer protocols and open standards, security, and development tools and languages. All capabilities and make-or-buy options must be evaluated in context of the enterprise—its goals as well as its propensity for risk-taking. Only with an appropriate planning can an organization move into the world of true integrated Web-based systems.

REFERENCES

1. Bughin, J. and Manyika, J., How businesses are using Web 2.0: A McKinsey Global Survey, *The McKinsey Journal*, 2007, available at http://www.mckinseyquarterly.com (accessed February 25, 2008).
2. Tarzey, B., Longbottom, C., and Keane, D., *Web-Enabled Applications and the Internet: Satisfying the Growing Expectations of Business Users*, Quocirca Insight Report, 2007, available at http://www.quocirca.com/pages/analysis/reports/view/store250/item4972/ (accessed March 11, 2008).
3. U.S. Census Bureau, *E-Stats*, available at http://www.census.gov/eos/www/2005/2005reportfinal.pdf (May 25, 2007).
4. Meier, A., Providing database migration tools: A practitioner's view, *Proceedings of the 21st VLDS Conference*, Zurich, Switzerland, 635–641, 1995.
5. Comella-Dorda, S. et al., *A Survey of Legacy System Modernization Approaches*, The Software Engineering Institute, Carnegie Mellon University, Technical Note, CMU/SEI-2000-TN-003, 2000, available at http://www.sei.cmu.edu/publications/documents/00.reports/00tn003.html.
6. Lin, C., Relational database conversion: Issues and approaches, in *High-Performance Web Databases: Design, Development, and Deployment*, Purba, S., Ed., CRC Press, Boca Raton, FL, 2001, Chap. 38.
7. Russom, P., *Complex Data: A New Challenge for Data Integration*, TDWI Monograph Series, the Data Warehousing Institute, 2007.
8. Guardalben, G., Integrating XML and relational database technologies, retrieved from http://www.hitsw.com (2004).
9. Sherif, M. H., *Protocols for Secure Electronic Commerce*, 2nd edn, CRC Press, Boca Raton, FL, 2004, Chaps. 3 and 5.

APPENDIX A: PRODUCTS MENTIONED IN THE CHAPTER

Apache
ASP.net
DB2
Evolve
Firefox
Internet Explorer
mySQL
NetWeaver
Opera
Oracle Database
Safari
SAP Enterprise Portal
SAP Exchange Infrastructure
SAP NetWeaver
SQL Server
StyleVision HTML Importer
Stylus Studio Enterprise XML Suite
Iternet Information Server
XMLSpy

APPENDIX B: COMPANIES MENTIONED IN THE CHAPTER

Altova
Apple
IBM
Microsoft
Mozilla
Opera Software
Oracle
Progress Software Corporation
SAP
Sun Microsystems
The Sombers Group
Vertex Interactive

17 Enterprise Systems Integration in Telecommunications

Lin Lin and Ping Lin

CONTENTS

INTRODUCTION

There has been a long and fruitful history of integration between telecommunications and IT applications. Indeed, the most prominent enterprise voice applications are all examples of this integration:

- Unified messaging (UM) blends voice mail and e-mail by providing a single user interface on a variety of devices.

389

- Contact centers (also known as call centers) make heavy use of enterprise databases to route customer calls to agents with suitable skill-sets and present all relevant information at the same time.
- Interactive voice response systems enable end-users to retrieve information from enterprise databases and possibly update them by phone.

In this chapter, we examine a series of models under which telecommunications and IT application integration takes place. We begin by discussing standalone telecommunications applications interacting with servers found in a typical IT infrastructure using standard protocols such as Internet Message Access Protocol (IMAP) and Simple Mail Transfer Protocol (SMTP). A typical example may be found in the integration of voice mail and e-mail systems to provide UM.

Next, we cover a form of integration based on the Web browser analogy. We first examine the Windows Telephony Application Programming interface (TAPI) to illustrate the issues involved in computer-telephony integration. These same ideas find expression in the more contemporary style of writing telecommunications applications based on Voice Extensible Markup Language (VoiceXML) and Call Control Extensible Markup Language (CCXML).

Following that section we describe a form of integration based on application servers. We start by introducing the Session Initiation Protocol (SIP), the standard for signaling on converged voice and data networks. The design of SIP has borrowed much from the HyperText Transfer Protocol (HTTP). There is a parallel in the Java world—just as Web applications can be structured as HTTP servlets, there are now SIP servlets for Java-based SIP applications.

The service-oriented architecture (SOA) is a mechanism for integrating distributed and heterogeneous applications that are starting to see more adoption in the IT industry. The last section of the chapter considers an aspect of SOA that is particularly relevant to the integration of telecommunications and IT applications—the orchestration of Web services and real-time communications.

UM: LOOSE INTEGRATION THROUGH STANDARD PROTOCOLS

In this section, we examine UM as an example of loose integration between telecommunications and IT applications through standard protocols.

UM FUNCTIONALITY

UM enables users to access messages in a variety of media including voice, fax, and e-mail through a single interface on a variety of devices. For instance, from a desktop or wireless phone, a user can play and record voice messages, listen to fax message headers and print fax messages, listen to e-mail messages, and reply by voice and receive notifications when voice, fax, or e-mail messages arrive. Similarly, from an e-mail client or Web browser, a user can play and record voice messages, view and compose fax messages, view and compose e-mail messages, and receive notifications when voice, fax, or e-mail messages arrive.

UM helps to save time and improve user productivity. A user can, for example, check both e-mail and voice messages from the PC, instead of checking e-mail messages from the PC and voice messages from the phone.

INTEGRATION ARCHITECTURES

In the enterprise environment, UM functionality is often achieved by integrating a UM system from a telecommunications vendor with an e-mail system from an IT vendor. There are two typical integration architectures, which are somewhat confusingly referred to as the "integrated" and the "unified" architecture, respectively. The UM server connects to the Private Branch Exchange (PBX, i.e., the enterprise telephone switch) in both of these architectures, but its position in the data network relative to the e-mail server is different.

- In the "integrated" architecture, shown schematically in Figure 17.1a, the UM server and the e-mail server are peer entities in the network. Voice/fax

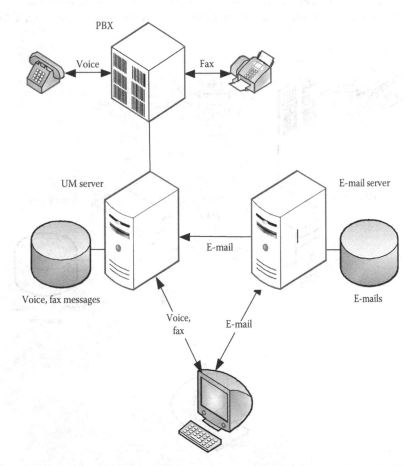

FIGURE 17.1a   Integrated UM architecture.

messages are stored and managed by the former, while e-mail messages are stored and managed by the latter. UM client software running on the user's PC or on a Web server communicates separately with both of these servers and merges the two streams of messages to present an integrated view to the end-user.

- In the "unified" architecture, shown schematically in Figure 17.1b, the e-mail server is the primary entity with which the UM client communicates, and the UM server feeds its stream of voice/fax messages into the e-mail server. The e-mail server is responsible for storing and managing all e-mail, voice, and fax messages, and for providing an integrated end-user view to the UM client.

COMPARISON OF THE INTEGRATED AND UNIFIED ARCHITECTURES

The integrated and unified architectures place significantly different requirements on server/network deployment and capacity/performance engineering.

- In the integrated architecture, the UM server is optimized to store voice/fax messages and to serve access requests for these messages from both UM

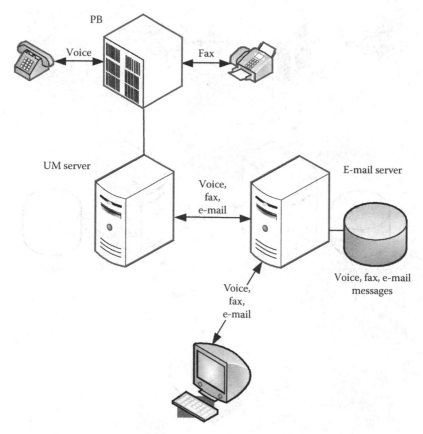

FIGURE 17.1b   Unified UM architecture.

clients and telephones. (Message stores in UM servers are generally designed to facilitate streaming of voice content.) There is no network traffic between the UM server and the e-mail server for message deposit or retrieval, since the UM server does not send its messages to the e-mail server. Data traffic pertaining to voice/fax message content only flows when users access these messages from UM clients or from IP phones.

- In the unified architecture, the voice/fax and e-mail messages for a given user are stored in the same mailbox on the e-mail server. UM clients connect to the e-mail server to access messages, while telephones connect to the UM server through the PBX. Although the same amount of data traffic flows when users access voice/fax messages from UM clients as in the integrated architecture, additional network traffic from the UM server to the e-mail server occurs whenever a voice/fax message is deposited or retrieved by (either IP or traditional non-IP) telephone or fax machine, since the UM server needs to send the voice/fax message to the e-mail server or fetch it from the e-mail server.

To provide additional availability beyond what the e-mail system can offer (since many users consider voice messages to be more timely than e-mails and have more stringent requirements on being able to access them "at all times"), the UM server in this architecture often includes the capability to buffer the incoming messages and possibly also to access a subset of cached messages when the e-mail server is down or unreachable.

More recently, some IT vendors have enhanced their e-mail systems to directly incorporate UM functionality. The architecture of these systems tend to be a variant of the unified architecture, in the sense that one of the servers in the system takes on the role of the UM server and interfaces (directly over IP or through a gateway) to the PBX and telephones.

INTEGRATION THROUGH STANDARD E-MAIL PROTOCOLS

UM integration can take place via standard or proprietary protocols and interfaces. Since almost all modern e-mail systems support standard Internet e-mail protocols in addition to the proprietary protocols/interfaces that they may offer, an Internet-standards-based approach to integration between voice/fax messaging and e-mail systems is advantageous in terms of its generality.

The discussion in this subsection is applicable to both the integrated and unified architectures with some differences as noted in the last paragraph.

Figure 17.2 shows the relationship between the key protocols and message formats that are used in standard Internet e-mail. The protocols illustrated in this figure are as follows:

- Post Office Protocol (POP) [1]: A protocol that enables an e-mail client to retrieve messages by downloading the messages in their entirety from an e-mail server. Once downloaded, messages are kept on the client and deleted from the user's mailbox on the server.

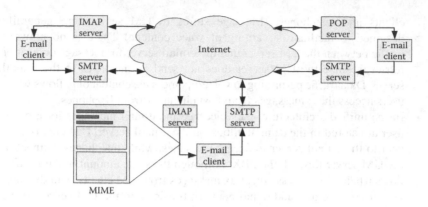

FIGURE 17.2 E-mail standards.

- IMAP [2]: An alternative to POP that enables an e-mail client to retrieve messages by first downloading just the header and body structure of each message, before selectively downloading the attachments. The messages stay in the user's mailbox on the server until they are deleted.
- SMTP [3]: A protocol used by an e-mail client to send messages.

The Internet e-mail messages conveyed by these protocols are encoded according to the Multipurpose Internet Mail Extensions (MIME) format [4]. A MIME message has an overall header and a body portion consisting of a number of body parts that in turn have their own headers and bodies. As an example, a fax message with voice annotation would have two body parts, one corresponding to the fax and one corresponding to the voice.

Figure 17.3 shows a sample integrated architecture based on standard Internet protocols.

The UM server shown in the above figure supports IMAP and SMTP and makes its store of voice/fax messages available to clients via these protocols. This enables the UM client to access the stream of voice/fax messages and the stream of e-mail messages by connecting to what appears to be two e-mail servers. The client interacts with the UM server by using IMAP to retrieve voice/fax messages and SMTP to deposit voice/fax messages, in the same way that it interacts with the e-mail server by using IMAP to retrieve e-mail messages and SMTP to deposit e-mail messages.

The IMAP protocol is preferred over POP for voice/fax message retrieval since it enables the client to download and present the MIME message header (which contains information about the sender, time sent, etc.) first without having to download the actual voice/fax component(s) that are packaged as body parts or attachments in the message. Also, since the IMAP messages stay in the user's mailbox on the server even after they have been pulled down to the client, it is easier to support multiple-client scenarios, for example, where a user listens to his/her messages selectively from the telephone and later on goes through them again from a PC-based UM client.

For brevity, we have not shown a sample unified architecture based on the same protocols. However, it should be mentioned that in this case the IMAP and SMTP

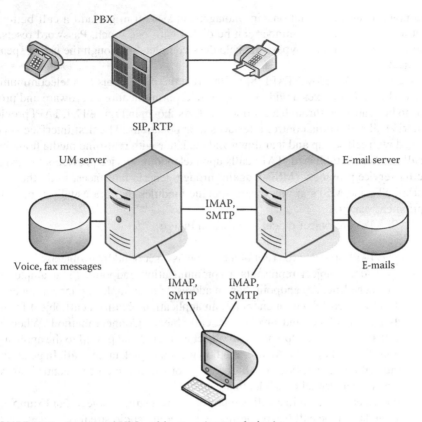

FIGURE 17.3 Integrated UM architecture (protocol view).

protocols are used between the UM server and the e-mail server, as well as between the e-mail server and the UM client.

VOICE BROWSERS

A Web browser displays HyperText Markup Language (HTML) documents that it fetched from Web servers. A request from the former triggers the execution of business logic in the latter; the document that is returned is often generated on the fly. This model forms the basis of a widely used style of integration between telecommunications and IT: the voice browser. Instead of HTML, a voice browser renders documents in VoiceXML [5,6] and CCXML [7]. As before, Web servers and the business logic they host supply these documents.

TELECOMMUNICATION APIs

The rationale behind VoiceXML and CCXML can be appreciated by considering procedural telecommunication APIs. These APIs enable IT applications to make use of the services of telecommunication networks to provide enhanced features. For example, a customer relationship management system might add a call button so that a customer's phone number can be dialed with one touch. Password resets, as another example, could bypass the help desk completely through the use of speaker verification.

We will use Windows TAPI [8] to illustrate the ingredients of a telecommunications API. TAPI enables a wide variety of telecommunications hardware and protocols to be controlled through a common API. As shown in Figure 17.4, TAPI provides generic call and media control interfaces to applications. The first interface is concerned with call set-up and tear down and the latter with real-time media flows once a call has been established. TAPI calls upon telephony service providers (TSPs) and media service providers (MSPs), again through generic interfaces, to do the actual work. TSPs and MSPs are hardware-specific modules that are usually supplied by equipment vendors.

TAPI 3.1's core object model is shown in Figure 17.5:

- The TAPI object is the root object. It owns a set of address objects.
- An address object represents a communication endpoint, for example, a telephone line. An endpoint has an address, for example, a phone number.
- To place a call from an endpoint, an application obtains a call object from its address object and invokes the call object's Connect method. When a call arrives at an endpoint, a call object is created and passed to the application. The call object's Answer method is used to pick up the call. In general, the call object provides methods for all of the common call control tasks that are performed on a telephone.
- Each media stream in a call is represented by a stream object. For example, a regular phone call has incoming and outgoing audio streams.

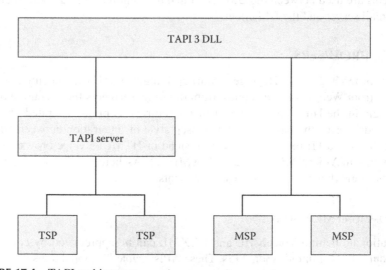

FIGURE 17.4   TAPI architecture.

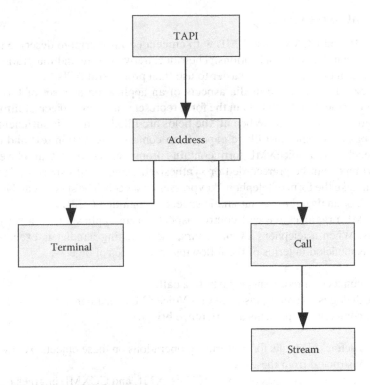

FIGURE 17.5 TAPI core object model.

- A terminal object is a source or sink for media streams. There are several classes of terminal objects, for example, headset, camera, file playback, file record, and so on. Media control consists of attaching terminal objects to stream objects, for example, after connecting a regular phone call between two people, a headset can be attached to both the incoming and outgoing streams of the call.

TAPI programming is event-driven. This is a reflection of the nature of the underlying processes. Call set-up usually involves alerting a real person and waiting for an answer; a relatively long period of time elapses between state changes. Call tear down is usually initiated by a person hanging up and can happen at any time. TAPI objects report these occurrences by raising events. Statically, a TAPI application contains a set of functions to handle events of interest. Dynamically, an event loop waits for events to arrive and executes the corresponding functions.

In summary, the following are the main elements of a telecommunications API:

- Hardware abstraction
- Call control interface
- Media interface
- Event handling

VoiceXML and CCXML

VoiceXML and CCXML use XML with embedded JavaScript to describe the logic in telecommunications applications. Their declarative nature and integration with a scripting language make them easier to use than procedural APIs.

VoiceXML models the media aspects of an application as a set of forms to be filled out by the user. Each field in the form represents a discrete piece of information that needs to be collected. When all the fields are filled in, there is sufficient data to invoke business logic. Just like a paper form contains instruction text and captions beside each box, a VoiceXML form contains prompt elements that are played to the user. Prompts can be prerecorded or synthesized using text-to-speech (TTS). User input can take the form of telephone keypresses or speech. The speech can be directly recorded, or analyzed using automatic speech recognition (ASR).

CCXML organizes the call control aspects of an application as a set of event handlers. When a telephony event occurs, the matching handler is executed. Call control is modeled in terms of the following three types of objects:

- A connection represents a party to a call.
- A dialog is a running instance of a VoiceXML document.
- A conference represents a conference bridge.

CCXML defines elements for performing operations on these objects. An event handler is constructed from these elements.

A voice browser consists of a pair of VoiceXML and CCXML engines that act as interpreters (Figure 17.6). They both fetch documents from a Web server. The VoiceXML interpreter controls ASR and TTS engines; VoiceXML can also be viewed as a generic interface to engines from different vendors. The CCXML interpreter controls signaling with the telephone network and the conference bridge. CCXML thus provides a generic interface to different signaling protocols.

There is a significant difference between Web and voice browsers. The former runs on client devices, and serves one user at a time. The latter handles calls from many telephones simultaneously, and runs on a server.

As an example of voice browser integration, we will voice-enable an online auction server with VoiceXML and CCXML. The goal is to allow the use of an HTTP request with the URL:

```
http://ccxml.auction.com/createsession
        ?uri=auction.ccxml&itemid=x&bidder=y
```

to trigger the following actions:

- Call a bidder at phone number y.
- Ask whether there is interest in placing a bid on item x at the current price.
- If there is interest, submit a bid from the same call.

When the CCXML interpreter at ccxml.auction.com receives the above request, it starts an instance of the CCXML document auction.ccxml running.

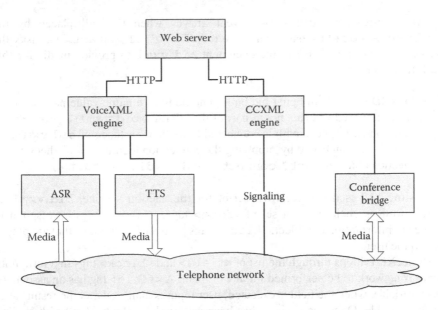

FIGURE 17.6   VoiceXML and CCXML architecture.

Listing 17.1 provides `auction.ccxml`, a CCXML script for auction service. Each set of `<transition>` tags enclose the handler for a particular event.

A `ccxml.loaded` event is the first to arrive when a document starts up. A call is placed to the bidder using the `<createcall>` tag in its handler, creating a connection object in the process. The JavaScript expression `session.values.bidder` picks up the phone number of the bidder from the URL that was used to invoke the document. The session object is a read-only global object that contains information specific to an instance of a document. In particular, `session.values` is an associative array or dictionary that holds all the name-value pairs from the invoking URL.

```
<ccxml>
  <eventprocessor>
    <transition event="ccxml.loaded">
      <createcall dest="session.values.bidder"/>
    </transition>
    <transition event="connection.connected">
      <var name="itemid" expr="session.values.itemid"/>
      <dialogstart src="'bid.vxml'" type="'application/
      voicexml+xml'"
        parameters="itemid" connectionid="event$.
        connectionid"/>
    </transition>
  </eventprocessor>
</ccxml>
```

LISTING 17.1   CCXML script for auction service (`auction.ccxml`).

A `connection.connected` event arrives when the call placed by the earlier `<createcall>` has been answered. The `<dialogstart>` tag asks the VoiceXML interpreter to run the document `bid.vxml` to provide media for this call. In particular,

- The ID of the item being bid on is sent along as a name-value pair of the form `itemid = x` (but not as part of the URL for `bid.vxml`).
- The bidder's speech path is connected to the new instance of `bid.vxml`. This is accomplished by supplying the connection identifier of his/her connection object (`event$.connectionid`) to `<dialogstart>`.

Listing 17.2 is the VoiceXML script for the auction service, `bid.vxml`. A single form is enclosed in a set of `<form>` tags. `<field>` tags correspond to pieces of information to collect. `<block>` tags produce instructions that are played out to the user.

VoiceXML loops through the list of `<field>` and `<block>` tags in a form until there is no work to be performed for any of them. A `<field>` tag has an associated item variable; when the field is executed, user input is analyzed and the result saved in the variable. Once the variable has been set, work on the field is finished. This model is extended to `<block>` elements as well. After execution (i.e., playing its prompt), a `<block>` element's (usually implicit) item variable is set, thus preventing it from running again.

The first `<block>` plays a message containing the description of the item being bid on and the current highest bid using TTS. This works as follows:

- The item ID passed in from `auction.ccxml` is retrieved using the JavaScript expression `session.connection.ccxml.values.itemid` and stored in the variable `itemid`.
- The auction server is queried for information on the item. The `<data>` tag sends an HTTP GET request with the following URL:

  `http://auction.com/inquire?itemid=x`

- The auction server responds with a small XML document that looks like this:

  ```
  <item id = x>
  <description>steel suspension bridge</description>
  <price> 0.01 </price>
  </item>
  ```

- The `<data>` tag saves this in the variable info. The document object model API is used to extract the text inside each tag; this is wrapped up in the JavaScript function `getval`. We defined `getval` using a `<script>` tag at the beginning of `bid.vxml`. The `<script>` tag allows an arbitrary piece of JavaScript to be embedded inside a VoiceXML or CCXML document.

- The contents of the `<prompt>` tag are played to the bidder after TTS conversion. The actual values of item description and price are inserted into the text fed to the TTS engine by the `<value>` tag. The `<say-as>` tag enclosing the second `<value>` tag causes the price to be treated as a dollar amount, that is, 0.01 would be read as "one cent" rather than "zero point zero one."

The `<field>` tag whose name attribute is "bid" is visited next:

- The bidder is asked whether he/she would like to make a bid. He/she can answer either by voice or by telephone keypad; the built-in grammar for Boolean variables can handle either.
- The VoiceXML interpreter stores the answer in the item variable `bid` and executes the contents of the `<filled>` element.
- If the bidder is not interested, we thank him/her anyway.

The `<field>` tag whose name attribute is "price" is visited next only if the bidder is interested (a field is executed only if its item variable is unfilled and its `cond` attribute evaluates to true):

- The bidder is asked for a price.
- The VoiceXML interpreter stores the answer in the item variable `price` and executes the contents of the `<filled>` element.
- The `<data>` tag submits a bid to the auction server by sending an HTTP GET to the following URL:

```
http://auction.com/bid?itemid=x&bidder=y&price=z
```

The identity of the bidder was not explicitly passed in from `auction.ccxml`, but was obtained from `session.connection.local.uri`—the number dialed from `<createcall>`.

- We confirm to the bidder that his/her bid has been placed.

The final `<block>` is visited regardless of whether a bid was placed. Unfailingly polite, we say goodbye to our bidder.

We make the following few observations from the example:

- Invoking a CCXML document via HTTP is the same as calling any Web application server.
- Caching considerations have an enormous impact on scalability. If `auction.ccxml` had invoked `bid.vxml` using a URL containing session-specific parameters, the VoiceXML interpreter would have to fetch and parse the document anew for every call (recall that a voice browser typically serves a small set of documents to many phones). Similarly, the common practice of generating documents on the fly using templates on the Web server has similar scaling issues.

```
<vxml>
  <var name="itemid" expr="session.connection.ccxml.
    values.itemid"/>
  <script>
    function getval(x,name) {return x.documentElement.
      getElementsByTagName(name).item(0).firstChild.
      nodeValue;}
  </script>
  <form>
    <block>
      <var name="info"/>
      <data name="info" src="http://auction.com/inquire"
        namelist="itemid"/>
      <prompt>
        This is auction dot com.
        The item <value expr="getval(info,
        'description')"/>
          is available for bidding.
        The current price is <say-as interpret-
        as="currency">
          <value expr="getval(info,'price')"/></say-as>.
      </prompt>
    </block>
    <field name="bid" type="boolean">
      <prompt>Would you like to place a bid?</prompt>
      <filled>
        <if cond="!bid">Thank you.</if>
      </filled>
    </field>
    <field name="price" type="currency" cond="bid">
      <prompt>How much?</prompt>
      <filled>
        <var name="bidder" expr="session.connection.
         local.uri"/>
        <data src="http://auction.com/bid"
          namelist="itemid bidder price"/>
        <prompt>Your bid has been placed.</prompt>
      </filled>
    </field>
    <block>
      Have a nice day!
    </block>
  </form>
</vxml>
```

LISTING 17.2 VoiceXML script for auction service (bid.vxml).

- In traditional Web pages, the lifetime of a page comes to an end after hitting the submit button on a form. The user interface is unresponsive between the HTTP request bearing the information from the form and a new page coming back from the Web server. The Asynchronous JavaScript and XML (AJAX) allows a Web page to stay alive while making HTTP requests through the XMLHttpRequest mechanism. VoiceXML's <data> tag is somewhat analogous to this.

APPLICATION SERVERS

In a client/server architecture, servers process requests received from clients over a network. While every server has its own unique business logic, common tasks recur in areas such as session life cycle and database transactions. An application server provides a run-time environment, or container, in which these tasks are handled. Business logic is packaged into components that run inside the container. When a new session starts up, the application server creates a new component instance for it. Requests that are part of existing sessions are routed to the correct instance.

Requests come in various forms, for example, HTTP GET/POST, J2EE (Java 2 Platform, Enterprise Edition)-style method invocation, or Web service call. An application server can have several containers, each holding components that handle one type of request. SIP [9,10] is the most widely used signaling protocol in Voice over IP (VoIP). Adding a container for SIP components to application servers is thus a way to achieve integration between telecommunications and IT. Specifically, telecommunication applications gain access to the same infrastructure that is used by IT applications. At the same time, converged applications, for example, those involving the use of both the Web and telephony, become readily available.

SESSION INITIATION PROTOCOL

The core function performed by SIP is the multimedia call set-up. This consists of two tasks that are as follows:

- Locating the called party. When a call is made to a logical address of record, it has to be directed to a physical address to which real-time media can be sent.
- Negotiating media settings. Both sides in a call have to agree on the media types (e.g., voice, video) to be exchanged and their compression settings.

SIP and HTTP messages look quite similar. All messages are text-based and consist of a series of headers and a payload. Request messages begin with a line containing a method and a uniform resource identifier (URI). URIs in SIP are usually of the form sip:user@domain or tel:phoneno. Response messages start with a line containing a three-digit return code that fall into the same classes as in HTTP (e.g., 200 means OK in both protocols).

Figure 17.7 shows how SIP is used to set up and tear down a call between two endpoints:

- Endpoint L sends an INVITE request to P. The payload of the request contains the media settings that L is offering to support.
- The phone starts ringing at endpoint P. A provisional response with a return code of 180 is sent from P to L.
- The phone is answered at endpoint P. A final response with a return code of 200 is sent from P to L. The payload contains media settings that P has selected from L's offer.
- An ACK request from L to P indicates that the final response has been received, completing a three-way handshake. The call has been set up and media starts flowing.
- Later on, P hangs up first and tears down the call by sending a BYE request to L.
- L sends a response with a return code of 200. The call has been torn down at this point.

Media settings are described using the Session Description Protocol (SDP) [11]. SDP supports a wide variety of media types, for example, audio, video, and instant messaging, among others. The set of rules governing the exchange of media settings is called the offer/answer model [12].

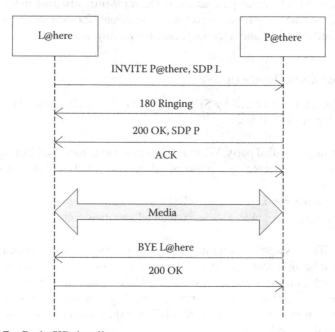

FIGURE 17.7 Basic SIP signaling.

As shown in Figure 17.7, SIP departs from a simple request–response between client and server in a number of ways:

- A single request can elicit more than one response.
- A node can act as a client some of the time and act as a server at other times. In SIP parlance, a node originating a request is called user agent client (UAC); a node terminating a request is called user agent server (UAS). It is even useful for a node, usually a network element, to act as both at the same time, carrying out upstream requests by sending new requests downstream. This is called a back-to-back user agent (B2BUA).

In a way of reminiscent of directory servers, there are classes of SIP nodes that add value not by terminating requests, but by intelligently forwarding or redirecting them:

- Proxy servers select one or more downstream nodes and relay messages between them and an upstream node.
- Redirect servers select a downstream node and ask the upstream node to contact it directly.

Figure 17.8 shows how a call is routed through a group of nodes using SIP. The call is directed to the logical address P@b.org. At the moment, the person with that address—we shall denote him/her as P—is sitting in front of a machine called there.b.org, so that is where the call should be sent.

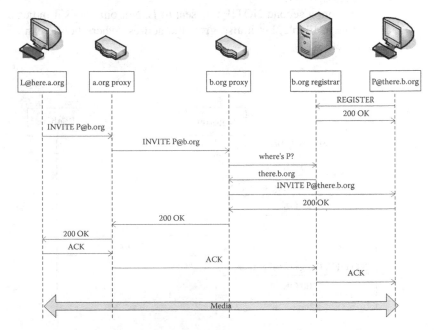

FIGURE 17.8 Call routing through SIP proxies.

- When P logs on at `there.b.org`, his/her user agent (UA), for example, an IP softphone, sends a SIP REGISTER message to `b.org`'s registrar. This establishes a mapping from `P@b.org` to `P@there.b.org`.
- When L calls P, his/her UA sends an INVITE request for `P@b.org` to his/her proxy server (the `a.org` proxy). Although it is in principle possible to go directly, a proxy server allows functions such as connection admission control (for maintaining of quality of service), least-cost carrier selection, authentication, and so on, to be controlled from a single spot.
- The `a.org` proxy forwards the INVITE on to `b.org`'s proxy.
- The `b.org` proxy consults `b.org`'s registrar to map `P@b.org` to a physical machine. It forwards the INVITE to `there.b.org`.
- P's UA puts `P@there.b.org` in the Contact field of the response. Assuming that the proxies do not wish to remain in the loop, L's UA can send subsequent requests directly to P's machine. While SIP messages go through proxy servers, media always flows directly.

Presence is another major usage of SIP. SIP contains a general event notification mechanism built around the SUBSCRIBE and NOTIFY methods [13]. Registrars, in addition to their role in call routing, may also act as presence servers to UAs. This mode of operation is shown in Figure 17.9:

- L wants to track P's presence status. His/her UA sends a SUBSCRIBE request with P's SIP URI to the registrar.
- P is not online at the moment. The registrar indicates this fact in its first NOTIFY message to L.
- When P logs on, a second NOTIFY is sent to L. Not only does it indicate that P is now available, but it also gives the address where he/she can be reached directly.

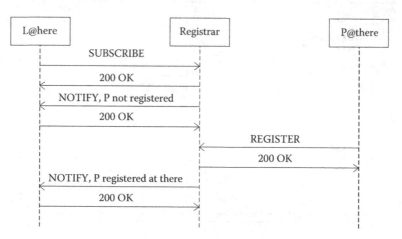

FIGURE 17.9   Presence through SIP event notification.

Many extant instant messaging systems, each with their own proprietary protocol, interwork through SIP.

SIP SERVLETS

Java's specification for application servers describe how components, irrespective of the protocol used for request and response, interact with their containers. These components are referred to as Java servlets.

HTTP servlets [14] are a type of Java servlet structured as a set of handlers, one for each type of HTTP method. A handler is passed a request message on entry and produces a response message on return. Handlers for GET and POST dynamically generate a Web page for the response and often execute business logic such as updating databases as well.

SIP servlets [15] are another type of Java servlet structured as a set of handlers. Because a SIP node can be both a client and a server, there are handlers for each class of response in addition to those for individual SIP methods. Furthermore, a request handler does not have to generate a response immediately on return.

HTTP is stateless, but it is often useful for higher-level applications that use the protocol to maintain a session. The ubiquitous shopping cart in online stores is a typical example. An HTTP servlet keeps the state of a session in an `HttpSession` object. When a request that is not part of an existing session arrives, the container creates a new `HttpSession` object and assigns it a session ID. Subsequent requests are then mapped to session objects by the session ID they carry.

In SIP, a sequence of related request–response transactions is a dialog. A dialog naturally models a call, but it is also applied to maintaining the SUBSCRIBE–NOTIFY associations used in presence. A SIP servlet keeps the state of a dialog in a `SipSession` object. The container creates a new `SipSession` object when it encounters the initial request of a dialog and uses the dialog identification mechanisms built into SIP to map messages to session objects.

There is a second level of session objects in SIP servlets. Because nodes such as proxies and B2BUAs can have multiple dialogs active at the same time, a `SipApplicationSession` object is used to collect related `SipSession` objects together.

HTTP servlets support a form of composition in which a request is processed by being passed along a chain of servlets. The container picks the first servlet in the chain by matching the request's URL against a series of patterns. Each servlet then passes the request on to the next one. This can be performed in one of two ways: forwarding or including. They differ in that the latter allows successive servlets to append to the growing Web page in the response.

SIP servlets also allow a request to be passed from servlet to servlet. This is enclosed within a higher level of routing in which requests are passed from application to application. A SIP application is a set of SIP servlets that are packaged together and deployed as a unit. The container asks a separate module called an application router for the next application in the chain. When a request is dispatched to an application, it is actually handed to a servlet designated as the main servlet. It may then be forwarded to other servlets in the same application.

The application router is intended to allow the deployer to flexibly compose SIP applications into a service offering. The SIP servlet specification only defines the interface between the container and the application router. The latter is not limited to only examining the request URI when determining which application to invoke. The application router also makes a determination of subscriber identity (i.e., for whom is the request being carried out) when making a routing decision. Finally, it should be noted that the application router is applied not only to external requests, but also to requests originating from within the container as well.

CONVERGED APPLICATIONS

The many similarities between HTTP and SIP servlets allow them to be used together in the same application fairly easily:

- The Web Archive (WAR) files in which HTTP servlets are packaged and the corresponding SIP Archive (SAR) files for SIP servlets have the same structure. In fact, both types of servlets can be present in a single file at the same time.
- A `SipApplicationSession` object can hold both `SipSession` and `HttpSession` objects.
- Under the SIP servlet specification, HTTP servlets have access to interfaces such as `SipFactory` for creating SIP requests and `SipSessionsUtil` for looking up `SipApplicationSession` objects by ID.

We give two examples of converged applications with both Web and telephony components. Click-to-call is a simple one: the HTTP servlet that handles the click spawns a SIP servlet to make a call.

A more sophisticated example is generalized call waiting. The user of this service wishes to conference a number of people, including him/herself, together at the same time. The list of people is entered into a Web page, and the service is armed. As soon as everyone's presence status shows available, calls are set up between each party and a conference bridge. At least three servlets are involved, which are as follows:

- An HTTP servlet handles the Web user interface.
- A SIP presence servlet monitors availability.
- A SIP conferencing servlet sets up the conference.

ORCHESTRATING WEB SERVICES AND REAL-TIME COMMUNICATIONS

There has been a lot of interest recently in integrating telecommunications functionality into IT applications by providing Web services APIs. In addition to the many proprietary or product-specific Web services APIs offered by telecommunications vendors, there are also a small number of standards such as the following:

- Parlay X [16], which provides a set of simple abstracted building blocks for incorporating telecommunication services into applications. Some examples of the capabilities offered include third-party call, call notification, short messaging, terminal status and location, multimedia conference, and so on.
- ECMA-348 [17], which provides a set of services for observing and controlling calls and telephony (endpoint and network) devices. Some examples of the capabilities offered include call control, monitoring, call associated features (e.g., digits, tones, user data sent along with a call), logical device features (e.g., forwarding, do not disturb), physical device features (e.g., button press, lamp status, display update), and so on.

Instead of discussing the functionality aspects of telecommunications Web services in more detail by drilling down further into specific APIs, this section will focus on the underlying issue of orchestrating Web services and real-time communications, since (in the authors' opinion) this issue affects the model for integrating telecommunications and IT applications in a fundamental way.

ORCHESTRATION

Orchestration enables a number of loosely coupled services in a SOA to be composed into a larger workflow and their interactions to be coordinated in the context of the workflow in an open, platform-independent manner.

Having been developed in the context of information technology, Web services orchestration is now being adopted for the coordination of real-time communications services (including telephony, video, and multimedia communications). It is being applied to both telecommunications-centric environments and, more importantly, to data-centric environments where real-time communications and nonreal-time information processing functions are integrated together as part of the same workflow.

In the rest of this section, we will compare two approaches for orchestrating workflows (using the word "orchestrate" in a broad sense to mean coordination of functions in general, vs. its more specific meaning in the context of Web services, in order to encompass telecommunications-oriented applications):

- Business Process Execution Language (BPEL), which is a representative of Web services orchestration in data-centric environments. A brief overview of this language will be given below.
- CCXML, which exemplifies orchestration in telephony and voice dialog applications. An overview of this language was provided earlier. For the purposes of the current discussion, an additional point of relevance is that since the external servers are performing the actual work in a CCXML application, CCXML can be seen as a domain-specific form of orchestration.

For a more detailed version of this discussion, the readers are referred to Ref. [18].

Business Process Execution Language

BPEL [19] is an XML-based language for Web services composition. A BPEL process provides a Web service interface; behind the scenes, it calls other Web services to do the actual work.

The Web services used by a BPEL process are referred to as partners. The relationship between process and partner is called a partner link and is defined by the operations that each side makes available to the other. In the Web Service Definition Language (WSDL), related sets of operations are grouped into port types. BPEL adds the notion of a partner link type, which typically consists of a pair of port types, one for each role (i.e., end) of a partner link (or a single port type for a unidirectional link).

The actual address of a partner cannot be hard coded into a partner link. An endpoint may be statically bound to a partner link when a process is deployed on a BPEL engine. It can also be assigned to a partner link in the course of process execution.

BPEL provides a number of activities, that is, statements, for interacting with partners:

- `<invoke>` sends a request to a partner and waits for a response.
- `<receive>` waits for a request from a partner. A matching `<reply>` sends a response.
- `<pick>` waits for one of a set of requests from a partner.

It also provides a number of structured activities to control the execution order of their child activities:

- `<if>`, `<while>`, and `<repeatUntil>` are similar to their namesakes in regular programming.
- `<forEach>` can not only be used as a sequential for loop, but also has the option of running its iterations in parallel.
- `<sequence>` executes a list of child activities in order.
- `<flow>` specifies a graph of activities. When an activity completes, its outgoing links fire. An activity whose incoming links have all fired becomes runnable.

A BPEL process models a stateful, long-running transaction. Each instance of a process has its own set of variables. The arrival of a message at a `<receive>` activity with the `createInstance` attribute set causes a new instance to be created.

BPEL and CCXML Compared

To compare BPEL and CCXML in more detail with respect to applications involving real-time communications, we will examine them in the context of the two following questions:

1. Do real-time communications services integrate into workflows in the same way as Web services in the data environment?

BPEL's focus is on the sequencing of activities to perform a task. CCXML's focus is on the interconnection of objects, while the real work of the system is the flow of media between the objects. This difference is manifested in programming style: procedural for the former vs. event-driven for the latter.

The design of Web services, including BPEL processes, generally follows a number of best practices for SOAs [20,21]. One of the principles that is particularly relevant to our current discussion is *coarse granularity*, that is, structuring into larger tasks or steps. Specifically, a well-designed service should expose a coarse-grained interface (i.e., one that consists of larger tasks or steps) to the functionality that it supports. Client-service communications should also be minimized by exchanging coarse-grained data types (i.e., larger groupings of data items) and doing composite tasks together where possible. This helps to keep response time within acceptable limits, since Web service invocations tend to have more overhead due to underlying tasks such as encoding and decoding of request and response messages in XML, and logging and monitoring for error recovery.

Real-time communications scenarios, on the other hand, tend to involve finer-grained asynchronous interactions (i.e., smaller incremental steps) among objects connected by signaling messages, and to have requirements for low-latency operation. Signaling messages are also not generally bundleable, that is, they cannot be batched. CCXML directly represents these types of interactions by reacting to events that come up in a call session, and generating events for consumption by other objects.

2. Are Web services orchestration mechanisms sufficient for the needs of workflows that involve real-time communications?

It is possible to model the style of asynchronous interaction captured by CCXML in BPEL. An <invoke> on an operation that has no output message will not block for a response. A <receive> on such an operation does not need to be paired with a <reply>.

At present, the types of external servers that BPEL and CCXML can talk to are different. The former is designed from the ground up for Web services; the latter simply accesses Web servers directly. However, the event I/O processor framework does mean that CCXML is not strongly tied to a particular protocol stack for interacting with the outside world, so it is possible to extend CCXML to use Web services as well.

BPEL requires that all partners of a process be enumerated, while CCXML has the ability to manipulate variable populations of objects such as connections. This limitation in BPEL may not matter in single-caller applications, but could be severely constraining in multicaller applications such as conferencing.

CCXML's core <eventprocessor> construct can be implemented in
BPEL by wrapping a <pick> activity in a <while> loop. A <pick>
consists of a set of <onMessage> elements, which behave like
<receive>. When a message comes in, the child activity of the match-
ing <onMessage> is executed.

In summary, there are some essential differences between the orchestration
mechanisms that are either required or would be the best fit for real-time communications, and the mechanisms provided by Web services.

A HYBRID APPROACH FOR CONVERGED APPLICATIONS

For converged voice-data applications involving both real-time communications and
nonreal-time information processing tasks, a hybrid approach can be taken in which
a set of related real-time communication flows described in CCXML are encapsulated in a coarse-grained Web service for the purposes of interworking with other
Web services orchestrated via BPEL. This enables each type of processing to be
orchestrated by a language that is best suited to its characteristics.

As a prerequisite of interworking, BPEL and CCXML need to be able to invoke
one another. For BPEL, this can be performed through a set of call control Web
service APIs. CCXML already has a basichttp event I/O processor that interacts
with external Web servers using HTTP POST, which could be further extended to
support Web services.

BPEL and CCXML can thus be seen as complementary tools in an orchestration
toolkit. When coordinating the actions of a set of data and communications servers,
a practical program would be as follows:

- Partition the problem into subproblems that are more suitable to BPEL or
  CCXML
- Design the portion in BPEL as a collection of Web services in the usual way
- Define Web service interfaces for the islands of CCXML so that BPEL can
  interact with them.

CONCLUSIONS

Much of the story of the integration between IT and telecommunications is really
about the profound impact of the Internet on the latter. The physical merger of the
telephone network into the data network in VoIP is a highly visible manifestation.
We suggest that much insight can be gained by realizing that there are more abstract
manifestations as well:

- Converged applications result by combining a telecommunications application with one from the Internet. Integration in media and signaling makes
  this possible. Starting from autonomous systems communicating via
  specialized computer-telephony interface links, data and telephony application elements can now run in the same application server.

- The best of these converged applications will blend the immediacy of voice with the high information density of the Web to achieve what neither can do on its own. For example, UM is the merger between nonreal-time voice mail and e-mail, and unified communications combines real-time telephony and instant messaging.
- Telecommunications borrow specific technologies from the Internet. MIME provides the organization for many multimedia message stores, and SIP draws not only its inspiration but also its syntax from HTTP.
- The Internet is also a source of architectural style. VoiceXML and CCXML use the same rapid development model as dynamic HTML. SIP servlets are modeled after HTTP servlets. Taking advantage of analogies with the IT world often facilitates the development of converged applications.

The integration between IT and telecommunications works by virtue of a shared heritage of tools and ideas from the Internet. Since telecommunications often involves finer-grained asynchronous interactions and latency-sensitive flows of real-time media, however, the deployment of Internet technologies in converged applications needs to take these aspects into account as well.

REFERENCES

1. Myers, J. and Rose, M., RFC 1939: Post Office Protocol—Version 3, May 1996, available at http://www.ietf.org/rfc/rfc1939.txt
2. Crispin, M., RFC 3501: Internet Message Access Protocol—Version 4 rev1, March 2003, available at http://www.ietf.org/rfc/rfc3501.txt
3. Klensin, J., Ed., RFC 2821: Simple Mail Transfer Protocol, April 2001, available at http://www.ietf.org/rfc/rfc2821.txt
4. Freed, N. and Borenstein, N., RFC 2045: Multipurpose Internet Mail Extensions (MIME) Part One: Format of Internet Message Bodies, November 1996, available at http://www.ietf.org/rfc/rfc2045.txt
5. Voice Extensible Markup Language (VoiceXML) 2.0, W3C recommendation, March 16, 2004, available at http://www.w3.org/TR/ccxml
6. Voice Extensible Markup Language (VoiceXML) 2.1, W3C recommendation, June 19, 2007, available at http://www.w3.org/TR/voicexml20
7. Voice Browser Call Control: CCXML Version 1.0, W3C working draft, January 19, 2007, available at http://www.w3.org/TR/voicexml21
8. Microsoft, Telephony Application Programming Interface, Version 3.1; MSDN Library, 2008, available at http://msdn.microsoft.com/en-us/library/ms734215(VS.85).aspx
9. Rosenberg, J. et al., RFC 3261: SIP—Session Initiation Protocol, June 2002, available at http://www.ietf.org/rfc/rfc3261.txt
10. Perea, R. M., *Internet Multimedia Communications Using SIP*, Morgan Kaufmann, Burlington, MA, 2008.
11. Handley, M., Jacobson, V., and Perkins, C., RFC 4566: SDP—Session Description Protocol, July 2006, available at http://www.ietf.org/rfc/rfc4566.txt
12. Rosenberg, J. and Schulzrinne, H., RFC 3264: An Offer/Answer Model with Session Description Protocol (SDP), June 2002, available at http://www.ietf.org/rfc/rfc3264.txt
13. Roach, A. B., RFC 3265: Session Initiation Protocol (SIP)—Specific Event Notification, June 2002, available at http://www.ietf.org/rfc/rfc/3265.txt
14. JSR 154: Java Servlet 2.4 Specification, Maintenance Release 2, September 11, 2007, available at http://jcp.org/en/jsr/detail?id=154

15. JSR 289: SIP Servlet Specification, Version 1.1, August 21, 2008, available at http://jcp. org/en/jsr/detail?id=289

16. ETSI ES 202 391: Open Service Access (OSA): Parlay X Web Services, Version 1.2.1, December 2006, available at http://portal.etsi.org/docbox/TISPAN/Open/OSA/ParlayX21. html.

17. ECMA 348: Web Services Description Language (WSDL) for CSTA Phase III, 4th edn, June 2009, available at http://www.ecma-international.org/publications/standard/Ecma-348.html.

18. Lin, L. and Lin, P., Orchestration in web services and real-time communications, *IEEE Commun. Magaz.*, 45(7), 44–50, 2007.

19. Web Services Business Process Execution Language Version 2.0, OASIS Standard, April 11, 2007, available at http://docs.oasis-open.org/wsbpel/2.0/wsbpel-v2.0.html.

20. Stal, M., Using Architectural Patterns and Blueprints for Service-Oriented Architecture, *IEEE Softw.*, 23(2), 54–61, 2006.

21. Shah, R. and Apte, N., Web Services: A Business Module Packaging Strategy, Prentice-Hall Professional Technical Reference online article, April 2004, available at www. informit.com/articles/article.aspx?p=170421&seqNum=2.

18 Leveraging Applications for Successful Customer Relationships

Kathleen Naasz

CONTENTS

This chapter focuses on Customer Relationship Management (CRM) and the importance of leveraging applications and processes to improve customer relationships from a sales, marketing, and contact center perspective.

CRM HISTORY: HOW DID WE GET TO WHERE WE ARE TODAY?

CRM is somewhat of an overused and misunderstood term. In order to understand how it applies in this chapter, the best way to think about it is to imagine an integrated system with customer-centric business processes, applications and their underlying infrastructure, and digital customer information to be used by businesses to acquire new customers, retain existing customers, and to get both categories to spend more money with a company. CRM is more than an application; it is a customer-centric philosophy with an integrated system of people, processes, and tools. If this definition does not help, let us add in a few more, so that you start off with a clear picture:

- From a marketing perspective, "CRM focuses on using information about customers to create marketing strategies that develop and sustain desirable long-term customer relationships" [1].
- From a systems perspective, "CRM uses information technology to create a cross-functional enterprise system that integrates and automates many of the customer-serving processes in sales, marketing and customer services that interact with a company's customers" [2].

From an individual perspective, we can see that it is more prevalent in our lives today than ever before:

- When we go online to order groceries for home delivery, the supermarket recognizes us, provides personalized specials of the week, and reminds us of our prior shopping lists.
- When we purchase an airline ticket via a contact center and then decide to choose the seat assignments online, the information is there, instantaneously.
- When a sales person visits an existing customer, he/she has information on past spending, preferred brands, and current needs.
- When a product manager is analyzing the product line, he/she is able to view the company's most profitable products and *most profitable customers.*

Perhaps taking a brief look at the history of CRM will help to remind us of the power of this application in today's digital world. In the 1980s, the introduction of more powerful databases and concepts such as data mining, data warehousing, and data models formed the foundation to capture customer data. Move forward about 10 years, and the next piece of the puzzle comes into play with a focus on business processes, including reengineering the process functions and aligning organizational roles to be more customer centric. Based on the requirements of the reengineered processes, the applications were then developed and, in many cases, custom-designed to be reliant upon supporting systems to maximize the output of the process. Process was the king and the systems were there to support it. It was in the 1990s that CRM became a known player in the business application space and was mainly characterized by sales force automation (SFA) applications. As processing power increased and the applications became more powerful, the emergence of several key players dominated the CRM market, mainly focused on large enterprises, delivering premises-based deployments:

- Oracle, extending to CRM from their financial module base and SFA.
- Siebel, with a stronghold in the customer services space.
- PeopleSoft, from a basis in human resources management and then extending into customer services and Supply Chain Management (SCM).
- SAP, best known for its Enterprise Resource Planning (ERP) strengths, also wanted a portion of the CRM pie.

Evolving hand-in-hand was the network that could handle more bits of information at ever-increasing speeds, and with the rapid increase in the number of Internet users, moved CRM from a "static" snapshot to a "real-time" relationship with customers via the Internet, and the term e-CRM appeared.

Even with all this evolution, CRM still had many skeptics at the turn of the latest century. Bad press regarding CRM implementations that were not considered successful, especially in large enterprises where the application was positioned as a panacea to solve every customer-related data issue, created a negative impression of CRM. In fact, in 2001, CRM had ranked near the bottom of a list of 25 possible tools global executives would choose and CRM sales dropped by 25% in 2002 [3].

Then the landscape of the big application providers was impacted by start-ups, such as Salesforce.com, providing an alternative to premises-based solutions and offering companies CRM as a service via Application Service Providers (ASPs). Due to this, the Gartner Group, a technology-based research firm, had to actually change the way it measured market share and based it on *total software revenue* rather than *new license revenue* due to subscription-based ASP models [4]. Mergers occurred, consolidating the industry, when Oracle acquired PeopleSoft in January of 2005 in a hostile takeover and then acquired Siebel in June 2006. According to a 2007 study [5], Oracle's Siebel solution was the leader in terms of implementations using external consultants and system integrators; however, the percentage of Siebel projects in 2006 (41%) was a decline from 2005 (47%), and this is mainly attributed to the disruption caused by Oracle's acquisitions and the potential use of on-demand solutions not requiring consultancy support.

Even after the changes in the landscape over time, the top two CRM vendors remain the SAP and Oracle as shown in the Gartner list of the top CRM vendors in Table 18.1. Although we have used global market data, it is important to note that the majority of implementations have been in Western economies (North America 53% and Europe 32%), with emerging markets counting for approximately 15% of the market [6]. This raises the question of "What is the cultural impact on CRM implementations?" As mentioned earlier in this chapter, CRM is a customer-centric philosophy. Thus, those cultures that embrace this approach are more likely to feel the need for an integrated CRM system and leverage it for its value.

TABLE 18.1
CRM Market Share Leaders

CRM Supplier	Market Share 2005 (%) [4]	Market Share 2007 (%) [6]
SAP	25.9	25.4
Siebel	17	
Oracle	6.4 (including PeopleSoft)	16.3 (including Siebel)
Salesforce.com	4.9	8.4
Amdocs	4.9	5.2
Microsoft	N/A	4.1

CRM'S FUTURE

Despite some publicized failures, CRM has shown steady growth based on the worldwide CRM total software revenue increase of 14% in 2005 [4] to 23% in 2007 [6]. With advances in technology and leveraging of CRM for business success, we are sure to see even more benefits from CRM in the next several years. Growth predicted by two key market research firms indicates that there is a large market for CRM. Forrester Research estimates that CRM revenues will grow at a steady 7% pace and reach $10.9 billion by 2010 [7]. AMR Research, which included all customer management applications in its study, predicts that the market will reach $18 billion by 2010 [7].

What will CRM be like in the next decade? Regardless of the name, you will still see companies leveraging technology and applications to maintain profitable customer relations. However, ways in which companies use CRM and interact with customers will need to be adapted for the online generation, "Generation Virtual." Generation Virtual prefers digital media channels and enjoys creating anonymous online personas. In order to build relationships with this generation, companies will need to change their approaches for customer acquisition and retention. It is recommended that companies "Collect persona data for product development, customer feedback, loyalty management, customer segmentation, campaign targeting and persona-group customer satisfaction management" [8].

Going forward, an area of continued growth will be CRM provided in an on-demand service model, now being termed Software-as-a-Service (SaaS). SaaS is a Web-based software purchased on a subscription basis. ASPs have been around for several years, so what makes SaaS new? The newness is more focused around what types of companies are using CRM in its SaaS model: larger enterprises. In the past, it was typically the smaller companies that took advantage of the SaaS model for several reasons, one being the flexibility to proceed without making a large capital investment. Although SaaS requires less capital investment and less consultancy service fees for selection, design, and implementation, it may also provide less customization and that may be acceptable for certain application components but not for others, such as targeted marketing campaigns. Oracle's Siebel CRM, which was classically a premises-based solution, launched *CRM On Demand* in October of 2003 and Microsoft released its Titan CRM on-demand code to about 300 partners in early 2007. Whether Titan will achieve a formidable market position against Salesforce. com is not fully known but the latest data, as was previously shown in Table 18.1, indicate that Microsoft is gaining in market share with 4.1%, although Salesforce.com still leads with 8.2%. Perhaps more telling is that these two companies are currently the fastest growing in the CRM space and both have on-demand solutions, thus supporting the trend toward growth in CRM on demand. DirecTV implemented an on-demand solution, along with other software applications, to provide mobile, real-time CRM data to its sales force. Some of the business benefits are captured in the following: "By mobilizing its on-demand CRM application, DirecTV has increased by 30 percent the number of accounts that can be visited weekly; improved frequency of sales data reporting from seven days to one; reduced service-request resolution from five days to three ... sales teams save more than 90 hours a week" [9].

CRM AS AN INTEGRAL PART OF ENTERPRISE SYSTEMS INTEGRATION

CRM is more than a business application; it is an approach, a system that leverages people, processes, and IT tools. It links the back-office customer databases with customer-facing interactions to the external (outside the enterprise) world. As illustrated in Figure 18.1, it is a system that is leveraged by the key enterprise functions of marketing, sales, and customer contact centers. It is not limited to use by these organizational functions, but more directly leveraged by them.

As shown in Figure 18.1, CRM uses software and supporting business processes to automate selling, marketing, and service functions. A CRM business application suite may have 50 or more components, such as campaign management, marketing analytics, opportunity and lead management, pricing applications, event-based marketing, contact management solutions, and chat and collaboration tools, just to name a few. In Hart's study [10] on the alignment of applications with business objectives, he indicates that 77% of the companies included had the analytics application software component. In its simplest definition, analytical CRM is the analysis of customer data, which is performed for a multitude of reasons with purposeful outcomes, but mainly used by marketing for trend analysis, segmentation and customer lifetime value analysis, and targeted campaigns. In the same study, the next most popular components were sales force opportunity and lead management applications

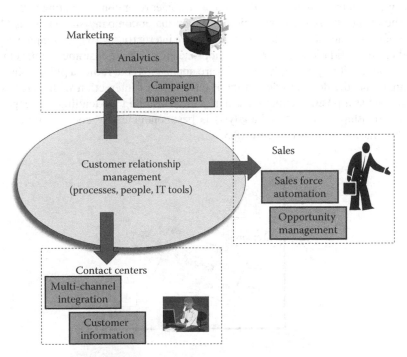

FIGURE 18.1   CRM leveraged by marketing, sales, and contact centers.

(68%) and contact center applications (56%), thus rounding out the triad of functions leveraging CRM the most often: marketing, sales, and contact centers.

CRM AND ITS IMPACT ON CUSTOMER RELATIONS

The previous section discussed CRM as an integral part of enterprise integration and the functional organizations that use it. This section will focus on CRM from the aspect of customer management. To bring it back to the basics, there are three main ways to generate customer revenue (as illustrated in Figure 18.2):

- Get customers to spend money with your company, such that you acquire them as a new customer.
- Get customers to continue to make profitable exchanges with your company over a longer period of time, thus extending the duration of the relationship.
- Get customers to buy more products from your company, thus expanding the share of wallet.

Businesses must continually nurture the relationships with customers and attract new ones, build trust and extend the duration of existing customer relationships, and expand the relationship to achieve a greater share of wallet, such that customers spend more across a greater set of products. CRM as a process for customer management has been more predominantly used in customer-retention strategies to extend and expand the relationship, rather than customer-acquisition strategies.

If we continue further down the path of customer retention (extending and expanding the relationship), the next logical question that a company should ask is "What type of experience does a customer have when interacting with our company?" This is where the validation of CRM as an approach to effective customer management is put to the test; it is not simply the software application, but rather a philosophy of the organization, the desire to determine if each point of interaction with a customer is conducted as a positive experience that will contribute to extending and expanding the relationship. This type of analysis is best conducted by considering customer touch points, as shown in Figure 18.3.

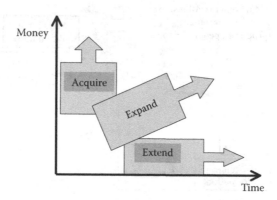

FIGURE 18.2 Customer management and revenue generation.

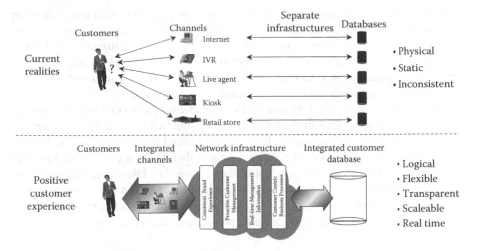

FIGURE 18.3   CRM at customer touch points.

   In the top part of the diagram, a company needs to document all of the ways that a customer may come into contact with the company; these points of contact are called "customer touch points." An analysis should be carried out to determine the effectiveness of each touch point on the customer experience. Prior to CRM, the processes and infrastructures supporting the touch points were fragmented, disparate, and often relied on separate physical channels containing static customer data that was not leveraged across multiple channels. Customers today require the flexibility that if they are using an Interactive Voice Response (IVR) system and they want to opt out to an agent, they can. Or if they have come in through the Internet and would like to switch to an agent to complete the transaction, they can "talk."
   In the CRM view at the bottom section of Figure 18.3, the channels are integrated and information can flow between channels with a consistent look and feel and with the customer making the decision as to how they guide themselves across the different channels in a way that enables them to conduct business on the customer's own terms. The CRM approach brings several key components together to achieve effective customer management. The first element is a consistent brand experience across channels. Have you ever searched a Web site of a well-known retailer for an item that you saw in the retailer's physical store, hoping to find a better deal? Many of us have taken advantage of the lack of consistency across channels. Companies leveraging CRM are able to put the data, systems, and processes in place to achieve a more consistent customer experience, regardless of the channel.
   The second element of CRM is to enable companies to do proactive customer value management. Companies have to manage mutually beneficial exchanges. Not only should the brand experience be positive and consistent from the customer's perspective, but also profitable from the company's perspective. The Royal Bank of Canada, the winner of the first international CRM industry awards, spent over $100 million on their CRM program and believes that it has helped them increase

revenue growth while also achieving cost savings [11], thus balancing customer needs and their business needs. One component of this balance is to engineer cost-effective channels that maximize the return from that customer relationship. Companies must do their homework to determine and understand the financial value of customer relationships. Companies need to extract value in terms of up-selling and cross-selling in order to expand the customer relationship.

The third element, and truly an enabling element for the former two, is real-time information, making sure that a company understands, in a real-time manner, the wants and needs of the customers. It also needs to send that information back to the people who make customer-oriented decisions so that they can continually fine-tune the service levels and also the content of the service. The last and most critical element is customer-centric business processes. If CRM does not rely upon processes designed and implemented around the value of a customer, it is not possible to actually provide customer management and a positive brand experience.

CRM AND ITS IMPACT ON MARKETING

In the previous section, we discussed CRM and its role in customer management, to acquire, extend, and expand customer relationships and along with the fact that the majority of companies purchased the analytics component of the CRM software; it is logical to expect a broad use of CRM in the marketing function. As we have mentioned, CRM is a critical component to retention and loyalty programs that build and sustain long-term customer relationships and the following facts remind us of how customer retention positively impacts business performance [12]:

- It costs six times more to sell to a new customer than an existing one.
- Boosting customer retention by 5% can boost profits by 85%.
- The odds of selling to an existing customer are 50%, a new one 15%.

What has not been discussed yet is how does CRM affect customer satisfaction? At the heart of the marketing concept is the customer and if CRM is going to positively impact marketing, then we need to show its positive impact on customer satisfaction. In a Mithas et al.'s [13] study, conducted on a cross-section of large U.S. firms, the use of CRM applications was positively associated with improved customer knowledge and improved customer satisfaction. Firms could enhance gains in knowledge by sharing their customer-related information with their supply chain partners. Another noteworthy finding from a preceding study supports having a focused CRM initiative in that "specific IT applications, such as CRM, that are directly involved in business processes affecting the customer experience may be much more effective in improving customer satisfaction than are aggregate IT investments" [14]. Therefore, companies that focus IT investments on customer-focused processes will see an increase in the customer satisfaction.

Another study that has helped to capture and publicize the positive impact of the broader category of CRM-related technologies on company performance was based on a sample of 172 U.S. companies. This study found that companies that have interactive customer contact, and capture and deploy customer information throughout the enterprise, tend to experience better customer satisfaction and customer-retention outcomes [15].

CRM has also been useful in identifying prospects for use in direct mail campaigns. Direct mail represents 19% of all advertising spend, the largest media category, and is an important vehicle in direct marketing [16]. CRM can identify prospects and track the implementation of a direct mail campaign.

CRM AND ITS IMPACT ON SALES

There are many applications that a sales organization may use, and to try capture them all here would never provide an up-to-date, comprehensive view; however, regardless of a particular vendor's solution, it is the SFA component of CRM that has increased sales force productivity and has laid the foundation for account segmentation based upon opportunity size (current or potential revenues and profit). In a study [17] of 301 users, they indicated the following key benefits from SFA:

- Keeping up-to-date customer contact information
- Providing sales related information to its remote staff
- Reducing search time for customer information
- Helping to identify future sales opportunities
- Improving work productivity

These benefits are typical of those stated when CRM is implemented effectively by a sales organization. Sales people today require real-time information with mobile access to it and the capability to be empowered by information to close a sale. The link from CRM to a workflow tool makes it even more powerful. Not only can sales leads be managed and tracked, but connecting to the business processes and supporting systems that track the sale from prospect stages to a closed deal, with the appropriate documentation and required approvals for compliance, are necessary in today's business world. Two examples of real-world applications will validate the effective use of CRM by the sales function. Siemens Medical Solutions leveraged its CRM program to drive operational integration of multiple sales channels [18]. They defined metrics such as opportunity win rates, quarterly budget attainment, and cost of sales to measure sales effectiveness. PNC Bank had announced in January 2008 its CRM program upgrade to allow a single view of sales channels. "Employee users in the retail network will have their daily job functions, such as new account opening, integrated into the CRM system" [19], which is a perfect example of integrating workflow into CRM.

CRM AND ITS IMPACT ON CUSTOMER CONTACT CENTERS

You may call them customer service centers, or call centers or customer support centers, in any case, they are the centers servicing a customer base and, in this chapter, we will call them customer contact centers. As the usage of electronic channels increases due to increased usage of the internet overall, it makes sense to view it as a contact center, rather than a call center, to represent an integrated view of contacts with a customer via a multitude of channels. Additionally, as companies drive costs out of operations, the costs of these e-channels are significantly lower than a phone channel (the actual cost of an agent-handled call varies by industry and is normally based on call length and associated agent salaries). As shown in Figure 18.3, customers may access a company via multiple channels. In order for the experience to be consistent and positive, whether they access via the internet or actually pick up the phone and call a toll-free number, the information needs to be up-to-date and accurate. All too often, the contact center representatives are not equipped with the latest information about customers, such as their most recent transaction, whether that had been at a retail store or over the internet. Even in recent years, the problem of disparate channels still exists, as evidenced in a Jupiter Communications study, 76% of retailers were unable to track their customers across channels [20].

Companies, having implemented CRM, found that it has indeed helped to improve and track customers, but it requires an integrated customer database for all contacts. A key step in the integration is a data model that brings together disparate customer information. Approximately 70% of the expense in a contact center is the labor: the people answering the phones and conducting chat sessions. If CRM can be leveraged to provide accurate data and a current view of the customer, then time will be saved and its associated dollars. Additionally, linking back to identifying the value of a customer and the associated profitability, contacts may be routed to the most appropriate and cost-effective servicing resource. If a customer is identified as giving low profit and low potential, they may be transferred to a more automated, cost-effective channel, such as an IVR unit, rather than a more costly "agent call." For example, Boise Cascade Office Products (BCOP) implemented a CRM system crossing all major functions and multiple channels to integrate across customer touch points, to personalize and improve the quality of all customer interactions, and increase the availability and application of customer information. This CRM strategy has been so successful in personalizing the customer experience that it received the first Gartner CRM Excellence Award [21].

APPROACHES TO ADOPTING CRM

We choose to use the term adopting, rather than implementing, to emphasize the need to have users actually incorporate CRM into their daily tasks rather than the idea of an IT staff implementing a system. A report found that companies who spent an average of $4.4 million on their CRM deployment were more likely to agree with the statement "CRM deserves the bad press it has often received" than companies who spent an average of only $2.0 million [11]. Could this be due to higher-priced projects having higher expectations that were never documented nor realistically quantified? Additionally, many of the early failures of CRM were due to over-hype by vendors, lack of buy-in from business owners, disconnect with business processes, and disparate customer data. It is from other companies' experiences that we can uncover the key mistakes to avoid.

There are many studies available that have tried to either prove or disprove that CRM positively impacts business performance and you can potentially find a study that aligns with your position, regardless of which side of the argument that you stand on. The important guideline is that each business must determine for itself the expected outcomes, in a realistic, quantifiable fashion, and then put the plans in place to achieve them, while monitoring and tweaking so that the expected benefits are truly achieved. It appears that the cases with the greatest dissatisfaction were those where the benefits were captured as qualitative hyperbolic executive statements, with no true quantified validation of anticipated results.

The author of this chapter has worked with several companies to develop customer-centric organizations, among the many steps that should be followed to effectively transform an organization to fully leverage CRM are as follows:

1. *Focus*: start with a narrow scope, in one distinct area, but with a vision of the overall solution. In this way, early progress can be shown and will provide momentum for the overall effort. Focus is necessary in order to achieve realistic changes and by limiting the scope, progress can be made, as long as linkages to other areas are part of the vision. If those linkages are not in place, rework may be needed to integrate it later on. For example, beginning with a marketing focus to determine the most profitable customers could be the starting initiative; however, the vision should include how that information may be used by the sales organization in later phases.

2. *Business case*: some companies will perform a business case to gain the approval for the application investment, but how many companies involve the business owners in the expectation-setting phase and the actual quantification of the business benefits? Many IT implementations are considered failures, not because they truly failed to operate, but because they "failed" to meet the expectations of the business owners, where many times those expectations were unrealistic. Therefore, it is important at the onset to capture the expectations in quantified terms, with documented time frames to measure against, and involvement by the business owners. This will help to dispel any emotional reactions, such as, "this application is not doing what you said it would." BCOP [21], mentioned earlier, determined the Return On Investment of its CRM initiative, thus contributing to its perceived success.

3. *Customer-centric business processes*: in order for users to fully leverage an application, it needs to be an integral part of their daily tasks. The business processes need to be defined in alignment with the application and the main focus needs to be the customer. As in Figure 18.3, a company should document a baseline of the customer touch points and then conduct an analysis of improvements needed.

4. *Integrated view of customer data*: many companies implementing CRM only paid attention to the front-end processes—and that is exactly what would happen if you stopped at item 3 above. Attention needs to be paid to the back-end corporate data and disparate customer systems to be pulled into a single view of customer information that is transparent across the enterprise.

SUMMARY

Whether CRM will still bear its name in the decades to come is not known. What is known is that an approach that focuses on the customer and aligning people, processes and tools to achieve increased revenue by acquiring, extending, and expanding customer relationships will exist. CRM has received mixed reviews based on failures to successfully plan and implement the solution in alignment with business expectations. For those companies that learn from the failures of others and successfully adopt a CRM solution, there are many studies that substantiate and quantify the potential benefits to a company's bottom line.

REFERENCES

1. Pride, W. and Ferrell, O.C., *Marketing*, Houghton-Mifflin, Boston, MA, 2008, p. 224.
2. O'Brien, J. and Marakas, G., *Management Information Systems*, 8th edn., McGraw-Hill Irwin, NY, 2008, p. 286.
3. Rigby, D.K. and Ledingham, D., CRM done right, *Harv. Bus. Rev.*, 82(11), 118–129, November 2004.
4. Gartner says worldwide CRM total software revenue increased 14 percent in 2005, Press Release, Stamford, CT, June 12, 2006 (www.gartner.com).
5. Thompson, E. and Goldman, M., *Commonly Deployed CRM Application Vendors in 2006*, Gartner Inc., Stanford, CT, June 22, 2007.
6. Gartner says worldwide Customer Relationship Management Market Grew 23 Percent in 2007, Press Release, Stamford, CT, July 7, 2008 (www.gartner.com).
7. Beal, B., CRM market to grow steadily, *CRM News*, November 14, 2006, p. 1.
8. Gartner Says Generation Virtual is Forcing CRM-Focused Companies to Transform the Way They Do Business, Press Release, Stamford, CT, February 19, 2008 (www.gartner.com).
9. Bailor, C., Mobile data gets better reception, *Cust. Relat. Manage.*, 11, 44, December 2007.
10. Hart, M.L., Customer relationship management: Are software applications aligned with business objectives?, *South African J. Bus. Manage.*, 37(2), 17–32, 2006.
11. Ang, L. and Buttle, F., CRM software applications and business performance, *J. Database Marketing and Customer Strategy Management*, 14(1), 4–16, 2006.
12. O'Brien, J. and Marakas, G., *Management Information Systems*, 8th edn., McGraw-Hill Irwin, NY, 2008, Chap. 8.
13. Mithas, S., Krishnan, M.S., and Fornell, C., Why do customer relationship management applications affect customer satisfaction? *J. Market.*, 69(4), 201–209, 2005.
14. Mithas, S., Krishnan, M.S., and Fornell, C., Effect of information technology investments on customer satisfaction: An empirical analysis, Working Paper, Ross School of Business, University of Michigan, Ann Arbor, MI, 2002.
15. Jayachandran, S. et al., The role of relational information processes and technology use in customer relationship management, *J. Marketing*, 69(4), 177–192, 2005.
16. Arens, W.F. and Schaefer, D., *Essentials of Contemporary Advertising*, McGraw-Hill Irwin, NY, 2006, Chap. 15.
17. Ekinci, Y., Gillett, P., and Stone, M., Deploying a CRM system in practice—Understanding the user experience, *J. Database Market. Customer Strategy Manage.*, 14(3), 195–224, 2007.
18. Camaratta, J., From theory to execution, *Market. Manage.*, 14(4), 16–19, 2005.

19. Adams, J., Systems integration: Command center CRM, *Bank Technol. News*, 21, 1, January 2008.
20. Murtaza, M.B. and Shah, J.R., Effective customer relationship management through web services, *J. Comput. Inform. Syst.*, 46 (1), 98–109, 2005.
21. Gartner Honors Boise Cascade Office Products (BCOP) With CRM Excellence Award at Gartner CRM Summit 2001, *Press Release*, October 2001 (www.gartner.com).

19 Radio-Frequency Identification Technology

Maria-Victoria Bueno-Delgado,
Esteban Egea-López, Javier Vales-Alonso,
and Joan García-Haro

CONTENTS

INTRODUCTION

Radio Frequency IDentification (RFID) technology enables the automatic identification of items by means of radio devices. Although this technology is usually considered a mere substitute of the nowadays ubiquitous barcode systems, it actually provides a rich variety of information flows for the benefit of enterprises in a wide range of application fields.

RFID technology has been gaining popularity over the last years due to the reduction in cost, increase of capabilities, and standardization efforts devoted to it. The number of companies and institutions actively involved in the development of this technology is an indication of the interest it arouses. Appendices A and B, respectively, list, in alphabetical order, the companies and the products discussed in this chapter.

Discussion of the various technical, practical, and economical issues around RFID technology would require a complete volume. In this chapter, we provide an overview of the basic principles and the major technical issues related to the technology itself and its standardization. We then consider issues related to the integration of RFID systems with the enterprise information infrastructure. We discuss the architecture of MEGASTAND that we developed as an example of an RFID middleware for tracking and tracing items in a commercial supply chain.

SYSTEM OVERVIEW

RFID enables the identification of distant objects or people by means of a radio-frequency (RF) communication link [1]. The communication takes place between a population of small devices called *tags* or *transponders*, attached to the items to be tracked, and one or more reader devices called *master, interrogator*, or simply *reader* that are placed in strategic areas. The tags identify the items it is attached to, whether people, animals, pallets, and so on. Compared with other identification technologies, such as barcodes, the main advantage of RFID is that identification can be automatic, with no human participation and without the need for a line-of sight link between the reader and the tags.

A tag is composed of an antenna and a simple electronic circuit with an electrically erasable programmable read-only (EEPROM) to store information about the object. When tags pass through the coverage range of the reader, they send their stored information back to the reader, thereby identifying the object. This communication is usually carried out by means of some communications protocol, such as ISO/IEC1800 [2], Electronic Product Code (EPC) [3], or others.

Although this is not a new technology, RFID technology is increasingly being adopted in a wide variety of applications to speed the real-time exchange of data between physical and logical entities in a network and to provide timely and more accurate information for animal identification, toll road control, checkpoint systems, security and access control, digital card mail, toy industry, and so on. These few examples of how RFID is being integrated in our daily life justify the interest for the implementation and deployment of this technology. The next sections summarize the major technical issues related to RFID.

Some History

RFID was born as the combination of radar and radio broadcast technologies. The first known work on RFID dates back to 1948: the landmark paper written by Harry Stockman "Communications by Means of Reflected Power" [4]. In the 1950s, different sectors started working on RFID for high range transponders, known as "Identification, Friend or Foe" (IFF), for the aeronautic industry. H. Stockman [4] and F.L. Vernon [5] contributed significantly to the evolution of RFID. In the 1960s, the EAS (Electronic Article Surveillance) used RFID to protect against thefts in large department stores. In the 1970s, RFID was progressively applied to logistics, transportation, vehicle tracking, livestock tracking, and in industrial automation. However, it is only in 1973, that the first RFID patent was filed by Charles Walton, a former IBM researcher, for a radio-operated door lock. Starting from the 1980s, commercial implementations in the United States focused on the access control and transport. In Europe, RFID was intended to industrial applications and short-range systems for animal control. In Japan, it was used for contactless payments in transportation systems (e.g., the FELICA card). RFID development took advantage of progresses in related fields: microelectronics, antenna design, software, and microprocessors. The fields of application of RFID were substantially extended thanks to companies like Texas Instruments or Philips that promoted the development and marketing of RFID devices.

Currently, the Auto-ID Center (now Auto-ID Labs) [6] is the leading organization for the development and implementation of RFID. The Auto-ID Labs is a consortium founded in 1999 by hundreds of companies, universities and research centers from all over the world. Auto-ID Labs consists of six laboratories located at different prestigious universities such as MIT (Massachusetts Institute of Technology) in the United States, the University of Cambridge in United Kingdom, the University of Adelaide in Australia, Keio University in Japan, Fundan University in China, and the University of St. Gallen in Switzerland. In 2005, the Auto-ID Labs, the European Article Number (EAN) International, the Uniform Code Council (UCC), and the large retail multinationals developed the EPC™ net and its components, EPCglobal Class-1 Gen-2 [7], which are the worldwide standard for RFID systems.

ADVANTAGES OF RFID VS. BARCODES

Regardless of the frequency employed, RFID has several advantages over the traditional ID-systems based on barcodes, a technology that started a revolution in automatic identification systems and in many industrial sectors. The main advantages of RFID compared with barcodes are as follows:

- *Read/write data.* Tags can store data about the object where they are attached to. Information can be written or read by a reader at distances that can reach up to a few hundreds of meters in the case of self-powered tags.
- *Storage capacity.* An RFID tag is able to store 30 times more data than a barcode. This means that several barcodes would be needed to store the same amount of information.
- *Environmental information.* Tags can obtain real-time information about the item to which they are attached through different sensors such as their temperature, the ambient humidity, and so on.
- *Simultaneous identification.* With traditional ID systems using barcodes, items must be read individually and manually to guarantee their successful identification. RFID provides simultaneous identification, which implies that the reader can simultaneously read a potentially large number of tags placed in its read range.
- *No line of sight limitations.* Tags can be identified without the need for line-of-sight communication, even in the presence of obstacles.
- *Resilience to forgery.* IDs with barcodes can be easily replicated, by simply scanning and printing them. On the contrary, copying an RFID tag requires a more complex procedure that involves accessing the tag data and replicating the EPC number stored on it.

Table 19.1 summarizes the main features that distinguish RFID from Barcode technologies.

COMPONENTS OF AN RFID SYSTEM

A typical RFID system consists of three components: (i) RFID transponders, also called tags, which are able to store data; (ii) one or more readers and antennas that work to facilitate data transmission and reception from the tags; and (iii) the processing software (middleware) (Figure 19.1).

TABLE 19.1

Comparison of RFID vs. Barcodes

Characteristics	RFID	Barcode
Writeable	Read/write	Read-only
Quantity of data	Up to Kbytes	Up to 100 bits
Read speed	Milliseconds	Seconds
Read distance	Up to 100 m	Line of sight with the reader
Data format standard	Few	Many
Dirt influence	No effect	Very high
Sight obstruction	No effect	Very high
Effects of degradation/wear	None	Susceptible
Unauthorized copy	Ciphering	Susceptible
Cost	Depends on the tag	Inexpensive

TAGS

In RFID systems, tags store information about the object they are attached to. This information includes its unique serial number (ID), its standardized identification codes, a history of transactions or measurements, for example, the temperatures monitored by a sensor, manufacturing date, expiration date, and so on. When tags are within the range of the reader, they transmit their identification data to the reader, which then stores them or process the information according to the particulars of the service or application.

There are many criteria to categorize RFID tags such as their size, the energy source, their durability, the operating frequency, the polarization, the communication

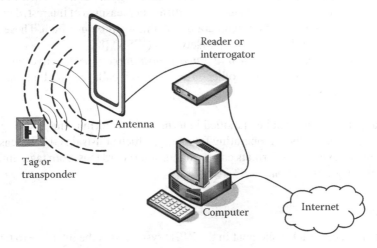

FIGURE 19.1 An RFID system and its components.

protocols, and so on. However, the most common way to classify tags is by their source of energy. Accordingly, tags can be active, passive, or semi-passive:

> *Active tags* have a fully autonomous power source that, in most of the cases, can be replaced. The cost of these devices is high because they incorporate complex circuitry with a microprocessor and a memory to read, write, rewrite, or erase data from an external device. The main advantage of active tags is the long reading distance, more than 100 m.
>
> *Passive tags* are simple and low-cost devices that do not incorporate their own battery and are excited by the electromagnetic waves emitted by the reader. This energy activates the tag's circuit and causes a response signal that stores the information in the tag's memory. The maximum range can vary from some centimeters to a pair of meters.
>
> *Semi-passive tags* have built-in batteries to power the tag's integrated circuit. The electromagnetic waves from the reader are only employed to activate the tags in coverage. Thus, semi-passive tags have a faster response time than passive tags.

Another classification of RFID tags is based on their read and write capabilities. Accordingly, tags can fall into one of following five classes [7]:

- Class 0: *Read-only tags*. This is the simplest type of tags with only read functionality. The data, usually a simple identification number, are written into the tag only once during the manufacturing process. Then, the memory is disabled for future updates.
- Class 1: *Write-once/read-only*. The tag's memory can be written by the programmer or by the factory only once. After this, tags can only be read.
- Class 2: *Read/write*. In these devices, data can be written and read by the user an arbitrary number of times.
- Class 3: *Read/write on-board sensors*. These tags are active or semi-active and contain on-board sensors to store different measures of interest, depending on the type of sensor (temperature, humidity, pressure, etc.). These tags may be used in Wireless Sensor Networks (WSN) [8].
- Class 4: *Read/write with integrated transmitters*. These active tags can communicate with each other. They are typically applied in *ad hoc* networks [9].

Finally, RFID tags can be classified in terms of their format and size. Tag size is strongly affected by the RF operating frequency, which constrains the dimensions of the antenna. Several tags formats can be found: smart card tags, coin tags, embedded tags, paper tags, and so on.

READERS

The RFID reader is a key element in the RFID system. It is the interface to tag information. The reader must be able to convert the data received from the tags into useful information for the final application. Readers can be classified according to the type of tag as follows:

- Readers for systems with active tags (denoted as active RFID systems) can be any such tag because active tags are able to communicate each other. This active tag must be connected to a computer or a network (wired or wireless) to dump the data received from other active tags in the range of coverage.
- Readers for RFID systems with passive tags (passive RFID system) have to meet a key requirement: their transmission power must be enough to excite the passive tags that they cover. The tags use a technique called *backscatter* to reply to the reader. Of course, this technique does not involve internal transmitters, and consists of reflecting the reader's carrier wave that is modulating the signal transporting the tag data of interest. Then, the reader detects the backscatter modulation, processes the signal, and reads the information sent by the tag.

Because readers for active RFID systems are less restrictive than those for passive RFID systems, this section will focus on the latter. Some selection criteria for commercial passive RFID readers are as follows:

- Standards of communication between a reader and the associated tags. There are many such standards today: EPC, International Organization for Standardization (ISO), proprietary, and so on, and the reader should support multiprotocol operation.
- Operating frequency: ultra high frequency (UHF), low frequency (LF), or high frequency (HF) (see below).
- Number of RF ports to connect antennas. Usually, one reader allows up to four antennas.
- Maximum power to each RF port. The antennas can be configured to transmit at different power levels.
- Networking to host protocol: RS-232, Wireless, Ethernet, and TCP/IP.
- Reader-to-reader connection. Readers must be able to coexist together in the same coverage area or in the same network.
- Fixed or portable reader. Readers can be (i) located at a fixed point of a strategic area to identify tags or (ii) portable. Portable readers (also called handled readers), collect the tag information, which in its turn is sent to an application by means of a wireless technology such as Wi-Fi, Bluetooth, and so on.

ANTENNAS

Antenna designs differ according to the operating frequency. For low-range applications, such as for the HF range, the antennas are embedded with the reader whereas, in UHF applications, antennas are external and are connected to it by a coaxial cable.

Irrespective of the operating frequency, some configurable antenna parameters must be tuned to get the optimal performance of the RFID system: operating frequency range, impedance, maximum transmission power, radiation pattern, number of ports, gain, and so on.

Polarization is another critical antenna parameter, which is application-dependent. Depending on the polarization, RFID antennas can be linear or circular. Selection of the appropriate polarization will reduce the interference between the antennas and the tags. Linear polarization antennas require that the tags be linearly polarized as well. These antennas have the best performance when the tag orientation is known and fixed. Circular polarization antennas radiate in a 90° pattern and are less sensitive to the tag's orientation, because in this case, radio waves propagate around obstructions better than in the case of linear polarization antennas. Therefore, this type of antennas is used when the tag orientation is unknown.

MIDDLEWARE

The term middleware refers to the software implementing the logic that glues RFID information with the backend enterprise information systems. This integration is the subject of the section on *RFID integration with enterprise information systems* (see later).

RFID middleware usually applies filtering, formatting, or rule-matching logic to the captured data before they are further processed by end applications.

OPERATING FREQUENCIES

The communication frequencies used by RFID systems, both passive and active, range from 125 KHz to 2.45 GHz depending on the application as shown in Table 19.2. The frequency of operation is directly related to the extent of the desired radio coverage.

TABLE 19.2

Operating Frequencies: Characteristics and Applications

Range Frequency	Read Range	Read Rate	Cost	Applications
Low (100–500 KHz)	Short	Low	Low	Access control, animal identification, inventory control, car immobilizer
Medium (10–15 MHz)	Short to medium	Medium	Medium	Access control, smart cards
High (850–950 MHz, 2.4–5.8 MHz)	Long	High	High	Railroad car monitoring, toll collection systems

Four carrier frequencies have been standardized as follows:

- LF: 125 KHz
- HF: 13.56 MHz
- UHF: 850–950 MHz
- Microwaves: 2.45 GHz

The International Telecommunication Union–Radiocommunication Sector (ITU-R) is responsible for the management of the frequency spectrum worldwide. It divides the world into three regions for the purpose of managing the global radio communication as follows:

- Region 1 is regulated by the Federal Communications Commission (FCC). This region includes Europe, the Middle East, Africa, and the former Soviet Union, including Siberia.
- Region 2 is regulated by CEPT (European Conference of Postal and Telecommunications) whose main responsibilities include frequency and output power assignment. The region includes North and South America and Pacific Rim East (comprising the countries located at the east coast of the Pacific Ocean).
- Region 3 is regulated by the MPHPT (Ministry of Public Management, Home Affairs, Posts and Telecommunication) of Japan. The region includes Asia, Australia, and the Pacific Rim West (comprising the countries located at the west coast of the Pacific Ocean).

RFID tags and readers usually do not require a transmission license, since they are Short Range Devices but have to comply with different local regulations to prevent interferences with frequencies in the Industrial, Scientific, and Medical Equipment (ISM) band. The frequency allocations per region as shown in Table 19.3.

NEAR- AND FAR-FIELD COMMUNICATIONS

Passive RFID communications can be categorized into near-field and far-field communications, according to the way that tags are powered from the reader:

- *Near-field communication.* The tag extracts the energy from a reactive magnetic field generated by the reader. Tags incorporate a small coil, where

TABLE 19.3
Regional Frequency Allocations for RFID

Region	LF (KHz)	HF (MHz)	UHF (MHz)	Microwave (GHz)
Region 1	125	13.56	868–870	2.446–2.454
Region 2	125	13.56	902–928	2.40–2.4835
Region 3	125	13.56	950–956	2.427–2.470

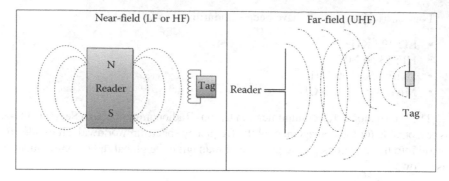

FIGURE 19.2   Near- and far-field methods of communication between reader and tag.

an electric current is induced by the magnetic field. The voltage between the two coil ends is rectified and coupled to a capacitor, so that the charge accumulated is used to power the tag (Figure 19.2). Near-field strategy is usually employed by RFID systems in the LF or HF bands.

*   *Far-field communication.* The tag extracts the energy from the incident electromagnetic radiation emanating from the reader's antenna after its capture by the tag's antenna. The difference of potential at the tag antenna causes a current to charge a capacitor so that the accumulated energy could power the tag. Far-field strategy is commonly employed by RFID systems in UHF and microwave bands.

The theoretical boundary between near- and far-field depends on the frequency used and is directly proportional to $\lambda/2\pi$, where λ is the wavelength.

MODULATION PROCEDURES

RFID systems operate according to three different modulation techniques. We briefly introduce each of them. For a more detailed explanation see Ref. [1]:

*   *Amplitude Shift Keying (ASK).* Amplitude modulation can provide a high data rate but with low noise immunity. For a given reference, a high amplitude is assumed as a "1" and a low one as a "0."
*   *Frequency Shift Keying (FSK).* This modulation uses two different frequencies to transmit data. For a simple reader, FSK provides very strong noise immunity, but the data rate achieved is lower than in other modulations.
*   *Phase Shift Keying (PSK).* This modulation technique is similar to FSK except that only one frequency is used, and the shift between "0" and "1" is accomplished by shifting the phase of the backscatter clock by 180°. PSK provides fairly good noise immunity, a moderate simple reader, and a faster data rate than FSK.

STANDARDS

Lack of standardization has traditionally been one of the main impediments of the wide scale adoption of RFID technology. Standards guarantee the interoperability between readers and tags of different manufacturers. However, the coexistence of multiple standards may cause the opposite effect by confusing the market.

In the past, each country used to set its own regulation for RFID frequencies and transmission specifications. The proliferation of local and regional standards prevented the worldwide adaptation of RFID technology. In recent years, several regulatory bodies, standard development organizations, and industry consortia, such as the European Telecommunications Standards Institute (ETSI), EPCglobal, and ISO, collaborated on a single global standard. Most of the current standards proposal today are the fusion of existing standards [10,11]. The most representative examples are as follows:

- EAN.UCC
- From ISO/IEC JTI/SC17: ISO/IEC 10536, ISO/IEC 14443, ISO/IEC 15693
- From ISO/IEC JT1/SC31/WG4: ISO/IEC 15961, ISO/IEC 15962, ISO/IEC 15963, ISO/IEC 18000
- From ISO/IEC JT1/SC31/WG3: ISO/IEC 18046, ISO/IEC 18047.
- EPCglobal Class-1 Gen-2

These standards will be discussed as follows.

EAN.UCC

In 2000, the EAN international organization and the UCC of the United States launched the Global Tag (GTAG) project. It was proposed to be implemented for tracking and logistics environments based on RFID. GTAG is based on open standards in the UHF frequency range to increase the data rate of RFID systems. Note: In 2005, the UCC changed its name to GS1 US.

ISO/IEC JT1/SC17

ISO and the International Electrotechnical Commission (IEC) have established jointly the standards for the physical characteristics of identification cards, the communication protocols at the physical layers, the transmission power, and so on. This work was conducted in JT1/SC17 (Joint Technical Committee 1, Sub-Committee 17) and resulted in the ISO/IEC 10536 international standards for contactless integrated circuit cards, ISO/IEC 14443 for proximity cards (contactless cards working at a distance up to 10 cm) and ISO/IEC 15693 for vicinity cards (contactless cards operating in the range from 10 cm to 1 m).

ISO/IEC JT1/SC31/WG4

ISO and IEC have also established the standard encoding rules for the data used in automatic identification. This includes the syntax of RFID tags, data formats, and so on. The work was carried by ISO/IEC JT1/SC31 (Joint Technical Committee 1,

Sub-Committee 31). The results include ISO/IEC 15961 (data protocol, application interfaces), ISO/IEC 15962 (data encoding rules and logical memory functions), ISO/IEC 15693 (unique identification of RF tags), ISO/IEC 18000 (air interface), and ISO/IEC 18001 (application requirements profiles) standards.

ISO/IEC JT1/SC31/WG3

Finally, ISO and IEC have worked on issues related to standard conformance to verify that the implementations have met the specifications. ISO/IEC 18046 defines the test method to measure the performance of RF tags and interrogators and ISO/IEC 18047 is the method for conformance testing of RFID devices.

EPCglobal Class-1 Gen-2

EPCglobal [7] was created in 2004 as a consortium to lead the development of industry-driven standards for the EPC that supports RFID. The membership of EPCglobal consists of industry leaders and organizations such as EAN International, UCC, The Gillette Company, Procter & Gamble, Wal-Mart, Hewlett Packard, Johnson & Johnson, Checkpoint Systems, Auto-ID Labs, and others. The main goal of EPCglobal is to increase the visibility and efficiency of supply chains and to improve the quality of the information flows between companies and their trading partners.

EPCglobal Class-1 Gen-2 is called "the worldwide standard for RFID systems" because it has been implemented to satisfy all the needs of the final customer, irrespective of the geographic location. Thus, an EPCglobal Class-1 Gen-2-compliant tag conforms with the following group of standards:

1. ETSI EN 302 208-1, EN 302 208-2
2. ISO/IEC Directives-2, ISO/IEC 3309, ISO/IEC 16961, ISO/IEC 15962, ISO/IEC 15963, ISO/IEC 18000-1, ISO/IEC 18000-6, ISO/IEC 19762
3. Code of Federal Regulations, Title 47: Telecommunication, Chapter 1: FCC, Part 15: Radio Frequency devices
4. EPCglobal: Tag Data Standards, EPCglobal: FMCG RFID Physical Requirements Documents, EPCglobal Class-1 and Gen-2 UHF RFID Implementation Reference

Figure 19.3 illustrates the standard format of EPC data. It consists of a unique identifier of 96 bits divided into three fields. The Header size is 8 bits long and contains a unique tag identifier. The GTIN (Global Trade Item Number) is the second field and comprises two subfields. The first is the identification number of the company or manufacturer ID (the EPCManager in Figure 19.3), which is 28 bits long and the second is the manufacturer's product ID (the ObjectClass) on 24 bits. Finally, a SerialNumber of 36 bits codes the information related to an individual item such as price, weight, expiration date, and so on. With its 96 bits code (note that 8 bits are devoted to the header), a total of 268 millions companies (2^{28}) can categorize up to 16 millions of different products (2^{24}), where each product category contains a maximum of 687 billion individual items (2^{36}).

The Auto-ID Labs has also promoted the so-called EPCglobal Network [12] with an ambitious purpose: to create a *global* network that provides visibility for target

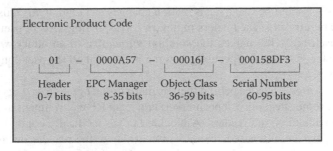

FIGURE 19.3   Standardized data format in an EPC.

items and to facilitate the product traceability in a supply chain by means of inexpensive RFID tags, readers, and a network infrastructure. More details are available in the section on EPCglobal Network (see later).

PRIVACY

The RFID technology raises concerns regarding the privacy issues for individuals and organizations because tags can be read by entities other than their owners and without the owner's knowledge [13,14]. RFID threats affect individuals and businesses. The main risk to personal privacy is that a tag with a unique identification number can be associated with a person. In the case of commercial entities, corporate espionage threat is the most important risk.

Policy solutions have been proposed to improve privacy protection in RFID systems [15,16]; they are, in general, difficult to implement and manage. Some of the technical solutions are listed here as follows:

- *EPC Kill.* The Auto-ID Center designed the EPC Kill command as a pro-privacy technology. The principle of this command is "dead tags do not talk" and so it is applied, for example, when tags pass through a checkpoint in a shop, they receive a "kill" command from the reader to deactivate themselves permanently. As an alternative to killing, tags can be attached to a product price tag and discarded at the point of sale.
- *Encryption.* The idea behind this solution is to store encrypted serial numbers into the tags. This alternative presents some problems regarding the distribution and management of keys. In addition, encryption does not protect from tracking because an encrypted serial number is, in essence, a static identifier that can help to track a tag.
- *Passwords.* Current tags have enough resources to verify pin codes or passwords. The idea is simple: a tag does not send information unless it receives the right password. The problem is that a reader would not know the password to send without determining the tag's identity beforehand. However, this approach would be applied in specific environments where only one reader interacts with a known population of tags.
- *Pseudonyms.* Besides the product data, tags store a list of pseudonyms that they could use to be identified by the readers, thus maintaining the customer

privacy. Each time that a tag is read, it changes its pseudonym. This mechanism requires that the readers maintain corresponding lists of pseudonyms for each tag. This makes the solution vulnerable to an attack where the same tag is scanned repeatedly to force it to reveal all the pseudonyms that it stores.

- *Blocker tags.* The idea behind them is that a group of tags (e.g., tags attached to consumer items in a supermarket) create an RF environment that is hostile to unauthorized readers. A blocker tag is specifically configured to be read-only by authorized scanners, for example, the readers installed in a given supermarket. This mechanism requires these readers to know ahead the tags to be identified.

ENERGY CONSUMPTION

RFID systems with active tags have some drawbacks in terms of energy consumption [17]. One of them is the need to save energy in order to increment the lifetime of the batteries, and thus, tag operation. In active RFID systems, the major sources of energy waste are related to radio communication issues [18]: namely collisions, idle listening, overhearing, and so on. When active tags are in the read range of the reader, they are listening to the channel and the radio is kept in the receiving mode, consuming energy. In Ref. [19], it is stated that idle listening is the dominant factor. Thus in RFID systems with active tags, as in WSN, one mechanism to save energy is to turn off the radios during periods of inactivity. This mechanism can be found in Refs. [18,20–22]. Other energy save mechanisms for WSN, such as Transmission Power Control (TPC), can be implemented in active tags. The goal of TPC is to select the optimum power transmission level to be employed in each packet delivery. The precise meaning of optimum depends, indeed, on the scope and objective. Some of the works proposed for TPC can be found in Refs. [23–28].

HARDWARE PLATFORMS

The supply of RFID hardware has steadily increased in parallel with standardization. In this section, a number of RFID vendors with offers based on the global standard EPCglobal Class-1 Gen-2 will be briefly introduced as follows.

- *Alien Technology* [29]. This company provides RFID solutions for UHF applications. Its product line includes tags, readers, and antennas for retail and government supply-chain operations, including suppliers of Wal-Mart and the U.S. Department of Defense.
- *Intermec* [30]. This company develops and manufactures wired and mobile computing systems, including RFID. Its product line includes tags, portable (handled) and stationary readers, printers, labels, RFID middleware, and so on. Also this company offers a complete RFID-based item-tracking and management system to the major and minor retailers.
- *Impinj* [31]. This company has contributed to the development of RFID standards for high-volume supply-chain applications. It works with partners

to develop a complete solution of tags, readers, modems, software, and system integration.

- *Samsys* [32]. This developer owns patents for multiprotocol and multi-frequency readers. Major retailers and manufacturers worldwide have been deploying SAMSys RFID readers to track the movement of tagged goods through the supply chain.
- *Symbol* [33]. Symbol technologies works in enterprise mobility, delivering products and solutions that capture, move, and manage information in real-time to and from the point of business activity. Radio identification technology is one of its fields of interest.

READER DEVICES

Readers come in a wide variety of sizes and offer different features. Moreover, readers can be fixed in a stationary position or be portable. Generally speaking, readers are classified into the following three groups [1]:

- *OEM readers.* OEM (Original Equipment Manufacturers) readers are intended for integration with the customer's own capture system.
- *Industrial readers.* Industrial readers are designed for harsh industrial environments, such as assembly lines and manufacturing plants. They have a standardized bus interface for simple integration between existing systems and provide various degrees of protection and ruggedness.
- *Portable/handled readers.* These readers are "mobile" in the sense that the user can change their location. They are usually equipped with a liquid crystal display and a keypad. Animal identification, devices control, and asset management are some of the applications of this kind of readers.

THE PROBLEM OF COLLISIONS IN RFID

A collision is said to occur when two or more devices interfere with each other. Passive tags are simple devices that are excited by a reader when they are in the reader's range. Therefore, they send their identification numbers without knowing if another tag is also simultaneously sending its own identification number. In contrast, active tags can incorporate carrier sense mechanisms to listen to the channel before transmitting their data, reducing the number of collisions.

Collisions can occur in a number of ways:

- Case of a single reader–multiple tags collisions. Multiple tags are in the reading range of the same reader and respond simultaneously. The reader detects the electromagnetic wave but is unable to interpret the signal received.
- Case of multiple readers–single tag collisions. Only one tag is in the read range of multiple readers. The interferences occur when the signal from a neighboring reader collides with the tag transmission.
- Case of reader–reader collisions. Multiple readers configured to work within the same frequency band, interfere each other and thus a collision occurs.

ANTI-COLLISION PROTOCOLS AT THE PHYSICAL LAYER

Numerous multiaccess and anti-collision protocols have been developed with the aim of separating the colliding signals. Frequency Division Multiple Access (FDMA), Time Division Multiple Access (TDMA), Space Division Multiple Access (SDMA), Code Division Multiple Access (CDMA), and Carrier Sense Multiple Access (CSMA) are available alternatives [1]. All of them are briefly reviewed in this section:

- *FDMA*. The channel is divided into different subchannels and the users are allocated different carrier frequencies. In RFID systems, this technique adds a cost to the readers, because they must provide a dedicated receiver for every reception channel. On the other hand, tags must be able to distinguish between different frequencies and they must be able to select the subchannels of interest.
- *TDMA*. The channel is divided into time slots that are assigned to the users. Due to its relative simplicity on the tag side, TDMA is the most extensively used anti-collision procedure.
- *SDMA*. This technique reuses certain resources, such as channel capacity in spatially separated areas. This technique can be applied to an RFID system as follows: in a scenario with two or more readers, the read range of each one is reduced but compensated by forming an array of antennas, providing then a large coverage area. The main drawback is the high implementation cost of the complicated array antennas system.
- *CDMA*. It consists of using spread-spectrum modulation techniques based on a pseudo-random code to spread the data over the entire spectrum. CDMA is the ideal procedure in many applications, for example, navigation systems, GPS, and so on. However, in RFID systems, this technique means more complex hardware in the tags and hence, higher cost.
- *CSMA*. This technique requires the tags to sense the channel traffic before sending their information. If there is no traffic, the tag starts to send. This mechanism can be only used with active tags because passive tags cannot monitor the channel.

Many of these solutions are not cost-effective due to the extra complexity of the tag. This is why solutions to the collision problem are typically sought at the media access control (MAC) layer. This solution is advantageous because the readers carry most of the burden due to the protocol complexity.

MAC LAYER SOLUTIONS TO THE COLLISION PROBLEM

When a number of tags are presents simultaneously in the coverage area of one or more readers, an appropriate MAC protocol can handle/avoid collisions caused by simultaneous transmissions. These protocols are now briefly presented as follows.

Single Reader–Multiple Tags (Tag–Tag) Collisions

When multiple tags are in the reading range of a single reader, each tag answers to a same reader simultaneously and collisions occur. One way to avoid these collisions is by having each tag respond at different times. To achieve this, an efficient medium access control protocol is necessary. The following protocols have been designed for this type of collisions.

Tree-Based Tag Anti-Collision Protocols

Tree-based anti-collision protocols put the computational burden the reader. The reader attempts to recognize a set of tags in the coverage area in several interrogation cycles. Each interrogation cycle consists of a *query* packet, sent by the reader, and the response of tags in coverage. If a set has more than one tag, a collision occurs. When a collision occurs, the mechanism splits the set into two subsets using the tags identification numbers or a random number. The reader keeps on performing the splitting procedure until each set has one tag. Tree-based protocols are not efficient when the number of tags to recognize is large due to the lengthy identification delay.

Tree based anti-collision protocols can be categorized into the following two groups:

- Query tree protocols [34–36] only need the tag's identifier number to carry out the anti-collision procedure. The protocol works as follows (Figure 19.4): the reader starts splitting a set of tags by sending a *query* packet with one bit set to 0 or 1. Tags in coverage receive the packet and those whose prefix matches the bit sent by the reader transmit their identification number. If there is a collision, the reader adds another bit set to 0 or 1 to the prefix of the last *query* packet and sends a new *query*. The mechanism continues expanding the *query* tree until a successful response occurs. This

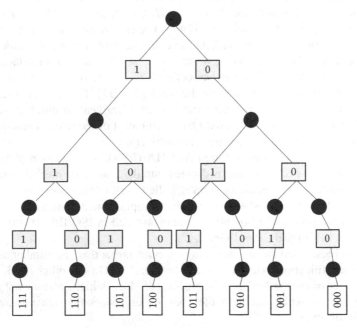

FIGURE 19.4 Query tree protocol.

means that a branch of the query tree has been built and one tag has been identified. Then, to identity the rest of tags, the reader must send new *query* packets with other combination of bits in the prefix until all tags have been recognized. Query tree protocols are also called "memoryless" protocols because tags do not need additional memory beyond the one required for the identifier number.

- Binary tree protocols [34,37,38] follow the same procedure that the query tree protocols introduced above but with additional complexity associated with a random number generator and a counter. These protocols operate as follows: the reader sends a *query* packet announcing that a time slot starts. If there is only one tag in range, it is successfully identified. Otherwise, tags in range respond in that slot and a collision occurs. The collided tags generate a random number that can be 0 or 1. Based on the particular value, the set of tags is split into two subsets of tags. The set of tags which generated the 0 value send their identifier number in the following slot. If there is more than one tag in the subset another collision occurs, and the subset will be split again. This procedure continues recursively until the subset is reduced to one tag, in which case the transmission will be successful.

ALOHA Protocols

ALOHA protocols can be classified into four main groups as follows.

1. The first one is the *Pure-ALOHA* [39] protocol which is the most simple anti-collision scheme for passive tags with read-only memory.
2. The second group is the *Slotted ALOHA* protocol [40]. Slotted ALOHA protocol is based on Pure-ALOHA. A tag can transmit only at the beginning of a slot. Therefore, packets can collide completely or not collide at all. The mechanism is as follows: the reader sends a packet announcing the number of slots (n) that tags can compete to use. Tags receive the data and then generate a random number between [0, $n \boxtimes 1$]. These number indicate the slots where each tag must transmit its identification number. Slotted-ALOHA outperforms Pure-ALOHA at the cost of requiring a reading system that manages slotted time synchronization.
3. The third group, Frame-Slotted-ALOHA (FSA), is a variation of Slotted-ALOHA. In FSA, the time is divided into discrete time intervals, but slots are confined in consecutive frames, called cycles. Each frame has a length of a fixed number of slots. FSA has been implemented in many commercial products, such as I-Code [41] and standardized in ISO/IEC 18000-6C [2] and in EPCglobal Class-1 Gen-2 [7].

   In FSA, when the number of tags is much larger than the number of slots, the identification delay increases considerably. On the other hand, if the number of tags is low and the number of slots is high, many empty slots can occur, which increase the chances of successful transmission and identification.

4. In Dynamic FSA (DFSA), the number of slots per frame is variable. Tags randomly choose a slot within the frame to send their information to the reader. When a frame finishes, an identification cycle concludes and the reader, following some rules, makes a decision about whether to increase/decrease/maintain the number of time slots per frame in the next identification cycle. According to Ref. [42], the optimum throughput in a cycle of a DFSA protocol is achieved if the number of tags t equals the number of slots n in that cycle, and this throughput is given by $n \times e^{\boxtimes} = 0.36$. Since the number of tags in range per cycle is unknown, first the reader must estimate the number of tags that are going to compete per cycle, possibly through the statistical information collected on a cycle-by-cycle basis or any heuristic methods. Then, the reader adjusts the frame size to guarantee the maximum throughput and minimize the identification delay.

The various anti-collision DFSA algorithms for RFID applications fall into the following categories:

1. *Frame-size-correction techniques*. These permits a direct adjustment of the frame size based on the number of collisions or the empty slots in the previous frame, without computing the expected number of tags to obtain the optimal frame size. For instance, the EPCglobal standard [7] and the method proposed by Lee et al. [43] use mechanisms of this kind to adjust the frame size on a per-slot basis and to force the tags to reselect their slots based on outcome of the previous selections (empty, successful, or collision).
2. Heuristics algorithms compute an estimation of the number of tags based on some heuristically derived formula [44–47].
3. Bayesian estimators of the expected value of frame size, given a known *a priori* tags distribution and the observed state of the previous frame. Refs. [48,49] are examples of this type, where the statistics derived from the past history are used to improve the estimation. The proponents show that the Bayesian estimator outperforms the estimation given by the other algorithms introduced above [45]. However, Bayesian estimators require the *a priori* distribution of the number of tags, which is not always available.
4. Maximum Likelihood (ML) estimators. In this case, the frame size is selected as the value that maximizes the probability of the observed sample. Knowledge of the number of empty, successful, and collision slots is used to improve calculation of the frame size. The ML algorithms proposed so far compute the frame size using an estimate of number of empty slots. The work by Cha and Kim [47] and the ASAP algorithm [50] falls in this category. ASAP [50] outperforms the schemes presented in Refs. [44,45,48,49], in terms of the average time for tag identification.

Single Tag–Multiple Readers Collisions
In this scenario, several passive tags are in the reading range of two or more readers. The interferences occur when the signal from a neighboring reader collides with the

tag transmission. The collision can be avoided if neighboring readers operate at different times or different frequencies; however, selection of different frequencies is not always possible with passive tags.

Some protocols that have been designed to avoid this type of collisions [51–54] are summarized below.

Colorwave

Colorwave [55] is an anti-collision TDMA protocol, where each reader selects a time slot to transmit (each time slot is a "color"). If a collision takes place, the readers involved choose a new time slot and send a small control packet to all their neighbors announcing the new time slot. Any neighboring reader with this "color" switches to a different color and sends a control packet to announce its new time slot. When the percentage of successful transmissions is below a certain threshold, the number of time slots to choose (number of colors) is increased. In contrast, if the percentage is greater than another certain threshold, the number of time slots to select is decreased. Note that these thresholds can take different values.

The PULSE Protocol

In the PULSE protocol, the readers use two different channels to minimize the number of collisions. The first is a data channel to communicate with the tags; the second is a control channel to communicate with the readers by means of beacons (control packets) [56]. A reader notifies its neighbors that it is going to identify tags by using a beacon packet to prevent interferences due to signals from its neighboring readers. To implement this protocol, the reader must be able to simultaneously receive on both channels. Additionally, the reader transmits at a higher power on the control channel than on the data channel to be also listened by the readers in range with its neighbors but not directly with it. This mechanism avoids the well-known hidden terminal problem (which occurs when the reader is within the transmission range from two or more readers that are not aware of each other) [57].

ETSI 302 208

ETSI EN 302 208 is a European Regulation that specifies the operation of RFID readers. It allocates the 865- to 868-MHz band for RFID deployment. This frequency is subdivided into 15 channels. This standard is based on CSMA [58] and introduces the concept of "Listen Before Talk" whereby the reader listens to the channel for a short time to ensure that the channel is idle before reading tags. Otherwise, it performs a random back off before retransmission.

EPCglobal Class-1 Gen-2

The EPCglobal Class-1 Gen-2 protocol is based on FDMA. The spectrum is divided into different channels and each reader selects a different frequency (channel) to transmit. However, this solution requires fairly sophisticated technology for passive tags because simple tag devices change their frequency of operation from the nominal frequency.

SINGLE READER–SINGLE READER COLLISIONS

Here, collisions occur when the signal of a neighboring reader causes interferences. They can be avoided by configuring neighbor readers to work at different times, frequencies, codes or by means of other hybrid medium access mechanisms. The anti-collision protocols proposed to solve these interferences are the same as single tag–multiple reader collisions.

Tables 19.4 and 19.5 summarize the anti-collision protocols introduced in this section.

RFID INTEGRATION WITH ENTERPRISE INFORMATION SYSTEMS

An RFID middleware is the set of software tools that integrates the RFID system with the existing enterprise information systems and its information exchanges with its partner companies. Thus, a tag identifier can be used to query the database of associates to obtain information about the items identified, such as shipment orders,

TABLE 19.4
Multiple Tags–Single Reader Anti-Collision Protocols

Protocol Category	Protocol Name	
Tree protocols	Query tree protocols	
	Binary tree protocols	
ALOHA protocols	Pure	
	Slotted	
	Frame-slotted	I-Code
		ISO/IEC-1800-6C
		EPCglobal Class-1 Gen-2
	Dynamic frame	Frame-Size-Correction
	slotted	Heuristics
		Bayesians
		ML

TABLE 19.5
Single Tag–Multiple Readers and Single Reader–Single Reader Anti-Collision Protocols

Protocol Category	Protocol Name
Based on TDMA	Colorwave
Based on FDMA	PULSE
	EPCglobal Class-1 Gen-2
	ETSI 302-208

invoices, repair logs, and so on. Indeed, many of the EPCglobal specifications define a standard middleware for RFID systems.

In the following, we first discuss briefly the desired functionality of RFID middleware. Afterwards, we discuss the requirements of global interoperation of RFID systems and introduce the concept of globally unique identifiers. A review of the EPCglobal Network is provided next. To conclude, we present the MEGASTAND architecture for middleware to track and trace and trace-specialized pallets.

FUNCTIONALITIES IN AN RFID MIDDLEWARE

From a general point of view, any RFID middleware should provide the following capabilities:

- *Data aggregation and filtering.* Middleware should extract, aggregate, smooth, and filter raw RFID data according to business rules. Appropriate programming models for event specification and processing rules are available [59].
- *Data-flow management and business process notification.* RFID middleware is also in charge of routing data to appropriate enterprise subsystems. Filtered and aggregated data are stored for later use and appropriate RFID events are stored in an event-repository. This repository is available to business applications that need a log of tagged-item activities, like tracking and tracing systems. In these cases, RFID data is stored for later queries while in other, real-time events are of interest, for example the occurrence of an unauthorized shipment or a low-stock alarm. Therefore, middleware should provide mechanisms for real-time notification of events to applications. Finally, if tags have write capabilities, the flow of data may be bidirectional, from the RFID infrastructure to business processes and the other way around. For instance, once a shipment order is ready, the middleware may send it to the proper reader to write it on a tag memory. Therefore, the middleware should route also data from applications to tags.
- *RFID device management.* These are the tools for remote monitoring and control of readers and other devices are usually also part of the middleware.

Despite vendors' claims, there is no general-purpose plug-and-play middleware solution and the general functionality must be tailored to the particulars of an application or an enterprise. As a final remark, it should be noted that RFID remains an immature and evolving technology, and therefore RFID middleware should be flexible enough so that it could be adapted to the future changes with minimal efforts.

The middleware functionality may be organized and deployed in different ways. For instance, RFID data may be stored and processed locally, that is, at the collection points, or at a central data center. This issue is highly application-dependent as we exemplify in the next section. Furthermore, the complexity of management of RFID devices can be considerably decreased if the middleware supports and benefits from the self-organization capabilities provided by some RFID equipment. This topic is also covered in the following section.

SYSTEM ARCHITECTURE

Two architectural issues are of concern at an early stage of the design. First, how will the middleware functionality be distributed between the data center and the edge of the network, that is, at factories, warehouses, retail stores, and so on. RFID equipment is already providing self-organization capabilities. If the middleware is able to take advantage of them, many management tasks can be automatically handled. We will next discuss briefly these two issues:

Edge Components and Edge Processing

The application-dependent questions relate to the filtering and storage of the acquired data, the local use of data, and device coordination and management. For instance, it is well known that data aggregation and filtering at the edge of the network reduce the processing required from the central servers. The architectural decisions concern whether the filtered information should be sent to the central server and at which frequency or it may be kept at a local event-repository. Should this be the case, would the distributed repositories be synchronized or remotely queried? Finally, in some scenarios, readers must coordinate themselves, so as to avoid reader–reader interference, for instance.

As an example, consider a tracking and tracing system for the control of a cold chain, where food containers are tracked and their temperature monitored. After a reader has smoothed the tag readings and verified that a given container had passed through a checkpoint, the acquired data may be sent to a central tracking application. The log of temperatures measured by the tag, however, can be stored locally. In cases where some sampled readings exceed the allowed limit, an alarm is raised so that the local workers could stop the container. This event is also reported to the central server. For a trace report, the central server queries the local repository, since the centrally stored tracking information indirectly allows knowing where this information for a particular period has been stored.

Self-Organization Capabilities

The deployment and maintenance of RFID devices may become a nightmare in a large-scale infrastructure. Devices with self-organization capabilities are already available and middleware should provide adequate support to them. Minimum required capabilities for self-organizing systems are as follows:

- *Discovery*: edge devices must be able to discover resources provided by the middleware, such as coordinators, gateways, local event-repositories, processing rule repositories, and so on. Conversely, the installed infrastructure must be able to discover new additions.
- *Self-configuration and upgrading*: new devices must be able to automatically retrieve configurations and upgrades.
- *Status monitoring and recovery*: devices must monitor themselves and report error conditions. Strategies for automatic recovery from failures should be available.

THE PRODUCT-CENTRIC APPROACH IN GLOBAL COMMERCE

The benefits of RFID increase when there is an improved item visibility, not only for the internal processes of a company, but also across company boundaries. However, the interoperability of RFID systems raises the question of how to manage and share the information of the product associated with a tag. In particular, in a complex trading scenario, different companies and business actors join and leave the process and may append or modify product information as business transactions take place. To illustrate, consider a manufacturer of industrial equipment using RFID tags in the various parts that constitute that equipment with readers throughout the production stages. At the end of each stage, a reader collects and records in a database the information related to the part that was just produced and writes on tags what have been done to equipment at the stage. When the equipment is finally assembled and shipped, it is loaded on a truck operated by a different company, a new actor in the global process. The truck load is recorded in a different database and the shipment order is written on the tag. Afterwards, the load is delivered to a sea carrier (which may want to check the shipment order) and then loaded in a container. This process continues until final delivery at a retailer. This example shows the degree of complexity involved in the automation of the management of product-related information.

A product-centric approach has been proposed as a scalable solution to the problem of shared management of product information [60], mostly for supply chains. The idea is for the participant enterprises to store and manage their own product-related information while granting others access to it in a controlled way. This approach is called product-centric because the product itself carries all its information. Actually, the identifier in a tag is used as a pointer to a database entry that keeps track of business transactions (shipment manifests or invoices) and item life-cycle information (version, modifications, or repairs).

For this mechanism to work properly in the general case, each item must have a globally unique identifier. Although there are several proposals on how to assign these identifiers [61], EPC codes are becoming the prevailing choice. As we will see in the next section, the EPCglobal standards specify a distributed procedure to link EPC codes to enterprise backend systems, with the Object Name Service (ONS) and an interface to share data between companies, the EPC Information Services (EPCIS).

EPCGLOBAL NETWORK

In the EPCglobal vision, the actors involved in a global supply-chain exchange RFID data to enable near-real-time tracking and status information on items, forming what is called the EPCglobal Network. The EPCglobal specifications were originally focused on increasing the visibility of items throughout the supply chain, but their adoption is rapidly making them a general-purpose set of standards for RFID systems. The set of EPCglobal specifications [7] fall into three categories: identify, capture, and exchange, as shown in Figure 19.5, although some of the documents may fit more than one category. The lower levels of the architecture (Identify and Capture) deal primarily with RFID devices, whereas the upper layers—Application-Level Events

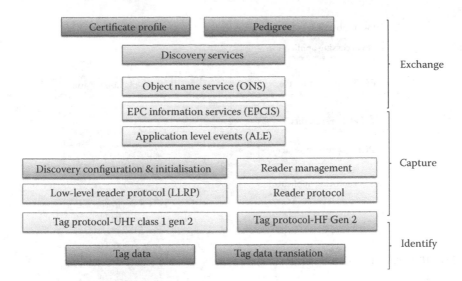

FIGURE 19.5 EPCglobal standards overview.

(ALE), EPCIS, and ONS—are for the exchange and can be considered part of an integration middleware. Certificate profile covers the issuance of X.509 certificates and their usage by entities in the EPCglobal network. Finally, Pedigree specifies an architecture for the maintenance and exchange of electronic pedigree documents for use by the pharmaceutical industry.

These specifications are mostly standard interfaces to be implemented by middleware components or RFID devices. The users (consumers, clients) of the higher levels are mostly business applications, like Enterprise Resource Planning (ERP) (not shown in Figure 19.5). These applications are referred to as EPCIS Accessing Applications in the EPCglobal notation. A user of EPCglobal specifications is called EPCglobal subscriber.

The ALE specification [59] provides a standard interface through which client applications can obtain the filtered *EPC observations* (the name used by EPCglobal to refer to tag readings). The EPCIS Capturing Software (Figure 19.6) can set up event processing rules and request filtered data. This interface allows the components to request data in synchronous or asynchronous mode and includes a flexible data model for specification of event filtering and grouping rules.

The EPCIS specification defines the standard interfaces for sharing of EPC data within and across enterprises (Figure 19.6). There are three interfaces: the Capture Interface, the Query Control Interface, and the Query Callback Interface, the latter two are represented in Figure 19.6 by the EPCIS Query Interface. The first one defines the delivery of EPCIS events from EPCIS Capturing Applications to other roles that consume the data in real-time, including EPCIS Repositories (an event-repository). An EPCIS Capturing Application provides business context by coordinating with other sources of information involved in executing a particular step of a business process. It understands the business processes in which EPC data

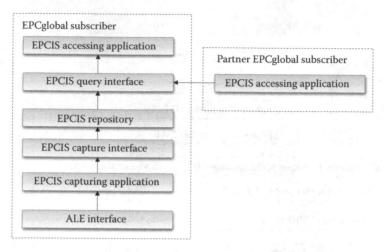

FIGURE 19.6   EPCIS architecture.

capture is involved, coordinates the information requested and received from the ALE interface, and routes this information to the appropriate enterprise systems. The Query Control and Callback Interfaces define a means to obtain EPCIS data subsequent to capture, typically by interacting with an EPCIS Repository. Finally, a number of bindings to these interfaces are defined, mostly based on XML messages over HTTP.

The ONS is a Domain Name System (DNS) to look up server addresses from a URL. Similar to the DNS, ONS servers are organized hierarchically, each company keeping its own local ONS. The role of the naming network service is to map EPC codes to (EPC codes were explained in section "EPCglobal Class-1 Gen-2") point to EPCIS Repositories. Basically, organizations announce their EPCIS services through their EPC codes to be looked up via ONS.

In the EPCglobal Network, readers collect EPC observations as items move through the chain. These observations are processed and passed to the EPCIS Capturing Applications (Figure 19.6). These applications add business context to observations and store the appropriate information for later use. The observations may be used internally or by trading partners. The ONS keeps a mapping between EPC codes and EPCIS servers. When an application needs some information about a particular EPC, it queries an ONS server to get the EPCIS server location information (IP address and port), and afterwards it queries the EPCIS server. The scope of the business information provided by EPCIS server is application-dependent. Figure 19.7 shows a simplified view of the EPCglobal Network architecture as described previously.

With this infrastructure in place, different companies along the supply chain may access real-time high-level business information about items provided by other companies, following the product-centric approach previously discussed. Although not already released, EPCglobal is working on the specification of discovery services,

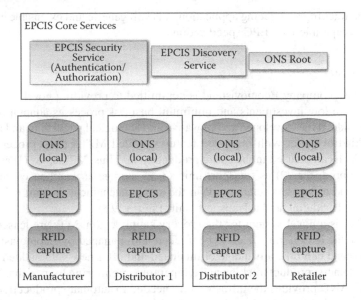

FIGURE 19.7 EPCglobal network simplified.

which would allow a company to discover all EPCIS repositories that may have data about a particular EPC.

COMMERCIAL AND OPEN-SOURCE RFID MIDDLEWARE

The number of vendors offering RFID middleware has dramatically increased over the last few years. Many of the most relevant software companies, such as SAP, Oracle, IBM or Microsoft already provide solutions, and so do a considerable number of smaller companies. Although RFID middleware can be found in many flavors, most of the products include EPC-compliant functionality since EPC specifications steadily settle as the industry standard. As a side effect, the standardization effort has paved the way for open source initiatives to release core middleware functionality, mostly EPC-based. To mention some of them, EPCIS and ALE implementations can be obtained from the MENTOR [62] project at the MIT or the Accada [63] project in Europe.

Hardware vendors are adding filtering, aggregation, and routing capabilities straight to reader devices, which can deliver the data in a variety of ways to fit in established enterprise systems.

MEGASTAND

MEGASTAND is an RFID middleware based on Web services used for tracking and tracing. In this section we summarize, as an example of RFID integration, the architecture, and design decisions of a novel Returnable Transport Unit called MT, which was developed by our research group [64]. Although the middleware is focused on a particular tracking and tracing application, it is still generic and extensible enough to become compatible with EPC specifications.

BACKGROUND

The Spanish company Ecomovistand is committed to providing novel value-added services with low investments and minimum business processes adaptation on the customer side. It has developed an innovative and ecological packaging and transport unit, a kind of pallet with improved features, called MT, for the grocery supply chain, which can be used in the entire product cycle. Thus, MT serves (1) as packaging at the producer, (2) as transport unit, (3) as storage at warehouses, and (4) as display stand at the supermarket, all in the same mechanical system, being thus a Returnable Packaging and a Transport Unit (Figure 19.8).

The MT is a novel system for the grocery supply chain. MTs are leased to customers; so the leased units need to be tracked and managed by Ecomovistand. But Ecomovistand can take advantage of this need and offer new value-added services to the customers: product tracking and temperature monitoring for perishable goods. MEGASTAND provides the infrastructure needed to automate product traceability and tracking as value-added services. It also let customers write additional information on tags, that is, middleware provide not only RFID read capabilities but also write functionality. Although Ecomovistand provides collected RFID data, the company neither integrates its products into the customer information framework, nor manages the customer systems. Hence, MEGASTAND is mainly an application for asset tracking and tracing, which provides an open interface for integration into customers IT systems. In short, RFID data is collected by Ecomovistand and served to its customers via standard interfaces. Customer can search and process RFID observations stored by Ecomovistand. They can also be notified directly when an event of interest occurs (the arrival of a particular batch to some site, for example). We refer to this functionality as a *read-type functionality*. Moreover, customer application can instruct RFID reader to write information in the tag memory after it is identified at a particular checkpoint. We refer to this functionality as *write-type functionality*.

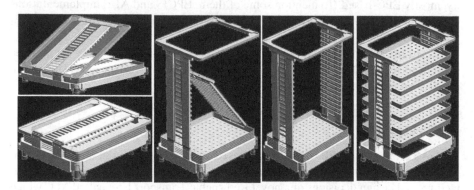

FIGURE 19.8   MT, a returnable transport and packaging unit.

Active RFID technology can provide the tracking support and value-added services to the MT. Active tags are useful for long-range readings as MTs are carried by forklifts and move through large, open warehouses and dock gates, temperature monitoring for perishable and full read/write capabilities. Temperature monitoring is a crucial value-added service. Hence, RFID tags must incorporate a temperature sensor. Finally, full read/write capabilities are necessary because the tags store in their memory the identifiers of the items loaded on the trays of the MT. This information must be updated (rewritten in memory) each time the load of the MT changes.

Active technology is more expensive than passive one. It is not cost-effective to install active tags in normal pallets, which are very cheap. However, since the MT is a high valuable asset, the increase of costs per unit due to the use of active tags with the desired capabilities can be justified and is quickly recovered by the added value functionality they provide.

MEGASTAND is the architecture of the middleware that integrates RFID captured data with the rest of the enterprise information systems.

MEGASTAND Architecture

We have developed customized active tag devices as well as an information support infrastructure called MEGASTAND, a middleware for managing, controlling, and exposing RFID data. This system could be implemented with other closed-loop asset management systems and with different RFID devices with reduced effort.

To accomplish this goal, we extend the service-oriented architecture (SOA) using the new concept called service-oriented device architecture (SODA) [65]. The SODA approach integrates a wide range of physical devices into distributed IT enterprise systems, by establishing a set of well-defined interfaces, regardless of the programming language and computing platforms on which they run. In our case, programmers deal with the RFID framework in the same way as they use business services in the SOA approach. SOA provides the abstract interoperability layers to integrate Ecomovistand information systems into with the customer's ERP system. The SODA extension supports the integration of different RFID devices into the information systems.

MEGASTAND consists of the following three different subsystems:

1. RFID subsystem: it includes active RFID devices and their software.
2. Middleware subsystem: it comprises database and application servers, and middleware software on the Ecomovistand side.
3. Control and Customer (C&C) subsystem.

Figure 19.9 illustrates these subsystems and their relation with physical devices as well as their physical location, for instance, the RFID subsystem is composed of readers and tags and located at the different supply-chain sites (factories, warehouses, retailer shops, etc.) sites. The Customer and Control Subsystems include both customer applications and the Ecomovistand control and management applications. These are the applications that use the middleware to access to RFID infrastructure and data. For instance, a customer ERP may interrogate MEGASTAND about the current location of a given batch of products carried by an MT. An Ecomovistand

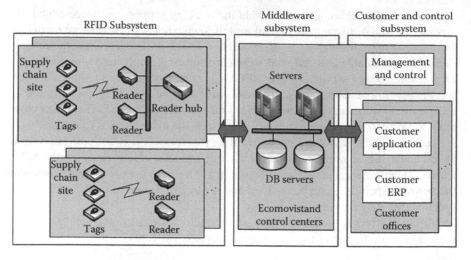

FIGURE 19.9   MEGASTAND architecture.

control application may interrogate MEGASTAND about the firmware version of a given reader. Components of the three subsystems are distributed between supply-chain sites (supplier and logistics warehouses, picking platforms, etc.), Ecomovistand Logistics Center, and customer offices.

The intersubsystem interactions are performed through Web Services Interfaces (WSI), as depicted in Figure 19.10. All of them provide a Web Services binding interface compliant with the core of W3C specifications (SOAP 1.2, WSDL 2.0 and, UDDI 2.0) [66] for accessing the different functionality via SOAP/HTTP.

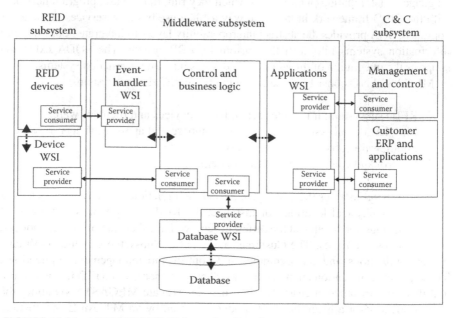

FIGURE 19.10   MEGASTAND Web services Interfaces.

Applications WSI

This interface provides the services offered to both control and customer applications. This is the main entry point to the MEGASTAND functionality, used to decouple it from its final representation, and the gate to the middleware binding framework between applications and RFID devices. There are two classes of service consumers for this WSI: on the one hand, Ecomovistand control and management applications. Control applications are used to manage the RFID infrastructure: monitoring of reader status, configuration of readers, and so on, whereas management applications are related to Ecomovistand business: management of MT stock, orders, invoices, and so on. On the other hand, customers may use this interface to retrieve information related to product location and routes, that is, tracking information, and monitored temperature, that is, tracing information. Customers can use this WSI in two ways: either by integrating the functionality directly into their own ERP or by using the *ad hoc* software provided by Ecomovistand.

Database WSI

This interface provides access to Data Base (DB) persistence services. This WSI acts as a hub for DB functionality. Future extensibility, as well as scalability and performance, are the desired features that motivate this interface.

Event-Handler WSI

RFID-generated events are passed to the middleware framework through this interface. It provides methods of communicating both raw RFID data and filtered events. Therefore, RFID readers and reader hubs must implement Web Services client applications, which are able to use SOAP/HTTP. This approach increases the complexity of the reader implementation compared with straight customized TCP connections (with Web Services, the reader must implement the HTTP protocol and create and parse SOAP messages). Despite this additional processing burden, we have adopted this approach for the following reasons:

- To minimize the problem of customer firewalls and proprietary technology. Readers are located in the customer sites, out of control of Ecomovistand. We do not rely on any customer technology other than HTTP infrastructure, which is a reasonable assumption.
- To support different RFID technologies. At the moment, we have developed our own tags and readers but other devices, such as EPC-compliant hardware, may be used in the future, and we expect they would support WS interaction.
- To provide RFID devices with the service discovery capabilities of SOA. We expect to use reader and reader hubs with different capabilities and sophistication. Once installed, these devices register and update their capabilities through this WSI.

Device WSI

The purpose of this interface is twofold: first, it decouples RFID hardware from its clients and exposes control functionality to manage the RFID framework. Second, it provides application access to filtered and consolidated data, in a very similar way as that specified by ALE, by subscribing to events of interest. Again, this approach requires the implementation of WS servers on the reader side, but we consider it worthy because of the reasons mentioned earlier in the discussion of the event-handler WSI. Together with the event-handler WSI, this interface extends the SOA to SODA.

This new extended architecture enables read-type and write-type functionalities. The functional requirements of the business model are achieved with read-type capabilities for package tracking and cold chain monitoring; product traceability is possible by storing and managing RFID data properly. Customers can either access relevant data directly via specific WS-client applications, or integrate it with their own ERP in a standardized way.

Write-type functionality supports other interesting applications. Let us first remark that efficient product traceability depends on the data model used [67]. MEGASTAND supports the use of a product-centric approach just by globally storing unique identifiers in the tags, such as EPC codes. In this way, this architecture is compatible with distributed product databases, for example, EPCIS. MEGASTAND gives the MT leasers the means to obtain the globally unique identifier for each item that MTs carry (an EPC code, for instance) so that they could query the appropriate backend systems. In fact, the use of read/write RFID tags provides additional flexibility, since not only product codes but also other product-related information could be recorded and modified/updated throughout the chain. The SODA approach facilitates such a functionality by providing a two-way interface between customers and products so that information that is relevant for the supply-chain operation could be appended. For example, at any given site in the chain, customers may add instructions about what should be done with a particular item at the next appropriate site—within the limitations of the available RFID tag memory—and send them through the Application WSI. The appropriate reader is instructed (by a command posted via the Device WSI) to store the information in the MT after its identification, to be accessed when needed later. Because tags carry information on the contents of the MT, it is also possible to use the data locally, without connecting to centralized information sites.

CONCLUSIONS

This chapter presented an overview of RFID technology and how it can be implemented for different services like animal identification, access control, or industrial automation. RFID is often considered just a substitute of traditional ID-systems based on barcodes. However, this technology shows an application potential that spans a wide range of fields and can be used in both local and global contexts.

The fundamentals of RFID systems have been introduced, as well as its components (readers, antennas, tags, etc.) and its operation mode. This chapter has been mostly focused on passive RFID, the most used and restrictive systems. The physical parameters that characterize an RFID system, such as modulation, polarization, modes to communicate (near- and far-field), and so on., have been outlined. Applications and features of a system according to its operating frequency have been shown. Among the available operating frequencies, LF, HF, and UHF, the latter will likely be the most employed in the near future because of its long range and high data-rate. Proposed anti-collision schemes and the energy source problems in RFID have been discussed. Finally, some issues related to privacy and security mechanisms have been shown. The consumers concerns about privacy have forced RFID providers to carefully develop appropriate mechanisms to ensure privacy and security. In fact, this is one of the most active areas of standardization at the moment.

The lack of standardization has traditionally been one of the limiting factors for the adoption of RFID technology. Therefore, a special attention has been devoted to the standards released over the last years to enable the deployment of cost-effective solutions. In this sense, the interoperability problems between manufacturers, hardware, and software developers are being overcome due to the EPCglobal standardization effort. EPCglobal is a worldwide organization that leads the development of industry-driven standards for RFID systems. It has released a set of specifications covering issues from physical to application level. During the last 4 years, these standards have been adopted by a considerable percentage of the RFID companies. Therefore, the more relevant and adopted EPCglobal specifications have been described along the chapter: in particular, the EPCglobal Class-1 Gen-2 protocol as physical/MAC layer protocol and EPCIS as middleware/application layer interface.

The integration of RFID systems by appropriate middleware components is a highly active field of development at the moment, especially those issues related to global interoperability of RFID applications. In fact, most of the recent standardization activities of EPCglobal are focused on application layer services offered by RFID systems. These topics have been discussed at the end of the chapter: the functionality of RFID middleware and the requirements for global interoperation of RFID systems have been explained, introducing the concept of globally unique identifiers and a review of the EPCglobal Network. Finally, a case of study of an RFID middleware (MEGASTAND) and its architecture has been discussed. It basically leverages WSI to facilitate integration of external RFID tracking and tracing functionality into enterprise systems as well as control and management of the RFID subsystem.

Adoption of RFID technology is still a complex task, which needs a great deal of implementation and integration effort. Even though it is a technology with a long history, it has been traditionally a proprietary one. The recent improvements and standards are not mature yet, though significant research opportunities have emerged to support its maturation and implementation. Despite this immature state, the market of RFID was worth around $300 million worldwide in 2007 and it has been predicted that will be worth $2.9 billion by 2009. Major retailers like Wal-Mart in the United States, Tesco in the United Kingdom, and the Metro Group in Germany are only some of a large number of industries that have recognized RFID may provide them competitive advantages by means of increasing product visibility and supply-chain performance. However, at the moment, in most of the cases only preliminary trials have been conducted. Retailers need active cooperation from their suppliers and manufacturers, since to get the most benefit out of RFID technology, tagging should be done from the very beginning in the business processes. Manufacturers, in turn, need to have a clear business case for RFID. It is, in the end, a question of how to share the cost and benefits of RFID adoption between the actors. On the other hand, software and hardware companies have not missed the market opportunity and are offering everyday more RFID solutions.

In summary, even though most of the actors agree on the potential and benefits of RFID technology, there is still a long way before seeing RFID operate in a truly global context. There are a number of important issues to be solved before regular adoption of this technology, particularly those related to privacy and consumer concerns and those related to interoperability of systems.

REFERENCES

1. Finkenzeller, K., *RFID Handbook: Fundamentals and Applications in Contactless Smart Cards and Identification*, 2nd edn., John Wiley & Sons, Chichester, UK, 2003, Chaps. 1–2, 1–7, and 11–28.
2. ISO/IEC 1800–6:2003(E), Part 6: Parameters for Air Interface Communications at 860–960 MHz, Final Draft International Standard ISO/IEC FDIS 18000-6, ISO, Geneva, Switzerland, November 2003.
3. Sarma, S., Brock, D., and Engels, D., Radio frequency identification and the Electronic Product Code, *IEEE Micro*, 21(6), 50–54, 2001.
4. Stockman, H., Communications by means of reflected power, *Proc. IRE*, 36(10), 1196–1204, 1948.
5. Vernon, F.L., Applications of the microwave Homodyne, *Trans. IRE Professional Group Antennas Propagat.*, 4(1), 110–116, 1952.
6. Documentation available on-line: http://www.autoidlabs.org, June 25, 2009.
7. EPC Radio-Frequency Identify protocol for communications at 868–960 MHz, Version 1.0.9: EPCglobal Standard Specification, 2004, available at: http://www.epcglobalinc.org/standards, June 25, 2009.
8. Akyldiz, I.F. and Kasimoglu, I. H., Wireless sensor and actor networks: Research challenges, *Elsevier Ad Hoc Networks*, 2(4), 351–357, 1995.
9. Jurdak, R., *Wireless Ad-Hoc and Sensor Networks: Protocols: A Cross-layer Design Perspective*, Springer-Verlag, New York, 2007, Chap. 2.
10. U.S. Department of Commerce, Radio Frequency Identification: Opportunities and Challenges for Implementation, US, Washington, DC, April 2005.
11. Kleist, R. et al., *RFID Labeling: Smart Labeling Concepts and Applications for the Consumer Packaged Goods Supply Chain*, 2nd edn., Banta Book Group, Printronix, Irvine, CA, 2005, Chap. 2.
12. EPCglobal Inc., The EPCglobal Network: Overview of Design, Benefits and Security, availavle at http://www.epcglobalinc.org, September 24, 2004.
13. Juels, A., RFID security and privacy: A research survey, *IEEE J. Select. Areas Commun.*, 24(2), 381–394, 2006.
14. Peris-Lopez, P. et al., RFID Systems: A survey on security threats and proposed solutions, *Proceedings of the 11th IFIP International Conference on Personal Wireless Communications-PWC06*, Lecture Notes in Computer Sciences, Vol. 4217, Springer-Verlag, Berlin/Heidelberg, 2006, 159–170.
15. Sarma, S. and Engels, D.W., RFID Systems, Security and Privacy Implications, Auto-ID Center White Paper, February 2003, available at: http://www.autoidlabs.org/researcharchive, June 25, 2009.
16. Juels, A. and Weis, S.A., Defining strong privacy for RFID, *Proceedings of the 5th Annual IEEE International Conference on Pervasive Computing and Communications Workshop* (PerComWorshops'07), White Plains, NY, 2007, 342–347.
17. ETSI-EN-302-208 V1.1.1 (2004-9), available online: http://www.etsi.org, June 25, 2009.
18. Akyildiz, I.F. et al., A survey on sensor networks, *IEEE Commun. Magaz.*, 40(8), 102–116, 2002.
19. Ye, W., Heidemann, J., and Estrin, D., Medium access control with coordinated adaptive sleeping for Wireless Sensor Networks, *IEEE/ACM Trans. Network.*, 12(3), 493–506, 2004.

20. Stemm, M., and Katz, R.H., Measuring and reducing energy consumption of network interfaces in hand-held devices, *IEICE Trans. Commun.*, E80-B (8), 1125–1131, 1997.

21. Lee, S.H. et al., Event-driven power management for wireless sensor networks, in *Software Technologies for Embedded and Ubiquitous Systems*, Lecture Notes in Computer Science, Vol. 4761, Obermaisser, R. et al., Eds., Springer-Verlag, Berlin/Heidelberg, 2007, 419–428.

22. Schurgers, C., Wakeup strategies in wireless sensor networks, in *Wireless Sensor Networks and Applications*, Li, Y., Thai, M.T., and Wu, W., Eds., Springer-Verlag, New York, 2008, Chap. 8, 195–217.

23. Zhou, F. et al., Evaluating and optimizing power consumption for anti-collision protocols for applications in RFID systems, *Proceedings of the International Symposium on Low Power Electronics and Design*, Newport Beach, CA, 2004, 357–362.

24. Kubich, M. et al., Distributed algorithms for transmission power control in wireless sensor networks, *Proc. IEEE Wireless Commun. Network.*, 1, 558–563, 2003.

25. Takagi, H. and Kleinrock, L., Optimal transmission ranges for randomly distributed packet radio terminals, *IEEE Trans. Comm.*, 32(3), 246–257, 1984.

26. Chen, Y., Sirer, E.G., and Wicker, S. B., On selection of optimal transmission power for ad-hoc networks. *Proceedings of the 36th Hawaii International Conference on System Sciences*, Waikoloa, HI, 2003, 300–309.

27. Egea-Lopez, E. et al., A real-time MAC protocol for wireless sensor networks: Virtual TDMA for sensors (VTS), *Proceedings of the 19th International Conference on Architecture of Computing Systems—ARCS 2006*, Frankfurt/Main, Germany, March 13–16, 2006, Lecture Notes in Computer Sciences, Vol. 3894, Springer-Verlag, Berlin/Heidelberg, 2006, 382–396.

28. Vales-Alonso, J. et al., Performance evaluation of MAC transmission power control in wireless sensor networks, *Comput. Netw.*, 51(6), 1483–1498, 2007.

29. Documentation available on-line: http://www.alientechnology.com, June 25, 2009.

30. Documentation available on-line: http://www.intermec.com, June 25, 2009.

31. Documentation available on-line: http://www.impinj.com, June 25, 2009.

32. Documentation available on-line: http://www.sirit.com, June 25, 2009.

33. Documentation available on-line: http://www.motorola.com/Business/US-EN/Business+ Product+and+Services/RFID, June 25, 2009.

34. Hush, D.R. and Wood, C., Analysis of tree algorithms for RFID arbitration, *Proceedings of IEEE International Symposium on Information Theory*, Cambridge, MA, 1998, 107.

35. Jacomet, M., Ehrsam, A., and Gehring, U., Contactless identification device with anti-collision algorithm, *Proceedings of the IEEE Conference on Circuits, Systems, Computers and Communications*, Athens, Greece, 1999, 269–273.

36. Law, C., Lee, K., and Siu, K., Efficient memoryless protocol for tag identification, *Proceedings of the 4th International Workshop on Discrete Algorithms and Methods for Mobile Computing and Communications*, Boston, MA, 2000, 75–78.

37. Shih, D. et al., Taxonomy and survey of RFID anti-collision protocols, *Elsevier Comput. Commun.*, 29(16), 2150–2166, 2006.

38. Myung, J. and Lee, W., Adaptive binary splitting: A RFID tag Collision arbitration protocol for tag identification, *Mobile Netw. Appl. J.*, 11(5), 711–722, 2006.

39. Leon-Garcia A. and Widjaja, I., *Communication Networks: Fundamental Concepts and Key Architectures*, McGraw-Hill, Boston, 1996, Chap. 6, Part 1, 368–421.

40. Weselthier, J.E., Ephremides, A., and Michaels, L.A., An exact analysis and performance evaluation of framed ALOHA with capture, *IEEE Trans. Comm.*, 37(2), 125–137, 1988.

41. Documentation available on-line: http://www.nxp.com/acrobat_download/other/ identification/1040616.pdf, June 25, 2009.

42. Schoute, F.C., Dynamic frame length ALOHA, *IEEE Trans. Comm.*, 31(4), 565–568, 1983.

43. Lee, S.-R., Joo, S.-D., and Lee, C.-W., An enhanced dynamic framed slotted ALOHA algorithm for RFID tag identification, *Proceedings of the 2nd Annual International Conference on Mobile and Ubiquitous Systems (MobiQuitous)*, San Diego, CA, 2005, 166–172.

44. Zhen, B., Kobayashi, M., and Shimizu, M., Framed ALOHA for multiple RFID objects identification, *IEICE Trans. Commun.*, E88-B(3), 991–999, 2005.
45. Vogt, H., Efficient object identification with passive RFID tags, *Proceedings of the 1st International Conference on Pervasive Computing*, Lecture Notes in Computer Science, Vol. 2414, Springer-Verlag, London, 2002, 98–113.
46. Chen, W.-T., An efficient anti-collision method for tag Identification in a RFID System, *IEICE Trans. Commun.*, E89-B (12), 3386–3392, 2006.
47. Cha, J. and Kim, J., Novel anti-collision algorithms for fast object identification RFID system, *Proceedings of the 11th Conference on Parallel and Distributed Systems*, Vol. 2, Fukuoka, Japan, 2005, 63–67.
48. Floerkemeier, C., Transmission control scheme for fast RFID object identification, *Proceedings of the Fourth Annual IEEE International Conference on Pervasive Computing and Communications Workshops* (PERCOMW'06), Pisa, Italy, 2006, 457–462.
49. Floerkemeier, C. and Wille, M., Comparison of transmission schemed for framed ALOHA-based RFID protocols, *Proceedings International Symposium on Applications and the Internet Workshops* (SAINT'06), Phoenix, AZ, 2006, 92–95.
50. Khandelwal, G. et al., ASAP: A MAC protocol for dense and time-constrained RFID systems, *EURASIP J. Wireless Commun. Netw.*, Article ID 18730, 2007.
51. Lai, W.K. and Coghill, G.G., Channel assignment through evolutionary optimization, *IEEE Trans. Vehicular Technol.*, 45(1), 91–96, 1996.
52. Kunz, D., Channel assignment for cellular radio using neural networks, *IEEE Trans. Vehicular Technol.*, 40(1), 188–193, 1991.
53. Duque-Anton, M., Kunz, D., and Ruber, B., Channel assignment for cellular radio using simulated annealing, *IEEE Trans. Vehicular Technol.*, 42(1), 4–21, 1993.
54. Ho, J., Engels, D.W., and Sarma, S.E,, HiQ Hierarchical Q-learning algorithm to solve the reader collision problem, *Proceedings of the International Symposium on Applications and the Internet Workshops*, Phoenix, AZ, 2006, 88–91.
55. Waldrop, J., Engels, D.W., and Sarma, S.E., Colorwave: An anti-collision algorithm for the reader collision problem, *Proceedings of the IEEE Wireless Communications and Networking Conference*, New Orleans, LA, 2003, 1206–1210.
56. Shailesh, B. and Iyer, S., PULSE: A MAC protocol for RFID Networks, *Proceedings of the Embedded and Ubiquitous Computing (EUC) 2005 Workshops: UISW, NCUS, SecUbiq, USN, and TAUES*, Nagasaki, Japan, December 6–9, 2005, Lecture Notes in Computer Science, Vol. 3823, Springer-Verlag, Berlin/Heidelberg, 2005, 1036–1046.
57. Tobagi, F. A. and Kleinrock, L., Packet Switching in radio channels: Part II—The hidden terminal problem in carrier sense multiple access modes and the busy-tone solution, *IEEE Trans. Comm.*, 23(12) 1417–1433, 1975.
58. Kleinrock L.and Tobagi, F.A., Packet switching in radio channels: Part I- Carrier sense multiple-access modes and their throughput-delay characteristics, *IEEE Trans. Comm.*, 23(12), 1400–1416, 1975.
59. ECPglobal Inc., The Application Level Events (ALE) Specification, version 1.0, available at: http://www.epcglobalinc.org, June 25, 2009.
60. Kärkkäinen, M., Ala-Risku, T., and Främling, K., The product centric approach: a solution to supply network information management problems? *Comput. Indus.*, 52(2), 147–159, 2003.
61. Främling, K., Harrison, M., and Brusey, J., Globally unique product identifiers—Requirements and solutions to product lifecycle management, *Proceedings of the 12th IFAC Symposium on Information Control Problems in Manufacturing (INCOM)*, Dolgui, A., Morel, G., and Pereira, C.E., Eds., St-Etienne, France, 2006, 855–860.
62. MIT EPC Net (MENTOR), available at: http://rolls.mit.edu/cs/, June 25, 2009.
63. Accada, EPC Network Prototyping Platform, available at: http://www.accada.org, June 25, 2009.

64. Alejandro S. et al., Tracking of returnable packaging and transport units with active RFID in the grocery supply chain, *Comput. Indus.*, 60(3), 161–171, 2009.
65. Deugd, S. et al., SODA: Service oriented device architecture, *Pervasive Comput.*, 5(3), 94–96, 2006.
66. W3C Web Services Activity, available at: http://www.w3.org/2002/ws
67. Främling, K. et al., Design patterns for managing product life cycle information, *Commun. ACM*, 50(6), 75–79, 2007.

APPENDIX A: LIST OF COMPANIES MENTIONED IN THE CHAPTER

Alien Technology
18220 Butterfield Blvd.
Morgan Hill, CA 95037, USA
Phone: +1 408-782-3900
http://www.alientechnology.com

Checkpoint Systems
Velázquez, 7, 3
28001 Madrid, Spain
Phone: +34 914-322-500
http://www.checkpointeurope.com

Ecomovistand
Polígono La Serreta
Gabriel Campillo s/n
30500-Molina de Segura, Murcia, Spain
Phone: +34 968-642-732
http://www.ecomovistand.com

Gillette
Prudential Tower Building
Boston, MA 02199, USA
Phone: +1 617-421-7000
http://www.gillete.com

Hewlett Packard
PO Box 10301
Palo Alto, CA 94303-0890, USA
Phone: +1 650-857-1501
http://www.hewlett-packard.com

IBM
1 New Orchard Road
Armonk, NY 10504-1722, USA
Phone: +1 877-426-6006
http://www.ibm.com
Impinj

701 N. 34th Street, Suite 300
Seattle, WA 98103 USA
Phone: +1 866-467-4650
http://www.impinj.com

Intermec
Avda. Diagonal 611–9
Barcelona, 08028, Spain
Phone: +34 934-104-576
http://www.intermec.com

Johnson & Johnson
One Johnson & Johnson Plaza
New Brunswick, NJ 08933, USA
Phone: +1 732-524-0400
http://www.jnj.com/

Metro Group
Schlüterstrasse 1
40235 Düsseldorf, Germany
Phone: 492-116-8860
http://www.metrogroup.de

Microsoft
One Microsoft Way
Redmond, WA 98052-7329,
  USA
Phone: +1 425-882-8080
http://www.microsoft.com

Oracle
Oracle Corporation
500 Oracle Parkway
Redwood Shores, CA 94065,
  USA
Phone: +1 800-223-1711
http://www.oracle.com

Philips
Philips Ibérica S.A.
María de Portugal 1
28050 Madrid, Spain
Phone: +34 902-888-784
http://www.philips.com

Procter & Gamble
One Procter & Gamble Plaza
Cincinnati, OH 45202, USA
Phone: +1 513-983-1100
http://www.pg.com

Samsys
1321 Valwood Pkwy, Ste 620
Carrollton, TX 75006, USA
Phone: +1 972-243-7208
http://www.samsys.com

SAP
3999 West Chester Pike
Newtown Square, PA 19073,
   USA
Phone: +1 610-661-1000
http://www.sap.com

Symbol
Motorola, Inc.
One Symbol Plaza
Holtsville, NY 11742-1300, USA
Phone: +1 631-738-2400
http://www.symbol.com

Tesco
PO Box 73, Baird Avenue
Dryburgh Industrial Estate
Dundee DD1 9NF, UK
Phone: 0845-600-4411
http://www.tesco.com

Texas Instruments
PO Box 660199
Dallas, TX 75266-0199, USA
Phone: +1 972-955-2011
http://www.ti.com

Wal-Mart
702 Southwest Eighth Street
Bentonville, AR 72716-8611, USA
Phone: +1 502-731-4000
http://www.wal-mart.com

APPENDIX B: LIST OF PRODUCTS MENTIONED IN THE CHAPTER

Product Name	Description	URL
Accada	EPC network prototyping platform (European Accada project)	http://www.accada.org
FELICA card	SONY contactless smart card system	http://www.sony.net/Products/felica
MENTOR	MIT EPC Net (MENTOR project)	http://rolls.mit.edu/CS/
MT pallet	Ecomovistand pallet described in this chapter	http://www.ecomovistand.com

20 Radio-Frequency Identification Applications and Case Studies

Daniel A. Rodríguez-Silva, Sergio Costas-Rodríguez, Francisco Javier González-Castaño, and Felipe Gil-Castiñeira

CONTENTS

INTRODUCTION

Radio-frequency identification (RFID) tags are considered by some to be the natural substitutes of traditional barcodes and it is obviously desirable that barcode-assisted applications should benefit from advanced RFID features. A clear example is library inventorying, where it is possible to place a tag containing different information (such as book title, author, description, price, reference code, etc.) on the back inside cover of a book. RFID offers numerous advantages over traditional barcodes [1,2]: (a) there are no line-of-sight requirements between the tag and the reader, (b) multiple tags can be read at a time, (c) the tag has a memory for temporal data, and (d) tag read time is lower than with barcodes. Thanks to these advantages and a gradual reduction in costs in recent years, the use of RFID is expanding, although the technology is still mostly used in systems integration.

Choosing the right hardware for an RFID application is no easy feat. The following sections are intended to provide the reader with some insight into how RFID technology can be applied in practice, given the current state-of-the-art. We illustrate it with a selection of case studies, taken from relevant projects.

CHARACTERISTICS OF RFID TAGS

FREQUENCY RANGE

RFID relies on inductive coupling in both low (LF) and high (HF) frequencies and radio-electric coupling at in the ultra high frequency (UHF) band. Each working

	Inductive			Radioelectric	
	LF	MF	HF	VHF	UHF
Wavelength	3000 m	300 m	30 m	3 m	0.3 m
Frequency	100 KHz	1 MHz	10 MHz	100 MHz	1 GHz
Typical RFID bands	125/134 KHz		13.56 MHz		860–960 MHz 2.4 GHz

FIGURE 20.1   RFID frequencies.

frequency has particular characteristics to be considered when selecting a system [3] (Figure 20.1).

The range of operation grows with the antenna size but larger antennas cause greater interference. In inductive coupling, the read range is generally small but effective, whereas in radio-electric coupling, the range of operation is greater but irregularly shaped and often discontinuous. (Nearby readers are also more likely to suffer from mutual interference.) LF tags need more antenna spirals than HF tags, although they can be compressed to a greater extent. UHF tags are simple to manufacture, but they must accommodate large antennas; their range is also limited by transmitting power. LF radiation penetrates through water and common liquids, unlike HF (which achieves so to a lesser extent) and UHF (except for inductively coupled near-field operation). LF radiation can penetrate thin layers of conductive metals, while HF and UHF are effectively shielded by them. LF tag operation is limited to low data rates, whereas HF and UHF tags can support tens or hundreds of kilobits per second.

Choosing the optimal operating frequency is very important for any application and requires careful consideration of the characteristics of the different frequency bands. For example, for cattle identification, UHF should be discarded due to the high water content in living beings. However, it may be appropriate for cramped locations, due to the small size of UHF reader antennas.

POWER SUPPLY

In terms of the power supply, RFID tags can be passive, semi-passive/semi-active and active [4] (Figure 20.2).

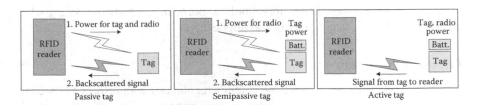

FIGURE 20.2   RFID tags and power supply.

Passive Tags

Passive tags are most common in RFID applications because of their price and size. They do not have an autonomous source of electrical power to drive the circuitry or a radio-transmitter of their own. They depend on the rectification of power received from the reader to support the operation of their circuitry, and modulate their interaction with the power transmitted from the reader in order to send information back (backscattered signal).

Semi-Passive Tags

Semi-passive tags have a local battery to power the tag circuitry (which can include sensors or volatile memory), but they still use backscattered communications for tag-to-reader communications. These tags are an interesting option for applications in which specific parameters (such as temperature, pressure, and position) need to be continuously monitored. Data are transmitted to the processing device by modulating the signal from the RFID reader (in the same manner as a passive tag).

Active Tags

Active tags have both a local power source and a conventional transmitter and are therefore equivalent to conventional bidirectional radio-communication devices. They are preferable when read range and speed are key factors, or when it is expected that large amounts of measurement may be transmitted at any time from any place, especially by moving objects. Although active RFID readers are cheaper than high-power passive readers, the corresponding tags are more expensive and battery recharging/replacement may be unfeasible in certain applications.

DATA ACCESS

Tags can also be classified according to how the information stored in the tag is accessed. There are three types of access modes [5] as follows:

- Read-only tags: information is stored when the tag is manufactured and cannot be modified. These tags usually only differ in terms of their identifiers.
- Write-once tags: the information they hold can only be saved once.
- Read-write tags: information can be saved and modified many times. These tags can store dynamic application-dependent information.

CRITERIA FOR TECHNOLOGY SELECTION

Based on the above, some key factors should be borne in mind when choosing which RFID technology best suits a particular application.

OPERATING FREQUENCY

The operating frequency depends on country regulations with respect to spectrum allocation. In general, higher operating frequencies increase the range between the tag and the reader, at the cost of a higher dependence on antenna directivity.

Possible nuisances such as interferences (by other readers in UHF) and noise (when using large antennas for HF) are other considerations. HF may seem preferable for access control systems due to the high liquid content in the human body whereas a multireader UHF system may be desirable for applications where large antennas are a nuisance for customers. Multiple antennas pointing in several directions can minimize the problem of body interception.

TYPE OF TAGS

Application requirements are an essential consideration when choosing the most appropriate tags. Active RFID tags have the longest range but they are expensive and need batteries that must be recharged or replaced. Semi-passive tags are adequate for collecting sensor data. For library inventorying, however, active tags are not suitable due to both their size and cost and the difficulties associated with installing a recharging infrastructure.

DATA ACCESS

It is important to decide how the data will be managed. Read-only tags are the cheapest option and may be sufficient in many applications provided that a database is indexed by tag identifiers. Tag encryption may be compulsory in access control applications, to protect user privacy.

TAG PHYSICAL DESIGN

Tag dimensions may be constrained by the operating frequency. In general, a larger size implies higher range (bigger inner antenna).

STANDARDS

Standards should be followed to avoid incompatibilities between applications and to facilitate scalability and updates (proprietary solutions are rare nowadays). Each standard has its own features. Examples of standards include ISO/IEC 18000, Electronic Product Code (EPC), and EPCglobal Class-1 Gen-2 [6].

ANTENNA

Antenna shape must be considered during the integration phase (arch antennas, e.g., are cumbersome in some industrial environments, such as the fishing industry). In general, a larger antenna has a longer range but is more sensitive to noise.

MATERIAL

The quality of components is related to the life and robustness of the devices used. The range of operating temperatures, for example, influence tag cost.

SURFACE

The composition of the items to be tagged is an essential consideration when choosing one technology or another. It is necessary to analyze whether the material will transmit, reflect, or absorb the radio-electric wave from the reader.

Paper and plastics are easy to tag as they are relatively transparent to RF signals.

Metal is a tricky surface because it can either strengthen the signal or block it completely. Careful placement and good antenna design improve tag performance (e.g., the metal surface can be used as part of the antenna). Water absorbs RF signals and tags should therefore be kept away from liquids as much as possible.

RFID INTEGRATION CYCLE

Once a hardware has been chosen for a given application, the integration cycle begins (Figure 20.3). This consists of a finding a balance between the practical constraints during actual usage and the application requirements. Based on this examination, a specific commercial product may be selected or, in extreme cases, a new RFID technology may be selected.

In a library, for example, it is necessary to detect the books left in a drop-off area fitted with a long-range RFID reader (requirement). However, some may be undetected due to their orientation (constraint), so it may be necessary to provide some physical references for the users to leave the books in certain "favorable" positions (updated requirement). In this case, it is not necessary to select a new technology.

RFID APPLICATIONS

A recent list of RFID applications can be found in Ref. [7]. These are applications that can be easily put into independent categories; however, the same technology can be used for different purposes within the same context, so that a single application may combine several RFID subapplications. A supply chain, for example, is made up of different stages (e.g., production, logistics, stock control), all of which can potentially be enhanced by RFID. In the next section, we distinguish between RFID general uses and application fields; Table 20.1 shows the relation between them.

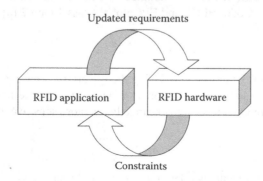

FIGURE 20.3   RFID integration cycle.

TABLE 20.1

Relations between RFID Uses and Application Fields

	Uses		
Application Fields	**Stock Control and Inventory**	**Tracking and Traceability**	**Security and Identification**
Production lines and manufacturing	High	High	Medium
Logistics	High	High	Medium
Object tracking	Medium	High	Medium
Real-time location tracking	Low	High	Medium
Supply chains	High	High	Medium
Access control	Low	Medium	High
Human, animal, and object identification	Low	High	High
Medical applications	Medium	High	Medium
Event management	Low	High	High
Law enforcement	Low	High	High
Documentation center management	High	High	High
Museums and exhibitions	Medium	Low	High

GENERAL USES OF RFID

RFID technology is currently applied in too many fields to list here. In this section, we provide some illustrative examples. Further information about RFID applications can be found in the literature, for example [1–3,7–9].

The nature of RFID technology permits the labeling of objects in order to perform operations or improve the applications in which the technology is used. We can distinguish three general categories, or uses: stock control and inventory, logistics, and security and identification.

STOCK CONTROL AND INVENTORY

Stock control, or inventory control, as it is also known, is used to determine and keep track of an existing stock continuously. It is applicable to every item used to produce a product or a service, from raw materials to finished goods. It covers stock at every stage of the production process, from purchase and delivery to usage and reordering. Efficient stock control means that the right amount of stock is available in the right place at the right time. It protects production from problems in the supply chain and avoids unnecessary costs.

RFID technology can be used to control the flow of items in large set-ups, typically warehouses, where it is necessary to manage large stocks levels. Individual

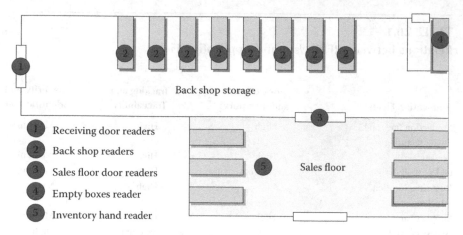

FIGURE 20.4 Read points in generic retail stores.

products and components can be identified and tracked throughout the supply chain, from production to point-of-sale. Each item is labeled with an RFID tag and readers can be placed at different points of the warehouse to detect the movement of goods and provide continuous inventory control (Figure 20.4).

One of the main applications of RFID stock control is in marketplaces where the continuous traffic of products is difficult to manage. RFID helps to reduce the problem of out-of-stocks (OOS), as was shown by the work of Hardgrave et al. [10]. Their studies showed that RFID reduced OOS by as much as 26% and in a comparison of test and control stores, the former outperformed the latter fourfold. An analysis of tagged vs. nontagged items (within the test stores) also revealed a threefold improvement for tagged items.

TRACKING AND TRACEABILITY

Logistics operations involve several processes such as the integration of information, transportation, warehousing, material-handling and packaging, and most importantly tracking and traceability.

Figure 20.5 shows the typical elements in a logistics application, which are as follows.

1. Production line logistics control system
2. Industrial logistics integration hub
3. Supply chain security control system
4. Cargo transportation management system
5. Logistics benchmarking management system
6. Enterprise efficiency evaluation and improvement system
7. Transportation and delivery support system
8. Electronic product code network and pedigree tracking system
9. Dynamic maintenance control system

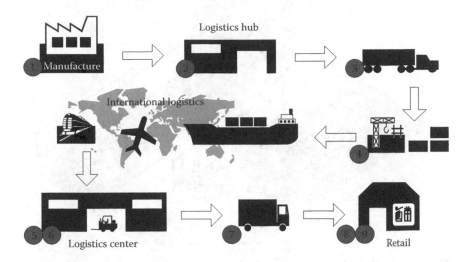

FIGURE 20.5 Elements of a logistic application.

Items can be tracked and traced by assigning unique identifiers to them. Once labeled, the information they contain can be read at different points as the items move through the supply chain. RFID readers can be installed at doors and gates or at entry or exit points to automatically detect when the merchandise reaches or leaves a controlled area. This information is then updated in the logistics database.

RFID tracking is not limited to industrial applications, however. It can be used also in the service sector, for example at sporting events to determine when spectators reach different checkpoints. Tracking can also be used in documentation centers to monitor items that are taken to reading areas or borrowed. As an extension of the industrial chain, it has been proposed to trace the food through RFID until the user's residence via packaging. When delivery is subject to deadlines, RFID is sometimes combined with real-time locating systems (RTLS).

SECURITY, IDENTIFICATION, AND ACCESS CONTROL

Security is an important concern in many applications. The need to authenticate the identities of persons or machines in certain areas in order to grant specific access permissions or privileges is very common in a number of situations. Individuals, for example, can be provided with an RFID identification badge. The best-known application in this area is access control, where RFID can provide an easy, efficient solution, which, in some cases, is transparent to the user. With RFID badges, users can be identified at much longer distances than with traditional technologies, and the information embedded in each badge can be repeatedly overwritten. The increased reading distance allows for easier integration with other tracking technologies such as surveillance cameras, which can be activated, for example, when an employee is approaching. Furthermore, multiple RFID badges can be read at the same time.

There are several ways of identifying users via RFID. As shown in Figure 20.6, (1) the user, wearing an RFID badge, is detected by RFID-enabled gates (*transparent*

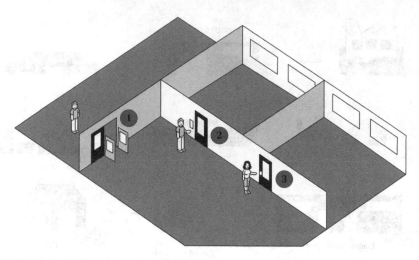

FIGURE 20.6   RFID for access control and security.

identification); (2) the user needs to pass his/her badge near an embedded RFID reader (*collaborative identification*); (3) the user, wearing an RFID wristband, is identified by an RFID reader on a door handle when he/she opens the door (*semi-transparent identification*).

The possibility of safely identifying a person wearing a badge has many interesting applications, particularly with relation to payment services. In hotels and resorts, for example, customer badges can contain information allowing access to different services. Another well-known access control application is electronic toll collection, where active tags are commonly used to increase reading range and effectiveness.

PRODUCTION LINES AND MANUFACTURING

A production line is a series of sequential operations in a factory, whereby raw or transformed materials enter a refining process to produce an end product that is suitable for onward consumption, or whereby components are assembled to make a finished article. RFID helps in this process by automatically tracking and identifying every component. It helps to match parts, saving costs and time, and convert production lines to just-in-time production systems. Vehicle, food and pharmaceutical manufacturing are some applications that have benefited from RFID, and Nissan, John Deere, and United Biscuits are good examples of firms that have implemented the technology.

LOGISTICS

As previously explained (see the previous section on Tracking and Traceability), tags allow items to be easily tracked, from their origin to their destination, and at any point in between. Tags may also hold relevant information about a particular item to ensure that it is treated in a special way (e.g., it could be a fragile good or have an imminent expiration date). This information ensures that item will be channeled to the appropriate exit point for onward shipping. RFID technology accelerates this process and eliminates human error. Kimberly Clark is an example of a company that uses RFID for logistics.

OBJECT TRACKING

Examples of object tracking applications include baggage management (Hong Kong Airport, Delta Airlines), waste and hazardous materials management, and sports event timing. It is relatively easy to install RFID readers on object tracking lines (Figure 20.7).

REAL-TIME LOCATING SYSTEMS

RTLS are fully automated systems that continually monitor the locations of assets and personnel. An RTLS solution typically utilizes battery-operated radio tags and a cellular locating system to detect the presence and location of the tags. The locating system is usually deployed as a matrix of locating devices across a space to determine the locations of the radio tags. In typical applications, RTLS can simultaneously track thousands of tags, and the average tag battery life can exceed five years. These applications include location of containers and cargo in docks and warehouses, or location of employees, contractors, and visitors in a facility (to assist in building evacuations, for instance).

SUPPLY CHAIN MANAGEMENT

A supply chain typically consists of a manufacturer, a retailer, and a distributor who uses logistics for transportation. Three types of tracking systems can be chosen: item-, case- and pallet-level tracking. RFID can be used in all cases to automate key processes, remove human intervention, and allow the straight-through processing of information [8,9]. Wal-Mart and Metro Group are some of the companies that claim to have successfully integrated RFID in their activities.

FIGURE 20.7   RFID for stock control and object tracking.

HUMAN AND ANIMAL IDENTIFICATION

The identification of subjects with embedded tags has many advantages in certain fields. RFID personal identity cards, for example, can hold more information than traditional ID documentation. They are also an interesting option for noncollaborative users such as children and elderly people, as they can be used to store information such as addresses or medical records (via bracelets or under-the-skin tags). RFID tags (placed under the skin or swallowed) can also be used in animals to replace traditional branding. Another widespread application is in the area of pet identification.

MEDICAL APPLICATIONS

RFID can be used in blood banks to ensure the correct selection of blood types by matching blood tags with a wristband worn by the patient. A similar procedure could be used in maternity wards to avoid mismatches between babies and mothers. RFID tags could also be used to manage medical parts (availability) and ensure that no surgical instruments are accidentally left inside the body after complex operations.

EVENTS MANAGEMENT

The management of large, complex events such as sports events (e.g., Olympic Games, marathons, and football matches), concerts, and exhibitions could be simplified by using RFID technology to help manage ticketing and access control processes or to track individuals by monitoring them at checkpoints. A good example of this is in ski resorts, where RFID badges automatically grant access to services such as equipment and locker rentals and the use of ski lifts.

LAW ENFORCEMENT

RFID can also be used in customs by placing tags in containers to be checked at control points. Another application is in cases of home arrest or women's protection. Potential attackers, for example, could be obliged to carry an RFID wristband that, if detected in a victim's home, would alert the authorities [11].

MANAGEMENT OF DOCUMENTATION CENTERS

Numerous services offered by documentation centers can be improved by RFID technology. Self-service operations (such as borrowing and returning books) can be implemented, for example, thanks to the ability of RFID systems to indirectly identify multiple objects at a time. A number of leading libraries, such as those in the Vatican and University of California at Berkeley, have implemented RFID-enabled services.

MUSEUMS AND EXHIBITIONS

The ability of RFID to identify items from a certain distance without the need for a direct line of sight between the reader and the item is an important feature of RFID technology. In museums and galleries, for example, pictures and works of art can be tagged to support automatic information systems for visitors carrying RFID-enabled personal devices. This is a great benefit for the visitor, who does not have to check and dial codes continuously to get information on the works. An access control system can also be used to limit access to temporary exhibitions.

CROSS-CLASSIFICATION OF RFID APPLICATIONS

As stated earlier, Table 20.1 relates the general uses of RFID to the most common areas of applications. In most cases, RFID can be used for different purposes within the same application field and this correspondence permits an assessment of the relative importance of the technology for a given application. In supply chains, for example, it can be used both for stock management and merchandise tracking, but much less for security and identification. In access control applications, RFID is used to identify individuals before allowing them into restricted areas; therefore, there is a strong correlation with its uses for security and identification; but tracking individuals and recording their movements is not always a concern.

RFID SPECIFIC CASE STUDIES

RFID IN GENERAL STORES: WAL-MART

Wal-Mart Stores, Inc. [12] is the world's largest public corporation of department stores by revenue, according to Fortune Global 500, 2007. Prior to the implementation of RFID technology, the company had an OOS rate of 8%, meaning that 1 out of 12 articles was not on the shelf when a customer wanted it, and this was one of the company's main reasons for adopting the technology. In June 2003, Wal-Mart launched its RFID initiative by issuing its first RFID mandate to its suppliers. In that mandate, the company required its top 100 suppliers to use passive RFID tags in cases and pallets. Tagging began in 2006 and soon 600 stores and 12 distribution centers were receiving RFID-enabled shipments.

Before RFID deployment, the process was completely manual. The attendants were responsible for checking all the shelves with a hand scanner, which built a picking list with the products to replenish (if available in stock). An inventory of available stock was also regularly kept to know when to order more products. This was a slow, tedious, and error-prone process when processing large amounts of merchandise (Figure 20.8).

RFID reader antennas have been added in Wal-Mart stores at four key points: the merchandise entrance, the back shop, the product container area, and the doors that communicate the back shop with the shop. More or less, the process is as follows:

- A box is unloaded from a truck. The RFID readers at the entrance read the tags and save the information in the store's inventory list.
- The box is carried to the back shop and placed in a container. The antennas read the box again and save the corresponding code in the stock list.
- When necessary, the box with the products is carried from the storage area to the shop. This is a proactive process as the decision depends on the sales

FIGURE 20.8 Merchandise management in a warehouse (without RFID). (Copyright iStockphoto.com, reproduced with permission.)

data from the cash registers and the stock list. When the box crosses the door, its code is removed from the stock list and added to the shop list.

- Once the products are sold, the empty box returns to the back shop. When the tag is read, again at the door, the code is removed from the shop list. This can be checked against the information from the cash registers.
- When the box is placed in the "empty boxes" container in the storage area, the corresponding antenna detects the tag and removes the code from the stock list.

The results grouped by the selling rates of the different products (sales velocity) are summarized in Table 20.2 [13]. The RFID system has no effect on products selling <0.1 units/day since these do not cause OOS situations due to their low sales. Products with rates of between 0.1 and 7 units/day showed an improvement of between 20% and 32% but those selling between 7 and 15 units/day performed best, with a reduction of 62%. Finally, there was no improvement for products selling over 15 units/day (uncommon) but the results were not conclusive. It is interesting to remark that over 90% tagged items sales were within 0.1 and 1 units/day. The aggregate reduction across all Wal-Mart stores for thousands of products is 30%, which is significant improvement.

RFID Vehicle Manufacturing: Thomas Built Buses

Vehicle manufacturing is a complex process with many tasks that can be automated with RFID technology. Thomas Built Buses [14] is one of the main bus manufacturers in the United States. The company grew very fast and evolved from its position

TABLE 20.2
OOS Reduction by Sales Velocity

Sales Velocity (units/day)	OOS Reduction (%)
<0.1	No reduction
0.1–0.2	32
0.2–0.3	32
0.3–0.5	20
0.5–1.0	36
1.0–3.0	29
3.0–7.0	32
7.0–15.0	62
>15.0	Inconclusive
Aggregate in the range of 0.1–15.0	30

Source: RFID Magazine: Impacto de la RFID en la rotura de stocks, 12 October 2006, http://www.rfid-magazine.com/_images/1278/02_Out_of_stocks.pdf

as a regional manufacturer to a leading national company with a 34% share of the U.S. school bus market, its main business.

Before the implementation of RFID, inventory updates on production lines (Figure 20.9) were made by manual scanning, a process which resulted in errors and caused a considerable delay in product availability.

The solution chosen to remedy this problem was an RFID traceability system for 40 stations connected to a database to register and store all movements and

FIGURE 20.9 Vehicle production line. (Copyright iStockphoto.com, reproduced with permission.)

relevant information. Fourteen RFID readers were used to trace movements along the production line and transmit information to the database through an intranet. Active UHF tags (915 MHz) were used throughout the whole manufacturing process, up to the point where the product is ready for delivery. When a work order is placed for a bus, a tag is attached to that bus with the order identification. As the bus progresses through the production line, the RFID readers collect the relevant information (such as location, entry, and exit times). With this system, it is simpler to produce custom products. At the end of the manufacturing process, the bus is taken to the pick-up area. This movement is automatically detected by the RFID system and the database is updated accordingly. The database indicates the exact location of the bus so that once it has been picked up, the tag is removed for reuse (over 100,000 times).

Experience has shown that the main benefits of the RFID system are as follows:

- Reduction in the time required to monitor production activities.
- Reduction in assembly errors due to human intervention.
- Improvement in quality of service. Each product is fully checked before delivery to ensure that it fulfills all the requirements.
- Reduction in total manufacturing time.
- Traceability support from start to finish, when the product is ready for pick up.
- Easy location of buses in the pick-up area.

RFID AT THE ROTTERDAM PORT

In modern large-scale ports, dozens of ships loaded with thousands of containers must be managed simultaneously (Figure 20.10). It is crucial to track these carefully because any mistake may send the merchandise to the wrong destination at a high expense. To

FIGURE 20.10 Container management in shipyards. (Copyright iStockphoto.com, reproduced with permission.)

speed up its processes without losing accuracy, Rotterdam port [15] decided to fully automate its container storage and recovery process by using automatic vehicles and cranes controlled by a central computer. The main difficulty with such a system is to know exactly where a given vehicle is at any time. Originally, inductive underground wires were used as guides, but this solution did not work. A simple wire failure or change in route implied major work and the interruption of port activity.

RFID technology provided a cheaper solution, which was not only more efficient and accurate but also yielded better logistics control. Furthermore, the use of passive transponders eliminated the need for power supply wires and batteries, meaning that the system was easier to install, more reliable, and free of maintenance. Finally, since the tags were embedded in the ground, the infrastructure was not affected by humidity or dirt.

The underground RFID transponders, positioned at a distance of 4 m from each other, form a matrix in the port terminals that serves as a reference for vehicle navigation since the tags hold unique (X,Y) coordinates. Since vehicle guidance requires high precision (3–10 cm), two antennas are attached to the vehicles so that they can calculate their relative position with respect to the transponders. The resulting precision is in the order of a centimeter, well within application requirements.

Thanks to this system, automatic vehicles and cranes follow their paths and pile containers with high accuracy, without the need for human intervention. The entire process is controlled by a central system that calculates the paths of all the vehicles. A vehicle only receives the direction changes it must follow and the system can stop one vehicle to give priority to another. There is no risk of collision, because all the vehicles have a set of sensors that can detect obstacles within a radius of 30 m.

Adopting RFID has increased the accuracy and reliability of Rotterdam port and saved costs and time by suppressing human intervention in tasks entailing risk.

RFID in Sports: Ironman Australia Triathlon

In sport races involving many participants, measuring individual times is a challenging task, but it is a task than can be simplified with RFID technology. To illustrate, over 1500 athletes took part in the 2006 Ironman Australia Triathlon [16] and it was necessary to accurately time these in the three stages of the race (3.8 km swimming, 180 km cycling, and 42 km running). To help achieve this goal, each athlete carried a 32-mm transponder on an ankle band (Figure 20.11). When a runner crossed a horizontal ground antenna at the start line of each stage, his/her time started to count, and when he/she crossed the horizontal antenna at the end of the stage, partial and total times were calculated and sent to a central server.

One of the main advantages of this system over traditional systems (in which humans measured times at the beginning and end of each stage) is that times are calculated individually for each athlete. This is particularly interesting for those who start the race several meters behind the start line.

Another major advantage is that antennas can be laid at intermediate points on the track to prevent cheating. The information relayed may also be of value for commentators. Note that the calculated times (average and total) are available for broadcasting almost in real-time.

FIGURE 20.11 Timing of marathons with RFID. (Copyright iStockphoto.com, reproduced with permission.)

Transponders are strong and impervious to dirt and humidity and can be used in any sport throughout the year. Furthermore, since sports applications rely on passive (battery-free) technology, the weight of tags is minimum and athletes are not aware of their presence.

ACCESS CONTROL: FIRA DE BARCELONA

Access control typically relies on passive technology, although long-range UHF systems with multiple antennas have been proposed for noncollaborative users to avoid body interception [17] (Figure 20.12).

Fira de Barcelona (Barcelona Trade Fair Center) has a tradition going back over 100 yr, when it held the 1888 Universal Exhibition. It organizes 80 trade fairs a year, drawing 30,000 exhibitors and some 3.5 million visitors.

The trade fair center installed a new access control system in 2006. The designed access point had to fulfill the needs of the various types of public and trade fairs as well as operate on-line and autonomously. The result was an access point equipped with a central processing unit, a 6-inch screen, and the following components:

1. An RFID proximity reader
2. An RFID Fast Pass reader
3. A bar code reader
4. A two-dimensional code reader (QR, DataMatrix)
5. A mobile phone reader
6. A ticket validator

The different devices permit many forms of accreditation for various types of trade fairs and public. The system is managed by Web-oriented software, which is

FIGURE 20.12   UHF access control in public spaces. (Courtesy of Quobis Networks SL.)

used to configure the access points and constantly monitor the operation of the devices. Access statistics, generated in real-time, allow immediate response in the event of overcrowding or system malfunction. With these access points, Fira de Barcelona has complete control of access to its facilities.

RFID in Electronic Toll Collection: E-ZPass

Electronic toll collection is a technological road pricing solution that minimizes delays (Figure 20.13). It determines whether passing cars are registered, alerts

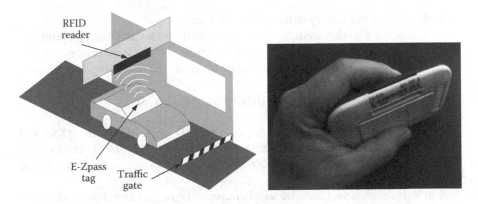

FIGURE 20.13   Electronic toll collection with RFID.

authorities if they are not, and automatically charges the accounts of registered cars without requiring them to stop.

E-ZPass is an RFID-enabled payment system that is used for collecting tolls on roads and bridges in many U.S. states [18]. Its purpose is to mitigate traffic congestion and delays, and is valid for cars driving between different states.

The car is automatically detected as it crosses below the RFID reader thanks to an active tag behind the rear view mirror. An E-ZPass installation consists of E-ZPass tags containing active RFID transponders (900 MHz) in each vehicle and readers (with long-range antennas) on traffic lanes, usually at toll-booths. When a car passes through the designated E-ZPass lane at the toll booth, its identifier is sent to a computer network to process the payment.

The benefits for the customers are clear as follows:

- No need to carry spare change
- No tickets or tokens
- Less waiting time at toll booths
- Toll discounts in some systems

Despite some hacking attempts and complaints from customers regarding the privacy of the system, E-ZPass ranks among the most successful RFID applications, with more than 10 yr of commercial use.

RFID IN LIBRARIES: THE LIBER-IMMS PROJECT

Large libraries are complex organizations that have to deal with huge amounts of items. The management of such volumes has relied on the use of barcode labels for a long time. These labels are cheap yet easy to damage. Even worse, the optimization of librarian tasks is constrained by the fact that item handling requires the manual alignment of a barcode reader with the tag. RFID seems like a suitable technology for library environments and may help to improve reshelving and inventory tasks as well as loan and return operations. An RFID library system (Figure 20.14) usually comprises the following items:

- RFID tags (for library items and user badges)
- Self-service workstations: a computer, an RFID reader and a receipt printer
- An administration desk: a self-service workstation plus card printer
- RFID-enabled return baskets to assist librarians in reshelving and related services
- Optional RFID antitheft gates (relying on item tags)

Typically, library systems employ passive RFID standards in the 13.56-MHz band, such as ISO/IEC 14443 (Proximity Card) and ISO/IEC 15693 (Vicinity Card). Current anti-collision protocols allow the simultaneous detection of a pile of books on a library tray.

Software developers, hardware suppliers, and service providers have collaborated in the development of library management systems (LMS) with RFID extensions.

FIGURE 20.14 Left: book tagging; center: self-service workstation; right: drop-off area.

Examples include Bibliotheca, Libramation, and Tagsys, and new systems are emerging continuously.

The LIBER-IMMS European project [19] was set up to quantify the benefits of using RFID technology in libraries. Its pilots were deployed in several libraries of varying profiles located in different countries. The project simultaneously collected data from traditional and RFID systems for an objective evaluation of RFID performance from two points of view: efficiency (time and cost) and user acceptance. The results [20] demonstrated that RFID improved many services, although users were more receptive to the technology than librarians, who were not keen to see the automation of certain processes.

Table 20.3 shows the results of RFID deployment in LIBER pilots over eight months. The most apparent benefit is in loans, where RFID-enabled operations were over three times faster than traditional operations with barcodes. Another advantage of the RFID system is the lower time to reshelf books, since they are easier to locate. A Personal Digital Assistant (PDA) equipped with an RFID antenna can read all the books in drop-off area simultaneously, and display a sorted list with reshelving instructions. A similar procedure can be used to determine if a requested book is

TABLE 20.3
Comparison of RFID and Traditional LMS

Criterion of Comparison	RFID LMS	Traditional LMS
Average time to tag a book (in s)	15	19
Cost of materials required to tag a book (in €)	0.52	0.2
Average time to reshelve a book (in s)	19	22
Number of books requested from the librarian	9.2	11.7
Average time to lend an item (in s)	16	58
Average time to return an item (in s)	14	15

located in the returning area (neither lent nor available), saving librarian time. However, returning operations are not necessarily faster: when the book is left in the drop-off area, the user must check on a screen if it was correctly read to get a returning ticket. With the traditional system, the book is given directly to the librarian.

The advantages of RFID for different library services can be summarized as follows:

- Membership: no identification mistakes, higher efficiency, improved safety.
- Lending: easy to use, do-it-yourself, no waiting time, no need for librarians, efficiency.
- Returning: no need for librarians, increase efficiency of utilization of library staff.
- Availability: time-saving; the customer knows the exact status of a book (on the shelf, in the lecture room, borrowed, etc.).

SUMMARY

RFID is a suitable technology that can improve many applications, especially those involving repetitive, manual tasks. It presents several clear benefits over barcode technology, the current dominant technology. There are many RFID hardware configurations to choose from, each with different characteristics to suit different applications. Indeed, the nature of an application may lead to hardware changes and new specifications during the RFID integration cycle. Despite the many benefits of RFID, however, it is not yet a plug and play technology. Although it may be difficult to integrate in same cases, as we have seen in this chapter, there are many success stories in diverse application fields.

REFERENCES

1. Sweeney, P. J., *RFID for dummies*, John Wiley & Sons, Indianapolis, IN, 2005, Chaps. 2 and 6.
2. Manish, B. and Shahram, M., *RFID Field Guide: Deploying Radio Frequency Identification Systems*, Prentice Hall PTR, Upper Saddle River, NJ, 2005, Chap. 13.
3. Finkenzeller, K., RFID Handbook. Fundamentals and Applications in *Contactless Smart Cards and Identification*, 2nd edn., John Wiley & Sons, Munich, Germany, 2003, Chaps. 5 and 13.
4. Dobkin, D. M., *The RF in RFID. Passive UHF RFID in Practice*, Elsevier, Burlington, MA, 2008, Chap. 2.
5. Hult, V. D., Puglia, A., and Puglia, M., *RFID-A Guide to Radiofrequency Identification*, John Wiley & Sons, Hoboken, NJ, 2007, Chaps. 2 and 5; Appendix A.
6. Chawla, V. and Ha, D. S., An overview of passive RFID, *IEEE Commun Magaz.*, 45(9), 11–17, 2007.
7. Polniak, S., *RFID Technology Applications: RFID Case Studies*, Ebook, Abhisam Software, available at http://www.bin95.com/case_studies/RFID_Technology_Applications.htm, 2007, last accessed July 13, 2009.
8. Myerson, J. M., *RFID in the Supply Chain. A Guide to Selection and Implementation*, Auerbach, Boca Raton, FL, 2007, Chap. 3.

9. Thornton, F. et al., *RFID security. Protect the Supply Chain*, Syngress, Rockland, MA, 2007, Chap. 2.
10. Hardgrave, C. B., Waller, M., and Miller, R., Does RFID reduce Out of Stocks? A preliminary analysis, Sam M. Walton College of Business, available at http://itri.uark.edu/91.asp?code=&article=ITRI-WP058-1105, 2005.
11. Gil-Castiñeira, F. J. et al., Personal microdevices for wide area Location via mobile gateways, *Proceedings of the MobileHCI'05*, Salzburg, Austria, September 2005, ACM, New York, pp. 381–382.
12. Wal-Mart website: http://walmart.com.
13. Hardgrave, C. B., Waller, M., and Miller, R., RFID's impact on Out of Stocks: A sales velocity analysis, Sam M. Walton College of Business, available at http://itri.uark.edu/91.asp?code=&article=ITRI-WP068-0606, 2005.
14. Thomas Built Buses website: http://www.thomasbus.com.
15. Port of Rotterdam website: http://www.portofrotterdam.com.
16. Ironman Australia Triathlon website: http://www.ironmanoz.com.
17. Costas-Rodriguez, S. et al., On the implementation of a multi-reader radio frequency identification (RFID) architecture, *Proceedings of the IEEE International Symposium on Industrial Electronics, 2007, ISIE 2007*, IEEE, Vigo (Spain), June 2007, pp. 2562–2566.
18. E-ZPass website: http://www.ezpass.com
19. Public liberary RFID_based system for interactive Internet and mobile messaging services, LIBER_IMMS project, available at http://ec.europa.eu/information_society/activities/eten/cf/opcdb/cf/project/index.cfm?mode=detail&project_ref=ETEN-517468, last accessed July 13, 2009.
20. Rodríguez-Silva, D. A. et al., Quantitative assessment of the benefits of RFID technology for libraries: A trans-European study, *Proceedings of the IEEE Workshop Automatic Identification Advanced Technologies*, AutoID 2007, Alghero, Italy, June 2007, pp. 128–133.

Section V

Standards

21 Information Modeling in Production Management: The ISO 15531 MANDATE Standard[*]

Anne-Françoise Cutting-Decelle,
Jean-Luc Barraud, Bob Young,
Jean-Jacques Michel, and Michel Bigand

CONTENTS

---

[*] J.J. Michel is currently the convener of the ISO TC184 SC4-SC5 JWG8 joint working group. Most of the authors of the chapter are experts of this group and delegates of their respective countries for the ISO TC184 SC4 and the ISO TC 184 SC5 international standardization committees.

INTRODUCTION

The primary inputs to production systems (PS) are requirements, concepts, systems parameters, raw materials, components, and management policies. Their outputs are finished products and their related information, including quality. This chapter shows how the use of standardized information models improves the management of the information in PS.

The performance of PS can be assessed from five points of view: planning, scheduling, simulation, control, and execution. Planning and scheduling is the process of allocating limited resources, in light of simulation studies, to production tasks on the basis of machine characteristics, production requirements, time of performance, production constraints, and economical factors. Through the use of control technologies, the control system determines the sequences of actions in the actual manufacturing process. One of the activities during the execution is to track the performance and provide feedback to the control system to adjust the control sequences.

The planning process is a recurring activity to seek the optimal scheduling of material flow on the basis of available data, internal or external data, subjective information, and sometimes with no information at all. The steps of planning, scheduling, control, and execution may be sequential or parallel. In many cases, by the time the system design is finished, the original requirements may have changed. This is why newer systems development methodologies are based on a rapid, concurrent prototyping with frequent feedback to validate the requirements. As explained by Frankovic et al. [1], such an approach requires the coordination of parallel activities and fast information acquisition and processing as well as efficient communication.

Standardized information models and the automated exchanges of data improve the accuracy of information sharing among all parties to the production, both within and outside the enterprise. Standards also facilitate the interoperability of software tools and they contribute to the integration of the production process into the product life management process.

First, we summarize the international activities that lead to the development of the ISO 15531 MANDATE (MANufacturing DATa Exchange) standard. The four information models of ISO 15531 are then presented. We describe how the joint use of these models enables a modular approach to the management of production and to the integration of all the information needed in production.

STANDARDS IN MANUFACTURING

The focus of manufacturing management is the flow of materials and products across the whole production chain starting with suppliers through manufacturers and assemblers to distributors and sometimes customers. The efficiency and accuracy of these exchanges can be enhanced by electronic communications, particularly, if the information handled during these exchanges is modeled and represented in a standard way.

The role of standardization in integration and its potential benefits vary according to the level and the type of integration:

- In the case of full integration, the standard is the software itself.
- In the case of integration by unification, the integration makes use of standardized components (constructs, partial models) and standardized interfaces.

- In the case of integration by federation (e.g., legacy software built around various products), standardized interfaces and communication standards may be used as well as standardized translators.

Three main categories of data are needed in manufacturing management: those related to time management, those related to resource management, and finally those related to the management of the manufacturing processes. Standards are particularly useful because they provide standardized components (enterprise models, partial models, constructs) that are shareable, reusable, and interoperable. They also convey and preserve the common part of the semantics included in the various enterprise (and inter-enterprise) applications. Data structuring in conformance with a given data model facilitates the management of databases built at the manufacturing management level, most of the time for historical and management purposes [2].

ISO STANDARDIZATION PROCESS

The different stages leading to the development of an international standard (IS) by the International Organization for Standardization (ISO) are as follows:

- Initial stage: working draft (WD).
- First standardization stage: committee draft.
- Further stages: draft international standard (DIS), and final draft international standard.
- Last stage: IS.

A voting procedure at the international level is necessary to go from one stage to another.

ACTIVITIES OF ISO TC184

ISO TC184 is one of the ISO committees responsible for "standardization in the field of industrial automation and integration concerning discrete part manufacturing and encompassing the applications of multiple technologies, that is, information systems, machines and equipments and telecommunications." This means that the standards developed are applicable to manufacturing and process industries, applicable to all sizes of business, to extending exchanges across the globe through e-business.

In manufacturing, standards are developed for system integration and to capture the enterprise semantics. The standards developed by the ISO TC184 and its different subcommittees cover various domains related to industrial automation and integration. Among the subjects covered are enterprise modeling, enterprise architecture, communications and processes, integration of industrial data for exchange, access and sharing, life cycle data for process plants, manufacturing management, mechanical interfaces and programming methods, part libraries, physical device control, product data, and robots for manufacturing environment etc. The Process Specification Language, an ontology-based language aimed at representing process concepts defined in ISO 18629-1 [3], is also within the scope of TC184.

The goal of SC4 is the creation and maintenance of standards that enable the capture of information comprising a computerized product model in a neutral form without loss of completeness and integrity throughout the life cycle of the product. The activity of the SC4 committee deals with standardization of the industrial data related to products including, but not limited to, geometric design and tolerance data, material and functional specifications, product differentiation and configuration, process design data, production data (including cost), product support and logistics, life cycle data, quality data, and disposal planning data. It also includes organizational data provided by relationships between enterprises or between components of a single enterprise for the purposes of supplier identification. The field of activities covers human resource data but specifically excludes business planning data, such as profit projections, cash flow, and any other personnel data or organizational data.

The main standards developed within the framework of ISO TC 184/SC4 and related to the management of manufacturing information are:

- The Standard for the Exchange of Product Model Data (STEP) (ISO 10303) designed for product data modeling based on the EXPRESS modeling language and on "integrated resources."
- Part Library (P-LIB) (ISO 13584) standard whose scope is the design and provisioning of parts library and components. This standard has been implemented, particularly in Japan, and is well suited to e-business. Currently, specific standardized catalogues are being developed for fasteners, cutting tools, measurement devices, and so on, often in joint collaboration with International Electrotechnical Communication (IEC).
- The ISO 15531 MANDATE standard, which builds on the previous standards to specify constructs or information models.

We now turn our attention to the management of PS using the ISO 15531 standard.

MANAGEMENT OF MANUFACTURING WITH THE ISO 15531 MANDATE STANDARD

MANDATE is an IS for the computer-interpretable representation and exchange of industrial manufacturing management data. The purpose is to facilitate the integration of industrial applications by means of common, standardized software tools. MANDATE is suitable, not only for a file exchange using a neutral format, but also as a basis for implementing and sharing manufacturing management databases and archiving. The standard is focused on, but is not limited to, discrete manufacturing.

ISO 15531 is a good example of the links between research and standardization, since the different models that it uses were initially developed as research topics. They were then proposed as New Work Items (NWI) to the Joint Working Group (JWG8) of the joint standardization committees ISO TC184 and subcommittees SC4 ("industrial data") and SC5 ("systems architecture and communications"). Once accepted as NWI, the different models have provided the "parts" of the standard, each of them going through the different stages of the standardization process at the international level.

ORGANIZATION OF ISO 15531

The standard is organized as a series of parts, each published separately. The various parts belong to the following series:

Manufacturing resources usage management data (3x series):

- ISO 15531-31: Resource information model: Basic concepts [4].
- ISO 15531-32: Conceptual model for resources usage management data [5].

Manufacturing flow management data (4x series):

- ISO 15531-42: Time model [6].
- ISO15531-43: Data model for manufacturing flow management [7].
- ISO DIS 15531-44: Manufacturing management information modelling for shop floor data acquisition [8].

All the parts of the MANDATE standard are written using the EXPRESS language of ISO 10303-11 [9], which is the language used for all standards developed by the ISO TC184 standardization committee. MANDATE Part 1 [10] provides a general overview and specifies the functions of the various parts of the standard and the relationships among them. Part 1 also specifies relations to the other standards developed within the framework of the ISO TC184 committee.

INFORMATION MODELS OF THE ISO 15531 MANDATE STANDARD

To date, the standard provides four information models: the resource usage management model, the data model for the management of manufacturing flows, the time model and the information model for the shop floor data acquisition systems. These models are described in this section. As stated earlier, these models were the subjects of research activities before being proposed as NWI to the ISO standardization process.

RESOURCE USAGE MANAGEMENT MODEL

The conceptual information model for resources usage management data consists of six logical modules [5]. They are: resource hierarchy (generic, specific, individual resource), resource characteristics and administration (administrative information), resource status (whether the resource is available), resource view (specific aggregation of resources), resource representation (physical values), and resource configuration. The different modules are illustrated in Figure 21.1.

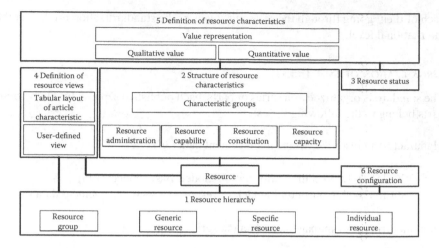

FIGURE 21.1 Overview of the resource information model of ISO 15531-32 [5]. (Copyright ISO, with permission.)

The term of "schema" as defined by the ISO 10303-11 EXPRESS language is a set of conditions and entities that establish a domain. The entity resource is the central element of the schema. A resource is characterized by different properties, which are organized in the schema in categories. Each category groups the features usually met in resource management software applications and corresponds to some required information about the resources.

A `resource` is the basic element for resource management. A resource can be generic, specific, or individual and may in turn be made of a number of other resources. A resource is not *a priori* related to any given activity; it exists and may be managed before any assignment to an activity, which is the typical case of human resources.

Resource properties are defined by references to external modules, or catalogues, structured using the ISO 13584 P-LIB standard [11]. The process properties and flow properties are defined by references to external modules or part catalogues, structured according to the ISO 13584 P-LIB standard.

Figure 21.2 shows the resource usage management schema, as defined in Part 15531-32 using the graphical representation of the EXPRESS language (EXPRESS-G) of ISO 10303-11 [9]. In this schema, the resource entity appears through its relationships with other entities; these relationships define its characteristics, such as the representation of the resource (qualitative or quantitative values) and the view of the resource (defined as a table of predefined values or user-defined values).

DATA MODEL FOR THE MANAGEMENT OF MANUFACTURING FLOWS

ISO 15531-43 addresses the modeling of data for the management of manufacturing flows as well as flow controls in a shop floor or in a factory [7]. This manufacturing flow model is provided in the context of various processes running simultaneously

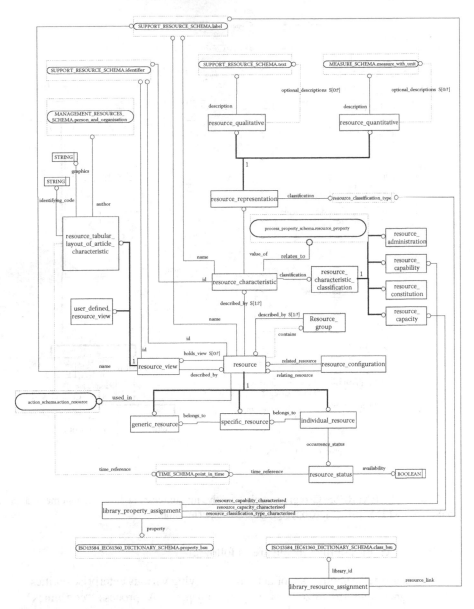

FIGURE 21.2 EXPRESS-G schema definition of the resource usage management model of ISO 15531-32 [5]. (Copyright ISO, with permission.)

and/or sequentially, providing one or more products and/or components and involving numerous resources as indicated in Figure 21.3. This part provides a way to model the data necessary to the management of the multiple complex flows among the different manufacturing processes of a factory. These flows include products, components, or raw material flows as well as services flows such as information flows [12].

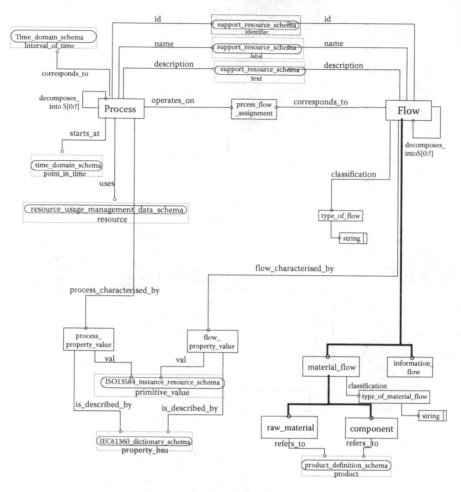

FIGURE 21.3 EXPRESS-G representation of the manufacturing flow management data schema in ISO 15531-43 [7]. (Copyright ISO, with permission.)

The main entities of the schema are as follows:

- Process: structured set of activities involving various enterprise entities, designed and organized for a given purpose. A process "consumes" resources, and is allocated a starting point (point in time) and a duration.
- Flow: motion of a set of physical or informational objects in space and time.

Flows are categorized into material flows and information flows. Both processes and flows are associated with properties defined in the P-LIB standard. They can be decomposed into sets of subprocesses and subflows, respectively. For compatibility with the ISO 10303 STEP standard, the names and identificators of process and flow entities follow the STEP naming rules and conventions.

TIME MODEL

One of the challenges of the time model of ISO 15531-42 is to propose a global representation to integrate different geographic regions, countries, and time zones into a common representation [6]. This model is particularly suited to the representation of scheduling applications.

The time model comprises two schemas: the domain property schema and the time domain schema (also called "time schema"). The domain property schema provides a generic topological structure applicable to any one-dimensional variable. The time domain schema is an instantiation of the previous generic structure to the "time" variable. We present here the time domain schema represented in Figure 21.4.

This schema provides a definition of concepts related to the time representation that are necessary for software applications mainly dealing with scheduling and manufacturing management operations. It enables multiple representations of time domains, intervals of time, points in time, and time units. A time domain is defined as a period, mathematically represented as a set of points in time. A point in time is defined by a selected location on the time axis, through the use of a time unit. Examples are the worked period within a year or the maintenance period of a machine tool.

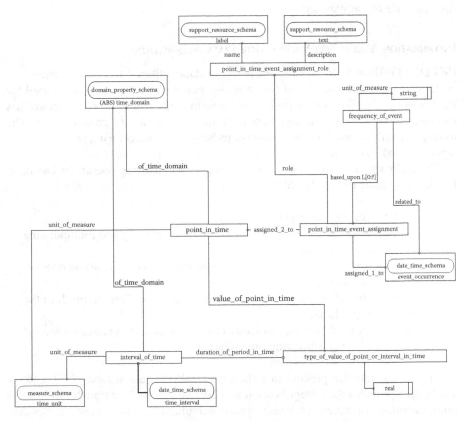

FIGURE 21.4   Time domain schema of ISO 15531-42 [6]. (Copyright ISO, with permission.)

A time domain may be finite or infinite. It may be bounded by one or two points in time. A time domain may be composed of other time domains (in a recursive relationship). A time unit is used to measure the duration in the related time domain.

Since the time domain and all its related subcategories define categories of sets of points only, another entity is needed to consider the length, the duration of a period in time. This concept is provided by the entity `interval_of_time`, whose duration is given by the type of value of point or interval of time entity.

The concept of frequency of events enables the characterization of the intervals of time separating event occurrences. Transformation rules between two time domains are provided through the entity `time_domain_relation`. These rules can be expressed either in terms of time units or in terms of change of origin (translation). These transformation rules are necessary to compare points in time in different time domains (e.g., a time domain defined with the months of the year, and a time domain containing the number of worked hours in a week).

The time model is a "new" standard: as such, there has not been to date a large enough number of implementations enabling to analyze the benefits and/or drawbacks of the approach. Notably, the model has not yet been tested against the requirements of the just-in-time approach in production and supply chain management. This is planned for the future and could be of a great interest to the approach followed in this fascicule of the standard.

INFORMATION MODEL FOR SHOP FLOOR DATA ACQUISITION

ISO DIS 15531-44 addresses the modeling of data collected from data acquisition systems at the control level and stored at the manufacturing management level for further processing [8]. Time stamping and time measurement by the data acquisition systems for control and management data are also taken into consideration. The model is mainly focused on the relationships between manufacturing process events, activities, and state changes.

Generally speaking, the functions related to manufacturing operations can be at five levels as indicated in IEC 62264-1 [13]:

- Level 0 is for the actual physical processes.
- Level 1 consists of the functions involved in the sensing and manipulating of the physical processes.
- Level 2 is reserved for the functions involved in the monitoring and controlling of the physical process.
- Level 3 is that of the functions for managing the work flows to produce the desired end-products.
- Level 4 is for the functions involved in the business-related activities needed to support the manufacturing organization.

The data acquisition process in a shop floor collects data at Level 2 (shop floor level), then provides their identification and content before their transfer to Level 3 (manufacturing management level). These manufacturing data concern devices, manufacturing batches, products or staff. They are used to compute the key performance indicators and to monitor the quality of operations. These data also enable the validation of shop floor models and scheduling through manufacturing scenarios proposed by simulation applications.

MODEL ENTITIES

The entities described in the conceptual model are generic enough to be specialized (refined description and instantiation) according to the use of the model within the enterprise, through the use of P-LIB libraries.

This part of the standard is currently under development. The guiding principles of the model are as follows:

- To address the lot of products or components to be produced.
- To include the information that is predefined and related to the equipment independently of its mode, status, and also independently of the work-order it operates.
- To address unexpected noticeable incidents that occur during the manufacturing process, such as the failure of a resource (whether equipment or human). The failure will have to be important enough to warrant recording.
- To know the result of a control.
- To be able to identify an anomaly detected on a product, semi-finished product, or subassembly. This detection leads to a discard of the concerned product.
- To know the level of stocks of products, components, or raw material, which are not on the fabrication line.

In the following section, we show the use of the standard in terms of products, processes, and resources management through the example of an industrial production management system.

APPLICATION OF THE MANDATE STANDARD

The APICS Dictionary defines Manufacturing Resource Planning (MRPII) as "a method for the effective planning of all resources of a manufacturing company. Ideally, it addresses operational planning in units, financial planning in dollars, and has a simulation capability to answer what-if questions. It is made up of a variety of processes, each linked together: business planning, production planning (sales and operations planning), master production scheduling, material requirements planning, capacity requirements planning, and the execution support systems for capacity and material. Output from these systems is integrated with financial reports such as the business plan, purchase commitment report, shipping budget, and inventory projections in dollars. Manufacturing resource planning is a direct outgrowth and extension of closed-loop MRP" [14].

In this section, we discuss the implementation of the models in an MRPII approach.

GENERICITY OF THE STANDARD

MANDATE provides a generic approach to some of the main concepts used in production management systems in terms of products, processes, and resources. It cannot be used without specializing or else tailoring the constructs of resources, time, processes, and flows developed in Parts 32, 42, 43, and 44 to the needs of the enterprise. Tailoring is possible through knowledge about the company, its history, the know-how of the enterprise, its added-value, and the skills of its personnel. Thus, ISO 15531 provides links to external component libraries: resource libraries, flow libraries, and process libraries. Most of the time, however, the knowledge is implicit, that is, not formalized or coded in a specific electronic format. This knowledge may also be embedded in a set of procedures often developed within the framework of a quality-based approach.

MANDATE does not target specific processes and resources. All information, characteristics, features, and catalogue data related to processes and resources are considered as external to the standard and are specified by the ISO 13584 P-LIB standard.

The development of P-LIB-based libraries, stored independently from any particular software tool, is a powerful way to record and to structure their know-how, activities, and skills. It is also a way to make this knowledge modular, thus more adaptable to new situations that companies may face in the future. Finally, it improves the interoperability of the different software applications used throughout the different departments and/or plants of the companies.

JOINT USE OF THE INFORMATION MODELS

Many companies realize that methodologies and "productivity tools" are essential to be competitive in manufacturing and comply with the relevant international quality requirements [15]. In this context, the MANDATE models bring an important contribution to the representation of information in the MRPII approach.

Figure 21.5 shows the main information models in an MRPII environment. The MANDATE models can be used to structure the information and the data exchanged at the functional interfaces (or "boxes") of the schema. It can contribute to the integration of the different functions of planning, scheduling, simulation, quality assurance, control, and execution. In this figure, various lines connecting the different functional blocks represent the flows of material (raw materials and subassemblies/components used to make the final products), in addition to process and flow information as well as resources information.

The industrial example shown in Figures 21.6 through 21.8 corresponds to the "assembly workshop" box of the Figure 21.5. In this case, all the data and information necessary for the Enterprise Resource Planning and Manufacturing Execution Systems applications of the manufacturing enterprise, including data acquisition provided by the shop floor are here stored into the Oracle DBMS.

Figure 21.6 illustrates the output of the manufacturing execution system, with the results for a given machine about a manufacturing order.

The following information is made available to other enterprise applications:

- Definition of the equipment (machines) that are production resources through the following attributes: name, resource number, genealogy: shop floor/line/cell/machine/station, phase.

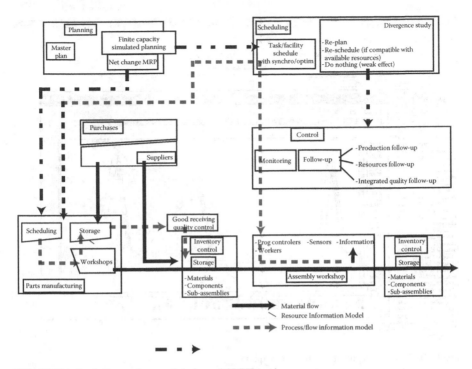

FIGURE 21.5   Information models in an MRPII environment.

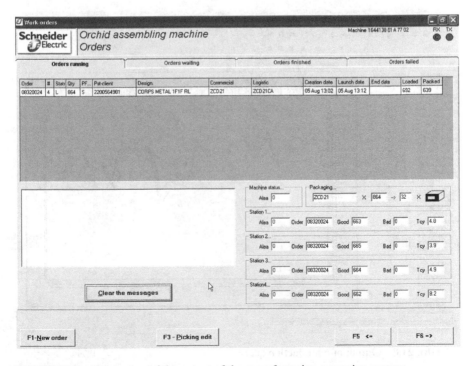

FIGURE 21.6   Illustration of the output of the manufacturing execution system.

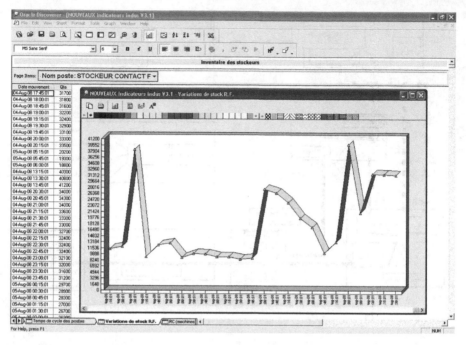

FIGURE 21.7   Output of an inventory query.

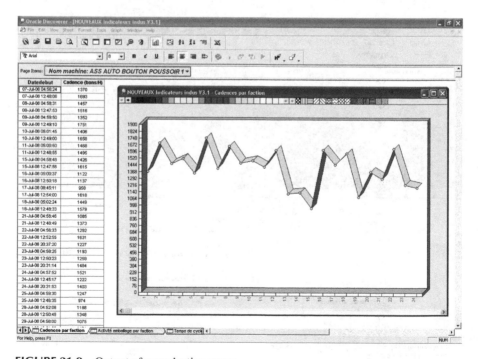

FIGURE 21.8   Output of a production query.

- Bills of materials providing intermediate stocks for the different assemblies (linked to the equipments).
- Manufacturing order.
- Resource scheduling (human and materials).
- Information related to supply chain management: packaging and dispatch.
- History of the data acquisition: production quantitative follow-up (quantities, time spent), qualitative follow-up (measures), and machines follow-up.

Figures 21.7 and 21.8 depict the output of queries made to the Oracle DBMS. These analyses are made possible by the integration of the relational database into the whole manufacturing execution system.

DISCUSSION

To date, in the domain of information representation and management, standardization committees have mostly concentrated on the semantics of the message to share, store, and exchange data, information, and knowledge. Besides, product data engineering is now mature and enterprises are more and more interested in the standardization of their whole information systems and architectures.

Although numerous standards are available and applicable at different levels of production management systems, their joint use highlights various problems, among which the lack of compatibility of the information models, the vocabulary used, not defined in the same way, even though the terms used are the same [16]. Ontology-based approaches are necessary to find the common "essence" of the information handled. Ontologies can be integrated into software interfaces, making it easier to convey a higher level of semantics for the exchanges.

Intelligent collaboration and integration in manufacturing are characterized by:

- The level of integration (physical, application, and business)
- The way of integration (top-down or bottom-up approach)
- The expected results (full integration, unification, and federation)
- The tools and methods implemented (enterprise organization integration, enterprise architecture, data integration, communication integration, and integration through interfaces and translations)

The methods for integration can be grouped into the following three categories:

- Data integration (integration through data models). This form of integration is addressed by the standards developed in ISO TC184/SC4 (Industrial data) [17,18].
- Organization integration (integration based on enterprise models, process models, decisional models): mainly addressed by standards developed in ISO TC184/SC5 (systems architecture and communications).
- Communication integration (integration based on network communication models and tools): also addressed by standards developed in ISO TC184/SC5 but IEC SC65 also addresses the same domain although with a different point of view.

The MANDATE standard provides an integration methodology applicable to production management systems. It is expected that its industrial usage will develop along with the physical instantiation of P-LIB catalogues. Although this will take time, the financial rewards can be substantial, provided that all information about products, resources, and flows are available in electronic formats. As an illustration, a study from the U.S. National Institute of Standards and Technology (NIST) in 2002, highlighted that the use of ISO 10303 (STEP) presently saves more than 120 million US$ per year and will save 900 million US$ per year in 2010 in the U.S. aerospace, automotive and ship-building industry [19,20]. The exact savings are obviously for the STEP standard; however, the interoperability problems mentioned in the document and their consequences in terms of cost also apply to all the standards developed within the framework of the ISO TC184 SC4 and SC5 committees.

In terms of perspectives for the future, several domains still need to be addressed, among which conformance checking, through the development of testing procedures in order to assess the reliability and the quality of the exchanges through the MANDATE models. It will also be necessary to guarantee the security of the exchanges, particularly for sensible or possibly confidential information.

Another important extension of the current work consists in the integration of the previous models into more generic business process modeling frameworks and approaches, such as the Capability Maturity Model Integration (CMMI), or the Information Technology Infrastructure Library (ITIL), thus leading to the development of integrated models valid for any enterprise.

Work has started and is currently on-going in the domain of the integration of quality standards in software collaborative projects, particularly on the use of CMMI and ISO 9001:2000 [21] with the objective of developing a unique quality reference framework integrating both CMMI and ISO 9001:2000. Some practical solutions for processes interoperability between the company and its offshore suppliers or clients have also been implemented to organize projects, particularly the exchange of documents.

SUMMARY

ISO 15531 defines a new paradigm in terms of managing the information of manufacturing systems through a systemic approach that integrates the concepts of product, process, and resource. The concept of integration is also an important characteristic of the standard.

An important theoretical principle that has guided the development of the ISO 15531 MANDATE standard is the use of system theory as the foundation of the modeling approach. MANDATE is process-based and provides process-related information such as the resources (used or consumed), the flow/activity management and of course, the sequencing and scheduling of these activities. The modular structure of the standard enables its use in different contexts of a manufacturing enterprise.

This approach is relatively new; most common software applications are product-focused. Another important feature is that it ensures the interoperability of product information and links to external part libraries. Finally, because the information described in the standard is generic, it can be used in a wide range of application domains.

It should be noted that in terms of industrial maturity, MANDATE is a young standard, whose development started recently and whose parts have not reached the IS status (necessary for sake of stability) at the same time. For this reason, the different models proposed by the standard have not been implemented at the same time.

REFERENCES

1. Frankovic, B., Budinska, L., and Dang, T.T., Creation of ontology for planning and scheduling, *Proceedings of the 3rd International Symposium of Hungarian Researchers on Computational Intelligence*, Magyar Kutatók 3. Nemzetközi Szimpóziuma, Budapest, Hungary, 2002.
2. Cutting-Decelle, A.F. et al., Utilising standards based approaches to information sharing and interoperability in manufacturing decision support, *Proceedings of the Flexible Automation and Intelligent Manufacturing Conference, 14th International Conference (FAIM04)*, Toronto, Canada, July 12–14, 2004, Ryerson University & National Research Council Canada, NRC Research Press, Toronto, Canada, 2004.
3. ISO 18629-1, Industrial automation systems and integration—Process specification language, Geneva, Switzerland, 2004.
4. ISO 15531-31, Industrial automation systems and integration—Industrial manufacturing management data—Resource usage management data: Resource information model: Basic concepts: Part 31, ISO TC184/SC4, Geneva, Switzerland, 2004.
5. ISO 15531-32, Industrial automation systems and integration—Industrial manufacturing management data—Resource usage management data: Conceptual model for resources usage management data: Part 32, ISO TC184/SC4, Geneva, Switzerland, 2004.
6. ISO 15531-42, Industrial automation systems and integration—Industrial manufacturing management data—Time model: Part 42, ISO TC184/SC4, Geneva, Switzerland, 2005.
7. ISO 15531-43, Industrial automation systems and integration—Industrial manufacturing management data—Manufacturing flow management data: Data model for manufacturing flow management: Part 43, ISO TC184/SC4, Geneva, Switzerland, 2006.
8. ISO WD 15531-44, Industrial automation systems and integration—Industrial manufacturing management data—Information model for shop data acquisition: Part 44, ISO TC184/SC4, Geneva, Switzerland, 2008.
9. ISO 10303-11, Industrial automation systems and integration—Product data representation and exchange—Part 11: Description methods: The EXPRESS language reference manual, Geneva, Switzerland, 1994.
10. ISO 15531-1, Industrial automation systems and integration—Industrial manufacturing management data—General overview: Part 1, ISO TC184/SC4, Geneva, Switzerland, 2004.
11. ISO 13584-1, Industrial automation systems and integration—Parts library—Conceptual descriptions—Part 1: Overview and fundamental principles, Geneva, Switzerland, 1997.
12. Cutting-Decelle, A.F. et al., A standardized data model for process and flow management: ISO 15535-43—A step towards CE in manufacturing, *Proceedings of the International Conference CE 06, Concurrent Engineering*, Vol. 15, No. 2, pp. 217–235, Sage Publications, London, 2007.
13. IEC 62264-1, Enterprise—control system integration—Part 1: Models and terminology, Geneva, Switzerland, 2003.
14. APICS Dictionary, 11th Edn., APICS, Alexandria, USA, 2005, pages and http://www.apics.org/default.htm, accessed June 2009.
15. Salazar, M.E., available at http://www.plant-maintenance.com/articles/ERP_concepts.shtml, 2006, accessed June 2009.

16. Michel, J.J., Trends and role of international standards for intelligent collaboration and integration in manufacturing, Workshop on Intelligent collaboration in the Supply Chain, Wolfson School of Engineering, Loughborough University, Loughborough, UK, May 13–14, 2004 (available from the author at idpiconseil@orange.fr).
17. ISO 10303-1, Industrial automation systems and integration—Product data representation and exchange—Part 1: Overview and Fundamental Principles, Geneva, Switzerland, 1994.
18. ISO 10303-41, Industrial automation systems and integration—Product data representation and exchange—Integrated generic resource—Part 41: Fundamentals of product description and support, 3rd Edn., Geneva, Switzerland, 2004.
19. NIST, Economic impact assessment of the International Standard for the Exchange of Product Model Data (STEP) in transportation equipment industries, Planning Report #02-5, Gaithersburg, ND, U.S. Department of Commerce, RTI Project Number 07007.016, 2002, available at http://www.nist.gov/director/prog-ofc/report02-5.pdf
20. NIST, Interoperability cost analysis of the U.S. automotive supply chain, Planning report #99-1, Prepared by Brunnermeier, S.B. and Martin, S.A., 1999, http://www.nist.gov/director/prog-ofc/report99-1.pdf, accessed June 2009.
21. Ferchichi, A., Bigand, M., and Lefèbvre H., An ontology for quality standards integration in software collaborative projects, *CAISE 2008, MDISIS Workshop*, Montpellier, France, 2008, available at http://sunsite.informatik.rwth-aachen.de/Publications/CEUR-WS/Vol-340, accessed June 2009.

22 Standards for International Trade and Enterprise Interoperability

P. G. L. Potgieser

CONTENTS

INTRODUCTION

International trade takes place within an organized framework according to well-defined rules, custom, and usage, adhered to by the key players, the traders. It can be seen as the result of a chain of interrelated activities or tasks with a specific purpose. This chain is also called a *business process*. Within a business process, a group of activities or tasks that logically belong together is called a *phase*.

A business process begins with the need of a customer and ends with the fulfillment of that need. It consists of many activities, from inquiry until the goods or services have been delivered and paid for. In order for a seller to find a buyer, for a sales contract to be signed (electronically or otherwise), for goods to be shipped by the producer and received by the consumer, for the payment to be made within the contractual deadline, the many steps in the business process have to take place within a pre-established system, on the basis of a functioning legal framework and technical infrastructure.

This framework of international trade can be structured into the macroeconomic level (country A to country B), the inter-governmental level (government of country A to government of country B), and the microeconomic level (a private company in country A to a private company in country B). While the macroeconomic level focuses on providing a legal framework for the flow of trade and services between countries, the microeconomic level focuses on the transactions between those engaged in commerce, that is, the trader-to-trader relationship. It is at the microeconomic level that most trade facilitation tools and technical standards are developed and implemented and it is at these standards (and in particular their development and application) at this microeconomic level that this chapter will focus.

There are potentially some 40 or more parties involved in international trade; these parties are usually referred to as "actors." This large number can be reduced to four actor-categories, as follows:

1. *Customer.* A party that acquires, by way of trade, goods or services.
2. *Supplier.* A party that provides, by way of trade, goods or services.
3. *Authority.* A statutory body existing within a jurisdiction and a specific area of responsibility that administers legislation to regulate trade and/or monitors compliance with existing legislation.
4. *Intermediary.* A commercial party that provides auxiliary services to customers, suppliers, or authorities.

For a better understanding, some of the roles possibly carried out by the actors in these four categories are listed in the Table 22.1, using the customary designations.

Although the physical transport and handling of goods constitute a flow made up of a straightforward series of activities, the corresponding information flow shows a more varied and complex pattern. In addition, the information flow involves more parties than the actual physical flow. To illustrate this, Figure 22.1 represents an overview of the SHIP phase. It depicts the preparatory activities that the actor types presented above generally need to carry out to ensure that goods are delivered to the agreed location after clearance by the appropriate authorities, once a supplier had accepted an order.

Some of the activities depicted in Figure 22.1 are obvious: "Supplier requests Export license from Authority," followed by "Authority responds" or "Transport booked with Intermediary (carrier or freight forwarder) by Supplier according to agreed delivery terms." Others may require more explanation; a purchase of goods for instance is predominantly perceived as a combined action of "Buyer," "Seller," and their respective "Banks" (for the necessary payments), as shown in Figure 22.2. But there are activities

TABLE 22.1

Actors in International Trade and Their Roles

Actor Type	Possible Roles
Customer	Buyer, Consignee,[a] Payer, Importer
Supplier	Consignor, Payee, Seller, Manufacturer, Exporter
Authority	Chamber of Commerce, Customs, Licensing, Receiving Authority, Standards Institute
Intermediary	Bank/Financial Institution, Broker, Carrier, Credit Checking Company, Export Agent, Freight forwarder, Import Agent, Insurer, Receiving authority

[a] The *Consignee* is the recipient of the goods or services ordered. *Buyer* and *Consignee* do not need to be the same for an order, but both have a possible role in the Actor type *Customer*.

that, while not abundantly visible in the purchase process, are nevertheless essential for the business process in question. "Intermediary (insurer) provides Supplier with Insurance Certificate (for Customer)" is an example of such an activity.

Referring to Figure 22.1, it is easy to understand that similar diagrams can be made showing groups of activities, for example, for the phase that precedes (i.e., where the goods or services are described and ordered) or follows (e.g., where the

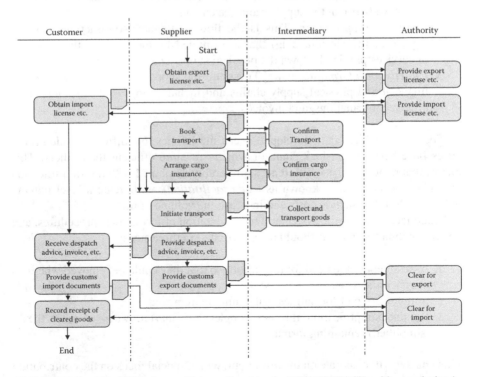

FIGURE 22.1   The SHIP phase of international trade. (©UN/CEFACT, with permission.)

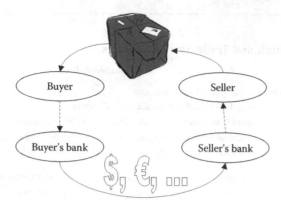

FIGURE 22.2   Goods purchase as a combined action of "buyer," "seller," and "bank."

goods or services that have been received are paid for) the SHIP phase. All these activities, consisting of the processes carried out by a variety of parties together, are called the (international) supply chain.

Looking at the supply chain from a different perspective, three parallel flows can thus be identified as follows:

1. *The physical supply chain.* Which consists of the flow of goods or services that move between the supplier and the customer.
2. *Financial supply chain.* This is the flow of financial transactions (e.g., payments, invoice financing) that are implied by the move of the goods or services physically down the physical supply chain.
3. *Underlying information flows.* These are the supportive flows of both the financial and physical supply chains and include things such as purchase orders, confirmations, and invoices.

The way in which trade developed over time implies that different trade procedures have been established, some of which are more efficient than others. This means that removing these differences, preferably combined with the simplification of trade procedures (also known as *trade facilitation*), will create a level playing field, to reduce transaction costs and increase the volume of trade.

Trade facilitation is the systematic rationalization of formalities, procedures, and documentation for trade. It should be approached in three steps:

1. Assessment of the need for formalities so that they could be removed where proven unnecessary
2. Simplification of formalities that cannot be removed
3. Routine simplification through simpler, or smarter, ways to meet the (simplified) remaining formalities

This chapter will elaborate on the third item, with a special focus on the contribution of standards to routine simplification.

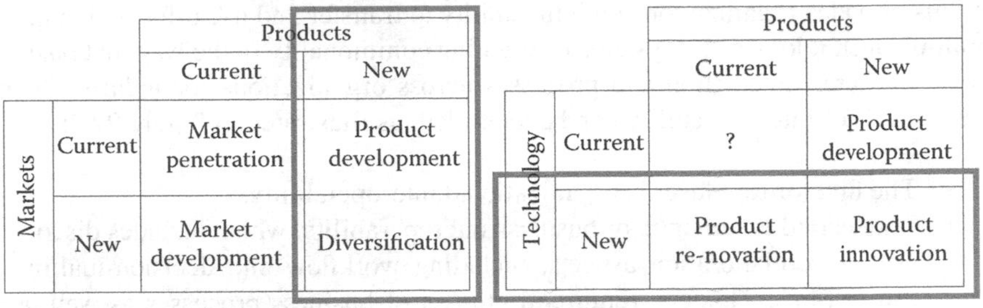

Markets		Products	
		Current	New
Current		Market penetration	Product development
New		Market development	Diversification

Technology		Products	
		Current	New
Current		?	Product development
New		Product re-novation	Product innovation

FIGURE 22.3 Business opportunities from application of standards.

Complying with global standards can generate significant savings in the supply chain as well as improve productivity; it can help identify growth opportunities for actors in the international supply chain. The evaluation is based on using the Ansoff Matrix. This is a tool typically used to help businesses select their product and market strategies and it is shown in the left-hand matrix of Figure 22.3. Manufacturers seeking growth would focus on the strategies labeled "Product development" and "Diversification." The right-hand matrix concerns the relationship Product vs. Technology. It indicates that, for new technologies, the use of standards contributes to product and service renovation as well as innovation by increasing their international acceptance so that business could compete in more markets around the world.

STANDARDS AND INTEROPERABILITY

Although, most organizations have traditionally focused on improving efficiencies of the physical supply chain, effective management of information flows is beneficial to all parties. With automated and electronic solutions, information could be processed faster and more accurately so that lead times could be reduced. A procurement process would also be quicker if purchase orders were managed electronically. Furthermore, if a company is able of forecasting its purchases and sales with a high degree of accuracy, it will gain a competitive advantage by the successful management of the supply chain.

Precise definition of the information flow is important because:

- Supply chains have become much more complex in the globalized economy. Information of the trade transaction is vital to reduce delays and costs. In recent times, there is also an increased need for governments to receive advance trade information for an automated risk analysis.
- The harmonization of processes and the simplification of cross-border procedures require clarity in the data required and provided. As documents are the core means to transfer data in international trade, the precise definition of the information in the trade document is important to simplify and harmonize processes.

The goal of *interoperability* is to allow information to be presented in a consistent manner between business systems, regardless of technology, application, or platform.

It thus provides organizations with the ability to transfer and use information across multiple technologies and systems by creating commonality in the way that business systems share information and processes across organizational boundaries. Three basic levels of interoperability can be identified, as illustrated in Figure 22.4:

- The first (or top) layer is organizational interoperability.
- The second is semantic or business interoperability, which includes discovery and collaboration aspects, including workflow and decision-making transactions. This can require alignment of business processes as well as operational synchronization of collaboration data.
- A third (and the lowest) layer is technical interoperability, which consist of the common methods and shared services for the communication, storage, processing, and presentation of data. This includes the technical foundations for a secure environment, compatible technical standards, and a common framework.

Preferably, organizations aiming for interoperability should first strive for interoperability at organizational level and then extend into business and technical interoperability. In practice however, this sequence is often reversed. Note that, although the economic advantages of the use of electronic data interchange (EDI) are widely recognized and its use is beneficial, the potential benefits of its use between two parties can thus only be reaped to their full extent if EDI is established as part of a program to achieve "interoperability" between these parties and this program thus involves all three layers in the appropriate sequence.

Currently, the lack of interoperability is the single most important impediment to e-business, particularly to the participation of small and medium enterprises (SMEs). Yet, the development of standards to facilitate interoperability requires a full understanding of the problem domain, which is usually of an inter-organizational nature. The correct and logical approach toward the development of standards to facilitate international trade would thus be by means of a comprehensive study of all informational and procedural requirements for the execution of trade, followed by the negotiation of—and agreement on—international standards for these purposes. However, this would undoubtedly be a task of the greatest complexity.

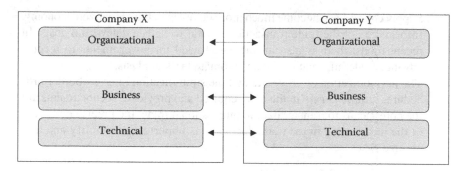

FIGURE 22.4   Levels of supply chain interoperability.

Standards developing organizations like United Nations Centre for Trade Facilitation and Electronic Business (UN/CEFACT) and International Organization for Standardization (ISO) have been working on this problem for years and have found ways to make this challenge manageable. Their related activities are carried out under a unique cooperative model: together with International Telecommunication Union (ITU) and International Electrotechnical Commission (IEC), they signed a Memorandum of Understanding (MoU) [1]. This MoU establishes a coordination mechanism to produce mutually supportive standards required in business transactions (data interchange and interoperability) as well as products design and manufacturing to meet the urgent needs of both the industry and the end-users.

Let us take a look at the way standards for the exchange of information in electronic form are developed to ensure that EDI and organizational procedures evolve together on a worldwide basis to avoid the multiplication of circumscribed "islands" of applications, different from each other that, in the end, would constitute as many barriers to trade.

The basic principles that UN/CEFACT used during the development of the United Nations Electronic Data Interchange for Administration, Commerce and Transport specifications for EDI—also known as United Nations Recommendation 25—are as follows:

- *Open cooperation.* The global dimension of international trade entails an open development process. Although this process can be especially elaborate and time-consuming (as it is based on consensus and requires the co-operation of a wide range of entities and cultures), it does secure the "buy-in" of parties and gives the results their universal acceptance.
- *Interrelationship between government and business.* Thorough analyses of business processes shows that many of the activities in a business process usually contain several elements (think of Value Added Tax) related to public administration and vice versa and hence the distinction between Business and Government—from a process point of view—vanishes.
- *Neutrality.* It is evident that a concerted development of international standards is less expensive than multiple conversion of concepts between various sectorial, national, or regional systems.
- *Involvement of end-users.* Standardization for the benefit of international administrative and commercial procedures addresses economic issues of a general and far more complex nature than most of the other standardization areas. As the needs of end-users are essential for achieving improvement, they have to be taken into consideration accordingly and reflected in the developments. This involves evolution, because the dynamic character of trade procedures means that they evolve over time. However, the involvement of end-users and SMEs is a challenge on its own; usually this is achieved through organizations that represent them. In general, getting the required interaction with these organizations makes it necessary that the benefits of the development and application of standards must be made clear in a direct, that is, nontechnical, way.

- *Role of governments.* The benefits of adopting standardized data exchange are potentially very high and can only be fully achieved by a coordinated and cooperative effort among all users to overcome divergent sectorial, local, or national solutions. As governments are also potentially major implementors through their public sector, they are sometimes essential if legislation needs to be harmonized in order to be able to use certain standards.

ELECTRONIC DATA INTERCHANGE

The introduction of data interchange using electronic means (instead of paper) is a major contribution to the effective management of information flows. However, thinking about information flows, it should be recognized that trade patterns are *not* static; also, new transport logistics concepts are developed that pose new information requirements.

Today, Internet solutions have the potential to provide for the establishment of an open market. This electronic market can provide for new opportunities for information sharing, service and support, and payment. As will be shown later in this chapter, a process can be set up (not only between businesses, but also between business and government or business and consumer) for specific purposes, defined *ad hoc* or for one time use, as opposed to business processes belonging to established and permanent business relationships. The introduction of new techniques for the compilation, exchange, storage, and retrieval of data supports these evolving methods and provides an unprecedented opportunity for changes in processes carried out by governmental and private participants in international trade. The new information technology supporting these techniques may, in fact, for a certain trade provide the actual means of delivery.

But all this implies that the introduction of EDI should not be a mere 1:1 substitution of paper documents by electronic messages, as that would practically freeze the current situation and make future developments difficult, if not impossible. The remainder of this chapter will focus on the way in which current standards, for example, the electronic interchange of data, are being developed, in such a way that it supports all of the above.

Using the definition of the European Commission [2], EDI is "the electronic transfer, from computer to computer, of commercial and administrative data using an agreed standard to structure an EDI message," where "an EDI message consists of a set of segments, structured using an agreed standard, prepared in a computer readable format and capable of being automatically and unambiguously processed."

A closer look at these definitions reveals the following key characteristics:

1. Messages are of predefined types, that is, the message functions are well defined and agreed in advance by sender and receiver.
2. Data are structured according to agreed standards, that is, they are in a form suitable for automatic validation and processing by computers.
3. Exchanges take place electronically without manual intervention between independent computer applications. This enables systems to automatically

make decisions according to rules defined by the business management, provided that the resulting business transaction satisfies the requirements by management.

4. User computers and applications shall be independent from one another. Each sender and/or receiver of messages for EDI shall have a maximum freedom in choosing his/her hardware, software, and other modules of his/her own computerized information system.

BUSINESS PROCESS MODELING IN DEVELOPING STANDARDS FOR E-BUSINESS

UN/CEFACT [3] has endorsed Business Process Modeling as the basis for future e-business standardization activities and to aid in the facilitation and simplification of international trade procedures. Business modeling provides a formalized way of describing how a business or market operates and thus enables a common understanding of the key features and requirements of that domain. UN/CEFACT uses their "BUY-SHIP-PAY" model of the international supply chain. This is a hierarchical model, which in its simplest form, involves the three key business processes—Buy, Ship, Pay—and the main actors—Customer, Supplier, Intermediary and Authority.

The BUY–SHIP–PAY model of the international supply chain is depicted in Figure 22.5 in a Unified Modeling Language (UML) representation. In general, this model aims to fulfill the following goals:

- A reference model for supply chain processes, which can be used as a reference for all parties engaged in the supply chain in order to assist in harmonization of trade processes and data, use of best practice, promotion, and training.
- Provide support for standardization projects. The model can clarify different understanding, define contextual information, and provide examples, which the standardization bodies can refer to.
- Act as an educational tool. It explains complex relationships and interrelations, gives the user various information like the context a transaction is executed in, or describes roles that a business partner needs to fulfill.

Although at first sight the model may look (too) simple, the hierarchical structure of the model means that all the activities in the international supply chain can be contained in a logical manner; for instance, all the activities as depicted in Figure 22.1 are contained in the "Ship" oval, reflecting the "SHIP" phase. So, even though the "BUY–SHIP–PAY" model recognizes only three processes at the highest level, it has the possibility to cover all process activities required in international trade in goods or services.

The international supply chain involves a large number of activities performed by a number of different parties. Depending on the terms of business, type of product, country, and market, and so on, as well as on the methods of operation of the buyer

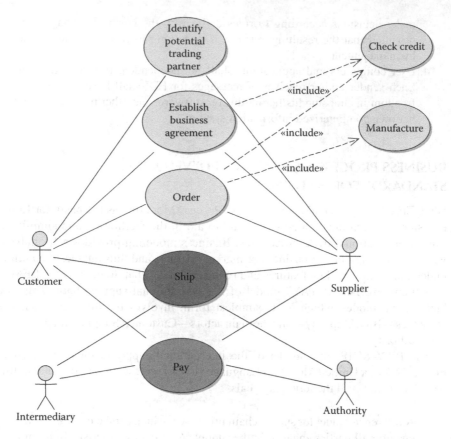

FIGURE 22.5 UML representation of the international supply chain. (©UN/CEFACT, with permission.)

and seller, one or more of these activities may at different times even be carried out by different parties. If the goal is to be able to automate not only the interchange of single messages, but also the entire business process from the first electronic message sent by the first actor, to the last one received by the last actor (identifying ALL actors and ALL the messages exchanged during the whole of the process), then an overall scenario is needed identifying what the comprehensive requirements of each actor are: which role each actor plays from the start of a process to its final conclusion. So, if a supply chain is to operate effectively and efficiently then the relationships, activities, and the information that has to be exchanged have to be clearly identified and managed. Only when seen from a message content point of view, the appropriate messages for the electronic exchange of data are defined, the full automatic exchange of these messages can be performed, automating the business process between traders. Here a precise, unambiguous definition of this data content of the electronic messages used is required in order to enable the development of applications supporting these automated processes.

REQUIREMENTS ON STANDARDS SPECIFICATIONS

Standards for EDI messages are developed by standardization organizations. The development method used must be able to fulfill certain requirements, where the most obvious areas follows:

1. It must (of course) be able to support the definition of the information, enveloped in electronic data messages, that actually needs to be exchanged between actors in order for their business processes to function.
2. It must be able to cope with evolution in the interaction among actors, while reusability of its deliverables must be possible; if not reusability of the EDI messages themselves then at least reusability of intermediate results of the development method, not to mention the development method itself.
3. The method should preferably focus on business essentials, where translation into actual messages used in the EDI can be left to an automated process.

Let us elaborate on some more on two of these aspects.

REQUIREMENTS ON IMPLEMENTATION METHODS

The actors whose necessities should be taken into account are active in very diverse sectors, such as: trade, banking, transport, manufacturing, healthcare, education, public administration, construction industry, and so on. So, there is a need for a development method that delivers results that are usable globally, that is, across all sectors and the world over. These requirements also include the necessity to identify the regulations and any requirement for legislative compliance, which are satisfied by current nonelectronic message-based solutions and would need to be met by any electronic business solution.

The functions where EDI is to be applied need to be identified in relation to the overall business: traditional boundaries and functions may be affected. Refer to Figure 22.1, the messages developed for exchange between Supplier and Intermediary should have a relation with the messages that are exchanged between Authority and Customer, as these exchanges fall within the same process and hence no different representations of data used for the same elements may occur.

The messages should be such that all requirements for cooperation between the parties are satisfied by the implementation of these messages, where implementation should be possible according to publicly available, nonproprietary standards or rules. In that case, there will be no need for private agreements in order to resolve ambiguities in exchanges. (The freedom to use private agreements in addition to and in the framework of a shared agreement is of course always available.)

In case this form of implementation cannot be achieved then:

• Bilateral agreements may be necessary between electronic business participants.

- Individual parties may have to support a range of different sets of inter-working facilities depending on the participants. These facilities must be ready to evolve across time, domains and technologies, thus loading each participant with increasing duties and problems.

Note that the introduction of the electronic form of data interchange should not limit the flexibility that parties require in their operation, for example, for delegating a part of their business—or (part of) the operation of the electronic services required to support that business—to subcontractors. In addition to that, exchanges of all information types need to be covered, as long as they are predefined, structured, and can be processed by applications at both ends. These not only include alphanumeric structured data, but may also cover the exchange of Computer Aided Design drawings, images, texts, voice recordings, and so on within a business transaction.

SERVICE DELIVERY AND THE SERVICE-ORIENTED ARCHITECTURE

There is another scenario for the application of electronic messages for data interchange. In contrast to Figure 22.1, where this interchange is used between actors in the supply chain (for the delivery of *goods*), this other form of interchange is used in the delivery of *services*.

In this context, a service is a function that is well-defined, self-contained, and does not depend on the context or state of other services. It is provided by a service provider and used by a service consumer; a service consumer can not only be a person, but also a system or application.

A single-service provider or multiple-service providers can deliver the service. In the latter case, they cooperate to offer a single service, each delivering a part of that service, while only one of them has the contact with the service consumer. The service provisioning to the service consumer is the result of the appropriate combination of service composing elements.

Figure 22.6 shows a service consumer (left) electronically sending a service request message to a service provider (right). The service provider electronically returns a response message to the service consumer. The request and subsequent response are defined in some way that is understandable to both the service consumer and service provider. This is the simplest form of implementation of what is called "the service oriented architecture" (SOA).

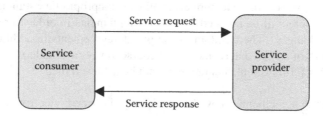

FIGURE 22.6   Basic service-oriented architecture.

There are three steps in providing and consuming a service:

1. A service provider describes its service using a standardized format, for example, XML (Extensible Markup Language). This definition is published in a directory of services, frequently referred to as a Registry. A registry would be freely accessible and can be searched in various ways to discover the services available for various organizations and their contact information.
2. A service consumer issues one or more queries to the registry to locate an available service. The result of these queries is in the form of part of the service description information originally provided by the service provider. From this information, the service consumer can determine how to interact (i.e., requests and responses) with the particular service provider. This information does not need to be limited to the description of communication requirements; it may also contain other information as, for example, information on trade agreements.
3. The service consumer uses this information to query the service provider. The service provider, in turn, can consult other service providers using the same mechanism available to the service consumer.

These three steps of registration, discovery, and use are schematically indicated in Figure 22.7.

A service provider can also be a service consumer if, to satisfy a service request, it needs information from another (or more) service provider(s). This is just a matter

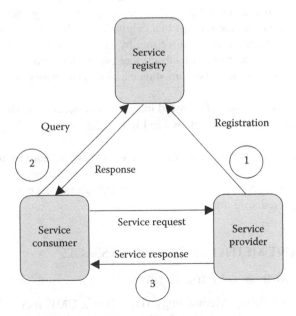

FIGURE 22.7   Service registration, discovery, and use.

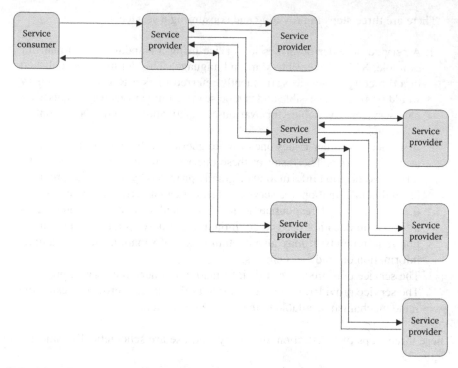

FIGURE 22.8   Nested interaction between a service consumer and service providers.

of issuing the appropriate service request to the required service provider at the right moment. The number of service providers invoked and the sequence may depend on parameters from the service request that originally reached the service provider. So the service may be composed at run-time, by means of invocation of subservices, where the number and sequence of subservices can be determined based on a profile of the service consumer, actual circumstances, history or result of a previous request, and so on.

Thus, the general picture of a nested interaction between a service consumer and service providers in the SOA is shown in Figure 22.8. Note that

- There are many other definitions, also used by other authors in this hand-book.
- The Service Providers shown in Figure 22.8 do not necessarily belong to the same (business) organization.

DEVELOPMENT METHODS FOR EDI MESSAGES

UN/CEFACT MODELING METHODOLOGY

UN/CEFACT's Modeling Methodology (UMM) is a UML modeling approach to design the business services that each party must provide in order to collaborate. It provides the business justification for the services to be implemented in a service-oriented (collaboration) architecture. The primary scope of UMM is to provide a perspective of business transactions limited to those aspects regarding the making of business decisions and commitments among organizations. The UMM provides a procedure for specifying (modeling) collaborative business processes involving information exchange among actors in a technology-neutral, implementation-independent manner.

This methodology is incremental, that is, it provides levels of specification granularity suitable for communicating the model to the various target audiences, including business practitioners, business application integrators, and network application solution providers. Application of UMM leads to UMM Business Component Libraries (Registries), where previously defined business processes will be registered. The lowest level of the registries contains the so-called "Core Components" that are used to structure the information exchanged between business partners.

UMM Views

The 2006 version [4] of the UMM consists of three views each covering a set of well-defined artifacts:

- Business requirements view (bRequirementsV)
- Business choreography view (bChoreographyV)
- Business information view (bInformationV)

The bRequirementsV is used to gather existing knowledge. It identifies the business processes in the domain and the business problems that are important to stakeholders. Stakeholders might describe intra-organizational as well as inter-organizational business processes. The result may be depicted in use case diagrams.

The bChoreographyV is used to define and document the global choreography between collaborating business partners in an inter-organizational business process. Within the bChoreographyV, the Business transaction view contains and documents the requirements of business transaction Use Cases, and their participating Authorized Roles.

The bInformationV presents the minimum information exchange needed to change the state of one or more business entities after the execution of a business transaction.

Business Component Libraries

The UMM specifies all information that needs to be captured during the analysis of an electronic commerce-based business process. The goal of the UMM is to understand and formalize the dependencies between partner processes for a problem domain. Historically, business partner communication methodologies have focused on modeling the business documents being exchanged while the UMM instead focuses on modeling the business actions and objects that create and consume business information. Previously defined business processes will be registered in the

UMM Business Component Libraries (Registries) to encourage the development of a common vocabulary and the reuse and integration of the components.

CORE COMPONENTS

The Core Components, as registered in the UMM Business Component Libraries, form a new approach to the well-understood problem of the lack of information interoperability between applications in the e-Business arena. A Core Component is a semantic building block used to construct all electronic business messages. The concept of the UN/CEFACT Core Components presents a methodology for developing a common set of semantic building blocks that represent the general types of business data in use today and provides for the creation of new business vocabularies and restructuring of existing business vocabularies, satisfying the requirements of tomorrow.

UN/CEFACT Business Process and Core Component solutions capture a wealth of information about the business reasons for variation in message semantics and structure. Where in the past, such variations have introduced incompatibilities, the Core Components mechanism uses this rich information to allow identification of exact similarities and differences between semantic models. The key concepts of Core Components Technical Specification cover two focus areas—Core Components and Business Information Entities.

BUSINESS INFORMATION ENTITIES

A Business Information Entity is the result of using a Core Component within a specific Business Context. When a Core Component is used in a real business circumstance, it serves as the basis of a Business Information Entity. Thus, what differentiates a Core Component from the corresponding Business Information Entity is the business context, which is a mechanism for qualifying and refining Core Components according to their use under particular business circumstances. In this way, Core Components can be differentiated to take into account any necessary qualification and refinement needed to support the specific business transaction.

UNIVERSAL FINANCIAL INDUSTRY FINANCIAL MESSAGES AND ISO 20022

A standards development method that has similar characteristics in terms of the use of a Registry, Business Process Modeling, and so on is used in the standardization of the ISO 20022 methodology prepared by the ISO Technical Committee 68 on financial services. International Standard ISO 20022 [5] is described in the document "ISO 20022 Financial Services—UNIversal Financial Industry message scheme." It includes five parts:

1. Part 1: Overall methodology and format specifications for inputs to and outputs from the ISO 20022 Repository.
2. Part 2: Roles and responsibilities of the registration bodies.
3. Part 3: Technical Specification—ISO 20022 modelling guidelines.
4. Part 4: Technical Specification—ISO 20022 XML design rules.
5. Part 5: Technical Specification—ISO 20022 reverse engineering.

ISO 20022 provides the financial industry with a common platform, including the required governance, for the development of messages in a standardized XML syntax, using a modeling methodology (based on UML) to capture. in a syntax-independent way, financial business areas, business transactions, and associated message flows. It is a well-governed process, where a so-called Registration Management Group and a Registration Authority play a pivotal role. The Registration Authority, for instance, maintains and publishes the Registry.

The ISO 20022 methodology also provides a set of XML design rules to convert the messages described in UML into XML schemas. Currently, the preferred syntax for all electronic documents is XML, but upon request from the financial industry, the design rules can later be extended to other syntaxes.

ISO 20022 METHODOLOGY

The ISO 20022 methodology for defining and standardizing business transactions and messages consists of the following five activities:

- *The Business Analysis.* The purpose of the Business Analysis is to understand the specific application for which ISO 20022 compliant business transactions and message sets are to be developed. The activity starts by modeling business users in terms of Business Actors and Business Roles to define the business processes and the business information they need. The result of this analysis will drive the requirements analysis and the identified information needs will be used later in the design and definition of the exchanged messages to include the needed data elements.
- *The Requirements Analysis.* Based on the Business Analysis activity, the communication problems for which an ISO 20022 compliant Business Transaction and Message Set is to be developed are defined.
- *The Logical Analysis.* The purpose of the Logical Analysis is to use the requirements to specify the details of the Business Transaction and Message Set under development. The definitions proceed independently of any physical implementation and include Message Flow Diagrams and Message Definitions.
- *The Logical Design.* The purpose of the Logical Design activity is to derive precise and unambiguous descriptions of the Message Components and Message Elements through formal descriptions that can be reused.
- *The Technical Design* delivers the physical implementation of Message Definitions and Message Rules in an appropriate syntax such as ISO 20022 XML. The purpose of the Technical Design is to produce a physical implementation of the Message.

These five activities are applied in an iterative and incremental way for the development of ISO 20022 compliant Business Transactions and Message Sets. Indeed, communities using another syntax may link the content of their Industry Message Sets to items already existing in the ISO 20022 Repository.

Under the ISO 20022 methodology, the complete models and the derived syntax output are stored in a central Repository (the ISO 20022 Repository). The ISO 20022 Repository as schematically indicated in Figure 22.9 offers industry participants access to the following.

- A financial Business Process Catalogue, containing
  - The description of the financial business model
  - The description of financial business transactions, including message definitions
  - The message schemes represented in an agreed syntax (such as ISO 20022 XML).
- A financial Data Dictionary, containing business concepts, data types, and message concepts used in business areas, business processes, business transactions, and message sets. The word "concepts" is used to indicate a Dictionary item within a specific context.

If the existing set of definitions stored in the ISO 20022 Repository does not address the business transactions and message of a particular application, the communities of users can agree on the new Business Transactions and Message Definitions and design them from the items registered in the Data Dictionary. To standardize their agreements, they submit them as proposals to the Registration Authority. The Registration Authority, with the support of so-called Standard Evaluation Groups (groups of people with knowledge on the specific matter), will validate the requests and update the ISO 20022 Repository as necessary and generate the corresponding ISO 20022 syntax output using the agreed ISO 20022 Syntax Design Rules for XML or for other future open syntaxes.

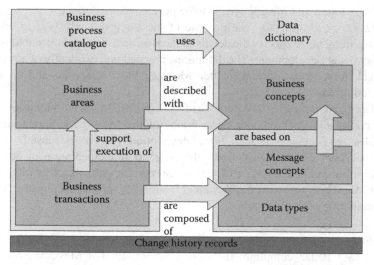

FIGURE 22.9   ISO 20022 Repository. (From http://www.iso20022.org/understanding_unifi. page. With permission.)

HARMONIZATION OF ISO 20022 AND UN/CEFACT

Figure 22.10 depicts, in a simple way, the physical supply chain, the financial supply chain, and the underlying information flows as mentioned previously, showing only the buyer and the seller and their respective banks. This picture, for obvious reasons, is often referred to as "the four-corner model."

It is noteworthy to say that the development of standards for messages for EDI supporting the *exchange of goods and services* (upper half of the figure) may be considered complementary to the development of standards for messages for EDI between banks supporting, for example, payments or additional services that can be offered by banks to their clients (lower half of the figure).

Both UN/CEFACT and ISO have recognized this and, as a result, an approach is followed leading to a convergence where Universal Financial Industry Financial (UNIFI) provides the financial portion of the UN/CEFACT repository. Figure 22.11 illustrates the main aspects of the long-term convergence goal, when the UN/CEFACT repository will be up and running and when the exchange of information with the UNIFI repository will be operational.

In Figure 22.11 a number of important users for the messages generated using the ISO 20022 method are indicated:

- ISTH—International Standards Team Harmonization is a group, formed in 2003, with members from the of IFX (Interactive Financial Exchange), TWIST (Transaction Workflow Innovation Standards Team), OAGi (Open Applications Group) and SWIFT (Society for Worldwide Interbank Financial Telecommunication). Its goal is to define a single "core payment kernel" for customer-to-bank payment initiation and status messages. All parties agreed to use ISO 20022, and all committed to include the messages in their own existing set of standards.

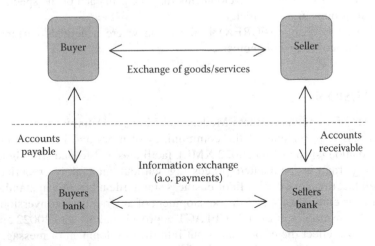

FIGURE 22.10 Information flows in the supply chain—a four-corner model.

A single ISO–UN/CEFACT approach

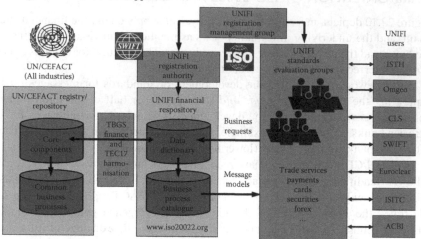

FIGURE 22.11   ISO UNIFI–UN/CEFACT long-term convergence goal. (Based on a presentation at www.iso20022.org)

- Omgeo—Omgeo is the global standard for efficiency, certainty, and confidence in post-trade operations.
- CLS—Continuous Linked Settlement is a unique process that enables cross border currency transactions to be settled intra-day.
- SWIFT—SWIFT is the Society for Worldwide Interbank Financial Telecommunication, a member-owned cooperative through which the financial world conducts its business operations.
- TBG 17 is the group within UN/CEFACT that is responsible for the harmonization of the various developments that occur in each of the specialized TBG groups [6] in parallel.
- Foreign Exchange (FOREX) is the arena where a nation's currency is exchanged for that of another.

CONCLUSION

Agreement of common Business Models and Message Definitions, which address the business requirements of the communities of users and include a common syntax solution (such as ISO 20022 XML), facilitates end-to-end straight through processing, that is, automated processing without manual intervention. It is expected that this new, dual split of business standard and technical standard will facilitate the convergence and the development of any required conversion mechanisms. The examples of the UN/CEFACT approach and the ISO 20022 approach shown above reflect the effort that is put into the development of messages to be used in the electronic interchange of information, among others for the benefit of "dematerialization of business processes" or (more in general) trade facilitation [7]. There are good reasons behind this standardization effort, to name a few:

- For sellers, developing and offering products and services based on International Standards means that they can compete on many more markets around the world without additional development burden.
- Customers are given a broad choice of offers if products and services are based on International Standards, where they can also benefit from the effects of competition among suppliers.
- For governments and trade officials, International Standards create "a level playing field" for all competitors on those markets. As opposed to the existence of divergent national or regional standards that can create technical barriers to trade.

However, there are hurdles that slow down the uptake and adoption of these new concepts and technologies that make the trading environment of market participants more efficient. One of these hurdles is indeed the inadequate level of awareness about the topics at business level, which in turn acts prohibitively on the participation in standardization activities and hence the formulation of business requirements (and their verification) that are needed to give guidance at the aforementioned activities. Hopefully, this chapter succeeded in unveiling some of these topics, needed to contribute to the required awareness and possibly to participation.

REFERENCES

1. Memorandum of Understanding on electronic business, 24 March 2000, available at http://www.itu.int/ITU-T/e-business/mou/mou.html, accessed on June 29, 2009.
2. European Commission, 94/820/EC: Commission Recommendation of 19 October 1994 relating to the legal aspects of electronic data interchange, *Official J.* L 338, 98–117, 28/12/1994, http://eur-lex.europa.eu/LexUriServ/LexUriServ.do?uri=CELEX:31994H0820: EN:HTML, accessed on June 29, 2009.
3. http://www.unece.org/cefact, accessed on June 29, 2009.
4. UN/CEFACT TMG, UN/CEFACT's Methodology (UMM), UMM Meta Model Foundation Module, United Nations Center For Trade Facilitation and Electronic Business, 2006, available at http://www.untmg.org/umm/spec/foundation/2_0, accessed on June 29, 2009.
5. (NEN-)ISO 20022, Financial Services—UNIversal Financial Industry message scheme, Part 1 (2004): Overall methodology and format specifications for inputs to and outputs from the ISO 20022 Repository, Part 2 (2007): Roles and responsibilities of the registration bodies, Part 3 (2004): Technical Specification—ISO 20022 modeling guidelines, Part 4 (2004): Technical Specification—ISO 20022 XML design rules, Part 5 (2004): Technical Specification—ISO 20022 reverse engineering, available at http://www.iso. org/iso/iso_catalogue/catalogue_tc/catalogue_detail.htm?csnumber=40337, accessed on June 29, 2009.
6. http://www.uncefactforum.org/TBG/TBG%20Home/tbg_home.htm, accessed on June 29, 2009.
7. European Free Trade Association (EFTA), Trader's ABC, A trade facilitation manual, Brussels/Geneva, 2006, available at http://www.efta.int, accessed on June 29, 2009.

23 Standards for Business-to-Business Electronic Commerce

Mostafa Hashem Sherif

CONTENTS

The electronic flow of commercial data was a direct consequence of the computerization of businesses as a way to increase operational efficiencies through automation. More recently, the adoption of the Internet in commercial applications has generated new types of exchanges, especially in the fragmented markets of small and medium enterprises.

This chapter summarizes the current status of business-to-business electronic commerce, often known as B2B e-commerce or e-business, from a standardization viewpoint. We start by reviewing the legacy protocols used in Electronic Data Interchange (EDI) and the various ways to manage their co-existence with new frameworks based on distributed processing and object-oriented designs. The focus is on communications based on the Extensible Markup Language (XML), in particular, the Electronic Business (using) XML* (ebXML) framework, Web services, and the various initiatives for financial services-oriented XML. We also underline attempts at harmonization and integration at the various standardization bodies.

STANDARDIZATION OF BUSINESS-TO-BUSINESS ELECTRONIC COMMERCE

The first attempts for business-to-business electronic commerce took place in the United States in the 1960s with the aim of improving the military supply logistics [1]. Civilian applications soon followed in railroad and truck transportation, civil aviation, international payments (credit transfers, credit cards, and the management of customs. As each industrial group was devising its rules for structuring data without consultation with others, the U.S. Transportation Data Coordinating Committee was formed to work on the convergence of the various specifications. Its first document, published in 1975, covered transport by air, by road, by railroads, and by maritime or river transport. Some time later, the food and warehouse industries in the United States issued their respective standards: UCS (Uniform Communication Standards) and WINS (Warehouse Information Network Standard). Finally, large automobile manufacturers, such as General Motors, and retailers and others with wide distribution networks, such as K-Mart, J. C. Penney, and the National Wholesale Druggists Association, imposed their own specifications on their subcontractors and their

---

* In some circles, the word using is added to distinguish the suite of modular specifications for the conduct of business on the Internet from the specific dialect of the XML that is used in electronic business exchanges. See www.ebxml.org/geninfo.htm.

billing agents. To avoid the proliferation of sector-specific or proprietary rules, the American National Standards Institute (ANSI) established in 1982 a common syntax across the different business sectors. This syntax for EDI is known as the ANSI X12 standard, which is widely followed in North America.

In the United Kingdom, the Department of Customs and Excise developed the first EDI for customs known as the London Airport Cargo EDP Scheme (LACES) at Heathrow Airport in 1971. The objective of this activity, known as the Simplification of International Trade Procedures, was to speed up the processing of documents used in international trade and produced the Trade Data Interchange (TDI), which was then submitted to the United Nations (UN) Economic Commission for Europe (UN/ECE) to facilitate international trade. UN/ECE adopted this document as the UN-TDI which evolved into the General Purpose TDI in 1981.

Although similar in form and function, the rules in North America and in Europe diverged in several important aspects, complicating the tasks of information systems developers as well as users (e.g., the subcontractors working for different groups on the two sides of the Atlantic). It was therefore necessary to investigate the possibility of reaching a worldwide standard. The experts from both sides met under the aegis of the UN Joint EDI initiative to reach a consensus and harmonize both standards. This endeavor generated a worldwide agreement known as the EDI for Administration, Commerce, and Transport (EDIFACT) language. This agreement was adopted by the UN in 1987 and then by the International Organization for Standardization (ISO), where it was given the identification ISO 9735. Teletransmission of customs forms using EDIFACT is regularly used within the countries of the European Union since the January 1, 1993, the date of opening the borders among member states.

BANKING APPLICATIONS

In parallel of the above activities, the Society for Worldwide Interbank Financial Telecommunication (SWIFT) was established in 1987 by 239 banks in 15 countries with the objective of relaying the electronic interbank messages related to international fund transfers. The aim was to replace paper and telex communications with electronic messaging. The SWIFT standard contains 200 messages that cover all aspects of international finance: cash, retail, large amounts, settlement of real estate transactions, currency operations, treasury, derivatives, international trade, and so on. Bringing the system into full operation, however, required considerable debugging efforts that lasted until the late 1990s.

AERONAUTICAL APPLICATIONS

SITA (Société Internationale de Télécommunications Aéronautiques—International Society for Aeronautical Telecommunications) was established in 1949 to serve the airline industry. Some time later, it established a network for the exchange of data concerning reservations, tariffs, passenger boarding, and so on according to the standards of the IATA (International Air Transport Association). These are CARGO-IMP (CARGO Interchange Message Procedures) for freight and AIR-IMP (AIR Interline Message Procedures) for passengers. Another SITA service allows the selection, purchasing, and localization of spare parts used in aviation. In 1994, SITA started to use both EDIFACT and ANSI X12 for the IFTM (International Forwarding and Transport Message) messages with the messaging protocol X.400. Currently, migration to a Transmission Control Protocol/Internet Protocol (TCP/IP) infrastructure is proceeding.

APPLICATIONS IN THE AUTOMOTIVE INDUSTRY

The worldwide automotive industry is organized around a small number of manufacturers (General Motors, Ford, Daimler, Toyota, Renault, etc.) that procure automotive components from several thousands of suppliers organized in a tiered structure. Figure 23.1 shows a three-tiered structure. Starting from the top, the first tier is formed by around 1000 entities that are supplied by the second tier of about 5000 firms. Lastly, the third tier comprises about 50,000 suppliers, generally small or medium enterprises that work simultaneously with several car manufacturers. Without standardization of the interfaces, the third tier suppliers would have to invest in training and maintenance of multiple programs for computer-aided design and communication to be able to work with the different automobile manufacturers with whom they partner.

In 1984, the European automobile manufacturers formed ODETTE (Organization for Data Exchange and TeleTransmission in Europe) for the exchange of information

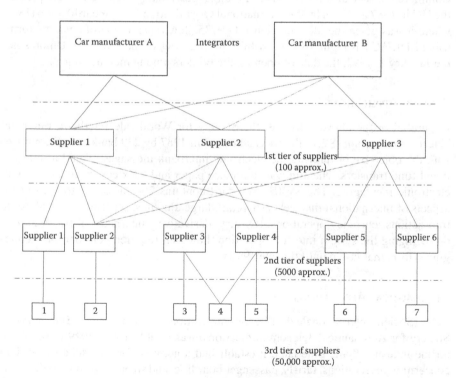

FIGURE 23.1 Hierarchical structure of the automobile industry as integrators and three tiers of suppliers. (Adapted from Sherif, M. H., *Protocols for Secure Electronic Commerce*, 2nd edn, CRC Press, Boca Raton, FL, 2004, pp. 174–181. With permission.)

between suppliers and car manufacturers. Part of its program involved the standardization of the content and the structure of the documents and the use of common transmission protocols according to the syntax of EDIFACT in ISO 7372. The North-American equivalent is the ANX® (Automotive Network eXchange), the network of the Automotive Industry Action Group (AIAG), which is based on the TCP/IP protocol stack. AIAG was formed in 1982 to define the rules for exchanging information among partners in the North-American car industry.

MISCELLANEOUS EXAMPLES

Retail distributors use the standard EAN (European Article Number) for the automatic identification of items which was discussed in Chapter 19. The multinationals in the area of industrial chemistry employ the procedures of the CEFIC (Conseil Européen des Fédérations de l'Industrie Chimique—European Council of Industrial Chemistry federations) in Europe and the CIDX (Chemical Industry Document Exchange) in the United States, and so on.

STANDARDIZATION, THEN AND NOW

In the 1980s, the focus of standardization was on the format and content of messages exchanged and EDI was concerned with the purchase of direct goods related to the production chain or to the service creation in a specific sector. Nonstrategic purchases (equipment and office furniture, travels, etc.), even though they represent the majority of purchases in volume, continued to be managed in the traditional way. Specialized software at each end performed the necessary format conversions, while providers of value added networks (VAN) were responsible for the details of the communication and its security, including the protocol conversion to and from the networks used within each trading organization. Private contracts (interchange agreements) defined the framework for bilateral electronic transactions: the technical and legal responsibilities of each party, the rules for authentication and identification of the various entities, and the ways to preserve and archive the electronic documents. Enterprise Resource Planning (ERP) systems were introduced later to integrate the back office and production planning systems with incoming orders.

An important limitation of the traditional representation of data in EDI is its reliance on alphanumeric characters, even though in many sectors, such as automobile or public works, there is a need to include other types of data such as drawings. Network convergence onto the TCP/IP protocol introduced the need to secure the transport of legacy EDI messages on the Internet and gave the opportunity to include all the objects of commercial transactions (text, graphics, images, sound, audio, and video) by using structured documents, first based on SGML (Standard Generalized Markup Language) defined in ISO 8879 and finally on the XML. Thus, standardization actually refocused on the following items:

- The coexistence of the traditional EDI with XML-based communication
- The integration of business-to-business communication with new developments in enterprise systems such as Enterprise Application Integration (EAI), ERP, Web services, and service-oriented architecture (SOA)

- The interoperability of businesses at the semantic level, because open communication and the global dimension of the Internet would bring together many organizations with dissimilar business procedures and scenarios

As a consequence, the architecture for business-to-business exchanges had to evolve from that of the traditional EDI. We will now review that traditional EDI.

X12 AND EDIFACT

In the traditional way of business-to-business electronic communications, data are extracted from the enterprise databases, converted to a mutually agreed format, and secured before transmission to the VAN that is connecting the business partners. At the destination, the received data are converted to the "in-house" format and then directed to the specific application that can process the data. The software that interfaces with both the transmission network and the internal systems and carries out the necessary format conversion and reorganization data is called "translator" or "converter."

As explained earlier, there are two different standards for structuring the content of documents into alphanumeric messages. X12 is the structuring method most frequently used in North America (United States and Canada), whereas EDIFACT is used in Europe. The differences between the two reside in the definitions of the various data elements, the syntax rules, as well as the procedures employed to secure the exchanges.

The basic units of an alphanumeric EDI exchange are *data elements* defined in a dictionary of elementary data. From a functional viewpoint, the data element is either a *service element* or an *application element*. Service elements contain the information that structures the transmission and are utilized in service segments. In contrast, application elements relate to the heart of the end-to-end transaction itself, that is, the data defined and agreed upon by the two parties of the transaction.

A *segment* is a logical set that includes a series of elements, simple or compound, and may include other segments. The order, content, the maximum number of repetitions of the constituents, and the way these repetitions should be organized are defined in the segment dictionary. To express a precise functionality, for example, a purchase order or a payment instruction, the segments are combined and organized in a *group of segments*.

Control (or service) segments are used to structure the content and to distinguish the various parties. The application data segments contain the application data organized by function. It is the entity in charge of managing the application that is responsible for specifying the coding and the organization of the application data segments.

A *transaction set* (X12) or *message* (EDIFACT) is the set of structured segments in the order defined in a directory of the corresponding standard messages. These messages represent functions that are common to all activity sectors.

SECURITY

Standardization of EDI security is relatively more recent. X12 transmissions use the security structures defined in X12.58 issued in December 1997. X12 can directly utilize the X.509 certificates delivered by a certification authority.

Security of EDIFACT follows ISO 7498-2 (1989). This standard is the outcome of the European research program TEDIS (Trade Electronic Data Interchange System), which lasted from 1988 to 1994. The services offered are message integrity, authentication of the origin, and nonrepudiation (at the origin and at the destination). Confidentiality is not offered explicitly, but may be constructed with the other services. EDIFACT security services can be offered in two ways: by sending security segments "in band" using ISO 9735-5 or "out-of-band" with ISO 9735-6, both adopted in 2002.

The management of EDIFACT certificates (inscription, renewal, replacement, revocation, delivery) as well as the generation, distribution, and management of keys is defined in ISO 9735-9. It should be noted that the EDIFACT certificates are different from X.509 certificates both in their format and in their method of management. However, a DEDICA (Directory-based EDI Certificate Access and Management) gateway allows access to secure EDI with X.509 certificates.

EDI SECURITY WITH MULTIPURPOSE INTERNET MAIL EXTENSIONS AND SIMPLE MAIL TRANSFER PROTOCOL

The need for transporting EDI messages with Simple Mail Transfer Protocol (SMTP) and Multipurpose Internet Mail Extensions (MIME) became more pressing as enterprises started to use the IPs in their networks. Various specifications defined in Request For Comments (RFCs) 2045 through 2049 show how to encapsulate these messages to include different object types. In addition, RFC 3335 describes how EDI messages could be protected with encryption and digital signatures using Pretty Good Privacy/MIME, Secure MIME, or Secure HyperText Transfer Protocol (HTTP).

Figure 23.2 summarizes the different protocol stacks for EDI messaging without security while Figure 23.3 depicts a synthetic view of the protocol stack for a secure EDI. In these figures, X.25, X.400, and so on refer to the ITU-T—formerly known as

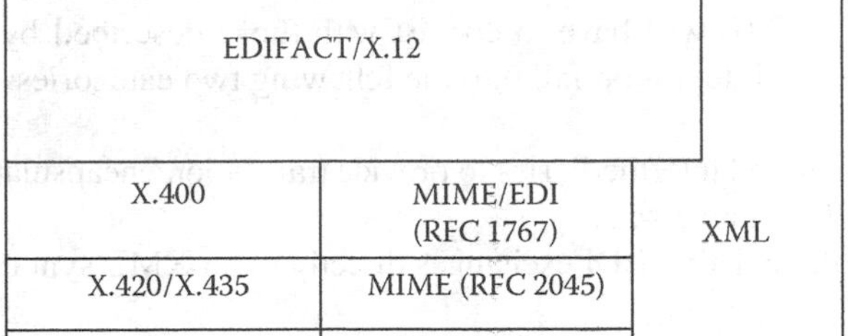

EDIFACT/X.12			
X.400	MIME/EDI (RFC 1767)	XML	
X.420/X.435	MIME (RFC 2045)		
X.411	SMTP (RFC 821)		
X.214–X.216	TCP		
X.25	IP		

FIGURE 23.2 Protocol stack for EDI messaging (without security). (Adapted from Sherif, M. H., *Protocols for Secure Electronic Commerce*, 2nd edn, CRC Press, Boca Raton, FL, 2004, pp. 174–181. With permission.)

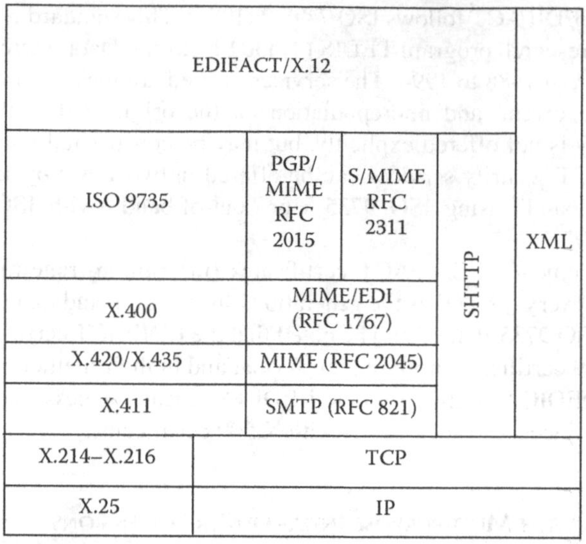

EDIFACT/X.12					
ISO 9735	PGP/ MIME RFC 2015	S/MIME RFC 2311		SHTTP	XML
X.400	MIME/EDI (RFC 1767)				
X.420/X.435	MIME (RFC 2045)				
X.411	SMTP (RFC 821)				
X.214–X.216	TCP				
X.25	IP				

FIGURE 23.3 Synthetic view of the protocol stack for secure EDI. (Adapted from Sherif, M. H., *Protocols for Secure Electronic Commerce*, 2nd edn, CRC Press, Boca Raton, FL, 2004, pp. 174–181. With permission.)

the CCITT (Comité Consultatif International Téléphonique et Télégraphique)—recommendations that are part of the EDIFACT specifications.

INTEGRATION OF XML AND TRADITIONAL EDI

Predictions that novel Internet-based platforms will rapidly supplant the traditional EDI in business-to-business commerce turned out to be incorrect. Although the volume of enterprise purchases over the Internet has expanded, EDI and private value-added networks continued to thrive and increased their revenues. However, as new industrial applications are now based on XML, it became evident that exchanges structured with XML will have to coexist with those described by the traditional EDI. Strategies for integration fall into the following two categories:

1. Use specialized intermediaries to provide translation/encapsulation services between EDI and XML.
2. Express the existing EDI exchanges directly in an XML syntax.

We now review the main efforts in each category and present RosettaNet, a totally independent e-Business activity that got folded into the mainstream of business-to-business communications.

EDI/XML TRANSLATION/ENCAPSULATION

In this approach, called "WebEDI," an intermediary is responsible for carrying the translation of EDI messages into XML dialogues (Figure 23.4). The traditional EDI

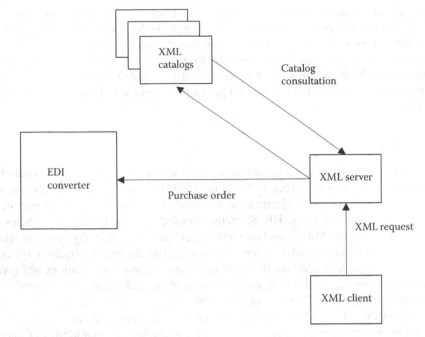

FIGURE 23.4   EDI/XML integration. (Adapted from Sherif, M. H., *Protocols for Secure Electronic Commerce*, 2nd edn, CRC Press, Boca Raton, FL, 2004, pp. 174–181. With permission.)

messages are encapsulated to display them on the client station with a simple browser. The end-user sees at the client station an electronic form to be filled through a browser. This arrangement takes into consideration prior investment in alphanumeric EDI. The disadvantage of this solution is that it rests on proprietary formats because the interface between the client and the server is not standardized.

XML EXPRESSIONS OF EDI

This is a pragmatic approach relying on the conversion of existing EDI messages into XML documents. Two approaches, in particular, warrant attention: XML Common Business Library (xCBL) and Universal Business Language (UBL).

XML Common Business Library

The xCBL initiative was started in 1997 by software companies such as Veo Systems and Commerce One to express EDI messages (X12 and EDIFACT) in the XML syntax. The documents covered include cost estimates, invoicing, payment, order tracking, shipment of goods, delivery, and so on. The work continued after Commerce One had acquired Veo Systems and resulted in Version 3.0, approved in November 2001, which served as the basis for UBL.

Universal Business Language

The UBL was developed by the Organization for the Advancement of Structured Information Standards (OASIS) consortium to facilitate the production of XML schemas for business operations starting with a library of EDI templates. This language was initially promoted by CommerceNet on the basis of Version 3.0 of xCBL. The first version of the specification codifies the transposition of the X12 and EDIFACT messages associated with the cycle purchase order/invoice into their equivalent in XML schemas [2]. A version of UBL, called OIOXML, is currently the only format recognized in Denmark for public procurement and for government ERP systems [3].

RosettaNet

The scope of the RosettaNet consortium, founded in 1998, was the supply chain for the electronics industry, a sector almost unaffected by the legacy EDI. The parties included manufacturers of electronic components (e.g., Intel), equipment manufacturers (e.g., Cisco Systems, HP, Siemens, Toshiba), system integrators, wholesale dealers (e.g., Ingram Micro), and retailers (e.g., CompUSA). The object was to allow tracking of the supply chain at any moment by linking the information systems end-to-end so as to coordinate the production and distribution capacities and avoid build-ups or shortages. All business processes, objects, and transaction models are described using PIPs (Partner Interface Processes). In 2002, the Uniform Code Council (UCC) absorbed RosettaNet. The UCC covers around 23 industries associated with the public warehousing and grocery industries. As mentioned in Chapter 19, the UCC changed its name to GS1 US in 2005.

NEW ARCHITECTURES FOR BUSINESS-TO-BUSINESS ELECTRONIC COMMERCE

The switch to TCP/IP networks in the mid-1990s initiated a wave of migration from proprietary to standard solutions. This led to a major redesign of the architectures of business-to-business electronic. Semantic interoperability was added to the list of requirements in the face of the heterogeneity of business models and processes [4].

In this new architecture, reusable components are built on the basis of domain information that represents the common requirements within a specific industrial or economic sector. These components are then stored in global depositories and referred to in a directory accessible on the World Wide Web. The directory points to repositories storing the potential partners' profiles, the processes, the exchange scenarios, and the data dictionaries. The dynamic discovery of the services, service providers, and agreements, and the potential partners are mediated through standardized protocols. Finally, at run-time, that is, when a specific transaction takes place, the exchanges follow a predefined "choreography" specified in the business process model. This new architecture is represented in Figure 23.5.

Depending on the starting point, we can distinguish two major ways to implement this architecture. The first evolved from the traditional EDI with the intent of exploiting the capabilities of XML and the World Wide Web; this is the ebXML framework. Another technology base is that of ERP and EAI, which leads to Web services as the building blocks for integrating electronic commercial exchanges within and without the enterprise boundaries. These two approaches are illustrated in Figure 23.6.

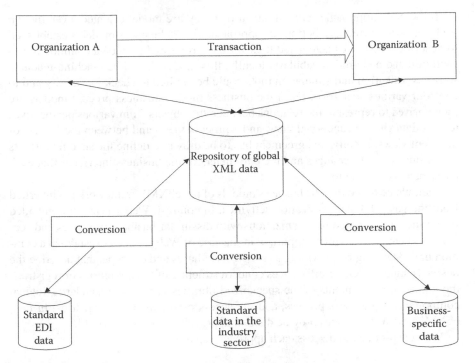

FIGURE 23.5 New architecture for the business-to-business electronic commerce. (Adapted from Sherif, M. H., *Protocols for Secure Electronic Commerce*, 2nd edn, CRC Press, Boca Raton, FL, 2004, pp. 174–181. With permission.)

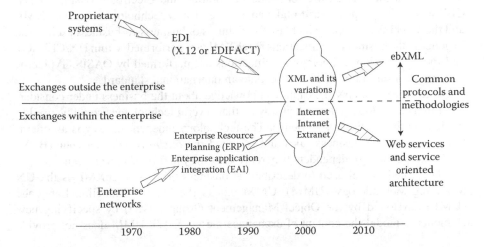

FIGURE 23.6 Convergences and divergences in collaborative applications inside and outside enterprises.

Today both approaches are similar in that they are model-oriented, even though Web services started as a bottom-up approach. First, a business model is established to describe the various actors and their business roles and provide a common representation and a shared vocabulary. Ideally, this model should be machine-readable so that verification and simulation tools could be applied to check its validity and to consider various scenarios. From the business model, business process models are then derived to represent the relations between the objects from various perspectives (e.g., a data view, a functional view, and a process view) and between the objects of different views. Finally, an agreement has to be drawn to define the specific formats of the business interchanges and the parameters of the business interfaces that each party has to conform to.

It should be noted that the business models of the ebXML framework are inherited from the past EDI standardization activities. In contrast, Web services are intended for a much wider range of organizations with dissimilar business processes and scenarios. Therefore, it is more important in the case of Web services to establish a common understanding by providing a set of vocabularies and concepts that describe the business logic [5]. Other differences concern structure of the directories or registries, the nature of the contents of the specialized libraries in terms of standards, logical components or business process, and the access protocols to the registries. In fact, ebXML and Web services provide distinct approaches for discovery [6].

We now proceed to discuss each approach separately.

ELECTRONIC BUSINESS (USING) XML

As stated earlier, ebXML is a model-driven open framework to ensure the interoperability of transactions among business entities based on the object-oriented methodology and consistent with the Open-edi reference model of ISO/IEC 14662. The specifications of ebXML were started jointly in September 1999 by the OASIS consortium* and the UN Centre for Trade Facilitation and Electronic Business (UN/CEFACT). The purpose was to take advantage of new technologies, such as XML and the World Wide Web, to increase the richness of business-to-business exchanges. In general, the business specifications for ebXML are performed within UN/CEFACT and the information technology specifications are performed by OASIS. Typically, they are then submitted to ISO to become an international standard.

As in Open-edi, ebXML captures knowledge about the business under consideration in a technology-independent way so that several technologies could be used to implement this business knowledge. The technology-independent way is an operational view of the business rules and is called the *business-oriented view* (BOV) while the technology-dependent way represents the *functional service view*.

The formal model used to describe the business process in ebXML is the UN Modeling Methodology (UMM). UMM adapts the Unified Modeling Language (UML) developed by the Object Management Group (OMG) by specifying new elements to model the content of exchanges messages [7]. UMM does not provide

---

* This consortium, founded in 1993, groups the main software developers and system integrators and focuses on Web services standards.

specific mechanisms for message exchange and does not specify the data to be exchanged. With this arrangement, several implementation technologies could correspond to the same specification. Further details on UMM are available in Chapters 12 and 22 of this book.

ARCHITECTURE OF ebXML

The ebXML is built on a directed peer-to-peer architecture with five major components and two perspectives. The BOV comprises the business scenarios and the core components. The business scenarios capture the business knowledge in the form of process models for the interaction between the parties of a transaction or an interaction. The core components are the basic building blocks used to construct all the interactions. The functional view consists of the following:

- The specific profile of the collaboration protocol as well as the agreements between the two parties on the various aspects of the transaction that are needed for its execution
- A registry of previously agreed information on objects, exchanges, and processes that could be reused
- A messaging protocol for communicating and exchanging data through standardized interfaces

These five parts are defined in a series of standards defined by UN/CEFACT, OASIS, and ISO, as listed in Table 23.1.

Business Scenarios

Typical business scenarios, such as catalogue consultation, purchasing, payment, delivery, and so on, are modeled using UMM. The corresponding business processes are described using an XML-based language called the Business Process Specification Schema (BPSS). Each process is described from the following three views:

- A business domain view to describe the context and the business sector where the process applies
- A business requirements view for the preconditions to execute the process
- A business transaction view reserved for the exchanged data at the semantic level

Core Components

The core components are the objects, messages, and data elements that are used for a given business sector as the building block for all processes, messages, and data exchanges. They are specified in UML and stored in a core components library. Agreements on these building blocks are reached at the international level under the auspices of the UN/CEFACT. They are then harmonized with those of other sectors to avoid duplication and encourage reuse.

The exchanged documents are formed from the core components, taking into account the business rules governing the exchange and the context of use. A Business

TABLE 23.1

Standards and Specifications of ebXML

Document Title	Source	URL	ISO
ebXML Technical Architecture Specification v1.0.4, 16 February 2001	UN/CEFACT and OASIS	http://www.ebxml.org/specs/ebTA.pdf	—
ebXML Business Process Specification Schema Technical Specification v2.0.4, 21 December 2006	OASIS	http://docs.oasis-open.org/ebxml-bp/2.0.4/OS/spec/ebxmlbp-v2.0.4-Spec-os-en.pdf	—
ebXML Collaboration Protocol Profile and Agreement Specification, Version 2.0, September 23, 2002	OASIS	http://www.oasis-open.org/committees/ebxml-cppa/documents/ebcpp-2.0.pdf	ISO/TS 15000-1:2004, Electronic business Extensible Markup Language (ebXML)—Part 1: Collaboration-protocol profile and agreement specification (ebCPP)
ebXML Messaging Services version 3.0: Part 1, Core Features	OASIS	http://docs.oasis-open.org/ebxml-msg/ebms/v3.0/core/os/ebms_core-3.0-spec-os.pdf	—
ebXML Message Service Specification Version 2.0, 1 April 2002	OASIS	http://www.oasis-open.org/committees/ebxml-msg/documents/ebMS_v2_0.pdf	ISO/TS 15000-2:2004, Electronic business Extensible Markup Language (ebXML)—Part 2: Message service specification (ebMS)
ebXML Registry Information Model (RIM) v3.0, May 2005	OASIS	Not available	
ebXML Registry Information Model (RIM) v2., April 2002	OASIS	http://www.oasis-open.org/committees/regrep/documents/2.0/specs/ebrim.pdf	ISO/TS 15000-3:2004, Electronic business Extensible Markup Language (ebXML)—Part 3: Registry information model specification (ebRIM)

Standard	Organization	URL	ISO equivalent
ebXML Registry Services Specification (RS) v3.0, May 2005	OASIS	Not available	—
ebXML Registry Services Specification (RS) v2.0, April 2002	OASIS	http://www.oasis-open.org/committees/regrep/documents/2.0/specs/ebrs.pdf	ISO/TS 15000-4:2004, Electronic business Extensible Markup Language (ebXML)—Part 4: Registry services specification (ebRS)
Core Components Technical Specification—Part 8 of the ebXML Framework, 15 November 2003, Version 2.01	UN/CEFACT	http://www.unece.org/cefact/ebxml/CCTS_V2-01_Final.pdf)	ISO/TS 15000-5:2005, Electronic Business Extensible Markup Language (ebXML)—Part 5: ebXML Core Components Technical Specification, Version 2.01(ebCCTS)
UML Profile for Core Components (UPCC), Version 1.0, Final Specification, 2008-01-16	UN/CEFACT	http://www.unece.org/cefact/codesfortrade/UPCC_UML-CoreComponent.pdf	—
UN/CEFACT's Modeling Methodology (UMM): UMM Meta Model—Base Module Version 1.0 Technical Specification, 2006-10-06	UN/CEFACT	http://www.unece.org/cefact/umm/UMM_Base_Module.pdf	—
XML Naming and Design Rules, Version 2.0, 17 February 2006	UN/CEFACT	http://www.unece.org/cefact/xml/XML-Naming-and-Design-Rules-V2.0.pdf	—

Note: All Web sites were last accessed on June 29, 2009.

Information Entity is made from the core components arranged in a specific business context. Changes to the core components do not affect the choreography. Similarly changes in the preconditions that affect the choreography, that is, the interchange agreement, do not ripple through to the data. With the separation of the business from the functional aspects, the information model is valid irrespective of the syntax used, for example, ANSI X12 or EDIFACT messages or XML documents.

Registry and Repository

The registry contains information about companies or organizations as well as definitions of the processes already defined for business collaborations, and the meta-information concerning the objects in a business collaboration, such as the messages to be exchanged, the data definitions, and formats. The Registry Information Model describes the internal data structure of the registry. The Registry Services (RS) describe the methods for accessing the registry via a browser over the Word Wide Web or via queries using Structured Query Language (SQL).

The repository is the actual database that stores the entries. It can be centralized or distributed on a geographic basis or per business sector or using both criteria. The RS specifications explain how to synchronize the various distributed data stores and how to retrieve the information.

Collaboration Protocol Profile and Agreement

The protocol profiles for collaboration describe the technical capabilities of the partners in a business transaction in terms of the services offered, the parameters of the connection, for example, the configuration and security parameters, the maximum delay before an acknowledgement is to be sent, the maximum number of attempts at a communication, and so on. For any given party, its business profile is based on the core components used in the interaction, the common business processes for the particular business sector, and the instant of the process model described in BPSS that is appropriate to the firm. Each company defines its profile in XML and stores it in the ebXML registry as a Collaboration Protocol Profile (CPP) as defined in the electronic business Collaboration Protocol Profile and Agreement (ebCPPA).

Companies find each other's profiles by querying the registry or by communicating directing. The technical agreements among the parties can be made automatically using an automatic matching process to determine if the two profiles can be matched and if so, create a technical contract that binds the two parties. The Collaboration Protocol Agreement (CPA) defines the technical parameters of the interface and the messaging services as specified in the CPPA. The CPA does not cover the legal aspects of the collaboration.

Message Service Specification

The message service (ebMS) concerns the messaging protocol and the structure of the messages to be sent securely over the World Wide Web. The ebMS has a payload outside the Simple Object Access Protocol (SOAP) body, that is, SOAP with Attachment (SwA), the messages or "payload." SOAP structures the exchanges in the form of requests and responses. The messages are XML documents formed of three

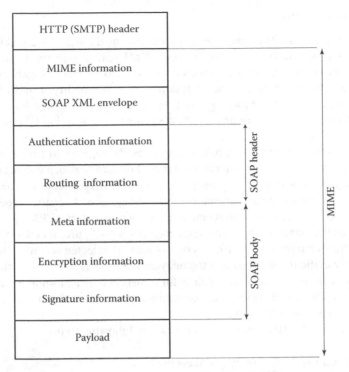

FIGURE 23.7 Structure of ebXML message specification (ebMS).

elements: an envelope, coding rules and conventions to make remote procedure calls and interpret their responses, and a payload. The envelope consists of a header and a body. The header supplies information for authenticating the exchange as well as routing information. The body contains the elements that are needed to interpret the exchanges as well as encryption and signature information. The transport protocol is usually HTTP, but ebMS can also be used on top of SMTP or FTP (File Transfer Protocol). ebMS adds security mechanism so that messages can be partially or totally encrypted and/or electronically signed to verify their integrity.

The structure of the MIME ebMS message with an SwA is shown in Figure 23.7, while Figure 23.8 illustrates the protocol stack of ebXML.

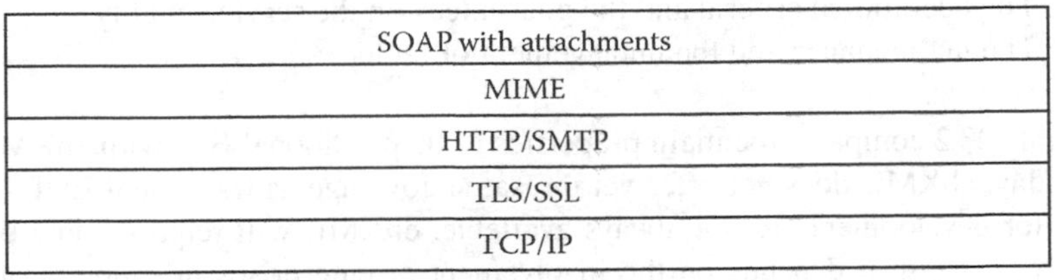

SOAP with attachments
MIME
HTTP/SMTP
TLS/SSL
TCP/IP

FIGURE 23.8 Protocol stack for ebXML.

ebXML OPERATIONS

Each business defines its business processes following the steps specified in ebXML and requests them to be registered in the ebXML global registry. It may have to modify some of its proposed definitions to conform to the rules already established or reuse an already existing process specification and modify it according to its proper usage. Alternatively, it may start by querying the registry for an existing specification to start with. In any event, it submits a conforming CPP to be registered and stored.

To establish collaboration, a business queries the registry to find a match to a specific profile or a specific scenario of interest. For each match, it contacts the associated party to propose an arrangement using the ebXML procedures. The proposed arrangement outlines specific scenarios and messaging and security requirements. Once both parties settle on an agreement, they document it in a CPA.

Based on the details of the agreement, each party configures its interfaces, called Business Service Interfaces. The core components are selected according to the context of the specific transactions and the relevant Business Information Entities.

If intermediaries are involved, such as for transportation and shipping, each party conducts similar negotiations with these intermediaries independently, because ebXML is a peer-to-peer arrangement.

In summary, ebXML operations comprise the following steps:

- Registration of each party and their profiles
- Discovery, where each party discovers the other's technical capabilities and negotiates an agreement
- Implementation, during which each party implements and configure an ebXML compliant application capable of carrying out the business collaboration described in the agreement
- Run time, where the business transaction takes place according to the choreography of the business process specification

The first three steps occur in the "design time" as depicted in Figure 23.9 [8].

For a fully operational ebXML system, some additional architectural decisions will have to be made, such as the following:

- The placement of the registries, directories, and repositories
- The procedures to verify the conformance of the stored components to the specifications
- The operational criteria and the guarantees on the service quality
- The maintenance and the management of faults

Table 23.2 compares the main properties of the traditional EDI with ebXML.

Today, ebXML does not offer yet the same coverage as traditional EDI and the tools for development are not always available. ebXML will require some time to mature, because it depends on the involvement of enterprises in supplying all the necessary blocks.

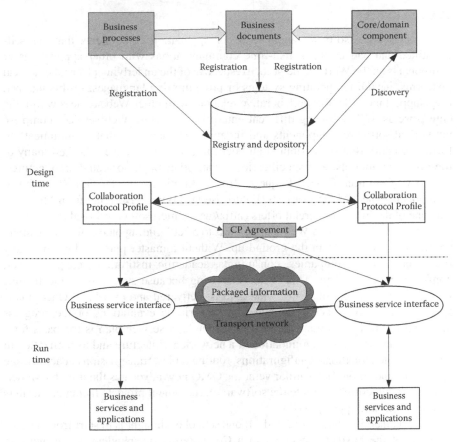

FIGURE 23.9 Technical operations of ebXML.

TABLE 23.2

Comparison of Traditional EDI and ebXML

Characteristics	Traditional EDI	ebXML
Design orientation	Documents	Processes
Nature of the links	Point-to-point	Peer-to-peer but allows multilinks
Interface configuration	Static and manual	Dynamic and automatic
Subject of standardization	Structured messages, data elements and segments	Methods, architectures, processes, objects
Technical negotiation	Manual	Automatic
Operation	Batch	Transactional
Orchestration of the exchange kinetics	Managed by each application	Managed by a choreography process

WEB SERVICES

Web services are software applications or application components that are self-contained and can establish real-time communications with other applications or components on the World Wide Web, irrespective of the underlying physical or logical platforms, including operating systems or programming languages. In this manner, they support more flexible collaborative relations with other Web services within the enterprise as well as among different enterprises. Because Web services comprise networked software components and independent machines that communicate to form one entity that is distributed and decentralized, they have inherited many of the concepts, models, and specifications from other object-oriented architectures: CORBA (Common Object Request Broker Architecture), DCOM (Distributed Component Object Model), or EJB (Enterprise Java Beans). BizTalk® from Microsoft was one of the first commercial offers (http://www.microsoft.com/biztalk).

The original concept of Web services was to offer building blocks for use in many applications starting from the ground up. Without a master plan guiding the many interested parties (companies, consultants, academic institutions, etc.), however, confusion rapidly set in. This is not surprising because successful projects start with a clear statement of needs, what is to be delivered and by whom. Once this is agreed, execution proceeds in phases with periodic evaluations of the progress achieved [9]. In telecommunications, for example, a service plan is the basis for a network plan, which is the foundation of a network architecture and its realization in terms of switch locations, configurations, routing tables, transmission capacities, site selections, and so on. In a similar vein, the OMG now advocates the use of a Model-Driven Architecture® to guide the software development projects facing constraints on cost, time, and quality [11].

As explained in Chapters 12 and 14, one school of thought is to start from a holistic view of the business specified in a Computation-Independent Model with an appropriate meta-modeling language, such as e3-value to capture the high-level knowledge about the business operations, rules, and terminology. Next, a Platform-Independent Model (PIM) is derived to describe the business process that would implement the business model in a technology-neutral manner. During this derivation, design alternatives can be considered. Alternatively, the starting point can be the PIM itself, described in the appropriate formalism such as UML. The PIM is mapped into several Platform-Specific Models for the inter-organizational business processes as well as the internal processes of each party in their own specific technology. Finally, the actual code and other deployment artifacts (documentation, diagrams, configuration files, tests files, release notes, etc.) are generated in target languages such as XML, Java, and so on [11–13]. Figure 23.10 shows an example for mapping the various model to the final code, as a particular development artifact.

As a new technology, there is a lot of ground work to cover and the number of specifications and standards related to Web services is impressive as shown in comprehensive treatments available elsewhere [14–16]. The focus here is on standards that have been approved by the main standard setting organizations involved, OASIS and the World Wide Web Consortium (W3C), to highlight some of the difficulties to achieve the integration of business-to-business applications.

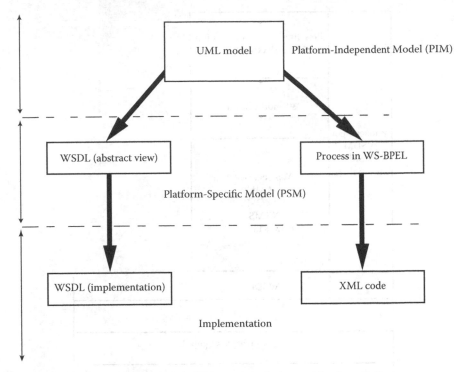

FIGURE 23.10   Model mappings in Web services design and implementation.

WEB SERVICES STANDARDS

The basic protocols of the Web services are as follows:

- Web Services Description Language (WSDL)
- Universal Description, Discovery and Integration (UDDI)
- SOAP

Additional protocols concern security, management, presentation, orchestration, routing and delivery of messages, and so on. Figure 23.11 is an attempt at presenting the protocol stack for Web services. It should be noted that there is not yet an agreement on how to present that stack, as shown in at least two instances ([16]; Figure 1.7 on p. 33 and Figure 7.1 on p. 218). We now present these various protocols.

WEB SERVICES DESCRIPTION LANGUAGE

WSDL is used to describe the operation interface to Web services (addresses, parameters, messages, and transport) so that they can be invoked in a client–server model of interaction. The description includes the operation that the service does and the protocols needed to access it on the World Wide Web. The description of the workflow internal to the state machine that represents the service (orchestration or service

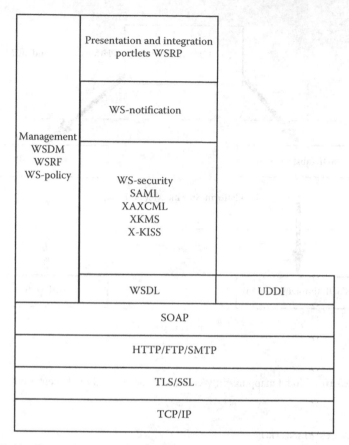

FIGURE 23.11   Protocol stack for Web services.

composition) is performed using Web Service Business Process Execution Language (WS-BPEL). The exchange of messages among the various BPEL machines according to the rules agreed by the various parties (choreography) is described with the WS-CDL (Web Services Choreography Description Language).

UNIVERSAL DESCRIPTION, DISCOVERY, AND INTEGRATION

UDDI describes a universal registry for the services, the businesses that offer them and their processes, organized in multiple ways, such as by name, by category, by geographic location, and so on. The aim is to have a uniform interface so that enterprises can discover potential trading partners and basic information about them irrespective of the technologies used to construct the subsuming directories and their geographic location. Thus, the WSDL files could be distributed over many sites and/or administrative domains, with the registry acting as a logical structure pointing to specific directories where the information resides.

SIMPLE OBJECT ACCESS PROTOCOL

SOAP defines the structure of the XML messages for communication in a decentralized, distributed environment. The messages are XML documents formed of an envelope, an optional header, a body, and fault information. They are typically transported using HTTP [14].

WS-Addressing provides a mechanism for exchanging end-point logical addresses to be inserted in the SOAP envelopes. WS-Eventing specifies ways to provide asynchronous notification of events (e.g., the events associated with shipping an order) and subscribe to an event notification service (e.g., when a process has completed), which are needed for event driven SOAs.

SECURITY

Security Assertion Markup Language (SAML) is a protocol from OASIS that describes, using XML documents, user profiles and the requests for authentication before authorizing the access of an individual or an object to a given service. It establishes equivalencies among administrative domains, each with its own policy for managing rights.

WS-Security specifications, also from OASIS, describe the conceptual and technical basis of integrity and authentication. When a user identifies itself to a SAML server, the latter includes a description of the user's access rights within a SOAP envelope to be forwarded to the servers of the remaining Web services within the same administrative domain. Thus, following the initial authentication, the user's access profile is propagated to avoid a second authentication in a process called SSO (Single Sign-On)—this is also called the "federated identify" of the user. The SAML structures are transported either using the POST method of HTTP or in SOAP messages. The elements used for authentication are defined using the SAML protocol. WS-Security provides support for multiple security token formats, multiple trust domains, multiple signature formats, and multiple encryption technologies. Among these tokens are X.509 certificates and Kerberos tickets.

The security of XML exchanges themselves is the subject of several recommendations and technical reports from the W3C. XML Encryption allows selective encryption by identifying the sections to be encrypted with specialized tags while the processing of signatures is specified in XML Digital Signature.

The management of encryption keys has its own set of specifications. XKMS (XML Key Management Specification) defines the public key infrastructure for Web services in two ways: XML Key Information Service Specification (X-KISS) and XML Key Registration Service Specification (X-KRSS). X-KISS provides a client with the possibility of avoiding the computational load of the security tasks such as encryption, signature, authentication, and so on, by delegating them to specialized servers with larger computational power. X-KRSS specifies the protocol to register data about public keys so that they can be made available to all secured services on the Web. XACML (Extensible Access Control Markup Language) defines the access rights to a Web service and the ways to manage them. It is worth noting that this specification overlaps with another non-W3C specification (WS-Authorization).

Additional OASIS security specifications include the following:

1. WS-Trust to describe the trust model of Web services.
2. WS-SecureConversation (Web Services Secure Conversation Language), which builds on the WS-Security and WS-Trust models to secure the communication among Web services.
3. WS-SecurityPolicy (Web Services Security Policy Language), which defines how to represent the security capabilities and requirements of a Web service in machine readable form so that the compatibilities of the policies could be determined automatically.

The main W3C security specifications are as follows:

1. The Web Services Policy 1.5—Framework (WS-Policy), which defines a framework for expressing the security constraints and requirements of Web services as policy assertions.
2. Web Services Policy 1.5—Attachment (WS-PolicyAttachment). A policy attachment is a mechanism for associating a policy with one or more policy scopes, a policy scope being a collection of policy subjects to which a policy applies.
3. Web Services Policy Assertions Language (WS-PolicyAssertions).

STANDARDIZATION

Table 23.3 summarizes the partition of standardization activities between OASIS and the W3C.

TABLE 23.3
Standardization Activities for Web Services

Technical Service	Protocol	Function	Standards Organization
Presentation	WSRP (Web Services for Remote Portlets)	Aggregation of contents among enterprise portals	OASIS
Process orchestration	WS-BPEL (Web Service Business Process Execution Language)	Description and modeling of business processes	OASIS
Choreography	WS-CDL (Web Services Choreography Description Language)	To specify the rules of the message exchanges based on a common agreement of the parties involved	W3C

continued

TABLE 23.3   (continued)
Standardization Activities for Web Services

Technical Service	Protocol	Function	Standards Organization
Transaction	WSTF (Web Services Transaction) which comprise the following: WS-Coordination WS-AtomicTransaction WS-BusinessActivity	The mechanisms for transaction processing and management	OASIS
	WS-Addressing	Mechanism to find and exchange the logical addresses	W3C
Messaging	WS-ReliableMessaging	To provide guarantees for the message delivery in the presence of network failures	OASIS
Distributed Management of Services	WSDM (Web Services Distributed Management)	End-to-end management of Web services	OASIS
	SAML (Security Assertion Markup Language) WS-Security WS-Trust Web Services Secure Conversation Language (WS-SecureConversation) Web Services Security Policy Language (WS-SecurityPolicy)		OASIS
Security	XML Encryption XML Digital Signature. XML Key Management Specification (XKMS) XML Key Information Service Specification (X-KISS) XML Key Registration Service Specification (X-KRSS) XACML (Extensible Access Control Markup Language) WS-Policy WS-PolicyAssertions WS-PolicyAttachment	See text	W3C

Finally, the Web Services Interoperability Organization (WS-I) (http://www.ws-i.org) is an industry consortium that IBM and Microsoft initiated in 2003. It is focused on providing guidance, recommended best practices and supporting test tools to ensure the interoperability of Web services.

FINANCIAL DIALECTS OF XML

Market pressures, competition, and in some cases regulatory demands have combined to create a situation where independent efforts to derive XML-based descriptions of financial transactions have multiplied leading to a large number of languages, some of which are listed in Table 23.4.

It goes without saying that the presence of many specifications in the same sector is a major cause of concern because it increases the cost and difficulties of interoperability to the point of putting the benefits of electronic integration into question.

TABLE 23.4
Some XML Derivatives for Financial Services

Acronym	Title	Remarks
FinXML	Fixed Income Markup Language	—
FIXML	Financial Information Exchange Markup Language	—
FpML	Financial Products Markup Language	Over-the-counter derivatives
FXML	Financial Exchange Markup Language	—
IFX	Interactive Financial Exchange	Synthesis of the OFX and Gold specifications for on-line presentation of financial information, electronic bill presentment, electronic banking, and so on
IRML	Investment Research Markup Language	—
MDDL	Market Data Definition Language	Description of marketing research
NewsML	Electronic News Markup Language	Multimedia financial news
NTM	Network Trade Model	Stock and risk evaluation
OFX	Open Financial Exchange	Online exchange of payment messages among financial institution. Used for electronic billing
RIXML	Research Information Exchange Markup Language	Document indexing
STPML	Straight Through Processing Extensible Markup Language	—
TWIST	Transaction Workflow Innovation Standard Team	Wholesale financial transaction and account administration; financial supply chain (ordering, invoicing, financing, etc.)
xBRL	Extensible Business Reporting Language	Financial reporting
XFRML	Extensible Financial Reporting Markup Language	—

This, in turn, has spurred initiatives to bring some order to the situation by paring the number of specifications. In 1999, under the influence of BITS, the technology group for the Financial Services Roundtable, the Open Financial Exchange (OFX) and Gold specifications were merged into the Interactive Financial Exchange (IFX), to provide a unique way for describing on-line presentations of financial information, electronic bill presentment, electronic banking, and so on. Then, in 2003, IFX, the OAGi (Open Applications Group), SWIFT, and TWIST (Transaction Workflow Innovation Standards Team) launched the International Standards Team Harmonization (ISTH) initiative to develop and promote a common "core payment XML kernel" that banks could use globally. In 2004, ISO 20022 was agreed to define the UNIFI (Universal Financial Industry) message scheme. Unfortunately, however, the specifications of ISO 20022 and the prescribed registration infrastructure are not totally consistent with the framework used for the ebXML. Furthermore, the ISTH covered only one of the many financial services (i.e., payment). This is why the activities under the umbrella of ISO 20022 have expanded to include other financial exchanges in addition to the task of merging the two payment approaches. The long-term roadmap for such a merger was presented in Chapter 21.

SUMMARY

Business-to-business communications depend on common conventions and agreements to insure the flow of information and its correct interpretation throughout the supply chain. This includes the integration of external inputs (orders, delivery notices, payments, etc.) with the internal information of the enterprise such as inventory controls or other management reports.

At each technology transition, the established conventions are subverted and economic chains are thrown into turbulence until new rules settle. As computers became essential to the daily routines of enterprises, new electronic messages had to be standardized and this led to the traditional EDI protocols of X12 and EDIFACT. Likewise, the transition to open networks and distributed computing is underlining the need for new designs and operational techniques to take advantage of the distributed and open nature of the Web. It takes time for the new ways to mature sufficiently so as to be deployed securely and reliably in real situations. There currently are many approaches, such as ebXML, Web Services or the various XML solutions in the financial section, that combine the same building blocks to end with conflicting answers that complicate business integration. Just like in the case of traditional EDI, several years of experimentation are needed to stabilize the situation. Based on past experience, we can expect that pressures to rationalize business operations will drive the various interoperability agreements that are essential for any new model for universal business-to-business commerce.

ACKNOWLEDGMENTS

I would like to express my gratitude to Mr. Peter Potgieser and Professor Jörg Müller for their thorough reviews and comments on an earlier draft. Of course, the remaining shortcomings are my own responsibility.

REFERENCES

1. Sherif, M. H., *Protocols for Secure Electronic Commerce*, 2nd edn., CRC Press, Boca Raton, FL, 2004, 174–181.
2. Bosak, J., UBL: A standards-based approach to ecommerce, in *The Standards Edge: Future Generation*, Bolin, S., Ed., Bolin Communications, available at www.thebolingroup.com, 2005, 397–409.
3. National IT and Telecom Agency, About OIOXML, available at http://en.itst.dk/architecture-and-standards/data-standardisation/about-oioxml, accessed on June 29, 2009.
4. Hasselbring, W., The role of standards for interoperating information system, in *Information Technology Standards and Standardization: A Global Perspective*, Jakobs, K., Ed., Idea Group Publishing, Hershey, PA, 2000, 116–130.
5. Dorn, J. et al., A survey of B2B methodologies and technologies: From business models towards development artifacts, *Proceedings of the 40th Hawaii International Conference on Systems Science* (HICSS'07), Big Island, HI, 2007.
6. Al-Masri, E. and Mahmoud, Q. H., Interoperability among service registry standards, *IEEE Intern. Comput.*, 11(3), 74–77, 2007.
7. Langlois, M., Favero, D., and Lesourd, M., *XML dans les échanges électroniques, le Framework ebXML*, Lavoisier, Paris, 2005, 223–247.
8. van Blommestein, F. B. E. and Potgieser, P. G. L., EbXML for Managers, ECP.NL/Interpay Nederland/Berenschot, 2005, available at http://www.cen.eu/CENORM/businessdomains/businessdomains/isss/activity/ebxml.asp.
9. Kerzner, H., *In Search of Excellence in Project Management—Successful Practices in High Performance Organizations*, John Wiley & Sons, New York, 1998, 59.
10. Bézivin, J. et al., MDA Components: Challenges and opportunities, in *Metamodelling for MDA*, York, England, November 24–25, 2003, available at http://www.sciences.univ-nantes.fr/lina/atl/www/papers/MDAComponents-ChallengesOpportunities.V1.3.PDF
11. Jézèquel, J.-M. et al., Le génie logiciel et l'IDM: une approche unificatrice par les modèles, in *L'ingénierie dirigée par les modèles*, Favre, J.-M., Estublier, J., and Blay-Fornarino, M., Eds., Lavoisier/Hermès-Science, Paris, 2006, Chap. 3.
12. Almedia, J. P. A. et al., An integrated model-driven service engineering environment, in *Enterprise Interoperability, New Challenges and Approaches*, Doumeingts, G. et al., Eds, Springer-Verlag, London, 2008, 79–89.
13. Hammoudi, S., Lopes, D., and Bézivin, J., Approche MDA pour le développement d'application internet sur des plates-formes services web—Modélisation, transformation et prototypage, *RSTI série ISI*, 10(3), 67–90, 2005.
14. Erl, T., Service-Oriented Architecture, A Field Guide to Integrating XML and Web Services, Prentice Hall, PTR, Upper Saddle River, NJ, 2004, 72–77.
15. Thomas Erl's WS-standards, available at http://www.ws-standards.com
16. Papazoglou, M. P., *Web Services: Principles and Technology*, Pearson Education Limited, Harlow, U.K., 2008, Chaps. 4–12.

Section VI

Management of Integration

24 Managing Implementation Issues in Enterprise Resource Planning Projects

Prasanta Kumar Dey, Ben Clegg,
and David Bennett

CONTENTS

INTRODUCTION

Globalization has made today's business more challenging with growing competition, increasing customer expectations, and expanding markets. This places pressure on companies to have more effective logistics operations by cutting cost across the supply chain, optimizing inventory, expanding product variety, improving delivery schedules, increasing quality, and reducing material flow time. Companies have come to realize that these challenges can only be met, and the necessary changes made, when they share information among their suppliers, distributors, and customers. In order to remain competitive, organizations are increasingly developing collaborative and/or strategic partnerships with their suppliers to share a common goal for the business. To accomplish these objectives, many companies are adopting Enterprise Resource Planning (ERP) systems.

ERP systems are designed to provide seamless integration of processes across functional areas with improved workflow, standardization of business practice, and access to real-time, up-to-date data. As a consequence, ERP systems are complex and implementing them can be a challenging, time-consuming, and expensive activity for any organization [1].

BACKGROUND

Although ERP systems gained popularity in the 1990s, their roots date back to the 1970s when, at that time, the focus was on manufacturing systems and traditional inventory control. Early software packages for resource planning were limited to the "shop floor" and known as Material Requirements Planning (MRP) systems, but as competitive pressures increased and users became more sophisticated, MRP was developed to include more indirect business support functions such as product costing and marketing.

In the 1980s, MRP evolved from being just a material planning and control system to a company-wide system capable of planning virtually all the firm's resources and became known as Manufacturing Resource Planning (MRPII) [2]. A major purpose of MRPII was to integrate the primary functions (i.e., production, marketing, and finance) and other functions (such as personnel, engineering, and purchasing) into a planning process to improve the efficiency of the manufacturing enterprise. However, as with its predecessor, MRPII still focused heavily on the manufacturing process.

The term ERP was first used to describe a business software system that was a further enhancement of MRPII, although a key difference between MRPII and ERP, as we now recognize it, is that ERP also strives to plan and schedule supplier resources based on customers' dynamic demands and schedules, while MRPII has traditionally focused on the planning and scheduling of internal resources.

The maturity stage occurred in the mid-1990s when "back office" functions such as order management, financial management, warehousing, distribution production, quality control, asset management, and human resources management were included in ERP. In more recent years, "front office" functions such as sales force and marketing automation, electronic commerce, and Supply Chain Management (SCM) systems were added. Nah et al. [3] define ERP as a packaged business software system that enables a company to manage the efficient and effective use of resources (materials, HR, finance, etc.) by providing a total integrated solution for the organization's information processing needs. Thus, the scope of ERP implementation encompasses what is often referred to as the entire value chain of the enterprise, from prospect and customer management through to order fulfillment and delivery. ERP often involves a customizable, standard application software, which includes integrated business solutions for the core processes (e.g., production planning, production control, and warehouse management) as well as the main administrative functions of an enterprise (e.g., accounting and human resource management). Presently, ERP vendors are striving to include Customer Relationship Management (CRM) and SCM functionalities and, as a consequence, some use ERP as an umbrella term for any integrated business software system for a broad range of corporate information, from the procurement of supplies to shop floor control and financial accounting.

BENEFITS OF ERP SYSTEMS

ERP systems solve the problem of fragmentation of information in large organizations by providing a unified view of the enterprise that encompasses all functions and departments and by ensuring the integrity of global database of all business records and reports.

The potential benefits of ERP include dramatic reductions in operating costs through lower inventories and working capital requirements, abundant information about customers' wants and needs, along with an encompassing view of the extended enterprise of suppliers, alliances, and customers as an integrated whole [4–6]. This is because of ERP systems' abilities to automate and integrate business processes across organizational functions and locations, to share common data and practices across the entire enterprise in order to reduce errors, and to produce and access information in a real-time environment to facilitate rapid and better decisions and cost reductions [1,7].

ERP systems' potential benefits can be classified as tangible or intangible. According to a Deloitte & Touche survey, tangible benefits refer to inventory reduction, reduction of personnel, increased productivity, improvements in order management, more rapid closing of financial cycles, reduction in information technology (IT) and procurement costs, improvement of cash flow management, increase of revenue and profits, reduction in transportation and logistics costs, reduction in the need for system maintenance, and improvement in on time delivery performance [8]. Intangible benefits refer to the increased visibility of corporate data, new or improved business processes, improved responsiveness to customers, reduction in cost, tighter integration between systems, standardization of computing platforms, increased flexibility, global sharing of information, improved business performance, and improved visibility across all levels in the organization. In particular, ERP systems can also be an instrument for transforming functional organizations into process-oriented ones [9].

ERP can also contribute to the implementation of the three generic competitive strategies of Porter (i.e., cost leadership, differentiation, or focus) [10]. From a cost leadership viewpoint, ERP systems aim to achieve the lowest cost of production and, in a differentiation strategy, it would contribute to the development of a unique product or service and long-term customer relationships, while in a focus strategy the contribution may be limited to certain segments (products, clients, or geographic markets).

Another way to look at ERP benefits is to group them into five categories, operational, managerial, strategic, IT infrastructure, and organizational [11]. Operational benefits include cost reduction, cycle time reduction, quality improvement, and so on. Managerial benefits relate to better resource management, improved decision-making, and planning and performance improvement. Strategic benefits include support for business growth, business alliances, building business innovations, and cost leadership. It also includes building external linkages. IT benefits are IT cost reduction and increased IT infrastructure capability. Organizational benefits relate to facilitating business learning and empowering and building common visions. Realizing these potential benefits is difficult and will be discussed later on using a risk management framework and a case study.

ERP ARCHITECTURES

Most current ERP systems are based on the client/server architecture [12] where the server stores the data, maintains their integrity and consistency, and processes user requests from the client desktops. Originally, the data processing load and the application logic were distributed between the server and the client [13]. Now, ERP vendors have moved to a three-tier architecture using browser/Web server architecture in order to reduce the load on the database [14], so there is a clear separation of functional components with a Graphical User Interface toward the user. With this flexible architecture, installation, customization, and extensions are possible in increasingly shorter time frames. Further details are available in Chapters 11 and 15 of this handbook.

ERP is an infrastructure that supports the capabilities of all other information tools and processes used by the firm [15]. Shehab et al. [16] observed that the key to achieving success with ERP is to ensure its implementation in a way that can facilitate the flow of information to effectively manage and integrate all business functions across the whole organization.

ERP systems have huge storage needs, massive networking requirements, and potential training overheads [17]. Also, ERP suites tend only to have one best-in-class application, so most organizations must face the issue that the selected ERP software may lack some functionality to support all other existing business processes. Customization of ERP installation is possible to a certain degree, although major modifications are complex, extremely costly, and usually impractical. A significant amount of organizational change is required to conform to the vendor's solutions, which is why organizations can spend three to seven times more on implementation than on purchasing the software.

Incompatibilities between organizational requirements and the ERP package cause three categories of "misfits" [7]: data, function or process, and output. Data misfits concern data formats and the relationships among entities that are represented by the underlying data model, functional or process misfits concern the operational procedures, and output misfits are incompatibilities in terms of presentation format and information content. The degree of misfit may be more severe outside traditional Western companies because most ERP packages reflect European or U.S. industry practices.

Once integrated into a company's IT backbone, which is a tremendous task in itself, the presence of an ERP package could present additional problems when there are changes in the business conditions (through organizational splits, acquisitions, etc.) to the point that the processes embedded in the ERP system may no longer be the most suitable. Modifications can also jeopardize the key benefits of integration, and consequently most companies that succeed in installing ERP systems subsequently reengineer their business processes to fit.

PITFALLS IN ERP IMPLEMENTATION

Although ERP systems can bring competitive advantage to organizations, there have been a number of prominent failures. For instance, Allied Waste Industries Inc. decided to discontinue a US$130 million system built around SAP R/3, while Waste Management Inc. called off a SAP installation after spending about US$45 million of an expected US$250 million on the project. Hershey Food Corp. has also held SAP accountable for order processing problems that hampered its ability to ship confectionery and other products to retailers around the peak Halloween season [18,19].

Even after an ERP system has gone live, there is a variety of ways in which organizational processes may still underperform. For example, they may generate an unacceptable level of errors, they may be unstable and have performance that is difficult to predict, or processes may fail in unpredictable ways and be difficult to troubleshoot and correct. Also, forecasts made with the sales planning component of the ERP system (the representation of the sales planning process) may be incorrect if the past is not a representative of the future. For example, in the case of FoxMeyer, a failed ERP system created incorrect orders that resulted in excess shipments costing millions of dollars [17–19]. Whirlpool experienced delays in shipments of appliances to many distributors and retailers. Other cases of ERP failure were reported at Boeing, Dow Chemical, Mobil Europe, Applied Materials, Kellogg, and Hershey [4,20]. One study indicates that 40% of all ERP installations achieve only partial implementation while 20% of attempted ERP adoptions are scrapped as total failures [21]. Another study reported that between 60% and 90% of ERP implementations do not achieve the return on investment identified in the project-approval phase [22].

Given that the technical capabilities of ERP systems are relatively well proven, the consensus is that planning issues constitute a major barrier to extracting their full benefits. Therefore, the justification of ERP systems needs to encompass not only economic and strategic benefits, but also the enhanced organizational capabilities. The complexity of ERP implementation should also be considered [23]: for instance, upgrading process from SAP R/2 to R/3 is a costly, time-consuming process [1]. In other words, the implementation of ERP software packages can disrupt organizations [7,23].

RISK FACTORS IN ERP IMPLEMENTATION PROJECTS

Despite the large number of installed ERP systems, academic research on the outcome of their implementation is relatively new with case studies mostly published in the popular press (e.g., *New York Times*, *Wall Street Journal*, etc.) and trade magazines. Reports about the implementation of ERP as a business change enabler to achieve competitive advantage has been a critical area of concern [24–27], and Davenport [1] was among the first to report on these challenges. The remainder of this chapter discusses ERP implementation using the Project Management Body of Knowledge (PMBOK) [28], which have six generic steps to manage risk in projects, which are risk management planning, risk identification, qualitative risk analysis, quantitative risk analysis, risk response planning, and risk monitoring and control. These steps can be customized to suit to a specific project's requirements. In recent years, several researchers have tried to identify the critical success factors for ERP implementation [29–32]. From the results of their studies, the risk factors during the various phases of ERP implementations can be summarized as shown in Table 24.1. These risk factors could be further categorized into project management processes, organizational transformation, and IT in order to suggest mitigating measures for each category.

Successful implementation of ERP systems can result from effective management of these generic risks, which have been collated from a high number and wide variety of ERP projects across industries.

CASE STUDY ON RISK MANAGEMENT FOR ERP IMPLEMENTATION

The following case study shows a customized project risk management framework that is based on the PMBOK as discussed above and has successfully supported the implementation of an ERP project in a UK-based energy service group (hereafter referred to as "the Group").

THE GROUP

The Group was formed following the privatization of the gas energy market in the United Kingdom and a subsequent de-merger of part of the business in 1997. It has since developed into an international business with a total turnover of GB£13.4bn. The Group employs over 30,000 people and has expanded globally through a strategy of acquisitions and partnerships in both Canada and the United States. More recently the Group has focused on entrance into the deregulating European markets.

As the Group had grown by acquisition and mergers, it now possesses an IT landscape consisting of disparate IT systems and disconnected processes. Accordingly, it has embarked on an ERP implementation and re-implementation strategy with SAP as the chosen ERP solution. The Group already had a suboptimal SAP implementation in parts of the business.

The Group adopted a phased approach focusing on the highest priority process areas first and gradually increasing the ERP modular footprint over a time scale of several years. The first two immediate priorities on its roadmap were on different process areas and these had different strategic drivers and business case models. However, there were several areas of commonality such as a common ERP platform (i.e., SAP), a common implementation methodology and approach, and a common approach to the project management team structure and management processes.

TABLE 24.1
Generic Risk Factors from the PMBOK: Project Phase and Risk Category

Project Phases	Project Management Processes	Organizational Transformation	Information Technology
		Risk Categories	
Planning	Inaccurate business case Unclear objectives Weak implementation team	Lack of management/executive commitments and leadership Lack of synergy between IT strategy and organizational competitive strategy Unclear change strategy	Lack of communication with the end-users Inadequate training plan for the users
Implementation	Inappropriate management of scope Lack of communication between ERP implementation team, ERP provider, and ERP users Poor contract management	Inappropriate change management Inappropriate management of culture and structure	Business process reengineering incompetence ERP installation incompetence Inappropriate selection of ERP software Inappropriate system integration Inaccurate performance data Inappropriate users training
Hand-over, evaluation and operations	Inappropriate contract closeout	Inadequate organizational readiness Resistance to change Lack of user training	Inappropriate system testing and commissioning Multi-site issues Lack of clarity on inspection and maintenance Inaccurate performance measurement and management framework

Source: Project Management Institute, *A Guide to the Project Management Body of Knowledge*, 3rd edn., Newtown Square, PA, 2004.

ERP IMPLEMENTATION PROJECT

The project that is the subject of this case study was a 10-mo business transformation initiative consisting of the implementation of a SAP ERP platform for finance, procurement, and HR processes with 1500 system users and 35,000 payroll records involved. To support its vision, The Group undertook this business transformation project to radically overhaul its back office systems and to reduce cost. The objectives were to achieve simplification, automation, standardization, and integration across the three functions. To have the three back office functions working in a fully integrated and largely automated way would provide an invaluable platform upon which the group could begin to develop much wider improvements based on a common and flexible backbone.

The project involved implementing SAP's "mySAP" ERP application suite (to support the HR and Finance), e-Procurement, and BW (Business Warehouse). Additionally, the new solution provided the platform from which the functions would transform their partnership with the rest of the Group's businesses. The overall solution was based on the SAP "Netweaver" open platform, allowing legacy SAP and non-SAP applications to be fully integrated. A multinational ERP consultant company was engaged to plan and implement the project understudy. They closely worked with the ERP provider and the Group's project management team from concept to commissioning of the project in order to ensure effective implementation and operations. The Group's project team, consultant project team, and ERP vendor's project team formed the core ERP implementation team. The Group's project team was formed through careful selection of experienced and capable people from both functional and IT group. Figure 24.1 shows the ERP project governance structure of the ERP project under study.

The project resulted in the migration of significant volumes of complex legacy data (250 m transactions with a GB£1.53 trillion value); the solution was successfully implemented and achieved its objectives to provide simplified and standardized processes across the back-office. The SAP ERP suite provided automated and integrated support for these processes.

RISK MANAGEMENT METHODOLOGY

The project employed a risk management framework to address issues of implementation. The stakeholders "risk" can be defined as a problem that may occur in the future, that has a scale of impact and a probability of occurrence, that needs to be managed by a mitigation strategy or a contingency action, and its occurrence has a potentially adverse effect on the program or the quality of its deliverables. The approach adopted was that the formal risk analysis would capture broad, generic risks to the project's success, which would manifest themselves in specific ways as the project progressed. An example of a broad, generic risk would be "The project fails to find the skilled, experienced resources it requires to meet its obligations on time," while a specific manifestation of this risk might be "the technical work group cannot identify a suitable internal candidate for its Testing Specialist vacancy, which represents a risk to the milestone that marks completion of testing." The project

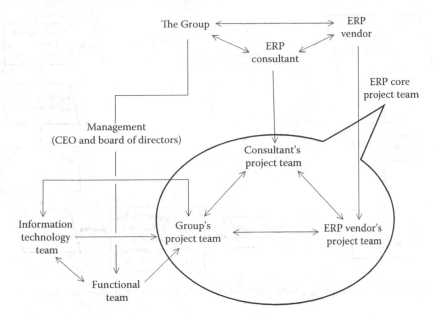

FIGURE 24.1 ERP project governance structure.

teams would then capture these individual manifestations and list them against the generic risk; a new risk would not be logged in response to such instances. If a new risk, that is, one not captured during the risk analysis, was identified while the project was underway, the Risk Log would be updated. Figure 24.2 presents an overview of the risk management framework that was used within the project under study in every phase.

The adapted risk management framework has five steps—identifying risk, logging risk, reviewing risk, managing risk, and closing risk. The following section describes each step.

Identifying Risk

A formal workshop was held in the project planning phase to review risks likely to occur. This involved representatives (middle-level management) of the Group's functional teams (human resource, finance, and information management) (i.e., the client), representatives of ERP vendor project team, three senior members (more than 15 years experience) of the Group's project management team, and the three senior members (more than 15 years of experience) of project management team of consultant. Project plans, various reports, and minutes of the meetings were reviewed by the members prior to the workshop. Additionally, the participants used their experience to identify risks. Although both ERP vendor and consultant companies were experienced in the risk analysis, it was the Group's first experience. The representatives of consultant and the ERP vendor using their prior experience developed a check list of project phase-wise risks that were expected for the project understudy.

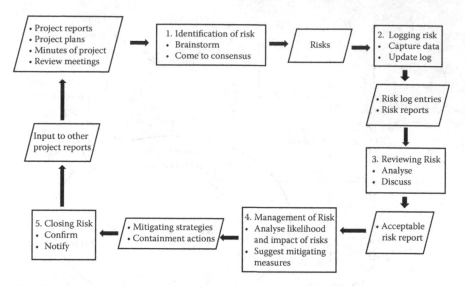

FIGURE 24.2   Risk management framework for the Group's ERP implementation project.

These risks were subsequently reviewed by both the functional and IT groups of the client organization in order to develop a final list.

Logging Risk

All risks were then recorded in the risk log and communicated to the concerned stakeholders. The project management team of the client and the consultant identified the more general project-wide risks and checked specifics for each function with the various functional teams. The functional teams were responsible for the identification of risks specific to their operations. The consultant project management team was responsible for updating the risk.

Reviewing Risk

On an ongoing basis, the risk log was updated with the status of key risks documented in weekly functional reports. This was the responsibility of each functional team. The representatives of both the Group's and consultant's project teams played active roles in policing this process by attending weekly meetings with functional team to check status, action dates, and to review if new risks were being missed.

Managing Risk

The likelihood and impact of each risk on project outcome were then determined with the involvement of the representatives of both The Group's and consultant's project teams and the ERP vendor and functional groups. They came up with mitigating strategies for each risk through brainstorming, which was conducted by the project manager of the consultant project team. This was formalized by a weekly review between the project management team of the Group and consultant. The project manager of the consultant's project team had overall responsibility for managing all risks and discussing closing actions, due dates, priorities, and risk impacts with the Group's functional and IT managers to ensure that risks were being actively managed. High probability and high impact risks were escalated up the governance structure of the Group's management to be analyzed and discussed within the weekly management meetings and were detailed in the weekly management reports. Should a risk be out of the control of the ERP project management team, it would be escalated further up the governance structure to the Executive Steering Committee (CEO and the Board of Directors) of the Group that provided the Executive sponsorship for the projects.

Closing Risk

All the risks were monitored closely along with the associated activities. They were closed as soon as the associate activities were accomplished. The occurrences and impacts of these risks were reported and archived for learning for forthcoming projects.

Tables 24.2 through 24.4 depict the project phase-wise risks that were actually identified in the first workshop for project risk analysis at the end of the planning stage. The risks were categorized into areas related to IT (hardware, software, network, and security), organizational transformation, and project management processes in order to entrust their mitigation to specific group of expert people in the organization.

TABLE 24.2
Risks for the Group in the Implementation Phase

Risk Factors	Impact	Likelihood	Category
Project resources required not available, for example, for training	H	M	Project management process
The project execution deviates from design/ principles	M	L	
"Quality" at risk due to time/cost drivers	M	H	
Risk that sponsor cancels the project	H	L	
Other projects that are happening in parallel within the business impact the ERP project	H	H	
Project team "burns out"	M	M	
Lack of resources available from within the business to fill specific roles	M	H	
Scope creep	H	L	
Delay in hardware procurement	H	M	
Project team turnover	M	M	
Plan is not achievable because of many concurrent activities	H	L	
Communication risk between the project and the business	M	L	
Inappropriate system testing	L	L	

continued

TABLE 24.2   (continued)
Risks for the Group in the Implementation Phase

Risk Factors	Impact	Likelihood	Category
Business resources required not available— Business resource may "overlap"	H	H	Organizational transformation
Legacy system change impact interfaces	H	M	
Legacy systems require changes which would be likely to delay the project	H	H	
Business inadequately prepared to take on new solution	M	L	
Fail to transfer knowledge (consultant to the business project resources)	H	M	
The business suffers "Change fatigue"	L	H	
Not meeting IT (hardware, software, network, security system) specifications	H	L	Information technology
Mismanagement of overall IT architecture	H	H	
Lack of resources in new technology areas being implemented due to their specialist nature	H	L	
Insufficient servers "horse power"	H	L	
Insufficient data base capacity within SAP for the volume of transactions being migrated across from the legacy systems	H	M	
Data cleansing does not meet the necessary requirements	M	H	
Telecommunication link with outsourcing partner fails, resulting in a lack of access to SAP by the offshore team	H	L	
SAP Profiles do not correspond to organization roles	H	L	
IT fails to resolve functional issues	H	M	
Decision on system architecture configuration selection is not taken on time	M	L	
The project end-user infrastructure fails to support deployment	L	M	
Insufficient training facilities available	M	M	
Failure to move toward SOX[a] compliance	H	L	

H, high; M, medium; L, low.

[a] The Sarbanes-Oxley Act (SOX) not only affects the financial side of corporations, but also affects the IT departments whose job it is to store a corporation's electronic records. The Sarbanes-Oxley Act states that all business records, including electronic records and electronic messages, must be saved for "not less than five years." The consequences for noncompliance are fines, imprisonment, or both. IT departments are increasingly faced with the challenge of creating and maintaining a corporate records archive in a cost-effective fashion that satisfies the requirements put forth by the legislation.

TABLE 24.3

Risks for the Group in the Handing-Over Phase

Risk Factors	Impact	Likelihood	Risk Category
Late decisions/sign-off	H	H	Project management processes
Organization fails to adopt change	L	L	Organizational transformation
The new system fails to reconcile business information	H	L	Information technology

H, high; L, low.

TABLE 24.4

Risks for the Group in the Operations Phase

Risk Factors	Impact	Likelihood	Risk Category
Failure to deliver benefits as outlined in the business case	M	L	Organizational transformation
Inadequate training	H	M	
Solution is not scaleable	M	L	Information technology
No disaster recovery arrangements	M	M	
The new system fails to provide appropriate financial information	H	M	
The information generated by the new system fails to comply with Data Protection Act (United Kingdom)	H	L	
System malfunctions after "going live"	L	L	

H, high; M, medium; L, low.

DISCUSSION

The Project Management Book of Knowledge (PMBOK) [28] proposes a six-step project risk management framework, in which the steps are risk management planning, risk identification, qualitative risk analysis, quantitative risk analysis, risk response planning, and risk monitoring and control. The Group adopted a customized version of the PMBOK risk management framework for this project which had only five steps (i.e., identification of risk, logging risk, reviewing risk, managing risk, and closing risk). Although planning had been carried out in the Group on how to pursue risk management at a high level up, until the adoption of this particular framework there had been no *detailed formalized* steps for risk management planning. As this particular project had been a great success, the risk management framework is now used across the whole of the Group and its related businesses for other similar projects. All large IT-based projects now start with a formal identification of risk, followed by the logging and the reviewing of them (in terms of "impact" and "likelihood"). In the customized version of the risk management framework, only analysis and response development are undertaken, whereas the PMBOK's framework would normally comprise of qualitative risk analysis, quantitative risk analysis, and risk response development. This change was made because the Group believes that explicit quantitative risk assessment at a relatively immature stage would infer artificial accuracy and create suspicion among the workforce. This lack of quantification, however, would be addressed in the future as risk assessment practices mature within the Group and become culturally accepted into the standard operating procedures. The last step of both the frameworks remains consistent with one another, although they are given different titles.

These ERP risk management practices accrued the following practical advantages for the Group:

Decision making was more systematic and less subjective.
The relative importance of each risk was made immediately apparent.
There was an improved understanding of the project through identifying the risks and thinking through "what-if" scenarios.
There was a powerful impact on management through the realization that there is a range of possible outcomes for a project.

The future quantification of risk management practices would include demonstrable financial opportunity cost savings based on these qualitative advantages for which the project team could be rewarded.

SUMMARY AND CONCLUSION

This chapter addresses the implementation issues of ERP projects. A review of the literature can identify the generic risk factors of ERP projects so that they can be classified by project phases as recommended by the PMBOK. In the case study presented in this chapter, we introduced a five-stepped risk management procedure adapted from the generic framework introduced by the PMBOK. Using the adapted risk management framework, the identification of the risk factors and their likelihood of occurrences and impact were found, without going through quantitative risk analysis.

The literature review revealed that the key success factors for ERP implementation are commitment from top management and selecting the appropriate systems and proper management of its integration with existing business information systems, including the reengineering of the business processes. Additionally, managing ERP project processes, managing IT, and managing organizational transformation all contribute significantly to the successful implementation of ERP projects.

In the Group's case study, the risk management framework was used proactively by all participating stakeholders for risk identification and analysis within each phase of the project *before* making decisions on project variables (e.g., resource deployment and allocations, implementation methodology selection, contractors and supplier selection, etc.). This made a significant difference to the level of risk experienced later on in the project.

In summary, it is commonly believed that ERP projects are technically complex, multidisciplinary, of long duration, and capital intensive; therefore, they are often thought of as highly risky projects. Although it is challenging to develop an accurate project plan at the beginning of any implementation project because of lack of information, dynamic risk analysis has been demonstrated to improve knowledge dissemination throughout a project and give better project delivery. Risk management practices may increase the project's cost initially in terms of deployment of extra human resources, and additional analytical activities. However, we argue that the benefits of these failure prevention activities more than outweigh the cost of the failure recovery activities, which are far more likely to occur and would have a greater impact on the project if the extra initial risk analyses had not been undertaken.

REFERENCES

1. Davenport, T.H., Putting the enterprise into the enterprise system, *Harv. Bus. Rev.*, 16(4), 121–131, 1998.
2. Wight, O.W., *Manufacturing Resource Planning: MRPII*, Oliver Wight Ltd. Publications, Essex Junction, VT, 1984.
3. Nah, F.F.-H., Lau, J.L.-S., and Kuang, J., Critical factors for successful implementation of enterprise systems, *Bus. Process Manage. J.*, 7(3), 285–296, 2001.
4. Chen, I.J., Planning for ERP systems: Analysis and future trend, *Bus. Process Manage. J.*, 7(5), 374–386, 2001.
5. Binder, M. and Clegg, B.T., Enterprise management: A new frontier for organizations, *Int. J. Prod. Econ.*, 106(2), 409–430, 2007.
6. Clegg, B.T., The growing importance of inter-company collaboration, *J. Manufact. Technol. Manage.*, 19(3), Editorial, 2008.
7. Soh, C., Kien, S.S., and Tay-Yap, J., Cultural fits and misfits: Is ERP a universal solution? *Commun. ACM*, 43(4), 47–51, 2000.
8. Callaway, E, *Enterprise Resource Planning—Integrating Application and Business Processes Across the Enterprise*, Computer Technology Research Corporation, Charleston, SC, 2000.
9. Al-Mashari, M. and Zairi, M., Supply chain re-engineering ERP systems: An analysis of a SAP R/3 implementation case, *Int. J. Phys. Distrib. Logist.*, 30(3/4), 296–313, 2000.
10. Porter, M.E., *Competitive Advantage*, Free Press/Collier Macmillan, New York, 1985.
11. Shang, S. and Seddon, P., A comprehensive framework for classifying the benefits of ERP systems, *Proceedings of Americas Conference on Information Systems (AMCIS)*, Vol. II, 1005–1014, Long Beach, CA, 2000.
12. Rao, S.S., Enterprise resource planning in reengineering business, *Bus. Process Manage. J.*, 6(5), 376–391, 2000.
13. Gupta, A., Enterprise resource planning: The emerging organizational value systems, *Ind. Manag. Data Syst.*, 100(3), 113–118, 2000.
14. Scheer, A.W. and Habermann, F., Enterprise resource planning: Making ERP a success, *Commun. ACM*, 43(4), 57–61, 2000.
15. Bendoly, E. and Schoenherr, T., ERP system and implementation-process benefits: Implications for B2B e-procurement, *Int. J. Oper. Prod. Manag.*, 25(4), 304–319, 2005.
16. Shehab, E.M. et al., Enterprise resource planning: An integrative review, *Bus. Process Manage. J.*, 10(4), 359–386, 2004.

17. Aladwani, A.M., Change management strategies for successful ERP implementation, *Bus. Process Manage. J.*, 7(3), 266–275, 2001.
18. Bailey, J., Trash haulers are taking fancy software to the dump, *The Wall Street Journal*, June 9, 1999.
19. Boudette, N.E., Europe's SAP scrambles to stem big glitches, *The Wall Street Journal*, November 4, 1999.
20. Bicknell, D., SAP to fight drug firm's $500M suit over R/3 collapse, *Computer Weekly*, September 3, 1998.
21. Trunick, P.A., ERP: Promise or pipe dream?, *Transport. Distrib.*, 40(1), 23–26, 1999.
22. Ptak, C.A. and Schragenbeim, E., *ERP: Tools, Techniques, and Applications for Integrating the Supply Chain*, CRC Press–St Lucie Press, Boca Raton, FL, 1999.
23. Kumar, K. and Hillegersberg, V., ERP experiences and evolution, *Commun. ACM*, 43(4), 22–26, 2000.
24. Volkoff, O., Using the structurational model of technology to analyze an ERP implementation, *Proceedings of Americas Conference on Information Systems (AMCIS)*, 235–237, Milwaukce, WI, 1999.
25. Piturro, M., How midsize companies are buying ERP, *J. Accountancy*, 188(3), 41–48, 1999.
26. Trunk, C., Building bridges between WMS & ERP, *J. Transport. Distrib.*, 40(2), 6–8, 1999.
27. Zuckerman, C., ERP: Pathway to the future or yesterday's buzz?, *J. Transport. Distrib.*, 40(8), 37–43, 1999.
28. Project Management Institute, *A Guide to the Project Management Body of Knowledge*, 3rd edn., Project Management Institute, Newtown Square, PA, 2004.
29. Mabert, V.A., Soni, A., and Venkataraman, M.A., The impact of organisation size on ERP implementations in the US manufacturing sector, *OMEGA*, 31(3), 235–246, 2003.
30. Al-Mashari, M., Al-Mudimigh, A., and Zairi, M., Enterprise resource planning: A taxonomy of critical factors, *Eur. J. Oper. Res.*, 146(2), 352–364, 2003.
31. Mandal, P. and Gunasekaran, A., Issues in implementing ERP: A case study, *Eur. J. Oper. Res.*, 146(2), 274–283, 2003.
32. Umble, E.J., Haft, R.R., and Umble, M., Enterprise resource planning: Implementation procedures and critical success factors, *Eur. J. Oper. Res.*, 146(2), 241–257, 2003.

25 Introducing Complex Technologies into the Enterprise: The Case of RFID

Mario Bourgault and Ygal Bendavid

CONTENTS

INTRODUCTION

Radio Frequency Identification (RFID) has received a lot of attention lately and many authors have been quite enthusiastic about it, calling it "the next big thing for management" [1], "one of the ten greatest contributory technologies of the 21st century" [2] with the potential to drive "the next revolution in supply chain management" [3], allowing "smarter supply and demand chain" [4] where RFID enabled "intelligent products" could take automated decisions "on their own destiny" to provide a mechanism for delivering automated and autonomous supply chain [5].

Despite this enthusiasm, RFID adoption by enterprises still raises some challenging and unanswered questions for both developers and potential adopters. Despite the substantial technological improvements over the last few years, the technology has not been universally accepted and is still in the era of continuous incremental changes [6]. Yet the proactive stance adopted by lead users in various industries indicates that the market is strongly inclined to move toward RFID adoption [7,8]. RFID technologies therefore represent a very interesting case for studying the introduction of a complex technological innovation into the enterprise ecosystem, where the early phases of the project, which remain fuzzy, involve a large number of stakeholders, each with different views of interests in the outcome. The aim of the research reported in this chapter is to explain how early phases of such a project can be structured to ease the adoption process by engaging a university laboratory to coordinate a local innovation network.

Instead of investigating the innovation process as outside observers, a group of researchers[*] chose to get involved and to head up the front-end phase of the adoption process from the inside. This led to the creation of a living laboratory designed to better understand the adoption of RFID by a group of supply chain members pursuing intra- and inter-organizational business-to-business process optimization. More particularly, this project involved setting up a group of key stakeholders, putting in place the technological infrastructure, and leading the front-end process up to the proof of concept. That phase was intended to identify and explore RFID-related opportunities, gather and screen ideas, transform selected ideas into a robust concept, and assess its commercial viability and technical feasibility. This is the phase of activities performed before the actual start of the project (i.e., "pre-project activities") to determine whether the organization should proceed with the development and invest in a pilot project [9].

Moreover, although early front-end innovation activities are often described as fuzzy, chaotic, unpredictable, and unstructured, the situation can be organized and managed, provided that managers are ready to accept its experimental nature and cope with uncertainty [10,11]. They need to understand that the output of such a process will be a stronger concept not only to plan the pilot, but also to define the methods and all the other issues surrounding the whole innovation project.

The chapter is organized as follows. We begin by presenting the basic concepts of RFID technology and recent related studies in the literature. Next we describe the

[*] The group comprised researchers from ePoly, the expertise center for electronic commerce at École Polytechnique (Montréal, Canada). The two authors are affiliated to the center. They wish to thank ePoly's leaders, Profs. Louis A. Lefebvre and Elisabeth Lefebvre.

research design in which the living laboratory approach was applied. This approach is further explored with emphasis on the front-end activities of RFID development and implementation within a real organizational context. The next section focuses on the key issues that emerged from the project. Finally, theoretical and practical contributions are presented, highlighting the role of a university-based laboratory in the innovation process.

RFID: AN ENABLING TECHNOLOGY FOR EMERGING APPLICATIONS

This section draws on the literature to relate the development and implementation of RFID technology to previous similar innovations especially in the information technology domain. While previous chapters (i.e., 19 and 20) put the emphasis on the technology itself, the following presents RFID as an emerging technology within a portfolio of enterprise information systems.

RFID has been classified as a wireless Automatic Identification and Data Capture (AIDC) technology [1,12]. RFID systems are generally used for electronically identifying, locating, and tracking objects. Whereas the earlier applications were mostly in the area of security, access control, and specialized tracking applications, they are now more diversified including supply chain automation, asset tracking, and consumer service. Along with other AIDC technologies such as biometrics, bar codes systems, infrared, and ultra sound, it represents a step in the continuously increasing sophistication of intra- and inter-organizational information systems (IOS) applications.

Compared with more mature and established AIDC technologies such as barcoding, RFID is seen as a major innovation as it allows the automatic bulk reading of any objects without any requirement for a line of sight, offers read and write functionalities, can operate in harsh environments, holds a superior data storage capacity, and provides a mean to for uniquely identifying each product. Indeed, in supply-chain management applications, RFID is positioned as the emergent technology for real-time tracking of each product, module, system, and eventually component, as they move along the various layers of today's supply chains. In the short-to-medium term, however, RFID has to be considered as a complementary technology to barcoding systems as both will co-evolve. For instance, in its Item Unique Identifier initiative launched in 2004, the U.S. Department of Defense uses 2D Data Matrix bar codes at the product and subproduct levels for life-cycle data visibility purposes and RFID tags for supply-chain receipt/track applications at the pallet, box, and item levels [13].

RFID architecture is basically composed of three layers, as depicted in Figure 25.1: (i) a tag, also called transponder,* containing a chip and a mini antenna, which is attached to or embedded in a physical object; (ii) a reader, either mobile with an integrated antenna or fixed with separate antennas that allows multiple tags to be interrogated and to respond at the same time; and (iii) a middleware application that

---

* Generally, while passive RFID tags are activated only when powered by the radio waves of the reader's antennas, other types of tags have on-board power (active transponders, active beacons, and semi-passive tags) that provide them with enhanced functionalities such as longer read range (up to 100 m), more memory, or links to built-in sensors, but at much higher costs (starting at $15 per active tag compared with 10–15 cents per passive RFID tag).

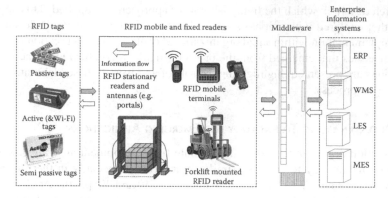

FIGURE 25.1   RFID technology infrastructure.

manages the RFID infrastructure and filters, aggregates, and routes the data cap-
tured. The latter component also interacts with other enterprise applications such as
Enterprise Resource Planning (ERP) Systems, Warehouse Management Systems
(WMS), Logistic Execution Systems, and Manufacturing Execution Systems.

When coupled with wireless technologies and linked to external networks, RFID
systems can automatically transfer very specific, accurate information inside and
outside the boundaries of the organization, allowing access to near-real-time information, anywhere, anytime. In a context in which multiple players are involved in the
delivery of a product or service, the importance of RFID as "a connective technology" [14] may support the emergence of novel electronic business models such as the
EPCglobal Network* [15], thus facilitating information management and inter-
organizational collaboration and enabling a better integration of the supply-chain
members [12,16]. With its high potential for extending the integration of information
flows upward and downward, RFID is likely to serve as a strong catalyst for agile,
flexible, and responsive supply chains.

Although some authors have dated the RFID concept back as far as the 1950s,
commercial activities integrating RFID technology started in the late 1960s with
applications such as electronic article surveillance [17]. Following decades of developmental work and large-scale deployment of applications such as electronic tolls,
the technology has only really attracted attention recently. Industry analysts now
predict a surge in RFID-related investments for the years to come, possibly reaching
$15 billion by 2012 [8].

Several reasons may explain the gradual, but steady growth of RFID popularity
in several industries. Reasons include nearly a dozen of trends or event depicted in
Figure 25.2 and explained hereinafter.

---

* The EPC (Electronic Product Code™) network is a set of technologies that ensure global interoperability and enable real-time, automatic identification, and sharing of information on items in the supply
  chain by allowing product data access on directories over the Internet [15]. The EPCglobal organization in charge of developing standards for data synchronization and communication of RFID data is an
  initiative of a number of research institutes and global organizations leading the development of worldwide standards for the EPC. The organization is part of a joint venture between GS1 (formerly EAN
  International) and GS1 US (formerly UCC—Uniform Code Council, Inc.).

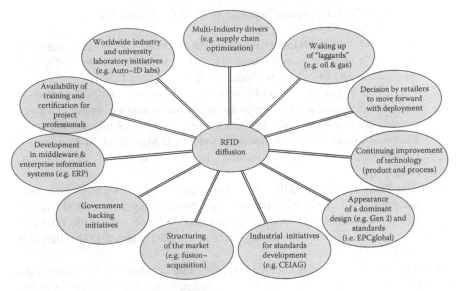

FIGURE 25.2   Trends influencing RFID diffusion.

These trends include the following:

1. The multi-industry drivers, such as (a) the continuing emphasis on supply-chain optimization within various industrial sectors such as the consumer goods, automotive, transportation and logistics, aerospace, and defense industries; (b) the need for increased efficiency within health-care services, (c) the requirement for preventing counterfeiting and diversion within pharmaceutical industry [7,18].
2. The recent and slow interest of "laggards" sectors such as oil and gas, chemical and mining, and so on, which represent a huge potential market [8].
3. The decision by major U.S. and European retailers and suppliers to move forward with the deployment of their RFID infrastructure (e.g., German Metro Group, Wal-Mart).
4. The continuing improvement of technology such as more effective types of tags and readers, enhanced anti-collision algorithms for readings tags in dense environments, innovative manufacturing processes for producing tags and antennas, and so on (e.g., Alien Technology and Impinj have new hybrid and more versatile tags enabling both near- and far-field reads in a single tag, while Mojix introduced its extreme long range passive ultra high frequency [UHF] technology covering 250,000 square feet of area, and pinpoint tag location in three dimensions, etc.) [19].
5. The appearance of a dominant design for RFID tags used for supply-chain applications (i.e., UHF 915-MHz Class-1 Generation-2 tags) [20], following the developments in ISO/EPCglobal standards such as the recent amendments to UHF RFID air interface protocol ISO/IEC 18000-6C [21]

and the EPC Information Services (EPCIS)* standard for real-time data sharing [22].

6. Initiatives by different industrial groups to reconcile various data standards (e.g., EPCglobal Consumer Electronic Industry Action Group, EPCglobal Healthcare, and Life Sciences Industry Action Group) [23].

7. The structuring of the market by major organizations with cross- and joint-licensing strategies and fusions and acquisitions to acquire "complementary technological assets" and strengthen their position in this market (e.g., Motorola-Symbol, Zebra-Wherenet, Honeywell-Metrologic Instruments).

8. Government initiatives, especially in Asian countries (e.g., Japan, Singapore).

9. The development of middleware and applications technologies that can take advantage of RFID capabilities and their proven integration in real-life settings [24]. This also includes complementary offers by enterprise information systems providers (e.g., SAP AII in the ERP market [25], Microsoft BizTalk® platform, etc.).

10. The development of specialized training and certification programs (e.g., Computing Technology Industry Association [CompTIA] RFID+™ Certification) providing companies with international, vendor-neutral certified RFID professionals [26].

11. The worldwide industry and universities initiatives to build up some laboratories such as the Auto-ID Labs, first at the MIT (Massachusetts Institute of Technology) and now around the world.

All of these initiatives suggest that the business environment is ready for RFID to be widely understood and adopted. The trend has reached the academic literature as well as witnessed by the large amount of papers recently published.

RFID ADOPTION AND IMPLEMENTATION: A VIEW FROM ACADEMIA

Since early 2000, with the building of the Auto-ID Center, Academia has definitely become interested in the RFID phenomenon, as witnessed by the constantly increasing number of papers in various related fields of research [2,27] including supply chain management (SCM), e-commerce, RFID technologies, ubiquitous, and intelligent computing environments (e.g., [2–5,14,28]). For instance, among the conceptual papers, as early as 2002, Zaharudin et al. [5] introduced the concept of "Intelligent Product Driven Supply Chain," where the events associated with product movements are at the origin of any transaction. Gunasekaran and Ngai [29], on the other hand, suggested that RFID technologies can facilitate the migration from "Built to Stock"

---

* The EPC Information Services (EPCIS) is an integral part of the EPCglobal Network. Its goal is to enable disparate applications to leverage Electronic Product Code (EPC) data via EPC-related data sharing within and across enterprises. EPCIS can be considered as a high-level middleware in the sense that it incorporates an understanding of the business context in which the EPC data were obtained [22].

to "Built to Order" models to make mass customization economically viable. More broadly, Pramataris [4] elaborated the concept of "smarter supply and demand chain" suggesting that introduction of RFID and the EPC Network are considered as the last step in the evolution of supply chain to enable more collaborative electronic business processes. Moreover, as a newly emerged IOS [30–32], RFID can be positioned as another step toward more integrated and more collaborative B-to-B e-commerce solutions to enable more efficient supply-chain practices [3,5,14,16,33].

From an adoption perspective, Sheffi [34] positions RFID's current state of development on a life-cycle model and speculates on the possible path to future adoption. From a technological ecosystem perspective, Adomavicius et al. [35] identified common patterns of technology evolution, using RFID as one of the examples of technologies, to provide insights into the Web of relationships among multiple technologies. The authors suggested that recent standards on RFID will foster interoperability and stimulate the development of new supporting technologies. Similarly, Quaadgras analyzed the emerging RFID ecosystem—based on announcements of alliances among firms—and the behavior of large, multi-line technology firms in this innovative, technology-based ecosystem. She suggests that "managers of technology firms need to understand not just the technology and the components, but the structure and dynamics of the ecosystem to determine where and how they want to compete ... especially for a new unproven technology" [36, p. 8].

More recently, Dew and Read [37] highlighted the role of focal points (e.g., the use the barcodes as a leverage for EPCs), leadership (e.g., the role of major firms such as Wal-Mart in creating a critical mass of adopters), and shared common information and knowledge as coordination mechanisms that may help organizational communities advance the network externalities that would encourage product adoption. Riggins and Slaughter [31] suggested that, when firms share similar mental models, they can collectively conceptualize their options with respect to IOS adoption, and decide more rapidly to adopt.

The adoption of RFID, as a collective action, has also been studied within multi-organizational alliance settings. For example, Yang and Jarvenpaa [30] focused on collective trust in the adoption of an RFID network as a newly emerged IOS. They suggested that, within an alliance, different social categories (i.e., formed by the differential use of RFID) play an important role in shaping group members' perceptions and beliefs about RFID systems as well as about each other, and their decisions about adopting the systems. Finally, Sharma et al. proposed a conceptual model to examine RFID adoption intent and level of expected integration. They found that two technological factors (perceived benefit and perceived cost) and one inter-organizational factor (power of the supply chain partner) have the most influence on adoption [32]. Whitaker et al. [38] built on a previous research on SCM and IOS to propose that firms with broad IT applications are more likely to adopt RFID. However, financial resources alone (i.e., IT budget) does not necessarily predict RFID adoption [38]. Others have investigated how technology ought to be implemented in corporate and network settings. In a case study of an RFID-based traceability system in an aircraft engineering company in Hong Kong, Ngai et al. [39] grouped eight critical success factors into the following categories: (i) high organizational motivation for improvement, (ii) implementation process, (iii) cost control, and (iv) effective university–industry interaction.

The authors also suggested 13 lessons learned at "strategic, management and operational levels." For instance, at the strategic level, the right partners must be selected based on their actual experiences and proven capabilities and the Return on Investment (ROI) in RFID deployment must take into account the indirect benefits and a clear business value. According to Loebbecke and Palmer [40], RFID pilot studies conducted in a German retail supply chain suggest that managers in charge of the implementation should carefully consider the following factors: (i) technical issues to ensure optimal reading rates; (ii) economic issues related to the selection of equipment; (iii) IT issues, addressing challenges such as information filtering and analysis; (iv) business process redesign for increased efficiency; but more importantly, (v) the "intelligent" use of RFID data. Wu et al. [41] and Li et al. [42] explored some technological obstacles to RFID adoption: RFID physics, the lack of a unified standard, challenges of the migration from barcodes to RFID, and other issues relating to intellectual property as well as the difficulty of making a business case by quantifying cost reduction and value creation.

Bhuptani and Moradpour [43] and Lahiri [44] emphasized the technical aspects in the business justification of an implementation project. For instance, Bhuptani and Moradpour [43] proposed a practical RFID project guide on how to implement and deploy an RFID system. Lahiri [44, p. 144] submitted a business justification method for determining roadmaps to plan a pilot project. Laubacher et al. [45] proposed an Activity-Based Performance Measurement tool for building the business case so that users could assess business performance at the three levels of activity, business unit, and corporation. In the same vein, Bendavid et al. [16] used the Supply Chain Operation Reference model as a framework to evaluate the impact and potential benefits of RFID technology in the supply chain. Finally, researchers built an "EPC/RFID calculator" to assist manufacturers in estimating the potential benefits from implementing RFID/EPC in their supply chain. This tool is now available as a subscriber tool on the EPC Global US Web site. Researchers from Stanford, MIT, Eindhoven University, and EPC Global US teamed to generalize the construct into the "EPC/RFID value model" to identify the contribution of EPC/RFID to individual business issues to assist companies in prioritizing their goals and their areas of implementation of the EPC/RFID.

The identification of critical factors does not necessary explain the process leading to adoption. Even at the level of technology, one must avoid minimizing the difficulties inherent in the systems to be developed. Some recent studies have addressed these issues concerning RFID, indicating that benefits are still questionable (e.g., [46]), and that some of what that has been written and speculated about this technology is misleading or simply not true [48,49]. In actual fact, it appears that some of the applications studied (e.g., self-service checkout, self-product replenishment, automated warehousing activities), while theoretically very attractive and potentially feasible, are quite challenging in the real world. Therefore, potential adopters could overestimate the technology's potential and develop unrealistic expectations, inevitably leading to future disappointments.

It is such context of fuzziness that created the opportunity for the group of researchers to initiate a project through a novel methodology, the living laboratory. The experiment is based on the hypothesis that, during the adoption and implementation of a technological innovation, neutral entities (such as a university laboratory) could act as intermediaries to develop, jointly with economic partners, a level of knowledge that would place those actors in a better position to understand and make the necessary decisions. This accompanying, catalyzing, integrating role that a third party can play to bring together actors would not easily come out of the classical contractual agreements with consultants or solution providers.

DESIGN OF A COLLECTIVE LEARNING EXPERIMENT IN THE LIVING LABORATORY

This section reports on the principles underlying the research strategy for assembling a group of firms to experiment with RFID technology as an enabler of collaborative supply-chain applications.

Because RFID adoption and implementation in the extended enterprise context represents a complex, multidimensional phenomenon, the research group initially planned to set up a network of industrial actors and help "create the phenomena that did not exist before" [50] at least locally. Therefore, the team of scholars did not restrict themselves to observing and documenting a phenomenon. Instead, they became active change agents embedded in a collaborative, project-oriented action research process [50]. This approach called for researchers to participate actively in a project in which real problems are tackled and a live case was investigated in real-time, as suggested by Coughlan and Coghlan [51]: "research in action rather than action about research, participative, concurrent with action, an approach to problem solving." Contrary to most cases of new technology implementation in which solutions are triggered by large firms,* the proposed research design called for a broader vision in which opportunities were to be shared and evaluated at all supply-chain levels in a neutral, university-based environment. In the specific case of RFID, this proved to be critical for the success of the project since an important element of realizing value from RFID is the level of business and technological integration within the group of internal and external supply chain members [52].

At the very beginning of the process, the context was too fuzzy for most of the firms involved. As one participant (Director, Operations Management) correctly put it, "consulting firms, vendors and even our WMS supplier are pressuring us to consider RFID technology as if we were already late in the process of adoption ... but we don't even know what exactly the technology is about ... and we don't want them to tell us." Leveraging on this timing, the research team adopted a proactive stance in order to explore these issues with influential lead users who were aware of the strong inclination by the market to move toward RFID adoption but who also knew that many critical questions were still pending. Because the industrial participants were not subject to the pressure one often finds in normal consultancy arrangements, their interest was more strategic in nature, focusing on questions such as: why consider the adoption of RFID technology? which layers of the supply chain should be included

---

* Most early RFID projects driven by large-group mandates primarily sought a "slap and ship" type of implementation in which RFID tags are simply attached to shipping containers rather than being integrated into an overall process.

in the newly developed business model? and which approaches should we use to conduct a safe implementation?

In more practical terms, the research team acted as a neutral, independent project initiator, integrator, and facilitator. As active intermediaries within the innovation process, the researchers performed multiple innovation intermediation functions such as those proposed by Howells [53]: (i) technology foresight and diagnostics, (ii) scanning and information processing to identify potential collaborative partners, (iii) knowledge processing by helping partners combine their knowledge, (iv) testing validation and training in laboratories, and (v) technology and application (pre) assessment and evaluation.

Because the researchers and the practitioners were jointly confronting issues that were not pre-identified (i.e., not driven by a planned pragmatic outcome such as a known transformational change), the inquiry process could be viewed as a value in itself [54]. In this sense, neither the researchers' assumptions nor their ways of thinking and acting were viewed as being necessarily right; they were also investigated during the research process. Many recent research projects have used the principle of collaborative inquiry of researchers and organizations [55], in e-commerce [56], innovation management [57], information systems [58,59], project management [60], and operation management [61].

The concept of living laboratory was used in Europe in recent years [62]. Loeh et al. [63] explained that this approach has been used to support different research settings and the use of a laboratory by private and academic partners for self-learning. Some of the applications are about testing virtual project management settings [64], the design and evaluation of ubiquitous computing research for human tracking [65], and location awareness in mobile computing environments [66]. The use of such laboratories for longitudinal experiments in realistic settings plays a central role for the management of front-end activities. This research strategy is also similar to other approaches, such as the following:

1. The use of social simulation games to manage change through experimentation and experiential learning: "(Where) the players can experience how the relationships between the activities in a business process are structured and how overall efficiency and quality of work can be improved through process changes" [67, p. 73].
2. Collaborative processes in the context of new product development (NPD) and R&D management. For instance, Nobelius [68] viewed that the management of R&D has moved from a technology-centered model to a more interaction-focused view based on collaboration with suppliers, clients, distributors, and other companies in various industries. Blonqvist et al. [69] introduced the approach of networked R&D management and shared innovation, which emphasizes firms' core competencies and dynamic capabilities. Here, collaboration is viewed as a meta-capability (i.e., knowing how to create, transfer, and use knowledge) for companies managing innovations in a dynamic business environment (as is the case for RFID technology). Cooperative R&D projects are conducted with internal parties and external complementary companies including universities and research institutes.

The co-learning approach within clusters of key partners is viewed as an enabler of both incremental and radical innovations, which become a source of competitive advantage. Similarly, Emden et al. [70] investigated co-development alliances where value creation comes by integrating and transforming disparate pools of knowledge related to a new product or service so that each party contributes significantly to the end solution.

3. Chesbrough [71] proposed an open approach to innovation to leverage internal and external sources of ideas. The underlying business model in which an idea travels from invention to commercialization provides access to new skills and knowledge (e.g., through research institutes) and complementary competencies and technologies, and allows cross-disciplinary and cross-organizational integration, as an essential element for a successful NPD. The author suggests that the ability to experiment with one's business model "requires the creation of processes for conducting experiments and for assessing their results ... (and) many companies simply do not have such processes in place" [72, p. 24].

RFID IMPLEMENTATION THROUGH A LIVING LAB

This section describes how the living laboratory was implemented. As illustrated in Figure 25.3, the project was conducted in a sequence of five major phases, starting with building agreements with organizations interested in the RFID technology and ending with a pilot study in a real-life setting. The research group was directly involved in the first four phases, during which the living laboratory was operational.

Despite the sequential presentation of the project, the iterative nature of the research process needs to be pointed out, as it reflects the complexity of what really happened as the activities unfolded.

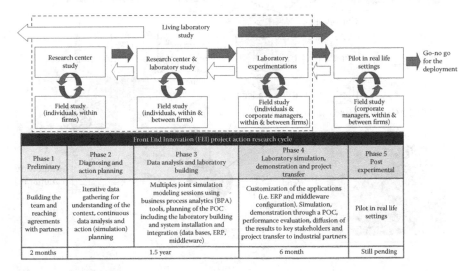

FIGURE 25.3   Managing the early phases of the project.

Preliminary Phase (1): Building the Team and Reaching Agreements with Partners

The objective of this preliminary phase was to set up a unified working group to investigate the concept of RFID. Following a conference held at the research center, the business case for potential strategic alliances for the project was presented and many potential partners in various industries were identified. Within each industrial subgroup, respondents were identified and more focused meetings were organized to negotiate the agreements. The agreements included ways to manage the alliance life cycle [73] including the creation of a research project in the public utility sector. As indicated in Figure 25.4, the living laboratory environment comprised the university research group, acting as an integrator, various industrial partners, and the technology providers.

Firm 1, a major North-American producer of electricity and a worldwide leader in the utility sector, and Firm 2, one of its first-tier suppliers were both looking to enhance their understanding of the potential of the RFID technology within their own supply chain. At the start of the project, the knowledge within both firms was mostly gathered at professional conferences, from specialized publications and through informal discussions with consultants. Within Firm 1 managers in charge of supporting the supply chain (distribution centers, logistics, stores, IT infrastructure, etc.) headed up the project within the company. The vice-president of Firm 2 and several operations managers were directly involved in the process.

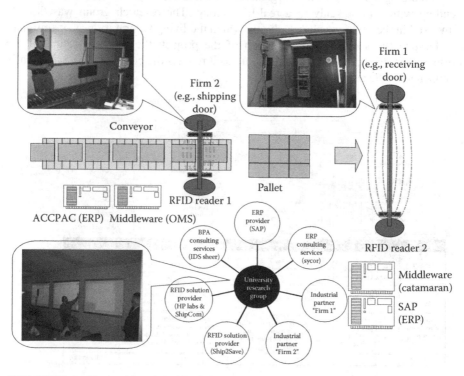

FIGURE 25.4   The multi-stakeholder living lab environment.

Central to the research process were the technology partners, whose contribution to the living laboratory was the provision of RFID and information system equipment and specialized resources such as technicians, consultants, and specialized training. This participation helped industrial partners and researchers to (i) gather data for understanding of the context (phase 2), (ii) build the laboratory (phase 3), and (iii) configure and customize the lab for the proof of concept (phase 4).

Three types of technology partners were involved in the living laboratory (bottom of Figure 25.4). First, HP Labs and Shipcom Wireless provided the RFID infrastructure including middleware to simulate Firm 1's internal divisions. Ship2Save provided a second RFID middleware application to simulate the environment of Firm2. Secondly, for the integration with enterprise systems, SAP provided its ERP software, which was hosted on local servers. A specialized consultant team from Sycor, in cooperation with personnel from Firm 1, configured a basic version of the client's ERP environment. Thirdly, the use of specialized Business Process Analysis (BPA) software (ARIS Toolset), and the training for its use was provided by IDS Sheer for the mapping, simulation, and analysis of the RFID-enabled scenarios.

Table 25.1 lists the expectations that were identified following a data collection exercise carried out by the researchers, through face-to-face discussions, e-mails,

---

TABLE 25.1

Initial Expectations of the Parties from the Collaboration

Initial Expectations of the Academic Institution

Understand the RFID phenomenon

Develop a methodology for managing front-end activities and define a roadmap to move from conceptual ideas to "real opportunities" for optimizing intra- and inter-organizational business processes in an SC environment

Assess the *business viability* and validate the *technological feasibility* of RFID-enabled SC in a controlled environment

Assess the *data analysis techniques* to understand how to evaluate the impact of RFID on business processes

Understand the *uncertainties related to RFID projects* by understanding (i) the variety of tasks and (ii) the degree of interdependencies within and between these tasks

Understand the *uncertainties related to the goals* (evolving motivation toward RFID interest), and *test the methods to reach these goals*

Understand *the uncertainties* related to market (client needs), technological (availability, stability), environmental (economic, ecological, social) and resource allocations

Access a *pool of expertise* by integrating technological and industrial partners in order to be able to build a proof of concept

Initial Expectations of the Technology Partners

For RFID solution providers (Ship2Save, HP Labs and ShipCom Wireless)

Based on the results of the proof of concept, *convince funding stakeholders* (potential clients) that the project is feasible and worth initial funding to proceed with a pilot, and eventually an implementation

Position themselves as *pioneers in the RFID* industry in Canada and gain access to a potential market in various industries (starting with this collaborative research)

---

continued

TABLE 25.1   (continued)
Initial Expectations of the Parties from the Collaboration

For the ERP provider (SAP)

    Gain *visibility* through a university alliance

    Demonstrate the *compatibility of their solution* with existing RFID solutions

    Insist on the importance of having a robust enterprise information system infrastructure to *be able to fully leverage on RFID technology*

For the ERP consulting services provider (Sycor)

    Develop expertise in ERP-RFID integration without "learning by doing" in real-life settings

    Commercialize this newly acquired expertise as a part of its offer in a booming market

For the BPA tool and consulting service provider (IDS Sheer)

    Gain *visibility* through a university alliance

    Understand *how its tool could be used* to help redesign RFID-enabled scenarios.

Initial Expectations of the Industrial Partners

For industrial partner Firm 1—client environment

    Demystify oversold benefits of RFID (as discussed in the press or by vendors)

    Build a "free" business case, and understand the real potential in the utility sector

    Understand the challenges and opportunities for an RFID development and implementation project

For industrial partner Firm 2—supplier environment

    Develop a *proactive stance toward a potential RFID mandate*

    Evaluate *opportunities for leveraging on such technology* to optimize its manufacturing/ assembling activities

and telephone conference calls. At the beginning of the project, the technology partners' expectations included gaining visibility through a university alliance, gathering RFID project knowledge (experience) that they would later be able to commercialize as part of their offer and also using the laboratory experiments as a commercial argument to leverage on when building and developing a business relationship with the industrial partners. Finally, the industrial partners' preoccupations were closer to those of the researchers, as they wanted to demystify the oversold benefits of RFID technology, as discussed in the press or by vendors, and to gain a more realistic understanding of the potential impact of the technology on their business processes along the supply chain.

PHASE 2: DIAGNOSING AND ACTION PLANNING

At this stage, the researchers were mainly involved with the individuals within industrial firms in gathering contextual data. Because of the nature of RFID technology as an enabler of radical innovation in supply-chain processes, when managing early front-end phases of NPD, problems and opportunities were mostly structured by individuals seen as the drivers of innovations within firms.

Through multiple field visits, on-site observation and semi-structured interviews with key respondents from each firm, various contextual data were gathered including detailed mapping of the supply chain, intra- and inter-firm business and operational processes, information systems infrastructure, and so on. Thus, information collected during Phase 2 clarified the rationale of the project so that the purpose and scope could be refined. Some of the questions that were answered are: which activities did the respondents identify as the most critical for investigating RFID potential? why? and how were these activities conducted in the existing systems?

During this phase, the industrial partners were mainly information providers and the RFID technology partners were consulted by the research group for specific technical questions, such as where are the "pain points" in the existing supply chain? How can these "pain points" be translated in business processes that can easily be shared among project stakeholders? Can RFID be used to automate the corresponding business processes? How? Is it possible for RFID readers to identify a specific type of product? In this specific environment? At this distance?

Because the selection of RFID infrastructure is primarily driven by (i) the targeted applications, (ii) the selected product to be identified and tracked, and (iii) the constraints specific to the physical environment,* HP had to participate to some extent to contextual data gathering. It then conducted the preliminary site survey to narrow the scope of the technological design considered for the implementation in a real-life setting, and to select appropriate arrangements for the laboratory demonstration.

Feedback to all project stakeholders was provided continuously by the research group, including, a mapping of selected business processes, preliminary data analysis and opportunity identification, and various basic conceptual models (e.g., for identifying RFID impacts). These outputs allowed adjusting the planning of further actions such as subsequent more specific data gathering, RFID-enabled scenario building, and simulation.

PHASE 3: DATA ANALYSIS AND LABORATORY BUILDING

In Phase 3, the industrial and technological participated in the development, building, evaluation, screening, and selection of RFID-enabled supply-chain scenarios. This phase allowed the industrial partners to understand and assess the impact and potential benefits the technology in terms of (i) business and operational process reengineering, (ii) changes in the information technology and network infrastructures, (iii) information sharing/synchronization between supply-chain members, (iv) human and physical resource reorganization, and finally (v) an organizational-wide strategy; in light of inter organizational supply chain applications.

One approach for collecting the requirements for the information systems was modeled on typical software projects (e.g., [74]), with an eye on experimentation, via

---

* The selection of RFID infrastructure depends on (i) the applications, which will be characterized by the distance of reading (how far?), the time frame for reading (i.e., dwell time) (how fast?), the number of tags to be read (how many?), and the volume of data to be transferred (how much?); (ii) the selected product to be identified and tracked, which will influence the choice of the technology with regard to the type of material (e.g., reflective material such as metal vs. absorptive material such as cardboard) and the level of tagging (pallet vs. box or item); and finally, (iii) the physical environment that has unique physical constraints influencing the level of interference, such as metal beams, specific level of humidity, distance between dock doors, presence of interfering electronic devices, and so on.

prototyping and iterative testing [75]. A second approach was partially based on the established methodologies in Business Process Reengineering (BPR) for integrating new technology [76]. Also, for the ease of communication among stakeholders, the business process language used a visual formalism to represent all the supply-chain departments and individuals, the processes to be carried out, the supporting information systems, and the different types of documents. With this common language, all parties could express their concerns, specify their needs, and clarify their objectives as the project progressed.

As a result of the brainstorming sessions, use case analyses, joint working sessions at the living laboratory, and selected scenarios were mapped in more detailed and populated with data, before being simulated and finally analyzed for their potential benefits. For this exercise, a BPA tool (Aris Toolset) was used. After several refinement rounds, a baseline version of the RFID-enabled scenarios was reached, providing the foundations for an innovative electronic business model. The new RFID-enabled business rules were configured in the middleware. The researchers formally informed all the project stakeholders of the final proposal for the proof of concept pilot so that they could elicit comments from their respective management.

PHASE 4: LABORATORY SIMULATION, DEMONSTRATION AND PROJECT TRANSFER

In this phase, the conceptual electronic business models proposed within Phase 3 was validated through a proof of concept in the research center laboratory (i.e., limited scope in controlled environment). Basically, this activity allowed the group to select an appropriate risk mitigation strategy and reduce the project's technical and commercial risks [77]. Dobni [78] pointed out that the proof of concept serves as a critical milestone prior to conducting a pilot study in a limited scope of the real environment. The required RFID infrastructure and IS system integration is presented in Figure 25.4.

To maximize the knowledge acquired during the experimentation, and to make the approach very practical, the researchers decided to control only some of the project's technical parameters (i.e., basic RFID infrastructure, limited integration, basic configuration, restricted application). All uncontrolled real-life issues were left open to change in building of the proof of concept. These included organizational issues (i.e., budget allocation, new contract negotiation, presence of unions, etc.), industrial issues (i.e., industry readiness, business relationship within the supply chain, market competitiveness), technological and standards issues (i.e., new technologies introduction, new standards, security threats, etc.), privacy issues (i.e., tracking of employees), and so on.

Moreover, because of the industrial partners' different interests in the project, two customized proof of concept sessions were held at the research center laboratory. The first focused on the potential benefits of optimizing the supply chain, while the second was IT integration, security, and infrastructure reliability. In order to ensure that the proof of concept would deliver relevant results, a "dry run" was conducted with the purpose of finding the right way to demonstrate the real potential and the limits of the technology. The RFID solution providers used this event to respond to a key concern of the industrial partners by convincing them that the proof of concept was worth mobilizing some of their key counterparts. In real-life, the results and analysis of the proof of concept constitute a milestone for the decision to go on (or not go on) with a pilot project. Similarly, two main objectives were sought in the living laboratory: (i) for the academic and industrial partners, to provide a concrete example of the benefits of the technology; and (ii) for the technological partners, to use this demonstration as a marketing tool for their companies' services.

After the proof of concept, the laboratory research center, which was initially positioned as the project leader, switched over to a more passive role (i.e., that of an observer). In the following phase of commercialization, the technological partners focused on the negotiation on a pilot project and an eventual live implementation. To date, Phase 5 is still pending, as a proposition derived from the proof of concept that the industrial partners are evaluating.

DISCUSSION

A recent survey by ChainLink Research [79] of over 1500 end-user firms on their RFID plans and experiences in several industries shows that firms have a much more cautious approach to RFID. As a result, pilot projects have become key parts of their roll-out of technology, which can take several years. Firms are making deliberate careful assessments of pilot results and weighing the benefits of moving on to larger initiatives. Earlier cases of complex, long, and costly implementations, as observed in the case of ERP and CRM, systems, may have contributed to creating this level of apprehension *vis-à-vis* new technology implementation. In this context, an improvement in the way front-end project are managed is definitely required.

The work carried out within the living laboratory allowed all parties to bring their knowledge up to a much more advanced level over the situation that prevailed at the very beginning. This section expands on this achievement by focusing on two aspects. First, a series of interdependent key dimensions and propositions that emerged from the project are identified. These dimensions help to describe the learning process that occurred as the project unfolded. Secondly, a list of positive side effects is reported based on the observations of each individual actor working with the laboratory.

EXPLORING THE KEY DIMENSIONS AND PROPOSITIONS THAT EMERGED FROM THE PROJECT

Toward Clear Goals Objectives

The project concerned RFID as an emerging technology whose possibilities are difficult to formalize in general. While some applications could easily be explained (e.g., automated warehousing), others were more abstract (e.g., customer engagement). Moreover, neither the methods supporting the development and implementation of these applications nor the goals of the project was clear. Because of the very limited number of RFID inter-organizational supply-chain implementations around the world, benchmarking opportunities were few, especially since RFID applications require a high level of customization (related to a firm's products, processes, physical environment, and IT infrastructure). This suggested that the demonstration of simple applications (e.g., receiving of products) on a limited number of products, with a minimum system configuration should be the first step before proceeding with further, more comprehensive applications.

Initially, the goal of the proof of concept was not clearly defined because all parties lacked a global view of the technology and of its potential applications and how it would fit in a specific organizational and industrial context. As the project progressed, however, goals emerged gradually as the stakeholders became familiar with the technology in their specific environments. This gradual emergence was reflected during phases 2 and 3 through multiple iterations to gather and analyze specific contextual data and propose RFID-enabled solutions developed to solve real-life issues, whether problems or opportunities.

This is consistent with prior research that showed that, where opportunities are difficult to delineate and customer requirements difficult to capture, alternative methods can be efficiently used such as goal-based business requirements (e.g., [80]) business-process-oriented requirements [81], collaborative scenario elicitation (e.g., [82]), and use case analysis (e.g., [83]), in which end-users should also be involved to ensure accurate requirements and a successful project [84].

Removing the fuzziness of the front-end phase was also accomplished through customer involvement in the early steps; as Alam [85] suggested in the context of new service development, and more broadly through the cooperation of internal groups such as senior management or functional groups, and external groups including customers, suppliers, and partners [10,86,87]. This approach, centered on the identification of shared purposes and visions, led to a better understanding of project environment uncertainty, clarifying the project target, improving the quality of early decision making [87], and contributing to the success of the project [88]. These results lead to the following propositions:

Proposition 1. In proof of concept experimentations, risks may be mitigated by restricting the number and the scope of the applications to be developed and validated.

Proposition 2. When objectives and goals are fuzzy, a variety of approaches are required for a better identification of customer requirements.

Performance Measures as Indicators of Required Applications

Undoubtedly, because of the unstructured nature of the front-end activities, the experiment showed that selecting the most appropriate applications to demonstrate and measuring their impacts in terms of performance improvement remains difficult. Product portfolio management techniques are difficult to implement at the early project stages, where ideas are not well structured. The difficulty of rapidly narrowing the focus of the research and developing propositions that could reveal the full potential of RFID created some tensions, as the technology partners were pushing for a proposal that could be used to program their equipment and deliver a solution. In order to manage this issue, a set of high-level, subjective, and qualitative measures needed to be suggested to assess the performance of the project deliverables (e.g., flexibility of the supply chain, agility, and capacity to respond to urgent deliveries, etc.).

This initial exercise allowed the project stakeholders to define some requirements, circumscribe the scope of the project, and agree on the initial applications to develop. It was only once this screening process was completed that a more detailed quantitative performance measures (e.g., inventory level, sourcing cycle time, asset utilization, etc.) were identified to assess the performance of the proposed applications and demonstrate how the goals of the project could be reached.

The initial intention to better understand how firms (potential users) can develop an understanding of the stakes, challenges, and benefits of implementing RFID in a supply-chain context also raised the level of difficulty, as conflicting goals were revealed when aligning intra- and inter-organizational objectives. The importance of incentive alignment had to be thought out at (i) the focal firm level, (ii) the supply chain level [16], and also (iii) between technology providers, reinforcing the role of the laboratory as a collaborative workspace for the negotiation of potential arrangements and their experimentation as a means to assess their commercial viability prior to real-life implementation, and so on or further negotiation.

Also, as the laboratory simulation was taking shape (phases 3 and 4), the business considerations at the origin of the RFID-enabled scenarios turned out to have considerable impact on the technological dimension of the project, suggesting that a systemic approach would help manage the interdependencies. This was reflected when the technology partners started integrating various electronic platforms (ERP and middleware) to simulate each site and the integration between the sites. Issues such as data standardization, access, sharing and flow represented challenging aspects of the project as RFID technology and the EPC network really appeared as a newly emerged IOS. However, bringing all the project stakeholders into the living lab greatly facilitated the communication process and allowed the group to resolve most of these issues as they arose.

> *Proposition 3.* For a project implemented in a supply-chain context to be successful, incentive alignments for collective performance improvement have to be thought out and be validated by a multidisciplinary team in a collaborative workspace prior to implementation.
>
> *Proposition 4.* Very early in the process individual participating in the preproject activities (i.e., proof of concept) needs to be trained to be able to champion the project in his/her own organization and push the innovation to a more formal corporate level decision-making process.
>
> *Proposition 5.* When the business and technological requirements are tightly coupled, the living laboratory approach appears to be an effective approach for concurrently and iteratively managing the project stakeholders' expectations.

From Creativity Management to Project Management

As reflected in management practices, the stakeholders moved from a very open and flexible style to a more systematic management style, where ideas and concepts had to be translated into objectives (phase 2), formalized through the building and validation of RFID-enabled scenarios (phase 3), and later tested in the laboratory (phase 4). The role of the researchers moved from that of innovative opportunity seekers, then technological and business integrators, to the "guardians of a Gantt chart." The challenge was therefore to maintain some flexibility throughout the project as goals and objectives became more tangible and formalized (e.g., [89]). This challenge was manifested when the team had to identify how to leverage on selected application in order to increase potential benefits. For instance, a "smart shelf" application would allow automated replenishment, while preventing theft and allowing real-time marketing for cross-selling opportunities. All these ideas were thought out early in the scenario-building process (phase 3), and were refined during working sessions with an emphasis on the identification of the required infrastructure for performing selected applications.

> *Proposition 6.* When managing the front-end of a project, some flexibility is necessary to allow creativity to be integrated into the requirement identification process thus ensuring a gradual transition from early to late front-end phase of the project.

From Formalized to Informal Business Relationships

Because the building of a proof of concept with other commercial partners, led by a research team, was not a widespread methodology among industrial firms, the living laboratory concept appeared more difficult to explain that the traditional model of using consultants. The researchers had to clearly position the role of the laboratory as a "learning space" to expand scientific and practical knowledge of RFID issues through a collaborative process that would evolve over time, from initial intent to full cooperation, through the building of a business case that would later be tested in a proof of concept, in a neutral and independent environment. This definition posited a fundamental distinction from consulting firms or solution providers, as it suggested that the researchers were better positioned to structure the project in the form of a learning organization.

As the project progressed, the business relationship among all the parties became more formalized. This transformation demonstrated the central role of the laboratory in the innovation phase as a hub for learning and collaboration that allowed the development of trust as a substitute for more formal rules of control [90]. Thus, the identification of a shared purpose underlay the success of the proof of concept by encouraging the willingness to share confidential data and to provide additional support.

From another perspective, during phase 2, it rapidly became evident that more technology partners than were initially identified would be required. Therefore, when building alliances, the selection of partners appeared crucial so the group could leverage the "recruitment" of additional members to build the collaborative platform. Indeed, selecting a major industrial partner (as potential user) facilitated the negotiations with RFID solution providers as it constituted a strong argument to convince them to join the platform. This preliminary platform, in turn, constituted a facilitator to convince the ERP consultants to embark and bridge the link between RFID infrastructure and ERP infrastructure. In essence, by acquiring all the actors one by one, the researchers had to handle a dilemma whereas the parties were waiting for sufficient incentives prior to embarking, leaving the project in wait-and-see mode—similar to real-life RFID implementations around the world [28].

Proposition 7. Selling the concept of living laboratory can be a very difficult task. Considering that the front-end of innovations involves the selection, recruitment, and active participation of multiple stakeholders with conflicting goals, it is necessary to concentrate on the common benefits.

Balancing Stakeholders' Expectations

Phase 4 of the project constituted a turning point in terms of delivering on promises and a cornerstone in convincing the industrial partners to proceed further with a pilot study. Because of the novelty of the concept, the researchers' role was again to manage the stakeholders' expectations and maintaining a balance between RFID solution providers eager to establish their presence in a flourishing market with minimal initial investment prior to client commitment to a pilot, and the industrial partners' ambitious requirements for the proof of concept. A preliminary dry run highlighted this issue when the RFID solution providers' commercial agents (satellite partners), who had a limited understanding of the whole research process, used the laboratory as a commercial demonstration.

The dry run underscored the diversity of the technology partners and the diverse interests of the industrial partners. For instance, while operations managers were interested in implementation costs and potential savings, the time frame for full deployment, and so on, the IT people were more concerned with frequency of use, communication methods, anti-collision protocols, encryption for security, middleware configuration and integration with existing IS, and so on. Clearly, the dry run highlighted the need to be focused so that the content would be adapted to the specific audience's interests. Therefore, the decision was made to conduct two customized proof of concept sessions, limiting the negative side effects of a cultural mismatch between all the parties.

Proposition 8. The living laboratory leaders have a fundamental role in the development of trust by their neutrality and independence throughout the process.

Knowledge Sharing

Turner and Müller [91] have proposed a revised definition of projects to expand the project output beyond the product/service delivered to include "beneficial objectives of change," and satisfying the project stakeholders. In that sense, the front-end phases of the RFID project could be considered a comprehensive technological and business approach to refine the management practices of potential early adopters of RFID technology and make them more competitive.

Indeed, along the project life cycle, the initial project knowledge was distributed among various poles of competencies, and no real collaboration would be possible before sharing some basic common undertaking on the entire project dimensions. For example, initially, RFID knowledge was centralized in the researchers and the solution providers. When this knowledge was shared with industrial partners, they were able to better understand the issues, challenges, and opportunities for realistic potential technology applications. Their primary motivations for RFID adoption were becoming clearer, bridging the gap between ideas and concepts and between concepts and system requirements. As the project evolved through phase 3, sharing the new common knowledge with supply-chain members gave everyone an opportunity to contribute to the goal of exploring new opportunities. These RFID-aware partners were then able to argue, ask very relevant technical and business questions, predict potential issues in the implementation, and so on.

> *Proposition 9.* For a collaborative project to be successful, all the project stakeholders need to share some time together to develop an understanding of each other's roles in the project, as well as a common knowledge of the technology to be implemented.
>
> *Proposition 10.* In the front-end of a new system development, a project and a product life-cycle views need to be considered in the assessment of the project feasibility and the commercial viability of the new system commercial and its impact on business processes and the supply chain.

Contributions of the Living Laboratory

In relation to the stakeholders' initial expectations and their contributions to the front-end innovation activities collaboratively performed in the laboratory, several positive side effects emerged. These were identified not only following a synthesis of observations and notes, mostly taken in the laboratory, during the multiple working sessions for the preparation of the proof of concept, but also afterwards, during lessons learned sessions, once the stakeholders had some distance from their personal involvement in the project. Table 25.2 lists these effects. Although outputs were

---

TABLE 25.2

Positive Side Effects of the Living Lab Approach

Some Observed Output (Side Effects) for the Technological Firms

Join a "co-development alliance," and *propose an integrated solution* for RFID deployment in a supply chain context

Remove the fuzziness of front-end innovation through multiple stakeholders' involvement

Access confidential data from key industrial stakeholders providing all the required information (tacit and explicit) to conduct an in-depth analysis and build a best business case

Understand the possible impact of RFID implementation on the particular interests of stakeholders in *refining an eventual business proposition* with the identification of other divisions that could directly benefit from the implementation of the selected RFID application

Refine their RFID offer with the adoption of a multidisciplinary (cross-enterprise) and cross-departmental approach where technical (R&D labs) and commercial people had to work together

Allow technological project members to *bridge the gap between project marketing and project management* by integrating all the stakeholders early in the project life cycle

Acquire knowledge (e.g., field specificities, preferred approaches for front-end of innovation projects) and *leverage on it in other RFID projects*. As other field and laboratory studies were conducted concurrently, similarities emerged and common concerns were highlighted, thus providing a means to *identify project patterns* that could eventually be treated in bundles of projects

---

continued

TABLE 25.2   (continued)
Positive Side Effects of the Living Lab Approach

Some Observed Output (Side Effects) for the Technological Firms

Realize that the *Canadian market* presents some inherent *specificities* compared to the U.S. market in terms of industrial stakeholders' readiness to adopt RFID and, most importantly, business practices, forcing them to refine their strategy

Realize the importance of the *living laboratory approach in a longitudinal perspective* for front-end of innovation projects, as a learning workplace for all stakeholders, including the ones providing the technology

Although the initial idea of HP Labs was to build the proof of concept and take back the laboratory infrastructure once completed, the research process revealed that the permanent existence of the laboratory would be necessary as a *window for potential commercialization*

Industrial stakeholders would meet again and again with internal clients to share their experiences and raise new issues and concerns regarding the *difficulty of clearly determining the end of the proof of concept* and the decision by an organization to move on to a pilot or implementation phase

Some Observed Output (Side Effects) for the BPA Software Provider

Contribute to refining its product offer by including some RFID functionalities that could be used as templates for RFID implementation, in their new version of Aris Toolset, and *reinforce its positioning* in the BPA landscape

Be at the forefront for leading the *fourth wave of BPR*

Some Observed Output (Side Effects) for the ERP Provider

While the SAP RFID middleware was not used for the laboratory simulations, the results *demonstrated that integration with a reliable back-office system* can guarantee the optimization of cross-organizational business processes (today, SAP has its own middleware, SAP-AutoID Infrastructure–AII)

Observed Output (Side Effects) for the Industrial Partners

Understand the benefits of collaboratively adopting the technology at a supply chain level

Be able to *assess the real impact of RFID technology* and the EPC network when considering various dimensions other than information system integration, such as the supply chain members' strategy, BPR and information flows, the organizational structure changes needed, and so on

Define a common ground for *incentive alignment* between multiple stakeholders managing performance: (i) at the department level, (ii) at the firm level, and (iii) at the supply chain level

Develop *managerial competencies* in the context of uncertain project situations involving multiple interdependent internal and external stakeholders

Some Observed Output (Side Effects) for the Academic Institution

Simulate RFID laboratory implementation (including ERP and middleware configuration) and provide valuable *hands-on experience* to allow a deeper understanding of RFID technology, front-end activities of innovation process, business process impacts, *potential benefits, and limitations* for deployment in real-life settings

Share the knowledge acquired among industrial communities and coordinate the adoption process by starting "the RFID bandwagon." Contribute to *building an initial "pool of lead users"* to position the region as an innovation pole for RFID application development

continued

TABLE 25.2   (continued)
Positive Side Effects of the Living Lab Approach

Some Observed Output (Side Effects) for the Academic Institution

Develop the researchers' *competencies in managing* the front-end phase of innovation projects involving
  leading-edge technologies and *leverage on* the first proof of concept to create similar experiences with
  other industrial partners in different industries, thereby significantly reducing the lead time from
  concept to proof of concept. While the first proof of concept (explored in this paper) took more than
  two years to build, the second one conducted in the retail industry with the same stakeholders (except
  for the industrial partners) took less than one year, highlighting the *learning curve concept*
Address the shortcoming of AIDC education and research, by integrating the knowledge gathered in the
  academic curricula
Build a *neutral collaborative platform* where the universities play a key role in the generation and
  diffusion of scientific and technological knowledge leading to innovation, where all members can
  mutually benefit from each other's *complementary competencies, skills, and technologies* and allow
  cross-disciplinary integration for successful NPD

observed for each specific stakeholder, several common benefits emerged for all partners, mainly in terms of understanding the front-end of RFID innovation projects:

All the parties developed a certain familiarity with the management issues
contextualized by multiple interdependent internal and external stakeholders in the
kind of dynamic project environment characterized by uncertain conditions that is
common to the implementation of leading technologies. While technology partners
may be familiar to some extent with such working conditions, the industrial partners
involved in this project learned how to deal with the fuzziness of the adoption process.
This gave participants an overall vision (i.e., systemic view of the project) that no one
stakeholder could have accessed individually. The research group was therefore
able to leverage on the first proof of concept in the utility sector to create similar
experiences with other industrial partners in different industries (e.g., retail), by significantly reducing the lead-time from concept to proof of concept.

As knowledge was gained, it strengthened the building of the business case and
allowed the team to refine the development of dynamic requirements. Because of the
nature of the project to be implemented in a supply-chain context, this exercise
helped to quickly understand the individual and collective impact of decisions on the
performance of RFID-enabled scenarios based on realistic considerations.

Finally, all the partners realized that technical and business dimensions are ultimately
interlinked in RFID projects, limiting the possibility of working sequentially and "forcing" industrial and technology partners into close collaboration. Although multiple technical issues were identified and resolved (e.g., optimization of the read rate, configuration
of the middleware, and integration with the ERP) during the living laboratory experiments, the business dimension (e.g., contractual management based on new RFID-
enabled applications) proved to be the trigger of the whole adoption process. Similar to
BPR projects, RFID implementation in a supply-chain context clearly emerged as a
business project in which the adoption of the technology is a means rather than a goal.

CONCLUSION

Adopting emerging technologies remains a challenging endeavor for many organizations. Part of this challenge come from the fact that limited, often contradictory information is available, so managers have difficulty getting a clear picture about the benefits and the overall cost and implications of a given technology. This was the case, many years ago, at the start of the ERP adoption wave. Today, the similar phenomenon can be observed, as the RFID technology develops and continues to gain interest within different industries. Traditionally, most companies would rely on third party (consultants, technology providers, etc.) in order to go through the fuzzy front-end phase of the adoption project. Such strategy is not without risk. Some adopters are reluctant to "get married" so early with services and technology providers which, in many cases, may not have as much competency and information that they claim.

This chapter explored a different way to manage the early phases of an adoption process. The leading role played by a not-for-profit organization—the university—proved to be key in helping firms to deal with the complexity of a new technology adoption in a neutral environment. Considering the distributed environment and the collaborative approach that are necessary for a technology like RFID to be deployed, the laboratory revealed a strong potential to help the stakeholders develop a mutual understanding of the technology, its potential impacts and the benefits that can be realistically expected, and the underlying concepts.

Overall, the chapter provides two sets of contributions. First, this study provides guidance on how to develop the business case for RFID adoption and implementation within and between organizations under uncertain market and technical conditions. Additionally, the living laboratory experiment demonstrates how a variant of the Triple-Helix (university–industry–government) model of collaboration [92] can be put in place even at the project level. Among the bulk of studies on industry–university collaboration, very few have focused specifically on the management of the early phases of a multi-stakeholder innovation project.

The study also contributes to our comprehension of the front-end phase of adoption projects, which is rarely discussed in the scientific literature. Many studies continue to be published about fuzziness in NPD projects. However, very few authors have explicitly applied such concept to adoption projects, even though they can represent a very high level of complexity for some companies. This chapter is therefore a partial answer to some questions raised by Turner [77] who highlighted the fact that, while front-end project activities (i.e., pilot studies) are widely used in real-life settings, almost nothing has been written about them in the literature. As Dobni notes, "while plenty of counsel (on innovation) exists on what organization should do, there is a shortage of 'how to' details" [78]. Because innovation projects typically involve *ad hoc* decisions and ill-defined processes, current models, and methodologies such as the current project management bodies of knowledge provide only partial guidelines for managing the front-end phases of innovation. This is particularly annoying considering that the latter represent one of the greatest weak points in innovative projects. In fact, effectively managing front-end activities is one of the most difficult challenges facing innovation managers, and where information requirement determination is one of the most difficult phases of information system design.

For practitioners who are engaged in projects with a high degree of uncertainty, there is certainly the need to move away from conventional methods of managing projects, and to accept the fact that early phases are fallible and may be longer that initially expected. The RFID project investigated in this chapter certainly falls in this category. It clearly represented a high degree of ambiguity, mainly because of confusion and lack of understanding by the various project stakeholders (i.e., clarity of the objectives and respective requirements). Projects like this also suffer from multiple sources of external environment uncertainties (e.g., technology, standards, ROI, security and privacy issues, etc.) and evolve through a very fragile equilibrium. In this context, project management requires alternative approaches based on stakeholder cooperation, which incorporate flexibility, tolerance, and vagueness [90,93]. To say the least, these attributes are not typical of the traditional control approaches. Hopefully, the approach presented in this chapter will lead to many more experiments of the kind, and help organizations to see and manage the complex adoption projects from a new perspective.

REFERENCES

1. Wyld, D.C., RFID 101: The next big thing for management, *Manage. Res. News*, 29 (4), 154–173, 2006.
2. Chao, C.C., Yang, J.M., and Jen, W.Y., Determining technology trends and forecasts of RFID by historical review and bibliometric analysis from 1991 to 2005, *Technovation*, 27 (5), 268–279, 2007.
3. Srivastava, B., Radio Frequency ID technology: The next revolution in SCM, *Business Horizons*, 47 (6), 60–68, 2004.
4. Pramataris, K., Collaborative supply chain practices and evolving technological approaches, *Supply Chain Manage. Int. J.*, 12 (3), 210–220, 2007.
5. Zaharudin, A.A. et al., The intelligent product driven supply chain, 2002. Available at http://www.autoidlabs.org/uploads/media/CAM-AUTOID-WH-005.pdf, accessed June 28, 2009.
6. Lefebvre, E., Bendavid, Y., and Lefebvre, L.A., Open innovation strategies in shaping technological progress: The case of RFID, *Proceedings of the European International Association of Management of Technology (EUROMOT)*, Nice, France, September, 2008.
7. Aberdeen, RFID in Retail: The Truth Behind the Hype, 2008. Available at: http://www.aberdeen.com
8. IDtechex, RFID Forecasts, Players and Opportunities 2008–2018, 2008. Available at: http://www.idtechex.com
9. Nobelius, D. and Trygg, L., Stop chasing the front end process. Management of the early phases in product development projects, *Int. J. Project Manage.*, 20 (5), 331–340, 2002.
10. Khurana, A. and Rosenthal, S.R., Integrating the fuzzy front end of new product development, *Sloan Manage. Rev.*, 38 (2), 103–120, 1997; reprinted in *Innovation: Driving Product, Process, and Market Change*, Roberts, E.B., Ed., Jossey-Bass., San Francisco, CA, 2002, 47–86.
11. Koen, P. et al., Fuzzy front end: Effective methods, tools and techniques, in *The PDMA ToolBook for New Product Development*, Belliveau, P., Griffin, A. and Somermeyer, S., Eds., John Wiley & Sons, New York, 2002, 2–35.

12. Fosso Wamba, S. et al., Exploring the impact of RFID technology and the EPC Network on mobile B2B eCommerce: A case study in the retail industry, *Int. J. Prod. Econ.*, 112 (2), 614–629, 2008.
13. U.S. Department of Defense, Item Unique Identification 101: The Basics, 2006. Available at: www.acq.osd.mil/dpap/UID/attachments/iuid-101-20060130.pdf
14. Kumar, S., Connective technology as a strategic tool for building effective supply chain, *Int. J. Manuf. Technol. Manage.*, 10 (1), 41–56, 2007.
15. Thiesse, F. and Michahelles F., An overview of EPC technology, *Sensor Rev.*, 26 (2), 101–105, 2006.
16. Bendavid, Y. et al., Key performance indicators for the evaluation of RFID enabled B-to-B eCommerce applications: The case of a five-layer supply chain, *J. Inf. Syst. E-Bus. Manage.*, 7 (1), 1–20, 2009.
17. Landt, J., *Shrouds of Time, The History of RFID*, AIM Publication, 2001. Available at: http://www.aimglobal.org
18. Computer economics, Radio Frequency Identification (RFID) adoption stalls. Computer Economics Report, February 2007. Available at: http://www/computereconomics.com.
19. Roberti, M., RFID 2.0, *RFID J.*, 5 (2), 40–43, 2008.
20. EPCglobal, EPC™ Radio-Frequency Identity Protocols Class-1 Generation-2 UHF RFID Protocol for Communications at 860 MHz–960 MHz Version 1.0.9, 2005. Available at: www.epcglobalinc.org
21. ISO/IEC 18000-6:2004, Information technology, Radio frequency identification for item management Part 6: Parameters for air interface communications at 860 MHz to 960 MHz, Geneva, 2006.
22. EPCglobal, EPCglobal Standards Development Process, Version 1.3, 2007. Available at: www.epcglobalinc.org
23. Wasserman, E., One RFID tag from cradle to grave, *RFID J.*, 5 (2), 28–33, 2008.
24. O'Connor, M.C., A guide to today middleware, *RFID J.*, 2007 Buyer's Guide to RFID Resources, 107–122, 2007.
25. SAP, SAP Solutions for RFID: Making adaptive enterprise vision a reality, 2007. Available at: www.sap.com/solutions/business-suite/scm/rfid/index.epx
26. Computing Technology Industry Association (CompTIA), Radio Frequency Identification (RFID+) certification, 2007. Available at: http://certification.comptia.org/rfid/default.aspx
27. Ngai, E.W.T. et al., RFID research: An academic literature review (1995–2005) and future research directions, *Int. J. Prod. Econ.*, 112 (2), 507–1010, 2008.
28. Reyes, P.M. et al., RFID: The state of the union between promise and practice. *Int. J. Integ. Supply Manage.*, 3 (2), 192–206, 2007.
29. Gunasekaran, A. and Ngai E.W.T., Build-to-Order supply chain management: A literature review and framework for development, *J. Oper. Manag.*, 23 (5), 423–451, 2005.
30. Yang, G. and Jarvenpaa, S.L., Trust and Radio Frequency Identification (RFID) adoption within an alliance, *Proceedings of the 38th Annual Hawaii International Conference on System Sciences (HICSS '05)*, Big Island, HI, USA, 2005.
31. Riggins, F.J. and Slaughter, K.T., The role of collective mental models in IOS adoption: Opening the black box of rationality in RFID deployment, *Proceedings of the 39th Annual Hawaii International Conference on System Sciences (HICSS '06)*, Kauai, HI, 2006.
32. Sharma, A., Citurs, A., and Konsynski, B., Strategic and institutional perspectives in the adoption and early integration of RFID, *Proceedings of the 40th Annual Hawaii International Conference on System Sciences (HICSS '07)*, Big Island, HI, 2007.
33. Choy, K.L. et al., Improving logistics visibility in a supply chain: An integrated approach with radio frequency identification technology, *Int. J. Integ. Supply Manage.*, 3 (2), 135–155, 2007.

34. Sheffi, Y., RFID and the innovation cycle, *Int. J. Logist. Manage.*, 15 (1), 1–10, 2004.
35. Adomavicius, G. et al., Understanding patterns of technology evolution: An ecosystem perspective, *Proceedings of the 39th Annual Hawaii International Conference on System Sciences (HICSS '06)*, Kauai, HI.
36. Quaadgras, A., Who joins the platform? The case of the RFID business ecosystem, in *Proceedings of the 38th Annual Hawaii International Conference on System Sciences (HICSS '05)*, Big Island, HI, 2005.
37. Dew, N. and Read, S., The more we get together: Coordinating network externality product introduction in the RFID industry, *Technovation*, 27 (10), 569–581, 2007.
38. Whitaker, J., Mithas S., and Krishman, M.S., A field study of RFID deployment and return expectations, *Prod. Oper. Manage.*, 16 (5), 599–612, 2008.
39. Ngai, E.W.T. et al., Development of RFID based traceability system: Experience and lessons learned from aircraft engineering company, *Prod. Oper. Manage.*, 16 (5), 554–568, 2007.
40. Loebbecke, C. and Palmer, J., RFID in the fashion industry: Kaufhof Department Stores AG and Gerry Weber International AG, fashion manufacturer, *Manage. Inform. Syst. Quart. Executive*, 5 (2), 15–25, 2006.
41. Wu, N.C. et al., Challenges to global RFID adoption, *Technovation*, 26 (12), 1317–1323, 2006.
42. Li, S. et al., Radio frequency identification technology: Applications, technical challenges and strategies, *Sensor Rev.*, 26 (3), 193–202, 2006.
43. Bhuptani, M. and Moradpour, S., *RFID Field Guide: Deploying Radio Frequency Identification Systems*, Sun MicroSys/Prentice Hall, Upper Saddle River, NJ, 2005.
44. Lahiri, S., *RFID Sourcebook*, IBM Press/ Pearson Education, Upper Saddle River, NJ, 2005.
45. Laubacher, R. et al., What is RFID worth to your company? Measuring performance at the activity level, 2006. Available at: http://ebusiness.mit.edu
46. GMA (The Grocery Manufacturers Association) and IBM Business Consulting Services, EPC/RFID: Proposed industry adoption framework manufacturer survey and pilot learning's to date, April 2006. Available at: http://www.gmabrands.com/publications/docs/appendixfinal.pdf
47. Cecere, L. and Suleski, J., What we have learned from three years of retail RFID pilots, *AMR Research Report*, 2007. Available at: www.amrresearch.com/Content/View.asp?pmillid=20358
48. Hardgrave, B.C. and Miller, R., The myths and realities of RFID, *Int. J. Glob. Logist. Supply Chain Manage.*, 1 (1), 1–16, 2006.
49. Moore, B., RFID: "Et tu, Brute?" Killing some RFID "truths", Association for automatic identification and mobility, March 2007. Available at: www.aimglobal.org
50. Kaplan, R.S., Innovation action research: Creating new management theory and practice, *J. Manage. Acc. Res.*, 10, 89–118, 1998.
51. Coughlan, P. and Coghlan, D., Action research for operation management, *Int. J. Oper. Prod. Manage.*, 22 (2), 220–240, 2002.
52. Curtin, J., Kauffman, R.J., and Riggins, F.J., Making the most out of RFID technology: A research agenda for the study of the adoption, usage and impact of RFID, *Inform. Technol. Manage.*, 8 (2), 88–110, 2007.
53. Howells, J., Intermediation and the role of intermediaries in innovation, *Res. Policy* 35, 715–728, 2006.
54. Coghlan, D., Practitioner research for organizational knowledge, *Manage. Learn.*, 34 (4), 451–463, 2003.
55. Shani, A.B., David, A., and Willson, C., Collaborative research: Alternative roadmaps, in *Collaborative Research in Organizations: Foundations for Learning, Change, and*

Theoretical Development, Adler, N.B., Shani, A.B., and Styhre, A., Eds., Sage, London, U.K., 2004.

56. Daniel, E. and Wilson, H.N., Action research in turbulent environments: An example in e-commerce prioritisation, *Eur. J. Market.*, 38 (3/4), 355–377, 2004.

57. Fricke, W. and Totterdill, P., *Action Research in Workplace Innovation and Regional Development*, John Benjamin's Publishing Co., Amsterdam, the Netherlands, 2004.

58. Baskerville, R.L. and Wood-Harper, T., Diversity in information systems action research methods, *Eur. J. Inform. Syst.*, 17 (2), 90–108, 1998.

59. Lau, F., Toward a framework for action research in information systems studies, *Inform. Technol. People*, 12 (2), 148–165, 1999.

60. Parker, D. and Mobey, A., Action research to explore perceptions of risk in project management, *Int. J. Prod. Perform. Manage.*, 53 (1), 18–32, 2004.

61. Naslund, D., Logistics needs qualitative research—Especially action research, *Int. J. Phys. Distrib. Logist. Manage.*, 32 (5), 321–338, 2002.

62. Eriksson, M. et al., Living labs as a multi-contextual R&D methodology, *Proceedings of the 13th ICE conference on Concurrent (Collaborative) Innovation*, Sophia-Antipolis, France, June 4–6, 2007.

63. Loeh, H., Sung, G., and Katzy, B., The CeTIM virtual enterprise lab—A living, distributed, collaboration lab, *Proceedings of the 11th International Conference on Concurrent Enterprising (ICE '05)*, Munich, Germany, 2005. Available at: http://www.veforum.org/apps/comm.asp?$1=407

64. Katzy, B. and Sung, G., Virtual project productivity—A management issue, in *Proceedings of the 13th ICE Conference on Concurrent (Collaborative) Innovation*, Sophia-Antipolis, France, June 4–6, 2007.

65. Intille, S. et al., Using a live-in laboratory for ubiquitous computing research, *Proceedings of the 4th Int. Conf. on Pervasive Computing (PERVASIVE O '6)*, Dublin, Ireland, May, 2006. Available at: http://web.media.mit.edu

66. LaMarca, A. et al., Place Lab: Device positioning using radio beacons in the Wild, *Proceedings of the 3rd International Conference. on Pervasive Computing*, Munich, Germany, 2005.

67. Smeds, R., Managing change towards lean enterprises, *Int. J. Oper. Prod. Manage.*, 14 (3), 66–82, 1994.

68. Nobelius, D., Towards the sixth generation of R&D management, *Int. J. Project Manage.*, 22, 369–375, 2004.

69. Blonqvist, K.M. et al., Towards networked R&D management: The R&D approach by Sorena corporation as an example, *R&D Manage.*, 34 (4), 591–603, 2004.

70. Emden, Z., Calantone, R.J., and Droge, C., Collaborating for new product development: Selecting the partner with maximum potential to create value, *J. Prod. Innovat. Manage.*, 23, 330–341, 2004.

71. Chesbrough, H.W., *Open Innovation: The New Imperative for Creating and Profiting from Technology*, Harvard Business School Press, Boston, MA, 2003.

72. Chesbrough, H.W., Why companies should have open business models, *MIT Sloan Manage. Rev.*, 48 (2), 21–28, 2007.

73. Dyer, J., Kale, P., and Singh, H., How to make strategic alliance work, *MIT Sloan Manage.t Rev.*, 42 (4), 37–43, 2001.

74. Wiegers, K.E., *Software Requirements, Practical Techniques for Gathering and Managing Requirements Throughout The Product Development Cycle*, 2nd edn., Microsoft Press, Redmond, WA, USA, 2003.

75. El Louadi, M., Galleta, D.F., and Sampler, J.L., An empirical validation of a contingency model for information requirement determination, *ACM SIGMIS Database*, 29 (3), 31–51, 1998.

76. Attram, M., Exploring the relationship between information technology and business process reengineering, *Inform. Manage.*, 41, 585–596, 2004.
77. Turner, J.R., The role of pilot studies in reducing risk on projects and programmes, *Int. J. Project Manage.*, 23 (1), 1–6, 2005.
78. Dobni, C.B., The innovation blueprint, *Bus. Horizons*, 49 (4), 329–339, 2006.
79. Grackin, A., RFID Checklist: RFID Markets and Solutions for 2008, ChainLink Research, October 2007. htttp://www.alienrfid.com/docs/RFID_Checklist_RFID_Mkts_ Solutions.pdf, accessed June 28, 2009.
80. Dardenne, A., Van Lamsweerde, A., and Fickas, S., Goal-directed requirements acquisition, *Sci. Comput. Program.*, 20 (1–2), 3–50, 1993.
81. Arao, T., Goto, E., and Nagata, T., Business process oriented requirements engineering process, *Proceedings of the 13th International Conference on Requirements Engineering (ICRE '05)*, Paris, France, 2005.
82. Hickey, A.M. et al., Establishing a foundation for collaborative scenario elicitation, *ACM SIGMIS Database*, 30 (3–4), 92–110, 1999.
83. Kaasinen, E., Tuomisto, T., and Välkkynen, P., Ambient functionality—Use cases, in *Proceedings of the Smart Objects & Ambient Intelligence Conferece*, Grenoble, France, 2005.
84. Kujala, S. et al., The role of user involvement in requirements quality and project success, *Proceedings of the 13th International Conference on Requirements Engineering (ICRE '05)*, Paris, France, 2005.
85. Alam, I., Removing the fuzziness from the fuzzy front-end of service innovations through customer interactions, *Ind. Market. Manage.*, 35, 448–68, 2006.
86. Kim, J. and Wilemon, D., Focusing the fuzzy front-end in new product development, *R&D Manage.*, 32 (4), 269–279, 2002.
87. Hong, P. et al., The role of project target clarity in an uncertain project environment, *Int. J. Oper. Prod. Manage.*, 24 (12), 1269–1291, 2004.
88. Zhang, Q. and Doll, W. J., The fuzzy front end and success of new product development: A causal model, *Eur. J. Innovat. Manage.*, 4 (2), 95–112, 2001.
89. Maiden, N. and Robertson, S., Integrating creativity into requirements processes: Experiences with an air traffic management system, *Proceedings of the 13th International Conference on Requirements Engineering*, Paris, Franc, 2005.
90. Atkinson, R., Crawford, L., and Ward, S., Fundamental uncertainties in projects and scope of project management, *Int. J. Project Manage.*, 24 (8), 687–698, 2006.
91. Turner, J.R. and Müller, R., On the nature of the project as a temporary organization, *Int. J. Project Manage.*, 21 (1), 1–8, 2003.
92. Etzkowitz, H. and Leydesdorff, L., The dynamics of innovation: From National Systems and "Mode 2" to a Triple Helix of university–industry–government relations, *Res. Policy*, 29 (2), 109–123, 2000.
93. Williams, T.M., Assessing and moving on from the dominant project management discourse in the light of project overruns, *IEEE Trans. Eng. Manage.*, 52 (4), 497–508, 2005.

26 Managing Virtual Project Teams: Recent Findings

Nathalie Drouin, Mario Bourgault, and Caroline Gervais

CONTENTS

INTRODUCTION

Recent developments in information and communication technologies (ICT) have spurred the rise of virtual teams as a new form of collaboration in project execution, particularly in industries where specialists from various functional units pool their talents, as in the software, aerospace, and telecommunications industries.

For over a decade now, studies have aimed at identifying, elements that structure and impact project teams when team members work at a distance. The research findings on virtual teams are varied and allow only a confused grasp of the situation, with no single, unifying definition of the virtual team. As a starting point to clarify the research findings and to understand the key underlying dimensions in virtual project teams, this chapter classifies the literature on virtual teams from three perspectives: virtuality, technologies, and management. A review of representative studies revealed a lack of consensus on what constitutes a virtual team. Even though, technologies are inextricably linked, and many key success factors for team performance have been identified. But what to do with all this information? Based on the literature review and our research conducted under the Canada Research Chair in Technology Project Management, we propose some key dimensions of virtual teams as well as several lessons learned to assist team leaders in managing virtual project teams in the section "Key Dimensions of Virtual Teams."

THREE LINKED PERSPECTIVES

PERSPECTIVE 1: VIRTUALITY

The notion of virtuality has assumed a preponderant place in the definition of the virtual work team, and the literature on virtual teams has mushroomed. However, a precise definition of virtuality in teams assembled for a common purpose is still lacking [1]. Are geographically dispersed teams the same as virtual teams? Do the terms global team, virtual transnational team, multicultural team, virtual group, and virtual organization all describe the same work unit?

As some authors do not clearly distinguish the different concepts [2,3], their studies lump various types of virtual groups together, with no differentiation. Early experimental studies compared face-to-face collaboration with computer-mediated interactions [4,5] and treated virtuality as an inclusive concept. Thus, the team was either face-to-face or virtual [6]. More recently, scholars have shifted away from this dichotomy and focused on the extent or degree of virtualness, recognizing that teams can be situated on a continuum of virtuality.[7] From the excellent literature review by Gibson and Gibbs [7, p. 453] we have identified three key points that summarize the state of the research on the notion of virtuality.

(1) *Virtuality is multidimensional* [1,8,9]. Virtual teams transcend geographic, temporal, and organizational boundaries. Some authors [10–13] restrict the definition of the virtual team to groups whose members are separated by at least a few kilometers, as opposed to the global virtual team [14,15], whose members are located in different countries and belong to different cultures. For other authors [16,17], the team qualifies as virtual if the majority of communications between team members are technologically mediated, irrespective of distance. Niederman and Beise [18] used temporal, spatial, and cultural dimensions to characterize virtual teams. Lipnack and Stamps [11] classified virtual teams according to distance and organizational boundaries, and identified four categories: colocated, colocated cross-organizational,

distributed, and distributed cross-organizational. Duarte and Snyder [10] added to the above criteria the notions of authority, cohesion, and team life cycle. When attempting to understand virtual teams, we should bear in mind that virtuality is a function of many dimensions, including cultural diversity, dependence on electronically mediated communication, and degree of geographical dispersion.

(2) *The number of studied dimensions varies.* Because virtuality is a multi-dimensional concept, the number of dimensions studied in the literature varies. For instance, Gibson and Cohen [1] considered two dimensions only: electronic dependence and geographic dispersion. Griffith et al. [19] addressed other dimensions such as the level of technology support, the percentage of time on task, and physical distance. Martins et al. [8] identified four dimensions: geographical dispersion, use of computer-mediated communication, temporality, and diversity. Shin [20] proposed that the degree of virtuality depends on the organization's (or team's) position with respect to four dimensions: temporal, spatial, cultural, and boundary. Chudoba et al. [21] contended that virtuality is governed by discontinuities in geography, time zone, organization, national culture, work practices, and technology. What this tells us is that various dimensions have been studied according to the authors' interests. However, there is no consensus on which dimensions are the most important.

(3) *The most commonly investigated dimensions.* Although there is no consensus in the literature on the most important dimensions, we can identify the most commonly investigated ones. The most frequently cited are geographic dispersion and electronic dependence [7]. A team with members who are distributed around the world and represent diverse organizations would therefore be more virtual than one whose members are located in the same geographic area and belong to the same organization. In addition, many articles explore virtuality through themes such as technology-supported distributed teams [2], computer-supported collaborative work [22], computer-supported inter-organizational virtual teams [23], computer-mediated communication [24], and technology-based projects [25]. Technology use is also widely addressed in the virtual team research. Technology issues are discussed more fully in the following section.

The second most commonly cited dimension is cultural diversity [24,26,27], or the fact that the virtual team contains members from different cultures. Team members express these cultural differences through their own sets of values, behaviors, conventions, beliefs, and so on.

We realize that a single sentence cannot cover everything of importance that has been written so far on virtual teams. As previously mentioned, virtuality is multi-dimensional and some of its key dimensions have been more investigated than others (i.e., geographic dispersion and electronic dependence). However, in the literature review, we found one definition that captures many of the critical dimensions and features of virtual teams. This definition, proposed by Martins et al. [8] has been retained for this chapter: "teams whose members use technology to varying degrees in working across locational, temporal, and relational boundaries to accomplish an interdependent task."

PERSPECTIVE 2: TECHNOLOGIES

Advances in ICT have facilitated distributed team collaboration, particularly for knowledge-intensive tasks. [10] Qureshi et al. [28] reported an explosive growth in distributed project management solutions, with market worth vaulting from $2 to $7 billion from 2002 to 2007. Data collected for the European project called Statistical Indicators Benchmarking the Information Society (SIBIS) [27,29] aptly illustrate this reality, particularly in countries such as Finland, Germany, and Great Britain, where over 50% of national companies provide ICT access (e-mail, the Internet, intranet) to their employees. E-mail exchange is particularly helpful to non-native speakers, who are more at ease with written than oral communications.

Many researchers in the areas of computer-mediated communication, computer-supported cooperative work, group support systems, and group decision support systems have focused on technological solutions that support e-collaboration, whereas researchers in group decision support systems have focused on the effects of technologies on work group behavior. Early studies on group support systems showed that decision quality is not affected by less rich media communication, despite lower satisfaction with various communication technologies compared to face-to face meetings [30, p. 90]. In fact, many researchers have found that effective communication is more dependent on the decision-making environment than on the communication tools [31,32]. More recent studies have shown that adding video to audio-based communication systems improves virtual team decision making over other collaborative technologies [30], and that a "leaner" medium such as e-mail can reduce conflicts [33]. Qureshi et al. [28] underscored that shared understanding is a prerequisite for effective decision making, greater efficiency, and optimal group attitude under stress, and that communication problems, whether caused by human or technological factors, considerably impair collaborative quality.

The technology perspective has generated many studies on virtual teams. However, technologies evolve at a very rapid pace, and new practices and behaviors are constantly emerging in response to innovations. It is important to keep in mind that early writings on virtual teams were published when the Internet was still in its infancy [34,35]. Since then, new technologies and applications (wikis, social networking, etc.) have emerged at an astonishing pace, and this trend should continue for the foreseeable future. New generations of workers will also bring new work patterns based on their own experience with new technologies. This should have a considerable effect on the way we look at virtual teams. Thus, technologies are and always will be inextricably linked to the concept of the virtual team.

PERSPECTIVE 3: MANAGEMENT

This perspective focuses on the key success factors that enhance virtual team effectiveness. When comparing the performance of traditional and virtual teams, most researchers [36,37] have considered the key success factors of traditional teams to see if they would still be applicable in the virtual mode [38–40]. Studies on key success factors and virtual team performance fall into two groups: those that demonstrate the effect of a specific variable on performance, and more exploratory studies that attempt to identify a range of key success factors. For example, Balthazard et al. [41] investigated personality traits as a specific variable affecting virtual team performance. Many others [42–45] agreed that good communication management ensures successful team work. Kirkman et al. [9] for their part, concluded that empowering virtual team members, for example, with more responsibility and decisional power, is positively related to team performance.

A few authors have attempted to identify a range of key success factors. For instance, Duarte and Snyder [10] identified seven critical success factors that were directly related to the virtual team performance: (1) human resources policies; (2) on-the-job education and development; (3) standardization of organizational and team processes; (4) use of collaborative and communication technologies; (5) organizational culture; (6) leadership support; and (7) competences of the team leader and members. Vakola and Wilson [46] recommended that organizations should (1) develop structures to facilitate information sharing; (2) implement appropriate performance management systems; (3) build an organizational culture that promotes participation (horizontal structure, open communication channels, employment involvement in decision making, employee motivation); (4) promote the development of a positive attitude toward change; and (5) develop a training program so individuals can acquire the competences required to work effectively in virtual mode. Thus, in order to effectively cope with the virtual mode, basic changes must be made to day-to-day activities at the individual, group, and organizational level. Bissoonauth [47] found that (1) team members' commitment, (2) perceived organizational support, (3) management support, (4) technological support, and (5) perceived benefits are critical virtual team success factors. Finally, from a survey of 150 project professionals involved in virtual project teams, Bourgault and Drouin [48] identified a list of 10 conditions that promote virtual team performance: (1) good communication processes, (2) availability of adequate technological tools and the training to use them, (3) trust throughout the project life cycle, (4) standardized team practices, (5) a common vision and goals, (6) strong and shared leadership, (7) team competence, (8) formal decision-making process [49], (9) shared information and know-how, and (10) support from upper management at all locations.

These disparate findings demonstrate that there is no single way to understand and manage virtual teams, although they certainly increase our knowledge and understanding of virtual teams. The next section attempts to unite all this knowledge in a framework designed to help managers identify the key components at play in virtual teams.

KEY DIMENSIONS OF VIRTUAL TEAMS

Based on the literature review and our research under the Canada Research Chair on Technology Project Management, this section proposes a framework grounded in the reality of team work rather than academic theory. The literature provides useful

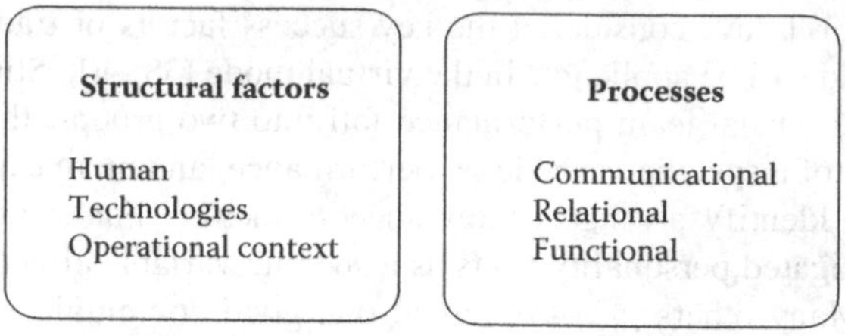

Structural factors	Processes
Human	Communicational
Technologies	Relational
Operational context	Functional

FIGURE 26.1   Key dimensions of virtual teams.

information to understand team work, but lacks a practical method to identify the key dimensions of the virtual team, which could be used as a guide for virtual team managers. We selected six key dimensions and grouped them into two categories: structural factors and team processes, as shown in Figure 26.1.

STRUCTURAL FACTORS

The structural factors are the conditions that shape the environment in which the virtual team operates. These factors have a direct influence on the effectiveness of communicational and relational processes as well as the team's overall management methods. The three groups of structural factors identified—human factors, technologies, and operational context—are discussed below.

Human Factors

This refers to the individuals that make up the virtual team, all of whom contribute their own attributes and commitment.

Individual Attributes

A virtual team may be formed when the required experts are not colocated. Because individual attributes shape the virtual team and influence the way it operates, it is worthwhile identifying these attributes. Some studies [20] indicate that certain combinations of personal attributes (e.g., flexibility and communicational skills) equip individuals to perform better in virtual teams. Katzenbach and Smith [50] pointed out that technical expertise, problem-solving and decision-making skills, and relational qualities are key attributes that enhance team performance. It is also recognized that teams with members with experience in distance collaboration generally ramp up more rapidly. Hertel et al. [42] grouped the key attributes into three categories: taskwork-related attributes (conscientiousness and integrity), teamwork-related attributes (cooperativity and communication skills), and telecooperation-related attributes (self-management, interpersonal trust, intercultural skills, and expertise in new media and groupware technology). Some authors added that team members should possess a minimum degree of agreeableness or conscientiousness in order to prevent conflicts [51,52].

Similar to colocated teams, virtual team members are selected for their professional and technical knowledge and expertise. However, in a virtual context, individual attributes also appear to make a key contribution to enhanced team performance. Beyond professional know-how, the importance given to individual attributes depends on the team's degree of virtuality. In other words, individual characteristics increase in importance, as the environment becomes more virtual [38].

Team Member Commitment

Commitment to a common team goal is now understood to be a prerequisite for team success [53]. However, team member commitment poses a challenge in a distributed context. Unlike face-to-face collaborators, remotely located workers have to process information through a multiplicity of channels and must depend on the abilities of other members to use them. It is also more difficult to define the structure of the work to be accomplished, because team members do not benefit from direct feedback from colleagues. Other factors that influence team member commitment are *ad hoc* participation in the virtual team, hidden agendas, and local motivating factors. *Ad hoc* participation could cause a member to become either overcommitted or less committed due to simultaneous involvement in a number of different work teams [16]. Hidden agendas and local motivating factors increase feelings of isolation in team members and can negatively affect the commitment of distance workers [53].

It is essential to recognize and manage individual differences in commitment and local interests, because they may conflict with the overall concerns of the virtual team and adversely affect team performance. Dubé and Paré [16] also suggested that noncommitment to the virtual team can be exacerbated if the member of a virtual team is also part of another traditional face-to-face team, as identification with the traditional team is usually stronger.

Technologies

The second structural factor concerns technologies. As explained above, ICT are inextricably linked to the notion of the virtual team. They constitute a structural factor because they mediate the communicational interactions of the team members, thereby facilitating team collaboration. ICT support remote interactions between team members as they carry out project tasks [8]. Managers can improve team performance by matching media characteristics with task needs. The theory of media richness [54] identifies two types of tasks: uncertain and equivocal. Uncertain tasks are those for which the executors lack the necessary information but can obtain it from other team members. Equivocal tasks are those for which the available information is ambiguous and open to varying interpretations, so that team members need to agree on a common meaning [55,56]. Consequently, team performance can be improved by using richer media for equivocal tasks and less rich media for uncertain tasks [54]. However, some researchers [31,32] have found that effective communication depends more on the environment than the actual communication tools. Beyond the need to match the media to the task type, the type or nature of the task also influences overall team functioning.

Technologies facilitate communication, information sharing, and activity coordination within virtual teams. Nevertheless, the rapid evolution of technologies as well as their adoption and utilization by virtual teams still pose challenges. We list below some potential technological irritants when operating in virtual mode.

- Collaborative technologies are considered costly and hard to justify.
- Virtual collaborators are not equally skilled in adopting and using technology.
- Compatibility, reliability, and security remain major issues.
- Implementation and updating are problematic issues, especially for occasional collaborations.
- Collaborative technologies generate unmanageable daily information flows. Virtual teams spend much of their time answering e-mails.
- Incentives and organizational support for virtual teams to adopt technologies are lacking.

Operational Context

Operational context is the third structural factor considered. The virtual work team operates within its own environment, that is, through the lens of a particular culture and using its own expertise and internal processes. Many factors can impede or facilitate virtual team effectiveness. Three operational factors are discussed here: the *cultural background* of team members, the *distribution* of the actors, and the *nature of the tasks* to be accomplished.

Cultural Background

A key factor for virtual team effectiveness is the appropriate management of cultural and functional diversity of its members [51]. Culture can be defined as "a set of deep-level values associated with societal effectiveness, shared by an identifiable group of people [8]," such that each group will have its own set of norms with which to filter and interpret information [57,58]. Teams with high cultural diversity may have difficulty building trust, and time may be needed for the team to work and communicate effectively [59].

Distribution of Team Members

Virtual teams can take many forms and configurations, depending on how the team members are distributed. This raises the issue of the consequences of being a member of either the central team or a "satellite" team that gravitates around it [60]. Authors have also addressed the consequences of team managers' locations and their relationships with other team members [60]. O'Leary and Cummings [60] noted that different arrangements of team members across sites raised different sets of issues, with implications for subgroup learning and conflict management [46]. For instance, relationships between team members and the project manager and between each other differ according to whether they are centrally located or at a satellite site [60,61]. Although virtual teams may enable continuous work, it may also create delays and necessitate greater coordination of activities.

Evaristo and van Fenema [26] focused specifically on distributed collaboration and developed a two-dimensional project typology based on the number of project sites and the size of the project portfolio (single or multiple projects). They defined seven project types, ranging from the traditional (one project, one site) to the multiple and distributed (several projects, several sites). These project forms are dynamic and evolve over time with the organization's needs. They noted that the chief difference between them lies in the relative difficulty in managing communications and coordinating the interdependent resources shared among sites [38]. The large variety of project configurations directly impacts the nature and structure of the project teams in charge. They also affect working methods and team governance, and team members must adapt to new operational methods to maintain performance levels [2,10,42,62].

There is little doubt that team member distribution is an influential factor. The greater the team distribution, the stronger the effect on team performance. However, the significance of team configuration for group functioning and performance is only starting to be discussed and formalized as an influential factor.

Nature of Tasks

The nature of the tasks to be accomplished influences the virtual team's overall functioning. For example, Hertel et al. [42] showed that virtual teams are better at performing production tasks, but seem to have more difficulty with decision-making tasks. This is because, in a computer-mediated decision-making process, more time is required, less information is exchanged, and the team's satisfaction with the decision is lower than in face-to-face teams. Task complexity also changes the virtual team's communicational dynamics. According to Bell and Kozlowski [6], less complex tasks require less collaboration and interdependence than more complex tasks, which require more synchronicity and communication to transmit richer and more detailed information. Finally, the degree of interdependence between the tasks to be accomplished influences the team's structure and processes [16]. The greater the interdependence between tasks, the greater the need for communication and coordination between team members [2,16]. This interdependence can either facilitate teamwork [9,42] or promote conflicts between members [42].

TEAM PROCESSES

Team processes encompass all the interactions that take place within the virtual team. By understanding the team's processes, the organization can exert some influence over the types of interactions that the team uses, as processes are strongly impacted by the various combinations and configurations of the structural factors. Three main groups of processes have been identified and are discussed below: communicational, relational, and functional.

Communicational

Communications coordination is a major challenge for virtual teams. Communicational processes refer to the interactions of team members to exchange information. Most virtual teams must cope with considerable distances, different cultures, and diverse organizational backgrounds. In such circumstances, individuals may not be mindful of the potential differences between their daily reality and that of their foreign collaborators [44]. This can lead to major misunderstandings, usually due to (1) inadequate information flow, (2) misinterpretation or unawareness of the importance of the information received, (3) different rhythms of message sending and checking, and (4) and misinterpretations of silence [44]. Thus, lacking information, understanding, and shared knowledge, individuals tend to make emotional rather than situational judgments about other team members [44]. For example, when a conflict arises, team members tend to blame their collaborators (emotional judgment) instead of considering the situation or the underlying causes (situational judgment). Moreover, the massive use of ICT by virtual teams creates its own set of problems. Hertel et al. [42] documented a number of studies showing that virtual conversations tend to exacerbate intragroup conflicts. The researchers noted that the anonymity afforded by some technologies opens the way to toxic or virulent interactions [63]. However, when team members anticipate a lengthy collaboration, this toxicity tends to disappear as anonymity is replaced by acquaintanceship [42]. Other authors found that the anonymity factor encourages people to couch their ideas in more objective terms, use more constructive criticism, and agree too readily due to personal feelings or the other person's status [42]. Furthermore, the study by Postmes et al. [24] showed that social influence is more powerful in groups when anonymity is preserved.

Relational

Relational processes refer to the socio-emotional interactions between virtual team members. Trust is one of the most frequently addressed topics in the virtual team literature [8,59,64]. Building trust within a group is a core process that is essential for collaboration [65], communication, and coordination [39], as well as overall team performance [40,59,66]. In the networks and virtual teams of the Information Age, trust is a prerequisite for productive relationships. However, trust is not so easy to establish in a virtual team, due to the diversity of disciplines and cultures and the lack of face-to-face interactions, all of which make it harder to establish the common ground that forges relationships [44,67]. Nevertheless, Jarvenpaa et al. [39] found that, in teams distributed across a number of different countries or departments, workers who managed to gain trust at the outset were perceived as people who could deliver on their promises.

Other relational processes, such as leadership and cohesion, have considerable influence on success, functioning, cooperation, motivation, and personal satisfaction in virtual teams [42,68]. Many aspects of leadership have been investigated, from the emergence of leadership in virtual teams [69] to the impact of leadership styles on project managers' management methods [6,67] and the identification of the main leadership behaviors and roles [6]. As for the development of cohesion, it appears to have a considerable influence on successful virtual teamwork, as it facilitates group functioning, encourages extra-role helping, and helps prevent employee turnover [42]. In addition, high cohesion motivates teams to improve their decision-making practices and use more open communication, and it generates higher personal satisfaction [68]. However, Dubé and Paré [16] contended that, due to the virtual team's relatively short life cycle, virtual team building can be more difficult than in traditional teams. Creativity is an emerging research issue in the study of relational processes. For example, Ocker [70] identified inhibitors of creativity in virtual teams, such as dominance and lack of shared understanding, as well as factors that fostered creativity, such as a collaborative work climate.

Functional

A prominent feature of the virtual team is that it must find new ways to adapt or replace traditional approaches in order to coordinate its work [55]. For example,

Maznevski and Chudoba [2], in their study on three global virtual teams, concluded that effective global virtual teams develop a rhythmic temporal pattern of interaction "structured by a definite beat of regular, intense face-to-face meetings, followed by less intensive, shorter interaction incidents using various media." Face-to-face meetings seem to benefit team functioning in terms of relations as well as the alignment and shared understanding of targeted objectives, roles, and team member functions [10,16,42]. The rhythm of face-to-face meetings varies with task complexity and interdependence [2,55], the team's capacity to communicate by electronic media [2], and the project life cycle, such that coordination is more intense at project start and end [55].

KEY DIMENSIONS OF VIRTUAL TEAMS: WHAT CAN WE LEARN?

Thus far, we have described the key dimensions of virtual teams. We noted that teams have different characteristics (diverse cultural backgrounds, expertise, technology infrastructures, and physical distance) that act as preconditions for the way that processes unfold. Structural factors influence the effectiveness of team processes. For example, physical distance between team members affects communications and relations between team members (communicational and relational processes). This suggests a range of actions, from promoting a better understanding of the cultural differences and abilities of team members (to enhance trust building) to using ICT to communicate and providing the appropriate communication tools. Task complexity and interdependency may impede coordination and communication between team members. These are only a few examples of the potential interactions between structural factors and team processes. But what can we learn from this? More specifically, which dimensions can help managers improve virtual team performance? We attempt to pinpoint the key lessons for managers seeking to improve virtual team performance. Five lessons are presented below.

LESSON 1: INDIVIDUALS ARE CENTRAL TO THE VIRTUAL TEAM

Individuals are central to virtual team work and virtual project success, but fulfilling that role depends on the members' individual attributes. Managers can start by knowing that certain combinations of personal and technical attributes influence the way virtual teams operate. For instance, it is essential to recognize and manage individual differences in commitment. Managers must therefore understand the role of the individual in virtual team success before recruiting team members. They should also identify the motivating factors that act to reduce feelings of isolation and foster commitment.

LESSON 2: TECHNOLOGY IS ONLY PART OF THE EQUATION

The emergence and widespread use of collaborative technologies for virtual team work has opened up opportunities for collaborative undertakings. Many researchers have highlighted the effects of technologies on communication, decision-making, and conflict in virtual teams. Although technologies can be used to improve information sharing and team interaction, effective management of these issues still depends more on environmental factors than technological tools. Moreover, teams may possess a range of the most sophisticated technologies, but technological ease of use remains a central concern in virtual team performance. When virtual teams encounter ineffective technologies, communication and coordination problems are liable to escalate, leading to dysfunctional behaviors.

LESSON 3: CULTURAL AWARENESS IS A MUST

Effective virtual team work requires cultural sensitivity on the part of team members. The socio-cultural environment in which the virtual team operates influences the interactions between the members. Awareness of and appropriate responses to cultural differences are therefore critical factors for virtual team effectiveness.

LESSON 4: OPERATIONAL FACTORS AFFECT TEAM PROCESSES

Virtual teams operate in specific contexts. The many factors that characterize this context can either impede or facilitate virtual team effectiveness. Lesson 3 raised the issue of cultural differences. Lesson 4 addresses team member distribution and the nature of the tasks to be accomplished. Team member distribution may not only enable the work to be accomplished continually, but also create delays and adversely affect working methods as team members adapt to new operational methods. Moreover, team distribution can create difficulties in managing communications and coordinating shared resources.

The complexity and interdependence of tasks require synchronocity, communication, and coordination between team members. Each member has a part to play in the overall team functioning. Operational factors impact the nature and intensity of the interactions, communications, and operations in virtual teams.

LESSON 5: FACILITATE AND SUPPORT TEAM PROCESSES

Effective virtual team performance is fostered by trust, good communicational processes, standardized practices, common vision and goals, and support by upper management. Managers should understand not only how the structural factors shape the virtual team environment, but also how these factors affect team processes. More specifically, they must develop the ability to identify the activities and mechanisms that support virtual team processes. For instance:

- Communicational and functional processes can be supported by mechanisms that help *facilitate the establishment of a common language between members* through the selection of key individuals; *facilitate information exchange* through clear definitions of the roles and responsibilities of team members as well as standardized processes; and *facilitate information access* through communication protocols.
- Relational processes can be supported by mechanisms that primarily act to *build trust and cohesion between members*, again through the selection of

key individuals; *facilitate management of political aspects of the project through greater team autonomy; and allow team members a better understanding of the cultural and situational issues of other team members* through informal communications management.

These key lessons show the importance of appropriately managing the structural factors that can limit effective team processes and team performance. To better understand team interactions in today's global climate, the impact of structural factors on team processes must be grasped, as well as the importance of appropriately adjusting virtual team activities. These lessons are starting points and are intended to assist managers in understanding the virtual team environment. Finally, we provide a list of questions to help managers connect the proposed key dimensions to the day-to-day realities of managing virtual teams.

Structural factors

- Human factors
  - ☐ What knowledge, skills, and abilities do my virtual team members need?
  - ☐ Beyond professional skills, what weight is given to their individual attributes?
- Technologies
  - ☐ How can I match task needs with the appropriate communication tools?
  - ☐ What kinds of incentives should I provide to team members to foster the use of technologies?
  - ☐ What kinds of technological training do my virtual team members need?
- Operational context
  - ☐ How complex is the task?
  - ☐ What is the physical distance between team members?
  - ☐ What level of coordination is needed between my team members?

Team processes

- Communicational and functional
  - ☐ How can I facilitate project activity coordination?
  - ☐ How can I facilitate the establishment of a common language between team members?
  - ☐ How can I facilitate information access?
- Relational
  - ☐ How can I build trust and cohesion between team members?
  - ☐ How can I facilitate the management of political aspects of the project?
  - ☐ How can I foster a better understanding of the cultural differences within the team?

CONCLUDING REMARKS

This chapter provides an overview of the recent scientific research on virtual teams. There is no consensus on a single definition of the virtual team even though many authors have investigated the impact of technology on virtual teams, whereas others have concentrated on defining the key success factors for virtual team management.

Based on recent literature reviews, we proposed a list of dimensions related to the performance of "virtual teams." These dimensions can be classified into two groups: structural factors and team processes. In a set of key lessons addressed to managers, we underscored that virtual teams face a number of challenges. Thus, many issues, including cultural sensitivity, the skills and knowledge of team members, team member commitment, the team's degree of "distributedness," and the selection of appropriate technologies, impact virtual team performance. In view of the progressively demanding environment in which most firms operate, virtual teams will be increasingly used as a way to tap resources and gain a competitive advantage, whatever their location.

Nevertheless, more theoretical development is needed, as there is still no unifying theory in the research on virtual teams. Practitioners who must deal with these challenges daily need a better understanding of the conditions and determining factors. It is hoped that this chapter provides a good starting point.

REFERENCES

1. Gibson, C.B. and Cohen, S.G., *Virtual Teams That Work: Creating Conditions for Virtual Team Effectiveness*, Jossey-Bass, San Francisco, 2003.
2. Maznevski, M.L. and Chudoba, K.M., Bridging space overt time: global virtual team dynamics and effectiveness, *Organization Science*, 11 (5), 473–492, 2000.
3. Gassmann, O. and von Zedtwitz, M., Trends and determinants of managing virtual R&D teams, *R&D Management*, 33 (3), 243–262, 2003.
4. Strauss, S.G. and McGrath, J.E., Does the medium matter? The interaction of task type and technology on group performance and member reactions, *Journal of Applied Psychology*, 79 (1), 87–97, 1994.
5. Huang, W.W. et al., Supporting virtual team-building with a GSS: An empirical investigation, *Decision Support Systems*, 34 (4), 359–367, 2002.
6. Bell, B.S. and Kozlowski, S.W., A typology of virtual teams, *Group & Organization Management*, 27 (1), 14–49, 2002.
7. Gibson, C.B. and Gibbs, J.L., Unpacking the concept of virtuality: The effects of geographic dispersion, electronic dependence, dynamic structure, and national diversity on team innovation, *Administrative Science Quarterly*, 51 (3), 451–495, 2006.
8. Martins, L.L., Gilson, G.L., and Maynard, M.T., Virtual teams: What do we know and where do we go from here? *Journal of Management*, 30 (6), 805–835, 2004.
9. Kirkman, B. et al., The impact of team empowerment on virtual team performance: The moderating role of face-to-face interaction, *Academy of Management Journal*, 47 (2), 175–192, 2004.
10. Duarte, D.L. and Snyder, N.T., *Mastering Virtual Teams*, Jossey-Bass, San Francisco, 2000.
11. Lipnack, J. and Stamps, J., *Virtual Teams*, John Wiley & Sons, New York, 1997.
12. Henry, J.E. and Hartzler, M., *Tools for Virtual Teams*, ASQC Quality Press, Milwaukee, 1997.

13. Lurey, S.J. and Raisinghani, M.S., An empirical study of best practices in virtual teams, *Information & Management*, 38 (8), 523–544, 2001.

14. Massey, A.P., Montaya-Weiss, M., and Hung, Y.-T.C., Synchronizing pace in asynchronous global virtual project teams, *Proceedings of the 35th Hawaii International Conference on System Sciences*, IEEE Computer Society, Los Alamitos, CA, Vol. 1, 14, 2002, available at http://www2.computer.org/portal/web/csdl/doi/10.1109/HICSS.2002.993869, last accessed on July 9, 2009.

15. McDonough III, E.F., Kahn, K.B., and Barczaka, G., An investigation of the use of global, virtual and colocated new product development teams, *The Journal of Product Innovation Management*, 18 (2), 110–120, 2001.

16. Dubé, L. and Paré, G., The Multi-faceted Nature of Virtual Teams, Working Paper, No. 02-11, HEC Montreal, Canada, 2002.

17. Johnson, P., Heiman, V., and O'Neil, K., The "wonderland" of virtual teams, *Journal of Workplace Learning*, 13 (1), 24–29, 2001.

18. Niederman, F. and Beise, C.M., Defining the "virtualness" of groups, teams, and meetings, *Proceedings of the 1999 ACM SIGCPR Conference on Computer Personnel Research*, ACM, New York, 1999, pp. 14–18.

19. Griffith, T.L., Sawyer, J.E., and Neale, M.A., Virtualness and knowledge in teams: Managing the love triangle of organizations, individuals, and information technology, *MIS Quarterly*, 27 (3), 265–287, 2003.

20. Shin, Y., A person-environment fit model for virtual organizations, *Journal of Management*, 30 (5), 725–743, 2004.

21. Chudoba, K.M. et al., How virtual are we? Measuring virtuality and understanding its impact in a global organization, *Information Systems Journal*, 15 (4), 279, 2005.

22. Huysman, M. et al., Virtual teams and the appropriation of communication technology: Exploring the concept of media stickiness, *Computer Supported Cooperative Work*, 12 (4), 411–436, 2003.

23. Majchrzak, A. et al., Technology adaptation: The case of a computer-supported inter-organizational virtual team, *MIS Quarterly*, 24 (4), 569–600, 2000.

24. Postmes, T. et al., Social influence in computer-mediated communication: The effects of anonymity on group behavior, *Personality and Social Psychology Bulletin*, 27 (10), 1243–1254, 2001.

25. Thamhain, H.J., Team leadership effectiveness in technology-based project environments, *Project Management Journal*, 35 (4), 35–42, 2004.

26. Evaristo, R.J. and van Fenema, P.C., A typology of project management: Emergence and evolution of new forms, *International Journal of Project Management*, 17 (5), 275–282, 1999.

27. SIBIS. 2003b. *e-Europe Topic Reports, Topic Report 2: Internet for research and development*. Available online at: http://www.sibis-eu.org, last accessed on June 25, 2009.

28. Qureshi, S., Liu, M., and Vogel, D., The effects of electronic collaboration in distributed project management, *Group Decision and Negotiation*, 15 (1), 55–75, 2006.

29. SIBIS. 2003a. e-Europe Topic Reports. Topic Report 5: Work, employment and skills. Available online at: http://www.sibis-eu.org, last accessed on June 25, 2009.

30. Baker, G., The effects of synchronous collaborative technologies on decision making: A study of virtual teams, *Information Resources Management Journal*, 15 (4), 79–93, 2002.

31. Zack, M.H., Interactivity and communication mode choice in ongoing management groups, *Information Systems Research*, 4 (3), 207–239, 1993.

32. Markus, M.L., Electronic mail as the medium of managerial choice, *Organization Science*, 5 (4), 502–527, 1994.

33. Sivunen, A. and Valo, M., Team leaders' technology choice in virtual teams, *IEEE Transactions on Professional Communication*, 49 (1), 57–68, 2006.

34. Malone, T.W. and Rockart, J.F., Computers, networks and the corporation, *Scientific American*, 265 (3), 128, 1991.
35. Davidow, W.H. and Malone, M.S., *The Virtual Corporation: Structuring and Revitalizing the Corporation for the 21st Century*, Harper Business, New York, 1992.
36. Powell, A., Piccoli, G., and Ives, B., Virtual teams: A review of current literature and directions for future research, *Database for Advances in Information Systems*, 35 (1), 6–12, 2004.
37. Mohrman, S.A., Cohen, S.G., and Mohrman, A.M., *Designing Team-Based Organizations*, Jossey-Bass, San Francisco, 1995.
38. Evaristo, R.J., The management of distributed projects across cultures, *Journal of Global Information Management*, 11 (4), 58–70, 2003.
39. Jarvenpaa, S.L., Knoll, K., and Leidner, D.E., Is anybody out there? Antecedent of trust in global virtual teams, *Journal of Management Information Systems*, 14 (4), 29–64, 1998.
40. Lee-Kelly, L., Crossman, A., and Cannings, A., A social interaction approach to managing the "invisible" of virtual teams, *Industrial Management & Data Systems*, 104 (8), 650–657, 2004.
41. Balthazard, P., Potter, R.E., and Warren, J., The effects of extraversion and expertise on virtual team interaction and performance, *Proceedings of the 35th Annual Hawaii International Conference on System Sciences*, IEEE Computer Society, Los Alamitos, CA, Vol. 8, 2002, 269. Available at: http://doi.ieeecomputersociety.org/10.1109/HICSS.2002.994426, last accessed on July 9, 2009.
42. Hertel, G., Geister, S., and Konradt, U., Managing virtual teams: A review of current empirical research, *Human Resources Management Review*, 15 (1), 69–95, 2005.
43. Sarker, S. and Sahay, S., Implications of space and time for distributed work: An interpretative study of US-Norwegian systems development teams, *European Journal of Information Systems*, 13 (1), 3–20, 2004.
44. Cramton, C.D., Finding common ground in dispersed collaboration, *Organizational Dynamics*, 30 (4), 356–367, 2002.
45. Suchan, J. and Hayzak, G., The communication characteristics of virtual teams: A case study, *IEEE Transactions on Professional Communication*, 44 (3), 174–186, 2001.
46. Vakola, M. and Wilson, I., The challenge of virtual organization: Critical success factors in dealing with constant change, *Team Performance Management*, 10 (5), 112–120, 2004.
47. Bissoonauth, B., Virtual project work: Investigating critical success factors of virtual project performance, Master's Thesis. Concordia University, Canada, 2002.
48. Bourgault, M. and Drouin, N., How's your distributed team doing? *PMI Virtual Library*, Project Management Institute, 2007. Available at: http://www.pmi.org/PDF/Member/Bourgault_final_121107.pdf, last accessed on July 9, 2009.
49. Bourgault, M., Drouin, N., and Hamel, E., Decision making within distributed project teams: An exploration of formalization and autonomy as determinants of success, *Project Management Journal*, 39 (S1), S97–S110, 2008.
50. Katzenbach, J.R. and Smith, D.K., *The Wisdom of Teams: Creating the High Performance Organization*, Harvard Business School Press, Boston, MA, 1993.
51. Zakaria, N., Amelinckx, A., and Wilemon, D., Working together apart? Building a knowledge-sharing culture for global virtual teams, *Creativity and Innovation Management*, 13 (1), 15–29, 2004.
52. Furst, S.A. et al., Managing the life cycle of virtual teams, *Academy of Management Executive*, 18 (2), 6–20, 2004.
53. Rennecker, J., Local Motives and Virtual Team Success: Inverting the Normative Views of Team Goal Commitment and Hidden Agendas, Case Western Reserve University, USA, Sprouts: Working Papers on Information Systems, Vol. 4, No. 5, 2004. Available at: http://sprouts.aisnet.org/117, last accessed on July 25, 2009.

54. Draft, R.L. and Lengel, R.H., Organizational information requirements, media richness and structural design, *Management Science*, 32 (5), 554–571, 1986.
55. Ramesh, V. and Dennis, A.R., The object-oriented team: Lessons for virtual teams from global software development, *Proceedings of the 35th Hawaii International Conference on System Sciences*, IEEE Computer Society, Los Alamitos, CA, Vol. 1, 2002, 18b. Available at: http://csdl2.computer.org/comp/proceedings/hicss/2002/1435/01/14350018b.pdf.
56. Dennis, A.R. and Valachi, J.S., Rethinking media richness: Toward a theory of media synchronicity, *Proceeding of the 32nd Hawaii International Conference on System Sciences*, Vol 1, 1017, 1999.
57. Adler, N.J., *International Dimensions of Organizational Behavior*, South Western College Publishing, Cincinnati, OH, 1997.
58. Hofstede, G., *Culture's Consequences: International Differences in Work-Related Values*, Sage Publications, Newbury Park, 1980.
59. Corbitt, G., Gardiner, L.R., and Wright, L.K., A comparison of team developmental stages, trust and performance for virtual versus face-to-face teams, *Proceedings of the 37th Hawaii International Conference on System Sciences*, IEEE Computer Society, Los Alamitos, CA, Vol. 1, 2004, 10042b. Available at: http://doi.ieeecomputersociety.org/10.1109/HICSS.2004.1265157, last accessed on July 9, 2009.
60. O'Leary, M. and Cummings, J., The spatial, temporal and configurational characteristics of geographic dispersion in teams, *Management Information Systems Quarterly*, 31 (3), 433–452, 2008. Available at: http://aisel.aisnet.org/misq/vol31/iss3/8
61. Evaristo, R.J. et al., A dimensional analysis of geographically distributed project teams: A case study, *Journal of Engineering and Technology Management*, 21 (3), 175–189, 2004.
62. Massey, A.P. et al., When culture and style aren't about clothes: Perceptions of task-technology "fit" in global virtual teams, *Proceedings of the 2001 International ACM SIGGROUP Conference on Supporting Group Work*, ACM, New York, 2001.
63. Baltes, B.B. et al., Computer-mediated communication and group decision making: A meta-analysis, *Organizational Behavior and Human Decision Processes*, 87 (1), 156–179, 2002.
64. Pinsonneault, A. and Caya, O., Virtual teams: What we know, what we don't know, *International Journal of E-collaboration*, 1 (3), 1–16, 2005.
65. Zolin, R. et al., Interpersonal trust in cross-functional, geographically distributed work: A longitudinal study, *Information and Organization*, 14 (1), 1–26, 2004.
66. Child, J., *Organization*, Blackwell Publishing, Oxford, 2005.
67. Panteli, N. and Duncan, E., Trust and temporary virtual teams: Alternative explanations and dramaturgical relationships, *Information Technology & People*, 17 (4), 423–441, 2004.
68. Misiolek, N.I. and Heckman, R., Patterns of emergent leadership in virtual teams, *Proceeding of the 38th Hawaii International Conference on System Sciences*, Hawaii, IEEE Computer Society, Los Alamitos, CA, 2005, Vol. 1, 49a. Available at: http://doi.ieeecomputersociety.org/10.1109/HICSS.2005.486, last accessed on July 9, 2009.
69. Bouas, K.S. and Arrow, H., The development of group identity in computer and face-to-face groups with membership change, *Computer Supported Cooperative Work*, 4 (2/3), 153–178, 1995.
70. Ocker, R.J., Influence on creativity in asynchronous virtual teams: A qualitative analysis of experimental teams, *IEEE Transactions on Professional Communication*, 48 (1), 22–39, 2005.

27 Salvaging Projects in Trouble

John P. Murray

CONTENTS

INTRODUCTION

According to an ancient proverb, "when the ox gets in the ditch, you do what you have to do to get him out." Too often, information technology (IT) application development projects fall into a ditch. When that occurs, organizations must direct every effort toward getting the IT ox out of the ditch.

One reality of managing IT applications projects is that the high probability that they will, at some point in their development cycle, fall into difficulty. That difficulty usually comes, or is at least formally recognized, well into the project life cycle. The project team then faces several issues:

- It must take steps to get the project back on track as quickly as possible.
- It must address to how to meet the project deadlines because the issues are being raised late in the project life cycle. There will be a push to get the project completed and some agreed-upon features and functions will be removed. Although in theory these features and functions will simply be "delayed," at least some of them will never be delivered.
- It must consider how to divide the project into phases, in an attempt to deliver something by the original deadline. The overall project deadlines will be extended to accommodate the new phased approach. In many IT installations, because of the new deadlines, one or more planned but not yet started projects for other areas will also be delayed.

627

Organizations typically make changes that will negatively affect the project's quality. Examples might include the following:

- Reduce the amount of testing required to ensure high quality. The project team might try to overcome current difficulties by showing some positive results, rationalizing that the once applications are in production, someone can go into the applications and conduct the delayed testing. In reality, this will probably not happen.
- Circumvent the normal project quality controls. The team might try to avoid strict adherence to development standards, arguing that they are now too time-consuming and will delay the project progress.
- Abandon project documentation processes, claiming no time to do that work because the project must meet its deadlines. Although documentation will be seen as being delayed rather than abandoned, it is highly unlikely that the documentation will ever be delivered as a completed package.

Beyond the issues related to acknowledging problems late in the development cycle, political concerns will arise. As the intensity to bring the project to completion grows, there will be an effort to place or avoid blame for the project's failure. Given the project team's already high stress level, this will only add to the problem and accomplish nothing concrete. In fact, taking such a tack negatively affects the morale and makes people reluctant to identify and present project-related problems from a concern that doing so will jeopardize their careers.

It is far better to direct the time and energy for placing blame toward improving the project. Later, after the project has been salvaged, the team can spend time in assessing the problems' causes and taking corrective action.

THE COST OF QUICK SOLUTIONS

The project team makes serious mistakes when it lowers the project's quality in an attempt to make up the lost time. Although the project is behind schedule and must be completed as quickly as possible, compromising with quality results in a short-term gain at the expense of a long-term loss. While the project might be completed more quickly, the IT product delivered will probably require considerable fine-tuning and general repair in the future to keep it going. In terms of overall project cost, attempting to build in quality after the fact will be more expensive than doing it right the first time around.

Too often, when a project is determined to be facing difficulty, the team moves to a series of "quick fix" solutions. When developers give in the pressure to meet the project deadline, they will try anything that appears to offer some type of improvement. Usually, applying these "improvements" in an uncontrolled manner, without thinking through all the issues, just make matters worse, and it becomes more difficult to correct the basic project problems. What happens is that the changes brought about by the improvements add one more layer of confusion to the project problems.

Although taking the time to do the work right when the project is facing difficulty will be very frustrating for everyone involved, the frustration will generally last only a short time, and then go away. However, attempting to retrofit quality into the system after it moves to production drags out for a long time, as does the accompanying frustration.

The only way to salvage a trouble project might be to work around normal project development practices. However, there will be costs attached such as the following:

- There will be a tendency to rush ahead with changes and adjustments before the team has a clear understanding for the problems' causes. Therefore, time and money will be wasted on problems that have little to do with the real project difficulties.
- The organization will probably see the staffing level as one cause of difficulty, and might therefore add more people to the project. However, this measure requires additional management time and attention to deal with the project's increased communication lines. Although bringing on more experienced people might be the right approach, this should be performed in a careful, controlled manner. Before adding staff to a project, the decision-maker must have a clear idea of why people need to be added, and their exact roles and responsibilities.
- There will likely be increased senior management attention directed at the troubled project—a mixed blessing. Senior managers can help cut through constraints to move the project forward and provide additional needed resources. However, they might have little understanding of the issues, yet be ready with quick (usually wrong) solutions.

In dealing with troubled IT projects, the easy answer is to avoid the situation. However, experienced IT project managers know that keeping projects out of difficulty is often beyond the project management team's control. And, although the most pragmatic approach to IT project management is to provide adequate project discipline and control from the onset so the project does not fall into difficulty, the issue being explored here is recognizing when a project is in difficulty and developing approaches that will bring the project back on track.

The key to successfully restoring troubled IT projects is to determine as early as possible in the development cycle that the project is beginning to deteriorate, and to then move quickly and decisively to take corrective action, assessing and installing the needed correction processes in a disciplined and controlled manner.

DETECTING PROJECT DIFFICULTIES

A difficult aspect of dealing with a failing IT project is to recognize that the project is indeed in trouble; this is all too often an emotional issue. Usually, those managing the project simply deny that the project has begun to slip (possibly in the sincere belief that it is not in trouble). Alternatively, they might admit to some slippage, but state that it will be made up and the project will be brought back on schedule.

It is exceedingly difficult to begin the correction process unless people accept that the project is in difficulty and understand steps that must be taken to make corrections. People will argue about whether the project is really in trouble, and why it got that way.

Such arguing is counterproductive because one argument will simply lead to others. Therefore, someone in authority must declare that the project is in difficulty.

When people are just beginning to recognize project difficulties, they will make little attempt to develop a recovery plan. Instead, they suggest that time (and perhaps additional effort) will help correct the problems. This approach often rests on a false assumption. In reality, management is depending on luck, rather than factual assessing the project's status.

Accurately assessing the project status is also difficult because, early on, project managers may have incorrectly reported the project as being on or ahead of schedule. After reporting favorable project progress, project managers will find it difficult to admit that the project is in trouble. Usually, however, believing that things will work out becomes an untenable position, as the project's failure becomes highly apparent to people outside the project team.

Once the project team recognizes that the project is in trouble, it can begin to work on correcting the problems and salvaging the projects. However, there must first be a clear understanding of the problems' causes. Unfortunately, when projects fall into difficulty, people tend to jump to an apparent solution without understanding the issues involved; this will only make the problems worse. A more effective approach is to investigate what went wrong and develop a solution that addresses the real problems.

A team that rushes to a solution without clearly understanding the causes of the difficulty usually addresses the problem's symptoms, rather than the problem itself. An example is when application testing uncovers a series of difficulties. The team may well assume that the problem stems from poorly written code, which shows up in testing. The obvious approach to improvement is to go through the code, find the errors, and make the needed corrections. However, while the code may seem to the problem, the trouble may be tied to the established testing processes, to the architecture of the software, or to the requirements themselves.

In this example, rushing to redo the code will not help; it will only make the problem worse. Where the issue is seen as poor coding, the team will waste both time and effort on "correct" flawed coding (which, in fact is not flawed at all). When the team discovers that the coding indeed was not the cause of the problem, the fix must be backed out, and the modified code retested. Thus, moving to an expedient but incorrect solution is the wrong approach to the problem.

STABILIZING THE ENVIRONMENT

Once the real causes of the problem have been identified, the team should verify that the apparent cause is indeed what needs correction. The final step in the process is developing a plan for making the needed corrections.

In salvaging the project, the team should avoid panic. Of course, there will be pressure to correct the problems and get the project back on schedule. And it requires determination and discipline on the part of the project manager to hold off pressure from other areas, while identifying the problem's causes.

An immediate step in bringing the project back on track must be to temporarily stop or freeze all project work. Because the cause of the problems is unknown, doing any work would simply add to the project problems. The idea is to contain damage to the project while looking for workable solutions.

What can project members do while the project is frozen? Of course, some team members will help investigate and verify the causes of project difficulty and help develop the improvement plan. In addition, some project areas can be fine-tuned in the interim. For example, the team can review documentation, bringing it up-to-date and clarifying it. The team can also review testing plans, both technical and business cases, developing and strengthening them. Developers can also examine project specifications and requirements, to determine if they are still correct, or if anything should be added. Finally, as a last resort, project team members can be temporarily shifted to other work within the IT department.

With large IT projects in particular, freezing the project may not be seen as a viable option because there are so many staff members working on the project. Managers might argue that everyone must be kept busy or those people taken off the project temporarily will be permanently lost to the project. In such cases, the project will likely be broken, with predictably unfortunate results. It is a poor reflection on management, when it is not an option to freeze a project to discover and correct the problem's causes, although there is a strong case for the freeze.

There may well be defensiveness on the part of those working on the trouble project, and strong pressure to get the project back on track. The stabilization process may involve appointing a new project manager. This can substantially benefit the project because the new person has no connection to the project and can therefore make objective judgments about what he/she is told and observes. In addition, a new project manager can more easily take a firm stance investigating what has occurred, before making project adjustments. Also, a new manager will not have preconceptions or assumptions about what is or is not causing the problems; such prejudgments can otherwise cloud the analysis.

FINDING THE ROOT CAUSE

As stated earlier, to avoid unnecessary arguments, someone in authority must declare that the project is in difficulty, that it will be frozen until the problems have been adequately investigated and understood, and that the process of correcting the situation can begin. Although this approach is not easy, particularly in light of mounting pressure, it is the right course of action.

Determining what has gone wrong will require patience. The key to a good diagnosis is asking the right questions, and testing the answers against the project's apparent conditions. Care must be exercised here because the answers will be based on subjective interpretation of the facts, or on beliefs, which may not necessarily be accurate. In addition, the atmosphere will be tense, thus people may be reluctant to admit that their work may have contributed to the difficulty.

For example, someone might state that testing the applications' changes are not part of the problem because the testing schedules have been met. Yet a testing review may reveal poor-quality testing processes. Although test plans were developed for both technical and business unit testing and those plans were followed, these plans overlooked some important conditions. Because the criteria were not sufficiently rigorous to meet the project requirements, some parts of the applications were flawed.

Should it be accepted that testing is not part of the problem, nothing will be done to verify testing quality, and testing problems will not be identified until later. Considerable time and effort may be spent on other areas of project difficulty before the true testing conditions are identified. The net result will be a delay in making the needed project improvements.

Although it is tedious to question and search for the correct answers to the causes of project difficulty, it must be done before conclusions about corrective actions can be reached. The first step is in understanding what has actually gone wrong, rather than what appears to have gone wrong. As possible causes are considered, there must be a mechanism to test these assumptions against reality. That mechanism is to ask probing questions and, where appropriate, require concrete proof of the statements being presented.

Once the problems have been identified, they should be prioritized as to their effect on the effort to bring the project back on track. A list of items that bear on the project difficulties should be developed in a short time. Then the items should be investigated to determine those that must be addressed immediately and those that can be set aside for correction at some later time.

Beyond identifying the problem issues and setting the correction priorities, the linkages between the identified items must be analyzed. The inherent complexity of IT projects tends to lock many parts of the project together; therefore, there must be assurance that correcting an item in one part of an application will not affect other processes negatively, whether in the same application or in a different one. This is another reason why the team should understand what went wrong before starting corrections.

DEVELOPING THE RECOVERY PLAN

Once the project problems have been identified and prioritized, a correction plan must be developed. The team must allow sufficient time for, and attention to, developing the plan to ensure that what it proposes will work. The goal is to establish a logical progression in the order of changes to ensure that, as the changes are applied, they would not disrupt either the preceding changes or some other area of the system. The team should avoid a process that forces backtracking to other parts of the applications to fix additional problems that the changes would have made.

The plan should also introduce control of the changes. Several basic rules can assist in establishing that control, including:

- A member of the project team should be assigned the responsibility of managing the application of the changes once they have been agreed and prioritized.
- Changes should be applied one at a time.
- Sufficient time (at least one processing cycle) should be set between successive changes.
- Two members of the project team—respectively, to IT and the business unit—must certify that the changes being applied are working correctly.

- A log should be maintained to track all the changes in the order in which they have been applied, as a method for tracking problems should they arise after the changes have been installed.

After the plan has been developed, it should be submitted to all the parties involved to solicit their comments. Consistency in the development and execution of the plan should be maintained, in the same manner that a consistent and disciplined approach was required to determine the causes of the project failure. When everyone involved has had an opportunity to respond, the plan should be base-lined and published and copies should be distributed to all project team members. Everyone should understand that, from this point on, the project will be managed according to the updated plan.

DEVELOPING A STRONG COMMUNICATION PROCESS

In a gaining control of a failing project, a clear communication process is absolutely critical. Communication should be addressed by regular meetings of the project team members and via written status reports that can be distributed outside the project team to those who need to be kept informed.

As part of the communication process, all outstanding issues should be recorded and their status tracked. These issues include identified problems, change requests (modifications to the applications within the scope of the project), status of the work in process, and all applications abnormalities. Each member of the project team should have specific assignments and they should provide updates on the progress of their work or the difficulties that they encounter during the project team meeting.

All members of the project team should meet daily, until the project manager decides that sufficient progress has been made at which time the project team would meet less frequently. There will probably be some resistance; IT people generally see meetings as a waste of time. However, if the meetings are well run, they will provide some real benefits. First, if everyone involved with the project is in the same room at the same time, hearing the same reporting status and problems, there is an opportunity for all opinions to be expressed. This can be helpful, especially, if the person that is presenting a potential solution does not understand its ramifications so that the solution may be unacceptable.

The list of outstanding project items must be maintained and updated to record problems as they arise, as well as the relevant solutions when they are found. In large projects with interdependent tasks, considerable effort may be spent just to maintain an understanding of what each participant is doing. Yet the effort is worthwhile, because it can avoid unpleasant surprises when it is discovered too late that some work has not even begun, when it was assumed to be in process, or even completed.

RECOMMENDED COURSE OF ACTION

Virtually, all IT projects encounter some difficulties during their development. Dealing with these problems as they arise and keeping the project on track should be handled as part of the normal course of project development. In such cases, although the project deadlines may need to be adjusted, the transition to the production environment for life-cycle management can be performed within a reasonable time frame and with a sufficient quality.

In dealing with IT applications' development projects that have fallen into difficulty, the emphasis must be on getting the work back on track as rapidly as possible. Accomplishing anything of substance requires the following three actions:

1. The team must admit that the project is in difficulty and that corrective action is needed.
2. The best approach is to shut down the project until there has been an assessment of the project's status and the issues associated with its failing behind schedule.
3. A plan must be developed to begin the correction process so that the project can proceed.

The key here is that the project recovery requires an accurate understanding of what has gone wrong, rather than what people might believe has gone wrong. It is only after the problems have been identified and understood, that the salvage process can begin.

Salvaging failing IT projects is a difficult process that calls for a strong management skill and patience, a belief that broken IT projects can be repaired and having the will to make that happen.

Section VII

Conclusions

28 The Future of Enterprise System Integration

Mostafa Hashem Sherif

CONTENTS

It is difficult to overrate the importance of system integration in modern enterprises as instruments of rationalization and reduction of transactional costs and informational asymmetries. The ability of a system or a product to work with other systems or products without extensive modifications is a key issue in manufacturing and service industries. For example, large automotive and aircraft manufacturers were the driving force behind the STEP (Standard for the Exchange of Product Model Data) standard to facilitate the exchange and interpretation of product among different systems for CAD (Computer-Aided Design) and CAM (Computer-Aided Manufacturing). Thus, the aim of enterprise system integration is to overcome the fragmentation of knowledge in functional silos, to avoid the duplication of data processing activities in various departments, and to share the information across the value chain linking suppliers with customers. The integration agenda is driven by the twin goals of efficiency and agility; redundant operations waste time and resources, increase the likelihood of errors, and impede the response to sudden shifts in business conditions. This is why system integration is implicit when people talk about Decision Support Systems, Executive Information Systems, or more recently, Business Intelligence.

Interoperability is typically sought at three levels: the data exchanges, the applications that process the exchanges, and the significance of the message exchanged for the communicating enterprises. The methods and procedures of achieving this integration depends on whether legacy systems need to be considered or the integration project could start from a green field, so that the target integration architecture is defined top-down starting with a proposed design or bottom-up from the existing heterogeneous systems to be brought under one umbrella. The first approach leads to a "platform innovation" while the second is an "architectural innovation" [1,2]. Platform innovations correspond to a transition to new technology that achieves a quantum leap in performance, such as is the case of Web Services or the service-oriented architecture (SOA). Architectural innovations provide new functional capabilities by rearranging the existing technologies in a new form to create a sustained competitive advantage [3]. In either case, system integration is a life-cycle activity to be evaluated in light of the emerging discipline of System of Systems (SoS) engineering.

SYSTEM INTEGRATION AS A CONTINUOUS PROCESS

In a networked and interconnect environment and given the role of information processing in modern institutions, system integration is not a one-shot endeavor but a continuous sequence of projects [4]. These projects will have to always consider whether the embedded base needs to be included. Whatever the decision, enterprise networks will always include heterogeneous systems and technologies that need to be accessed. Even if business conditions remain stable, technological evolutions and hardware and software upgrades must be rolled-out, with as minimum perturbations as possible, whether for internal users or to outside customers. This activity is frequent enough to have generated its own jargon: "forklift upgrade" to indicate that the old system is completely replaced and "swivel chair integration" when the operator uses a swivel chair to switch from one terminal to the other to reenter the same data over and over again [5]. Other sources of imposed change are internal reorganizations as well as mergers, acquisitions or divestitures, or changes in operating routines to adapt to market trends and to the competitive outlook.

As explained in Chapter 7, the TM Forum has come up with the eTOM (Enhanced Telecomm Operations Map) model that groups the major operations business processes in a modern enterprise into three categories: enterprise management; strategy, infrastructure and product, and operations. The focus of "enterprise management" is the processes at the enterprise level, such as the overall strategy, finances and asset management, disaster recovery, research and development, human resources, and so on. The other two categories can be implemented at the business unit level. The first is for the development of products and services (planning, marketing, technology infrastructure, supply chain development, and management). The second relates to life-cycle operations in terms of fulfillment, quality assurance, computer networks and applications for operational support, customer and supplier management, billing, and so on. This general map can guide the simplification and automation of enterprise functions, even outside the telecommunications industry.

Many current research activities aim at developing process design modeling tools for the totality of the life cycle, that is,

- Formal description of business models and process models that could be used for simulations to identify potential bottlenecks as early as possible.
- Workflow tools to automate the execution of process transactions and events.
- Engines for implementing the business rules outside the main program so that the operations could be changed at run-time without touching the code itself.
- Business Activity Monitoring tools for business performance management, to track and record the performance measures that could be used later to improve the operations and/or the design. These measurements may go under the name of key performance indicators and can be presented in the form of a *balanced scorecard*.

In theory, this methodology could help businesses assess their current situation and readjust their processes accordingly by rearranging their workflow and/or modifying their business rules to reproduce the development artifacts automatically.

The IT Infrastructure Library (ITIL) (www.itil.org) is a compendium of best practices in the form of comprehensive task lists, recommended process flows, and system quality requirements issued by the U.K. Office of Government Commerce, then adopted as the British Standard BS 15000 and finally standardized worldwide as ISO/IEC 20000 in December 2005. It provides an integrated approach to the delivery of managed services. ITIL V2 considers three levels: strategic, tactical, and operational. The strategic-level relates to qualitative and quantitative performance measures of the IT services and their definitions in Service-Level Agreements. The processes at the tactical level are for the provisioning, installation, and financial management (billing, accounting) and network engineering. This includes capacity management, service continuity and trouble management, and availability management. Finally, the components at the operational-level relate to the day-to-day customer facing and network facing activities such as customer care, fault management (incident reporting and trouble tracking), change management, and configuration management. Many of these processes are common to public networks as well.

ISO/IEC 20000 differs from ITIL in that it includes a new component for "Business relationship management and supplier management," combines service continuity and availability management in one process, and eliminates the service-desk function [6].

The new generation of the ITIL documents "ITIL V3" takes a life-cycle approach, as opposed to the process-oriented approach of the previous version. It builds on the principles of Total Quality Management to ensure continuous learning and improvement.

Finally, the itSMFI (http://www.itsmfi.org) is an organization that promotes IT service management "best practice," standards, and qualifications since 1991, when the U.K. chapter started.

WHO DOES SYSTEM INTEGRATION?

Project management methodologies can be readily adapted to system integration projects to bring them under control. Accordingly, to conduct a successful system integration, the scope must adapt to the situation at hand. Organizations must be realistic in setting their goals in light of an honest examination of their capabilities to understand which functions to keep, which to outsource, and what is the best way to manage the integration project.

There are telltale signs of a system integration projects in trouble. Some of these relate to the organization of the enterprise; others to the project management structure, to the capabilities of the technology, or to the execution itself. The causes that lead to failure are well documented in the project management body of knowledge. Chapter 24 provides a confirmation by showing that the lessons learned from a recent project are consistent with what can be garnered from the literature, which is in turn very similar to what was stated in the first edition of the handbook [7]. In other words, how to achieve success is known and the reasons for failure are also known, provided there is a willingness to apply the necessary discipline to benefit from past experience.

SYSTEM INTEGRATION AND SoS ENGINEERING

SoS engineering is an emerging interdisciplinary approach focusing on making individually developed, managed, and operated systems function as autonomous constituents of one or more SoS to provide appropriate functional capabilities to each of them. Its scope covers the context of use and the associated political, financial, legal, technical, social, operational, and organizational factors, including the stakeholders' perspectives and relationships, and their influence on SoS development, management, and operations. The ultimate goal is to have an SoS that can accommodate changes to its conceptual, functional, physical, and temporal boundaries without significant effect on operations.

SoS engineering originated in the development of complex weapon systems for the U.S. Department of Defense (DoD). The DoD sponsors a SoS Engineering Center of Excellence operated by Concurrent Technologies Corporation, a nonprofit organization, to develop a formal SoS engineering methodology. The *International Journal of System of Systems Engineering* was launched in 2008 to advance the relevant knowledge.

SoS engineering is associated with the concept of a *metasystem* (systems of systems) "comprised of multiple embedded and interrelated autonomous complex subsystems that can be diverse in technology, context, operation, geography, and conceptual frame. These complex subsystems must function as an integrated metasystem to produce desirable results in performance to a higher-level mission subject to constraints" [8]. The metasystem and its relation to the various constituent subsystems can be best understood in terms of competition and symbiosis as discussed in Chapter 2.

In enterprises, the SoS methodology could be used to track the information flow, to assess the impact of changes to system requirements, budgets, schedules, and so on, and to perform trade-off studies among alternative solutions [9]. The goal of enterprise system integration would be the design, analysis, and evolution of metasystems to produce the desired outcomes of agility and efficiency. The metasystem [e.g., the Enterprise Resource Planning (ERP) architecture] provides a framework for the structure for the integration and its management and coordination functions to cover both legacy and new technology systems.

One civilian application where SoS engineering can be of help is in the field of computerized health care. The sharing of electronic medical documents among institutions is expected to increase to help in emergencies, in the management of chronically ill patients or those requiring long-term care. Both Japan and Korea have developed comprehensive national plans for a "ubiquitous network society" where people and "things" are always connected by access networks at any time and at any place. In Japan, the emphasis is on meeting citizens' daily needs and resolving their issues and problems including their interactions with the government offices [10]. This has implications on the interoperability among different networks as well on the management of the various services offered. For example, an IT-enabled medical, healthcare, and care-giving system to support the aging population involves the coordination and orchestration of many services and service providers (physicians, pharmacists, nurses, etc.) and is constrained by regulations, government supervision, and constraints to optimize service personalization at the lowest cost. For example, the delivery of controlled drugs to private residences requires secure networks with several levels of authentication and identification. Currently, hospital information systems can use one of several data exchange protocols such as HL7 (Health Level 7) and the IHE (Integrating the Health Care Enterprise) initiative aims at use and adapt existing standards to manage the workflow and the patient's information within a hospital. What would be needed is a much larger integration of all actors at the community or city level to form a Community Health Information Network or an Integrated Delivery Network [11,12]. This network would be responsible for the collection, processing, exchange, storage, and retrieval of clinical and administrative data related to comprehensive health care. It would encompass patients, physicians, nurses, technicians, pharmacists, hospital administrators, insurance providers, social security personnel, and so on. One obvious advantage would be to avoid multiple data entries and to reduce errors through automation, for example, by computer-aided pharmacy systems that dispense prescriptions in large hospitals. In a nonprofit environment, the main goal would be improved clinical diagnosis, more efficient patient follow-up, and long-term services to the chronically ill or the elderly. The for-profit sector would probably add as an objective to increase the returns to the shareholders. Thus, the objectives of such networks would vary according to the nature of the health-care system.

PLANNING FOR SYSTEM INTEGRATION WITH SoS ENGINEERING

One advantage of using the language of SoS engineering is that it provides a good starting point for recognizing and addressing the challenges of enterprise system integration. The rough consensus is that SoSs have the following characteristics [13–16]:

1. Emergent properties
2. Autonomous operations
3. Interconnected constituents
4. Ambiguous/changing boundaries
5. Multiple contexts and influences
6. Dynamic stakeholder relationships within the same SoS

Let us consider how these properties could affect enterprise system integration.

EMERGENCE

This property is that knowledge of a complex system, while always incomplete, evolves and improves with experience as the SoS is deployed and new properties are discovered following an unanticipated interaction. Another aspect is that the understanding of the whole system cannot be gained by extrapolating the behavior of each entity, because the interactions among the subsystems may introduce new unexpected aspects, as the experience gained during the implementation of ERP systems has shown.

AUTONOMY

This property means that individual constituents make independent choices and that decisions are decentralized. However, because the constituents are networked they are not autarkic; their interfaces have to conform to communication standards and, if possible, their applications have to agree on shared meanings to ensure semantic interoperability. In fact, legacy systems were built independently and, in SOA and for Web services, the various services group self-contained functions.

INTERCONNECTION

In integrated systems, elements are interconnected and the increased interactions among autonomous systems require coordination and standardization. In SOA, the communication is through an Enterprise Service Bus. As discussed in Chapter 1, interconnectivity is the first step in a process that ends by the optimization of performance. This optimization should be for the SoS as a whole and individual systems should not be pursuing local objectives at the expense of sum.

One of the arguments made in Chapter 2 is that in a world that is increasingly interconnected, changes outside an SoS may bring change and that these changes are best understood through the paradigm of Darwinian evolution.

FLUID BOUNDARIES

As a consequence of the emergency property, boundaries, whether temporal, special, or conceptual are ambiguous, fluid, and negotiable. Thus, their delineation is subject to value judgments and depends on the balance of power of the various stakeholders. They are susceptible to dynamic environmental shifts (e.g., mergers, splits, acquisitions, reorganizations, etc.). Globalization, for example, has also a direct effect on the management of project teams (virtual teams).

When enterprises open their boundaries (e.g., through the use of open source software), they contribute to making their boundaries more fluid. Also, as argued in Chapter 2, the management of products and services beyond the point-of-sale, particularly when third parties are involved, additional externalities are added to the metasystem.

As a consequence, the SoS (or the metasystem) must be adaptable and have sufficient intelligence to evolve.

MULTIPLICITY OF CONTEXTS

The context comprises the circumstances, factors, conditions, and patterns that both enable and constrain a complex system of solution, the deployment of that solution, and the interpretation. This is important in the case of varying legal environments and regulatory compliance.

ERP packages have implicit assumptions that may not be applicable in all contexts. For example, assumptions that bandwidth is plentiful and that it is available from fixed lines is not generally valid outside the main cities of industrialized countries. Modified architectures will be needed to squeeze as much information as possible into the available bandwidth or to adapt the application to satellite transmission. This mode of communication has its own advantages and disadvantages; for example, multicast solutions are more readily available with satellites but the package default parameters need to be changed to accommodate the additional transmission delays.

Finally, if sensors with multiple sensing capabilities become wide spread, as anticipated in Chapter 2, then the whole value chain including production, delivery, and customer care will have to be adapted to the various contexts of use.

DYNAMIC STAKEHOLDERS RELATIONSHIPS

With diversity, there may be multiple purposes and objectives at the various integration levels: the individual, the departmental, or that of the enterprise. These differences may be tacit, unmentionable, and a source of later conflicts.

As discussed in Chapter 2, the interactions among the constituents with each other, as well as with the outside parties, offer opportunities to increase the overall value of the metasystem by encouraging a more efficient management of resources.

CHALLENGES AND RESEARCH DIRECTIONS

It is sometimes stated that a complex SoS can never be completely understood: "to believe that you have the answers is to have already made the mistake" [13]. The implication is that the needs of a globalized, service-centric economy can never be totally satisfied and that the integration of hardware, software, people, and processes is always done with imperfect knowledge. In addition, the environment itself adds a certain degree of uncertainty,

THE REGULATORY PUSH FOR FUNCTIONAL SEPARATION IN TELECOMMUNICATION

Whenever economic cooperation and integration are being planned, the standard-ization of the interfaces, the interoperability of applications, and the integration of existing systems or those under development need to be considered. For example, the European Commission is considering the "functional separation" of vertically inte-grated telecommunications companies, that is, that they separate their network infra-structure from their service business. The assumption is that vertical integration provides the ability and incentives to discriminate against competitors, as evidenced in the enduring market power in access and backhaul networks. The thinking is that, by splitting the network from the services, competition would be stimulated. Without judging on the merit of this assumption, the benefits and costs of such an approach need to be considered in terms of the lessons learned from the past cross-enterprise integra-tion in recent years in terms of quality control, fault management, and provisioning.

RISK MANAGEMENT

The nature of the risks in an SoS is considerably different from the risks in individ-ual subsystems, because the large number of possible interactions increases the vulnerability to interruptions due to the failure of the weakest link. During the implementation of the integration project, the high degree of interdependence with other large internal or external projects may end with a critical path that is outside the project control. During operation, just-in-time delivery amplifies the conse-quences of the failure of a single supplier upstream. As an example, the 2008 finan-cial crisis has shown how problems that started with mortgage failures in the United States cascaded into a global credit crunch.

The novelty of the integration techniques makes the project susceptible to the lack of available functional or managerial expertise. Model-Driven Engineering, for example, requires intimate knowledge of the firm processes and a mastery of new techniques and languages that remain confined to a limited circle of experts. Long schedules increase the project exposure to changes in the scope of the project, shifts in the strategy of the firms, variations in the standards, or technology migrations.

Technology risks may arise from unreliable hardware or faulty software, particu-larly if time pressures lead to insufficient system testing. Another category of risks has its origin in defective standards or incorrect standard implementation either in the product itself or in the setting of the interface parameters.

Finally, in an unstable environment, supplier's risks arise from failure of delivery of high-quality product because of changes in the status of the supplier's team due to outsourcing, mergers, splits, and so on.

The increase in complexity has important implications regarding the maintenance and the security of the integrated system. Several decades of sheer individualism have introduced new categories of risk when "discarded employees"—to use the dehumanizing terminology currently in vogue—may be tempted to get even by disrupting the system. For example, a network administrator may change the system's passwords to effectively lock everyone, as happened in San Francisco's Department of Telecommunications and Information Services [17]. Policies in place to reduce such risks would probably introduce additional overhead, which can affect the agility that was required in the first place.

EDUCATIONAL CHALLENGES

System integration projects are large, complex, and risky. They demand a highly skilled and disciplined project team, a dedicated project manager with business and technological insights, and a methodology to track the execution and performance. System integration is multidisciplinary and relies on technical expertise in manufacturing, telecommunications, process engineering, software development, enterprise modeling in addition to domain-based business knowledge, and a mixture of synthetic and analytical skills. The demand of such a cross-functional expertise is expected to grow, even though it is not clear where such specialized training could be offered. In many engineering programs, whether in academia or in industry, designing systems and writing code are more valued than testing and debugging systems to put them to work together [18]. Vendor-certified training aims at building solutions with their respective products. Although MBA programs have started to include management of technology in their curricula, the training does not include the estimation of the costs and effort associated with the integration of two or more incompatible IT systems. As a consequence, this evaluation rarely figures in the assessment of potential mergers or acquisitions. In short, many academic institutions are not equipped to address cross-disciplinary programs, even though there are serious attempts, particularly in Korea, China, and Japan to include standards as part of the engineering curriculum [19].

It is possible that, by stimulating a research agenda on complex designs, the sponsorship of the DoD would encourage formal academic training on systems integration. Another model could be to promote a professional certificate similar to the approach that the Project Management Institute took to promote the project management profession.

LACK OF AGREEMENT ON THE TERMINOLOGY

In the field of system integration, the typical mode of operation is that industry consultants and software companies forge new terms and promote them to show the uniqueness of their products. Next, researchers reuse the terms to seek funds for their research proposals. At the next round of the cycle, a new terminology is advanced with hyperboles and extraordinary claims. As a consequence, "there is very little agreement as to what actually constitutes a systems integration project and systems integration services. Integrators themselves disagree about what constitutes systems integration, and few can define it in contractual terms rather than a substantive service" [4, p. 731]. The use of a common terminology is important for a shared understanding and for devising common ways for dealing with issues and responding to issues, particularly in the case where activities are outsourced.

REFERENCES

1. Abernathy, W. J. and Clark, V. B., Mapping the winds of creative destruction, *Res. Policy.* 14(1), 2–22, 1985.
2. Sherif, M. H., *Managing Projects in Telecommunications Services*, John Wiley & Sons, Hoboken, NJ, 2006, 23–25.
3. Porter, M. E., *The Competitive Advantage of Nations*, The Free Press, New York, 1990, 45–49.
4. Mische, M. A., Choosing a systems integrator, in *Enterprise Systems Integration*, 1st edn., Wyzalek, J., Ed., CRC Press, Boca Raton, FL, 2000, Chap. 56, p. 873; 2nd Edn, Myerson, J. M., Ed., Auerbach Publications, CRC Press, Boca Raton, FL, 2002, Chap. 59, 731.
5. Saxtoft, C., *Convergence. User Expectations, Communications Enablers and Business Opportunities*, John Wiley & Sons, Chichester, 2008, 124.
6. Cater-Steel, A. and Toleman, M., Education for IT service management standards, *J. IT. Stand. Standard. Res.*, 5(2), 27–41, 2007.
7. Mische, M. A., Symptoms of a terminally ill systems integration project, in *Enterprise Systems Integration*, 1st edn., Wyzalek, J., Ed., CRC Press, Boca Raton, FL, 2000, Chap. 55, 831–857.
8. Keating, C. et al., System of systems engineering, *Eng. Manage. J.*, 15(3), 36–45, 2003.
9. Carlock, P. G. and Fenton, R. E., System of Systems (SoS) enterprise systems engineering for information-intensive organizations, *Syst. Eng.*, 4(4), 242–261, 2001.
10. DTI, Exploiting the broadband opportunity: Lessons from South Korea and Japan, Global Watch Mission Report, December 2005.
11. Beuscart, R. et al., Systèmes d'information et réseaux de soins, in *Présent et avenir des systèmes d'information et de communication hospitaliers*, Degoulet, P. et al., Eds, Springer-Verlag, Paris, France, 2003, 201–210.
12. Klein, L. A. and Neumann, E. L., *Integrated Health Care Delivery*, Nova Science Publishers, Hauppauge, NY, 208.
13. Sauser, B. and Boardman, J., Taking hold of system of systems management, *Eng. Manage. J.*, 20(4), 3–8, 2008.
14. DiMario, M., Cloutier, R., and Verma, D., Applying frameworks to manage SoS architecture, *Eng. Manage. J.*, 20(4), 18–23, 2008.
15. Keating, C. B., Padilla, J. J., and Adams, K., System of systems engineering requirements: Challenges and guidelines, *Eng. Manage. J.*, 20(4), 24–31, 2008.
16. System of Systems Engineering Center of Excellence, Brochure, available at http://www.sosece.org, downloaded on December 25, 2008.
17. Clapperton, G., Pull the plug on a specialist and run the risk of IT theft, *Financial Times*, January 19, 2009, p. 10.
18. London, S., Battling the bugs, *Financial Times*, August 27, 2002, 12.
19. De Vries, H. J. and Egyedi, T. M., Education about standardization: Recent findings, *J. IT. Stand. Standard. Res.*, 5(2), 1–16, 2007.

Index